MAGILL'S LITERARY ANNUAL

2010

MAGILL'S LITERARY ANNUAL 2010

Essay-Reviews of 200 Outstanding Books Published in the United States During 2009

With an Annotated List of Titles

Volume One
A-LIT

Edited by
JOHN D. WILSON
STEVEN G. KELLMAN

SALEM PRESS
Pasadena, California Hackensack, New Jersey

Cover photo: Courtesy, U.S. Senate

∞ The paper used in these volumes conforms to the American National Standard for Permanence of Paper for Printed Library Materials, Z39.48-1992 (R1997).

Library of Congress Catalog Card No
ISBN (set): 978-1-58765-655-2
ISBN (vol. 1): 978-1-58765-656-9
ISBN (vol. 2): 978-1-58765-657-6

FIRST PRINTING

PRINTED IN THE UNITED STATES OF AMERICA

CONTENTS

CONTENTS

PUBLISHER'S NOTE

Magill's Literary Annual, 2010 is the fifty-sixth publication in a series that began in 1954. Critical essays for the first twenty-two years were collected and published in the twelve-volume *Survey of Contemporary Literature* in 1977; since then, yearly sets have been published. Each year, *Magill's Literary Annual* seeks to evaluate critically 200 major examples of serious literature, both fiction and nonfiction, published during the previous calendar year. The philosophy behind our selection process is to cover works that are likely to be of interest to general readers, that reflect publishing trends, that add to the careers of authors being taught and researched in literature programs, and that will stand the test of time. By filtering the thousands of books published every year down to 200 notable titles, the editors have provided busy librarians with an excellent reader's advisory tool and patrons with fodder for book discussion groups and a guide for choosing worthwhile reading material. The essay-reviews in the *Annual* provide a more academic, "reference" review of a work than is typically found in newspapers and other periodical sources.

The reviews in the two-volume *Magill's Literary Annual, 2010* are arranged alphabetically by title. At the beginning of both volumes is a complete alphabetical list, by category, of all covered books that provides readers with the title, author, and a brief description of each work. Every essay is approximately four pages in length. Each one begins with a block of reference information in a standard order:

- Full book title, including any subtitle
- *Author:* Name, with birth and death years, where available
- *First published:* Original foreign-language title, with year and country, when pertinent
- Original language and translator name, when pertinent
- Introduction, Foreword, etc., with writer's name, when pertinent
- *Publisher:* Company name and city, number of pages, retail price
- *Type of work:* (chosen from standard categories)

Anthropology
Archaeology
Autobiography
Biography
Current affairs
Diary
Drama
Economics
Education
Environment
Essays
Ethics
Film
Fine arts
History
History of science
Language
Law
Letters
Literary biography
Literary criticism
Literary history
Literary theory
Media
Medicine
Memoir
Miscellaneous
Music
Natural history
Nature

Novel	Psychology	Sociology
Novella	Religion	Technology
Philosophy	Science	Travel
Poetry	Short fiction	Women's issues

- *Time:* Period represented, when pertinent
- *Locale:* Location represented, when pertinent
- Capsule description of the work
- *Principal characters* [for novels, short fiction] or *Principal personages* [for biographies, history]: List of people, with brief descriptions

The text of each essay-review analyzes and presents the focus, intent, and relative success of the author, as well as the makeup and point of view of the work under discussion. To assist readers further, essays are supplemented by a list of additional "Review Sources" for further study in a bibliographic format. Every essay includes a sidebar offering a brief biography of the author or authors. Thumbnail photographs of book covers and authors are included as available.

Four indexes can be found at the end of volume 2:

- Biographical Works by Subject: Arranged by subject, rather than by author or title. Readers can locate easily reviews of biographical works—memoirs, diaries, and letters in addition to biographies and autobiographies—by looking up the name of the person covered.
- Category Index: Groups all titles into subject areas such as current affairs and social issues, ethics and law, history, literary biography, philosophy and religion, psychology, and women's issues.
- Title Index: Lists all works reviewed in alphabetical order, with any relevant cross references.
- Author Index: Lists books covered in the annual by each author's name.

A searchable cumulative index, listing all books reviewed in *Magill's Literary Annual* between 1977 and 2010, as well as in *Magill's History Annual* (1983) and *Magill's Literary Annual, History and Biography* (1984 and 1985), can be found at our Web site, **www.salempress.com**, on the page for *Magill's Literary Annual, 2010*.

Our special thanks go to the editors for their expert and insightful selections: John D. Wilson is the editor of *Books and Culture* for *Christianity Today*, and Steven G. Kellman is a professor at the University of Texas at San Antonio and a member of the National Book Critics Circle. We also owe our gratitude to the outstanding writers who lend their time and knowledge to this project every year. The names of all contributing reviewers are listed in the front of volume 1, as well as at the end of their individual reviews.

COMPLETE ANNOTATED LIST OF TITLES

VOLUME 1

VOLUME 2

COMPLETE ANNOTATED LIST OF TITLES

CONTRIBUTING REVIEWERS

Michael Adams
City University of New York Graduate Center

Richard Adler
University of Michigan-Dearborn

Thomas P. Adler
Purdue University

M. D. Allen
University of Wisconsin-Fox Valley

Emily Alward
Henderson, Nevada, District Libraries

Charles L. Avinger, Jr.
Washtenaw Community College

Dean Baldwin
Penn State Erie, The Behrend College

Carl L. Bankston III
Tulane University

Milton Berman
University of Rochester

Cynthia A. Bily
Adrian, Michigan

Margaret Boe Birns
New York University

Franz G. Blaha
University of Nebraska-Lincoln

Pegge Bochynski
Salem State College

Harold Branam
Savannah State University (retired)

Peter Brier
California State University, Los Angeles

Thomas J. Campbell
Pacific Lutheran University

Edmund J. Campion
University of Tennessee

Henry L. Carrigan, Jr.
Northwestern University

Sharon Carson
University of North Dakota

Mary LeDonne Cassidy
South Carolina State University

Dolores L. Christie
John Carroll University

C. L. Chua
California State University, Fresno

Richard Hauer Costa
Texas A&M University

Frank Day
Clemson University

Francine A. Dempsey
College of Saint Rose

Robert P. Ellis
Worcester State College (retired)
Northborough Historical Society

Thomas R. Feller
Nashville, Tennessee

Rebecca Hendrick Flannagan
Francis Marion University

Roy C. Flannagan
South Carolina Governor's School for Science and Mathematics

Donald R. Franceschetti
The University of Memphis

Raymond Frey
Centenary College

Jean C. Fulton
Landmark College

Ann D. Garbett
Averett University

Janet E. Gardner
University of Massachusetts, Dartmouth

Leslie E. Gerber
Appalachian State University

Sheldon Goldfarb
University of British Columbia

Sidney Gottlieb
Sacred Heart University

Karen Gould
Austin, Texas

Lewis L. Gould
University of Texas, Austin

Jay L. Halio
University of Delaware

Diane Andrews Henningfeld
Adrian College

Carl W. Hoagstrom
Ohio Northern University (retired)

John R. Holmes
Franciscan University of Steubenville

Joan Hope
Palm Beach Gardens, Florida

Jeffry Jensen
Glendale Community College

Fiona Kelleghan
University of Miami

Steven G. Kellman
University of Texas, San Antonio

Howard A. Kerner
Polk Community College

Grove Koger
Boise, Idaho, Public Library

Margaret A. Koger
Boise, Idaho

James B. Lane
Indiana University Northwest

Timothy Lane
Louisville, Kentucky

Eugene Larson
Los Angeles Pierce College

Leon Lewis
Appalachian State University

Thomas Tandy Lewis
St. Cloud State University

Bernadette Flynn Low
Community College of Baltimore County-Dundalk

R. C. Lutz
Madison Advisors

Janet McCann
Texas A&M University

Joanne McCarthy
Tacoma, Washington

Andrew Macdonald
Loyola University, New Orleans

Gina Macdonald
Nicholls State University

Margaret H. McFadden
Appalachian State University

S. Thomas Mack
University of South Carolina-Aiken

David W. Madden
California State University, Sacramento

Paul Madden
Hardin-Simmons University (emeritus)

Charles E. May
California State University, Long Beach

Laurence W. Mazzeno
Alvernia College

Vasa D. Mihailovich
University of North Carolina

Timothy C. Miller
Millersville University

Robert Morace
Daemen College

Daniel P. Murphy
Hanover College

John Nizalowski
Mesa State College

Holly L. Norton
University of Northwestern Ohio

Robert J. Paradowski
Rochester Institute of Technology

David Peck
Laguna Beach, California

Marjorie J. Podolsky
Penn State Erie, The Behrend College

Cliff Prewencki
Delmar, New York

Maureen J. Puffer-Rothenberg
Valdosta State University

Edna B. Quinn
Salisbury University

Thomas Rankin
Concord, California

CONTRIBUTING REVIEWERS

R. Kent Rasmussen
Thousand Oaks, California

Rosemary M. Canfield Reisman
Charleston Southern University

Mark Rich
Cashton, Wisconsin

Dorothy Dodge Robbins
Louisiana Tech University

Bernard F. Rodgers, Jr.
Bard College at Simon's Rock

Stephen F. Rohde
Los Angeles, California

Carl Rollyson
City University of New York, Baruch College

Joseph Rosenblum
University of North Carolina, Greensboro

John K. Roth
Claremont McKenna College

Marc Rothenberg
National Science Foundation

Barbara Schiffman
Vanderbilt University

Barbara Kitt Seidman
Linfield College

R. Baird Shuman
University of Illinois, Urbana-Champaign

Thomas J. Sienkewicz
Monmouth College

Charles L. P. Silet
Iowa State University

Amy Sisson
Houston Community College

Roger Smith
Portland, Oregon

Ira Smolensky
Monmouth College

George Soule
Carleton College

Maureen Kincaid Speller
University of Kent at Canterbury

Theresa L. Stowell
Adrian College

Paul Stuewe
Green Mountain College

Paul B. Trescott
Southern Illinois University

Jack Trotter
Trident College

William L. Urban
Monmouth College

Sara Vidar
Los Angeles, California

Shawncey Webb
Taylor University

Thomas Willard
University of Arizona

John Wilson
Editor, Christianity Today

James A. Winders
Appalachian State University (retired)

Scott D. Yarbrough
Charleston Southern University

Author Photo Credits

Chinua Achebe: *Rocon/Enugu, Nigeria*; Buzz Aldrin: *Courtesy, NASA*; Aharon Appelfeld: ©*Jerry Bauer*; Ludovico Ariosto: *Library of Congress*; Margaret Atwood: ©*Washington Post; reprinted by permission of the D. C. Public Library*; Paul Auster: ©*Jerry Bauer*; Amiri Baraka: *Library of Congress*; Samuel Beckett: ©*The Nobel Foundation*; Wendell Berry: *Dan Carraco*; T. Coraghessan Boyle: *Courtesy, Allen & Unwin*; Philip Caputo: ©*Stephen Ellis/Courtesy, Simon & Schuster, Inc.*; Michael Chabon: ©*Patricia Williams/Courtesy, Random House*; Michael Connelly: *Courtesy, Allen & Unwin*; E. L. Doctorow: ©*Barbara Walz*; Rita Dove: *Fred Viebahn*; Richard Flanagan: *Peter Whyte*; Diane Glancy: *Courtesy, University of Arizona Press*; Louise Glück: *James Baker Hall/Library of Congress*; Albert Goldbarth: *Michael/Pointer/Courtesy, Graywolf Press*; P. D. James: *Courtesy, Allen & Unwin*; Ha Jin: *Kalman Zabarsky*; Ismail Kadare: *Sophie Bassouls/Sygma*; Barbara Kingsolver: *Annie Griffith Belt/Courtesy, Allen & Unwin*; Alexander McCall Smith: *Chris Watt/Courtesy, UCLA*; Alice Munro: ©*Jerry Bauer*; Vladimir Nabokov: *Library of Congress*; Amos Oz: ©*Miriam Berkley*; Jayne Anne Phillips: ©*Jerry Bauer*; Reynolds Price: *Margaret Sartor*; Philip Roth: ©*Nancy Crampton*; John Updike: ©*Davis Freeman*

A. LINCOLN
A Biography

Author: Ronald C. White, Jr. (1939-   )
Publisher: Random House (New York). 796 pp. $35.00
Type of work: Biography
Time: 1809-1865
Locale: Illinois; Kentucky; Washington, D.C.

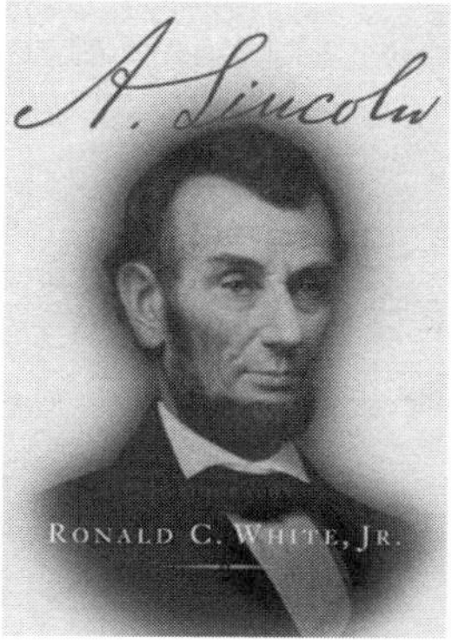

This biography of the sixteenth U.S. president incorporates new perspectives regarding Abraham Lincoln's formative years and development, including the role of his religious beliefs in shaping his life and work

Principal personages:
ABRAHAM LINCOLN (1809-1865), sixteenth president of the United States
MARY TODD LINCOLN (1818-1882), Lincoln's wife
JEFFERSON DAVIS (1808-1889), president of the Confederacy during the Civil War
STEPHEN DOUGLAS (1813-1861), Lincoln's Senate rival in 1858, debates with whom first brought Lincoln to national attention
ULYSSES S. GRANT (1822-1885), final commander of the Union armies during the Civil War
JOHN NICOLAY (1832-1901), Lincoln's secretary and a source of early material about the president
WILLIAM SEWARD (1801-1872), Lincoln's political rival for the presidential nomination and subsequent secretary of state

There have been an estimated sixteen thousand publications about the life and times of Abraham Lincoln, and a number of comprehensive biographies appeared during the Lincoln bicentennial birth year of 2009. Thus, while Ronald C. White, Jr., is among the most important of contemporary Lincoln scholars, it is reasonable to question whether *A. Lincoln: A Biography* stands out from the sizeable collection of analogous material. White provides a fresh approach by integrating Lincoln's "log cabin" origins with his religious views to develop a more comprehensive account of the politician's influences. He traces the effects of these influences both on his early political career and on his years in the White House.

Lincoln's early years have long been a subject of his numerous biographies. He was born February 12, 1809—the same day as Charles Darwin, the towering nineteenth century scientific figure—in Kentucky, not Illinois, which is sometimes mistaken for Lincoln's birthplace. His earliest recorded English ancestor, Samuel Lincoln, arrived in New England in 1637, one of thirteen thousand people who left Europe during that decade. Samuel Lincoln's descendents traveled progressively farther south and west, moving through New Jersey, Pennsylvania, Virginia, and eventually Kentucky, where

Ronald C. White, Jr., is the author of two previous best-selling histories about Lincoln: The Eloquent President *(2005) and* Lincoln's Greatest Speech *(2002). White has taught at several universities, is a fellow of the Huntington Library in California, and has presented hundreds of lectures on Lincoln.*

the future president's grandfather and namesake, Abraham Lincoln, settled near what is now Louisville. Lincoln's grandfather was killed during a Shawnee raid, leaving the six-year-old Thomas Lincoln fatherless. A man of average height, Thomas Lincoln was a typical young pioneer of the day—an active (Baptist) church member, a member of the local militia, and a man who believed the path out of poverty was through the accumulation of property. When he was twenty-six years old, Thomas Lincoln married Nancy Hanks in 1806. They moved to Elizabethtown, where Thomas built a log cabin on property he owned. Their first child, Sarah, was born the following year, followed a year later by Abraham.

In his 1860 autobiography, Lincoln described his family as "undistinguished." Neither Thomas nor Abraham himself had any more than a rudimentary formal education—which was hardly atypical for the time. Though he had purchased land equivalent to three farms, Thomas Lincoln became a victim of the indeterminate surveying methods used in many of the regions west of the mountains. Titles were frequently in error, and sales routinely involved overlapping properties. Like many of the settlers in the region, Lincoln lost title to the property he had purchased. Rather than disputing the issue in court, the Lincolns moved to Indiana.

Two major issues influenced the early settlers to the region and ultimately shaped the thinking of the future president. One was the search for open land. The other was that of slavery. Slaves were owned by relatives or households in the families of both of Lincoln's parents. Little is recorded concerning Thomas and Nancy Lincoln's feelings about slavery, but indirect evidence suggests that both opposed the practice.

White's contribution to the Lincoln story begins with this story of the future president's roots. The biographer attempts to answer questions about Lincoln's interior thoughts and beliefs, such as his true feelings about slavery and African Americans. He also addresses much more personal inner questions, such as Lincoln's feelings about his wife Mary and their marriage. In some respects, White discusses these questions in the context of twenty-first century culture and attitudes.

Dissection of Lincoln's evolving private thoughts is a challenge. His law partner, William Herndon, considered Lincoln "the most . . . shut-mouthed man that ever existed." Mary Lincoln burned much of their correspondence before leaving for Washington. As White points out, however, while Lincoln kept no diary, he did compose and keep a large volume of notes on whatever subject was on his mind at the time. Many of these primary sources were later used by Lincoln's secretary John Hay in the biography he composed following the president's death.

White arguably addresses Lincoln's view of religion in greater depth than do other biographers, discussing both Lincoln's beliefs and the role those beliefs played in shaping his political and personal life. Lincoln invoked religion and God in his most important speeches, including the Gettysburg Address and his second inaugural address. Religion was a portion of what White calls the future president's "intellectual curiosity." Relatively uneducated, at least by modern standards, Lincoln nevertheless read widely—poetry, history, books addressing morality, and the Bible. Anecdotal evidence supports the notion that Lincoln practiced the morality about which he read. A friend of Lincoln, David Turnham, described how Lincoln, while walking home after a full day threshing wheat, encountered a sleeping drunk on the road. Lincoln carried the man to a home, built a fire, and kept the man warm.

The family of the young Abraham Lincoln joined the Little Pigeon Baptist Church in Indiana, though Lincoln himself did not become a member. That he did not was unusual. White's view is that Lincoln's intellectual curiosity instilled a sense of questioning in the young man's mind, including a need to question religious denominations in which he saw rivalry rather than a source of comfort. Lincoln's skepticism of organized religion was likely influenced by his readings of political philosopher Thomas Paine and poet Robert Burns, both of whom attacked either the Church (Paine) or particular teachings (Burns). White describes one occasion on which a paper Lincoln wrote expressing some of his views was thrown into a fire by a friend, presumably to save Lincoln from embarrassment in their small town.

Lincoln's estrangement from any organized church later created problems when he was preparing to marry Mary Todd. The Todd family had members in both the Presbyterian and Episcopal churches; both churches would have been skeptical of Lincoln, who considered himself a deist. Mary later joined the First Presbyterian Church in Springfield, partly in an attempt to reprise the religious experience of her own youth. Her impetus for joining was the comfort provided to her by the church's minister, the Reverend James Smith, following the death of the Lincolns' son Eddie in 1850. Lincoln himself began to attend services on a more regular basis as well. During the final illness of Thomas Lincoln, Abraham's words of comfort to his father reflected the words of consolation he likely heard from the Reverend Smith's sermon following the death of Eddie. The Lincolns continued their membership in the Presbyterian Church after moving to Washington, joining the New York Avenue Presbyterian Church.

White refers to Lincoln's description of a "people's God" in his second inaugural address: "Both [North and South] read the same Bible and pray to the same God, and each invokes His aid against the other." Lincoln's view of God was perhaps best expressed in his farewell address to the people of Springfield as he left for Washington. White points out that 63 of the 152 words Lincoln spoke then described the role of God. White argues that Lincoln believed in a personal God, one who was present at the beginning of the country and who would accompany Lincoln to Washington.

Lincoln's significance as the sixteenth president derives from the two defining events of his political career: his view toward slavery and the African American people and his role as commander in chief during the four bloody years of the Civil War. By modern standards, Lincoln's view toward African Americans was decidedly mixed and certainly reflected the racism of the times. Lincoln repeatedly indicated he did not consider African Americans to be the equals of whites; he even considered the possibility of repatriation of slaves back to Africa. Lincoln's view of slavery, however, was clear, and during his debates with his political rival Stephen Douglas he reiterated the point that, while African Americans might not be his social equals and while he might not approve of an African American as his wife, "in her natural right to eat the bread she earns with her own hands . . . she is my equal, and the equal of all others." One anecdote, likely apocryphal, holds that a young Lincoln, upon observing the treatment of slaves at a Mississippi River dock, stated that if he ever had the opportunity to end the practice he would do so. True or not, the story accurately depicts Lincoln's view toward the practice.

While the causes of the Civil War were complex, the issue of slavery remained the single most important divisive factor between Northerners and Southerners. While Lincoln may have detested slavery, it was also his view that, under the Constitution, he was unable to arbitrarily end the practice. Several books address in detail the evolution of Lincoln's thinking, resulting in emancipation, and White provides a clear overview of that process: Lincoln's original idea was a "compensated emancipation," the idea that owners would receive payment in return for the gradual emancipation of their slaves. The idea failed, both because of the potential cost and because of the policy's social implications. The widening war made the issue largely moot as well.

The Emancipation Proclamation was released following the Battle of Antietam in September, 1862. The timing resulted from the advice of Secretary of State William Seward; emancipation would take effect on January 1, 1863. White addresses the question of exactly which slaves were emancipated, as the edict only affected regions beyond the control of the Union army. Lincoln recognized the consequences of making the highly controversial proclamation a war measure: It would not only spell the beginning of the end for a practice that had divided the country since its birth but also, at least in the minds of some, change the war into one for freedom. It is often overlooked that the Emancipation Proclamation had the additional significance of allowing African Americans to join the military.

Lincoln's role as commander in chief has been discussed in greater detail than in *A. Lincoln* in the numerous books dedicated wholly to that subject. White describes the path Lincoln followed in often vain attempts to find a man capable of leading the Union armies. In an army often dominated by politics, Lincoln's first choice as commander of the Army of the Potomac, General George McClellan, proved highly capable of training an army but woefully inept at actually using it. At times, McClellan seemed more interested in becoming a dictator than in winning the war. Lincoln's patience and his willingness to allow his generals significant leeway has no better example than his dealings with McClellan. In time, however, even Lincoln gave up, replacing each commander who failed to do the job until he found Ulysses S. Grant. Lincoln barely had time to relax following the surrender of Robert E. Lee to Grant in April, 1865, before he was assassinated.

Many excellent authors have covered the highlights of Lincoln's life and presidency. White provides with a view of the man, his private thoughts and beliefs, and the impact of those beliefs on his life.

Richard Adler

Review Sources

American History 44 no. 2 (June, 2009): 69.
Booklist 105 (January 1-15, 2009): 38.
Journal of American History 96, no. 2 (September, 2009): 549-550.
Kirkus Reviews 76, no. 22 (November 15, 2008): 1195.
Library Journal 133, no. 20 (December 1, 2008): 139.
The New York Review of Books 56, no. 14 (September 24, 2009): 58-60.
The Washington Post, February 8, 2009, p. BW03.

THE AGE OF WONDER
How the Romantic Generation Discovered the Beauty and Terror of Science

Author: Richard Holmes (1945-)
Publisher: Pantheon Books (New York). 552 pp. $40.00
Type of work: Biography, history of science
Time: 1769-1840
Locale: Great Britain

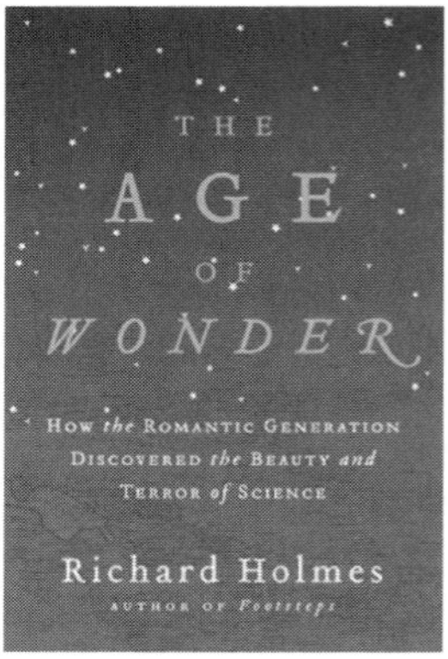

Holmes provides sequential biographies of some of the key figures in British exploration and science during the Romantic period, highlighting their impact on the literature and poetry of the age

Principal personages:

SIR JOSEPH BANKS (1743-1820), early explorer of Tahiti, later president of the Royal Society
GEORGE GORDON, LORD BYRON (1788-1824), poet with a lively interest in science, acquainted with Herschel and Davy
SAMUEL TAYLOR COLERIDGE (1772-1834), poet, essayist, and opium addict
SIR HUMPHREY DAVY (1778-1829), chemist, inventor, and lecturer at the Royal Institution
MICHAEL FARADAY (1791-1867), chemist and physicist, Davy's assistant and successor at the Royal Institution
CAROLINE HERSCHEL (1750-1848), German-born English astronomer, one of the first two women elected to honorary membership in the Royal Society
SIR FREDERICK WILLIAM HERSCHEL (1738-1822), German-born English astronomer and musician
MUNGO PARK (1771-1806), Scottish physician and explorer
MARY SHELLEY (1797-1851), novelist and essayist, known principally as the author of *Frankenstein*
PERCY BYSSHE SHELLEY (1792-1822), her husband, a poet and essayist
SIR BENJAMIN THOMPSON, COUNT RUMFORD (1753-1814), Massachusetts-born English scientist, inventor, and adventurer

Richard Holmes's *The Age of Wonder* examines the late eighteenth and early nineteenth centuries, a time of remarkable discovery and intellectual ferment in Great Britain. Nicolaus Copernicus's *De revolutionibus orbium coelestium* (1453; *On the Revolutions of the Celestial Spheres*, 1939) had already delivered a blow to the human ego, demonstrating that the universe did not literally revolve about humanity. This initial revolutionary insight was developed by subsequent explorers, astronomers, botanists, and physiologists, whose work revealed that the world was vaster, older, and more varied than earlier thinkers might have imagined. Holmes makes a distinction between the first scientific revolution—led by aristocratic scholars who wrote in Latin and, in England, held membership in the Royal Society—and the second scientific revolution, characterized by exploration and open to a broader literate public, including women.

Richard Holmes has written extensively about the Romantic period. His Shelley: The Pursuit *(1974) received the Somerset Maugham Award, while* Coleridge: Darker Reflections *(1998) was a* New York Times Book Review *Editors' Choice.*

According to Holmes, the second scientific revolution, or "age of wonder," falls between 1768, when Captain James Cook began his circumnavigation of the globe on the HMS *Endeavour*, and 1831, when Charles Darwin began his own voyage around the world on HMS *Beagle*. Scientific discoveries of the period helped shape its literature and poetry, which in turn defined the mental and emotional world, as well as the public image, of the "scientist," a term that would be coined a few years later. The personages participating in this revolution are many, and Holmes focuses on two, Sir William Herschel, who with his sister greatly broadened the scope of astronomy, and Sir Humphrey Davy, a physician's apprentice who became one of the most important chemical discoverers and expositors of science to the public.

Tying together much of Holmes's narrative is the career of Sir Joseph Banks, who, as president of the Royal Society from 1778 to 1820, was in a unique position to know about and encourage scientific developments throughout England. The Royal Society—founded in 1662 and enjoying, at least nominally, the patronage of the monarch—was then, as now, the most prestigious scientific society in England. Under Banks, it became the key organization in recognizing and supporting scientific achievement.

Holmes argues that the age of wonder was characterized by a number of interrelated trends. Government, in the person of the monarch, became active in providing financial support and recognition for scientific projects. Working-class individuals found various means of pursuing scientific careers. Training in classical Latin and Greek was no longer indispensible for the natural philosopher. Institutions such as the Royal Institution were established to popularize scientific concepts. Women could make scientific contributions without using pseudonyms, and popular books about science were penned by both male and female authors.

Poets and other writers during this period wrote about scientific developments and often socialized with scientists. Scientists, including the key individuals in Holmes's narrative, often wrote and sometimes published verse and speculative prose themselves. Throughout the age, new ideas on religion were propagated. Some scientists became freethinkers, others remained conventionally religious, and some vacillated between these extremes.

Holmes begins his story with the exploration of Tahiti in 1769 by Banks, who accompanied Cook at his own expense as the *Endeavour*'s botanist. Banks was a classically educated Englishman of independent means who, before his departure, was considered to be the fiancé of Harriet Blosset, a proper young Englishwoman. However, his voyage, and perhaps the relaxed sexual mores of the Tahitians, increased his yearning for adventure to the point that he begged off the engagement on his return, precipitating a scandal.

Scandal notwithstanding, Banks was invited to Windsor in August of 1771 and quickly formed a friendship with his near contemporary, King George III. By 1773, he was in effect the director of the Royal Gardens at Kew and was cohabiting with a young woman named Sarah Wells. In 1778, he was elected president of the Royal Society and began courting an heiress, Dorothea Hugessen, after "tactfully and generously" parting from Wells. The great adventurer Banks suffered recurrent attacks of gout beginning in 1787, eventually becoming chair-bound. His physical incapacity did not limit his enthusiasm for science and discovery, which he encouraged as president of the society for forty years.

One of the first major scientific personalities to emerge during Banks's tenure was William Herschel. A German-born musician, astronomer, and telescope builder, Herschel settled in Bath in 1766 when he obtained the post of organist at Bath Chapel. He was joined by his sister Caroline Herschel in 1772. William's interest in music theory led him to study optics and to build his own telescopes, which eventually surpassed those at the Royal Observatory in Greenwich in quality. William trained Caroline as his assistant, and together they recorded extensive and very precise observations of the night sky. In 1781, William discovered the planet Uranus, the first new planet since ancient times, which he originally proposed to name after George III. He was promptly made a member of the Royal Society, awarded its Copley Medal, and granted a salary as the king's astronomer.

In 1785, Herschel announced plans to build a telescope of unprecedented power, a Newtonian reflector 40 feet long and 5 feet in diameter. One of Banks's signal achievements was persuading King George to fund the entire construction and then provide four years' operating budget. While the big telescope was under construction, Caroline discovered a comet on her own and described it in a letter to the secretary of the Royal Society. The discovery was promptly confirmed at the Royal Observatory, and Caroline's letter was published in the *Philosophical Transactions of the Royal Society*. This rare publication by a woman correspondent confirmed Caroline's standing as an astronomer in her own right and made her something of a celebrity.

Over the course of his highly productive career, Herschel studied distant stars and nebulas, arguing that the nebulas were in fact located far beyond the Milky Way galaxy. This would be confirmed by the telescopic researches of Harlow Shapley and Edwin Hubble in the twentieth century. Herschel also occasionally gave free rein to speculation, proposing in a 1795 paper that the interior of the Sun was cool enough to be inhabited.

Humphrey Davy, a lad from rural Cornwall, began his career as apprentice to physician Thomas Beddoes, who quickly recognized his talent. In 1798, Davy was appointed to the Pneumatic Institute, founded by Beddoes to research and popularize the medicinal uses of gases. There, he discovered the properties of nitrous oxide as an anesthetic and intoxicant. Among the individuals to experience nitrous oxide intoxication were Davy himself and the poets Robert Southey and Samuel Taylor Coleridge, who became close friends. After three highly productive years, Davy took the post of assistant lecturer and director of the chemical laboratory at the Royal Institution, which had recently been founded by Count Rumford. He remained associated with the institution for the rest of his life.

While the Herschels explored the skies and explorers such as Mungo Park turned their attention to South America, Africa, and the South Pacific, a further revolution in chemistry, physiology, and ultimately physics was taking place. The Italian Luigi Galveni discovered biological electricity, and his compatriot Count Alessandro Volta invented the Voltaic pile, or battery. Volta's pile provided the first dependable source of continuous electric current. Davy wasted no time in putting the new technology to use. He chose "Galvanism" as the topic for his inaugural lecture at the Royal Institution and performed some spectacular demonstrations involving sparks and explosions. The demonstrations greatly entertained his audience, which was more aristocratic and included more ladies than had been anticipated.

Davy had become a scientific showman, even a star. Later, he would develop friendships with George Gordon, Lord Byron, Percy Bysshe Shelly, and Mary Shelley. The demonstrations of biological electricity performed under Davy's auspices played a role in inspiring Mary's novel *Frankenstein: Or, The Modern Prometheus* (1818). Michael Fraraday, a young bookbinder's apprentice also attended and was inspired by Davy's lectures. Faraday took very detailed and neat notes, with illustrations, bound them at his place of work, and presented them to Davy as his application for a position.

Davy made Faraday his apprentice, thus beginning one of the most famous and troubled apprenticeships in scientific history. Faraday proved to be a quick study and was soon delivering lectures on his own. He made a number of chemical discoveries and, despite a complete lack of formal training in mathematics, conducted fundamental research in electricity and magnetism. Among Faraday's many discoveries was the law of electromagnetic induction, which allowed the development of the large-scale electric generators upon which the modern energy economy came to be based.

In 1815, Davy was urged by the Coal Mines Safety Committee to look into the problem of the gas, or "fire damp," explosions that took the lives of groups of miners with some regularity. Before the invention of the electric light, miners were dependent on flames for illumination, and the flames from the miners' lamps could ignite methane gas in the mines. Davy and Faraday worked on the problem almost exclusively for three months. They determined the chemical nature of the gas and the critical concentration necessary for an explosion to occur. The eventual result was the Davy safety lamp, a mesh-enclosed flame that could exchange gas with the surrounding atmosphere and burn the methane within the mesh, without ever becoming hot enough on the surface to ignite the gas outside the mesh.

Despite their common working-class origins, Davy and Faraday accepted their success on very different terms. Holmes describes Davy as a persistent flirt who may have had a number of affairs with prominent women before settling into a more conventional marriage. Faraday, by contrast, was a member of the fundamentalist

Sandemanian sect, lived modestly, and would eventually decline Queen Victoria's offer of a knighthood. Davy became a fellow of the Royal Society in 1808 and its president in 1820, succeeding the infirm Sir Joseph Banks. Faraday became a candidate for membership in 1823 but was blackballed by Davy. After several attempts, he was elected in 1824, with Davy casting the only dissenting vote.

Holmes provides extensive appendixes in his volume, including more than seventy short biographies of scientific and literary figures of the period, as well as a detailed bibliography for each chapter. While professional historians of science will already be acquainted with much of his material, this book will be a useful starting point for students and teachers of either the sciences or literature. The twentieth century worked a separation between these two realms of knowledge, as the humanities and the science became institutionally separated as what C. P. Snow would describe in 1959 as "the two cultures." *The Age of Wonder* confirms, however, that the gap between these cultures was often remarkably small during the Romantic period and that it was in fact a modern invention.

Donald R. Franceschetti

Review Sources

Booklist 105, no. 21 (July 1, 2009): 17
Contemporary Review 291, no. 1694 (Autumn, 2009): 398
Economist 392, no. 8639 (July 11, 2009): 86-87
Harper's Magazine 319, no. 1911 (August, 2009): 73-74
Kirkus Reviews 77, no. 11 (June 1, 2009): 593
Library Journal 134, no. 9 (May 15, 2009): 95
New Criterion 28, no. 1 (September, 2009): 66-68
New York Review of Books 56, no. 13 (August 13, 2009): 15-18
The New York Times, July 9, 2009, p. 1.
The New York Times Book Review, July 19, 2009, p. 1.
The New Yorker 85, no. 24 (August 10, 2009): 81.
Publishers Weekly 256, no. 22 (June 1, 2009): 1.
Wilson Quarterly 33, no. 4 (Autumn, 2009): 107-109.

ALL OTHER NIGHTS

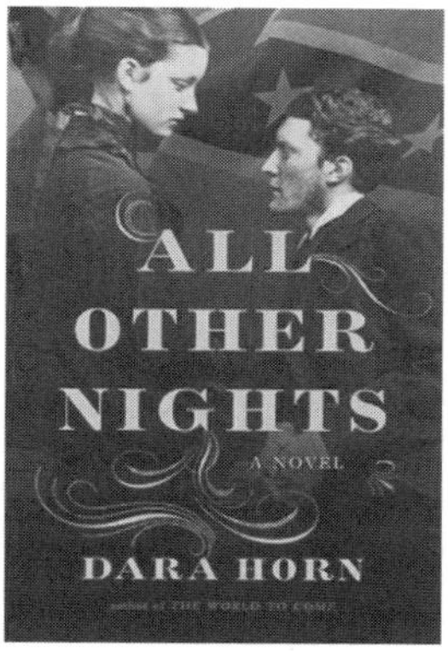

Author: Dara Horn (1977-)
Publisher: W. W. Norton (New York). 363 pp. $24.95
Type of work: Novel
Time: 1861-1865
Locale: New York; New Orleans; New Babylon, Virginia; Holly Springs, Mississippi

This Civil War tale follows the life of a young Jewish American spy as he deals with assignments that ask him to betray those closest to him and that challenge his understanding of his own identity

Principal characters:
JACOB RAPPAPORT, a young Jewish American soldier serving as a spy for the North
CHARLOTTE LEVY, the oldest Levy daughter, who is suspected of being a Rebel spy and who has been engaged numerous times
EUGENIA (JEANNIE) LEVY, the second Levy daughter, whom Jacob is sent to marry because she is suspected of being a spy
PHOEBE LEVY, the third Levy daughter, a talented wood-carver
ROSE LEVY, the youngest Levy daughter, who is skilled in wordplay
PHILIP LEVY, father of the girls who are suspected of being spies
HARRY HYAMS, Jacob's uncle and the instigator of an assassination plot against Lincoln
JUDAH BENJAMIN, second in command of the Confederacy

Jacob Rappaport, the protagonist of *All Other Nights*, has led a privileged life as the son of a wealthy businessman in New York. He has been given everything he needs; however, Jacob's confused relationship with his father has run the gamut from hero worship, to embarrassment, to frustration. In the beginning years of the Civil War, Jacob has begun to recognize that he is no more than a trophy for his father to show off to his business acquaintances. When his father agrees to marry Jacob off to the developmentally handicapped daughter of one of his colleagues, Jacob decides that he must break free. He runs away to join the Union army.

During his first few months serving the Union army, the nineteen-year-old Jacob is called to the office of three prestigious generals. In his youthful conceit, he is convinced he is going to be promoted. Instead, the generals reveal their knowledge of his family connection to Harry Hyams, a Jewish Rebel who is allegedly part of a plot to assassinate Lincoln. They assign Jacob the task of removing this danger to the president and send him to New Orleans to kill his uncle. Jacob struggles with memories of Hyams as a gentle, loving man who seemed to care more for him than his own father had. He has difficulty seeing his uncle as a danger to the country.

Once he reaches New Orleans, hidden in a barrel and dressed as a Rebel soldier,

Dara Horn was chosen as one of the Granta *Best Young American Novelists in 2007. She has also won the the Edward Lewis Wallant Award, the Reform Judaism Prize for Jewish Fiction, and the National Jewish Book Awards' First Time Author Award.*

Jacob goes to his uncle's home and joins in a Passover Seder. Jacob's conflict becomes more complicated when he finds out that Judah Benjamin, the second in command of the Confederacy, plans to join the Hyams family for the ceremonial meal. He wonders if he should poison Benjamin, one of the most powerful figures in the South, rather than his uncle. However, after overhearing his uncle arguing in favor of assassinating Lincoln while Benjamin rejects the plan, Jacob realizes that his uncle is enough of a villain to be a threat to the country, so he takes the opportunity to add poison to Hyams's drink.

Returning to New York, Jacob is admonished by his superiors for killing his uncle rather than Benjamin. Their disregard of his guilt over poisoning a man that he had held in high regard reinforces Jacob's confusion about patriotic duty versus humanity. His ability to follow orders despite the personal cost, however, leads to a second assignment. He is sent to New Babylon, Virginia, to infiltrate the family of Philip Levy, one of his father's business associates. Levy has four daughters, and the oldest two are suspected of spying for the Confederacy. Jacob's assignment is to marry Eugenia, the second daughter.

Upon entering the Levy home, he is immediately confused by the Levy women. The eleven-year-old Rose speaks only in word puzzles. She twists everything she is told or that she wants to communicate into code. Phoebe, a fifteen-year-old, has taken up the scandalous hobby of wood carving. Eugenia (Jeannie), has been a professional actress, performing in front of audiences of hundreds. The oldest daughter, Charlotte (Lottie), has been engaged numerous times, even to several men at the same time, but she has never married.

Despite his bewilderment at the women's behavior, Jacob revels in the family life of the Levys. He infiltrates the heart of the family, gaining the father's trust and helping him run his business. As he thinks he is building Philip's trust, he watches the women closely for evidence of espionage. His failure to discover their plots is relieved only by accident when he finds a coded message revealing his identity as a spy. He destroys the message just before his marriage to Jeannie.

At the wedding ceremony, the Levy family's life changes. William Williams, Jeannie's former beau and fellow spy, threatens to unmask and then kill Jacob. Philip Levy saves Jacob by shooting Williams himself. He is immediately sent to prison. Jacob holds the family together during their father's incarceration and learns several things. First, Jeannie reveals the women's espionage on their wedding night. Then, Philip tells Jacob that he has known all along that Jacob was a spy and has wanted a man who would save Jeannie and her sisters from the dangers of spying. Shortly after Philip's incarceration, Charlotte discovers Jacob's identity and turns him in to the authorities, so he must flee for his life.

Desperate to keep Jeannie safe, Jacob reports that Charlotte is the spy when he returns to the Union generals. His efforts result in the arrest of Charlotte and Jeannie and the disappearance of Phoebe and Rose. Immune to his protestations of Jeannie's innocence, the generals send Jacob to Mississippi, where he will be away from notice. On his way to the new post, Jacob reads a news article that reports the death of his wife. He withdraws emotionally, functioning only as needed to survive. He is overwhelmed with guilt at his role in delivering the woman he loved into the prison where she died. Meanwhile, Jacob's assignment in Mississippi ends when he almost dies in an explosion. He is disfigured in both face and body and sent home to his parents to die. Upon recovering enough to function, he resumes a role in his father's firm.

A period begins in Jacob's life when he is forced to mature. He reconnects with Philip Levy, who reveals that Jeannie is alive. He implores Jacob to find his daughters and give them a message. Ironically, this plea coincides with another undercover assignment from the generals. Jacob is sent back to the South with orders to infiltrate Judah Benjamin's office. He does this with some ease and takes the role of a trusted clerk to Benjamin. He serves until the night Benjamin and other Confederate officials flee Richmond on the eve of the war's end.

Jacob discovers Jeannie's location and is reunited with her in a scene that is almost anticlimactic. He has become deserving of Jeannie partly because he is now physically inferior to her, as he has always been emotionally and intellectually inferior. The impending end of the war further frees Jacob from the need to make any true decisions.

Dara Horn delves into the realm of feminism in history, as she models the Levy sisters after a number of female spies from the Civil War. The novel's limited omniscient narrative focus on Jacob, however, somewhat restricts the impact of the women's lives and sacrifices. Because Jacob's previous relationships with women have been limited to those with his mother, his aunt, and his handicapped fiancé—women who were submissive to the men in their lives—Jacob's expectations of a woman's place reinforce a patriarchal mind-set. This is changed only marginally as Jacob is immediately confronted with four independent, strong, thinking women upon reaching the Levy home. Jacob is sure the young Levy women are insane. His opinion begins to evolve as he lives with the family and falls in love with Jeannie.

The issue of slavery is a central theme in this novel about the Civil War. Though a Union soldier, Jacob does not have strong views against slavery when he enters the Army. He is first confronted with hatred from slaves in his uncle's home, where the slaves are insubordinate and where one slave observes him adding the poison to his uncle's drink but does not interfere. Life with the Levy daughters, whose mother was shot by a slave, further complicates his opinions of the institution.

Philip Levy's willingness to rescue a slave who is imprisoned with him confounds Jacob until he meets the man and purchases his freedom at Philip's urging. This slave, ironically, saves Jacob's life by providing him with safe passage back to the North when Charlotte reveals his identity to the authorities. Later in the novel, Jacob recognizes the intelligence of slaves when he becomes Judah Benjamin's aide.

One of the most striking aspects of the novel is the revelation of the Jewish American involvement in the Civil War. Jacob's religious heritage is a key element in his ability to infiltrate the South. Among other connections, he realizes the irony of the

Passover recitation—which celebrates the release of the Jews from their enslavement in Egypt—as he plots to kill his uncle. Further, he is able to connect with Judah Benjamin because Benjamin recognizes him as a fellow Jew.

The novel meanders, sometimes slowly, through a period of four years and often includes superficial characters. Readers follow Jacob from immature conceit; to depressed maturity, after he reads the false report of Jeannie's death; to scarred hero, after he is trapped in an exploding building. Despire the narrative's focus on Jacob, his motivations seem superficial throughout. He spies because he is told to do so. Though he loves Jeannie, he marries because he was ordered to do so. He learns that slaves are human because Philip Levy is able to forgive and ask for another man's freedom. He even searches for his wife because his father-in-law implores him to find his daughters. Jacob rarely takes initiative to do anything for himself.

Jeannie's personality is equally frustrating at points. When readers first meet her, she is outspoken, flirtatious, and brave. She is seemingly an active part of a spy ring involving all three of her sisters. She performs publicly in theaters and the homes of the wealthy. However, at the end of the novel, she disappoints by returning to Jacob with the excuse that her previous actions had only been a result of her sister's influence. Though she had been an important part of the Confederate war effort, she confesses that the war had never been her driving force.

Theresa L. Stowell

Review Sources

Booklist 105, no. 16 (April 15, 2009): 29.
Kirkus Reviews 77, no. 5 (March 1, 2009): 42.
Library Journal 134, no. 6 (April 1, 2009): 70.
Los Angeles Times, April 12, 2009, p. 7.
National Post 11 (May 16, 2009): WP13.
Publishers Weekly 256, no. 5 (February 2, 2009): 29.
Wall Street Journal, April 4, 2009, p. W8.
Washington Post, April 14, 2009, p. C06

AMERICAN RADICAL
The Life and Times of I. F. Stone

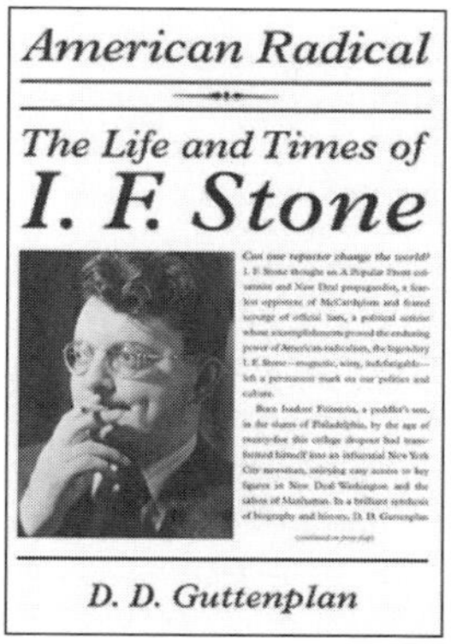

Author: D. D. Guttenplan (1957-   )
Publisher: Farrar, Straus and Giroux (New York). 570 pp. $35.00
Type of work: Biography
Time: 1907-1989
Locale: United States

An intellectual biography of American political journalist I. F. Stone, with emphasis on the broader political contexts that shaped Stone's work and legacy as an independent radical reporter

Principal personages:
I. F. STONE, independent radical journalist
ESTHER ROISMAN STONE, his wife
J. EDGAR HOOVER (1895-1972), director of the Federal Bureau of Investigation, 1935-1972
JOSEPH MCCARTHY (1908-1957), U.S. senator from Wisconsin, 1947-1957
FRANKLIN D. ROOSEVELT (1882-1945), U.S. president, 1933-1945

As a skilled journalist writing political biography, D. D. Guttenplan uses *American Radical: The Life and Times of I. F. Stone* to advance his own arguments, which are aimed squarely at the present day. He sees a critical press as essential to healthy democracy, while independent journalism is perpetually endangered by the machinations and obfuscations of entrenched political power. I. F. Stone's life and work as an American political thinker and iconoclastic journalist demonstrate for Guttenplan "the compatibility of [Stone's] beloved Jefferson and his equally beloved Marx," and he seeks through this biography to show that an extended study of one remarkable life can illuminate the tensions inherent in history while sparking fresh political insight and the energy for democratic political action.

Guttenplan does not argue that the legacies of Thomas Jefferson (1743-1826), philosopher of the American Revolution, and Karl Marx (1818-1883), philosopher of socialism, coexist easily in either the history of the United States or the life of I. F. Stone, nor does he ignore the deeply contradictory historical trajectories of these legacies. He does, however, show that Stone's life and work demonstrate that it was, and remains, possible in the United States to fuse and nurture the best elements of both political traditions while standing up to challenge the worst historical developments evolving out of each. *American Radical* is not only a meticulously detailed analysis of an exemplary twentieth century life but also a book seriously engaged with political realities of the twenty-first century. A cover-to-cover reading will reward a variety of readers holding an extremely wide range of political perspectives.

D. D. Guttenplan writes regularly for the Nation, *as well as various magazines and journals in the United States and Europe. Guttenplan is the author of* The Holocaust on Trial *(2002). He received a doctorate in history from the University of London.*

I. F. Stone was born Isadore Feinstein in 1907 to Jewish immigrant parents whose struggles with pressures to assimilate shaped Stone's lifelong stance as an essentially skeptical and "outsider" social critic. Guttenplan's sketch of Stone's childhood shows clearly the formation of this future reporter's critical interpretive lens, while highlighting the Yiddish cultural atmosphere of Stone's upbringing and his precocious early passion for books, ideas, writing, and left-oriented politics. Guttenplan very effectively draws out key formative moments for Stone's life within the broader historical context of early twentieth century American culture and politics.

Stone's lifelong critical engagement with the American and international left is described in extended detail throughout the book, which not only relates that engagement to his work as a political journalist but also forcefully argues that Stone is best understood, not primarily as an iconic journalist, but rather in broader terms as a political thinker, writer, and activist. For decades, Stone worked with, argued with, and criticized his political allies and opponents across the spectrum of American and international politics. He worked on and wrote about issues related to labor organizing, economics, the Great Depression, the New Deal, the Popular Front, World War II, the Korean War, African American civil rights, the formation of Israel, the resulting displacement of Palestinians, the Vietnam War, and the New Left.

One of Guttenplan's several significant journalistic accomplishments in *American Radical*, in addition to his own exhaustive archival research, is represented in the collection of interviews he conducted for the book. The list of his interviewees presents a fascinating portrait of twentieth century intellectual history. It includes thinkers as diverse as Isaiah Berlin, Murray Kempton, Victor Navasky, Arthur Schlesinger, Jr., Clancy Sigal, Paul Sweezy, Edward Said, and Andrew Kopkind.

Guttenplan spends considerable narrative time analyzing two key dimensions of Stone's political involvement. First, he places Stone's writing and activism in relation to left politics generally to Stone's evolution more specifically as an American radical responding to the Soviet Union, the Popular Front against international fascism, and American communism. Second, Guttenplan catalogs Stone's ferocious and lifelong defense of civil liberties in opposition to efforts by the U.S. government to suppress free speech, especially the free speech and free press of those Americans on the Left or liberal-left.

Stone was a democratic socialist for most of his life, and, like many on the American left, his assessment of the Soviet Union and especially of Stalin and later the Cuban Revolution vacillated between early optimistic support and later full-scale critical condemnation. As Guttenplan extensively documents, Stone was right in the middle of key political conflicts and shifts among American leftists from the 1930's until his death in 1989, and much of the persisting controversy about Stone's career and legacy has swirled around his participation in a host of political activities in addition to his writing.

As *American Radical* makes clear, what is less debated and utterly consistent is Stone's long advocacy for civil liberties. During the 1940's and 1950's, he resisted directly investigations launched by the House Committee on Un-American Activities and the persecutions of leftist and left-leaning American citizens by Senator Joseph McCarthy and others, as well as ongoing efforts by Federal Bureau of Investigation (FBI) director J. Edgar Hoover to harass activists on the left and in the labor and Civil Rights movements. Even when Stone sharply criticized the Communist Party and dismissed American incarnations of Marxism-Leninism and Stalinism, he defended the First Amendment freedoms of communist activists and writers. In the wake of his lost confidence in the Soviet Union and the Cuban Revolution, Stone did not abandon his commitment to socialism in democratic forms. In fact, his life serves as a reminder of the long existence of a democratic left in the United States.

American Radical places Stone's journalism squarely within these political crosscurrents related to free speech, political dissent, and democratic criticism of government. The biography charts the intellectual context and evolution of Stone's writing, from his early years writing for smaller independent political papers to his work on the *New York Post*, *PM*, the *Nation*, the *New York Review of Books*, and especially his own paper, *I. F. Stone's Weekly*, which Stone published from 1953 to 1971. Guttenplan extensively documents Stone's well-known willingness to question official versions of events, to track down documents in obscure files, and to criticize openly players across the political spectrum. Guttenplan's account of Stone's seemingly indefatigable labors on behalf of democratic dissent creates an implicit argument for the continued importance of such work.

Indeed, a key strength (and occasional weakness) of *American Radical* is Guttenplan's truly impressive detailing of historical context, events, people, and issues related to Stone's life and work. There are moments in the book where detail derails the focus a bit too much, and readers may return from an extended digression a bit weary from too much tangential information. Most of the time, however, Guttenplan's meticulous detail builds the book as an exemplary intellectual biography, with all the depth and historical illumination possible in the best of the genre. In many sections, readers are happily rewarded for their patient attention with glimpses of American historical events that are too often forgotten.

For example, Guttenplan links the landmark Supreme Court desegregation case *Brown v. Board of Education* (1954) with an account of activist educator Myles Horton being hauled out of Senator John Eastland's anticommunist hearings in New Orleans in 1954. Horton, a Christian socialist who had studied at Union Theological Seminary in New York City, was also a founder of the Highlander Folk School in Tennessee, which also became a target of FBI harassment. The Highlander Folk School was started in 1932 as a community school for labor organizers, but it was also a place where Rosa Parks, Martin Luther King, Jr., and other civil rights activists received training in nonviolent activism prior to their more public careers. Through a short narrative interlude drawing the links between these people, places, and events, Guttenplan also illuminates the links in American history between labor and civil rights organizing, while reminding readers of the twin perils of suppressed free speech and repressed civil liberties.

A second strength of *American Radical* is Guttenplan's effective rhetorical engagement with contemporary American political life, which he accomplishes by framing particular episodes in Stone's life in ways that are suggestive of persisting issues and problems facing citizens and journalists in twenty-first century democracies. This rhetorical use of Stone's biography is especially evident as Guttenplan analyzes Stone's journalistic work related to the Korean and Vietnam wars. In these sections, Guttenplan highlights Stone's indictment of coopted journalism, his impatience with failed Democratic Party liberalism and political quietism among American citizens, and his repeated warnings about the potentially catastrophic consequences of these failures for American civil liberties at home and foreign policy abroad.

In his chapter "An American Tragedy," Guttenplan foregrounds Stone's persistent investigative dismantling of official deception related to American military intervention in Vietnam. He offers this account from *I. F. Stone's Weekly*, written after Stone's visit to Saigon in 1966:

> To watch the young Ivy Leaguers arriving briskly at the Embassy of a morning is to feel oneself on the eve of the Harvard-Yale game. The team spirit is bursting out all over; it demands optimism; patriotism is equated with euphoria . . . Under the supposed benevolence of our policy one soon detects a deep animosity to the Vietnamese and a vast arrogance. We assume the right to remold them, whether they choose to be remolded or not.
>
> It is significant that those like Gen. Lansdale and Colonel John Paul Vann who would approach the Vietnamese as people soon find themselves sidetracked, suspect and frustrated. The machine instinctively reacts against the human, and what we are running, or what is running us, is a bureaucratic war machine.

Guttenplan introduces the quote with this phrasing: "[Stone] evoked, unforgettably, the tone of empire, American-style." Readers of *American Radical* who have also read dissenting journalistic accounts of the 2003 U.S-led invasion and occupation of Iraq or who have read books such as *Imperial Life in the Emerald City: Inside Iraq's Green Zone*, by Rajiv Chandrasekaran (2007), will find themselves invited via Guttenplan's prose to translate Stone's language across time and place, to more recent wars and their tragic landscapes.

American Radical has been extensively reviewed and will continue to draw political interest as the legacy of Stone's work is debated by new generations of readers and journalists. The lingering controversy over Stone's alleged but unproven link to Soviet agents has distracted some reviewers from the sweep of Stone's life. Guttenplan offers a fair and duly considered discussion of that controversy toward the end of *American Radical* and argues that it would matter very much to have final resolution to the question of Stone's integrity and honesty.

> The attacks on Stone help to remind us not just of what he was, but of what he represented—an independent radical who kept hold of his ideals, and kept faith with his comrades, without renouncing his freedom to speak his mind. Destroy that credibility, and you have destroyed more than a man, more than a reputation. But grant his credibility—grant him the compatibility of his beloved Jefferson and his equally beloved Marx—and I. F. Stone remains, even in death, a dangerous man.

It seems clear that after such a lengthy exploration of Stone's life as that of an exemplary independent radical—and given that he ends *American Radical* with an explicit call for a revitalized, critically independent, and activist public—Guttenplan is himself convinced of Stone's integrity. While not ignoring the contradictions and controversies of the past, *American Radical* is rhetorically pitched to the present and future, concluding with the suggestive argument that it would be wise to follow Stone into the better legacies of both Jefferson and Marx.

Sharon Carson

Review Sources

Columbia Journalism Review 48, no. 2 (July/August, 2009): 60-61.
The Economist 391, no.8631 (May 16, 2009): 90.
The New York Review of Books 56, no. 14 (September 24, 2009): 79-82.
The New York Times, July 5, 2009, p.BR12.
The New York Times, July 10, 2009, p.C26.
The New York Times Book Review, July 12, 2009, p. 18.
Publishers Weekly 256, no. 12 (March 23, 2009): 53.
Village Voice, June 2, 2009, p. 32.
The Wall Street Journal 253, no. 125 (May 30, 2009): W8.

ANGELS AND AGES
A Short Book About Darwin, Lincoln, and Modern Life

Author: Adam Gopnik (1956-)
Publisher: Alfred A. Knopf (New York). 211 pp. $24.95
Type of work: Biography, history
Time: 1809-1882
Locale: England; United States

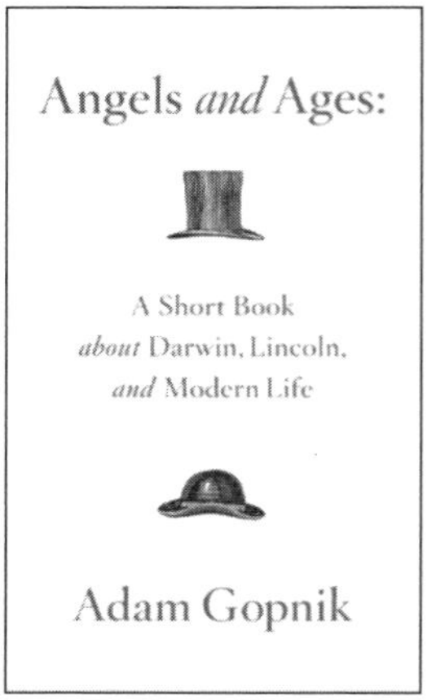

This study of the nineteenth century reveals significant and surprising parallels between the lives of English biologist Charles Darwin and U.S. president Abraham Lincoln

Principal personages:
CHARLES DARWIN, English biologist and theorist of evolution
EMMA WEDGWOOD DARWIN, his wife
ANNIE, Darwin's second child and his favorite
ABRAHAM LINCOLN, president of the United States
WILLIE, Lincoln's favorite child
EDWIN STANTON, Lincoln's friend and secretary of war

Most readers of *Angels and Ages* will recognize Charles Darwin and Abraham Lincoln as two of the great men of the nineteenth century, a century that produced many great men. Darwin posited a theory of evolution. Lincoln, his contemporary, served as president of the United States during the Civil War and in 1862 issued the Emancipation Proclamation. Few readers, however, would have thought to compare these two men. Adam Gopnik does, however, with significant results. The comparison begins with the fact that both were born on the same day, February 12, 1809. This observation might have seemed to be a gimmick if made by another writer, but it does not in Gopnik's hands.

Darwin grew up in the beautiful county of Shropshire in western England. He was a conventional-appearing man from a well-to-do and intellectually prominent family; his grandfathers were the biologist and poet Erasmus Darwin and the potter and liberal advocate Josiah Wedgewood. Gopnik stresses that, besides becoming well-read in biology, geology, and poetry, Darwin's peculiar strength was to look at things—especially living things—with great intensity and sensitivity. He compares Darwin's powers of close observation to those of John Ruskin in *The Stones of Venice* (1851-1853).

In addition to Darwin's powers of observation, Gopnik argues, the biologist had an ability that many good observers lack: He was able to think productively about what he saw. He concluded that the old view, that God created everything at once, was false, and he replaced it with a theory by which elementary life-forms developed over time by adapting to new circumstances. Those forms that did not adapt perished. Those that did adapt lived on. This portion of his theory Darwin called "natural selection." Darwin's evolutionary theory pointed to no moral or spiritual force or plan driving life's development. God was not mentioned.

Adam Gopnik has been a New Yorker *writer since 1986. In 1995, he became the magazine's Paris correspondent. His essays from Paris were collected as* Paris to the Moon *(2000). He has written a children's novel,* The King in the Window *(2005).*

After his trip to the Galapagos to study various species, Darwin was silent for many years, perhaps thinking that the world was not ready for his revelations. Perhaps he did not want to offend his very religious wife Emma. (In the end, Emma read what he wrote and made helpful comments.) In these years and later, Darwin was not idle. He theorized that adaptation was made possible by living organs changing their functions, as when the bladders of fish become the lungs of mammals. He continued his scientific research.

Darwin performed this research, not in the Pacific, but in his own backyard, at his house just southeast of London, where he studied worms. In *The Formation of Vegetable Mould, Through the Action of Worms, with Observations on Their Habits* (1881), Darwin wrote:

> Worms have played a more important part in the history of the world than most persons would at first suppose. . . . When we behold a wide, turf-covered expanse, we should remember that its smoothness . . . is mainly due to all the inequalities having been slowly leveled by worms. . . . It may be doubted whether there are many other animals that have played so important a part in the history of the world as have these lowly organized creatures.

Darwin knew there would be great resistance to his idea. As Gopnik puts it, "There isn't a special providence in the fall of a sparrow, but try telling that to the sparrows."

Darwin was so great a scientist that he knew his theory was not final. It did not yet account adequately for intermediate species, as he had found no evidence of slow mutations between primitive and advanced organisms. In his writing, he tried to give conflicting theories their due by summarizing them as sympathetically as he could and by inviting discussion. He was also limited by the fact that deoxyribonucleic acid (DNA) had not yet been discovered; he could not figure out how traits were inherited.

An important aspect of Gopnik's thesis concerns prose style. Darwin and Lincoln both instinctively departed from the rather formal language of those who wrote earlier in the century, to write in less florid and sparer styles. Darwin chose to write, not in the accepted polysyllabic professional style, but in a style that any literate person could read. He could inspire and argue as well. He particularized everything and allowed his generalizations to rise from the details. What was more, he was a gifted storyteller, much like the great Victorian novelists, such as his friend George Eliot. Thus, he helped form a prose style for the modern democratic and liberal age.

In assessing Darwin's achievement, Gopnik thinks that the theory of natural selection would have emerged soon even if Darwin had not proposed it. Because Darwin's style made his ideas understandable and because he told the story of these ideas so dramatically, however, he allowed the theory of evolution to be accepted must faster than it might otherwise have been.

Gopnik's treatment of Lincoln develops from his title. When Lincoln died in a small room across from Ford's Theater, his friend and secretary of war Edwin Stanton made a remark that has been variously recorded as either "Now he belongs to the ages" or "Now he belongs to the angels." In other words, now Lincoln will be part of history—or part of God's heaven.

Gopnik details many telling parallels between Lincoln's and Darwin's life. Unlike Darwin, Lincoln was American and was famously born into poverty in a log cabin in Kentucky. He trained himself in the law. He rose to prominence as a lawyer and then as a legislator. He married a woman who was much higher socially than he was. Like Darwin, he knew great sadness: His favorite son Willie, like Darwin's favorite daughter Annie, died young. Both Lincoln and Darwin were opposed to slavery, but Lincoln had to contend with John Brown. Brown's code of action was Southern, nearly feudal in its concern for revenge and honor.

Gopnik argues that Lincoln was driven by what he knew best: He had a passion for law. He was against war and violence, but when the law, the federal union, was violated, he responded with force. He did not sign the Emancipation Proclamation because slavery was illegal (it was legal in many states) but because secession went against the law. To die in battle, for Lincoln, was not to die in an aristocratic game, but rather in an act of sacrifice. Darwin's universe had no God. For Lincoln, God was not the God of justice and mercy but the fierce God of the Old Testament. (Gopnik is very interesting on how new secular customs regarding the treatment of the dead evolved during the Civil War. These customs sought to ennoble the actions of the fallen. Black clothes were emphasized, and embalming was developed.)

Like Darwin, Lincoln wrote in a new prose style. Unlike earlier writers such as Ralph Waldo Emerson and Henry David Thoreau, Lincoln employed a style that was plain, moving to monosyllables. Gopnik uses as an example of this monosyllabic tendency The Gettysburg Address: "the world will little note . . . what we say here . . . " This address was lampooned—probably because its brevity and its style offended the president's old-fashioned critics. Earlier, Lincoln had defeated Stephen Douglas in debate, partly because his spare style was appealing to a democratic audience, whereas Douglas's oratory was heightened in the traditional fashion.

Lincoln's style differed from Darwin's. Lincoln was influenced by the Bible, Mark Twain, and William Shakespeare. Like Harry Truman almost a century later, he was fascinated by the toxic effects of ambition as dramatized in Claudius, the fratricidal usurper in Shakespeare's *Hamlet, Prince of Denmark* (pr. c. 1600-1601, pb. 1603). Claudius reflects on murdering his brother and asks "May one be pardoned and retain th' offence?" Claudius was clear-sighted enough to understand that one could not.

Lincoln's effect on his world was immense. Gopnik considers what might have happened if he had not been assassinated. For one thing, the postwar Reconstruction would likely have been much different. The freed slaves might not have been forced to become essentially serfs. Restrictive laws might not have been passed. As it was, Lincoln's death froze him in time. His transformation into a saint of liberty was due in part to the fact that he was cut down in midlife. The effects of Lincoln's memory, functioning as a symbol of liberty, were not as potent in the United States as they were in Europe. In Great Britain, the symbol of Lincoln's martyrdom to liberty helped pass the Reform Bill of 1867; in France, it helped shape events following the fall of the Second Empire, as the French sought to determine the best form of government to replace that instituted by Napoleon III.

Angels and Ages is a brilliant book. It explains the cultural history of the nineteenth century in an original and persuasive way. One paragraph of Gopnik's contains as many arresting and compelling ideas as a whole chapter of most books of this kind. Moreover, Gopnik succeeds in doing what literary criticism often tries to do, but fails: he shows how ideas are intricately tied to the styles in which they are expressed. He also demonstrates that—in the case of his two stylists—both their ideas and their style point ahead to the modern era.

Gopnik practices what he preaches. His own style is lucid and forceful. He regularly backs up his points with specific examples. Perhaps his most moving passage is the one connecting Lincoln's idea of liberty to events in France later in the century. Gopnik writes that "The Statue of Liberty, though it has been incorporated into our history of immigration, stands in New York Harbor as a testament from one free country to another that liberty, after two thousand years, really does light the harbor. When we look at it, we should see our grandparents arriving. But we should think of Lincoln too." Not many history books end like that.

George Soule

Review Sources

Booklist 105, no. 8 (December 15, 2008): 4.
Kirkus Reviews 76, no. 23 (December 1, 2008): 1241.
Library Journal 134, no. 1 (January 1, 2009): 99.
New Scientist 201, no. 2694 (February 7, 2009): 49.
The New York Times Book Review, February 1, 2009, p. 11.
Publishers Weekly 255, no. 46 (November 17, 2008): 54-55.
Wired 17, no. 1 (January, 2009): 64.

THE ANTELOPE'S STRATEGY
Living in Rwanda After the Genocide

Author: Jean Hatzfeld (1949-)
First published: La Stratégie des antilopes, 2007, in France
Translated from the French by Linda Coverdale
Publisher: Farrar, Straus and Giroux (New York). 242 pp. $25.00
Type of work: Current affairs, ethics, history

Hatzfeld's third book about the 1994 Rwandan genocide uses testimony from Tutsi survivors and Hutu perpetrators to assess how they are coping with the devastation that both links and divides them

Principal personages:
EUGÉNIE KAYIERERE, Rwandan genocide survior
JEAN HATZFELD, documenter of the genocide and its aftermath
INNOCENT RWILILIZA, another survivor, Hatzfeld's friend and interpreter
IGNACE RUKIRAMACUMU, one of the perpetrators of the genocide whom Hatzfeld interviews

No crime is more human or inhumane than genocide, the intended destruction of one national, ethnic, racial, or religious group by another. Other creatures do not make and enact such catastrophic plans. In particular, genocide is alien to the fleet-footed and vulnerable antelopes that are widespread in Africa. Nevertheless, it becomes clear that *The Antelope's Strategy* is an apt title for Jean Hatzfeld's latest report about Rwandan life after the 1994 genocide.

Hatzfeld's chapter "Forest Exploits" focuses on Eugénie Kayierere, who "gave the most prodigious athletic performance" ever known to him. This performance took place not in a sporting event but in a five-week run for her life in the Kayumba Forest during April and May of 1994. Kayumba Forest stands on the hills above Nyamata, a town about twenty miles south of Kigali, the Rwandan capital. In 1994, the Nyamata district was a Tutsi-dominated region in the small, predominantly Christian country—the most densely populated in Africa—whose people numbered approximately eight million. Some 85 percent of the population was Hutu.

Systematic killing of Tutsis began in Nyamata on April 11, after Juvénal Habyarimana, the Hutu president of Rwanda, was assassinated in a missile strike against his airplane. The identity of the strike's perpetrators is still under dispute. However, the April 6 attack inflamed preexisting ethnic prejudices and violence, as the extremist Hutu leadership feared that a Tutsi takeover was imminent. Thus, Hutu troops, supported by militias known as *interahamwe* ("those who attack together") and soon augmented by large numbers of local Hutu men, unleashed a planned—and in their eyes justifiable—slaughter of the Tutsi people, whom Hutu propaganda dehumanized as "cockroaches."

Born in Madagascar, the son of Jews who fled the Holocaust, Jean Hatzfeld is a journalist and prize-winning author who concentrates on upheavals in Eastern Europe, the Middle East, and Africa. He is best known for his accounts of the 1994 genocide in Rwanda, featuring testimony from the survivors and perpetrators of that crime.

Genocide engulfed the Nyamata district, as frenzied massacres left fifty thousand Tutsis dead. Five of every six Tutsis in the region were murdered, including five thousand who were killed in or around Nyamata's main church and an equal number who met the same fate in another church at nearby Ntarama. By May 12, the genocide in Nyamata was over, as Hutus fled from the troops of the Rwandan Patriotic Front (RPF), who returned from exile to take control of the country. The RPF arrived too late, however, to prevent the national death toll from reaching 800,000. Nearly all of the dead, including moderate Hutus and about one-third of Rwanda's eighty thousand Twa (commonly known as Pygmies), were butchered by machetes wielded by tens of thousands of Hutus.

Two of Hatzfeld's earlier books documented this history. Concentrating on the Nyamata district, *Dans le nu de la vie: Récits des marais rwandais* (2000; *Into the Quick of Life: The Rwandan Genocide—The Survivors Speak*, 2005; better known as *Life Laid Bare: The Survivors in Rwanda Speak*, 2006) presented testimony by Tutsi survivors. *Saison de machettes* (2003; *Machete Season: The Killers in Rwanda Speak*, 2005; also as *A Time for Machetes—The Rwandan Genocide: The Killers Speak*) was Hatzfeld's stunning account of ten Hutu men from the Nyamata area—friends and neighbors, mostly in their twenties and thirties—who became machete-wielding killers, hunting their Tutsi prey day after day in the marshes and hills and profiting from the loot that mass murder brought them.

Eventually captured, tried, and imprisoned in the penitentiary in Rilima, not far from their homes, these killers spoke with Hatzfeld freely, if not always honestly. They anticipated neither release from their sentences nor further recriminations resulting from the testimony they gave him. In early January, 2003, however, President Paul Kagame decreed that thousands of perpetrators whose confessions had been accepted and who had served at least half of their prison sentences would be released from captivity. By early May, most of Hatzfeld's interview cohort was home again. Throughout Rwanda, known perpetrators and survivors of their onslaughts had to live together. Hatzfeld felt compelled to return to Rwanda, reestablish contact with friends and acquaintances in the Nyamata district, and document how the Hutu-Tutsi encounters were unfolding in the genocide's aftermath. Those decisions led him to tell Eugénie Kayierere's story, a vital part of his book's message according to Hatzfeld, and to reflect on the antelope's strategy.

Hatzfeld notes that his earlier books scarcely mentioned the killings in Nyamata's hilltop forests, sparse with "thorny shrubs and stunted eucalyptus trees." Unlike the thick marshes in Nyamata's lowlands, Rwandan hilltop forests such as the one at Kayumba lack hiding places. Hatzfeld estimates that equal numbers of Nyamata's Tutsis fled to the marshes and to the forests to escape their Hutu predators. However, those who survived in the slime and muck of the swamps far outnumbered the few who escaped the Hutu killers in the forested hills. Hatzfeld thinks that only "twenty people out of six thousand survived the hunting expeditions in the Kayumba Forest." One was Innocent Rwililiza, who became Hatzfeld's trusted interpreter and close friend. Two others, the only women among them as far as Hatzfeld knows, were Eugénie Kayierere and Médiatrice, "then a desperate little eleven-year-old who sneaked back down the hill after twelve days to lose herself amid the Hutu population of Nyamata."

When the killings began in the Nyamata district, Eugénie and her husband ran for their lives but lost each other in the panic. Surrounded by *interahamwe*, Eugénie and some of her neighbors hid in the bush for four days, not moving even to relieve themselves. On the move at night, they reached the forest, where thousands of Tutsis sought refuge. Hutus had carried out pogroms against Tutsis before. Some Tutsis thought that the violence soon would subside, making it possible for them to return home. Their hopes proved too optimistic.

For five weeks, a lethal routine brought Hutu hunters—sometimes two thousand of them—to the forest at 9:00 each morning. Tutsis who had not been "cut" by 4:00 in the afternoon might live another day, but staying alive required outrunning the killers. As Innocent put it, "We ran for about six hours during the day. Some days threatened more than others, but never, never, was there a day without an attack."

Chances for survival were minimal at best and nonexistent for the elderly, young children, and mothers with babies. These chances depended not only on stamina and speed but also on sticking together with those who knew the terrain or tactics that might confuse the hunters. "You had to latch onto a gang that kept up its morale," says Eugénie, but "when the killers seemed to be upon us, we'd scatter in all directions to give everyone a chance: basically, we adopted the antelope's strategy." (A variation on this strategy was also employed in Rwanda's marshes, in imitation of antelopes called *sitatungas* that may elude danger because they are able to run fast in the muck or submerge themselves in the swamp water.)

Eugénie recalls "the hiss of the machetes swiping at your back." She thinks she escaped more by luck than by strategy or speed. One day, she recalls, "I was trapped by a neighbor I'd known for a long time. Our eyes locked so suddenly that his first blow missed me, and I ran off." Another time, when she ran from 9:00 A.M. to 3:00 P.M.—"sprinting, dodging, leaping"—her group started with one hundred members and ended with thirty survivors. "We knew we were racing toward death," she adds, "but we wanted to dodge through life for as long as possible."

Hatzfeld takes the title of his book from Eugénie's comment about the antelope's strategy and calls her story vital to his message. He neither emphasizes nor discounts that her narrative contains elements of a "happy ending." Eugénie survived the genocide, found her husband alive, established a popular cabaret filled nightly with folks drinking *urwagwa* (banana beer), and gave birth to the first of her six children only ten months after returning from the forest. With those children at the center of her attention, she says that "the genocide simplified happiness for me."

Eugénie does not forget the genocide's brutality or the people who were "chopped up so viciously." She thinks it dishonors and humiliates the dead to give "details about how they were stripped naked or cut short, how they dragged themselves along, how they pleaded for mercy, how they screamed or groaned or vomited or bled." Without her saying so, however, such details afflict her "simplified happiness," a point crucial to Hatzfeld's message and to the antelope's strategy in post-genocide Rwanda.

Neither the antelope's strategy nor the book's message brims with hope about reconciliation, justice, or trust—three of the most challenging themes threaded through the book. Government policy, international influence, and everyday necessities in post-genocide Rwanda suppress Tutsi desires for revenge and Hutu regrets that the genocide was incomplete. Hatzfeld finds Tutsis and Hutus living and working together, even to some extent socializing and worshiping together. This civility is not superficial, for Tutsis and Hutus need each other to sustain a viable economy in Rwanda, but relationships and respect between Tutsis and Hutus do not yet run deep enough to assuage the grief and grievances that linger and fester after all that happened in Rwanda's swamps, forests, and other slaughter sites.

The *gaçaça* proceedings, which in Nyamata began on Thursday mornings in 2002, seem to be an exception to this rule. *Gaçaça*, meaning "soft grass," refers to the locations where tribal people's courts sat for centuries until they were largely supplanted by colonial courtrooms. When the genocide left Rwanda's justice system in ruins, the government reinstituted *gaçaça* deliberations, hoping that their organized encounters between perpetrators and survivors would advance accountability, rebuild trust, enhance reconciliation, and restore at least some sense of justice.

These aims are essential if Rwandan life is to move beyond its genocidal past. To some extent they are being achieved, but Hatzfeld's conversations with Tutsis and Hutus underscore that success is sporadic and fragile. While time's passage will bring some mending to Rwanda, Hatzfeld suggests that many of Rwanda's wounds are beyond healing. The ongoing predicament is how Tutsis and Hutus will live together in those circumstances.

The antelope's strategy contributes to the dilemma. Tutsis and Hutus continue to "run" in their ethnic groups. As the past pursues them into the future, those groups stick together, but unavoidably individuals must go their own ways, as Eugénie said, to give everyone a chance. That dynamic means that the genocide remains—one could even say continues—inside individuals, ultimately leaving them alone to cope with its memories and effects as best they can. The results of that struggle do little to encourage trust, reconciliation, or hope for justice.

A survivor named Berthe Mwanankabandi speaks for many in Nyamata when she says that "justice finds no place after a genocide." Innocent Rwililiza tells Hatzfeld that when Tutsis "talk among ourselves, the word *forgiveness* has no place," even though the international humanitarian organizations active in Rwanda insist on the importance of reconciliation. Ignace Rukiramacumu, one of the killers interviewed by Hatzfeld, claims that "convincing a Tutsi you are telling the truth is impossible," and his fellow perpetrator, Alphonse Hitiyaremye, adds that "the real truth, the atmosphere, if I may say so, cannot be told."

A survivor named Claudine Kayitesi would agree with Alphonse. "The future has already been eaten up by what I lived through," she laments with profound awareness of how much is lost "when you cannot trust those who live close by." Appropriately, Hatzfeld offers no one-size-fits-all summation for the personal testimonies in his book; their perspectives and contents are diverse and at times conflicting. *The Antelope's Strategy*, however, moves unrelentingly to a telling conclusion: trust between Tutsis and Hutus, tenuous as it has long been, remains damaged beyond repair by the genocide and its aftermath.

Hatzfeld's message is as sober as it is vital: the cost of genocide is incalculable. Innocent says that living through the genocide brought him "no enriching knowledge," but he has learned "to be ready for anything, to think on the alert. . . . I always want to know what's going on behind what's going on." *The Antelope's Strategy* runs in those directions, making the book incisive about ethics as well as about history and current events.

John K. Roth

Review Sources

Booklist 105, no. 11 (February 1, 2009): 12.
Kirkus Reviews 77, no. 2 (January 15, 2009): 69.
New Criterion 26, no. 6 (February, 2008): 64-69.
The New Republic 240, no. 16 (September 9, 2009): 35-42.
Publishers Weekly 256, no. 1 (January 5, 2009): 40-41.

THE ANTHOLOGIST

Author: Nicholson Baker (1957-   )
Publisher: Simon & Schuster (New York). 245 pp. $25.00
Type of work: Novel
Time: 2008
Locale: A farm outside Portsmouth, New Hampshire

In Baker's novel, writer Paul Chowder muses on poetry, and on life while trying to write an introduction to an anthology of rhymed poetry he has been commissioned to compile

Principal characters:
PAUL CHOWDER, poet, anthologist, and blocked writer
SMACKO, his dog
ROZ, the woman who shared his home for eight years, but who left because he was going nowhere
NANETTE, his nearest neighbor, who is going through a divorce
RAYMOND, her son
CHUCK, her new boyfriend
VICTOR, a poet and housepainter
TIM, his friend
MARIE, a friend of Tim

The dust cover of Nicholson Baker's *The Anthologist* displays the words "A Novel" in very small type after the title. The small font seems appropriate because, although there is a definite narrative thread throughout the work, on the whole it reads much more like an essay as that form was originally conceived by Michel Eyquem de Montaigne: a leisurely, wandering exploration of a theme or idea. In this case, the focus is poetry, rhymed and unrhymed. Baker's novel also resembles Montaigne's essays in that Baker represents a mind in conversation with itself, a thinker who diagnoses and anatomizes his own mind as he goes. Although this approach is risky, the narrative voice is likable, despite being frustrating and self-absorbed at times. Over all, the voice is whimsical, witty, knowledgeable, and sympathetic, so reading the novel comes to seem like reading the journal of a very dear friend, a guilty pleasure.

Baker's protagonist, Paul Chowder, is a middle-aged poet who is not writing. He has been commissioned, and received an advance, to put together an anthology of rhymed poetry (he himself writes free verse) and write an introduction. With much angst, he has managed to decide which poems to include, but he cannot bring himself to write the introduction. He lives on a farm that he has inherited, and he has set up his study in the loft of the barn, where he goes to struggle with his demons. His failure to write has led Roz, his live-in girlfriend of many years, to leave him in frustration, and

Nicholson Baker has published six novels and received a National Book Critics Circle Award for his nonfiction book Double Fold: Libraries and the Assault on Paper *(2001). He lives with his wife and two children in South Berwick, Maine.*

it has also placed him on the brink of bankruptcy.

The action of the novel is mostly an account of Chowder moving from place to place on the farm, from barn to hayloft, from brook to stream, looking for his muse. He also makes a brief foray into playing badminton with a friendly neighbor, her lover, and her son, and he does some manual labor for the same neighbor to earn a bit of money. He cares for his dog Smacko and very occasionally sees his former lover. He does a reading in Cambridge. He goes to a poetry conference in Switzerland and gives a master class. The suspense in the novel is generated by the question of whether he will ever write his introduction.

The delight of reading *The Anthologist* comes from Chowder's musings on poetry—rhymed and unrhymed, metrical or not—including rants on iambic pentameter (according to him, a French form not appropriate to English); discourses on the counting of beats, including rests; and thoughts on some of the greatest poems of the past and present, as well as some of the greatest poets from Horace, through Geoffrey Chaucer, to John Ashbery. To say that Chowder's ideas about poetry are at times eccentric is to make an understatement, but they are also informative. For example, he has a revelation about the translation of Horace's *carpe diem* as "seize the day." According to Chowder (and, by extension, Baker), the proper translation is "pluck the day," an insight that leads him to produce a page and a half of commentary on typos, mistranslations, and the true meaning of Horace's poem, all of which is both elegant and edifying.

The title of Chowder's anthology is *Only Rhyme*, an allusion to the novelist E. M. Forster's famous epigraph to *Howards End* (1910), "Only connect." Chowder's dilemma is that although he connects totally with poetry, there is nothing much else he is connecting with, try though he may. He sleeps in his bed accompanied only by piles of his favorite poetry collections, which are strewn between the sheets. He is utterly blocked in his own writing, spending days watching reruns of sitcoms such as *The Dick Van Dyke Show* and *Friends*. He decides that the sitcom is a new, underappreciated, and totally American art form.

Chowder is so distracted by his major losses—of his girlfriend and his ability to write—and by his pending loss of everything he owns through bankruptcy that he injures himself, not once but three times. He cuts his finger in a series of freak accidents, beginning with carrying a computer down a flight of stairs. These accidents serve to underscore his problem: He cannot write, so he injures the digits with which he writes.

Occasionally, one of Chowder's rants will seem a bit too easy, too cute, or simply not clever enough to sustain itself, but most of his opinions are fresh, witty, and revelatory. Another device that is less successful, though, is his spotting of famous dead authors in various places around his town and elsewhere: Edgar Allen Poe in a laundromat in Marseilles, France, Theodore Roethke walking up the street with just one shoe on, Algernon Charles Swinburne at a bookstore. These minor quibbles do not detract from the cleverness of the novel as a whole, nor from the wealth of insight it offers not only into the world of poetry but also into the world of the frustrated writer, the blocked poet, and the author who recognizes that he will always be second tier and therefore never become immortal.

Chowder has opinions on everything that pertains to poetry, not just rhyme, rhythm, and meter. He has his favorite poets, favorite magazines (*The New Yorker* is his holy grail), and favorite styles and rhythms. He makes a list of "People I'm jealous of" that includes such disparate individuals as Sinead O'Connor, Jon Stewart, Lorenz Hart, and Billy Collins, the former poet laureate whom he marvelously sums up with "Charming, chirping crack whore that he is." It is hard to resist such a narrator. Although at times he appears too opinionated, too agonized, or too depressed, his comments are so interesting and informed that one reads on and wishes him well, hoping that in the end, once he finishes his introduction, he will find love and happiness and someone to pick the fleas off his beloved dog.

Baker knows his readers, especially those who peruse, ponder, and collect books of poetry. As Chowder says in an attempt to cheer himself up and reestablish his place in the world: "I think I'm going to go to RiverRun Books and look at the poetry shelves. When I see new books for sale there that I already own, it makes me happy. It makes me feel that there's part of the world that I really understand." Chowder's understanding is quite real: Although one might disagree with his opinions at times, the extent of his knowledge is both broad and deep. He has lived a life steeped in poetry and feels the need to share it with others.

The text of the novel features a number of postmodern elements—although some of these elements date back to Lawrence Sterne's *The Life and Opinions of Tristram Shandy, Gent.* (1759-1767; commonly known as *Tristram Shandy*), published in the eighteenth century. The book is self-reflective, but, beyond that, it also has musical notes incorporated into it to allow readers to hear the songs that Paul Chowder makes up to prove his points about the rhythmic qualities of poetry. In addition to sightings of dead poets, it incorporates conversations with people who are not there. Baker has his main character offer not only advice on how to read and understand poetry; definitions of poetry; and insights into the work of Latin, English, and American poets throughout the centuries but also tips on how to write poetry (although, with himself as an example, Chowder does not always strike one as a reliable narrator).

What finally frees Chowder is a trip to a poetry convention in Switzerland, before which he visits Roz and asks her if he should have an affair while there. He is trying unsuccessfully to be light and flirtatious. However, after she advises him not to, she tells him that she loves him. While at the conference, he gives a master class. His main piece of advice during it is to find the best moment of a day and write about it. Then, having quoted Amy Lowell, who called poetry a young man's job, he bursts into tears. Although he apologizes, the outburst ends his session.

Afterward, Chowder climbs up a mountain and, while sitting on a bench, becomes aware of a certain slant of light, which is the best moment of his day. (He does not have an affair, as there is no chance to.) When he begins his trek home, he is suddenly free of his block. He writes twenty-three poems on the airplane back and, once home, sits down to write the introduction to his anthology. He finishes it in three days, sitting at his kitchen table in the same shirt the whole time. After that, he calls Roz. Though she will not move back in with him right away, she invites him to dinner. He starts restoring his finances by painting houses. Summer is over and so is his drought.

Chowder's introduction to the anthology is almost the same length as Baker's novel. Thus, almost inevitably, the novel seems to become the introduction with which Chowder has been struggling. It certainly would serve in many ways as a suitable introduction to rhymed poetry, one from which a student of poetry would benefit. As in Montaigne's essays, Chowder's dialogue has taken place with the ideal reader, as it is with himself. For anyone who loves poetry, this novel is a pleasure not to be missed.

Mary LeDonne Cassidy

Review Sources

Booklist 105, no. 21 (July 1, 2009): 25.
Kirkus Reviews 77, no. 13 (July 1, 2009): 671.
Library Journal 134, no. 13 (August 1, 2009): 64.
New Statesman 138, no. 4966 (September 14, 2009): 46.
The New York Review of Books 56, no. 16 (October 22, 2009): 22-24.
The New York Times, September 10, 2009, p. 7.
The New York Times Book Review, September 6, 2009, p. 10.
The New Yorker 85, no. 29 (September 21, 2009): 95.
Publishers Weekly 256, no. 21 (May 25, 2009): 33.
The Times Literary Supplement, August 21, 2009, pp. 5-8.

ARDENT SPIRITS
Leaving Home, Coming Back

Author: Reynolds Price (1933-)
Publisher: Charles Scribner's Sons (New York). 408 pp. $35.00
Type of work: Autobiography
Time: 1955-1961
Locale: Great Britain; United States

This third volume of Price's autobiography is a graceful and elegiac view of his life in the 1950's as a Rhodes Scholar at Oxford University and his return to his native South to teach writing and literature at Duke University

Principal personages:
REYNOLDS PRICE, a novelist and short-story writer
DAVID CECIL, one of Price's mentors at Oxford
HELEN GARDNER, an aloof Oxford don who fascinates Price
MICHAEL JORDAN, Price's closest friend at Oxford
EUDORA WELTY, a fellow Southern writer who acknowledges Price's talent early in his career
STEPHEN SPENDER, one of Price's literary mentors
JOHN GIELGUD, a famous British actor who befriends Price
MATYAS, a British academic who becomes Price's lover

Ardent Spirits begins its narrative just after Reynolds Price's father has died of lung cancer at fifty-four and Price has been awarded a Rhodes scholarship to study in England at Oxford University. Already determined to be a scholar and writer, the precocious Price embarks on his first major journey. He is concerned about leaving his mother and younger brother but also driven to make his mark by ambitiously attempting to write both short fiction and a major study of Milton's poetry.

Academia never quite suits Price, even though he will remain in it all his working life. Thus, his academic study of Milton seems in this memoir to be more an idea than a fully realized project. Price seems far more engrossed in his fiction—even when he puts off writing it to fulfill academic requirements. As narrator, Price provides wonderful insight into his younger self, the budding young writer trying to make a name for himself who nearly gets into serious trouble when two journals accept the same story for publication.

Although Price studies hard at Oxford, he also engages in a full social life, making a few lifetime friendships and taking the time to tour Italy with a British friend. Price portrays himself as an earnest young man already encouraged by major writers such as Eudora Welty and renowned scholars such as Lord David Cecil. Cecil comes alive as a caring teacher very much attuned to his student's sensibility. He is also an excit-

Reynolds Price has taught at Duke University since 1958. His novel A Long and Happy Life *(1962) won the William Faulkner Award, and his novel* Kate Vaiden *(1986) won the National Book Critics Circle Award.*

able lecturer who inadvertently spits on his students. Oxford don Helen Gardner, on the other hand, is inscrutable. She seems inexplicably to thrive among many male scholars who do little to make her welcome. Price clearly wishes that she had opened up to him during his time at Oxford, but her very mystery speaks volumes about the repressive Oxford milieu, which the outgoing Price negotiated with surprisingly little angst. By contrast, Price treats Welty with too much reserve. A literary icon, she appears without much color in the memoir, as though Price—in an effort to preserve her privacy—has censored his otherwise candid commentary on his friends and acquaintances.

Although only in his early twenties, Price has already secured an agent. He keeps an eye on the literary world, even as he adopts the mannerisms of a British scholar. Price describes Great Britain as a country still recovering from the ravages of World War II. Compared to the culinary sophistication Britain would later flaunt, the land in *Ardent Spirits* serves bland food, lacks central heating, and is populated with people who wash rather infrequently. At Oxford, Price puzzles over the lack of showers for students and the mysterious absence of toilet paper dispensers, but he treats these shortcomings with considerable understanding. He is there, after all, to learn from the world's greatest scholars and writers—although he is noticeably eager to leave for his Italian vacation.

Thus, Price lives a bifurcated life in England, juggling academics with social and literary endeavors. A young man of extraordinary poise, he makes friends with literary greats such as Stephen Spender—who becomes a lifelong friend—and with famous actors such as John Gielgud. The latter emerges as a sensitive, openhearted man who welcomes the young American. Even with the distractions of his busy social life, Price manages to earn a B.Litt degree and to return home a success.

Price deals with his homosexuality in a straightforward way, while acknowledging that, during the years he was at Oxford, this was hardly a subject that could be broached in public in England—or even among close friends. Some of Price's male friendships seem charged with sexual tension, but Price describes only one long-term relationship with a British academic. In a highly amusing incident, Spender dines with the distinguished American critic Lionel Trilling, who is the object of some amusement for Price's British literary friends because Trilling published a book about the novelist E. M. Forster without realizing that his subject was homosexual. According to Price, Spender clearly wanted to sleep with him, although the details of Spender's advances to the young writer form no part of Price's narrative. Price seems eager to avoid accusations that he has sensationalized his autobiography.

Critics have noted that homosexual themes and characters do not appear often in Price's nearly forty published books. Price has responded that his concern has been with extended families and long-term relationships that most often occur in the heterosexual world. Then, too, he admits that he has wanted to reach audiences that might very well have no particular interest in the lives of homosexuals. As a practical matter, in other words, he has wanted to appeal to as many readers as possible.

David Leavitt and Edmund White, two writers openly identified as gay, have taken exception to Price's comments in their reviews of his autobiography. White has even suggested that Price's fiction might have been better if it had reflected the same degree of effervescence that suffuses *Ardent Spirits*. For whatever reason, however, Price has not wanted to make his sexual orientation an integral part of his creative work, even though it emerges as an important determinant of his experiences in his autobiography. Perhaps because Price sensed as early as the age of seven what his sexual orientation would be, homosexuality per se was never an issue that caused him grief. Indeed, his early attraction to literature and his reading of the gay novelist Andre Gide seem to have steadied Price, reinforcing an identity with which he seems always to have been comfortable. Price does get exercised, however, over the term "gay." Like many homosexuals of his generation, he dislikes the term because he believes it suggests a frivolity and irresponsibility that has been attached to gays, especially in the wake of the AIDS epidemic. He prefers the term "queer."

Price's friendship with Michael Jordan is presented as without sexual implications—just a deep bond that the two men maintained long after their Oxford years and without the encouragement of proximity. Jordan seems to have provided a kind of anchor for Price, the cruiser and man about town, although Price never puts it this way. Perhaps he sees such assessments as too facile, too abstracted from his actual experience. Price simply allows the story of his relationship with Jordan to unfold in its natural order without undue speculation about its meaning.

After returning to the United States, Price accepts a three-year contract at Duke University, expecting that he will have to look elsewhere for employment once his contract expires. However, the English Department chair, impressed with Price's fiction, suggests that his plan to move and to earn a Ph.D. will not be necessary if Price continues to produce work of such high quality. The memoir ends as Price returns for another year at Oxford—not to earn a degree but to work on his fiction and renew the rewarding friendships that he formed three years earlier.

The American portion of *Ardent Spirits* seems a little flat compared to the section recounting Price's journey of discovery at Oxford and on the Continent. (At one point in Rome, he is misdirected to a brothel and mistakes it for a pension.) Although Price mentions students such as Fred Chappell and Anne Tyler who would go on to become noteworthy writers, he again seems entirely too circumspect (as he was with Eudora Welty) when he ventures so close to home. Not even creative writing seems to inspire Price. He doubts the utility of teaching writing since he sees it as an activity best cultivated by the independent minded in solitude. His down-to-earth advice to writers is that they keep regular hours and concentrate on daily output.

Price avoids delving into his experience of academic routins and the backbiting and paranoia common in English departments. Duke University, Price's lifetime employer, is accorded a level of discretion that lessens the problems plaguing even the best academic departments. Certainly this seems to have been Price's experience. If in this period he had significant contact with the Duke faculty, he does not divulge what it was. Missing from the American section are enticing cameos such as those set in England. Price recounts W. H. Auden leaving his Oxford rooms in a shambles (the British would refer to such behavior as shambolic), and he details encounters with the witty essayist Cyril Connolly and the cheerfully encouraging Sonia, George Orwell's widow.

Price takes his title from a remark Thomas Jefferson made about the "ardent spirits" (hard liquor) he kept only for those friends who required them. The title seems an appropriate one for a life spent with lively and engaging friends. Price has enjoyed—indeed required—the company of such ardent spirits, and, as an ardent spirit himself, he writes a narrative full of ebullience and joie de vivre. Questions arise, however, as to whether the memoir is entirely accurate. Indeed, Price himself raises this question, alluding to controversies involving other memoirs that have turned out to be more fiction than fact.

Price acknowledges the fallibility of memory and writers' tendencies to embroider stories, yet at the same time he claims considerable accuracy for his own version of events. In part, he relies on his letters, which form a record that he has used to reconstruct this period of his life. He apparently writes, moreover, without fearing contradiction from those who are still alive and could dispute his recollections. He seems confident that he has not distorted the past. This confidence may derive from his level-headed prose, which is devoid of the melodrama and searing revelations that have undone other memoirs. Unlike the authors of those works, he seems unmotivated to manipulate chronology or invent details in order to heighten the human interest of his narrative. Instead, he seems entirely content with the accretion of details and episodes that do not succumb to embellishment so much as to the nuanced style that Price has perfected.

Carl Rollyson

Review Sources

Booklist 105, no. 17 (May 1, 2009): 56.
Boston Globe, May 24, 2009, p. 7.
Kirkus Reviews 77, no. 7 (April 1, 2009): 366.
Library Journal 134, no. 6 (April 1, 2009): 76.
Los Angeles Times, May 24, 2009, p. E5.
The New York Review of Books, July 2, 2009, pp. 22-23.
The New York Times, May 13, 2009, p. C4.
The New York Times Book Review, May 17, 2009, p. 8.
Publishers Weekly 256, no. 13 (March 31, 2009): 42.
Washington Post, May 4, 2009, p. 9.

THE ART INSTINCT
Beauty, Pleasure, and Human Evolution

Author: Denis Dutton (1944-)
Publisher: Bloomsbury Press (New York). 278 pp. $25.00
Type of work: Philosophy, fine arts, music, literary criticism, anthropology, science
Time: Prehistory to the early twenty-first century

An exploration of the origins of the arts within the context of Darwinian evolutionary science and the ways that this intellectual perspective changes contemporary art theory and criticism

Denis Dutton begins *The Art Instinct* by asserting that most art history, criticism, and theory of the last century has been premised, either explicitly or (more often) implicitly, on the idea that artistic production falls in the category of "learned behavior." Culture, including the arts, has appeared to exist in "a realm of free creativity" that falls into "the uncontested domain of the humanities untouched by biology." Recently, Denis says, this viewpoint has been changing in ways that affect critics' understanding of the underlying foundations of the arts. Evolutionary psychology has introduced lines of inquiry and methodology that are applicable to studying the place of the arts within an evolutionary context. Even more, the fields of anthropology and ethnography offer both evidence and theory that can help situate the artistic impulse and art production within an evolutionary framework. For example, the work of cultural anthropologist Ellen Dissanayake in books such as *Homo Aestheticus: Where Art Comes From and Why* (1992) and *Art and Intimacy: How the Arts Began* (2000) has delved into these issues. The theory of evolution has also found its way into literary theory and criticism as "literary Darwinism."

None of these evolutionary explorations into the origins of various art forms has yet brought together their ideas to form a broad philosophy of art. *The Art Instinct* takes on that ambitious project. Dutton's thesis is that art is a natural instinct in humans. He argues that the arts are evolutionary adaptations that, in Darwinian terms, were necessary for the survival and evolutionary development of humans. It may seem from a modern perspective that the arts belong to a more rarefied category of activity that demands high levels of complex abilities in both artistic creation and appreciation. Dutton, however, believes that all artistic experiences rest on deep foundations in the evolutionary origins of the human animal. His book embraces all of the arts, including the visual arts, music, dance, drama, and literature. To examine his premise, Dutton takes a global cross-cultural approach. His examples range from the earliest prehistoric evidence of art to contemporary multimedia art and technology.

In the first four chapters, Dutton lays the groundwork for his study by discussing

Denis Dutton is a professor of philosophy at the University of Canterbury, Christchurch, New Zealand. He the founder and editor of several Web sites, including Arts & Letters Daily, *and a journal,* Philosophy and Literature.

several basic features of art. The chapter "Art and Human Nature" brings together views ranging from Greek philosophy to evolutionary psychology to introduce the idea that art seems to be a universal capacity of the human mind. This propensity toward art does not, in and of itself, prove that art reaches the Darwinian standard of a trait that contributes to the survival of the species. However, the universality of the arts in human culture suggests for Dutton the possibility that art springs from deep evolutionary roots.

In the chapter "What Is Art?" Dutton establishes a method for examining the nature and basic characteristics of art, not by trying to define art, but rather by "treating art as a field of activities, objects, and experience that appears naturally in human life." He presents twelve "cluster criteria" that appear universally in the arts throughout the historical and global spectrum of human culture. These criteria are: direct pleasure, skill and virtuosity, style, novelty and creativity, criticism, representation, special focus, expressive individuality, emotional saturation, intellectual challenge, art traditions and institutions, and imaginative experience. He points out that each of these twelve characteristics, taken individually, overlaps with nonart experiences. A significant cluster of the criteria are needed for an object or activity to qualify as art.

Chapter 4, "'But They Don't Have Our Concept of Art,'" confronts the arguments of various art theorists and anthropologists about cultural relativism, a view that different cultures have distinct concepts and practices of art that do not translate cross-culturally. In part, some of these positions arise in response to what might be regarded as the hegemony of Western cultural values. In each case, Dutton rebuts these arguments to demonstrate that the art instinct is, indeed, universal and cross-cultural.

Finally, beginning with Chapter 5, "Art and Natural Selection," Dutton arrives at the centerpiece of his thesis: that the arts arise from evolution of the human species in the terms that Charles Darwin set forth in his most famous work, *On the Origin of Species by Means of Natural Selection: Or, The Preservation of Favoured Races in the Struggle for Life* (1859). Much of this chapter is concerned with the process of categorizing human traits or activities as either adaptations or by-products of adaptations. As Dutton explains:

> The gold standard for evolutionary explanation is the biological concept of an adaption: an inherited physiological, affective, or behavioral characteristic that reliably develops in an organism, increasing its chances of survival and reproduction.

Some, perhaps most, evolutionary psychologists would classify the arts as by-products. Dutton, in contrast, would like to put the arts in the category of adaptations, thereby situating the arts firmly within the "gold standard" of Darwinian evolutionary science. However, he appears to back away from this position when he first questions then abandons the very distinction between adaptations and by-products in the context of the arts.

Dutton says:

> My arguments are built on the idea that a vocabulary of adaptions versus by-products cannot make sense of the ancient origins and present reality of aesthetic and artistic experience.

Rather, his evolutionary aesthetics is based on the importance of "reverse-engineering" the artistic experience to help find and understand how the underpinnings of the arts "directly address and satisfy ancient, persistent interests and longings." Of all the arts, he says, the literary art of fiction has the most potential to be seen as an evolutionary adaption. In the chapter "The Uses of Fiction," Dutton identifies three adaptive advantages of fiction that could plausibly contribute to the survival and reproduction of the human species from the Pleistocene era. First, fictional stories provide low-risk rehearsals for life experiences and thus are "preparations for life and its surprises." Second, fictional stories can have didactic purposes of conveying information. Third, fiction can expand the mind in ways that encourage social interaction and "provide regulation for social behavior."

These features of stories and storytelling do support the argument that fictional production could have provided humans with evolutionary advantages. However, two major problems remain to be addressed in establishing a case for "evolutionary aesthetics." First, all of the arts, not just fiction, need to be considered. Second, the arts would need to contribute to the reproduction of the species by sexual selection. Dutton expands his inquiry into both of these issues in the next chapter, "Art and Human Self-Domestication." He addresses the apparent problem that all of the arts utilize and often emphasize lavish display, excess, ornamentation, and other traits that are costly in terms of both resources and human effort. Such excessive efforts to achieve what appears to be beauty for its own sake contradicts the economy and functionalism required for natural selection for survival.

In *The Descent of Man and Selection in Relation to Sex* (1871), Darwin struggled with an analogous problem in the animal kingdom: the famous example of the peacock's tail, which seems to serve only to make the male peacock more vulnerable. However, when considered from the standpoint of mating and sexual selection, the tail indicates to the peahen not so much attraction as fitness, "a signal of health and high-quality genes." Dutton expands on this idea, augmenting it with arguments put forward by the evolutionary psychologist Geoffrey Miller in *The Mating Mind* (2000) to advance the proposition that the evolutionary roots of art contain elements of this same social function of sexual selection, which has integrated the need for displays of beauty and extravagance into the human mind.

In the last three chapters, Dutton takes on various problems and issues in aesthetics to show how "evolutionary aesthetics" can unravel some of these conceptual tangles. One chapter examines three problems: artistic intention, forgery, and the twentieth century artistic movement known as Dada. In each case, however, Dutton's analysis seems to be only tangentially connected with a Darwinian view of aesthetics. As a result, his conclusions fail to persuade. In the example of Dada, Dutton evaluates Marcel Duchamp's *Fountain* (1917)—a urinal displayed on a plinth—to ascertain whether his system of cluster criteria would classify the work as art. For each of the twelve criteria, the conclusions end up being ambiguous. In talking about the direct pleasure criterion, for example, Dutton says that the urinal as object "would supply no pleasure in perception, direct or indirect." However, he also says that "as a Dadaist gesture . . . the object can be a source of great pleasure." Discussions of the other cluster criteria in relation to *Fountain* are similarly inconclusive.

One important element of Darwinian evolutionary science is contingency. Dutton examines this issue in the chapter "The Contingency of Aesthetic Values." Contingency in cultural terms means that culture is a "mental blank slate" where "accidents" of history and locale combine with "free creativity" to produce the broad field of culture in which the arts play a large role. In Darwin's theory of evolution, the biological aspects of human nature are also products of contingency arising from random mutation and selection. While it would seem that contingency forms a common ground that unites biology and culture, Dutton seems to continue to separate the two. He concludes that "art may seem largely cultural, but the art instinct that conditions it is not."

A book of such sweeping scope has both strong and weak points. One difficulty is that, although Dutton grounds his ideas about evolution on the work of Charles Darwin, he never fully explains what Darwinism is. The first several chapters focus on establishing Dutton's concepts about art, and indeed, these chapters, especially when developing cluster criteria for discussing the arts, are some of the best parts of the book. An additional chapter that thoroughly engages the basic concepts of Darwinian theory and the development of those concepts since their introduction would have provided a stronger intellectual foundation for Dutton's exploration of evolutionary aesthetics.

As it stands, it is difficult to determine in some cases the extent to which Dutton fully embraces evolutionary theory. Sometimes, Dutton seems to be arguing that the arts are adaptions and not by-products of adaptions or cultural contingencies. At other times, Dutton seems to move away from a strict adherence to the Darwinian position. For example, Dutton's ideas about the place of sexual selection as a component of the art instinct is controversial. Dutton admits, especially in the case of music, the explanatory element of sexual selection "misses a great deal of the art itself as we understand it today." Taken overall, the book presents a new and challenging way of looking at the arts. Many of Dutton's ideas about evolutionary aesthetics introduce stimulating ideas and insights about not only the origins of the arts but also how humans experience the arts in their present and constantly evolving forms. *The Art Instinct* is filled almost to overflowing with many new ideas to explore and debate in the future.

Karen Gould

Review Sources

American Scholar, February 24, 2009, pp. 121-125.
Booklist 105, no. 9/10 (January 1, 2009): 34.
Commentary 127, no. 4 (April, 2009): 74-76.
Kirkus Reviews 76, no. 21 (November 1, 2008): 1146.
New Scientist 201, no. 2693 (January 31, 2009): 44.
The New York Review of Books 56, no. 15 (October 8, 2009): 22-24.
The New York Times Book Review, February 1, 2009, p. 12.
Philosophy and Literature 33 (2009): 204-220.
The Times Literary Supplement, March 20, 2009, pp. 10-11.
The Wilson Quarterly 33, no. 2 (Spring, 2009): 109-110.

BAADER-MEINHOF
The Inside Story of the R.A.F.

Author: Stefan Aust (1946-)
First published: Der Baader-Meinhof Komplex, revised edition, 2008, in Germany
Translated from the German by Anthea Bell
Publisher: Oxford University Press (New York). 478 pp. $29.95
Type of work: History
Time: 1960's-1970's
Locale: West Germany and Berlin

Aust provides a detailed account of the activities of the Red Army Faction (RAF), a group of urban terrorists operating in Berlin and West Germany for more than a decade

Principal personages:
Andreas Baader, cofounder and leader of the RAF
Ulrike Meinhof, a leader in the RAF
Gudrun Ensslin, a leader in the RAF
Jan-Carl Raspe, a key participant in the RAF
Holger Meins, a key participant in the RAF
Irmgard Müller, a key participant in the RAF
Peter Jürgen Boock, a leader of the second-generation RAF
Brigitte Mohnhaupt, a leader of the second-generation RAF
Hanns Martin Schleyer, a businessman kidnapped by the RAF

In the 1970's, it was not uncommon for German travelers to exit the autobahns (freeways) only to be brought to a dead stop by a cadre of law enforcement officials. Cars waited in line while officers armed with automatic weapons made a thorough search of the passenger compartment, trunk, and undercarriage. This scene was reminiscent of something one might have expected to see in one of Eastern Europe's police states. The West German government found such drastic measures necessary, however, to counter the most serious internal threat since the rise of Adolf Hitler's National Socialist Party nearly half a century earlier: the Red Army Faction (RAF).

From 1970 until 1977, this band of armed urban guerrillas terrorized the citizens of West Germany and West Berlin, conducting a series of bank robberies, car thefts, kidnappings, and even murders of public officials. The RAF carried out these attacks in the name of armed revolution against a state that its leaders declared to be nothing more than a corrupt and dictatorial reinstatement of the fascist regime that had led Germany into World War II. Frequently referred to by law-enforcement and political officials as the Baader-Meinhof gang, the group was led by Andreas Baader, a disaffected ne'er-do-well who lived outside the law in order to combat the many social ills he believed were plaguing West Germany and other Western nations. Joining Baader in the inner circle of RAF leaders were Ulrike Meinhof, a leftist journalist who eventually abandoned her family (including twin daughters); Gudrun Ensslin, the daughter of a Protestant pastor; and a handful of other young radicals, including Jan-Carl Raspe, Holger Meins, and Irmgard Müller.

Stefan Aust is a journalist and former editor of Der Spiegel, *one of Europe's most popular magazines. He is the author of more than a dozen books on recent German history and culture.*

Baader's active participation in criminal activities was relatively brief. In the late 1960's, ostensibly to protest the government's support of right-wing regimes and activities against oppressed peoples throughout the world, he organized a small group of like-minded individuals to call attention to what he perceived as the State's drift back toward fascism. A 1967 visit to Germany by the shah of Iran provided the impetus for Baader to launch a crime spree that eventually landed him in prison.

At this point, Baader might have been considered little more than a common criminal and a nuisance to law-enforcement officials, who were relieved that he was now in custody. In 1970, however, Ulrike Meinhof was recruited by Baader's followers to help organize a plot to break him out of jail. For the next two years, Baader and Ensslin, who was his girlfriend and the second in command of his fledgling organization, built up the group's membership and carried out crimes against key organizations within the West German state.

Baader also found a highly visible international target for his anger in the United States' involvement in Vietnam. After the U.S. government mined Hanoi harbor and began bombing North Vietnam, he escalated his group's activities to include bombings in which a number of innocent civilians were injured and even killed. This loss of life did not seem to bother Baader, although some members of the group took issue with the indiscriminate nature of the RAF's activities. Meanwhile, Meinhof began composing a series of political tracts laying out the intellectual foundations to justify the RAF's actions. Over the next few years, a number of disaffected young people found this leftist propaganda and the lure of life outside the law attractive. Among them were Peter Jürgen Boock and Brigitte Mohnhaupt, who became leaders within the RAF.

German law enforcement quickly infiltrated the RAF. Within months after Baader was freed from prison, members of his gang were being arrested and incarcerated. By the end of 1972, all the leaders were in custody, and for the next five years the German government systematically developed a case against them for their terrorist activities. Eventually, all of them were brought together in the high-security Stammheim prison outside Stuttgart. While the government was building its case, lawyers for the jailed RAF leaders assisted their clients in communicating with members of the group who were still conducting operations. Surprisingly, as late as 1975 when the trial of Baader and his associates began, a notable portion of the West German population saw some justice in their complaints against the state.

The government's decision to conduct the trial of the RAF's leaders outside the public gaze only fostered suspicions that the defendants were being treated unfairly.

Records of the proceedings demonstrate, however, that RAF leaders were decidedly uncooperative with the court—and sometimes with their own attorneys. Complicating the proceedings for the government, Meinhof committed suicide while the trial was in progress. After more than a year, Baader and his chief lieutenants were found guilty of a string of crimes and sentenced to long prison terms.

Prompted by the court's decision, RAF members still at large staged two bold actions intended to force the German government to release the incarcerated leaders. Under Boock and Mohnhaupt's leadership, in the fall of 1977, RAF members kidnapped Hanns Martin Schleyer, head of the West German Employers' Association. The RAF also assisted a group of Middle Eastern terrorists in the hijacking of a Lufthansa jetliner en route to Frankfurt from Mallorca. Over the next few days, the aircraft flew to several countries before landing in Mogadishu, Somalia, where German commandos stormed the plane and freed the passengers. When this news reached the jailed leaders, Baader and Raspe took their own lives by putting guns to their heads, and Ensslin managed to hang herself. Müller plunged a knife into her chest but survived. When news of this mass suicide was made public, the RAF executed Schleyer.

How four high-profile prisoners in solitary confinement in a maximum-security prison were able to obtain the weapons they needed to commit suicide is just one of the many mysteries veteran German journalist Stefan Aust solves in *Baader-Meinhof: The Inside Story of the R.A.F.* Aust has had a lifelong interest in the RAF, and he published his first book about the group in 1985. In fact, the 2009 *Baader-Meinhof: The Inside Story of the R.A.F.* is a reworking of that 1985 volume, *Der Baader-Meinhof Komplex* (*The Baader-Meinhof Group: The Inside Story of a Phenomenon*, 1985), a detailed account of the group's activities published within a decade of their leaders' suicides.

Aust began his career at *Konkret*, a socialist periodical for which Ulrike Meinhof had worked before going underground in 1970. In retelling the story of the RAF in this extensively revised edition, Aust makes use of new documents that came to light after the publication of the first edition, most notably files made available when the East German government fell in 1989. *Baader-Meinhof* reveals the extensive role played by Stasi, the East German's secret police organization, in facilitating the mayhem created by the RAF. Aust also details the extensive relationships built between Baader's group and various Middle Eastern terrorist organizations, particularly the Popular Front for the Liberation of Palestine, which helped train several of the original members of the RAF and participated with them in the ill-fated airplane hijacking attempt in 1977.

Baader-Meinhof is written as a series of vignettes, loosely organized to follow the chronology of the gang's activities from 1970 through 1977. Aust concentrates on what people did and said, avoiding extensive speculation about the ideology that motivated hundreds of disaffected young men and women to go underground and follow the caustic yet charismatic Baader. Undeniably, however, Aust's account of the RAF is a group portrait. Dozens of young radicals are introduced, as Aust offers a brief description of their upbringings and reasons for joining the urban guerilla group before launching into a narrative of their actions. More attention is naturally paid to the group's leaders. Separate chapters are devoted to discussing their backgrounds and offering some insight into their motives for joining Baader in active struggle against the state.

A careful reading suggests that Aust has formed opinions about several of the RAF's leaders, although he seldom states these opinions directly. For example, Holger Meins is portrayed as a committed follower whose belief in the cause led him to heroic self-sacrifice: He died during a hunger strike staged by the prisoners at Stammheim (during which Baader had food smuggled to him). Gudrun Ensslin is presented as a thoughtful, sensitive individual whose dedication to Baader served as motivation enough to engage in acts of terrorism—but whose belief in her cause ran on a parallel track with her sensitivity for others' feelings.

In what might seem a surprising twist, Ulrike Meinhof is treated quite sympathetically, albeit within limits. Aust goes out of his way to separate her from the group intellectually, presenting her as someone whose thoughtful criticisms of the state motivated her to actions that seem at times totally out of character. He even quotes extensively from her letters to her two daughters to suggest that her maternal instincts ran deep, even if her commitment to radicalism ran deeper. Nevertheless, Aust reminds readers that Meinhof was quite adept at carjacking and participated willingly, even enthusiastically, in a number of violent criminal actions. Aust has virtually no sympathy for Baader, whom he portrays as self-aggrandizing, pompous, callous, and egomaniacal, evincing virtually no concern for anyone but himself. In many respects, Baader appears to be a classic sociopath.

As Aust notes in his final chapter, the deaths of Baader and his closest associates in 1977 did not end the group's terrorist activities. For the next twenty years, remaining RAF members continued to carry out bombings, kidnappings, and even murders. Not until 1998 was there any indication that the group had officially disbanded and that the people of Germany were finally free from the threat posed by this homegrown guerrilla force. By that time, there had been a change in Germany's government. Ironically, it was not the democratic state in West Germany that fell but instead the totalitarian socialist establishment in East Germany, the same regime that had assisted the RAF to bring terror to the streets of Berlin, Cologne, Frankfurt, and other German metropolises. Despite Baader's best efforts, capitalism and democracy won out in the end.

Laurence W. Mazzeno

Review Sources

Booklist 105, no. 14 (March 15, 2009): 4.
Christianity Today 53, no. 3 (March, 2009): 62.
Library Journal 134, no. 6 (April, 2009): 72.
Publishers Weekly 256, no. 13 (March 30, 2009): 29.
Wall Street Journal 253, no. 77 (April 3, 2009): A15.
Washington Post, April 12, 2009, p. B7.

BACK TO THE GARDEN
The Story of Woodstock

Author: Pete Fornatale (1945-)
Publisher: Simon & Schuster (New York). 303 pp. $24.99
Type of work: History, music
Time: 1969, especially August 15-18
Locale: Bethel, New York

Based on the recollections of dozens of participant observers, a legendary rock-and-roll disc jockey reconstructs the story, and considers the legacy, of the 1969 Woodstock Music and Art Fair

In *Back to the Garden*, Pete Fornatale reconstructs the story of the Woodstock Music and Art Fair, August 15-18, 1969 (known to most people simply as "Woodstock" or the "Woodstock Music Festival"). He assembles hundreds of eyewitness statements from participant observers into a roughly chronological account of the festival's legendary three days of "peace and music." While Fornatale's roster of witnesses includes a handful of ordinary spectators, it is heavily weighted toward Woodstock's movers and shakers. These include such luminaries as John Roberts and Joel Rosenman, the neophyte entrepreneurs who financed the Woodstock festival; Michael Lang and Artie Kornfeld, who put the festival together; John Morris, the beleaguered (and by all accounts heroic) production manager of the festival; Sam Yasgur, son of Max and Miriam Yasgur, on whose farm the festival took place; and Michael Wadleigh, the filmmaker who made the Academy Award-winning documentary that has immortalized Woodstock for many millions of viewers in the United States and around the world.

Fornatale, who was not present at the event, also provides testimony from numerous artists who performed at the festival, some triumphantly, others far less so. He strings together these eyewitness accounts (based on interviews conducted for the book, as well as published sources) with his own somewhat modest narrative. The accounts and the story combine to create a picture of an event that was conceived as a profit-making venture, narrowly averted disaster, and became one of the major cultural events of the mid-twentieth century.

Just how this seemingly miraculous outcome came about is one of the themes of Woodstock, as it exists both in the American public consciousness and in Fornatale's book. Woodstock was planned as a three-day music festival to be held in rural upstate New York, originally in the town of Wallkill. The audience was projected to number between 50,000 and 200,000 people. Upon learning the crowd would be so large, officials at Wallkill pulled out of their agreement just a few weeks before the festival was scheduled. This left the organizers with tens of thousands of tickets sold and no place to hold the event.

Pete Fornatale became a groundbreaking disc jockey in New York City in 1969. In 1983, he won the Armstrong Excellence in Broadcasting Award. He has written Radio in a TV Age *(with Josh Mills, 1980),* The Story of Rock 'n Roll *(1987), and* Simon and Garfunkel's Bookends *(2007).*

This first stage of near disaster was averted when Max Yasgur offered to rent part of his farm in Bethel for the festival. Nevertheless, the change of venue had its costs, putting preparations for the festival permanently behind schedule. In addition, the festival organizers far underestimated the throngs of music fans that would attend the festival. While no precise estimate of the festival's peak audience has been made, it is generally agreed that the number of attendees climbed into the range of one-half million people. This throng led to the second and far more serious stage of near disaster: a severe shortage of the food, water, medical supplies, and sanitation facilities needed to service a crowd the size of a decent-sized city's population. In fact, the Bethel area was declared a disaster area by Sullivan County, though casualties were ultimately kept to a minimum.

As Fornatale details, the flood of people arriving for the festival also led to three additional problems. Attempting to sell tickets at the gate or separate ticketed from unticketed attendees became a logistical nightmare. Potential conflicts arose between the invading hippie horde and the local residents, who were anything but hippies. Similarly, potential conflicts arose among audience members, who were forced to stay in cramped quarters without ample supplies. The organizers dealt quickly with the ticket issue, reading the situation accurately and declaring the proceedings to be a "free concert." The problem of culture clash between concertgoers and townsfolk was resolved by the principals involved: Both groups found the graciousness to make the best of the situation, with hippies displaying respect for their hosts and townsfolk showing great generosity toward their bedraggled interlopers. Meanwhile, little violence broke out among the audience members, because the crowd overwhelmingly acted in accordance with the values of the 1960's counterculture, enjoying the music, getting high on drugs, and "making love not war."

The situation was further helped by the fact that crowd control was managed by members of the Hog Farm, a commune that had provided similar services in a noncoercive way at previous events. Police and other officials also suspended the enforcement of drug laws and other regulations that would have put them at odds with the audience and the festival organizers. Even the U.S. Army cooperated by flying in emergency medical supplies. In sum, the organizers, government officials, festival attendees, and locals all behaved prudently and compassionately. As a result, and despite the additional failure of the weather to cooperate (there were sporadic rainstorms throughout the weekend, causing Woodstock to be closely associated with mud), there was little or no violent crime, no riots, and no mass starvation. In short, the people involved achieved a small miracle of human cooperation.

Fornatale describes the effects of logistical problems on the performers as well as the attendees. Like the other people involved, performers faced transportation challenges and shortages of food and drink (though, apparently, not of illicit drugs). In addition, there were serious problems with equipment and serious safety issues because of the weather. Some of the performers succumbed to these conditions, but others responded with festival-saving performances. These latter included Richie Havens, who got the concert off to a late but rousing start after previously scheduled performers had either failed to appear, refused to go on, or been in no shape to perform. Country Joe McDonald, Melanie, Arlo Guthrie, and Joan Baez all helped to set a nonviolent and antiwar political tone for the proceedings. Santana, Sly and the Family Stone, The Who, Ten Years After, and Jimi Hendrix all provided memorable artistic highlights that helped keep the crowd focused on the music rather than their own discomforts.

In return, many of these artists received important boosts to their careers. For example, Santana had not yet released a record album when they performed at Woodstock. With a legendary Woodstock performance under the group's belt, their first album was a winner even before it was released. Melanie and Ten Years After also had their careers propelled forward. On the other hand, artists such as the Incredible String Band missed an opportunity to expand their fortunes. Some established stars, such as The Who and Jimi Hendrix, merely deepened their already legendary status.

Fornatale, a longtime New York City disc jockey, is both an aficionado of and a significant figure in the rock music business. He devotes ample text to assessing the relative experiences of the performers, as well as the effects Woodstock had or failed to have on their careers. Nor is he hesitant to express his own views on which artists made good choices or mistakes along the way—and which had good or bad fortune through no fault of their own. As a result, many readers will learn things about their favorite muscians and other performers that they did not know before.

Fornatale is less thorough and also less direct in his assessment of what, after all the media hype and myth-making, Woodstock has actually meant to American society. Like the creators of the Woodstock movie, he gives a balanced view of what went on, registering the positive aspects of the festival—connected with the collective triumph over adversity—as well as its negative aspects, such as mass drug overdoses, the utter dependence of Woodstock attendees on the kindness of strangers, and the self-destructive behavior that would bring early deaths to prominent Woodstock figures such as Jimi Hendrix, Allan "Blind Owl" Wilson, and Janis Joplin. Overall, it is clear that Fornatale wants to believe that something significant happened at Woodstock. This is indicated by the book's inclusion of an enthusiastically pro-Woodstock foreword by Country Joe McDonald. McDonald pleads—perhaps only playfully—for a return to the 1960's.

Ironically, McDonald's plea signifies the failure of Woodstock as a transformative event in American history: If Woodstock had successfully transformed American society in accord with the values of the 1960's counterculture, then a plea to return to those values would be superflous. Even so, the spirit of Woodstock is a part of American identity forty years after the event. To be sure, the cultural and political stew of which the spirit of Woodstock is a part is hopelessly complex and dauntingly fluid. It is probably unrealistic to expect anyone to sum up exactly what the United States is and where it is going. Thus, it is equally unrealistic to expect any author to say conclusively what Woodstock means or will mean.

What Fornatale does provide is a lot of different (sometimes contradictory) perspectives on what happened forty years ago at Woodstock and what it has meant to different people, most of whom played a role in making Woodstock happen. To gain a better understanding of the audience's point of view, one would be well served to complement Fornatale's book with *Woodstock Revisited: Fifty Far Out, Groovy, Peace-Loving, Flashback-Inducing Stories from Those Who Were There* by Susan Reynolds. For the nuts and bolts of how Woodstock came together, the text of choice would be *The Road to Woodstock* by Michael Lang. Fornatale's version has its own unique place in the Woodstock literature, however. As a young disc jockey in 1969, Fornatale brought great passion to his work. He strung songs together in a way that made his audience listen carefully to, and think hard about, their lyrics. He often found artistic pay dirt in places others had deserted. He was, for example, a big supporter of Brian Wilson and the Beach Boys when, for most other progressive disc jockeys, they had become passé and worthy only of smug dismissal. For Fornatale, the musical awakening of the late 1960's was all about opening minds, not closing them. Indeed, listening to Pete Fornatale in 1969 was very much like attending Woodstock, only without the mud, excrement, and body odor. In that light, Fornatale's take on Woodstock conveys special significance, particularly for those who have tuned into his radio shows over the last four decades.

Ira Smolensky

Review Sources

Boston Globe, July 19, 2009, p.5.
International Herald Tribune, August 8, 2009, p. 18.
New York Daily News, July 7, 2009, p.24.
The New York Times Book Review, August 9, 2009, p. 6.
Publishers Weekly 256, no. 26 (June 29, 2009): 118.

BAD MOTHER
A Chronicle of Maternal Crimes, Minor Calamities, and Occasional Moments of Grace

Author: Ayelet Waldman (1964-)
Publisher: Doubleday (New York). 213 pp. $24.95
Type of work: Memoir

An offering of motherhood, its joys and impossible goals, on the altar of public opinion

In *Bad Mother*, Ayelet Waldman asks whether it is possible in contemporary society to be a good mother. The women's movement of the twentieth century promised women emancipation from the traditional monochromic roles of secretary, teacher, nurse, wife, mother, and grandmother. It promised the freedom to succeed both in marriage and in business, achieving results on a par with one's partner and one's professional peers. Sharing in the tasks of taking out the garbage or screwing in a Molly bolt, as well as in the accomplishments and rewards of the workplace, has become an expected norm for married couples. Such multitasking for success takes its toll, however. Motherhood is still an idealized role that is likely to make every actual mother feel guilty for not living up to its image. Young professional mothers exhaust themselves in simultaneous pursuit of perfection in career and caregiving. Waldman, a former public defender and workplace mom, addresses this issue with humor, pain, and good sense.

Waldman observes that visions of the ideal mother generally begin in the starry-eyed hopes of the mother's mother, who passes on her own model of motherhood—one that she herself could not match—to her daughters. The author speaks of her own mother, a member of the women's movement, who advocated and instilled values of freedom and self-determination in her daughter. As she notes, "My mission as her daughter was to realize the dream of complete equality that she and her fellow bra burners had worked so hard to attain." There was no other narrative available to Waldman. Just as abused children become abusive adults, girls take on the models of how to be a wife and mother from their own mothers' values and actions.

In addition to all the feminist goals presented to the author, her good Jewish mother predictably expected grandchildren—but not too many. She embraced her daughter's career and her maternity, at least until Ayelet became pregnant with her fourth child. Her mother's reaction was not positive, demonstrating the extent to which mixed signals can complicate the mother-daughter relationship.

Waldman also describes her relationship with her mother-in-law, a relationship she believes fits a universal template. One reads with understanding and empathy as the author describes her tussles with the mother of her novelist husband, Michael Chabon. When Chabon takes his mother to lunch each week, Waldman resents the

Ayelet Waldman writes for The New York Times, *Salon.com,* Elle, *and other publications. Born in Jerusalem and raised in Montreal and New Jersey, she lives now in Berkeley, California, with her novelist husband Michael Chabon and their four children.*

time he spends with her. When they dine together as a threesome, she continually and triumphantly reminds the older woman that Chabon is now connected more closely to his wife than to his mother. The "couple" is the hegemonic unit, and Waldman describes a universal competition between two women for the same man, "the stuff of sitcom jokes and Greek tragedy." She recognizes that the future holds a reprise of this war for her, when her son finds his own wife and she becomes the mother-in-law.

Waldman grew up in an era shaped by *Free to Be . . . You and Me* (1972), a record album that challenged the gender stereotypes used to educate children. The recording and the 1974 television special it inspired helped motivate her and many others to share homemaking responsibilities and to put the husband-wife relationship first. Public owning of this position has brought the author many negative comments from women who angrily suggest that her children should be taken away from her (because good mothers put their children first), as well as inquiries from men seeking advice on how to improve their own wives by purchasing lingerie. Waldman's response to the latter is to suggest that a turn at emptying the dishwasher will do more for a couple's sex life than changing their underwear.

Waldman emphasizes that equal involvement in marital tasks and parenting is not a matter of the man helping out the woman—still seen as the sole primary caregiver—but of owning the equality of responsibility. Even married couples of a former era, those old enough to have parented the author and her husband, may learn a new way of thinking about their relationships from Waldman's experience. They may also find her opinions threatening.

The author asserts that every woman has an innate calling to be part of the "Bad Mother Police." Violators of good motherhood seem to be everywhere: the Parent-Teacher Association (PTA), the supermarket, even in one's own home. Although the author has owned the title "bad mother" for herself, this designation does not keep her from searching out and condemning others of her kind wherever she goes.

Waldman chronicles her assessment of bad mothers she has encountered and at the same time lists criteria that qualify a woman for accolades as a good mother. She concludes that the prototypical good mother—whether a neatly starched Mary Poppins, who never loses her composure or her charges, or a 1950's June Cleaver, who remains crisp and smiling at all times—simply does not exist in real life. Despite its impossibility, though, the image of perfect motherhood endures, resembling a latent virus waiting to infect the most competent woman with frequent eruptions of pathologic guilt over her supposed inadequacy.

Waldman suggests that the single defining characteristic of "good motherhood" is self-abnegation. Women—even the most emancipated modern women—continue to beat themselves up for not reaching impossible goals. Others follow their lead and do the same. Mothers are the cozy rug upon which family members wipe their feet in comfort and confidence, and still, the mothers never quite measure up.

No book on motherhood would be complete without a foray into the actual physical reality of carrying and caring for babies. The author does not disappoint. She describes the inevitable exigencies of pregnancy and early motherhood, including bloated ankles, breast pumps, and baby bowel movements. For Waldman, the context of these mundane experiences is her career. She gains the sympathy of juries as she waddles very pregnant into the courtroom and is helped into a chair by her solicitous client. She takes maternity leave but eventually decides to be a stay-at-home mom. Women who have undergone pregnancy, early motherhood, and the juggling of multiple roles will identify. Women who have tried to retrieve their milk in privacy—a sometimes heroic feat—will laugh at the descriptions of Waldman in her office or in the cramped confines of an airplane trying to do so.

The book deals with spousal and maternal issues ranging from the trivial to the tragic. Waldman recounts her own struggles with on-time arrival of the preschool snack and the disappointment of trying to place refrigerator magnets on nonmagnetic modern appliances. She agonizes about the fact that her children love dodgeball, a childhood game that gives permission to bully. She wonders what the choice of Halloween costume by each child means. As an aspirant to perfect motherhood, she struggles to accept being the parent of a "loser" on the athletic field or of a "cereal box" on Halloween. She describes her children overhearing the arguments between herself and her husband as well as their marital lovemaking, and she worries about how to teach her children the meaning of sex in the contemporary world. A box of candy-colored condoms in her children's bathroom is part of the plan.

Perhaps the most poignant chapter is the one in which she deals with "Rocketship." Pregnant with her third child and all packed to go on an idyllic family vacation to Hawaii, Waldman discovers that she may be carrying a boy with Down syndrome. "Rocketship," the name her older son has given the baby, has genetic trisomy and therefore is not expected to fulfill the promise of the perfect child born to the perfect mother. The description of the couple's intense fact-finding about the possibilities, debating what to do, and eventually making the decision about whether to terminate the pregnancy will demand sympathy of readers.

Although they may not always agree with the author's positions (on topics including abortion, giving up a career, producing a large family, and condoning and practicing premarital sex), women of all ages can find something in this short volume. For contemporary grandmothers, the book offers insight into how the current generation of parents thinks. Many such grandmothers did not themselves face the daunting task of juggling career, car pools, and caregiving. Many past mothers, unlike the author, did not have to navigate the murky waters of their own history of multiple premarital sexual partners as a background for teaching their children about prudent sexuality. Nor did they have the options of the birth control pill or legal abortion. For contemporary mothers coping with the experience of raising a family larger than today's norm, Waldman offers some degree of wisdom. She offers a large dose of identification, at least with the challenges if not the conclusions of parenting.

Waldman concludes the book with her hopes for her children, that they might avoid the ideologies and dangers of modern American society. She knows that these children are not naïve but trusts that they will remain innocent. She wishes for them a faith in people and a hope for justice. She sees a world of promise, even in what she sees as the bleak realities of the present. Finally, this "bad mother" occasionally entertains a hope for another child for herself. While she longs for that wonderful smell and feel of babies, however, she concludes that four is enough.

It is difficult to think about a book on motherhood as a page-turner, but *Bad Mother* manages to be just that. In many ways, it tells the story of a traditional Jewish mother, often the butt of caricature and jokes. In a more profound way, though, it tells the extraordinary tale of a modern Jewish mother who puts her relationship with her husband first. As the dust jacket avows, a good mother "is never too tired for sex." If she is, though, at least she knows it is fine: Good enough is enough.

Dolores L. Christie

Review Sources

The Atlantic Monthly 304, no. 5 (December, 2009): 86-101.
Booklist 105, no. 16 (April 15, 2009): 14.
Kirkus Reviews 77, no. 8 (April 15, 2009): special section, p. 8.
The New York Times Book Review, May 10, 2009, p.7.
The New Yorker 85, no. 19 (June 29, 2009): 76-79.
Newsweek 153, no. 22 (June 1, 2009): 13.
Publishers Weekly 256, no. 11 (March 16, 2009): 52.

THE BARD
Robert Burns, A Biography

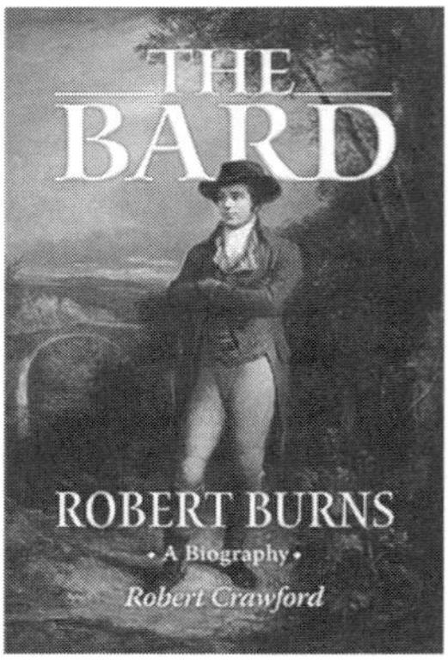

Author: Robert Crawford (1959-)
Publisher: Princeton University Press (Princeton, N.J.). 465 pp. $35.00
Type of work: Biography
Time: 1759-1796
Locale: Scotland

Published on the 250th anniversary of Burns's birth, Crawford's biography traces the many influences on Burns's poetry and thought; Crawford also explores the writer's various relationships and his efforts to provide for himself and his family

Principal personages:
ROBERT BURNS, poet
WILLIAM BURNES, the poet's father
AGNES BROWN, the poet's mother
JEAN ARMOUR, the poet's wife
AGNES MCLEHOSE, the poet's close friend, whom he addressed as Clarinda
JOHN MURDOCH, Burns's tutor
MARGARET CAMPBELL, one of Burns's loves, the "Highland Mary" of his poems
JAMES JOHNSON, editor of *Scots Musical Museum*

Britain in the eighteenth century wanted an unlettered poet, one who derived inspiration directly from nature rather than from books. Stephen Duck, the thresher poet patronized by Queen Caroline, filled this need in the 1730's. Similarly, the fictional third century poet Ossian, largely the creation of James McPherson, enjoyed immense popularity in the latter half of the 1700's and well into the 1800's. Even before Robert Burns published his first volume of poems, he began calling himself a "bardie," a diminutive of "bard," reflecting his desire to cast himself in this mold of the untutored writer.

In a verse epistle to the Scottish poet John Lapraik that Burns wrote on April 1, 1785, "Gie me ae spark o' Nature's fire,/ That's a' the learning I desire." Henry McKenzie in his magazine *The Lounger* praised Burns as a "Heaven-taught ploughman," further fostering the image that the poet himself was cultivating in Edinburgh at the time. He even dressed the part, wearing boots rather than shoes to social events, just as Benjamin Franklin in Passy wore a coonskin cap to create the illusion that he was a provincial among sophisticates. Burns at that time struck the sixteen-year-old Sir Walter Scott as rustic and plain, as well as intelligent, dignified, and self-confident. While Burns did not attend college, he was not "fancy's child warbling his native wood-notes wild," any more than was William Shakespeare, about whom John Milton wrote those words. Robert Burns, Jr., noted that his father's library contained the works of Geoffrey Chaucer, Shakespeare, Edmund Spenser, Milton, Alexander Pope, Oliver Goldsmith, Molière, Voltaire, and Jean-Jacques Rousseau.

A founding editor of Verse *(1984), Robert Crawford has been a professor of modern Scottish literature at the University of St. Andrews since 1989. He has won the Scottish Arts Council Book Award for* Identifying Poetry *(1993) and again for* Spirit Machines *(1999). He is a fellow of the Royal Society of Edinburgh.*

Robert Crawford devotes much of *The Bard* to discussing the various literary influences that shaped Scotland's best-known and most enduring native poet. Crawford observes that Burns's poetic education began almost at his birth. His mother sang old Scottish songs to him, and his grandmother recited Scottish folktales. Burns remembered these later in life. He also recalled another relative, Betty Davidson, who had a vast stock of tales of the supernatural. Burns's "Halloween" (1785) pictures a grandmother telling stories; "Address to the Deil" (1785) consists of a collection of folktales. Burns's formal education began when he was six. Crawford shows how fortunate the future writer was to have eighteen-year-old John Murdoch as his tutor.

At school, Burns memorized works that stayed with him into adulthood. He read Arthur Masson's *Collection of English Prose and Verse* (1781), which included works by the Scots James Thomson and John Home, whom Burns admired. After Burns left school to help his family work on their farm, Murdoch continued to supply the boy with books, including an English grammar and the poems of Alexander Pope. Burns's early letters quote from Pope, who also supplied models for Burns's letters in verse. Pope's poetry provided the epigraphs for "Holy Willie's Prayer" (1799) and "The Twa Herds: Or, The Holy Tulzie" (1784). In the summer of 1773, Burns spent a few weeks with Murdoch studying French. Burns returned home with a French dictionary and a copy of François Fénelon's *Les aventures de Télémaque* (1699; *The Adventures of Telemachus, the Son of Ulysses*, 1699). With these two books and Murdoch's lessons, Burns taught himself to read French.

Burns's father secured books from the Ayr Library Society, and Burns was a voracious reader. Nelly Miller, who dated Robert's younger brother William, said that she always saw Robert with a book in his hand. Among the first works he read was William Hamilton's *Life and Heroic Actions of the Renown'd Sir William Wallace, General and Governor of Scotland* (1722). One of Burns's most famous poems begins, "Scots, what hae wi' Wallace bled," which adapts lines that Hamilton ascribed to the Scottish leader. John Newbery's *Letters on the Most Common, as well as Important Occasions in Life* (1756) introduced Burns to important British authors of the early eighteenth century, especially Joseph Addison. Burns attributed his knowledge of manners, literature, and criticism to Addison's journal *The Spectator* (1712-1715). Yet another significant book from Burns's youth was a collection of English songs. Crawford quotes Burns's statement that he pored over these poems.

Two of the most important literary influences on Burns's poems were Allan

Ramsay and Robert Fergusson, whose writings Burns encountered about 1784. Crawford cites Burns's description of Fergusson as "my elder brother in Misfortune,/ By far my elder Brother in the muse." Fergusson died in an asylum at the age of twenty-four. In 1786, Burns urged the erection of a tombstone for Fergusson and wrote two epitaphs for the dead author. In one of these, he applied to Fergusson the epithet that Mackenzie had used for Burns, "Heaven taught," thus linking himself with the older man. From Fergusson, Burns took the title of bardie. Fergusson had written about peasant life and folk festivals and had employed the Scots vernacular. Fergusson and Ramsay both used the Standard Habbie stanza, supposedly named for the bagpiper Habbie Simson. This stanza consists of six lines, in which lines 1-3 and 5 are long and lines 4 and 6 are short. The four long lines all rhyme, as do the two short lines. Standard Habbie became the Burns stanza, and Fergusson's subjects and language became Burns's as well.

Crawford shows that Burns drew inspiration from life as well as from books. As Crawford notes, Burns wrote and adapted many love songs to express his passion of the moment. In the summer and early fall of 1775, he was at Kirkoswald, where he met Margaret Thomson, to whom he addressed his "Song, composed in August" (1783). The love songs addressed to Highland Mary were inspired by Margaret Campbell. Margaret Chalmers served as Burns's muse for "My Peggy's Face" (wr. 1787). His affair with Ann Park expressed itself poetically as well as physically; their daughter, Elizabeth, was born in March, 1791, a month before his wife, Jean Armour, gave birth to Burns's son William Nicol. "Lovely Davies" (1791) refers to Deborah Duff Davies, another woman to whom Burns was drawn.

Burns's amours got him into trouble with the Church. He and Elizabeth Paton, who gave birth to his daughter, another Elizabeth, in May, 1785, had to sit on the "cutty stool" in Tarbolton kirk for three Sundays. This event prompted a poem, and Burns satirized religious conservatives in a variety of other verses. "Holy Willie's Prayer," unpublished in Burns's lifetime, pretends to be a dramatic monologue by the conservative William Fisher, who attacks the unrighteous while at the same time confessing to his own sexual indiscretions. "The Holy Fair" (1785) describes an annual gathering of churchgoers to receive Communion. For Burns, this event is also an occasion for drinking and "haughmagandie" (sex). "To a Louse" (1786) attacks the hypocrisy of those Burns characterized as the "unco guid," the supposedly uncommonly good, who are in fact as flawed as anyone else.

Crawford's final chapter is titled "Staunch Republicans," reflecting Burns's liberal views about politics as well as religion. Crawford does not gloss over the contradictions in Burns's behavior. In 1786, Burns was having a hard time earning a living, and he resolved to emigrate to Jamaica. The post he secured was that of assistant overseer on a slave-holding plantation. In 1792, he composed "The Slave's Lament," supposedly spoken by a Senegalese slave in Virginia and sympathizing with the plight of the captive. Burns's political views accommodated both Jacobite and Jacobin sentiments. He lamented Scotland's loss of independence and the Hanoverian succession that ended the Stuart monarchy. At the same time that he mourned these monarchs who believed in the divine right of kings and in their absolute power, Burns wrote poetry celebrating the American Revolution, George Washington, and the French Revolution that abolished royal rule. In March, 1795, he joined the Royal Dumfries Volunteers, a home guard to protect the country against invasion by the French. He was also at that time circulating "A Man's a Man for A' That" (1795), a ringing declaration denouncing aristocratic pretension and championing the universal brotherhood of people. That poem contains the line "Its comin' yet for a' that," a translation of the French revolutionary cry *ça ira*. Crawford justifies Burns's occasional antirevolutionary behavior by arguing that, as a tax collector, he had to limit his prorevolutionary utterances. Burns's ambivalence even about his job manifests itself in his poem "The De'il's Awa wi' the Exciseman" (1792).

Burns's poetry and sexual exploits suggest that he would have fit in well with the people he describes in "The Jolly Beggars" (1785). Crawford indicates, however, that Burns suffered repeated bouts of depression. One of his earliest poems bears the title "Prayer under the Pressure of Violent Anguish" (wr. 1784). In "On a Scotch Bard Gone to the West Indies" (1786), he writes of being the victim of misfortune and suffering a broken heart. "Gloomy December" (1791) laments his separation from Agnes McLehose.

Crawford thus presents a complex character, refusing to gloss over his faults but also noting why his poetry still matters. He shows a man of deep passion who wrote beautifully about love but was hardly faithful to his wife or even his lovers; while pursuing Agnes McLehose, he slept with her servant and had a child with that young woman. He was attracted to cultivated, middle- and upper-class women but slept only with servants and the uneducated. He wrote rollicking lyrics but often battled feelings of despondency. He wrote about and believed in the equality of all while working as a tax collector for a Tory government at war with revolutionary France. Crawford successfully shows all these facets of Robert Burns and thereby makes the man and his poetry live for his readers.

Joseph Rosenblum

Review Sources

Booklist 105, no. 9/10 (January 1, 2009): 35.
Daily Mail (London), January 23, 2009, p. 64.
Daily Telegraph (London), January 24, 2009, p. 19.
London Review of Books 31, no. 5 (March 12, 2009): 3-5.
New Criterion 27, no. 10 (June, 2009): 80-82.
The New York Review of Books 56, no. 17 (November 5, 2009): 47-49.
The New Yorker 85, no. 1 (February 9, 2009): 109.
Times Higher Education, January 20, 2009, pp. 46-47.
The Times Literary Supplement, January 16, 2009, pp. 3-5.
The Washington Post, January 27, 2009, p. A2.

THE BELIEVERS

Author: Zoë Heller (1965-   )
Publisher: Harper (New York). 352 pp. $25.99
Type of work: Novel
Time: 1962; 2002
Locale: London; New York City

After noted radical lawyer Joel Litvinoff is felled by a stroke, the lives of his wife and three children unravel, but they eventually achieve significant psychological and spiritual transformations

Principal characters:
JOEL LITVINOFF, high-powered New York City radical lawyer
AUDREY LITVINOFF, his equally left-wing British wife
ROSA and KARLA LITVINOFF, their daughters
LENNY LITVINOFF, their adopted son
KHALED, Egyptian newsstand owner
CHIANTI, African American teenager
BERENICE MASON, Joel's mistress

Joel Litvinoff exists at the center of his family in Zoë Heller's *The Believers*, but early in the novel he is rendered insensible by a stroke, leaving a void that intensifies and accelerates a family crisis. Before his debilitating stroke, Joel put himself in a difficult situation by agreeing to defend Mohammed Hassani, an Arab American who is accused of being a member of a terrorist cell. Because Joel is an atheist, there is some casuistry in his defense of his client as an apolitical religious Muslim. His strategy requires him to display strong religious beliefs despite his disdain of religion. Instead of spirituality, Joel grounds his beliefs in the politics of revolutionary socialism. He has been known to return invitations to Jewish religious ceremonies with "there is no God" scrawled on them.

It is thus ironic that Joel seeks to cleanse his client of any political convictions in favor of his religious identity. Joel may have been softening his hard-left stance for some time, however: He has been keeping an African American mistress, Berenice Mason, who has New Age religious inclinations. The two have a son, Jamil. When Joel's already irritable wife Audrey discovers the affair, she is outraged. She realizes that Berenice is not merely one of her husband's familiar sexual dalliances. Instead, she has been there to provide a perspective otherwise missing in Joel's life. It is as if he were not only cheating on his wife but also cheating on his own political ideology.

If a new center replaces the sidelined Joel, it is Audrey. She began her life with Joel as an unformed British teenager, but she has evolved into a hard-boiled radical, perfectly willing to defend the September 11, 2001, attacks on the United States as an example of justifiable political retaliaton against American power. Her husband was a "red diaper" baby; his formative influences as a child included a Workers' Children's Camp at which songs of praise to Stalin were sung around the campfire. However, Audrey, a convert to her husband's cause, is now more of a true believer. Audrey is the most controversial character in this novel, by dint of her sheer unpleasantness. Priding herself on her utter honesty and on the purity of her politics, Audrey has undergone a sad hardening process as she has aged; she is less a beacon and a standard for her humanitarian causes and more a self-righteous shrew in whom the milk of human kindness has completely disappeared. At times, in fact, she appears to be on the verge of madness.

Zoë Heller is the author of two previous novels, Everything You Know *(1999) and* What Was She Thinking? Notes on a Scandal *(2003), which was shortlisted for the Man Booker Prize in 2003.*

Audrey's is not the novel's ruling consciousness, however. Instead, Heller draws her readers to the perspectives of Audrey's daughters, Karla and Rosa. Rosa, clearly and somewhat comically named for the famous radical Rosa Luxembourg, had formed her identity very much in compliance with that of her progressive father. Like Audrey, she has positioned herself to the left of Joel, accusing her father of ideological timidity and choosing to reside for several years in socialist Cuba. By the end of this sojourn in what she hoped to be a socialist utopia, however, Rosa has completely lost her faith in her father's political ideology. No longer a convinced socialist, she also begins to feel that her upbringing has left her surprisingly unformed and unsophisticated.

Working with underprivileged young girls in New York City does nothing to restore Rosa's faith. In fact, she finds she cannot bear the way in which she believes the ideologies of both sexual revolution and the self-esteem movement have corrupted her charges. She finds Chianti, one of the girls in her program, particularly incorrigible. She especially finds the salacious choreography Chianti has created for her dance project upsetting not only in itself but also because of the welcome it receives on the part of her more liberal coworkers. Unhappy with what she perceives as the sleazy sexuality of youth culture and unsatisfied with her own sex life, Rosa finds herself returning to her parents' religious roots in Judaism.

Shunning the more modern forms of Jewish faith, Rosa finds herself drawn to Orthodox Judaism, even as this interest throws her into crisis since there are aspects of this faith that seem to undermine her hard-won feminist identity. Her father's stroke, his subsequent death, and the general unraveling of her family and all their previous identities bring Rosa to a crossroads. She is inspired to once again leave home, this time choosing not the Cuba of her parents' socialist dreams but instead their worst nightmare—an Orthodox community in Israel. For Rosa, this choice provides her with a faith and a sense of belonging grounded in the tradition of her own family's past. She is convinced that this return to the faith of her forebears will give her life the meaning and purpose she can no longer find in her former, more modern political convictions.

Rosa's sister Karla is both less political and less religious than is Rosa. Like her sister, however, Karla has been raised to work in social services. Overweight and lacking in self-confidence, Karla—clearly and comically named after Karl Marx—is suitably married to a union organizer and is a social worker in a hospital, but she is far from happy. Her husband would like to start a family, but Karla not only has difficulty conceiving but also is not particularly interested in motherhood. When she stumbles into an affair with Khaled, the Egyptian man who runs the hospital newsstand, it becomes clear that her life, like Rosa's, is at a crossroads.

Indifferent to politics, Khaled is a nominal Muslim whose true beliefs include astrology and esoteric Enneagram charts. They are beliefs of which Karla's parents would wholly disapprove. None of this, however, matters to Karla; it is Khaled's empathic personality to which she responds. Choosing love over a compliance that has left her secretly seething and mysteriously liberated by her father's death, Karla impulsively abandons her plan to join her husband and family for Joel's memorial service in Manhattan and instead hops a subway to Khaled's borough. As the train barrels away from the platform into the dark tunnel, it becomes a perfect metaphor for Karla's brave decision to leave the old, the familiar, and the disappointing for the greater possibilities inherent in the new and unknown.

The third child of the Litvinoff family is the adopted Lenny, whose mother, a 1960's-style radical, has been imprisoned for bank robbery since he was a baby. Unlike the girls, the raffish Lenny has no interest in social service, having struggled with drug addiction and general aimlessness for most of his adult life. His recent return to yet another rehab program, under the guidance of a strangely angelic carpenter named Dave, seems to have made a major difference in his life. His testy stepmother Audrey loves Lenny dearly and probably best of all, but she is nevertheless a major obstacle to his recovery. As an atheist, she belittles the spiritual aspects of his twelve-step program, unwittingly making it more likely that drugs will continue to control Lenny's life. Audrey's general harsh vitriol is directed toward her children, her friends, and even the doctors and nurses who are looking after Joel. Eventually, it seems to poison even herself. She sinks into squalor, as her always recalcitrant cooking and housekeeping degenerate to such an extent that, both physically and psychologically, she seems to have sunk into an abyss of her own making.

One of the points of Heller's beautifully developed novel is that things and people change. As Rosa returns to her ancestral religious roots, as Karla finds happiness with a Muslim shopkeeper, and as Lenny turns a corner into sobriety, so Audrey is miraculously and mysteriously transformed by the very thing she had fought tooth and nail to prevent: her husband's death. While her husband seemed at one point utterly necessary to the very integrity of her personality, his death seems to emancipate Audrey in surprising ways, as it emancipated Karla. Joel's death actually inspires the cynical Audrey to turn affirmative, as she invents a new role for herself as Joel's loyal widow, the keeper of his flame. Amazingly grateful, Audrey not only celebrates Joel's achievements but also genuinely understands and appreciates the degree to which Joel permitted her to share his own good life.

In the wake of Joel's death, Audrey begins a foundation in his name, and at his memorial service she invites all his liberal and left-wing friends to commemorate his good deeds. In keeping with the narrative's satirical perspective, however, the memorial service is over the top and preposterously ideological, featuring a program that culminates in the congregation singing the anthem of international socialism. Despite the service's relentless secularity, the influence of Lenny may be felt in the fact that it takes place in a Christian church, the famous and politically progressive Cathedral of St. John the Divine. Appropriately, the service features an Audrey who seems suddenly the very soul of Christian charity. Having previously behaved in a heartless and ugly way toward Joel's patient mistress, she publicly proclaims her new familial friendship for Berenice and Jamil, virtually from the pulpit. Audrey's political beliefs have been sustained, but they seem to be inching closer to an alliance with the progressive wing of Christianity; more important, Audrey is no longer the "wicked witch of the West Village," and has relaxed into a more open and accepting perspective that has allowed her to age gracefully into a far more generous friend and mother than she was in her jaded middle years.

In the end, Audrey gives her blessing to everyone—Rosa, Karla, Lenny, Berenice—as a significant page has been turned in the life of all the book's major characters. Significantly, this is a family that has decentered and dispersed; no longer under one tent, the family scatters to various locales and comes to be shaped by diverse perspectives, none of which can be said to reflect the previous, purely radical vision that was the foundation of Audrey and Joel's marriage. While only Rosa has officially embraced a faith rooted in her own family traditions, all of the family's members have developed spiritual beliefs or affinities, whether involving Judaism, Islam, Christianity, New Age philosophy, or twelve-step therapies. While this novel is as much about the dismantling of political beliefs as it is about their perpetuation, there is a spiritual optimism in its concluding embrace of various religious perspectives that recalls the early socialist faith in the future that was so much the ground of Joel's own convictions.

Both satiric and empathic, this entertaining novel asks some serious questions. Heller not only examines the current condition of one of the last century's most powerful political ideologies but also does so within the intimacies of family life and human relationships. As a result, her novel is at heart a psychological exploration of what happens when losing one's politics is equivalent to losing one's religion and of how such a crisis can represent an awakening and an opportunity for personal exploration and transformation.

Margaret Boe Birns

Review Sources

The Boston Globe, March 8, 2009, p. C5.
The London Review of Books, November 6, 2008, pp. 35-36.

Los Angeles Times, March 2, 2009, p. E1.
The New York Review of Books, April 9, 2009, pp. 48-51.
The New York Times, February 26, 2009, p. C1.
The New York Times, March 3, 2009, p. C1.
The New York Times Book Review, March 8, 2009, p. 9.
The Times Literary Supplement, September 26, 2008, p. 23.
Toronto Star, March 3, 2009, p. E2.

THE BIG BURN
Teddy Roosevelt and the Fire That Saved America

Author: Timothy Egan (1954-)
Publisher: Houghton Mifflin Harcourt (Boston). Illustrated. 324 pp. $27.00
Type of work: History
Time: 1910
Locale: Washington, D.C.; Bitterroot Mountains, Idaho and Montana

Egan presents a popular history of the origins of the United States Forest Service, and its heroic but doomed battle against a massive firestorm in 1910

Principal personages:
THEODORE ROOSEVELT, president of the United States, 1901-1909
WILLIAM HOWARD TAFT, president of the United States, 1909-1913
GIFFORD PINCHOT, first chief of the United States Forest Service
ED PULASKI, forest ranger

Timothy Egan's *The Big Burn: Teddy Roosevelt and the Fire That Saved America* is an engaging account of a 1910 forest fire that burned an area in the northern Rockies the size of Connecticut and took dozens of lives. Egan is a winner of the National Book Award for a popular history of the 1930's Dust Bowl, and he knows how to vividly evoke character and spin a tale. When he is writing about the heroic efforts of forest rangers and firefighters to combat the flames of the Big Burn, he is on sure ground and his narrative is dramatic and compelling.

Egan's account of the fire takes up only about one-third of the book, however, and his sections on the political background to the Big Burn prove much less satisfying. Egan's portrayal of Theodore Roosevelt, William Howard Taft, and the Progressive Era is simplistic and one-dimensional. He settles all too often for a portrayal of "good guys" fighting "bad guys" that would be more appropriate for juvenile literature. He leaves out crucial aspects of the story of the rift between Roosevelt and Taft, his chosen successor. He also oversells the significance of his subject. The great Northwestern blazes of 1910 did not save America. In the end, then, Egan's book obscures as much as it reveals of the political forces operating through the smoke of the Big Burn.

Egan insists on referring to Roosevelt as "Teddy," a name the president loathed. He did not appreciate being called by a diminutive that evoked the children's toy that was named after him. Egan's use of the nickname is a telling indication of the superficiality of his understanding of Roosevelt. An immediate verbal caricature, it is of a piece with his general depiction of the president, startlingly reminiscent of the grinning, toothy, Rough Rider who graced contemporary political cartoons. One constantly expects Egan's Roosevelt to shout "Bully" and charge up the hall stairs.

Timothy Egan is a Pulitzer Prize-winning journalist and the author of five books. His The Worst Hard Time *(2006) won a National Book Award for nonfiction.*

Egan sees the well-born Roosevelt as a traitor to his class who defended workers and challenged big business and the wealthy. This is a crude interpretation of Roosevelt's Square Deal, which sought to balance the interests in American society. Although famed as a trustbuster, Roosevelt made a crucial distinction between good and bad trusts; he never led a crusade against corporate America. Even during his Bull Moose campaign for the presidency in 1912, one of Roosevelt's closest associates was George Perkins, a partner of financier J. P. Morgan.

Egan writes with more authority about Roosevelt's conservationism. Roosevelt played a critical role in protecting great tracts of land from immediate exploitation, as Egan says. Even here, however, Egan obscures the strong connections between Roosevelt's love of the outdoors and his less currently fashionable concerns about hunting, war, and "race suicide." Roosevelt wanted to preserve ground where men could test themselves as their pioneer forebears had, resisting the deadly corruptions of an urbanized, consumerist society. As Egan grudgingly acknowledges, Rooseveltian conservationism was concerned with preserving resources for future generations, not precluding future development.

Egan's treatment of Taft is little better. Invariably, when Taft makes an appearance in the book, mention is made of his girth. While Roosevelt is portrayed as a trim and fit liberal, Taft is a fat and languid conservative. Taft was no politician, and he soon felt out of place in the White House. He made many mistakes in his first year of office and never mastered the art of public relations. Nevertheless, he was an able chief executive with a progressive record that gets no mention in Egan's book.

As a conservationist, Taft set aside twice as much public land in his single term in office as did his energetic predecessor in over seven years. Taft deserves the title of trustbuster far more than Roosevelt does. His Justice Department launched over three times as many antitrust suits in his four years as president. In fact, it was Taft's decision to bring an antitrust suit against U.S. Steel in 1911 that led to the decisive rupture in his relations with Roosevelt. The suit mentioned a deal made by U.S. Steel that Roosevelt had personally approved.

The Rough Rider regarded the Justice Department's action against U.S. Steel as a personal affront, and he soon resolved to challenge Taft for the Republican presidential nomination. Egan leaves the impression that Roosevelt ran against Taft in 1912 because of differences over conservation. His fixation on the Big Burn and the battle for America's woodlands leads Egan to distort the political history of the Roosevelt and Taft Administrations. In his version of progressivism, the tail wags the dog.

Fortunately, Egan's weakness in laying out the political background of his story is balanced by the strength of his account of the formative years of the United States Forest Service. The central figure in his book is Gifford Pinchot, Roosevelt's chief forester. Pinchot was born to wealth, the family fortune ironically rooted in the lumber industry. Financially secure, Pinchot devoted himself to the study of forestry. He became a leader in a field few understood. He befriended the great naturalist John Muir and became passionately devoted to protecting the American wilderness from reckless commercial exploitation.

The crucial relationship of Pinchot's life was his friendship with Roosevelt. Both men were avid outdoorsmen; they also shared impatience with the politics of business-as-usual in Washington. Pinchot became a sparring partner and speechwriter for Roosevelt. He was a kindred spirit the president could count on for companionship in either a constitutional or a convivial conversation. Pinchot's reward was access to power. Roosevelt gave Pinchot an opportunity to act on his ideals, making him the first chief of the Forest Service.

Pinchot threw himself into his work with single-minded devotion. Unlike his mentor, he had not married and started a family. Pinchot was once engaged, but his fiancé died of tuberculosis in 1894. Egan recounts that, for the next two decades, Pinchot was convinced that the spirit of his lost love visited him regularly—not as an ethereal presence but in a form so tangible that he could carry on conversations with her about policy. Egan notes this strange psychic phenomenon in Pinchot's life but does not otherwise comment on it. In other hands, this might be taken as an indication that Pinchot was mentally unbalanced. For Egan, it seems to be one more measure of his hero's driven nature. Pinchot was a man determined to make the world conform to his vision of it.

Certainly, this was the case in his management of the Forest Service. He stamped his personality on it so indelibly that his early corps of specially chosen and trained forest rangers called themselves "Little G.P.s." Pinchot carefully picked his forest rangers. Many were products of the Ivy League, especially a program in forestry at Yale University. Pinchot demanded that his rangers write well; they also had to pass grueling tests in outdoor living, animal care, shooting, and carpentry.

The first generation of forest rangers was expected to patrol huge ranges of woodland, building their own cabins and stations. Pinchot entertained rangers in his Washington home as they trained for their assignments, imbuing them with his own sense of dedication to defending America's woodlands. Morale was very high in the Forest Service. This was important because, under Roosevelt as well as Taft, forest rangers were poorly paid and had to provide their own, horses, saddles, rifles, and boots.

Pinchot faced entrenched opposition in Congress from powerful politicians who saw the Forest Service as an obstacle to economic development in the West. In an effort to justify his fledgling agency, Pinchot made fire control a priority of the Forest Service. This was a mission that lumber men and conservationists alike could embrace. Rangers soon were stamping out brush fires that seemed to threaten ancient timber.

Pinchot's maneuver, while politically shrewd, set the stage for the Forest Service's futile battle in 1910. He, however, would not be there to command his rangers. He engaged in a ferocious dispute with Taft's secretary of the interior, Richard Ballinger, over the opening of some public land to commercial use. Taft finally fired Pinchot early in 1910. Pinchot immediately joined the peregrinating Roosevelt overseas to tell his mentor his version of events, and the affair strained relations between the former and incumbent presidents.

The summer of 1910 in the mountain woodlands where Montana and Idaho meet was unusually dry. On July 26, an electrical storm started over one thousand fires. Almost a month later, the number had doubled. On August 20, a western wind known as a Palouser blew in and stoked the fires into a rapidly moving inferno. Caught in the advance of this firestorm were forest rangers, Army troops, and hundreds of immigrant laborers hired to fight the fires and protect the wildcat towns in the region that housed miners and lumbermen.

Egan masterfully describes the efforts of the firefighters to survive in the terrifying conditions of the resulting perfect storm of flame. There were many heroes in this desperate struggle for survival. Ed Pulaski, a forest ranger, was widely acknowledged as the greatest of these heroes. He saved most of his force of fifty firefighters by leading them through the blaze to a mineshaft that gave them cover. Pulaski himself suffered severe injuries that stayed with him for the rest of his life. By the time the fire died down, around eighty men had died, and a huge stretch of the Bitterroot Mountains had been burned over.

Roosevelt and Pinchot used the Big Burn as an occasion to criticize the conservation policies of the Taft administration. Roosevelt talked of the fire on the famous swing through the prairie states during which he laid out his "New Nationalism." Pinchot argued that, had the Forest Service been better supported and funded, it could have prevented the disaster. Given the titanic natural forces at work, this was an absurd claim. Nevertheless, the trauma of the Big Burn shaped the governing ethos of the Forest Service for generations. As veterans of the fire rose in the service, firefighting became an obsession.

Increasingly, the Forest Service cooperated with the logging industry, protecting trees so they could be harvested for commercial purposes. Only recently has the Forest Service acknowledged the ecological folly of preventing all fires, which are nature's way of renewing forests. Pinchot himself came to acknowledge this. After a successful career in politics, during which he served two terms as governor of Pennsylvania, he revisited the western forests and recognized that fires were not a force that human beings could hope to control. Egan ends his account on a note of grace, pointing out that, whatever the errors of Pinchot and other early leaders of the Forest Service, the forests that they sought to protect still remain for future generations to treasure.

Daniel P. Murphy

Review Sources

Booklist 106, no. 1 (September 1, 2009): 25.
Kirkus Reviews 77, no. 15 (August 1, 2009): 96.
Library Journal 134, no. 16 (October 1, 2009): 94.
The New York Review of Books 56, no. 17 (November 5, 2009): 44-46.
The New York Times Book Review, November 1, 2009, p. 14.
Publishers Weekly 256, no. 31 (August 3, 2009): 38.
The Wall Street Journal, October 21, 2009, p. A21.
The Washington Times, October 12, 2009, p. 17.

BIRDSCAPES
Birds in Our Imagination and Experience

Author: Jeremy Mynott (1942-   )
Publisher: Princeton University Press (Princeton, N.J.). 367 pp. $29.95
Type of work: Natural history, philosophy, science, sociology

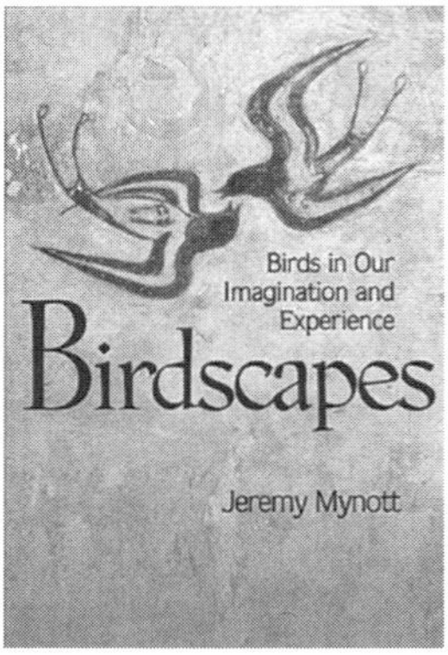

Mynott sets out to determine what humans appreciate about birds and what that appreciation teaches humans about themselves

In the Preface to *Birdscapes*, Jeremy Mynott expresses his intention to let readers follow the twisted and indirect path he himself took to reach his conclusions, rather than presenting a streamlined path—purged of false starts and dead ends—in the manner of most studies of this sort. While it is doubtful that he includes all of the nonproductive thought processes he toyed with in writing the book, he certainly includes some of them. Even when it is time to draw conclusions, in the last paragraphs of the last page of the book, Mynott fails to answer the questions that he set out to explore—why people like birds and which characteristics of birds draw people to them.

Instead of stating broad, general conclusions to these questions, Mynott declares that people can lose themselves (and then find themselves) in a number of activities or interests, from art to travel. He concludes that wondering about birds is one such activity—and a good one. Earlier, on the previous page, he explained his feelings with regard to the paucity of precise answers in his study, saying that he learned a great deal in the process of writing the book and he is now "confused in more interesting ways."

These are appropriate, even refreshing conclusions, especially in light of a secondary expectation Mynott held. He anticipated that he would learn some basic things about human nature in his exploration of human-bird relationships. This may have been the primary purpose for the book, to use human interest in birds to understand humanity. At any rate, he explores both ideas throughout the book, hypothesizing about which characteristics of birds interest and charm humans and why, as well as exploring what these observations and hypotheses might teach people about themselves.

Mynott explores very different attitudes and activities involving birds, ranging from hunting and eating them to watching and listening to them. To Mynott, most human interactions with birds suggest basic human characteristics. Using these suggestions, he explores human nature as an extension of the bird-human interaction. Each chapter begins with a description of one of Mynott's many bird-watching experiences. The experience exemplifies the focus of the chapter and initiates its discussion.

Each chapter considers one or more reasons for loving birds, including their association with a particular memorable experience or favorite landscape. Mynott argues that it is really the total experience or the total landscape that is remembered fondly and that that total context stimulates the love of the birds that were integral parts of the whole.

A bird-watcher for most of his life, Jeremy Mynott has traveled widely to observe birds and bird-watchers. He is especially interested in the songs and calls of birds and has studied them in depth. He has worked as the chief executive of the Cambridge University Press.

Mynott posits several other possible reasons that people appreciate birds. Some enjoy the challenge of identifying specific species. Some simply find birds' construction and coloring beautiful and take pleasure in looking at them. Some appreciate their songs. Some are struck by the wonder of flight. Those humans who wish they could fly may be attracted to birds, though simultaneously jealous of them, for their ability to fly. Mynott is unable or unwilling to pin down a single characteristic of birds that gives them such favor with humankind, and he suggests, from time to time, that combinations of many bird characteristics are responsible for human ornithophilia.

Mynott suggests that each of the reasons for loving birds plays a part in or is parallel to human endeavors and interests that do not involve birds. For example, in the chapter on sound he presents an argument that, while vision is considered to be the most fundamental sense, it may be no more important than hearing. He relates this arugment to birds by pointing out that in some contexts, forests in full leaf for example, bird-watchers must use their hearing more than their vision, finding and identifying birds by their songs and calls rather than by their appearance. He muses that in these situations, the exercise might be better called "bird listening" instead of "bird-watching." Outside the birding context, Mynott quotes Helen Keller saying that loss of hearing was a greater hardship to her than loss of sight. He thus wonders why aural cues are subordinated to visual cues in bird-identification field guides.

Mynott explores some ornithologic and birding history. He discusses the early American bird artists, including John James Audubon and Alexander Wilson, who stimulated the rise of North American ornithology. In addition, he considers the formal nomenclature that has developed for birds; scientific and common names are both discussed. In keeping with his determination to generalize the human response beyond that to birds, Mynott develops a philosophy of nomenclature that is broader than bird names. He concludes that the names humans use in many contexts may be less random and more meaningful than is commonly believed.

Mynott includes an interesting consideration of the role of "rarity" in bird-watching. The bird-watchers who keep lists of the birds they have seen value the ability to add rare birds to those lists. Because rare bird species will, by definition, seldom be available for observation and counting, birders sometimes exert extreme effort to see them. Responding regularly to the presence of a rare species is called "twitching" and the responder is called a "twitcher."

Mynott argues that some of this reaction to rarity is shallow and artificial. For example, sometimes a bird is discovered by someone else and advertised on a rare bird alert network. Twitchers then travel to the discovery site by following the instructions provided in the announcement, wait in a line at the site, and look through a telescope that has been provided and focused on the bird by someone else. Mynott denies that these twitchers deserve credit for such "sightings." He sees the same type of shallow, artificial attention to rarity exhibited in contexts other than ornithology, such as by collectors. He tells of a rare-book collector who bought a second copy of a book he already owned and burned the copy in order to keep it out of the hands of other collectors.

Several topics recur at different points in the book. Mynott notes and discusses the extensive roles birds have played in symbolism, folklore, and mythology. He also explores birds' contributions to the problem of anthropomorphism in scientific writing. Anthropomorphic verbiage assigns human characteristics and thoughts to birds and other animals and is frowned upon in scientific circles. Mynott agrees that it is a bad practice, but he is sympathetic with the argument that it is sometimes easier and more direct to use terms that could be interpreted anthropomorphically in scientific discourse, rather than contorting one's speech in order to avoid the suggestion of anthropomorphism.

At one point in this discussion, Mynott discusses "ornithomorphism" (a neologism meant to be an antonym of anthropomorphism), in which bird words are used in the description of human activities. He provides such examples as "eagle-eyed" and "craning one's neck," among others. He repeatedly expresses concern at the fact that some birds have charisma while others seem to lack it and that charismatic species receive more attention and protection than uncharismatic species. Often, a charismatic species is neither as much in need of protection nor any more deserving of attention than its less charismatic compatriots. To make this point, Mynott describes some unpleasant characteristics of the most charismatic birds in Great Britain, those chosen as the people's favorites in various polls.

Some of the anecdotes Mynott uses to support his arguments are interesting in their own right. One of the more intriguing examples is the story of Beatrice Harrison, her cello, and the skylark that volunteered to sing along when she played the cello in a woodlot. The skylark's acompaniment was so impressive that the pair was featured on British television. There is some skepticism that the skylark was actually harmonizing closely with the cello, but it was clearly singing along in response to the instrument.

Another such anecdote is included in the description of human attempts to present birdsongs and calls so that they can be easily learned. Mynott discusses attempts to describe birdsongs verbally and in sonograms, to record them for playback, and otherwise to learn and emulate these songs. He concludes that it is difficult, that sonograms are useful if a learner has the patience to understand them, and that playback of recorded birdsongs is very helpful. In this context, he describes an effort to generate artificial but accurate birdsongs: Songs were recorded then played back at a slower speed and set to music at that slower, human tempo. The musical score produced by transcribing the slowed birdsong was then played at the faster speed of actual birdsong, and it greatly resembled the original birdsong.

Mynott lives in Great Britain and writes primarily about the birds of the British isles. However, he does describe some of his and other bird-watchers' experiences in North America, Australia, and elsewhere, so the book is not restricted to discussion of British birds. The principles Mynott explores are germane to any geographic location. His secondary familiarity with American birds might have contributed to the few errors found in the work, such as Mynott's assertion that the field sparrow is in sharp decline or his outdated assertion that the Baltimore oriole has been combined with another species. None of these oversights detracts seriously from the book, which is well written and carefully edited.

Mynott transitions between chapters and sections nicely, and every so often he inserts a paragraph summarizing his past argument and previewing the next section. His refusal to draw a conclusion that declares one or a few bird characteristics to be the attractant that draws people to birds is both appropriate and refreshing. There is no single, easy-to-identify set of bird characteristics that attract humans. Instead, different birds in different contexts and different landscapes are attractive to different people for different reasons or different combinations of reasons.

Four appendixes, a list of abbreviations, extensive notes on each chapter, a thorough general index, and an index of the birds mentioned in the book all add to the volume's usefulness. Fifty-seven black-and-white illustrations and eight color plates serve to clarify various points in the text. Reviewers have been favorably disposed toward the book.

Carl W. Hoagstrom

Review Sources

The Guardian, April 18, 2009, p. 8.
The New Yorker 85, no. 10 (April 20, 2009): 113.
Pittsburgh Post-Gazette June 28, 2009, p. DD-2.
Science 325, no. 5947 (September 18, 2009): 1501.
Times Higher Education, May 14, 2009, p. 50.
The Times Literary Supplement, September 11, 2009, p. 23.

BLAME

Author: Michelle Huneven (1953-)
Publisher: Farrar, Straus and Giroux (New York).
291 pp. $25.00
Type of work: Novel
Time: 1980-2001
Locale: Los Angeles, California, and vicinity

A story of guilt and redemption, in which a brilliant young history professor's life is changed by her involvement in a fatal automobile accident and her subsequent prison sentence

Principal characters:
PATSY MACLEMOORE, a tall, blond history professor and an alcoholic
CAL SHARP, a kindly, elegant lawyer, the guiding spirit of local Alcoholics Anonymous groups
BRICE, Patsy's one-time boyfriend, a charming wastrel
JOEY HAWTHORNE, Brice's niece
GILLES, Cal's nephew, former lover of two famous artists
IAN SASAKI, a taciturn artist and professor
LEWIS FLETCHER, an intense comparative literature adjunct
EILEEN SILVER, Patsy's therapist
MARK PARNHAM, widower and father of the accident victims, a civil engineer

Los Angeles as a literary landscape has long been the territory of gritty detective stories and tragic or comedic tales of the glittering denizens of Hollywood. However, the area is also home to quite a few novelists who explore dilemmas of the human heart occurring in lesser-known parts of the region. Michelle Huneven's novel *Blame*, which tells of the personal price extracted for a random event, plays out in three environments unfamiliar to most readers: a woman's prison, the subculture of Alcoholics Anonymous, and the old-money enclaves of Altadena and Pasadena, which have changed very little during the decades of the metropolitan area's explosive growth.

Six months after Patsy MacLemoore successfully defends her dissertation and earns a Ph.D., she enters the custody of the California correctional system. She has just pled guilty to two counts of criminal negligence resulting in loss of life. The plea bargain was the best deal her attorney Benny could get; she had several prior convictions for driving while under the influence of alcohol and was driving with a suspended license when she hit two Jehovah's Witnesses, a mother and daughter, in her own driveway. Patsy herself remembers nothing about the accident. She only knows that she blacked out then awakened in jail, finding her joking query, "What'd I do now?" met with stony silence.

Michelle Huneven was born in Altadena, California, where she still lives. She studied at Grinnell College and the Iowa Writers Workshop. Huneven is the author of two earlier novels, Round Rock *(1997) and* Jamesland *(2003).*

Patsy enters prison overwhelmed with guilt and dread. Benny has warned her that prison is horrible, and it is. All around her are metallic sounds and shrieking. The solitude she expected to experience in confinement never materializes: She is always surrounded by other women prisoners, many of whom babble constantly. The food is so bad that she stops eating. She loses thirty pounds in her first month in prison and is only saved from starvation when Gloria, an older woman who functions as a sort of den mother to her fellow prisoners, gets Patsy a job working in the kitchen. There, she can filch saltine packets and occasionally eat an apple or banana. When she is moved to a medium-security unit, Patsy survives on food from the commissary, which she likens to a badly stocked convenience store. She buys ramen noodles, tuna, and expired crackers that she can consume in her dormitory.

Patsy knows she must give up drinking. She refuses the rotgut concoctions others sneak into prison, but for a long time she also turns down Gloria's invitations to join the prison's Alcoholics Anonymous (AA) sessions. The sheer lure of alcohol is still too seductive for her to face giving it up for a lifetime. Eventually, she does attend the sessions, drawn as much by the genuine laughter and camaraderie found there as by the prospect that her attendance may later help her gain parole.

Patsy's self-denial goes beyond food and drink. Racked with remorse, she resolves to live a better life, to not be cruel in word or deed, and to make a difference. For the last year of her sentence, she is assigned to a fire camp in the hills above Malibu. Despite the bone-wearying work of chopping brush and the occasional danger of fighting wildfires, it is "easier time" than prison. From camp, she can see vistas of the sea and mountains; the food is actually good, cooked from scratch on-site.

Patsy's release comes in June, 1983, two months earlier than expected. She is given a long list of conditions she must meet in order to be released. Patsy's former boyfriend Brice, her most faithful visitor in prison, has arranged for some of them. He secures an apartment for her at the Lyster, a formerly fashionable apartment building that he manages. Her department head at Hallen College has already assured her that she will have a teaching job in the fall. Because she needs to show that she is working immediately, she takes an English as a second language (ESL) summer teaching assignment at a nearby school. She also has to attend frequent AA meetings—ninety meetings in ninety days, says Knock-Knock, her parole officer. She must also to be prepared for Knock-Knock to drop by and check on her any time.

The following year is possibly the most eventful of Patsy's life. Her adjustment to freedom, though welcome, is equally as traumatic as was that to prison two years before. Patsy is unused to having a whole apartment to herself and to being sociable without the buffers of liquor and the hilarity it provides. Formerly, she had a sharp wit and a reputation as the life of the party, but now she has become subdued and even shy. Fortunately, Brice proves a more reliable friend than he was a lover. He and

Gilles, who has moved in with him, often invite Patsy to dinner and provide rides to AA meetings. Patsy also follows up on Knock-Knock's recommendation of a therapist and finds in Eileen Silver a wonderful confidant who helps her work through depression and other life issues.

Patsy resolves to take things slowly with her emotions. For a while she dates Ian and to her shock finds herself burning with erotic impulses. They go out to dinner and to a few movies, but Ian does not want to talk much, and their friendship settles into a pattern of twice-weekly late evenings of sex. It is not what Patsy wants, but she is not even sure what sort of relationship she is capable of at this time. Then, Cal Sharp comes into her life.

Cal is a legend in AA circles, a rich, good-looking man who always has a helping hand for anyone trying to rebuild their life. Most women in AA cherish a secret crush on him, for his accepting attitude and his intense blue eyes, but he is also more than twenty-five years older than Patsy. When he first asks her to exercise his late wife's horse, she believes he is only helping provide a new AA member with a useful task.

Patsy's life rapidly becomes complex. Gilles is hospitalized, an early acquired immunodeficiency syndrome (AIDS) patient. Ian's status in Patsy's life remains undefined, and the challenges of climbing back onto the tenure track at Hallen absorb her. Outwardly, Patsy is doing great—and Cal tells her so—but inside, she is not so sure. Being with Cal feels like being wrapped in a warm glow of approval and emotional support. Before either of them quite intends, marriage looms as the logical next step. Patsy rationally examines the implications of such a choice, from acquiring stepchildren to the consequences for her own hopes for the future. At least, she thinks she is being rational. She decides that Cal is the best man she has ever met and she will be able to deal adequately with any problems resulting from their marriage. They marry less than a year after her release from prison.

Cal's encouragement and wealth make it possible for Patsy to do good, as she resolved to do. She keeps in touch with Mark Parnham, who while she was imprisoned inexplicably forgave her for causing the death of his family, and she helps pay his son's college expenses. She and Cal tell their stories at innumerable AA meetings, where they are treated like royalty. As the years go by, Patsy's academic career advances. She publishes two books and earns offers to speak and study overseas, yet the guilt from her past is never quite assuaged. It does not help that, in a season of discontent, she thinks she has found her soul mate in Lewis, a fellow academic, but cuts off their friendship as a potential threat to her marriage.

Then, two decades after the event, evidence emerges that Patsy was not the driver during the fatal crash. She follows up this initial evidence, examining all relevant information with a historian's caution. Once she has confirmed that she was not responsible for the Parnhams' deaths, she reacts with joy and relief. Inevitably, though, she also undergoes a major reexamination of her life choices, seeking to understand how they have been shaped by a mistaken belief in her own guilt.

As fate would have it, the age difference between Patsy and Cal has finally caught up with them. Cal is almost eighty and content to stay home watching television while Patsy pursues her own professional goals. Further, Cal's youngest daughter, the snappish March, has moved into their house with her entire family. Given her husband's laziness and her toddlers' needs, they appear poised to stay indefinitely.

Cal is charmed at being surrounded with grandchildren in his old age. Patsy feels displaced in her own home. The final blow comes when Cal, unlike Patsy's friends and colleagues, insists on downplaying Patsy's newly revealed innocence. At first, he grumbles about it being hearsay evidence. When he can no longer do so, he dismisses her prison time and enormous guilt by saying, in effect, that it does not matter because the experience got her to stop drinking. To Patsy, this feels like the ultimate betrayal. She buys a small house in a mountainside neighborhood and moves into it, ready to live her life on her own terms.

Blame is not a tightly structured novel, in which cause and effect make certain events inevitable. As one reviewer notes, it is more like real life, in which things just sort of happen. In accordance with this pattern, the most significant event in Patsy MacLemoore's life is something that did not happen—at least, not in the way she believes it did. The somewhat random string of resulting events seems appropriate for such a story.

Critical reviews of the book have been overwhelmingly positive, with good reason. Huneven uses words, metaphors, and incidents with a near-perfect touch. Her presentation of character never rings false. Even background details are carefully observed and gracefully described. The author catches the qualities of the Los Angeles-area sky at different hours precisely, and neighborhood sounds convey the inner life of a street or cul-de-sac.

A few criticisms are common to several reviewers; some are valid, some less so. Many note that the prologue focuses on twelve-year-old Joey Hawthorne, adrift in the old Bellwood hotel while her mother is dying of breast cancer. Patsy MacLemoore is a peripheral actor in this scene. When the main narrative opens a year later, a reader's attention suddenly has to shift to Patsy, the book's central character. This strategy violates most advice given to novelists. One can only guess that Joey's continuing role in Patsy's life—as the discoverer of the truth about the accident and perhaps as a sort of substitute daughter figure—motivates the opening.

No quotation marks are used for dialogue in *Blame*. While this lack is bound to annoy some readers, it functions to wrap conversations in a woozy blanket, suggesting first the effects of alcohol on Patsy then her distancing from the other prisoners' chatter. Even after her release, Patsy never feels fully a part of the world.

Only two minor story points do not ring true, a good record for any novelist. One might speculate about the real errand of the accident victims. They were hit at dusk after leaving flyers at Patsy's door. Jehovah's Witnesses usually "witness" from door to door during the daytime, especially on Sunday mornings. Also, given interdepartmental rivalries, it seems unlikely that a history professor would be teaching a course on the works of literary figures such as Willa Cather and Edith Wharton, as Patsy does.

The publisher has been criticized for hinting at the crucial turning point in the book cover's notes. One can make a case, though, that the story's real peripeteia—or emotionally stunning reversal—comes afterward, in Cal's unsympathetic reaction to Patsy's exoneration. These few quibbles aside, *Blame* is a novel full of extraordinary insights and grace.

Emily Alward

Review Sources

The Atlantic Monthly 304, no. 3 (October, 2009): 114.
Booklist 105, no. 21 (July 1, 2009): 27.
Library Journal 134, no. 13 (August 1, 2009): 68.
Los Angeles Magazine 54, no. 9 (September, 2009): 72.
The New Yorker 85, no. 33 (October 19, 2009): 87.
People 72, no. 12 (September 21, 2009): 65.
Publishers Weekly 256, no. 20 (July 20, 2009): 122.

BLOOD'S A ROVER

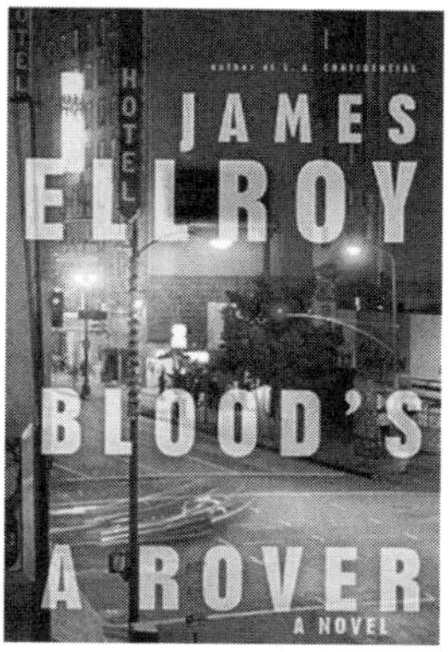

Author: James Ellroy (1948-)
Publisher: Alfred A. Knopf (New York). 639 pp. $28.95
Type of work: Novel
Time: 1968-1972
Locale: Los Angeles; Dominican Republic

In the third volume of James Ellroy's Underworld U.S.A. trilogy, following American Tabloid *and* The Cold Six Thousand, *Ellroy tells the story of three men who struggle to surface through the mire of late 1960's and early 1970's police, government, and underworld corruption*

Principal characters:

DWIGHT HOLLY, an FBI agent
WAYNE TEDROW, JR., a former policeman who becomes an agent for reclusive billionaire Howard Hughes
DON "CRUTCH" CRUTCHFIELD, a young private investigator
KAREN SIFAKIS, an informant to Dwight and also his lover
JOAN KLEIN, a left-wing underground activist
MARSHALL BOWEN, an undercover police officer used by Dwight to infiltrate a militant African American organization
SCOTTY BENNETT, a vicious and corrupt Los Angeles police detective
JEAN-PHILLIPPE MESPLEDE, a French mercenary and anti-Castro agent who participated in the assassination of John F. Kennedy
MARY BETH HAZZARD, wife of a murdered African American activist

James Ellroy's novel *Blood's a Rover* is the final installment in the author's Underworld U.S.A. trilogy. The first novel, *American Tabloid* (1995), covered the abortive American attack on Cuba and the Bay of Pigs crisis in 1963 as well as its aftermath and the assassination of President John F. Kennedy. The second novel, *The Cold Six Thousand* (2001), further detailed the interweaving of government agencies such as the Central Intelligence Agency (CIA) and the Federal Bureau of Investigation (FBI) with organized crime and led up to the assassination of Martin Luther King, Jr. *Blood's a Rover* picks up soon after the end of *The Cold Six Thousand*, further relating the struggles, both external and internal, of former police officer (and onetime vigilante) Wayne Tedrow and his friend, FBI agent Dwight Holly, from 1968 through 1972.

Stylistically, *Blood's a Rover* is similar in cadence to *The Cold Six Thousand.* Ellroy uses slang and short, choppy sentences with very little setup or description to develop his story; very few paragraphs are longer than three sentences. Ellroy employs the staccato rhythms and beats of everyday speech—and particularly the slang of the period covered in the novel—to keep the pace of the lengthy, 639-page novel rapid and edgy. While the style can be wearying, it is unique and speaks to Ellroy's willingness to challenge the tropes of detective fiction, as his plots have always dem-

A native of Los Angeles, James Ellroy has written thirteen crime novels, including L.A. Confidential *(1990),* White Jazz *(1992), and* American Tabloid *(1995), as well as essays, short fiction, screenplays, and the 1996 memoir* My Dark Places. *Many of his works have been adapted into films.*

onstrated. In a strategy also similar to that the previous novels, Ellroy primarily divides his narrative between three characters: Wayne, Dwight, and Donald "Crutch" Crutchfield. Much of the tension of the novel takes the form of dramatic irony; readers realize that a fact discovered by one of the protagonists would be revelatory to another protagonist, but readers cannot be sure whether those characters' paths will intersect in the right time and way.

Like its two predecessors, *Blood's a Rover* is a book that bores down through the surface happenings of American history and posits a tumultuous, interwoven, and complicated underworld of dark ambitions and hidden manipulations. As in the previous novels of the trilogy, as well as the earlier novels of Ellroy's L.A. Quartet, *Blood's a Rover* makes use of real-world public and underworld figures. Ellroy appropriates and offers characterizations of J. Edgar Hoover, the legendary founder of the FBI; Hollywood actor Sal Mineo; Howard Hughes, the famously reclusive and troubled billionaire; President Richard Nixon; and notorious underworld figures such as Sam Giancana, Santo Trafficante, Jr., and Carlos Marcello. Ellroy's portrayal of Hoover is particularly unkind, depicting him as a man obsessed with subjugating African Americans and making use of the national fear of communism to build his own power base.

Two of the novel's three protagonists previously appeared in *The Cold Six Thousand.* Dwight Holly returns as J. Edgar Hoover's subtle and tough "enforcer." He is joined in the narrative by former policeman Wayne Tedrow. Dwight previously helped Wayne in a vendetta against the man who raped and killed his wife. In taking his revenge, Wayne found himself in the debt of powerful people. Doing the bidding of various underworld and right-wing interests (including Hoover) in the previous novel, the two men helped bring about the assassinations of Robert F. Kennedy and Martin Luther King, Jr. In *Blood's a Rover*, Dwight, still in the FBI and still working primarily for Hoover on clandestine operations, is tasked with infiltrating and bringing down any of the various militant African American groups rising to power in the late 1960's, such as the Black Panthers or (in the case of the novel) the Black Tribe Alliance (BTA) and the Mau Mau Liberation Front (MMLF).

Wayne, on the other hand, uses his notoriety as a former vigilante and the son of a notorious right-wing personality to ingratiate himself with the reclusive billionaire Hughes. Wayne becomes a go-between for Hughes in contact with a triumvirate of Mafia leaders: Giancana, Trafficante, and Marcello. While helping Dwight in his various machinations, Wayne is also tasked with getting Hughes to buy more property in Las Vegas and to eventually begin development (again in collusion with the underworld) in the Dominican Republic.

The novel's third protagonist, "Crutch" Crutchfield, is a young private eye who is making a name for himself as a surveillance expert, able to film and record clandestine trysts and meetings. Engrossed as he is in voyeurism, and obsessed with older women, Crutch is reminiscent of earlier Ellroy characters such as Bucky Bleichert of *The Black Dahlia* (1987) and the author's self-portrait in his memoir, *My Dark Places* (1996). Despite his initial naïveté, Crutch is talented at finding suspects and recording them without their knowledge.

In some ways, *Blood's a Rover* is the most traditional of the three Underworld U.S.A. novels, in that the structure of the entire lengthy book is centered and grounded by a famous armored-car robbery of emeralds that occurred in 1964. Various characters throughout the novel become obsessed with finding the emeralds; additionally, single emeralds from the robbery occasionally appear in African American communities of Los Angeles. The robbery itself, obscure as it is, slowly works to intersect the lives of Dwight, Wayne, and Crutch.

At the same time, the novel is a strident departure from most of Ellroy's earlier books. Typically, Ellroy characters may be brave but are almost never heroic; instead, his detectives, agents, and policemen work in their own self-interest. Their need to solve crimes is less about catching criminals and more about building up their own reputations. Initially, *Blood's a Rover* seems to be cut from the same cloth: Dwight is willing to cover up murders and steal important information for Hoover; Wayne works for Dwight and has no compunction about working for the Mafia; Crutch feels no pangs of remorse for taking pictures and films that will be used in blackmail. The primary trajectory in *Blood's a Rover*, however, brings all three men to crave atonement for their misdeeds; each decides to make up for past crimes and to work to change the future, and at least two of the three face serious consequences for their changes of heart. The novel's title comes from A. E. Housman's poem "Reveille":

> Clay lies still, but blood's a rover;
> Breath's a ware that will not keep.
> Up, lad: when the journey's over
> There'll be time enough to sleep.

In the same way that the speaker in the poem warns that things must be accomplished in lives all too brief, so do Wayne and Dwight work to make differences in the world they helped create.

All three men are led through their internal changes by women. Initially, Dwight uses his lover Karen Sifakis, a left-wing peaceful activist and professor, simply as an informant. Eventually, though, she leads him to the enigmatic and magnetic Joan Klein, a subversive leftist underground worker who has sought for years to counteract the right-wing machinations of men such as Hoover and Nixon. Like Karen, Joan agrees to inform on violent crimes to Dwight in exchange for help for her friends and political favors. Additionally, Wayne becomes involved with Mary Beth Hazzard, a woman whose husband was killed in part to cover up a crime committed by Wayne himself and whose son has been missing for years.

Wayne and Dwight are both haunted by their pasts. Wayne, particularly, is unable to forget the damage he has done, partly out of fury and partly out of the manipulation of power brokers. Even as he is supposed to be helping his trio of Mafioso leaders develop casinos in Haiti and the Dominican Republic, he begins helping the communist resistance instead. Wayne's integrity and raw need for change make an impression on Dwight, and, as Wayne develops, Dwight does too. Before long, each is being led by Joan to work increasingly for her gains while they strive to keep their changing affiliations secret from the likes of Giancana, Trafficante, and Hoover.

For much of *Blood's a Rover*, the plot is fragmented and scattered, and it seems doubtful that the various strands will ever tie together. Wayne's actions in Haiti and the Dominican Republic seem to have little to do with Dwight's work in having a young African American policeman, Marshall Bowen, infiltrate the BTA and MMLF. At the same time as Crutch is employed by Wayne's sometime partner, the French mercenary Mesplede, Crutch still follows the original case that led him to Wayne and Dwight, searching for a blackmailing woman who turns out to be one of Joan Klein's partners. Appearing throughout the text is the vicious and predatory detective Scotty Bennett, whose single-minded quest to recover the emeralds lost in an armored-car robbery five years earlier is clearly less about justice and more about his avarice. The emeralds and Joan, however, provide the anchors for the plot, and slowly but surely the various plot lines tighten into a dense and complex knot of entanglements. In a sense, the development of the characters' consciences—from both a political and a moral perspective—mirrors the growth of the United States throughout the decade of the 1960's that is covered in the Underworld U.S.A. trilogy. The nation and the characters evolve from a ferocious adherence to the status quo to a slow if grudging progress.

Even as the cynical and savvy Wayne and Dwight are manipulated by Joan Klein, Crutch comes to understand how everything ties together. Of them all, Crutch is the survivor, the one who understands how to play his part without having to pay an irrecoverable price. Crutch does not have the blood on his hands that Wayne and Dwight have on theirs, nor are his actions scrutinized as theirs are. Taking their cues from Joan "the Red Goddess," the men in *Blood's a Rover* ultimately have to transform themselves into men they can live with being.

Scott D. Yarbrough

Review Sources

Booklist 105, no. 19/20 (June 1, 2009): 4.
Economist 392, no. 8649 (September 19, 2009): 98.
Kirkus Reviews 77, no. 15 (August 1, 2009): 46.
Library Journal 134, no. 12 (July 1, 2009): 81.
New Statesman 138, no. 4974 (November 9, 2009): 55-56.
The New York Review of Books 56, no. 16 (October 22, 2009): 50-52.
The New Yorker 85, no. 31 (October 5, 2009): 79.
The Paris Review 190 (Fall, 2009): 37-69.
Publishers Weekly 256, no. 26 (June 29, 2009): 110.
Rolling Stone, October 15, 2009, 60+.
The Times Literary Supplement, October 30, 2009, pp. 19-20.

THE BLUE HOUR
A Life of Jean Rhys

Author: Lilian Pizzichini (1965-)
First published: The Blue Hour: A Portrait of Jean Rhys, 2009, in Great Britain
Publisher: W. W. Norton (New York). 322 pp. $29.95
Type of work: Literary biography
Time: 1890-1979
Locale: Dominica, West Indies; England; Paris and Juan-les-Pins, France; Vienna, Austria; Budapest, Hungary

This portrait of the author of Wide Sargasso Sea *is more an evocation of Jean Rhys rather than a detailed, scholarly examination of the facts of her life. Omitting any analysis of her novels, it focuses on Rhys as a troubled and troubling woman*

Principal personages:
JEAN RHYS (born ELLA GWENDOLINE REES WILLIAMS), a writer
WILLIAM REES WILLIAMS, her father
MINNA REES WILLIAMS, her mother
META, her childhood nurse
CLARICE WILLIAMS, her aunt
LANCELOT SMITH, her first serious lover
JEAN (or JOHN) LENGLET, her first husband
LESLIE TILDEN SMITH, her second husband
MAX HAMER, her third husband
MARYVONNE LENGLET, her daughter
FORD MADOX FORD, a famous British author, her lover
STELLA BOWEN, Ford's common-law wife
SELMA VAZ DIAS, an actress

Toward the end of Jean Rhys's life, after one of her many arrests for assaulting neighbors, disturbing the peace, and so forth, a local newspaper published an article about Rhys's latest clash with the law under the headline "Mrs. Hamer Agitated." One of the neighbors with whom she was feuding, when informed of Rhys's identity, refused to believe it, saying that she was an impostor "impersonating a dead writer called Jean Rhys." Lilian Pizzichini's biography of Rhys, *The Blue Hour*, reveal that its subject was a violent drunk. She beat her husbands as well as her neighbors, and she seemed to have a perpetual chip on her shoulder. She suspected others and their motives, even when they tried to help her—perhaps especially then.

The biography thus reveals an unpleasant side of an author known for *Wide Sargasso Sea* (1966) and other novels about suffering, vulnerable women. Pizzichini attempts to defend Rhys, arguing that the author had "good reason to be angry" be-

Lilian Pizzichini won the 2002 Gold Dagger Award for her memoir about her grandfather, Dead Man's Wages: Secrets of a London Conman and His Family. *She has worked for the* Literary Review *and the* Times Literary Supplement *in England and has been a writer-in-residence at several prisons.*

cause of the many difficult external circumstances she faced. In taking this approach, Pizzichini sets herself against a previous biographer of Rhys, Carole Angier. For Pizzichini, Angier was too judgmental and sought inappropriately to pathologize Rhys, diagnosing her as a "borderline personality." Even Pizzichini, though, ends up using words such as "paranoid" to describe her subject.

In fact, a glance at Angier's 1990 biography, *Jean Rhys: Life and Work*, reveals that—differences in tone notwithstanding—the two biographies are very much alike. Pizzichini suggests that Angier sits in judgment while she, Pizzichini, is sympathetic and understanding. In fact, however, Angier is quite sympathetic as well, though admittedly less prone to explaining things away.

By talking of how Angier's research uncovered the facts of Rhys's life and laid the groundwork for later biographers, Pizzichini also makes it sound as if Angier had produced a work of dry scholarship in contrast to Pizzichini's livelier, more impressionistic approach. It is true that Pizzichini's narrative is almost novelistic, evoking Rhys as a character and eschewing scholarly methodology. There are no footnotes in *The Blue Hour*, while Angier provides copious notes in her book. However, Angier's biography, while perhaps more scholarly, also attempts to be novelistic, adopting a chatty, informal tone marked by the use of the first person.

A close comparison of the two biographies reveals even more similarities. Pizzichini says Angier's book was "a departure point for my own researches," but she does not seem to have departed very far from Angier. She tends to report the same incidents, using the same quotations from newspapers and other accounts, and even lifts phrases from her predecessor.

Here, for instance, is Pizzichini's account of the experiences of Rhys's first husband after being released from prison:

> Lenglet spent the next two years tramping around Europe. He became a sandwich man in Lucerne, sold newspapers in Berlin, was a publisher's courier in Frankfurt, and when all else failed, he scraped a living as a street musician.

Here is Angier's account of the same incident:

> He spent most of the next two years tramping around Europe, becoming a sandwich man in Lucerne, selling newspapers in Berlin, carrying books for publishers in Frankfurt; and when he couldn't get even such lowly jobs, passing round his hat as a street musician.

There are also differences between the two accounts. Angier's book is more than twice the length of Pizzichini's. Partly, this is because Angier devotes several chapters to analyzing Rhys's novels, whereas Pizzichini barely discusses the novels at all: Pizzichini's focus is almost exclusively on Rhys as a person, rather than as a writer.

This approach might have pleased Rhys, who according to Pizzichini preferred being admired as a woman rather than as a writer.

Indeed, one striking suggestion to emerge from Pizzichini's biography is that Rhys was not particularly driven to write, and authorship was not the essence of her being. True, Pizzichini notes, Rhys often felt best when writing, but as a child she did not aspire to a writing career, and she took it up only at the suggestion of her aunt when she received a setback in her attempts to become an actor. Even after starting to write, Rhys returned to the stage (she never progressed beyond chorus girl roles, however). She also spent time as an artists' model.

Rhys let all her careers go when she met her first serious lover, Lancelot Smith, who kept encouraging her to pursue the theater even while she was abandoning her career aims in order to devote herself to their relationship. Later, she turned seriously to writing when she was short of money—and even then only when encouraged by others, including the well-known author Ford Madox Ford. For a dozen years, she worked as an author, producing four novels and a collection of short stories, but then she stopped publishing for almost thirty years, though she long had the idea to write what became her most famous novel, *Wide Sargasso Sea.* She first thought of it in 1939, at the end of her twelve-year productive period, but she did not begin working on that novel, or anything else, until the mid-1950's, when once again she received outside encouragement.

In a way, therefore, Pizzichini's omission of literary analysis and focus on Rhys's personality may represent an attempt to be true to Rhys's nature. Pizzichini's book holds one's attention. She writes very well, in an impressionistic way, and does not get sidetracked into irrelevancies. She also presents a portrait of Jean Rhys that seems to ring true even if some of her facts may not be accurate—she tends to simplify at times. She speculates on her subject, as do many biographers, but those speculations in Pizzichini's hands tend to acquire the status of fact rather than conjecture.

Sometimes Pizzichini is simply wrong, as when she says Rhys mailed off the manuscript of *Wide Sargasso Sea* the day after her third husband died. In fact, according to Angier, the husband died March 7, and in April and May Rhys was still working on the manuscript. She mailed it on May 21. This is an odd error for Pizzichini to make because it puts Rhys in a worse light than the truth would, but this version of events makes for a romantic flourish in her prose, and she seems to value such flourishes. *The Blue Hour* is more a literary work than a scholarly one. Instead of accumulating detail on her subject, Pizzichini selects those impressions that are most suggestive or evocative. She attempts to reach her subject in this manner, where Angier attempted to use details gleaned from Rhys's fiction to make deductions about the author. Neither biography may represent the final word on Rhys. Perhaps there can be no final word, because Rhys kept herself too secret.

What does emerge in Pizzichini's book, though, is a sense of Rhys as someone who alienated all who sought to help her. She would fail to recognize the aid she received until it was gone then denounce the friends and caregivers she drove off for ceasing their aid. Despite Pizzichini's attempts to defend her subject, Rhys comes across as almost dedicated to frustrating herself and then blaming the world for her frustrations. For a novelist, she seems strikingly lacking in self-awareness.

Rhys saw herself as weak and vulnerable, yet she was the one assaulting husbands and neighbors. No doubt, she felt weak and vulnerable inside, but Pizzichini seems to go too far in sympathizing with Rhys when she says that her later relations with men arose from early fantasies of male cruelty and female submission. Especially in her last two marriages, the reverse seems to have been the case.

Interesting patterns do emerge in the account of Rhys's relationships. She seems to have been drawn to men who, like her father, were unable to provide enough money for their family. Her husbands' schemes and businesses tended to collapse, leaving them broke, and two of them were sent to prison for shady dealings. She seems to have been drawn to weak, ineffectual men and to men with little respect for the law.

Rhys herself often chafed against the rules of society. On arriving in England from Dominica, she found the conventions in her new land, along with the rules at her schools, to be stifling. England in general she found gray and ugly, remembering her homeland with nostalgic regret, thinking of its heat and its lush vegetation. When she had been on Dominica, however, she had fantasized about going to England, and after emigrating she visited Dominica only once, finding herself miserable there. She never seemed to be content where she was; she was always complaining. Even when *Wide Sargasso Sea* made her famous, she complained that her fame came too late.

In a way, Pizzichini suggests, Rhys was most satisfied during her brief stay in prison, for there she could feel vindicated. In prison, she could feel the world was conforming to her expectations, whereas outside prison the helpful people she encountered disrupted her view of humanity as purely self-seeking and dangerous. It is sad to think of Jean Rhys fighting imaginary enemies all her life, and it is this feeling of sadness and waste that one takes away from Pizzichini's biography. Those seeking fuller details about Rhys's life, and especially about her writings, will be best served by looking at Angier's biography, but those who simply want to get a sense of what Jean Rhys may have been like will find Pizzichini's biography a fascinating read.

Sheldon Goldfarb

Review Sources

Booklist 105, no. 13 (March 1, 2009): 14.
Kirkus Reviews 77, no. 3 (February 1, 2009): 68.
Library Journal 134, no. 7 (April 15, 2009): 92-93.
Literary Review, May, 2009, pp. 19-20.
Publishers Weekly 256, no. 7 (February 16, 2009): 123.
Spectator 310, no. 9432 (June 6, 2009): 37-38.
The Times Literary Supplement, July 24, 2009, p. 5.
The Wall Street Journal, May 15, 2009, p. W2.

THE BOOK OF NIGHT WOMEN

Author: Marlon James (1970-)
Publisher: Riverhead Books/Penguin Group (New York). 417 pp. $26.95
Type of work: Novel
Time: The late eighteenth and early nineteenth centuries
Locale: Jamaica

Women slaves on the Montpelier sugar plantation plot secretly at night to raise an insurrection against the violent and cruel British owners

Principal characters:
LILITH, a mulatto slave with mysterious powers
HOMER, the slave woman who heads the plantation household
JACK WILKINS, overseer of Montpelier
HUMPHREY WILSON, the young master of Montpelier
ISOBEL ROGET, a Creole woman from the Coulibre plantation involved with Humphrey
ROBERT QUINN, a friend of Humphrey and Wilkins's replacement as overseer

Marlon James's novel *The Book of Night Women* portrays the Montpelier estate, a sugar plantation in Jamaica where the slaves outnumber the white owners by thirty-three to one. Mindful of the 1791 takeover of St. Domingue by Toussaint L'Ouverture and the Jamaican history of bloody slave uprisings, the whites rule by terror. The barbaric treatment of the slaves includes such tortures as burning alive, chopping off the feet of runaways, brutal whippings for minor offenses, and other punishments too gruesome to describe. Slaves know that their lives are worthless in the eyes of their owners; they can be easily replaced at the slave market in Kingston. James's unrelenting depiction of violence and explicit descriptions of sexual abuse of women have disturbed many readers and critics. However, as the author has said, historical records offer ample evidence of the savagery of plantation life of that time.

Into the enclosed world of Montpelier is born Lilith, the green-eyed daughter of overseer Jack Wilkins, who names her for the first wife of the biblical Adam. Lilith's fourteen-year-old mother, whom Wilkins raped, dies giving birth in a blood-filled scene that portends the role of blood throughout the story. Six women slaves who are secretly plotting an uprising at night believe that Lilith was born with demonic powers that threaten danger. Patrick Wilson, the dead plantation master, gave these women names from Greek mythology. Five of them—Gorgon, Pallas, Hippolyta, Iphegenia, and Callisto—are half-sisters fathered by Jack Wilkins; several have inherited his green eyes. Homer, the only African-born of the six, commands the house-

Marlon James was born in Kingston, Jamaica. His first novel, John Crow's Devil *(2005), was shortlisted for the Commonwealth Prize and was a finalist for the* Los Angeles Times *Book Prize. He is professor of literature and creative writing at Macalester College in St. Paul, Minnesota.*

hold slaves and is the most powerful black woman on the plantation. Mutilated by a brutal whipping that caused a miscarriage, she was used by the master as breeding stock, producing two children who were sold and met early deaths at the hands of their owners. Homer, outwardly compliant, is ruled by her desire to avenge her children; she has nothing more to fear.

In the wake of Wilson's death, his widow teeters at the edge of insanity, while the plantation descends into chaos. Humphrey, Wilson's son, is summoned from Europe to restore order. He replaces Wilkins, making his Irish companion Robert Quinn the new overseer.

The narrator, whose identity is withheld until the final chapter, speaks in Jamaican dialect, a risky choice by the author. However, once this voice is established in the first pages, the lyrical speech patterns seduce readers into accepting the compelling story. Several times, the narrator begins a chapter with this mantra: "Every negro walk in a circle. Take that and make of it what you will." The slaves of Montpelier understand that their lives are circumscribed by the dictates of their masters: They have no choices.

Montpelier is a nightmare for the slaves, whose work enriches its British owners. The whites, separated from the conventions of British society, exercise unrestrained power over their slaves, whom they treat as animals. In an early chapter, two slaves die from a mysterious bloody flux. The terror-stricken slaves attribute this event to Obeah, African black magic, and refuse to go into the fields. The overseers choose a random victim, a young girl, and slowly burn her to death while the slaves are forced at gunpoint to watch. Order is outwardly restored, but the slaves' resulting hatred and thirst for revenge fuel the brewing insurrection.

The British landowners, shunned by polite society, have their own caste system. They regard the Irishman Quinn as an inferior, little better than a slave. He is tolerated by Humphrey, as he harbors a dark secret about Humphrey's past. Meanwhile, Isobel Roget, the daughter of the civil servant of the Coulibre plantation, is a Jamaican-born Creole. Mistress Wilson is horrified by the looming possibility of a marriage between Humphrey and a woman of such dubious ancestry.

The slaves, in turn, have secrets and enmities among themselves. From the lowest field hands, fed starvation rations and worked to death, to the house slaves, who fare marginally better with food and clothing, they establish their own hierarchy. The "johnny-jumpers," slaves given unlimited freedom to punish others by the master, rape and whip fellow slaves at will. In the hills, Maroons, roaming bands of escaped slaves, are paid by the whites to hunt down runaways.

Lilith, at fifteen, is beautiful and headstrong and believes herself superior to the other slaves. Homer watches with scorn as Lilith attempts to ingratiate herself with the white family. She warns: "Lord knows what happen when a nigger girl not content with her lot." Homer includes Lilith in the nighttime plotting, although the other five hate her and fear that she will betray their cause.

When a Johnny-jumper attempts to rape Lilith, she murders him with his own cutlass. The night women dispose of the body; Homer brings her to the main house under her protection. Lilith, despite dire warnings from Homer, attracts the attention of Mistress Wilson, who assigns her to serve at table for the plantation's New Year's banquet. Vain and consumed by her own self-importance, Lilith commits a misstep that changes her life: She spills scalding soup on Isobel Roget's chaperone, severely burning her and disrupting the dinner party. Humphrey beats Lilith with his fists, then turns her over to be gang-raped by white overseers. Isobel, driven by a desire for vengeance, takes satisfaction in ordering Lilith's beating with the bullwhip for several weeks until Jack Wilkins intervenes. Lilith becomes known as the woman with the quilt on her back.

Although it will be difficult for readers to summon any sympathy for the unspeakable behavior of the white plantation owners, James successfully develops complex psychological portraits that make them believable characters. Moral distinctions between good and evil are clouded, as even the whites are revealed to be capable of unaccountable acts of compassion. Slaves, meanwhile, victims who should elicit readers' sympathy, are capable of savage cruelty toward other slaves.

James also includes instances of humor amid the horror. Homer teaches Lilith to read with the only book available, Henry Fielding's *The History of the Adventures of Joseph Andrews, and of His Friend Mr. Abraham Adams* (1742; commonly known as *Joseph Andrews*). Quinn continues her education with Edmund Spenser's *The Faerie Queene* (1590, 1596). Lilith's disingenuous commentary on the behavior of these fictitious narratives provides some lighter moments in the otherwise unrelenting darkness.

After the banquet disaster, Lilith is sent to Coulibre to serve at Isobel's whim—Isobel's strategy for keeping her enemy under her control. Lilith is terrified when the young slave Dulcey, her coworker in the kitchen who serves the master's perverted sexual desires, is beaten to death by Mistress Roget in a fit of jealousy. One day when Isobel is away, Lilith explodes under her silent burden of terror. While she is assisting Master Roget in his bath, he forces her into a sexual act. She responds by drowning him. When the mistress approaches, Lilith pushes her over the balcony to her death. Crazed by the fear of discovery, Lilith sets fire to the house, burning two slave women and the Rogets' two young children to death. In the confusion that follows, her claim that she was in the barn milking the cow when the fire started is believed, but only by the whites. Several slaves are tortured into false confessions and executed, including the innocent Francine, who is burned to death. Lilth's murderous powers become legendary among the slaves.

Lilith, who sees herself as less than human, begins to mature into an individual capable of highly intelligent distinctions of moral reasoning. She is, in her own word, "perplex" about questions that trouble her. Roget, a murderer and rapist, deserved to die, as did his wife, who was equally guilty of terrible cruelties. She believes that the two boys, who would have become cruel masters like their parents, also deserved death. Nevertheless, Lilith's nights are haunted by the vision of a shadowy, dark woman, and she is tormented by the smell of the burning bodies. She charges herself with the murder of seven people, including the three innocent slave women whose deaths she has caused.

Isobel, meanwhile, is driven insane by the ghastly deaths of her family. She begins speaking wildly in slave dialect and makes nighttime journeys into the brothels and opium dens of Kingston. Although she and Humphrey are having a sexual relationship, she cannot convince him to propose marriage.

In an unexpected turn in the narrative, there is a temporary respite, an incongruous love story. Robert Quinn takes Lilith into his house as his mistress and housekeeper. He treats her as though she were a white woman, begging her to call him by his Christian name and calling her "Lovey." His gentle lovemaking awakens her sexual response, which was deadened after her earlier rapes. Even while they make love, though, he feels the scars on her back from the whippings that he sanctioned. Lilith, growing confident in her new knowledge of love, begins to imagine herself differently. Homer, scornful of her trust in a white man, asks who she thinks she is. She responds, "Me think me is Lilith," yet she understands what Quinn cannot: He will always be the master and she the slave.

In contrast to these tender scenes of romance, Homer's plans for the uprising, three years in the making, are coming to fruition. She intends to kill all the whites and establish African-style villages throughout the island. Secret communications among slaves from several plantations have set the day for the revolt. It will take place in the midst of the cane harvest, when most slaves will be in the fields, where they can kill the overseers and escape in the night. Homer orders Lilith to join in the conspiracy, but Lilith refuses, telling Homer that she cannot commit any more murders and predicting that the revolt cannot succeed. Homer, unforgiving in her thirst for revenge for the deaths of her children, will not listen. Lilith's warning fails.

When the uprising begins, Lilith attempts to protect Quinn by drugging his food and hiding him. Mistress Wilson, the johnny-jumpers, and at least ninety-four whites from the rebelling plantations are killed, their bodies mutilated in barbaric acts of revenge. Inevitably, however, the insurrection is put down by British soldiers with their superior numbers and weapons.

The horrors of the insurrection and its aftermath are described in explicit detail in the final section of the book, "Gehenna." Lilith, watching as the plantation house burns, runs to the safety of Jack Wilkins's house. When she protects him by facing down the rioters, they retreat in terror, fearing her evil powers. This act saves her from the fate decreed by Humphrey Wilson's vengeance: The surviving rebels are placed in spiked cages alongside the road to die slow, agonizing deaths. Robert Quinn is killed during the revolt despite Lilith's efforts to save him. Isobel, already pregnant, is brutally raped and left to survive as best she can in the ashes of Montpelier.

The narrative voice is finally revealed as that of Lovey Quinn, the daughter of Quinn and Lilith. She assumes the traditional African role as witness and storyteller, charged with honoring the lives of the night women who died in the uprising. She pieces together the story as given to her by her mother and an unnamed "blind niggerwoman in the bush." Either Homer has survived, or she serves as a tutelary spirit who witnesses to the truth. In the words of the chant repeated through the story, the circle within which every African walks is complete. As Lilith foresaw, Homer's thirst for vengeance was the fatal flaw that blinded her to the truth that the slave insurrection would fail, marking the full circle of tragedy.

James has created, out of historical fact and soaring imagination, a compelling world of such horror as to give readers nightmares. Still, as several critics have said, this is a story that needs to be told. Slavery, as history shows, has the power to corrupt both those who own other human beings and the slaves themselves, who prey on one another. This tale of racism and ethnic strife carries a warning that transcends its time and place. When one group refuses to acknowledge the humanity of the other, primitive savagery beyond rational belief can be the only result.

Marjorie Podolsky

Review Sources

The Boston Globe, Living Arts, May 12, 2009, p.4.
Chicago Tribune, Books and Media, February 14, 2009, p.1.
Essence, March, 2009, p.60.
Library Journal 134, no. 12 (July 1, 2009): 52.
Library Journal 134, no. 3 (February 15, 2009): 94.
Miami Herald, March 1, 2009, M6.
The New York Times Book Review, March 1, 2009, p.7.
The Washington Post, February 17, 2009, p. C9.

THE BOOK OF SAMUEL
Essays on Poetry and Imagination

Author: Mark Rudman (1948-   )
Publisher: Northwestern University Press (Evanston, Ill.). 270 pp. $18.95
Type of work: Literary criticism

Rudman assesses the literary achievement of a wide range of authors, examines their influence on other writers (including himself), and provides autobiographical accounts of his travels inspired by their works

The essays in *The Book of Samuel*, most of which have appeared elsewhere previously, put forth a thought-provoking and sometimes maddening mélange of reflections on a variety of writers. The book is replete with insights into these writers' works, intermingled with autobiographical vignettes that do not always obviously connect to the subjects ostensibly under consideration. Mark Rudman serves as a chatty and knowledgeable tour guide through the works he investigates, but his free-form presentation will frustrate those seeking a thesis or a cohesive argument. Readers seeking to revisit Rudman's reflections will also be frustrated by the absence of an index.

The opening chapter, "On the Road, Touch and Go, with D. H. Lawrence" responds to a letter from Gary Adelman of the University of Illinois asking Rudman's opinion of Lawrenace, the author of *Sons and Lovers* (1913), *Women in Love* (1920), and *Lady Chatterley's Lover* (1928). The Cambridge scholar F. R. Leavis regarded Lawrence as the most important early twentieth century novelist, but Lawrence's reputation has declined over the decades with the rise of feminist and postcolonial criticism. Rudman nonetheless champions Lawrance's work in all genres: short stories, novels, poems, letters, and nonfiction. According to Rudman, Lawrence rebelled against the modernist concern with form. Rudman maintains that Lawrence's poetry is imperfect but not flawed. All Lawrence's writing seeks immediacy, movement rather than fixity. According to Rudman, Lawrence, who wrote *Studies in Classic American Literature* (1923), took Walt Whitman as his model. Much of this chapter deals with Rudman's retracing Lawrence's footsteps through Italy as set out in *Sketches of Etruscan Places* (1923). Lawrence admired the vitality of the Etruscans, which he contrasted with Roman commercialism. Rudman finds the book still a useful guide, as well as a beautifully written text.

Rudman argues that William Carlos Williams is the American poet closest in spirit to Lawrence, as well as the most original U.S. poet. Like Lawrence, Williams was not a slave to form. Instead, he allowed form to evolve from content. Williams was influenced by Lawrence's *Classics in American Literature*, and Lawrence favorably reviewed Williams's *In the American Grain* (1925) in an essay that appeared in *The*

Nation. There, Lawrence praised Williams's concentration on Americans' energy, a quality that Lawrence admired in the Etruscans.

Poet and translator Mark Rudman teaches at New York University. His collection Rider *(1994) won the National Book Critics Circle Award, and his work has appeared in many periodicals, including* The Atlantic Monthly, Harper's Magazine, The New Yorker, *and the* London Review of Books.

In a typically thought-provoking insight, Rudman claims that Williams focused on the sounds of words in the same way that nineteenth century realists emphasized personal appearance and furnishings. Rudman shows that Williams was aware of the slipperiness of language. The title of "By the Road to the Contagious Hospital," published in *Spring and All* (1923), suggests that the hospital not only is for those with contagious diseases but also is itself contagious. Rudman also shows through example how shifting the emphasis from one word to another in Williams's poems can alter their meaning. Though Williams's language is simple, it expresses complex truths, whether about mourners at a funeral or about spectators at a baseball game. Like Lawrence, Williams is, according to Rudman, undervalued. Harvard poetry professor Helen Vendler ignored Williams in her anthology of American verse.

Rudman finds a strong strain in Williams reminiscent of William Shakespeare, particularly when his poems express skepticism similar to that expressed by Shakespeare's character Hamlet. Walt Whitman provides another influence on Williams. Rudman reflects that some of Whitman's best poems derived from his experience nursing soldiers during the Civil War. Williams, a physician, tended the sick every day. Such work, Rudman reflects, forces a writer outside the self. It may also have contributed to Williams's focus on the physical, such as the thighs of a policeman's wife ("The Cold Night," 1921) or the gravel in a park (*Paterson*, 1946-1958). Williams contended that there are no ideas but in things, yet objects gain significance through Williams's imaginative renderings.

John Keats, too, trained in medicine, and Rudman finds in Williams's open vowel sounds echoes of that Romantic poet. Keats's example also taught Williams to compose rapidly. Rudman links Williams's poignant "The Sparrow" (1955) to Keats's observation in a letter that, when he sees a sparrow, he partakes of the bird's existence. The Roman poet Catullus also famously wrote about the pet sparrow of his beloved Lesbia, a possible source that Rudman ignores.

Rudman admires Williams for rejecting form. A theme that pervades the book is Rudman's argument with modernist emphasis on that element. Rudman links Williams's poems to Jackson Pollack's paintings. Neither is amorphous, but form evolves in the process of creation. Rudman also admires playfulness, a quality that he finds in Williams and Samuel Beckett, whom he treats later in the book. Rudman argues that this element has cost Williams readers who believe that poetry should be serious.

Rudman turns next to American poet Hart Crane and British novelist Malcolm Lowry, both of whom were, like Lawrence, drawn to Mexico. Both also killed themselves, though Lowry may have had some assistance from his wife. Crane hoped to write a verse history of the Spanish conquest of Mexico, a project that defeated him. Rudman argues that Crane failed because he tried to plan the work rather than allow it to emerge spontaneously. Rudman contrasts the failed poem with Crane's masterful letters from Mexico that record his immediate experiences. Both Crane and Lowry, Rudman argues, sought perfection and thereby created masterpieces, but they left themselves no opportunity to progress.

Rudman concedes that he initially objected to what he regarded as the overly intellectual qualities of the poetry of Czesław Miłosz. Miłosz's prose works, however, made Rudman more receptive to the spontaneity and risk-taking of his verse. In discussing Miłosz, Rudman focuses on what the Polish poet calls "apokatastasis," or restoration, the idea that things exist both within and outside of time so that nothing is lost. Himself a translator of Boris Paternak and Bohdan Antonych, Rudman reflects on Miłosz's good fortune to have his poems translated into English by Robert Haas and Robert Pinsky. Fine poets themselves, they have reproduced Miłosz's sounds as well as his sense. In contrast, Joseph Brodsky has not been so fortunate in his translators. One of the best features of Rudman's idiosyncratic book is its generous and incisive sampling of the works of the writers it discusses. Rudman reveals himself to be an excellent anthologist, using his selections to entice readers to seek out more works by the authors he treats.

Rudman says of T. S. Eliot what Statius says to Virgil in Dante's *Purgatorio* (c. 1320; *Purgatory*, 1802): Through him, he became a poet. Rudman argues that Eliot's attempt to convey wisdom through verse hurt his later poems. Still, he admires Eliot's late *Four Quartets* (1943) for its ability to transcend time. Rudman contrasts Lawrence's cultivation of anxiety in his writings with Eliot's attempt to escape it. Rudman observes that, while Eliot seemed to be the embodiment of conventionality in his dress and mien, his poetic language was original.

Rudman's book takes its title from the final section, which examines the work of three Samuels: Samuel Johnson, Samuel Taylor Coleridge, and Beckett. Rudman is so enamored of these writers that he named his son Samuel for them. As disparate as the three writers at first blush appear to be, Rudman connects them through their fascination with conversation. Coleridge wrote conversation poems, for example, while Johnson was noted for his brilliant talk. Rudman ascribes Coleridge's failure as a poet to his loss of William Wordsworth's friendship, the failure of Coleridge's marriage to Sarah Fricker, and Coleridge's inability to gain the love of Sara Hutchinson. As a result of these events, Rudman believes, the poet had no one with whom to communicate. Coleridge continued to produce volumes of prose, but, for Rudman, his lectures on William Shakespeare and the *Biographia Literaria* (1817) are poor consolations for the poems that Coleridge failed to create. Rudman regards the *Biographia Literaria* as an attempt by Coleridge to act as Wordsworth's publicist. Rudman attributes Wordsworth's poetic achievement to his conversations with his sister Dorothy. He also maintains, with less plausibility, that Johnson, too, turned to prose as a lesser substitute for poetry.

Rudman quotes Robert Lowell's report of Delmore Schwartz's comment that if a poet can get people talking, his work will succeed. Robert Frost, T. S. Eliot, and Ezra Pound achieved that goal. Beckett's central problem, Rudman argues, was solitude. One of the Irish-born writer's last works is called *Company* (1980). Isolation leads to silence, a situation reflected in the title of *"Fin de partie," suivi de "Acte sans paroles"* (pr., pb. 1957; *"Endgame: A Play in One Act," Followed by "Act Without Words: A Mime for One Player,"* 1958).

Another Samuel enters the final chapter, the director Samuel Fuller, whom Rudman admires. This chapter turns into even more of a grab bag than the others, as Rudman discusses his son's first encounter with the poetry of Robert Frost, a horseback riding incident when Rudman himself was ten, and the lives and works of Ernest Hemingway and William Faulkner. Perhaps Rudman seeks to create a sense of conversation akin to Coleridge's, which famously rambled but always stimulated.

The Book of Samuel concludes with a tribute to the Chilean poet Nicanor Parra, whom Rudman met in 1972. Rudman already shared Parra's objections to modernism and neo-Romanticism, strictures that inform much of *The Book of Samuel* and that may explain the work's free-form construction. However, Rudman at twenty-three still admired Romantic writers such as John Keats and modernists such as Pablo Neruda, whom Parra regarded as outdated remnants of the nineteenth century. Parra wrote a book called *Antipoems* (2004), which Rudman links to Parra's background in physics. Parra's poems resemble antimatter and reflect his rejection of the lyric and of the closure that characterizes so much earlier verse. These reflections on antipoetry form a fitting conclusion to what might be seen as a book of antiessays that also lack a sense of ending, inviting further reading and reflection.

Joseph Rosenblum

THE BOOK OF WILLIAM
How Shakespeare's First Folio Conquered the World

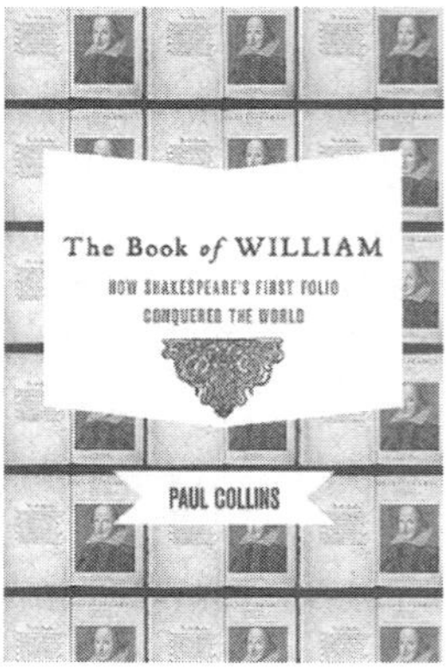

Author: Paul Collins (1969-)
Publisher: Bloomsbury (New York). 246 pp. $25.00
Type of work: Literary history
Time: 1623-2006
Locale: London, England

Evaluation of the first collected edition of Shakespeare's plays, which preserved the work of England's most famous playwright, including much that could have been lost, and which also began a great industry of Shakespeareana

Principal personages:

WILLIAM SHAKESPEARE (1564-1616), the most famous writer in the English language
WILLIAM JAGGARD (c. 1568-1623), the London printer chosen to produce the First Folio
SAMUEL JOHNSON (1709-1784), English essayist, critic, and editor of Shakespeare's works
HOWARD STAUNTON (1810-1874), a chess virtuoso and editor of the first facsimile of the First Folio
HENRY CLAY FOLGER (1857-1930), a book collector and founder of the Folger Shakespeare Library

Paul Collins's *The Book of William* presents a literary history of William Shakespeare's First Folio. One of the most valuable books in the world, its importance is represented among other places in Umberto Eco's novel *The Mysterious Flame of Queen Loana* (2005). The novel's narrator, a publisher who is unable to work and deeply in debt, suffers a massive stroke on discovering that his grandfather's battered copy of Shakespeare's plays is in fact a First Folio edition.

Such discoveries, though rare, are not unheard of. Since the first census of First Folios was taken in the mid-nineteenth century, new copies have turned up at the rate of about one per year. Some have been in attics, others in cupboards and storage sheds, and a few out in the open in uncatalogued private libraries. Rumors of still others emerge periodically, to be pursued by any number of booksellers and collectors.

Collins reveals that, to date, some 230 copies of the First Folio have been identified, and their individual flaws and markings have been noted in great detail. There must be an upper limit to those remaining to be found since the print run of the 1623 publication was limited by statute to two thousand copies and most of those were probably consumed in the Great Fire of London in 1666. It is increasingly rare for a First Folio to be sold on the open market, and the asking price is likely to increase.

When a private library in London put its copy up for auction in 2006, the book sold for a record 2.5 million pounds, the equivalent at the time of 8 million dollars. The auctioneer remarked that the sum represented approximately one-third of the library's net worth; the librarian said the proceeds would make it possible to preserve the library's eight thousand other rare books.

A former editor for McSweeney's Books, Paul Collins is a professor of English at Portland State University. He has written on autism, the used-book trade, and Thomas Paine.

Collins attended the auction, fascinated by the allure of old books and determined to write a popular history of Shakespeare's First Folio. The title of his book is well chosen, for this first posthumous edition of Shakespeare's plays is as close as one can come to the words as he wrote them. It was edited by two surviving shareholders in the King's Men, the acting company that made Shakespeare a rich man. The texts were based on acting copies in the company's possession, not on the pirated copies printed during the author's lifetime, and they included a good many plays that might otherwise have been lost. Many literature students purchase the Norton facsimile of the First Folio to see how Shakespeare's contemporaries saw the text, and some actors use the Applause facsimile to eliminate the stage directions, scene descriptions, and other insertions that have been made over the centuries.

Collins's subtitle, on the other hand, is pure hyperbole, as the author would be the first to concede. First Folios are bargains compared to paintings by Rembrandt or Vincent Van Gogh. Even in the world of printed books, the First Folio sold at Sotheby's is not the most valuable book known. A Gutenberg Bible, for example, has sold for 3.3 million pounds, and a first edition of Geoffrey Chaucer's *The Canterbury Tales* (1387-1400) has commanded 4.7 million pounds. However, a more accurate subtitle, more strictly limited to the auction that Collins attended, would be much longer, and he intends his book to be accessible to a wide reading public.

Collins strikes a breezy tone, contracting words when, for example, he shows sympathy for "every high schooler who's suffered through a Shakespeare assignment." He uses such vernacular adjectives as "dorky" and "legit"; calls Shakespeare's hometown a "tourist trap" (as may well be the case); and calls the playwright "Bill" (as was not the case: until the nineteenth century, the standard nickname for William was "Will," and Shakespeare punned on that name in Sonnet 130). He notes that the folio's editors divided the plays into acts and scenes, in the manner of Roman plays studied in grammar schools such as the one Shakespeare attended briefly. They thus gave a classical appearance to comedies and tragedies originally organized by scene alone. Collins follows suit, dividing his book into acts and scenes rather than chapters and sections. By adapting the five-act structure of the Shakespearean drama, he makes it easy for readers familiar with Shakespeare to grasp the overall structure of his story.

"Act I" is set in London and describes the auction at Sotheby's interspersed with portrayals of the print shop of William Jaggard and son, where the First Folio was produced. Collins provides details of the paper Jaggard chose for the job and of the folio format in general. The section also includes information about the second, third, and fourth folios that followed Jaggard's 1623 folio over the next half century. Each edition corrected perceived errors in prior editions and added new texts attributed to Shakespeare—wrongly attributed, in almost every case.

"Act II" continues in London and describes the fiercely competitive market in new editions of Shakespeare's collected works—a market created by England's first copyright law in the early eighteenth century. The poet Alexander Pope thought the First Folio useless and made as many corrections to it as he could; Lewis Theobald, his rival, considered the First Folio to have the highest authority and corrected Pope's corrections whenever possible. Samuel Johnson, who compiled the first authoritative dictionary of English words, owned Theobald's heavily annotated copy of the First Folio and followed Theobald's lead.

Johnson's introductory essays in the several volumes of his edition of Shakespeare's works helped shape the way that people read and understood the plays. They also had the immediate effect of reversing the value placed on earlier editions. First Folios began selling for more than the original selling price of one pound. They became collectors' items.

Given the structure of *The Book of William* and its analogy with the plays' dramatic structure, one might expect the story of the First Folio and its readers to reach a crisis at this point in the text. Curiously enough, that crisis occurs with the invention of photography and the production of the first facsimile edition between 1857 and 1860. The facsimile was the work of Howard Staunton, a chess master who helped standardize and popularize the game. Rather than diminish the demand for original First Folio copies, as one might suppose, Staunton's facsimile edition greatly increased that demand by putting members of the general reading public in contact with a monument of English printing comparable to the King James Bible of 1611. As demand increased, so did the number of known copies. Exhibitions of First Folios were held, and soon a census of known copies was published.

The crisis of "Act III," then, involves the scarcity of a desired commodity. What began as a story of artistry preserved by fellow actors and interpreted by poets and essayists who turned their hands to editing ends up as a story of acquisition. At this point, the story leaves England and begins to follow the money.

"Act IV" focuses on Henry Clay Folger, a lieutenant of John D. Rockefeller in the Standard Oil Trust. Folger bought a cheap reprint of Staunton's facsimile when he was a student at Amherst College and formed a lifelong fascination with Shakespeare. When he became a rich man, Folger used his wealth to buy books, and his focus was always on First Folios. Most of those he acquired were kept in warehouses, much like proven oil reserves, while Folger bought up land on Capitol Hill in Washington, D.C., and laid the plans for a great library dedicated to the works of Shakespeare and his contemporaries.

Folger became the first person known to have two First Folios of his own, and by the time of his death he owned seventy-two, more than half of all the copies then known. The endowment of the institution he founded, however, was harmed by the recession of the early 1980's: Despite new acquisitions and construction to house them, the Folger Shakespeare Library had to place itself in trust to Folger's alma mater. By then, investment capital was concentrated in Japan, where the Tokyo Globe Theater opened in 1988. Japanese audiences flocked to see *Hamlet, Prince of Denmark* (pr. c. 1600-1601, pb. 1603) performed by visiting English actors, as well as its translation as *Hamuretto*, performed by their native counterparts. The play about the conflicted Danish prince resonated with the post-World-War-II generation in Japan.

"Act V" thus discusses Japanese collectors of First Folios. The founding president of Meisei University in Tokyo began collecting Shakespeare editions in the mid-1970's. By the time he died, his university had the second-largest collection of First Folios in the world, next only to the Folger Library's. Since then, the Meisei library has expanded its collection to include first folios of Geoffrey Chaucer and Ben Jonson, the direct ancestors of the Shakespeare First Folio. Collins traveled to Japan to examine a First Folio once owned by the benefactor of Harvard's Houghton Library. Heavily underlined throughout, it is the First Folio known to have textual notes made by one of Shakespeare's contemporaries—a man Collins identifies tentatively as a mathematics professor at the University of Aberdeen.

Here, Collins writes, "*Exuent*"—"all exit"—but his book does not conclude with the narrative. Instead of the usual scholarly apparatus of endnotes and bibliography, he provides a twenty-page essay on further readings, arranged in the same five-act sequence. There is also a two-page list of acknowledgments. Together, these supplements identify Collins's major sources of information. They take readers through the steps of his research and provide enough detail that the sources can be tracked down through an Internet search engine such as Google or a database such as WorldCat.

Shakespeare might have called Collins "a snatcher up of unconsidered trifles," for, like Autolycus in *The Winter's Tale* (pr. c. 1610-1611, pb. 1623), he cannot resist the odd item. Like his other books of nonfiction, *The Book of William* is chock-full of curiosities—details easily overlooked in a more strictly serious study. He discusses flakes of piecrust that a subeditor found in Johnson's copy of the First Folio, lost copies—such as that of a Spanish diplomat whose entire library was consigned to the rag pile or that of a Chicago collector whose books were destroyed in the fire of 1871—and a tavern built on a site where early editions of the plays were edited.

Shakespeare scholars may be surprised that Collins says nothing about the spelling found in the First Folio or the varied attempts to make sense of it. Collins resists citing Theobald's most famous correction, perhaps the most famous correction ever made to Shakespeare's text. Pope had omitted the apparently random phrase "a Table of greene fields" from the description of Falstaff's death in *Henry V*. Theobald emended it to read "a' babbled." Ever since then, the great comic character has been said to die babbling of England's greenery.

Early reviewers have appreciated the globe-and-century-hopping approach that Collins takes, though with some reservations. While *The New York Times Book Review* has called it amusing and *Library Journal* has termed it a welcome addition to the more serious studies it cites, *Commonweal* compares it unfavorably to Jack

Lynch's *Becoming Shakespeare* (2007), a longer book that provides a more comprehensive view of Shakespeare's "afterlife." The book has a few outright errors, such as referring to *The Merchant of Venice* (pr. c. 1596-1597, pb. 1600) as "*A Merchant of Venice*," and it would benefit from the addition of a general index. Nevertheless, it is a lively introduction to a subject that should interest more readers in the legacy of Shakespeare's works.

Thomas Willard

Review Sources

Booklist 105, no. 21 (July 1, 2009): 13.
Commonweal 136, no. 17 (October 9, 2009): 24.
Kirkus Reviews 77, no. 9 (May 1, 2009): 69.
Library Journal 134, no. 10 (June 1, 2009): 100.
The New York Times Book Review, October 4, 2009, p. 18.
Publishers Weekly 256, no. 18 (May 4, 2009): 42.

CAHOKIA
Ancient America's Great City on the Mississippi

Author: Timothy R. Pauketat (1961-)
Publisher: Viking (New York). 194 pp. $22.95
Type of work: History
Time: 1050 to the early twenty-first century
Locale: The banks of the Mississippi River, near modern-day St. Louis, Missouri

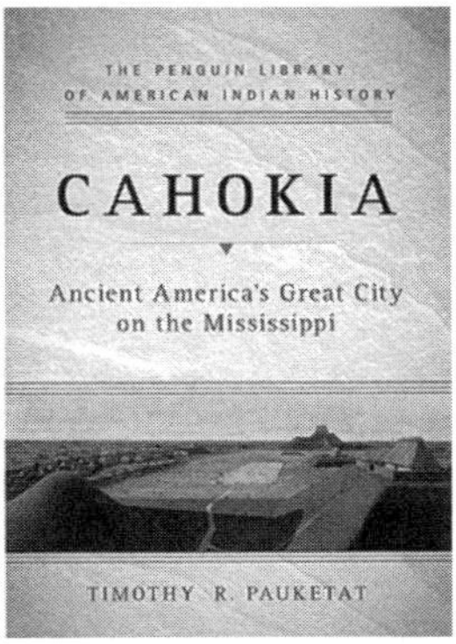

The story of a Native American city that flourished more than a thousand years ago and whose inhabitants built more than two hundred pyramid mounds

In *Cahokia*, Timothy R. Pauketat argues that Cahokia was the one true city of ancient America north of Mexico. It was as large as London in its day and was the capital of what Pauketat describes as "a most unusual Indian nation." Cahokia—no one knows what its inhabitants actually called it—lay in the Mississippi bottomlands, close to modern St. Louis, Missouri. The Cahokia Mounds State Historic Site now protects the eighty mounds that remain from this ancient city, and they are designated as a World Heritage Site. At least sixty other mounds, and probably more, were destroyed in the nineteenth and early twentieth centuries, during the building of St. Louis.

Cahokia was originally North America's largest pyramidal mound site, possibly containing as many as two hundred mounds, including the third-largest pyramid in the New World. Most of these pyramids were packed into an area five miles square, and they were surrounded by thousands of houses and broad plazas. At the height of its importance, Cahokia may have been home to at least ten thousand people, with another twenty to thirty thousand living in the surrounding area.

For a long time, no one was entirely clear who had built the mounds. Although it was clear that they had been built by human hands, it was believed that, rather than being constructed by Native Americans, they had been made by a lost race of moundbuilders. This hypothetical race would have traveled along the American frontier west of the Allegheny Mountains, through the Ohio Valley and the Mississippi trench, constructing the mysterious mounds. They then would either have been wiped out by warlike Native Americans or else have migrated into Central America, where they would have become the Aztec and the Maya. However, as Pauketat notes, the work of archaeologists and historians has begun to question long-held beliefs about Native Americans, suggesting that they were not necessarily as ecologically sensitive, peaceful, and mystical as was previously assumed. The emerging picture of Native Americans indicates that they were perfectly capable of building a city and developing an elaborate culture.

Pauketat is particularly interested in the founding of Cahokia, which seems around 1050 to have sprung suddenly into being—what he calls the "big bang" theory. Al-

Timothy R. Pauketat is a professor of anthropology at the University of Illinois, Urbana-Champaign. His previous books include Chiefdoms and Other Archaeological Delusions *(2007) and* Ancient Cahokia and the Mississippians *(2004).*

most overnight, the buildings that formed what is now called Old Cahokia were taken down; the area was leveled; and the elaborate pyramids, streets, and houses of New Cahokia were constructed, creating what Pauketat argues was a new capital city. He notes that for this project to achieve such rapid growth in so comparatively short a period of time would have required a good deal of cooperation, not to mention strong leadership and a large population. Pauketat thus argues that the Cahokia civilization was either built on consensus or based on an ideology that legitimized the rule of the few in the eyes of the many.

Whatever their governmental structure, the Cahokians made rapid and drastic changes to their lives. Pauketat theorizes that a supernova in 1054, documented in the New World but not noted elsewhere, may have been the impetus behind the change. The Mississippian culture developed rapidly and then spread across the American Midwest into the South and onto the Great Plains. Its influence can be traced in buildings and artworks, suggesting that there was an elaborate dissemination of Cahokian culture, which was copied by local artists and builders in turn. The reasons for the culture's spread remain unclear. Pauketat suggests that in the dissemination of the culture was associated in some way with chunkey, a game widely played among different Native American groups for centuries, which seems to have arisen first in Cahokia.

There is evidence that the Mississippi supported a prosperous society prior to the development of New Cahokia. This earlier society comprised unified family groups based in small villages. The population of the area was not large, and it sustained itself through hunting and through growing and gathering crops. There were festivals throughout the year, and the villages were neither socially isolated nor culturally insular.

Pauketat argues that influential people in the larger villages, in particular Old Cahokia, drew people to them because of their success. He speculates that intermarriage with foreigners may have brought with it new ideas, leading to the development of the mound-building culture. It has even been suggested that people traveling from Mesoamerica brought with them the idea of mound-building (though it has also been suggested that, after Cahokia collapsed, the Cahokians traveled southward into Mesoamerica).

Much of what is known about Cahokia is based on the extraordinary work of a dedicated group of archaeologists who have worked throughout the twentieth century to recover evidence of the mounds. Awareness within white culture of the mounds' existence goes back further: In 1811, Henry Marie Brackenridge described them in detail in a letter to Thomas Jefferson. His account laid emphasis on the numerous mounds and their ordered arrangement. Remarkably, before this, the mounds had gone unnoticed by observers, although there had been European settlement in the area for many years.

Modern Cahokian archaeology began with the arrival in the St. Louis area of Preston Holder, who began to draw together earlier work on the various mounds in order to make some sense of the information already gathered. Holder established a protocol for working on the mounds and their associated houses, stressing attention to detail during digging.

Holder and the archaeologists who came after him often worked under intense pressure to record information, struggling in desperate conditions, only one step ahead of encroaching bulldozers as they tried to excavate archaeological sites before builders moved into them. Sometimes, they dug well into the night, working by the light of car headlamps. Often, they had to abandon work when the weather deteriorated and winter set in. The pressure of the work was such that more than one of the workers turned to drink. The quantity of material they found was immense, but retrieving it was only the beginning of the job. Everything then had to be cleaned and analyzed.

While it had long been assumed that Cahokia had been a ritual center, the work of Holder and his successors, in particular Melvin Fowler, revealed the elaborate nature of some of the rituals practiced there. Archaeologists recognized and excavated special mortuary mounds in which they discovered high-status burials. These included the "beaded burial," in which a corpse had been laid on an elaborately decorated cloak.

Some of the burials were associated with human sacrifice. In particular, fifty-three women were discovered in a carefully organized mass grave. Pauketat notes that this grave is comparable with the royal burials in the cemetery at Ur. He observes that it is clearly the result of planned killings, carried out within a complex society that must have condoned such rituals.

It is difficult, however, to discern exactly how Cahokian society was organized. Pauketat speculates on a number of possibilities, using examples drawn from elsewhere in the Americas. Such elaborate burials may represent a bloodline eliminated for dynastic reasons, ritual sacrifices designed to provide social cohesion, or sacrifices to ancestors or gods in which participants impersonated ritual figures. Pauketat cannot offer a clear answer, although he surveys the various possibilities in detail. In particular, he provides a close examination of the myth of the Twin Heroes, a story found in various forms from Central America right into the Midwest, and he considers its implications for Cahokia.

Pauketat makes a dense argument regarding the Twin Heroes myth, and he draws on a wealth of material in support of his claim. However, some of it, particularly the connection he forges with the Gottshall Rockshelter in Wisconsin, remains somewhat controversial. He argues that women were important within the Cahokian society, which he believes was constructed on matrilineal lines. This argument is somewhat sketchy, however, relying heavily on the presence of so many female sacrifices. Their presence is further discussed when he theorizes about foreign groups being drawn into the orbit of Cahokia and possibly providing sacrificial subjects.

The final great mystery of Cahokia is what happened to the city and its inhabitants. Archaeological evidence suggests that it flourished and was highly successful for several hundred years, before disappearing almost as suddenly as it had sprung up. Evidence further suggests that the city emptied very rapidly, its people dispersing almost without a trace. There are indications that groups from Cahokia scattered and settled, taking with them elements of their distinctive culture, but the dispersal was wide. The city's residents seem to have left in small groups and become absorbed into other native tribes and cultures.

Pauketat argues that traces of the Cahokian culture within other native groups persisted into the sixteenth and seventeenth centuries. It is almost impossible at present to determine what happened to the people as a whole. Remarkably, there are no stories in the oral histories of neighboring tribes to account for the city's foundation or for its later disappearance, and Pauketat proposes the possibility of a concerted act of intentional forgetting, for reasons unspecified.

Debate persists as to how the Cahokian culture first came into being. Although it appears to share certain similarities with Mesoamerican cultures, particularly in its apparent veneration of the Twin Heroes, no Mesoamerican artifacts have ever been found in Mississippi (with the exception of a few flakes of obsidian). It has been suggested that the similarities between the two cultures emerge from the experiences of a shared background or from a general diffusion of ideas. However, more recently, it has also been suggested that ideas from Mesoamerica were brought into the Mississippi Valley not by land but by sea and river, with Mesoamericans traveling along the coast of Texas and then upriver.

This theory does not address the continued lack of artifacts, although some researchers are now suggesting that certain styles of Northern American knife in fact originate in Mesoamerica and might have been brought to the Mississippi by travelers. Many of the mysteries surrounding the foundation and later destruction of Cahokia remain unsolved. It may never be known whether the city's foundation was precipitated by the supernova of 1054 or whether it was shaped by the needs of ritual cults. Nonetheless, the work of archaeologists, historians, and anthropologists such as Pauketat point to the possibility of even more remarkable discoveries waiting to be made, leading to a fuller understanding of the lives of the mound-builders of Cahokia.

Maureen Kincaid Speller

Review Sources

Booklist 105, no. 21 (July 1, 2009): 23.
Kirkus Reviews 77, no. 11 (June 1, 2009): 598.
Wall Street Journal, August 28, 2009, p. W6.

CAN POETRY SAVE THE EARTH?
A Field Guide to Nature Poems

Author: John Felstiner (1936-)
Publisher: Yale University Press (New Haven, Conn.). Illustrated. 396 pp. $35.00
Type of work: Literary history, literary criticism

A series of essays engaging British and American poems of the past two centuries that respond to the natural world, demonstrating how environmental concerns were central to the poets' visions of human existence

While there are arguably more people writing competent if not exceptional poetry than at any time since the advent of modern English, there appears to be a paradoxical decrease in the prominence and influence of the poet as a figure of importance in the American cultural community. More than half of U.S. states have a designated poet laureate, but the people occupying these positions are rarely recognizeable to the states' inhabitants. One factor in this separation is a displacement between the approach of academic commentators and the reasons that literate nonprofessionals read poems.

John Felstiner, a professor of literature at Stanford University, addresses this disjunction in *Can Poetry Save the Earth?* by selecting and discussing nature poems, primarily from the Romantic era to the present. He begins with one of the first nature poems, the biblical book of Genesis, and concludes with the work of one of the most accessible contemporary poets, the pioneering environmental visionary Gary Snyder. These framing selections emphasize a sacred regard for the planet and an encompassing secular engagement with the matter and materials of everyday experience. In his discussions of poems, their authors, and the cultural contexts from which the poems evolved, Felstiner intends not only to answer the question his title poses in the affirmative but also to develop a positive argument for a parallel query: Can an awareness of one's environment lead to a deeper involvement with all that a poem can provide?

Felstiner's introductory chapter demonstrates his method. It begins with an enthusiastic brief for poetry itself, including familiar quotes such as William Carlos Williams's impassioned proclamation in "Asphodel, That Greeny Flower," that

> It is difficult
> to get the news from poems
> yet men die miserably every day
> for lack
> of what is found there

An important facet of "the news" referred to is the history of the destructive misuses of land, water, and living creatures in the United States since the arrival of Europeans

John Felstiner is a professor of English at Stanford University. His award-winning translations of Pablo Neruda and Paul Celan have been highly praised, and his biographical and critical study, Paul Celan: Poet, Survivor, Jew *(1995) is regarded as the definitive work on the poet.*

on the continent. This volume's convival conversation about poets and their work—marked by neighborly descriptions of poets such as the "boisterous" Dylan Thomas, the "peasant poet" John Clare, and the "Missouri-born T. S. Eliot"—shifts toward a professional historian's rigorous, informative account of continental dispoilation stemming from a fundamental misunderstanding of how to live in harmony with the landscape.

By the end of the opening chapter, Felstiner has effectively illustrated humanity's devastating disregard for environmental necessities with many statements from the historical record. He has also juxtaposed these statements with observations from poets to demonstrated the ways that a mindful awareness of language—the essence of poetry itself—is a part of a way of seeing that results in an understanding of the natural world. This perspective is one of the reasons he calls his book a "field guide," linking the explorer's report on phenomena to the poet's image-making vision of the cosmos. The heart of Felstiner's project is a celebration of the capacity to see, understand, and appreciate the "human universe" (in the poet Charles Olson's term) through language—in conjunction with a guided response to the natural universe calling on all of the senses.

The linkage between the perilous condition of Earth's ecological systems and the endangered or neglected state of poetic discourse beyond a coterie of devotees and initiates shapes Felstiner's program. In his preface, he declares his intentions to address "every sort of reader," an ambition common to guidebooks written by experts whose desire to share their knowledge is fired by enthusiasm and fueled by a diligent application of all their senses to the focus of their attention. The book follows the pattern of reports from the field, echoing Robert Duncan's observation about "the opening of the field" in the mid-twentieth century, when conceptions of poetry and the poet moved outward from what has been called "academically sanctioned formalism" toward a poetics that had its origin in Walt Whitman's work.

In this sense, Felstiner calls for a return to a primal impulse that paralleled the perspective of the English Romantic poets, while introducing an American voice and the vision of a different landmass. Olson characterized the New World by saying, "I take SPACE to be the central fact of man born in America. . . . I spell it large because it comes large here. Large and without mercy." It is through this "SPACE" that Felstiner, in collaboration with the poets whose work is an interaction with its dimensions, intends to guide his readers.

By beginning his discussion with the book of Genesis, Felstiner asserts that the environment, in its largest sense, is fundamental to human existence. The focus on the familiar in the lines of the King James Version of the Bible, with an emphasis on God's judgment that the creation of the earth was "very good," establishes the sacred center of what Felstiner calls "Singing Ecology unto the Lord." Felstiner is not just gathering poems that sing in praise of the natural world, however. He notes that, where the Old Testament offers humans "dominion over the fish of the sea, and over the fowl of the air," the word "dominion" stems "from the same Hebrew root as 'tyrant,' an ominous gift," but he emphasizes that the "Hebraic legacy also ordains stewardship." Just as the poems he explores are guides to the natural world, Felstiner's close and clear readings are designed to be guides to the poems. Each of the forty compact chapters chooses one or two poets and moves within their poems to reveal and illuminate the poets' relationship with their environment.

Recognizing that the primary component of poetic communication is an aural one, Felstiner has included sixty color and black-and-white images in the volume; a full range of response to the environment calls on all of the senses. The abundance of visual material in electronic form now available, the extensive array of digital videos that can bring the poet in performance almost anywhere, has taken poetry beyond the book, just as print took poetry beyond the poet's speaking voice. This development does not make a book less valuable, but it certainly alters the expectations of what a book can be. In spite of Felstiner's hope that he will reach "every sort of reader," a realistic assessment by the Yale University Press would indicate that libraries—especially those affiliated with universities—will be the ones most likely to acquire the book.

As an ultimate goal, a paperback prepared for courses with an accompanying compact disc would be a welcome outcome of Felstiner's project. Visionary professors have already chosen the book as a teaching text, but this imaginative utilization depends on too many factors to be assured. As a start, Felstiner's illustrations, including "many printed here for the first time," are an added enticement. He argues, "As long as we know, poetry has aimed to enlighten and delight. So have the visual arts, honing our perception." With the practice of printing on paper itself endangered, the incorporation of images represents part of a sound strategy for preservation.

Many of the book's illustrations recapitulate a tradition central to Anglo-American literary history. They include a reproduction of a page from John Keats's manuscript for "To Autumn," the frontispiece for Walt Whitman's 1855 edition of *Leaves of Grass* (1855, 1856, 1860, 1867, 1871, 1876, 1881-1882, 1888-1889), the poet young and confident facing the world; a daguerreotype of Emily Dickinson and two pages of her manuscript for "A narrow Fellow in the Grass"; her penmanship is strikingly different from Keats's, but both are intensely personal. Among the book's less familiar images, there is a sketch by Gerard Manley Hopkins signed "Balagas, Isle of Man, Aug. 12, '73"; a group of climbers on Mount Rainer in 1922, with Marianne Moore "third from right"; and a photo by Una Jeffers of Robinson Jeffers and Edna St. Vincent Millay at Hawk Tower, an unexpected alliance.

Twelve pages of reproductions in color, superbly reprinted, are set in the center of the volume. They include William Blake's awesome conception of "Creation" from *Europe: A Prophecy* (1794); Ansel Adams's photograph of Big Sur for the cover of Robinson Jeffers's *Not Man Apart* (1965); Stanley Kunitz walking in his garden; and an oil painting by Derek Walcott from *Breakers, Becune Point* (1995). Two prints from Japanese scrolls, meanwhile, point to the sources of Gary Snyder's poetry.

For some readers, these images alone would be worth the price of the book. It is the words, however, written, spoken, and sung, that are the essence of a poet's response to and recreation of the whole earth and beyond. The chapter that concentrates on the anonymous medieval lyric "Western Wind" is crucial for Felstiner's contention that "speech in the beginning brings all into being." Likening human speech to the voice of God in Genesis, Felstiner maintains that "secular nature poetry lives if not by the grace of God then by the grace of language."

Felstiner's close reading of the sound patterns of what he calls a "late medieval fountainhead of the English lyric tradition" leads readers syllable by syllable through the query in the couplet and the prayer closing the quatrain, alert to nuances of rhythm, measure, cadence, and rhyme. It then shows how the sonic structure of "Western Wind" is echoed in Dickinson's "The Brain is wider than the sky" and in poems by Percy Bysshe Shelley and Keats. The reading concludes with a discourse on metaphor as motion, citing Bob Dylan's well-known assertion about an answer "blowin' in the wind."

This chapter could be seen as a template for the entire text. It is rife with references to other poems that expand one's understanding of the work under scrutiny, defining and illustrating the terminology that is the vocabulary of poetic discourse. It then moves smoothly toward an intricate examination of how and why a poem operates in a linguistic and cultural field. The cultural component is a crucial element in Felstiner's reclamation project, because his representation of the lives of the poets as environmental expeditions supports the book's premise. Thus, William Wordsworth and Dorothy Wordsworth are placed in "England's semi-wild Lake District," and Samuel Taylor Coleridge is there with them and walking in the Alps. Whitman exists on the road in America; Dickinson is in New England, her mind everywhere; Robert Frost situates himself in New England; and William Carlos Williams inhabits the American language in one of the book's strongest chapters. Many other American poets are placed across the continent, leading up to Gary Snyder in the Sierra Nevada, building a house, voyaging across the Pacific, and seeming at home on all the surfaces of the globe.

Felstiner concludes the book with a chapter that operates as a capsule biography of Snyder, who is presented as an epitome of the poet as environmental activist, mariner, terrainer, and congenial companion in multiple endeavors. Allen Ginsberg spoke for many when he said in a letter that Snyder is "the only one with a strong sense to find what need be done." Felstiner follows Snyder's path as "avid hiker-climber, redneck [his word] logger, seaman, and firewatcher, Amerindian anthropologist . . ." in a long list that winds up with Snyder declared the inheritor of many of the poets cited in previous chapters.

Snyder's characteristically astute endorsement of the book on its back cover, praising Felstiner's "deep reflections" on poets "seeing the actual world" and telling "the story of the earth" is an accurate assessment of the book, which is not only a "field guide" but also, like Edward Thomas accompanying Robert Frost in the Glouscestershire countryside, a companion one would like to walk with when exploring new places or revisiting fond familiar ones.

Can Poetry Save the Earth? is the kind of annotated anthology that returns the reader to a poet's complete works and, like any valuable collection, implicitly invites readers to consider what other poets could have been included. The too-often ignored Appalachian region might have been represented by Charles Wright, for instance, and, while William Butler Yeats is always worth attention, Seamus Heaney's excavations of Ireland's soil would have been a fitting complement to the poets herein. The "boisterous" Dylan Thomas's invocations of the Welsh countryside would also seem to have been a natural choice. Thoughts along these lines are a testament to what Felstiner's book accomplishes and another of the reasons why it would be appropriate for compilers of introductory textbooks to follow its form, content, and aspirations.

Leon Lewis

Review Sources

Geographical 81, no. 10 (October, 2009): 57-58.
Science 326, no. 5949 (October 2, 2009): 48.
The Times Literary Supplement, April 24, 2009, p. 28.
World Literature Today 83, no. 6 (November/December, 2009): 75-76.

THE CANAL BUILDERS
Making America's Empire at the Panama Canal

Author: Julie Greene (1951-)
Publisher: Penguin Press (New York). 475 pp. $30.00
Type of work: History

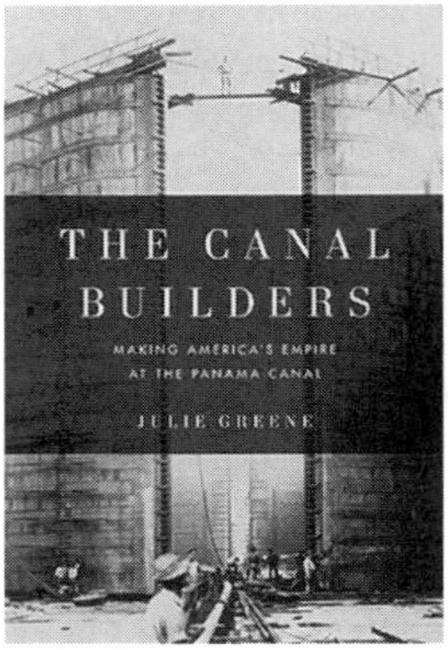

A prominent historian describes the daily experience of the workers who constructed the Panama Canal, as well as the social structure created for them

In January, 2009, when Barack Obama became the first African American president of the United States, another unprecedented event also took place: Elizabeth Alexander recited her poem "Praise Song for the Day," celebrating the workers of past generations—including slaves—who created the American infrastructure; "who laid the train tracks, raised the bridges,/ . . . built/ brick by brick the glittering edifices . . ." While workers like those honored in Alexander's poem might well have constructed the building where Obama was sworn in, historically their contributions have been little noted. More common is the sentiment of the poem "Dedication," composed by Robert Frost for John F. Kennedy's inauguration in 1961 and forecasting "The glory of a next Augustan age."

In the same vein, histories of the Panama Canal have typically emphasized the engineering feats involved in its construction and the glory reflected on the political and professional leaders who promoted the project. A celebrated 1906 news photograph, featured in at least three major books on the history of the canal, shows a white-suited President Theodore Roosevelt atop a giant Bucyrus steam shovel at the building site. The picture, says University of Maryland historian Julie Greene, "telegraphed to the world the importance of the Panama Canal project." Like Alexander, Greene shifts attention from the planners to the builders: "Absent from the picture," she notes, "are the thousands of workingmen who actually dug the canal."

Greene details the lives of those workers in *The Canal Builders: Making America's Empire at the Panama Canal*. Her account of their daily experience seeks to supplant, or at least supplement, the "tale enshrined in popular memory and innumerable histories and novels" about "breakthroughs in medicine, technology, and science and wise engineering decisions" which, "according to traditional accounts of the project, allowed the United States to succeed where France had failed" in its attempt to build a canal during the 1880's. Greene's additional goal is to demonstrate that it was the "human rather than the technological or scientific dimensions of the project" that presented the greatest challenge to the project's leaders. The tremendous size and diversity of the workforce—up to sixty thousand workers from some 105 countries around the world—created an unprecedented test of efficient social order in the Canal Zone.

During the construction period, from 1904 to 1914, the popular image of the Canal Zone—fostered by contemporary journalists—was one of an ideal progressive society, a model of efficiency and social justice. Progressives of the era believed that the strong government role in the canal project validated theories of "scientific socialism," of highly productive government-run ventures that also delivered social services to workers and the community. Expectations ran high: The zone was to offer "a display of America's domestic strengths in a world setting" and "progressivism for the world."

Julie Greene has authored Pure and Simple Politics: The American Federation of Labor and Political Activism, 1881-1917 *(1998) and coedited* Labor Histories: Class, Politics, and the Diversity of the Working-Class Experience *(1998). She is a founding editor of the journal* Labor.

Greene evaluates this image, drawing on a large amount of newly unearthed archival material to show that nothing turned out as expected for either the project managers or the laborers. Workers came from all over the world anticipating high wages, a healthy diet, and comfortable living quarters. The project leadership, in turn, expected a docile, manageable workforce. In reality, employees were divided into two categories: those paid in gold and those paid in silver. The "gold" workers—typically white American skilled craftsmen—received better wages and living accommodations, while "silver" workers—mostly unskilled laborers from outside the United States—tended to receive lower wages and often substandard living quarters. If the system was not racist to begin with, it became so in time, owing to continual reclassification of individuals or groups of workers along racial lines.

Death from disease or accidental injury was an everyday occurrence in the Canal Zone. More than five thousand workers perished before the project was completed. Managers also faced unexpected obstacles. The workers whom management expected to be so tractable—especially those from Spain and the West Indies—proved resourceful in getting around the rules and fomenting labor strife when they felt shortchanged. In response, the project's leaders took a divide-and-conquer approach toward workers.

Greene argues that there is a strong connection between the racist, exploitive treatment of the Panama Canal workers and the rise of U.S. imperialism generally. This rise was fostered by victory in the Spanish-American War of 1898, which established the United States as a world power. As Greene sees it, the patronizing attitude toward other countries of larger-than-life figures such as Roosevelt and George Washington Goethals, the final chief engineer of the canal project, was mirrored in the Americans' attitudes toward Canal Zone workers.

Greene's chapter titles pinpoint the vital issues looming throughout the construction period. For example, the chapters "A Modern State in the Tropics" and "Progressivism for the World" detail the quest for economic and political efficiency that was a hallmark of the era's progressive movement. Greene reveals anew the coercive side of progressivism that is often at odds with the movement's democratic ideals. The progressive tactic of placing power in the hands of professional administrators such as Goethals often meant reducing the power of individual citizens. Those workers who were not U.S. citizens—such as the numerous ones from Jamaica and Barbados—seemingly had no power at all over their own lives. Greene notes that such attitudes about citizenship persist in the present: On a recent cruise through the Canal Zone, she found the ship's crew racially divided between Europeans and Filipinos, as each group received significantly different living and working conditions and rates of pay.

The chapter titled "Silver Lives" shows how the International Canal Commission (ICC), the project's governing body, "searched the globe for a source of tractable workers. They settled on the West Indians as the most obedient workers they could feasibly bring to the Canal Zone," but, she continues, "Once on the isthmus, West Indians set out to shape the world around them." Finding the employer-provided food almost inedible, they opted to live outside the Canal Zone in Panamanian cities, where they could choose their own fare. They also frequently changed jobs and locations in search of better working conditions and higher pay. Sometimes, they also changed their names to avoid fines, imprisonment, or deportation—all common penalties for abandoning their old jobs.

Stymied by the West Indians' subtle strategies, which Greene says the ICC never truly grasped, canal officials began to recruit Spaniards instead as a more biddable source of labor. As recounted in Greene's chapter "Lay Down Your Shovels," Spanish laborers posed even greater challenges to management. Part of the difficulty stemmed from their indignation at being classified as "silver" workers along with the West Indians, to whom they felt superior. In this case, the divide-and-conquer strategy toward workers backfired on management, culminating in strikes and a major riot in 1912. Greene concedes that the strategy "also created a barrier to more widespread solidarities that might have empowered canal workers [and] given rise to a more potent labor movement."

A major strength of *The Canal Builders* is its powerful portrayal of the racial arrogance and economic exploitation that underlay the idealized canal project. However, the account is hampered by Greene's perception—not original with her—of the canal project as a type of proving ground for America's design to dominate the world. The new route between the Atlantic and Pacific oceans gave the United States tremendous military and commercial advantages, but Greene implies that the canal, in itself, served as the origin of a drive to global dominance. It was more likely a reflection of aspirations already long established. Moreover, Greene does not make a case that the hard lot of Canal Zone workers was worse than that of laborers in the United States, whose shameful working conditions were documented, for example, in Upton Sinclair's *The Jungle* (1906), which dealt with the Chicago meatpacking industry. The difference between Chicago and Panama lay primarily in the unjustifiable boasts about the Canal Zone as a workers' haven.

Greene rightly rebuts the myth of the canal as wholly an epic achievement of top-echelon engineers and managers. However, Greene wrongly implies that hers is the only history of the canal that looks beyond engineering marvels to the plight of the workers. For example, she characterizes David McCullough, author of the seminal 1976 volume *The Path Between the Seas: The Creation of the Panama Canal, 1870-1914* as fixated on the success of American engineers in confronting landslides and floods and on their development of a particularly strong and durable form of concrete for the canal locks. "The canal, he concluded, is 'an extraordinary work of civilization.'" McCullough himself may have helped create this false impression of his book through a series of interviews and public speeches. The book itself, however, takes a comprehensive approach toward the challenges of design, engineering, and disease control, in addition to the plight of the workers and the unjust, often racist, solutions to labor issues employed by management. He describes "canvas cot[s] in an unfurnished, often miserably small room with five or six others . . . for unskilled black workers" and the "meager, monotonous, high-priced" food provided to them in the zone. Even Matthew Parker's *Panama Fever* (2007), which generally celebrates the American triumph of engineering, includes an extensive chapter on racial and economic injustices in the Canal Zone—and Roosevelt's dismay over those injustices. Thus, Greene is not alone in calling attention to the struggle of unskilled workers.

The epigraph to Greene's book is Bertolt Brecht's poem "Fragen eines lesenden Arbeiters" (1936; "A Worker Reads History," 1947).

> Who built the seven gates of Thebes?
> The books are filled with the names of kings.
> Was it the kings who hauled the craggy blocks of stone? . . .

This passage does for the canal project what Elizabeth Alexander's poem did for President Obama's inauguration. Greene, as she asserts of herself, "tells a different story." The story she tells is the story of the workers, their enormous diversity, their long journeys from other parts of the world in search of opportunity in the Canal Zone, their work and their leisure, their dwelling places, their squabbles with neighbors, their social life, and even their daily diet. There is more: Greene is, after all, a scholar, and her skill with anecdotal detail is reinforced not only by the previously unrevealed archival material with which she works but also by extensive scholarly annotation and an appendix that sorts the Canal Zone's labor population by country of origin and gender. Greene portrays many individuals whose contributions to what Roosevelt called "the greatest work of the kind ever attempted" might not otherwise be fully chronicled. Without her meticulous depiction, these thousands of workers in the period 1904-1914 could be forgotten. That is enough to make *The Canal Builders* as significant an achievement as that of the people whose lives Greene portrays.

Thomas Rankin

Review Sources

Booklist 105, no. 11 (February 1, 2009): 12.
The Economist 390, no. 8620 (February 28, 2009): 89.
Foreign Affairs 88, no. 3 (May/June, 2009): 176-177.
Kirkus Reviews 76, no. 23 (December 1, 2008): 1241-1242.
Library Journal 134, no. 3 (February 15, 2009): 116.
The New York Times Book Review, March 29, 2009, p. 11.
Times Higher Education, April 2, 2009, p. 49.

CASTLE

Author: J. Robert Lennon (1970-)
Publisher: Graywolf Press (St. Paul, Minn.). 234 pp. $22.00
Type of work: Novel
Time: 2006
Locale: In and near Gerrysburg, in upstate New York

A man returns after a considerable absence to his hometown in upstate New York and is beset with a series of mysteries and inexplicable threats

Principal characters:
ERIC LOESCH, a man in midlife who returns home and purchases an old house and surrounding woods
DOCTOR AVERY STILES, a former professor at a local university who knew Loesch in his childhood and had a profound effect on the boy
BRIAN LOESCH, Eric's janitor father, who worked at Stiles's university
CYBELE LOESCH, Eric's deeply depressed and dysfunctional mother

J. Robert Lennon's *Castle* begins innocently enough, as Eric Loesch returns to his rural hometown and purchases a rundown house and 612 acres of adjoining forest. Loesch buys the land on an impulse and begins the process of restoring the property and presumably settling in to familiar surroundings. However, the familiar quickly becomes dangerously unfamiliar.

Loesch is something of a handyman and methodically restores the dilapidated property and begins exploring his densely forested land. For the most part, he keeps to himself, but when he does interact with residents in nearby Gerrysburg, insults and misunderstandings abound. Loesch has a knack for alienating everyone, including his older sister when she drops by for a visit.

Loesch is obsessed with a giant rock in the center of his property, and when exploring the woods he becomes horribly disoriented and fascinated with a pure white deer. When the title to his property arrives, he discovers that the rock and a small surrounding parcel belong to an owner whose name has been obliterated. Eventually, he discovers the identity of the owner—a former professor at nearby SUNY Milan who disappeared years ago.

A series of bizarre events and threatening omens ensue, and Loesch is convinced someone has invaded his privacy and is threatening him. During one of his explorations, he discovers that a castle has been built adjacent to the giant rock. While investigating the structure, he is knocked unconscious, and he awakens to find himself incarcerated in a cage at the hands of a septuagenarian professor.

At this point, the novel oscillates between incidents from Loesch's childhood, when he was used as a subject for personality experiments by the bizarre professor, and his present adventures in the woods. Details of his troubled childhood, his parents' dreadful marriage and deaths, and his recent past overwhelm Loesch. Some of the mysteries about his unsociability are explained, as he comes to terms with his past.

J. Robert Lennon is the author of The Light of Falling Stars *(1997),* The Funnies *(1999),* On the Night Plain *(2001),* Pieces for the Left Hand: One Hundred Anecdotes *(2005),* Happyland *(2006), and* Mailman *(2003), his greatest critical success. He teaches writing at Cornell University.*

The novel's title invites comparisons with Franz Kafka's last, unfinished work, *Das Schloss* (1926; *The Castle*, 1930), and although the two novels are markedly different, they do share a surreal similarity. Lennon's novel appears straightforward on the surface, until Loesch attempts to plumb the mystery of the anonymous owner of the adjacent property. When he receives a letter bearing only the name Doctor Avery Stiles, the narrator remarks that "the sight of those words caused my stomach to turn over" (93). This remark comes with no context to explain it.

Other surreal occurrences gradually mount until readers realize that the seemingly straightforward narrative is no longer so straightforward. In his few encounters with locals, Loesch reveals himself to be thoroughly inept socially. In response to their affable, inquisitive remarks, the protagonist is defensive and downright confrontational, and his responses are utterly inappropriate. Still another odd occurrence involves the appearance at key moments of the mysterious white doe that guides Loesch to safety. These scenes are simply inexplicable, as are the strange noises, half-opened doors, and shadowy presences in and around the house. Along with Loesch's fear of his basement, these episodes provoke questions that are never conclusively answered. Furthermore, the shifts between the present and past and the series of flashbacks that gradually predominate the story create an unsettling lack of narrative stability. These odd dislocations, however, appear to be Lennon's point. The past and present merge in the text, and a clear division between reality and fantasy is never established.

In many respects, *Castle* can be read as an inverted bildungsroman wherein the gradual movement from youth to maturity is displaced by a tracing from midlife to the protagonist's early beginnings. Roughly the first half of the novel exists in the present, as Loesch establishes his connections with his new house, and a good deal of attention is given to the mundane matters of renovating and setting up a new home. As Loesch explores the nearly impenetrable surrounding woods and the mystery of his neighbor's deed, readers similarly explore his tangled childhood. His family life is nothing short of horrific. He witnesses his parents' ceaseless quarrels and sorrows and his sister's rebellion and separation from home.

Loesch's father submits the boy, against his wife's objections, to the stern professor's experiments. These events match the oft-repeated pattern of an initiate in a bildungsroman being instructed by a surrogate parent in the ways of the world and the means of his eventual survival. As young Pip in Charles Dickens's *Great Expectations* (serial, 1860-1861; book, 1861) is frightened and aided by the mysterious convict Magwitch, Loesch is terrified and abused by Stiles, who inflicts his version of B. F. Skinner's radical behaviorism on the boy. Through punishments, coercion, and the torture of small animals, Stiles believes he is imparting major lessons to his subject. He warns the impressionable boy,

> . . . you will have to free yourself of all personal sentiment. A day will come when misplaced empathy could lead, I'm afraid, to your death. In what we think of as the civilized world—a world, I must inform you, Eric, that is soon to collapse into chaos and lawlessness—it is a virtue to do no harm. In the world to come, it will be a skill as valuable to you as the ability to start a fire, or build a shelter.

Despite the professor's most perverse efforts, Loesch has not been equipped with strengths and abilities as much as with resentments and proclivities for violence and misanthropy. In the end, his strengths are revealed to be deeply intertwined with his greatest weaknesses.

To the consternation of many reviewers, *Castle* is difficult to categorize, being neither a gothic tale, nor a traditional suspense novel, nor a hair-raising thriller. It is, by turns, each of these, as well as a psychological exploration of the deep recesses of the mind and heart. Like almost any psychiatric patient, Loesch and his own motivations are mysteries to himself. His alienation from others, which he views as a matter of preference rather than emotional incapacity, is a hint at his obtuseness. While hardly a typical Freudian analysis, the novel does explore a young man's difficulties with his father, his sympathy for his mother, and the complicated connections to his personal past.

The enigmatic white doe exists as a creature native to upstate New York and possibly a prophetic beast from Native American lore, but it is also a projection of something far more personal to the protagonist. It is a symbol of Loesch's innocence and vulnerability, that fragile self he was forced to abandon years ago. The identification is nowhere more evident than when the creature guides him to safety, "I felt as though the woods were mine—that I knew every twig, every bramble and pebble, every handful of earth, by heart. It was as though I were dreaming." This is the one figure that can rescue him at his most confused moments and the only physical presence for which he has any empathy or concern.

The numerous irresolvabilities of the novel—whether Loesch's father deliberately or accidentally killed his wife and then committed suicide, whether the professor has lived in the woods for decades after his dismissal from the university, whether he captures the protagonist on his last foray into the woods, whether he is killed at the end, and what exactly happens to Loesch in the concluding scene—have less to do with external events and explanations than they have to do with the protagonist's internal journey. He must confront the recesses of his own mind, which is oppressed by the dreadful burdens of his past.

The novel's major weakness issues from the concluding chapters concerning Loesch's military adventures in a detention center in Iraq. The attempt to fuse the topical atrocities of Islamic prisoners subjected to torture in the prison at Abu Ghraib with the tale of Loesch's emotional and psychological dislocation is a bit too pat. His service is presented as the culmination of the professor's behavioral experiments and his attempts to fashion Loesch as an empowered, unsympathetic warrior. Even as the answer to the novel's grand secret, however, these sections advance little. Loesch is a desperate, troubled soul who can find no peace until he confronts his own grief and contradictions, and the overly dramatic template of combat atrocities is unnecessary to dramatize pain and psychological dissolution.

In spite of this fault, Lennon is a clever writer who makes good use of the first-person narrator. The reader constantly questions the protagonist's reliability, and such dubiousness creates much of the novel's suspense. In relating events, Loesch does not dissemble or misrepresent, though he often withholds information for the sake of dramatic tension. When the narrator confronts Stiles, his "nemesis," on the edge of the great rock, he remains dense, though readers can see matters with greater clarity. The scene is reminiscent of many from doppelgänger stories, such as Edgar Allan Poe's "William Wilson" (1839), in which the protagonist finally confronts and does battle with his twin. Stiles clarifies the issue and the tensions in the novel when he says, "The fact is, Eric, that you cannot restore your own life by killing me. Furthermore, your life doesn't need to be restored. . . . It merely needs to be seized. And my life—my life was never here to be taken."

The clues have been available all along, and the mystery of Loesch is finally dispelled.

David W. Madden

Review Sources

Booklist 105, no. 13 (March 1, 2009): 22.
Kirkus Reviews 77, no. 4 (February 15, 2009): 168.
Library Journal 134, no. 5 (March 15, 2009): 95.
Los Angeles Times, April 5, 2009, p. E7.
The New York Times Book Review, May 24, 2009, p. 17.
The New Yorker 85, no. 20 (July 6, 2009): 85.
Publishers Weekly 256, no. 4 (January 26, 2009): 99.

CATCHER
How the Man Behind the Plate Became an American Folk Hero

Author: Peter Morris (1962-   )
Publisher: Ivan R. Dee (Chicago). 386 pp. $27.50
Type of work: History
Time: 1850's to the early twentieth century
Locale: United States

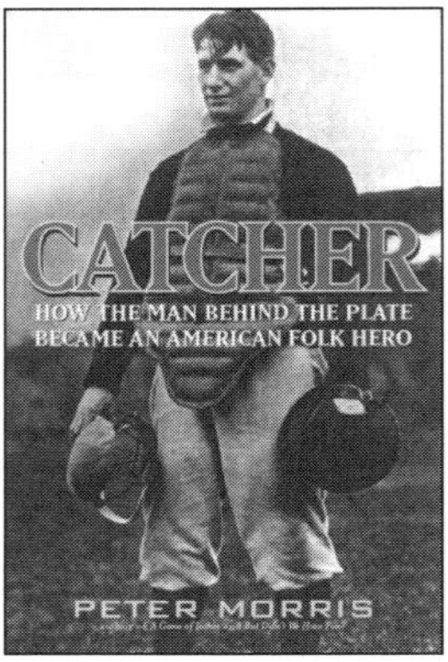

A sprightly history of the catcher's changing role, from baseball's formative years to the beginning of the modern era

Principal personages:
JIM "DEACON" WHITE, a catcher, perhaps the greatest professional baseball player of the nineteenth century
HENRY CHADWICK, an influential sportswriter
NAT HICKS, a leading catcher of the 1870's
CHARLEY BENNETT,
BUCK EWING, and
MIKE "KING" KELLY, the three leading catchers of the 1880's

Peter Morris has established himself as the leading historian of early baseball. With *Catcher: How the Man Behind the Plate Became an American Folk Hero*, he consolidates that reputation. Morris traces the evolution of the catcher's role from baseball's beginnings into the early twentieth century. Along the way, he connects changing perceptions of the catcher to larger changes in American society (sometimes persuasively, sometimes not). The story he tells is entertaining, unpredictable, and thoroughly absorbing.

Morris begins with a prologue of sorts, recounting the experience of Stephen, a young man born in 1871. Bright, slight of stature, fiercely competitive, and somewhat alienated, this young man loves baseball and in particular the catcher's position. He is good enough to be the starting catcher for Syracuse University, which he attends before dropping out to become a journalist and, before long, a novelist. Morris reveals with a flourish that he is describing Stephen Crane, author of *The Red Badge of Courage: An Episode of the American Civil War* (1895).

In Morris's telling, Crane's "obsession with being a baseball catcher" is not simply an interesting bit of trivia. Rather, Morris argues, Crane in this respect stands for his generation: "Mastery of the intricacies of the [catcher's] position was seen by American boys who came of age in the 1870's and 1880's as the ultimate embodiment of courage, leadership, resolve, and daring—in short, it was their initiation into manhood." Morris frames this assertion with a rapid overview of American conceptions of heroism from the colonial era to the late nineteenth century. He acknowledges his debt to the work of historian Richard Slotkin for this overview. Some readers, finding this account of the "American hero" heavy on clichés, may be tempted to stop right there. That would be their loss, however, for even if one rejects the notion of an entire post-Civil War generation of boys desperately in search of a way to enter manhood, Morris is thoroughly convincing when he argues that, for many young men of this era, the catcher had an aura that attracted admiration and emulation.

Peter Morris is the author of several books on the history of baseball, including Baseball Fever *(2003),* A Game of Inches *(2006),* Level Playing Field *(2007), and* But Didn't We Have Fun? *(2008). He is a former national and international Scrabble champion.*

Morris traces that aura to the 1850's, when baseball—still in its formative stage—came in two primary flavors: the New York Game and the Massachusetts Game. There were a number of differences between the two (both in rules and in style or attitude), but among the most salient was that in the Massachusetts Game the pitcher and catcher had greater impacts relative to the other positions in the field. At the same time, in the Massachusetts Game, the catcher—who was positioned much closer to the batter than was his counterpart in the New York Game—was far more vulnerable to injury. It was in part for this reason, Morris suggests, that by the end of the Civil War the New York Game had become dominant. Another concern was the fear that it would be too easy to throw games if only two positions were inordinately important for their outcomes.

In the New York Game, the pitcher had a role very different from the likes of Walter Johnson, Bob Feller, Sandy Koufax, and Tim Lincecum. The rules specified that the ball was to be pitched underhand. The pitcher's job was to put the ball in play. The catcher typically stood well behind the batter, hands protected (if at all) by thin gloves no thicker than today's batting gloves that generally covered the palms. The technique was to stand with legs slightly bent, hands cupped together, ready to catch the ball with the fingers (rather than on the palm, as would later catchers equipped with mitts). It was not a particularly inspiring role.

Even as the New York Game became generally accepted, changes were underway. Pitchers, growing restive under the restrictions, began to deliver the ball a bit higher, then higher still. Before long, average scores decreased as pitchers began to be more dominant. Meanwhile, catchers, who had already begun to move closer to the batter in certain strategic situations, now had to deal with much faster pitches. A fast pitcher could only be effective with a battery-mate who was able to handle his deliveries. (As Casey Stengel put it, in a line that Morris uses for the book's epigraph, "You have to have a catcher or you'll have a lot of passed balls.") At the same time that the catcher became much more subject to injury (Morris includes photos of veteran catcher's hands), the demand for outstanding skill at the position skyrocketed.

Thus were born the first two archetypes Morris proposes: "The Catcher as Tough Guy," stoically absorbing brutal punishment to his hands (not to mention his chest and legs—anywhere the ball might land with great force) and "The Catcher as Indispensable." Flourishing teams whose catcher was injured sank into mediocrity overnight. From these archetypes proceeded a third, "The Catcher as One in a Million." There was, Morris shows, a "mystique" associated with the position, expressed in various forms (including the notion of a special affinity between certain catchers and pitchers).

By the mid-1870's, baseball was ruled by the pitcher-catcher combination even more thoroughly than had been the case in the heyday of the Massachusetts Game. Scoring became scarcer than ever. For some observers, the nadir came in 1877 with a twenty-four-inning scoreless tie in a game between Harvard University and a professional team. The reaction against so-called scientific baseball became an outcry. Rule changes helped redress the balance. The pitching mound was moved farther from home plate, and a livelier ball was introduced (a move that would be repeated in the early twentieth century).

Meanwhile, protective devices were introduced that made catchers less vulnerable (and hence more easily replaceable). The catcher's mask was introduced in 1876 by a Harvard student, James Tyng, and refinements on his design soon followed. First used in a professional game in 1877, the mask was in general use by the following season. Several years later, in 1883, Detroit catcher Charley Bennett wore a chest protector made by his wife. Soon thereafter, inventor William Gray (who later created the pay telephone) devised an inflatable padded protector. By the end of the 1884 season, most major league catchers were wearing chest protectors. Finally, between 1884 and 1886, catchers began to change their technique, using primitive mitts to catch the ball on the palm instead of cradling it in the fingers. By 1888, mitts resembling the modern version were in use.

Although these innovations won quick acceptance, they also provoked a great deal of scorn from sportswriters, fans, and catchers of the old school. Morris shows how these changes affected the image of the catcher in the popular imagination, very much for the worse. This was true despite the fact that—even with a mask, a chest protector, and a stout mitt—the catcher was still subject to injury and wear and tear in a way that other players simply were not.

Part of what makes Morris such an enjoyable historian is a certain obsessive determination in following trails uncovered in his research, even when they seem to be leading rather far afield from the main line of his argument. One example in this book is the chapter titled "The Catcher as Desperado." Noticing a number of cases in which catchers or former catchers committed odd crimes or otherwise acted in aberrant fashion, Morris wonders if repeated blows to the head or a single particularly drastic blow (of a sort that many catchers suffered) could account at least in part for this pattern. The increased attention now being given to the long-term effect of concussions among players in the National Football League lends some credence to the argument. Morris cannot resist following this chapter with an entire chapter devoted to the particularly bizarre case of one catcher who ran amok: "Harry Decker, the Don Juan of Shaven Head."

The 1890's, the decade in which Stephen Crane played catcher briefly at Syracuse, saw a decline in public esteem for the position. The decline owed in some degree to the protections afforded the catcher, but it also suggests that not as many outstanding players were gravitating to the backstop in those years. Morris notes that, even during the 1880's, of the three leading catchers of the period—Charley Bennett, Buck Ewing, and Mike "King" Kelly—only Bennett was a catcher pure and simple. In the course of their careers, both Ewing and Kelly (the only two nineteenth century catchers in the Hall of Fame) played more than half of their games at other positions.

In the first two decades of the twentieth century, however—the beginning of the modern era for major league baseball—catching enjoyed a renaissance, as the position was redefined in ways that have not radically changed since then. There were changes in technique, the most significant of which was adopting the now familiar crouch behind the plate. Before the twentieth century, the vast majority of catchers stood with knees slightly bent, in a stooped posture. The crouch allowed the catcher to deal more effectively with new pitches such as the spitball (pitches that tended to break downward out of the strike zone) while protecting himself from injury. The crouch also allowed catchers to shield their signals to the pitcher and the infielders. Apart from these and other changes in technique, the role of the catcher as the field general—not previously unknown, but not so definitive of the position—was fully established during this period. It was an era, Morris notes, when a number of the most outstanding managers were former catchers, setting a precedent that endures to this day.

Following the main text of his book, Morris includes an appendix in which he makes a very strong case that Jim "Deacon" White should be in the Hall of Fame along with Ewing, Kelly, and the other great catchers already enshrined. He then provides endnotes—almost seventy pages of them and worth every page. Morris the tireless researcher, Morris the raconteur, and Morris the fan meet happily in these notes, which readers will find particularly worthwhile.

John Wilson

Review Sources

Christianity Today 53, no. 9 (September, 2009): 82.
Publishers Weekly 256, no. 8 (February 23, 2009): 47.

CHEEVER
A Life

Author: Blake Bailey (1963-)
Publisher: Knopf (New York). 770 pp. $35.00
Type of work: Literary biography
Time: 1912-1982
Locale: Boston; New York City and Westchester County, New York; Rome, Italy

An exhaustive and insightful study of one of the leading American short-story writers of the twentieth century, a man whose happiness was always shadowed by self-doubt

Principal personages:
JOHN CHEEVER, a short-story writer and novelist
MARY WINTERNITZ CHEEVER, his wife of forty-one years
SUSAN CHEEVER, their first child, a writer, author of the memoir *Home Before Dark* (1984)
BENJAMIN CHEEVER, their older son, also a writer, editor of *The Letters of John Cheever* (1988)
FEDERICO (FRED) CHEEVER, their third child, a law professor
MALCOLM COWLEY, *The New Republic* editor who helped Cheever early in his career
WILLIAM MAXWELL, Cheever's editor at *The New Yorker* for many years

John Cheever was one of America's most acclaimed writers in the middle decades of the twentieth century. He wrote more than 500 short stories and published 121 of them in the country's premier periodical for short fiction, *The New Yorker*, between 1935 and 1981. He was the subject of a *Time* magazine cover story in 1964 on the occasion of the publication of his second novel, *The Wapshot Scandal*, and thirteen years later appeared on the cover of *Newsweek* when his fourth novel, *Falconer* (1977), was published. His collected stories won the National Book Critics Circle Award, the National Book Award, and the Pulitzer Prize in fiction in 1979, and several stories were made into films (such as "The Swimmer") and teleplays ("The Housebreaker of Shady Hill").

Cheever traveled the world as a famous American writer and was particularly revered in Soviet bloc countries. Despite his apparent successes, Cheever was tormented by private demons and filled his voluminous journals with detailed descriptions of his loneliness and self-pity. He loved the rituals of family life but showed little affection for his wife and three children. He could be a charming and witty raconteur, as well as a mean, pompous bore. A chain smoker and alcoholic for most of his adult life, he was tormented by his own bisexuality and hated homosexuals.

Blake Bailey's *Cheever: A Life*, which was a finalist for the 2010 Pulitzer Prize in biography, is an exhaustive study of Cheever that explicates the gap between his public self and his private hell and does much to explain how Cheever's inner conflicts were forged into his art. The story of Cheever's life is not always pretty, but it is compelling, and the biographer employs both empathy and insightful analysis.

Blake Bailey published a biography of novelist Richard Yates in 2003 and edited the two-volume edition of John Cheever's works published by Library of America in 2009. He has written for The New York Times, *the* New York Observer, *and* Slate.

Cheever would often brag about his family's distinguished New England lineage, but their notable accomplishments ended long before Cheever was born in 1912. His father was a failed salesman who Cheever believed detested his second son. His mother was a gift-shop owner who showed him little tenderness. Cheever felt his childhood was miserable, never finished high school, and soon fled Quincy, Massachusetts, for Boston and then for New York. He befriended editor Malcolm Cowley and other writers and artists, including photographer Walker Evans, poet E. E. Cummings, and novelist Josephine Herbst. On the basis of his early fiction, Cheever was invited to the artists' colony at Yaddo, near Saratoga, New York, in 1934, the first of many visits over the next half century. (It is significant that Cheever, who at the end of his life was on the colony's board of directors, called Yaddo "the only place I've ever felt at home.") His first *New Yorker* story was published in 1935, and his career was launched.

Cheever worked on the Federal Writers' Project in Washington, D.C., and then New York to help support himself at the end of the 1930's. His story "Frere Jacques" (1939) was published in *The Best Short Stories of 1939*, and by 1940, with the help of *New Yorker* fiction editor and friend William Maxwell, he was averaging almost a story per month in the magazine. A year later, his first collection of stories, *The Way Some People Live* (1941), appeared. The same year, he married Mary Winternitz. He spent three and a half years serving in World War II, mostly in writing units. His first child, Susan, was born in 1943; his first son, Benjamin, was born five years later; and his last child, Federico, was born in 1957.

By the late 1940's, Cheever had become one of the best fiction writers at *The New Yorker* (along with J. D. Salinger and Irwin Shaw) and thus in the United States. "The Enormous Radio" (1947), one of his best stories, was published during this time. Cheever's marriage was not happy, however, in part because of his drinking and his conflicted sexuality, and he felt frustrated that he could not finish a novel. In 1951, the Cheevers moved from New York City to Scarborough, Westchester County, New York, near the street that would inspire the title of one of the best novels about postwar suburbia, Richard Yates's *Revolutionary Road* (1961).

Cheever's second collection of stories, *The Enormous Radio, and Other Stories* was published in 1953, and he began to produce the "Shady Hill" stories about upper-middle-class suburban life (including "The Five-Forty-Eight," 1954, and "O Youth and Beauty!" 1953) for which he would become famous. Bailey argues that these stories contained "a tone of detached gaiety—a tone most characteristic of Cheever's mature greatness, a playfulness that would lead him at last to *The Wapshot Chronicle*," Cheever's first novel, published in 1957. Cheever's apparent success, however, disguised his alcoholism (he was now often drunk before lunch), his impotence, his deteriorating marriage, and his terror of homosexuality. His success did lift the Cheevers from genteel poverty. Cheever's "The Country Husband" (1954) won first prize in the O. Henry Awards, was included in *The Best American Short Stories of 1954*, and was adapted for *Playhouse 90* on the Columbia Broadcasting System (CBS). Film rights to his "The Housebreaker of Shady Hill" (1956) were purchased by Metro-Goldwyn-Mayer (MGM) for twenty-five thousand dollars.

The Wapshot Chronicle won the 1958 National Book Award, but it also alienated Cheever from some of his Scarborough neighbors, who felt he had mined their lives for his satirical, often eccentric characters. In 1961, the Cheevers moved to Ossining, a few miles up the Hudson River. Cheever's success continued: He published more stories—including "The Swimmer" (1964), perhaps his most famous—and placed some in better-paying magazines such as *The Saturday Evening Post* and *Playboy*. He also published more short-story collections (for example, *The Brigadier and the Golf Widow*, 1964) and his second novel, *The Wapshot Scandal* (1964).

Cheever had an affair with the actress Hope Lange and traveled to Russia (with his *New Yorker* colleague John Updike, among others), but his successes could hardly mask what Bailey calls throughout this biography Cheever's *cafard*, a French term for melancholy and boredom. In the late 1960's, he made his first visit to a psychiatrist. The doctor diagnosed him as "egocentric," "narcissistic," and "evasive," but for the next ten years he would continue to cripple himself with alcohol and his wife would begin to find her own life outside their marriage. He taught at nearby Sing Sing prison, as well as at the University of Iowa and Boston University. Finally, however, his drinking prevented him from functioning. Updike had to take over his classes at Boston University in the spring of 1975, and his younger son Federico was often his caretaker at home.

A series of hospitalizations for seizures and heart problems finally led to Cheever's sobriety. In 1977, he published *Falconer* (based in large part on his Sing Sing experience) and appeared on the cover of *Newsweek*, an issue that included an interview with him conducted by Susan, then a staff writer at the magazine. Bailey writes that *Falconer* was "a tabulation of his own singular afflictions, ordered as a parable of sin and redemption," but it did not resolve Cheever's own inner torments. His sobriety seems to have released his homosexuality, and he entered into a series of relationships with younger men, but these canceled neither his loneliness nor his self-pity. *The Stories of John Cheever* was published to great acclaim in 1978 and garnered a number of awards, including his first Pulitzer Prize, but his acquisition of wealth and status only made him more affected and boring. In one of his most telling journal entries, Cheever wrote,

> I was born into no true class, and it was my decision, early in life, to insinuate myself into the middle class, like a spy, so that I would have an advantageous position of attack, but I seem now and then to have forgotten my mission and to have taken my disguises too seriously.

Cheever died of cancer in 1982.

As Bailey notes, Cheever felt some remorse about his treatment of his children and tried to confess his sins to them toward the end of his life. It was only after his death, however, that they had recourse to his journals and could read his account of an anguished inner life. Susan wrote the powerful memoir *Home Before Dark* in 1984 as her own catharsis of her childhood, and Ben edited *The Letters of John Cheever* (including graphic letters to lovers of both sexes) in 1988 to make his own peace with his father. The journals were sold to Knopf and excerpts were published in *The New Yorker* in 1990 and 1991 and as a book in October, 1991. The critic Jonathan Yardley called them "the record of a man so enchained within the prison of self that he was never able to embrace others, even those he most loved."

Cheever's story is a sad and depressing one, yet Bailey keeps readers interested by focusing on his fiction and its relationship to his life. There is no question that Cheever was one of the greatest practitioners of the American short story: He has been called the American Anton Chekhov, a reference to the great nineteenth century Russian writer, and Yardley calls Cheever's stories an "essential monument of American literature." Examples such as "The Country Husband" and "The Swimmer" continue to be included in anthologies of short fiction. His novels, however, have slipped in critical estimation, and Bailey pinpoints the problems with structure and sentimentality that account for this slippage. Like William Faulkner, Cheever was an autodidact who mythologized certain American landscapes and whose "tone of remote pessimism" captured a mid-century moment in American life.

Bailey details Cheever's relationships to other important twentieth century writers and identifies his place among them. Cheever resented the writer whom he perhaps resembled the most, his *New Yorker* colleague John Updike. In the end, however, they were friendly, and Updike gave the eulogy at Cheever's funeral. Just before his own death, Updike reviewed Bailey's biography of Cheever in *The New Yorker*. The contemporary writer toward whom Cheever was most magnanimous was Saul Bellow, perhaps because the two writers wrote for different audiences. (Mary Cheever has another explanation for their closeness, Bailey writes: "They were both women haters.")

Cheever detested the experimental fiction of John Barth, Donald Barthelme, and others who started to crowd him out of *The New Yorker* in the late 1960's and the 1970's, but he lived to see their postmodernist star fade. Bailey understands that Cheever's talent came out of his inner conflicts: an insatiable need for love and approval, a split personality, and ambivalence toward the world. In Cheever, memory and imagination were not two faculties but one, Bailey argues, which is why a study of his life necessarily entails a study of his literature—or, as Bailey's volume shows, why an understanding of the literature can start in the life.

David Peck

Review Sources

Booklist 105, no. 5 (November 1, 2008): 4.
The Economist 390 (March 14, 2009): 86-87.
Harper's Magazine 318 (April, 2009): 71-76.
Kirkus Reviews 76, no. 23 (December 1, 2008): 1232-1233.
Los Angeles Times, March 8, 2009, p. 1.
The New York Times Book Review, March 15, 2009, p. 1.
The New Yorker 85, no. 4 (March 9, 2009): 73-75.
Publishers Weekly 255, no. 47 (November 24, 2008): 45.
Time 173, no. 13 (April 6, 2009): 64.
The Wall Street Journal, March 7, 2009, p. W8.

CHRONIC

Author: D. A. Powell (1963-   )
Publisher: Graywolf Press (St. Paul, Minn.). 79 pp. $20.00
Type of work: Poetry

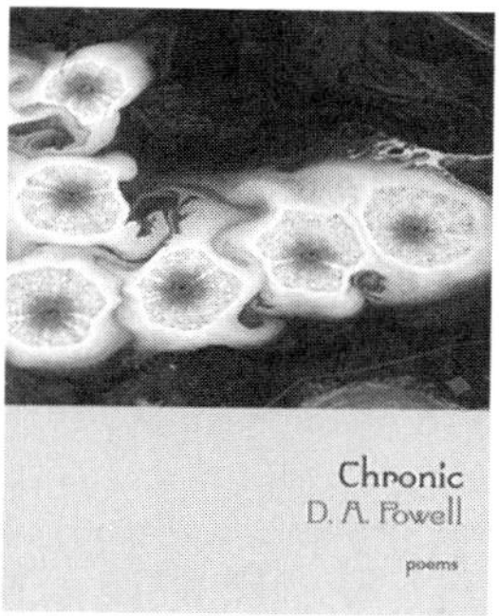

A striking poetic examination of how to survive tragedy and heartbreak in a world where AIDS, turmoil, and personal angst seemingly are always close at hand

Although born in the South, D. A. Powell has come to be identified more with the West, especially California. He studied at the prestigious Writers' Workshop at the University of Iowa. After graduating from the program, Powell began a teaching career that has included stints at several universities, including Columbia University, San Francisco State University, and Harvard University. Since 2004, Powell has taught at the University of San Francisco as a member of its English department.

Powell's first poetry collection, *Tea*, was published in 1998. He wrote powerfully about the acquired immunodeficiency syndrome (AIDS) epidemic in this volume, and he has gained a reputation for taking chances as a poet. Through his experimentations, Powell is able to mix a variety of poetic techniques. His reputation as a poet worth watching mature continued to grow with the publication of his second collection, *Lunch* (2000), and his third collection, *Cocktails* (2004). He was praised by critics and readers alike for his originality and poetic dexterity. Powell's first three collections can be read as a trilogy on living as a gay person in a world where AIDS has ravaged the human landscape. The poet understands that it is never easy to be gay or African American in the United States. Powell is both, and he constantly is wrestling with his place in contemporary American culture.

For all the tragedy and confusion surrounding the world that he inhabits, Powell still has not given up on life. As a person and as a poet, he can take pleasure in beauty, in playfulness, and in heated sexuality. Even with all the pitfalls, the health concerns, and the betrayals he encounters, Powell seeks dignity, poetic justice, and fulfillment in love. Powell is adamant that one should take full advantage of both the spirit and the carnal. It is striking that he examines what it means to be happy and how one should resolve issues of sadness and contempt.

Having to live with human immunodeficiency virus (HIV) on a daily basis remains close to the surface in *Chronic*, as it has in his earlier collections, but in this volume he broadens his approach, looking for new connections. Powell first learned that he was HIV positive while he was a student at the Iowa Writers' Workshop. Always a fierce advocate for what love can offer, he refused to withdraw from the social scene.

As in his previous collections, Powell does not capitalize the words of poems in *Chronic*. He also likes to employ short stanzas, usually no more than two or three

D. A. Powell teaches at the University of San Francisco and is the author of four critically acclaimed poetry collections, including Tea *(1998),* Lunch *(2000), and* Cocktails *(2004). In 2009, he published* By Myself: An Autobiography *(coauthored with David Trinidad).*

lines each. The poet is very adept at giving his poems catchy titles. In this new collection, Powell employs such wonderfully intriguing titles as "gospel on the dial, with intermittent static," "confessions of a teenage drama queen," "the expiration date on the world is not quite the same as the expiration date on my prophylactic," and "chia pet cemetery." For the poems "cinemascope" and "centerfold," Powell employs fold-out pages, so those poems' forms mimic their subject matter. Powell makes use of long lines in order to hold readers' attention for as long as possible. He believes that poetry must suspend the quick fix, the easy resolution. The richness of a Powell poem is in the words pressed together for emotional impact. His three earlier collections have been compared to Dante's *La divina commedia* (c. 1320; *The Divine Comedy*, 1802). This comparison represents high praise for any poet, and Powell has continued in *Chronic* to hone his craft.

While Powell has doubts about the validity of Christianity, he does not shrink from making use of biblical references in his verse. He uses the Christian perspective as a mirror to which his vision can be compared. No matter what tradition he may reject, the cultural vortex cannot be denied or removed from the frontal cultural lobe. He acknowledges that the mythology has not been shed, so it has not been removed from the poet's playbook.

Powell believes in the need to reference cultural icons in order to make a larger point. For all that is different, that is without comprehension, Powell wishes to be a member of the poetic community in good standing. This community includes Dante and T. S. Eliot, alongside many others whose poetry would seem to be at opposite ends of the poetic spectrum. Poets are linked to other poets no matter the starting point, no matter the cultural invectives, and Powell wishes to be aligned with the poetic chronology. Within the poetic continuum, there is more room than even Powell would imagine could be found. He does not lose his place on the spectrum merely because he is a gay African American.

In each of his collections, Powell has energized his audience with his passion and vision. Touching, bold, bitter, harrowing—each of the words can be used to describe Powell at his best in his latest collection. Divided into three sections, *Chronic* focuses on the power of memory and the tricks that it can play on the life of an individual. He takes aim at those who have wronged him in poems that are instantly recognizable. Powell also can be as touching as any poet writing, and it becomes obvious through his work that love and disease are closely related: Both are chronic.

Powell opens the collection with an epigraph from Virgil, taken from *Eclogue IX*. The ancient poet is melancholy about how "Time robs us of all, even of memory." Loss is part of the human condition, but, as the epigraph indicates, one of the roles that the poet can play is as the recorder of what has transpired, what humans have done. It is possible to celebrate life even in the face of death. Powell has spoken about how this volume came to be, about the gathering of poems. For any poet, it is not always clear at the outset what sort of grouping or collection will come out of the writing process. A poet must wrestle with the forces of the writing in order to locate what is at the center of the creation, the whole. For Powell, this "revelation came very late." The title poem was one of the last poems he wrote before he knew that a narrative cohesion existed for the manuscript that had been growing. Until this revelation, he believed that there were only "irreconcilable tensions" between the individual poems. Fortunately, Powell came to the conclusion that his poems about "love, loss, incurable illness, hope, the precipitous moment in history that we habit" truly could hold together and belonged to the same continuum of poetic thought.

Divided into "Initial C," "Chronic," and "Terminal C," the collection presents readers with a balancing act between "loss" and "hope." It also seems to balance upon the letter *c*. This letter of the alphabet appears in as either the first letter or the last letter of every title in the collection. Powell seemingly chose *c* in an arbitrary fashion, but he knew that there was something about the letter that meant something larger, something transcendent. He recognized that *c* is "the opening of a parenthetical statement," "the musical note that sounds like an ending," "the center of our grading system," "an echo of the ocean," and much more. None of these reasons alone held sway with Powell, it was a combination of several complex reasons that made him stick with his chosen *c*. It became obvious to him that "we live in the age of the complex," and the letter *c* is critical to the discussion.

With these tools and more, the poet attempts to construct a vision or, more correctly, myriad visions that express the world in all of its incarnations. Powell feels a bond also with the natural world, with the world of "the seasons, the trees, the vines, the bees, and the animals." Powell focuses on the uneasy relationship that humans have with their environment. He has stated that "we see our own deciduous selves mirrored in the landscape." Through engagement in the process of living, through a love for the power of poetry, Powell attempts to acknowledge the struggles of living without succumbing to them. He does this through eloquent wordplay, expressing sensibilities that have one foot in the traditions of the past and one foot squarely planted in the present.

The collection opens with the poem "no picnic." The poet's powers of observation are on display in this poem, with

> plain cloth cast upon the cool banks, the mere warbling frogs
>
> an interrupted repast, uninterrupted pile of leavings
>
> the parallax of bodies which are and are not ours.

It can be discerned that life is really "no picnic," no easy exercise. One of the last poems of the third section, "scenes from the trip we didn't take to the antarctic," opens with "your inability to phone says it all: whitecaps frozen in a touchless curl/ the space in the lungs where breath catches and falters" and ends with

say it with me, sunshine: today, brainscan; today, x-ray
today, complete metabolic panel with platelet differential
today, urinalysis; today, liver biopsy; today, preparing the body

at the last station, the sepulcher was empty and you asked why
beyond this numbing terrain, frozen white cell: phantom laughter
didn't you hear it all along? or did you think it was just the wind.

The journey is difficult, and there are no easy answers. Terror can strike at the heart, whether one is reaching out for love or in the throes of facing the end of life. Powell has stated that "much of art, and much of life, is simultaneously funny and horrifying." At the root of both is "surprise." Even with a "surprise," there is still a persistent recognition that no one can shake off what the Earth suffers from, what each person suffers from. The best that a person can do is do battle day by day.

The poet presents this predicament, this seemingly incurable situation, yet does not leave readers without hope or a course of action. There still remains, for Powell, good reason to struggle against what touches each person day after day. There are reservoirs that exist within memory, mythology, science, history, and religion that can be tapped. They can be called upon to serve as a shield against the chronic curse. The journey toward an end, a little death, and the ultimate monumental death can be handled with dignity. Taking inspiration from Walt Whitman, Frank O'Hara, Gertrude Stein, and John Ashbery, Powell continues in *Chronic* to construct astonishing poems that speak eloquently about "loss" and "hope."

Jeffry Jensen

Review Sources

The London Review of Books 31, no. 18 (September 24, 2009): 30-31.
Los Angeles Times, February 15, 2009, p. F7.
Poetry 193, no. 6 (March, 2009): 555-563.
Publishers Weekly 256, no. 3 (January 19, 2009): 41-42.
The Virginia Quarterly Review 85 (Spring, 2009): 215.

CHRONIC CITY

Author: Jonathan Lethem (1964-   )
Publisher: Doubleday (New York). 467 pp. $27.95
Type of work: Novel
Time: The early twenty-first century
Locale: New York City, especially the Upper East Side of Manhattan

The protagonist of this simultaneously surreal and satirical novel begins to understand himself and the nature of reality in a city that experiences multiple disasters

Principal characters:

CHASE INSTEADMAN, a former child television actor living an empty life in Manhattan
JANICE TRUMBULL, his fiancé, an astronaut trapped in space
PERKUS TOOTH, a manic pop culture theorist
BILLER, a homeless man Perkus helps, who later finds Perkus an apartment
RICHARD ABNEG, an aide to Mayor Arnheim of New York
LAIRD NOTELESS, a famous sculptor
GEORGINA HAWKMANAJI, a wealthy woman with whom Abneg becomes involved
OONA LASZLO, a ghostwriter with whom Chase falls in love
STRABO BLANDIANA, an acupuncturist and New Age guru

Chronic City is at once satire and science fiction, a novel about contemporary New York City that uncovers the city's glamour, its fantasy qualities, and its essential emptiness. The protagonist of the novel, Chase Insteadman, is a former child star who lives on the residuals from his role years before in the popular *Martyr & Pesky* television series. He now has no real job, except perhaps as a guest at fashionable dinner parties.

Chase is a one-dimensional character (as his last name, "instead-of-a-man," implies) who skates on the surface of life until he meets Perkus Tooth, a former rock critic who was famous for posting political broadsides around the city. Perkus draws Chase into his bizarre world of esoteric compact discs and digital videodiscs, while he deconstructs the conspiracies he senses lurking behind contemporary life. (For example, Marlon Brando, according to Perkus, is still alive, and the font of *The New Yorker* magazine controls its readers). Perkus smokes a lot of dope with Chase and also suffers from cluster headaches.

The two friends inhabit a very small patch of Manhattan's Upper East Side, rarely venturing beyond their apartments or the Jackson Hole restaurant where they consume the giant cheeseburgers that form the staple of Perkus's diet. Chase soon persuades Perkus to visit Strabo Blandiana, a New Age guru and acupuncturist, to treat his headaches. In the treatment rooms, Perkus has his first glimpse of a chaldron, a beautiful

Jonathan Lethem is the author of a number of previous novels, including Motherless Brooklyn *(1999) and* The Fortress of Solitude *(2003), and several collections of short stories and essays. He received a MacArthur Fellowship in 2005.*

vase giving off a mystical aura that leads Perkus and then his friends Chase and Richard Abneg (with whom he attended Horace Mann High School) to try to purchase one on eBay. All of them are caught up in the mystique of the chaldrons, but for Perkus the vases are also one of the keys to understanding reality.

Chase is supposedly engaged to Janice Trumbull, an astronaut with whom he shared a brief adolescent romance while growing up in Bloomington, Indiana. Janice is now trapped on the space station *Northern Lights*, stuck in a zone of Chinese mines. Janice's letters to Chase are published in the city newspapers, making Chase the object of public sympathy, but Chase has almost forgotten Janice. He falls in love with Oona Laszlo, who used to help Perkus with his broadsides and is now a ghostwriter working on the autobiography of Laird Noteless.

Noteless is a sculptor who builds giant installations as chasms in the city. Oona and Chase visit one such construction pit, called *Fjord*, a giant hole in the ground above Harlem, to conduct research for Oona's book. Meanwhile, other craters have appeared in Manhattan because a giant tiger is terrifying the city. Richard, an aide to the mayor of New York, explains that the "tiger" is really a tunneling machine brought in to finish a subway line that has gone berserk and wanders the city at night destroying buildings. In the long scene that brings this early exposition to a close, a large dinner party at the mayor's residence, Perkus discovers a chaldron in a niche in a wall and then disappears.

In the second half of the novel, the many mysteries raised in the first half are only partially solved. Perkus's apartment is been condemned after the "tiger" destroys the nearby Jackson Hole, and he is saved by his homeless friend Biller, who secretly installs him in the Friendreth Canine Apartments. In this dwelling-house devoted solely to dogs, Perkus shares an apartment with a three-legged pit bull named Ava, who is recovering from the loss of her leg after a policeman shot it in a drug raid.

Ava and Perkus appear to have rescued each other, but the old Perkus soon reemerges, riffing on his conspiracy theories about contemporary culture. When Chase finally tracks him down, Perkus begins to spin out the epiphanies he has gained from the chaldrons: He claims that all New Yorkers are living in a theme park and that the multiple urban disasters (such as the building-eating tiger, a gray fog that covers the city, a pervasive chocolate smell, and massive blizzards) are parts of a virtual reality that is being controlled by outside powers. They are all, in effect, players in a computer game being run by someone else. Perkus is also physically sick, however, and when Chase and Richard finally rush him to a hospital, it is too late. He dies of internal bleeding.

In the conclusion of the novel, Chase uncovers the truth of Perkus's rants, that he actually is an actor in a script someone else has written. Among other revelations, he discovers that Oona has been ghost-writing the letters to Chase printed in the newspapers because Janice probably died months ago in an explosion of the space station. The drama is being played out for publicity, to build public morale at a time of multiple disasters in the city. Further, Chase is living not only on residuals but also on checks from something called the Manhattan Reification Society, which is clandestinely paying him to play the empty roles he inhabits, such as Janice Trumbull's lonely fiancée and the charming dinner party guest.

Thus, the novel's characters are players in a kind of virtual reality, as Perkus realized. Their world is a computer game like the popular Web site Yet Another World, but one that they take to be real. Even the chaldrons, it turns out, are not real but holograms created by multiple laser lights. Chase dismisses Oona—who is really the Janice of her letters, as Janice and the chaldrons are Chase's illusions—and takes in Ava. He begins a relationship with another writer named Anne Sprillthrall and joins a combat unit in a Yet Another World video game. Chase in the end appears to have accepted his own identity and the city's reality—or unreality. He acknowledges the illusion and even joins it. "The world was ersatz and actual, forged and fake, by ourselves and unseen others."

Chronic City is at once surrealistic and satirical, but the different parts do not always blend together easily. Jonathan Lethem's first novels were science fiction, and elements of that genre permeate this work, from Janice's space station letters to the ravaging tunnel machine beneath the city's streets. There are other pits in the city, however—notably the public sculptures Laird Noteless builds, like his *Fjord*, but also the mayor (whom Chase calls "a black hole"), Jackson Hole (which becomes one), the empty chaldrons, and even Chase, who says, "I'm truly a vacuum filled by the folks I'm with." The parallels point to the satire Lethem is creating in the novel.

Everything in the city is layered, for beneath the shallow surface of this urban scene another world exists. Perkus Tooth gets Chase to question reality and to see that they are all living in a giant computer simulation. Even the tiger, it turns out, is a city operation, creating distractions to keep the public's attention from the real disasters in New York. (The popular Tiger Watch Web site allows concerned residents to follow the nocturnal wanderings of the rogue tunnel machine.)

Perkus gains some of his insights after his encounters with the chaldron, which is recognizable for "its sublime and superb *thingliness*," and these objects point to another satirical angle. The Manhattan Reification Society—which not only pays Chase's checks but also supports the canine apartments where Perkus ends up living for free with Ava—points to a Marxist analysis of contemporary life. In the superficial world Chase inhabits, everything and everyone has been turned into an object—they have been "reified" by contemporary life in "this world of commodities and cartoons"—and permanent and lasting human values have been lost. The characters, in other words, are not only shallow actors in some scripted reality television show, but they are also objects to be purchased and used. (At one elegant dinner party, Chase is auctioned off as a premium in a charity fundraiser; Perkus, Richard, and Chase try to buy a chaldron by outbidding others in an online auction.)

The only objects in the novel that rise above this reification, strangely, are animals. Chase watches a flock of birds circle a church spire throughout the novel, and at its end he makes an accidental pilgrimage and finds both church and flock. Richard Abneg is involved in a dispute with his apartment managers over his treatment of an eagles' nest. Perkus and Oona work late on a new broadside centering on a photo of a polar bear on an ice floe meant to symbolize isolation. Finally, Ava, the three-legged pit bull, comes into the lives of Perkus and Chase and helps rescue both of them from themselves. (The coincidences in the novel point to a lame and unimaginative virtual reality, however: Ava has lost her leg, paralleling Janice's loss of a foot that is amputated when she develops a tumor in space.) People in *Chronic City* inhabit a superficial world filled with television reruns and gossip—possibly scripted by others—but animals at least act out their natural roles.

Lethem has always been a writer able to carry the sounds of New York: Both *Motherless Brooklyn* (1999) and *The Fortress of Solitude* (2003), his best novels, are filled with vivid descriptions of the city and characters with distinct voices, and *Chronic City* follows their lead. For example, Chase comments on his city, saying

> To live in Manhattan is to be persistently amazed at the worlds squirreled inside one another, the chaotic intricacy with which realms interleave, like those lines of television cable and fresh water and steam heat and outgoing sewage and telephone wire and whatever else which cohabit in the same intestinal holes that pavement-demolishing workmen periodically wrench open to the daylight and to our passing, disturbed glances. We only pretend to live on something as orderly as a grid.

Lethem's Perkus has a voice as distinct as any in contemporary fiction. In the last part of the novel, it is even punctuated on the page by the hiccups that foreshadow his imminent death. Lethem is one of the best writers in capturing New York, a mimic of social mores and manners in a line of writers that stretches from William Dean Howells (*A Hazard of New Fortunes*, 1889) at the end of the nineteenth century through Stephen Millhauser (*Martin Dressler*, 1996) and Tom Wolfe (*The Bonfire of the Vanities*, 1987) at the end of the twentieth. *Chronic City* has moments of insight and humor, but it does not hold together at the end as one novel, nor, finally, does it compete with its predecessors.

David Peck

Review Sources

Booklist 105, no. 22 (August 1, 2009): 7.
The Christian Science Monitor, October 25, 2009, p. 25.
Kirkus Reviews 77, no. 12 (June 15, 2009): 624.
Library Journal 134, no. 13 (August 1, 2009): 69.
Los Angeles Times, October 18, 2009, p. E.9.
The New Republic 240, no. 19 (October 21, 2009): 48-53.
New York 42, no. 28 (August 31, 2009): 64-65.
The New York Times, October 13, 2009, p C1.
The New York Times Book Review, October 25, 2009, p. 1.
Publishers Weekly 256, no. 31 (August 3, 2009): 27.
The Wall Street Journal, October 15, 2009, p. 13.

COLD
Adventures In the World's Frozen Places

Author: Bill Streever (1961-)
Publisher: Little, Brown (New York). Illustrated. 292 pp. $24.99
Type of work: Natural history, history of science, environment
Time: Human history, particularly 2006-2007
Locale: Alaska and worldwide

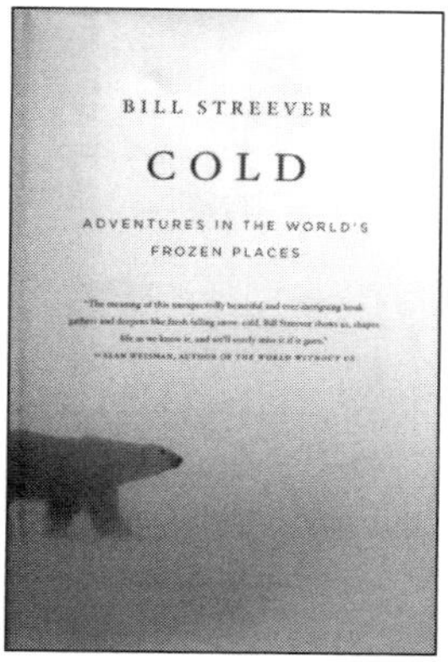

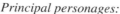

Streever explains how most living creatures on Earth are affected by and cope with cold and with winter and tells the history of polar explorations and the science of cold

Principal personages:
BILL STREEVER, American biologist
ADOLPHUS W. GREELY, American explorer of the North Pole
ROBERT FALCON SCOTT, British explorer of Antarctica
ROALD AMUNDSEN, Norwegian explorer of Antarctica and leader of the first expedition to reach the South Pole
HEIKE KAMERLINGH ONNES, Dutch physicist and Nobel laureate, a pioneer in cryogenics

Bill Streever tackles many subjects in *Cold*, an engaging, wide-ranging history-cum-journal. These include winter survival; catastrophic weather; polar expeditions; scientific studies of thermodynamics, including the search for absolute zero; glaciation; hibernation; the cycle of ice ages; and climate change. His nonlinear text does not, however, discuss these topics straightforwardly, chapter by chapter. Only Streever's journal entries are in chronological order, while biographical narratives and scientific histories are interspersed among them. These interwoven narratives may be relinquished early, only to be amplified in later chapters. The journal, meanwhile, covers Streever's life from July, 2006, to June, 2007.

Streever's journal recounts more than one occasion on which he exposed himself to conditions that would have been fatally cold had he not been able to extricate himself from them. Each chapter offers information about cold weather and its effects, as well as human effects upon the weather. The book begins by demonstrating what happens to the human body under extremely cold conditions. In a summer swim in the thirty-five-degree waters of Prudhoe Bay, in northernmost Alaska, Streever describes his sensations to a companion, who times his immersion for five minutes. Within moments, Streever's extremities become numb. At three minutes, he begins to shiver. At four minutes, his skin seems to sting and burn. The seconds pass, his muscles tensing, his mind wandering. After spending five minutes in the bay, it takes him two hours to regain a feeling of warmth.

Biologist Bill Streever is the Environmental Program studies director for BP Exploration (Alaska) Inc. and chairman of the North Slope Science Initiative's Science Technical Advisory Panel. He is the author of several books and numerous journal articles.

Streever's narrative alternates facts with drama, geographical data with animal behavior, mortality statistics with stories of heroics and loss. For example, he reports that Barrow, Alaska, has the coldest average yearly temperature of any community in the United States, just under 10° Fahrenheit. Then, he elaborates that it is the home of arctic foxes and polar bears and also among the oldest permanent settlements in the country. When starving European explorers first appeared in what would become Barrow, Native Americans there were flourishing. Their name for the site was "a place for hunting snowy owls." Elsewhere, Streever juxtaposes the fact that a cumulonimbus cloud can hold 500,000 tons of water with accounts of an English youth who was killed by a falling icicle in 1776 and of a 1974 incident in which an eighteen-inch block of ice fell from an airplane and smashed into the hood of a woman's car.

Each chapter includes diary entries. In February's chapter, for example, Streever informs readers of the then-current temperatures in several American cities. He reports that a thawed creek has flooded an Anchorage office building and ruined its computers and that, at an Alaskan zoo, a brown bear woke up and opted to go lie out in the sunshine. After establishing background details, he summarizes conversations with scientists, conference attendees, miners, friends, and family members as he travels the world to research the present and history of cold temperatures.

Particularly arresting are Streever's accounts of tragedy, which he begins describing within the first few pages as he treads water in Prudhoe Bay. He encapsulates episodes that he will expand upon later, including the Adolphus Greely expedition to the Arctic in 1883; the School Children's Blizzard of January, 1888; and Robert Falcon Scott's disastrous 1910 race to the South Pole, which he lost to Norwegian explorer Roald Amundsen. When Streever goes into detail, drawing upon pioneers' journals and contemporary newspaper accounts, armchair explorers may shiver and wonder what drove those men (they were always men) into such unlivable terrains and horrifying conditions. Streever writes, "When one reads past the stoicism and heroics, the history of polar exploration becomes one long accident report mixed with one long obituary."

Greely was a U.S. Army officer who was put in charge of twenty-five men sent to Ellesmere Island, in far northern Canada, just west of Greenland. Only six members of the expedition survived; the rest died of starvation, drowning, or freezing—except the one whom Greely ordered shot for stealing food. It is likely that some of the dead were cannibalized. Two rescue attempts failed. When the survivors were finally reached in 1884, a rescuer wrote that one of the men in the tent had had both hands and both feet amputated because of frostbite; a spoon had been tied to the stump of his right arm. That man, Corporal Joe Elison, was still alive. He died several days after the rescue.

Streever documents that Greely, a recipient of the Medal of Honor, was held responsible for another crisis and failure. In charge of the Weather Bureau (now known as the National Weather Service), Greely issued a prediction for January 12, 1888, a relatively warm day. He said that a cold front was indicated for the American Plains states. The bureau underestimated the front that was approaching. A blizzard struck the Dakotas, Nebraska, Montana, Wisconsin, and elsewhere, covering a vast area within six hours. Several thousand people, horses, and cattle were caught outdoors in a snowstorm that granted zero visibility.

Of the several hundred victims of the storm, so many were children that the calamity was called the Schoolhouse Blizzard, or the Children's Blizzard. Streever describes the reported experiences of several survivors and explains, clearly and at length, exactly what happens to the human body when frostbite and hypothermia occur. Beyond the physical symptoms, apathy, amnesia, and what is vernacularly called "cold stupid" thought patterns afflict the mind and cause self-destructive behavior.

In the "January" chapter of *Cold*, Streever recounts stories beyond those of explorers and civilians: Untold soldiers have been ordered into and died in impassable weather conditions. Macedonian conqueror Alexander the Great was blocked by snow when he tried to invade India. U.S. president George Washington's twelve thousand Continental Army soldiers suffered greatly at Valley Forge, Pennsylvania, during the winter of 1777-1778, becoming "an army of skeletons." French emperor Napoleon Bonaparte's assault on Moscow, Russia, in 1812, was a disaster at –35° Fahrenheit, and German chancellor Adolf Hitler's similar attempted assault in 1941 caused the death of one-quarter of a million German soldiers at even colder temperatures.

Streever's book is not merely a history of catastrophe, however. He describes with admiration the attempts of the famous polar explorations of Roald Amundsen (which met with success), Richard E. Byrd (which first failed then succeeded), and Robert Falcon Scott (which toward the end amounted to pure tragedy). He explains the many ways in which measurements of cold temperatures have been standardized, most prominently by German physicist Daniel Fahrenheit, Swedish astronomer Anders Celsius, and British physicist Baron William Thomson, Lord Kelvin. His discussion of the obsessive scientific race to find the coldest temperature that could be created in laboratories—absolute zero—is both entertaining and alarming (the invention of dry ice ended in tragedy for a laboratory assistant).

Scientists who receive particular attention in *Cold* include British chemist and physicist James Dewar (inventor of the Dewar flask, not of the whiskey) and Heike Kamerlingh Onnes, among whose many achievements was liquefying helium in 1908. This was an impressive feat, given that helium goes from gas to liquid (or, rather, superfluid) at less than 7° Fahrenheit above absolute zero.

More amusing (and certainly less horrifying than other anecdotes) are Streever's accounts of the various inventions and reinventions of the icebox: Clarence Birdseye, whose last name is familiar in the grocery store, played a role. Streever also discusses the Dutch "part scientist, part alchemist, part showman, part con man" Cornelius

Drebbel, who promised King James of England that he could air-condition Westminster Abbey. Streever suggests that Drebbel managed to do so temporarily with some chemical tricks, but with no continuously operating machinery at work. In his "September" chapter, Streever visits Windsor Castle in England, hoping to meet with Queen Elizabeth II in order to ask about her heating bills. He writes philosophically that it was "a shame that my interview was refused."

Streever excels at metaphors, which makes his book accessible to general readers. He rarely waxes poetic but has a gift for visual details:

> On a global scale, seen from a distance, it might be said that the polar regions suck in the heat of the tropics, swallowing the world's warmth. The equatorial regions shed heat south and north, like a Weddell seal steaming as it lies on the Antarctic ice, or like a moose panting, overheated and uncomfortable, its hot breath projecting vaporous shadows against the snow.

His history of the natural and synthetic fabric industries is full of interesting anecdotes. He explains, for example, that musk ox wool is the warmest fabric known, while cotton can kill because its fibers hold water.

Describing domestic shelters as the outermost garment for people (or animals), Streever explains how igloos and quinzhees are built. He shows that such structures fashioned from ice, like animals' dens, are more permanent and favorable than are buildings constructed from materials imported to the Arctic from southern climes. Dens and igloos are not subject to frozen pipes, mildew, brittle metal and plastic parts, corrosion from salt and sand, or indoor carbon monoxide. Thousands of American houses are ruined each year because they were not planned with a proper understanding of the mechanics of freezing and melting.

The last chapter focuses on climate change. At the time of *Cold*'s publication, Streever reports, one-fifth of Earth's land is frozen in permafrost and four-fifths of its freshwater is frozen. These numbers will change as the global average atmospheric temperature increases. The melting of glaciers is good news for archaeologists, who can discover fossils and even preserved bodies of humans and mammoths in newly exposed ice. Streever provides a good selection of quotes from scientists and industrialists on both sides of the argument of whether the Pleistocene Ice Age is ending.

Cold includes pencil drawings and maps that usefully supplement this globe-spanning history. Less helpful for students is the "Notes" section, which includes bibliographic citations but no referral to the pages in question. A standard bibliography and endnotes section would serve better, while the subjective commentaries augmenting these notes should not have been relegated to an endnotes section: They would perfectly reinforce the stories within the main text. On the other hand, one great convenience of Streever's bibliography is that he includes universal resource locators (URLs) to primary documents whenever he can.

Cold will remain a classic of its type and of interest to general readers. It might serve well as a companion volume to Bernd Heinrich's *Winter World: The Ingenuity of Animal Survival* (2003), which focuses on northern animals but shares many of the same concerns. Streever's is a well-researched and well-written book and belongs in most libraries. Many of the scenes it describes, particularly of human triumphs and losses, will remain with readers for a long time after they finish reading.

Fiona Kelleghan

Review Sources

The Economist 392, no. 8642 (August 1, 2009): 73.
Harper's Magazine, August, 2009, pp. 73-74.
Kirkus Reviews 77, no. 12 (June 15, 2009): 650.
Library Journal 134, no. 8 (May 1, 2009): 97.
Los Angeles Times, August 3, 2009, p. D-8.
The New Scientist 203, no. 2718 (July 25, 2009): 49.
The New York Times, July 24, 2009, p. 21.
The New York Times Book Review, July 26, 2009, p. 1.
Publishers Weekly 256, no. 17 (April 27, 2009): 121.

COLLECTED POEMS

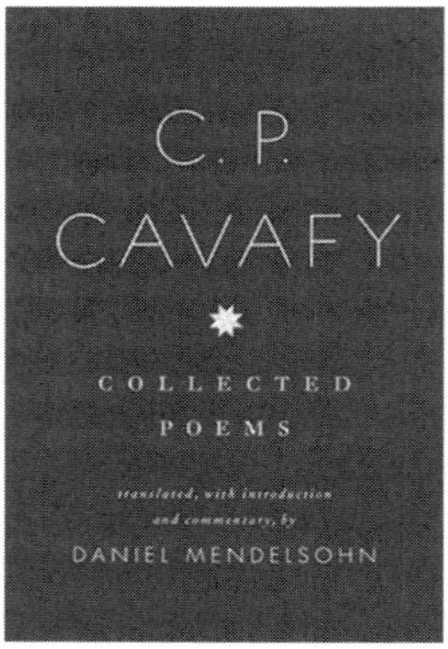

Author: C. P. Cavafy (1863-1933)
Translated from the Greek by Daniel Mendelsohn
Introduction and commentary by Daniel Mendelsohn
Publisher: Alfred A. Knopf (New York). 547 pp. $35.00
Type of work: Poetry

A translation by a noted memoirist and historian of Cavafy's published, repudiated, and unpublished poems, together with an introduction and extensive notes

When he died in 1933, C. P. Cavafy was virtually unknown outside a small circle of friends and admirers. Since then, however, his reputation has grown to the point that he is regarded as one of the two or three greatest Greek poets of the twentieth century. Now, Daniel Mendelsohn has added his versions of Cavafy's poems to an ever-growing body of English translations.

Cavafy was born in the Mediterranean port of Alexandria, Egypt, in 1863. Although the city was Egyptian, Cavafy's parents were Greek, members of a large ethnic community that lived and flourished far beyond Greece's nominal borders. Cavafy's father was a wealthy and successful merchant, but his death when the child was only seven forced the family to live on the generosity of far-flung relatives. As a result, Cavafy spent five years in England before returning with his mother to Alexandra. Subsequently, he led an outwardly uneventful life. He worked as a clerk in the Irrigation Office of the Egyptian Ministry of Public Works from 1892 until 1922 and continued to live with his mother until her death in 1899. Cavafy seems to have had his first homosexual experience (with a cousin) when he was twenty. Back in Alexandria, he developed the habit of slipping out after eating dinner with his mother to have sexual encounters with other men. According to one acquaintance, he also rented a room in a brothel.

Cavafy began writing poetry in his teens, but for the most part it was conventional and derivative. As Mendelsohn makes clear in his comprehensive introduction, Cavafy's early influences included two French literary movements—the Parnassians, who stressed the doctrine of "art for art's sake," and particularly the Symbolists, who elevated poets to a kind of elite status. One early poem by Cavafy bears the pointed title "But Wise Men Apprehend What Is Imminent," contrasting such privileged figures with those "in the street/ outside" who "hear nothing at all." With time, however, Cavafy was able to meld a number of more personal factors—his troubled sexuality, his identity as a Greek living outside Greece, his memories of the lost splendors of his childhood, and his sense of the even greater splendors of the vanished Hellenic world—into a body of ironic, elegiacal work.

Most of Cavafy's poems are short, with few extending beyond two pages. Aside from their allusions, they are also relatively straightforward, although they incorporate subtleties that defy easy translation. The poems Cavafy wrote during his maturity may be grouped into two general categories: the historical and the erotic. Many deal with familiar historical (or mytho-historical) figures, such as Achilles—the Greek hero of the Trojan War—or the Roman emperor Julian, known as "the Apostate." More frequently, however, the figures are obscure, such as rhetorician Theodotus of Chios or Seleucid dynastic victim Orophernes.

C. P. Cavafy was born in Alexandria, Egypt, where he spent most of his adult life employed as a minor government functionary. He shared his poetry with friends and admirers, but it was only after his death in 1933 that he came to be recognized as a distinctive and innovative poet.

The Roman soldier and statesman Mark Antony, whose troops had been defeated in battle by Octavian (the future Emperor Augustus), appears in one of Cavafy's earliest and most memorable poems, "The God Abandons Antony." The poem is set in Cavafy's native city on the last night of Antony's life. Miraculously, the doomed man hears the music and tumult of the invisible procession of the god Dionysus, to whom he had once compared himself and who now is deserting him. The poet counsels Antony not to fool himself into thinking that he is dreaming, but "like someone brave" to "listen with deep emotion" to the "exquisite instruments of that initiate crew/ and bid farewell to her, to Alexandria, whom you are losing." The story, according to Mendelsohn's helpful note, is taken from an account by ancient Greek biographer Plutarch.

One of Cavafy's finest and most famous poems, "Ithaca," draws a lesson from the long voyage home made by Greek hero Odysseus (Ulysses) after the Trojan War. The poem counsels the traveler to "hope that the road is a long one,/ filled with adventures, filled with discoveries." When the traveler finally arrives, he or she must remember that "Ithaca gave you the beautiful journey;/ without her you wouldn't have set upon the road./ But now she has nothing left to give you." After all, "As wise as you will have become, with so much experience,/ you will understand, by then, these Ithacas; what they mean."

Most of Cavafy's other poems deal openly (although never explicitly) with homosexual desire and experience. "In the Entrance of the Café" recalls a moment in which the speaker's attention is drawn to the

> lovely body that looked as if
> Eros had made it using all his vast experience:
> crafting with pleasure his shapely limbs;
> making tall the sculpted build.

In many cases, the experience seems predestined for incorporation into a poem and may even strike readers as nothing more than pretext: "Their Beginning" opens with what might strike most readers as an ending: "The fulfillment of their illicit pleasure/ is accomplished." One of the partners in the act takes away something more: "Tomorrow, the day after, or through the years he'll write/ powerful lines, that here was their beginning."

There are also a few mature poems that do not fit comfortably into either category. The first work in the collection, "The City," is of this type, and it ranks as one of the most haunting works about ennui ever written. "'I'll go to some other land,'" muses its unnamed speaker, "'I'll go to some other sea./ There's bound to be another city that's better by far.'" The poem, however, asserts, "You'll find no new places, you won't find other shores." It concludes with the chilling judgment, "Just as you've destroyed your life, here in this/ small corner, so you've wasted it through all the world."

Mendelsohn maintains that it is a mistake to divide Cavafy's poems into such categories as "historical" and "erotic" and asserts that the poet's single, overriding subject is time. However intriguing the point, readers may feel instead that Cavafy has collapsed time, allowing him to treat both ancient and contemporary events as elements of a vast continuum. Mendelsohn allows as much, speaking of the manner in which Cavafy weaves past and present, and he goes on to explain why some of the poet's effects are liable to be lost on readers of English. During Cavafy's lifetime, there were essentially two Greek languages—the "demotic," or everyday language of the people, and *katharevousa*, a formal, invented language of the intelligentsia designed to preserve Greek in its purest form. Cavafy started out writing in *katharevousa*, switched to demotic in 1893, and subsequently mixed the two. Mendelsohn duplicates the effect—which conveys the interplay of ancient and modern—by mixing Latinate with simpler, more direct Anglo-Saxon words. He also discusses in detail the poet's other stylistic methods and describes the manner in which he himself has rendered them into English.

Aside from a few unimportant works of his youth that appeared in journals and the like, few of Cavafy's poems were published—in the accepted sense of the term. Instead, Cavafy printed individual poems or small selections for circulation among friends and acquaintances and often revised the works afterward. ("The City," for instance, is the product of fifteen years of revision.) A few thin volumes saw wider distribution, but the first commercial edition of his work—consisting of 154 poems that would come to be known as "the Canon"—appeared two years after his death.

Besides the Canon, Mendelsohn includes twenty-seven poems that Cavafy repudiated and a group of seventy-seven poems (including three in English) that he retained but never published. Of the second group, one was written when the poet was in his early teens and another, "From the Drawer," in 1923, when he was sixty. The unpublished works contain few surprises, as Cavafy's concerns remained relatively constant throughout his adult years. Dealing with an old photograph, "From the Drawer" recapitulates one of the poet's constant themes, and its three central lines might easily stand as the summation of his erotic outlook: "Those lips, that face—/ ah if only for a day, only for an/ hour their past would return."

One of Cavafy's friends, the eminent British novelist E. M. Forster, memorably described him as a "Greek gentleman in a straw hat, standing absolutely motionless at a slight angle to the universe." Forster had met Cavafy in Alexandria during World War I and went on to introduce the poet to the English-speaking world in one of his essays. John Mavrogordato published the first substantial collection of Cavafy's works in English in 1951. Later readers, however, may have first encountered Cavafy as a shadowy presence in *The Alexandria Quartet* (1957-1960) by British novelist and travel writer Lawrence Durrell, who included his own translations of Cavafy's poems in two of the volumes.

The past few decades have witnessed a growing number of English translations, including those of Rae Dalven, Edmund Keeley and Philip Sherrard, and Theoharis Constantine Theoharis. Mendelsohn's volume contains more works than those of any of his predecessors (in some cases by only a slight margin), and it includes a number of additional features, such as a page on the pronunciation of Greek and Byzantine names, a roster of the most important historical characters Cavafy treated, and a short list of books in English for further reading. The translator's notes to specific poems run to more than 160 substantial pages.

There is never a definitive translation of a work. Words in one language inevitably possess shades of association that their seemingly exact equivalents in other languages do not. Translators may choose to emphasize exact sense over sound, or sacrifice a degree of meaning in order to reproduce the poet's rhyme and meter, although they commonly strive to capture both. Although Cavafy eschewed most poetic devices, his language is not as prosaic as previous translators have suggested. As Mendelsohn explains, Cavafy deployed a subtle rhyme scheme in "The City," one that allowed him to underline the inertia imprisoning his subject. Wherever possible, Mendelsohn says, he has attempted to reproduce such effects in English.

Mendelsohn states in his introduction to *Collected Poems* that he has included all of Cavafy's known works in the form, with the exception of five poems translated from other languages. He adds, however, that a second volume—*The Unfinished Poems* (2009)—prints his translations (the first in English) of thirty drafts that the poet left in various stages of completion at the time of his death. Although there will inevitably be further translations of Cavafy, Mendelsohn's skill and range are likely to make these volumes the translations of choice for some time to come.

Grove Koger

Review Sources

Booklist 105, no. 14 (March 15, 2009): 38.
Boston Globe, June 7, 2009, p. C5.
Harper's Magazine 318, no. 1908 (May, 2009): 71.
New Criterion 27, no. 8 (April, 2009): 4-8.
The New Republic 240, no. 10 (June 17, 2009): 39-45.
The New York Times Book Review, April 19, 2009, p. 19.
The New Yorker 85, no. 6 (March 23, 2009): 70-75.
Publishers Weekly 256, no. 11 (March 16, 2009): 44.

COLUMBINE

Author: Dave Cullen (1961-)
Publisher: Twelve Books (New York). 417 pp. $26.99
Type of work: Sociology
Time: April 20, 1999
Locale: Columbine, Colorado

Cullen, an acknowledged national authority on the massacre at Columbine High School on April 20, 1999, explores events leading up to the massacre, examines the psychological makeup of the perpetrators, and presents in chilling detail an account of the massacre itself

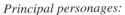

Principal personages:

ERIC HARRIS, a senior at Columbine High School
WAYNE HARRIS, Eric's father, a retired Air Force major
KATHY HARRIS, Eric's stay-at-home mother
DYLAN KLEBOLD, a senior at Columbine High School
TOM KLEBOLD, Dylan's father, a geophysicist employed by oil companies and later founder of Fountain Real Estate Management
SUE KLEBOLD, Dylan's mother, a reading specialist, later Tom's partner in Fountain Realty
FRANK DEANGELIS, principal of Columbine High School

Adolf Hitler was born on April 20, 1889, and, although he has been classified as a monster by mainstream U.S. society, many socially dysfunctional people have found in him someone with whom they can identify. His birthday and the days close to it have become rallying points for many dissidents, who have marked the day in a variety of violent and destructive ways. April 19 has also become an important date for many dissenters opposed to what they perceive to be governmental authority and oppression. It was on this day in 1993 that agents of the Federal Bureau of Investigation (FBI) stormed the Branch Davidian compound near Waco, Texas—an event that resulted in eighty deaths, including those of twenty children. Two years later, on April 19, 1995, Timothy McVeigh, seeking vengeance for the Branch Davidian attack, parked a truck loaded with explosives outside the Murrah Federal Building in Oklahoma City and detonated its lethal load. The explosion killed 168 people.

According to Dave Cullen's *Columbine*, Eric Harris and Dylan Klebold spent over eighteen months planning their own massacre, which was to take place at Columbine High School on "Judgment Day," their designation for April 19. They had to move the date of their attack to April 20 when the person from whom they were buying ammunition was late in delivering it. The two boys determined that the optimal time for their strike was during the school's most popular lunch period, which began at 11:10 A.M.

Eric, after closely observing Columbine's traffic patterns, found that the lunchroom had its largest concentration of students at 11:17 A.M. He and Dylan planted pipe bombs there and in various other places, including one diversionary bomb three miles from the school to distract the police. According to their plan, the bombs would have their greatest explosive impact in the school's cafeteria, where they were set to explode between 11:16 and 11:18 A.M. Had their timing mechanisms worked, the Columbine massacre, which killed twelve students and one faculty member, would have exceeded by far the 168 fatalities caused by McVeigh's attack on the Murrah Federal Building. Eric had discussed exceeding the toll of the Oklahoma City disaster.

Dave Cullen, a prize-winning journalist, is the leading authority on the Columbine tragedy and its two perpetrators. He has also written about such controversial topics as evangelical Christianity, popular culture, politics, and gays in the military; for his work on the latter topic, he won a GLAAD Media Award.

When much-publicized mass murders, such as the Murrah Federal Building bombing or school shootings, focus attention on those who participate in them, often other people who view themselves as social rejects are tempted to gain the sort of notoriety that such violent acts generate. When teenagers are involved, they often feel that they have been bullied in school or have been rejected in one way or another by their classmates or their families. Eric and Dylan both reacted very negatively to rejection. People with such a mind-set may retreat into a protective carapace and appear to be withdrawn or sullen. On the exterior, they may be polite and acquiescent, even though they may seethe below the surface. Many might be termed "injustice collectors."

Cullen conducted extensive research to uncover the psychology and motives of Eric and Dylan. On the surface, these two teens seemed quite atypical of what most people would perceive to be severely disturbed youths. Although they dressed idiosyncratically in black trench coats, they came from stable, relatively affluent families. They were bright, and both maintained high grade point averages through high school. Although they were not as socially active as many adolescents are, they had friends and, only three days before their assault on Columbine High School, both had attended the senior prom. The night before the massacre, the two ate dinner with classmates at the Outback Steakhouse, Eric's favorite restaurant.

Nevertheless, as early as July, 1997, Dylan wrote in his journal about killing. Eric's Web site also contained suggestions of what was to come and had caused him to be reported to the police. Later in the same year, Eric, Dylan, and another classmate were suspended from Columbine High School for breaking into school lockers. A month afterward, Dylan wrote in his journal about a killing spree. In January, 1998, Eric and Dylan were arrested for breaking into a van. In March, they were sentenced for this crime to enter a juvenile diversion program. Eric had begun seeing a psychiatrist shortly after being arrested and, at about this time, a pipe bomb was found near his house.

Shortly after that incident, Wayne Harris discovered his son had a pipe bomb. By May, 1998, Eric began keeping a journal that outlined his intention to mastermind a massacre. By November, 1998, Eric was writing in his journal about his sadistic rape fantasies. By January, 1998, both boys drew up detailed plans for an attack on Columbine and wrote about it in each others' yearbooks.

Although Eric maintained an "I hate" list on his Web site, he and Dylan were less focused on individual potential victims than they were on wiping out large numbers of people indiscriminately. The school principal, Frank DeAngelis, was genuinely well liked by the students, including Eric and Dylan. He interacted well with his staff as well as with parents. A hands-on administrator who voluntarily did lunch duty in the cafeteria, he viewed this service as a means of getting to know his students better. On Judgment Day, he would normally have been in the cafeteria, but that day he was in his office conducting an interview when the massacre began.

Hearing the commotion, DeAngelis left his office and, after he heard gunshots, saw Eric and Dylan brandishing guns. A shot shattered the trophy cabinet behind DeAngelis. Groping desperately to find the keys that would open the locked door of the gymnasium, he fished the right key out from several lookalike keys on his chain and herded a number of students into the gymnasium, thereby saving their lives as well as his own.

The boys had expected their pipe bombs to explode between 11:16 and 11:18 A.M. They positioned themselves in the school's parking lot so that they could observe the explosions. When their bombs failed to detonate, the two pulled their shotguns from their duffel bags at 11:19 A.M. and strapped them to their bodies. When one of them, presumably Eric, shouted "Go," they began firing into the crowd. They found the massacre exhilarating and laughed maniacally as they pumped bullets into their classmates.

By 11:23 A.M., four minutes after the onset of the shooting, Dylan had shot five of his classmates; Eric had shot the others. Bodies lay bleeding in the school's hallways, its library, and the cafeteria, whose blood-splattered walls bore mute testimony to what had happened. At about this time, the crime was reported by the 911 operator, and Deputy Neil Gardner sped into the parking lot, his emergency lights flashing.

As more police officers, including a special weapons and tactics (SWAT) team, gathered, no one knew where the two shooters were. The police had to proceed slowly among the dead and wounded because it was possible that Eric and Dylan were laying in wait to resume their killing. It was not until after 3:00 P.M. on that Tuesday that the attackers' bodies were found and terrified people could emerge from hiding without fearing for their lives. Even then, most of those who were hiding had no way of knowing that the two killers were dead.

In the wake of the disaster, there was speculation that Dylan, always the follower, had changed his mind about killing himself and that Eric had shot him. Cullen puts this notion to rest in his description of the aftermath of the shootings. He writes, "Most of the bodies lay under tables. The victims had been attempting to hide. Two bodies were different. They lay out in the open, weapons by their sides. Suicides, clearly. The SWAT team had descriptions of Eric and Dylan. These two looked like a match. It was over." The time was 3:15 P.M.

As the police gathered, Eric shot at them, by now hoping he and Dylan could go out in a blaze of glory, suicides by cop. When the police did not respond as Eric probably had hoped they would, he retreated into the southwest corner of the library, a small island of order amid the chaos. Dylan followed. One of them, probably Eric, lit a fuse to ignite a Molotov cocktail. He then put the shotgun into his mouth. Cullen writes,

> Eric fired through the roof of his mouth. . . . He collapsed against the books, and his torso slumped to the side. . . . Dylan's blast knocked him flat on his back and strewed his brain matter across Eric's left knee. Dylan's head came to rest just beside it.

In retrospect one can recognize that Eric and Dylan were like low-rumbling volcanoes, close to erupting. It must be remembered, however, that both boys were maintaining good grades in school and that both held down part-time jobs at Blackjack Pizza, where they were regarded as two of the most dependable employees of the establishment. When the pizza parlor was sold, they were among a small body of former employees to be retained. Just four days before the Columbine massacre, Eric was promoted to shift manager.

Against this backdrop, it was easy to dismiss suggestions that Eric and Dylan presented an imminent danger to anyone. Much earlier, they had decided what they would do and when they would do it. Nevertheless, they lived lives that seemed future-oriented, hardly the lives of people on the brink of killing themselves and as many others as they could take with them.

Dylan, who had been admitted to the University of Arizona, had recently visited the campus with his father to secure housing for the fall semester. He spoke to some of his friends about his future plans. Eric deceived his parents into believing that he anticipated joining the Marines, a plan his father supported. On the Thursday before the massacre, a Marine recruitment officer met with Eric and his parents in their home.

Searching for motives to explain the kind of violence that these two young men planned and approached with almost surgical precision, Cullen points to an essay about the Nazis that Eric wrote for his English class in October, 1998. Less than four months later, Dylan submitted to his English teacher a disturbing story about killing. What most people did not know was that in November, 1998, Eric and Dylan bought two semiautomatic shotguns at a gun show. Two months later, when both were still participating in the diversion program to which they had been sentenced, Eric and Dylan bought another gun, this time a powerful TEC-9, from a petty crook and drug pusher who also promised to sell them ammunition.

Cullen is to be commended for the scope and balance of his study, a project that took a decade to complete. His writing and research are exemplary.

R. Baird Shuman

Review Sources

Booklist 105, no. 15 (April 1, 2009): 9.
Commentary 127, no. 6 (June, 2009): 64-66.
Kirkus Reviews 77, no. 4 (February 15, 2009): 180.
Library Journal 134, no. 5 (March 15, 2009): 117.
New York 42, no. 14 (April 27, 2009): 66-67.
The New York Times Book Review, April 19, 2009, p. 13.
Publishers Weekly 256, no. 8 (February 23, 2009): 44.
Vanity Fair, May, 2009, p. 60.
Wall Street Journal, April 18, 2009, p. W8.

THE CRADLE

Author: Patrick Somerville (1979-)
Publisher: Little, Brown (New York). 204 pp. $21.99
Type of work: Novel
Time: 1997; 2008
Locale: Wisconsin; Minnesota; Indiana; Illinois; Hawaii

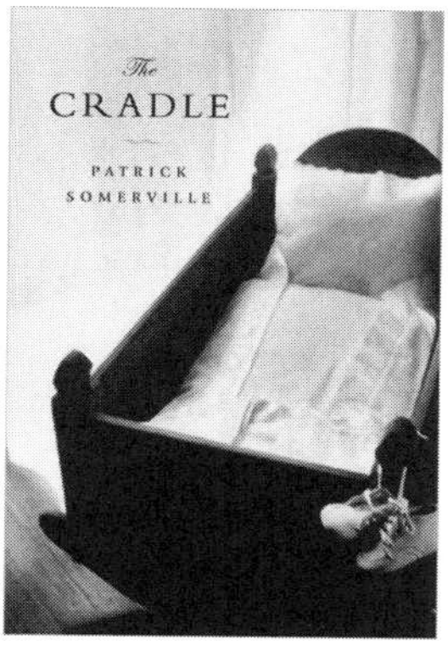

What begins as a quest for a long-lost cradle ends with the healing of old wounds and the restoration of broken familial relationships

Principal characters:

MATTHEW (MATT) BISHOP, a blue-collar worker, devoted husband, and orphan
MARISSA FRANCIS BISHOP, his pregnant wife, abandoned as a teenager by her mother Caroline Francis
GLEN FRANCIS, Marissa's father, a fifty-seven-year-old office worker and Caroline's ex-husband
JOSEPH (JOE) ROBERTS (later JOE BISHOP), the five-year-old son of Caroline and Darren Roberts and the adopted son of Matt and Marissa
RENEE OWEN, an author of children's books and a poet
BILL OWEN, her husband
ADAM OWEN, their nineteen-year-old son, a soldier deployed to Iraq
MARY LANDOWER, Caroline's half sister, now living in Antarctica
HANNAH PRICE, Matt's contact in Sturgeon Bay, Wisconsin
"ANCIENT" SYLVIA, a resident of Green Bay, Wisconsin, and a friend of Mary Landower
BRIAN, her reclusive, sixty-year-old son, a computer expert
DARREN ROBERTS, Caroline's husband and Joe's self-absorbed father, now living in Walton, Minnesota
SUSAN ROBERTS, Darren's alcoholic mother and Joe's grandmother, a resident of Rensselaer, Indiana

Patrick Somerville's debut novel, *The Cradle*, begins as the story of a quest for a specific object, the antique cradle from which the book derives its title. However, after that particular cradle has been found and then lost again, it becomes clear that the cradle is more than a narrative device. It symbolizes the yearnings of children for parents they have lost or by whom they have been rejected, and, even more profoundly, it stands for a rebirth, a return to innocence that can make possible the reestablishment of broken family ties.

At first, *The Cradle* appears to present a straightforward narrative: Matt Bishop and his wife Marissa Francis Bishop are living near Milwaukee in St. Helens, Wisconsin, in June of 1997. Marissa, who is eight months pregnant, has become convinced that her baby must have the very same cradle in which she herself slept as an infant. Unfortunately, she does not know where the cradle is. When Marissa was fif-

Patrick Somerville is the Simon Blattner Visiting Assistant Professor of Creative Writing at Northwestern University. He is the author of the short-story collection Trouble *(2006), and his short fiction has also appeared in* One Story, Epoch, *and* The Best American Nonrequired Reading, 2007. The Cradle *is his first novel.*

teen years old, shortly after her mother Caroline had deserted her and her father, there was a robbery at the Francis home. One of the things that disappeared was the cradle. Marissa and her father Glen have always assumed that Caroline arranged the robbery. Thus, it seems likely that she still has the cradle, and Marissa has decided that Matt must find the cradle for her, even though it means that he will have to take time off from his job at the Delco chemical plant.

Matt objects to this plan. Anticipating the expense of raising a child, he has been trying to build up the family's savings, primarily by working double shifts at the plant. He does not want to lose that extra income. Nevertheless, Marissa is adamant, and Matt feels that he has no choice but to do as she wishes. Matt has personal reasons for trying to make Marissa happy. His own childhood was miserable. He never knew his parents. Instead, he lived in an orphanage and in foster homes, where he suffered abuses that he tries not to remember. As a result, Matt has resolved to do whatever it takes to make his own marriage last so that his child will have the loving home and the security that he never had. He is committed to making his wife happy, even if to do so he must set off on what seems to him a quixotic mission.

In its second chapter, the novel moves suddenly to the year 2008, to suburban Chicago, and to a new set of characters who do not seem to have any connection with those previously introduced. Renee Owen, a successful author of children's books, is consumed with worry because, despite her vehement objections, her son Adam has volunteered for military service and is headed for Iraq. The only hint of a possible connection between the two plots comes at the end of the chapter, when Renee and her husband Bill see a television report of a horrendous explosion at the Delco plant near Milwaukee.

The story shifts back to 1997 and Matt's mission, which from this point on dominates the narrative. In fact, only three of the fourteen remaining chapters are set in 2008. From the third chapter on, the focus is on Matt's adventures as, like an epic hero, he moves from place to place searching for his equivalent of the Golden Fleece. As in an epic, he begins his quest with the help of a well-wisher: His father-in-law Glen slips a paper to him on which is written the address of Caroline's half sister, Mary Landower, in Sturgeon Bay, Wisconsin. Presumably, Mary will be able to put Matt on Caroline's trail.

However, also like an epic hero, Matt meets with one obstacle after another. When he arrives at the address Glen gave him, he finds that Mary no longer lives there. She has sold her house to an elderly woman, Hannah Price, and though Hannah admits that she knows Mary's new address, she will not give it to Matt until he completes a set of tasks. Sweeping down spiders, carrying bags of birdseed, and mowing the lawn are not as difficult or as dangerous as the tasks assigned to traditional epic heroes, but they are obstacles in Matt's way, since he knows that he must find the cradle before Marissa gives birth. After Matt finally finishes the work Hannah has assigned him, she keeps to her bargain and gives him the address of Mary's new home in nearby Green Bay, Wisconsin.

Speeding to Green Bay in the pickup truck that serves as his steed, Matt again fails to find Mary Landower. Instead, he encounters an ancient, witchlike woman called Sylvia who lives in a house so dilapidated that it could well house supernatural beings. From Sylvia, Matt learns that Mary is in Antarctica. However, Sylvia offers to help Matt in his quest, and she takes him upstairs to the room where her troll-like son Brian performs "magic" with his computers. Brian manages to make contact with Mary, who appears on his screen like a disembodied spirit. From Mary, Matt learns that Caroline is in Indonesia and that her ex-husband Darren Roberts lives in Walton, Minnesota. At first, it seems that Matt's quest is over: Darren admits that the cradle is in his basement. However, once he realizes how important it is to Matt, Darren begins to bargain, and Matt arranges to pay $750 for something that Darren admits he stole.

When Darren mentions that the cradle was last occupied by a baby born to Caroline and him five years ago, Matt's quest takes on a new dimension: He must find Marissa's half brother, who has been deserted by his mother and then dumped by his father on his paternal grandmother. Like other epic heroes, Matt cleverly outwits his antagonist. He tricks Darren into drinking himself into a stupor, searches his papers, and finds his mother's address.

When Matt appears at Susan Roberts's home in Rensselaer, Indiana, asking about Joe, he discovers that the child is filthy and seemingly mute. Marissa urges her husband to bring Joe home immediately, and Susan is only too happy to get rid of the child. On his way back to St. Helens, Matt stops at Darren's house to arrange to adopt Joe. Again in the epic tradition, Darren says that he will consent only if Matt gives the correct answer to a riddle. Matt refuses to play his game, for, as he points out, Joe is not an object, but a real person. Surprisingly, Darren capitulates. This episode highlights one of the themes of *The Cradle*: that no object, whatever its associations, is as important as a human being.

Though much of the humor in *The Cradle* comes from Somerville's use of epic conventions, the novel could hardly be called a mock-epic. Structurally, it differs from the traditional epic in that, though there are flashbacks to the past, notably Matt's memories of childhood abuse, there also periodic leaps into the future, to 2008. Moreover, epic heroes are men of action, not given to psychological analysis. While heroes such as Odysseus and Hector love their wives, they do not try to read their minds. By contrast, Matt is a thoroughly modern hero. After he sets off on his quest, he devotes hours of driving time to attempting to comprehend why Marissa is so obsessed with the cradle. Somerville traces Matt's thought processes, showing how he comes to see that, in Marissa's mind, the loss of the cradle is associated with the end of her parents' marriage: Only when it is once again present by her bed can she feel that her own marriage will last.

Since Matt, too, is determined to make their marriage last, he comes to an understanding of the cradle's importance to his wife. Later, however, both Marissa and

Matt see that the cradle is not as important as they had thought. To make room in his truck for Joe, Matt has to move the cradle out of the passenger seat and tie it in the open bed. As a result, it is stolen. When Matt returns home without the cradle, however, its loss does not seem to matter to Marissa, for she now knows that real people like Joe are always more important than inanimate objects.

Thus, though Matt and Marissa do not even know of his existence until the novel is well along, Joe has an important role in what turns out to be less a quest for an object than a quest for wisdom. It is Joe who links the subplot with the main plot, the future with the present. Halfway through the book, Renee informs her husband that she had an illegitimate son. Near the end of the novel, a grownup Joe takes the first step toward reuniting Renee with Matt, who turns out to be her lost son. It can be assumed that, with the new understanding of human nature that fatherhood has brought him, Matt will forgive his mother for abandoning him and that her expanded family will bring Renee the happiness she seeks.

The critical response to *The Cradle* has been generally favorable. The author is praised for his deft handling of a complex plot, for his skill in creating characters, and for using humor to enliven a book that is essentially serious. Even after the cradle Matt sought has disappeared from his truck, even after Marissa has forgotten about it, the idea of the cradle remains important in Somerville's novel, for it represents the fragile innocence that can be protected and preserved only by families committed to the values it represents.

Rosemary M. Canfield Reisman

Review Sources

Booklist 105, no. 13 (March 1, 2009): 22.
Kirkus Reviews 77. no. 3 (February 1, 2009): 4.
Library Journal 134, no. 1 (January 1, 2009): 81.
The New York Times, March 9, 2009, p. 4.
The New York Times Book Review, March 15, 2009, p. 11.
Publishers Weekly 256, no. 3 (January 19, 2009): 36.
St. Louis Post-Dispatch, March 15, 2009, p. F8.

CROSSERS

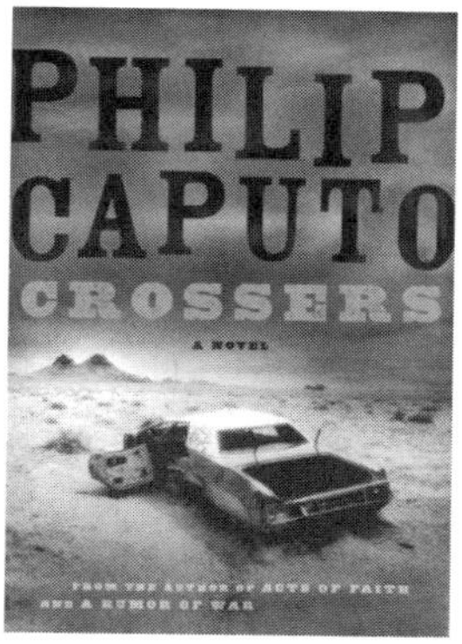

Author: Philip Caputo (1941-)
Publisher: Alfred A. Knopf (New York). 448 pp. $26.95
Type of work: Novel
Time: 1903-2003
Locale: New York, New York; New Canaan, Connecticut; Arizona; Mexico

In Caputo's novel, a recent widower moves to Arizona seeking solace only to find himself caught up in violence related to drug trafficking

Principal characters:

GIL CASTLE, a Wall Street financial analyst
AMANDA CASTLE, his wife, killed in the September 11, 2001, terrorist attacks
BLAINE ERSKINE, his cousin, a rancher
MONICA ERSKINE, Blaine's wife
BEN ERSKINE, Blaine and Gil's grandfather, a lawman
JEFF ERSKINE, Ben's brother, a cattleman
JOSHUA PITTMAN, their uncle, a justice of the peace
T. J. BABCOCK, a friend who fights alongside Ben in the Mexican Revolution
YNEZ YBARRA BABCOCK, his wife, a Mexican rebel
GRACE CASTLE, Ben's daughter and Gil's mother
MIGUEL ESPINOZA, a border crosser
GREGORIO BONHAM, also known as EUCLID J. CARRINGTON and THE PROFESSOR, a Mexican policeman who works for a drug cartel
YVONNE (LA ROJA) MENÉNDEZ, leader of a Mexican drug cartel
JULIÁN MENÉNDEZ, her son
JOAQUÍN CARRASCO, leader of a Mexican drug cartel
TESSA MCBRIDE, Blaine and Monica's neighbor, a rancher and painter
BETH MCBRIDE, her daughter, a soldier serving in Iraq
TIMOTHY FORBES, a reporter in the 1920's
SAMANTHA, Gil's Irish setter

In eight novels and several volumes of nonfiction, Philip Caputo has explored issues related to violence, war, terrorism, exploitation, and masculinity. His characters constantly find themselves tested by forces over which they have no control. A growing number of novelists have tackled the tragedy of the September 11, 2001, terrorist attacks and their consequences. Some have focused on the larger issues the attacks raised, while others have concentrated on their specific effects on individual characters. *Crossers* takes the latter approach. Unable to overcome his grief at losing his wife in the Twin Towers attack, Gil Castle moves to his family's Arizona ranch only to discover that greed, violence, and inhumanity are inescapable.

Caputo makes *Crossers* both challenging and rewarding by interweaving the fifty-

Philip Caputo is a Pulitzer Prize-winning journalist whose books include A Rumor of War *(1977), a memoir of his combat experiences in Vietnam, as well as the novels* Horn of Africa *(1980),* DelCorso's Gallery *(1983),* Indian Country *(1987),* Equation for Evil *(1996),* The Voyage *(1999), and* Acts of Faith *(2005).*

six-year-old Gil's tale with that of his Arizona ancestors, primarily his grandfather Ben Erskine, a legendary lawman and "the last ember of the true Old West." Caputo hints early on that Ben's actions, which include killing twelve men, will have effects on Gil and others, but he delays revealing the connections between the past and the present until their consequences begin to unravel lives. This structure causes *Crossers* to have a greater emotional impact than it would have had if it had been told in chronological order. The novel is an epic account of how little things can change over the course of a century. Villains are different, but ethical dilemmas remain as murky as ever.

Ben is thirteen in 1903, conducting himself as if he is living in the legendary Old West. Sent on an errand into Mexico by his uncle, Joshua Pittman, Ben kills a Mexican in self-defense and throws the body down a mine shaft. This event is one of several instances of subtle irony employed by Caputo. The reckless Ben, compelled by an unquestioned code of rugged manliness, reflects little on his actions, and a similar case of self-defense will have unexpected effects on his grandchildren and on the family of his victim. Joshua tells Ben, "It is a terrible thing to kill a man, even when it is justified," but the boy is deaf to this lesson. Caputo skillfully connects this small-scale personal war with the events of September 11 without belaboring the point. People kill other people for complicated reasons, and even when they feel they are justified because of religious, political, and family concerns, morality is corrupted in ways they could not have foreseen.

Caputo imparts to Ben Erskine's chapters a sense of verisimilitude and historical sweep by presenting them as transcripts of a 1966 oral history project in which Ben's life was recounted by those who knew him. Ben is repeatedly shown as a man with an unwavering code: "having solved so many crimes, having survived so many dangers, he begins to think of himself as a favored of the gods, as bulletproof. . . . He comes to believe in his own legend." Caputo manages to make Ben both larger-than-life and humanly flawed. While some worship him as a hero, his daughter Grace, Gil's mother, has conflicted feelings about the man she sees as an anachronism. Timothy Forbes, a newspaper reporter, thinks Ben became a lawman to avoid becoming a criminal.

Running parallel to Ben's story is the much less adventurous life of his grandson, senior vice president for the world's fourth-largest investment firm. Caputo emphasizes their differences from the beginning of the novel. While his friend T. J. Babcock describes the charismatic Ben as "relaxed and coiled at the same time," Gil has "the patrician severity of a Florentine prince," though "his looks lacked the voltage to draw second glances from women." After the death of Amanda, his beloved second wife, Gil no longer feels energized by New York's financial district or managing half a billion dollars in assets.

Despite being encouraged by his counselor and his two daughters to move on with his life, Gil cannot escape the past, which clings "to him like a second skin." Unable to understand the motives of the September 11 terrorists, Gil can find little comfort beyond reading Roman Stoics such as Seneca. After a year of mourning, he realizes that "his whole benign life and the faith it was founded on, that reason triumphs in the end, had been beautiful illusions." Contemplating suicide, Gil is saved by thoughts of what would happen to Samantha, his seven-year-old Irish setter, who is more a partner than a pet.

Considering himself "merely passing time rather than living a life" and knowing he will go mad if he continues on his current path, Gil accepts an invitation from Monica Erskine, the wife of his cousin Blaine. She offers him a chance to live in an adobe cabin built by Jeff Erskine, Ben's brother, in Patagonia, Arizona, near the border with Mexico. Taking early retirement and giving away much of his fortune to charities, Gil goes to Arizona hoping for rest and recovery. He begins to rise out of his misery when he finds himself falling for a neighboring rancher, Tessa McBride, who paints western landscapes. The lusty, buxom Tessa invigorates Gil. They also share burdens related to September 11, for Tessa's daughter Beth is serving with the U.S. Army in Iraq.

Patagonia, however, is far from the peaceful paradise Gil envisioned. Blaine's sprawling ranch is used as a highway for criminals transporting drugs and illegal aliens into the United States. Matters begin to unravel when Gil rescues Miguel Espinoza, an abandoned border crosser who has witnessed the brutal murder of two men smuggling marijuana.

One of Caputo's major themes in *Crossers* is the effect of chance on people's lives. Ben and T. J. join Pancho Villa's army because a flyer for gringo recruits happens to blow into their path. In rescuing Miguel in the desert, Gil helps advance a chain of events already set in motion:

> it had the quality of fate, as if the course of his life and Miguel's were destined to meet. Break one link, and he would not be here with his cowboy cousin and a Navaho tracker and a Mexican vaquero and two dead strangers.

Fate, in which Ben strongly believes, is a major factor in several of the novel's pivotal events.

Crossers contrasts two ways of coping with the complexities of modern life. Blaine is eager to return both to the Old West and to his Vietnam days by loading his guns and taking off after the bad guys. Gil is more contemplative, hoping some civilized means of sorting out problems will arise, while recognizing that this attitude may be inadequate, as the deaths in the desert remind him of how sheltered his life has been. Caputo implies that, while neither approach is entirely wrong, neither is applicable to all circumstances either. He sets up a situation in which Gil's resolve will be tested without trivializing his characters or themes by suggesting that violence is necessary to allow a man to discover his true self. One of these themes is the impossibility of escaping the consequences of one's actions, even when they are the result of the deeds of others. Given a gun and taking target practice, Gil wonders if he can shoot anyone.

Caputo's villains are more compelling that his heroes, even Ben. The man who calls himself the Professor is an American. A Georgetown University graduate, a former Drug Enforcement Agency officer, and a captain in the Mexican Federal Judicial Police, he also works for one of two rival drug cartels. He uses his law enforcement position to weaken the rival cartel by accumulating information to convey to the cartel's leader, Joaquín Carrasco. Able to pass for an Anglo thanks to his English father, the Professor is known as Gregorio Bonham in Mexico and as Euclid J. Carrington across the border, where the Central Intelligence Agency (CIA), presented as being involved in drug trafficking, hopes to settle a score with him.

Both loving and hating America, fitting uneasily into two cultures and on both sides of the law, the Professor enjoys fluctuating between identities. He justifies his actions working for the drug cartel because it improves the lives of those living in Carrasco's field of operations. Moreover, he sees the United States as "a nation of lazy, superficial, Web-surfing fools playing video games, alienated from the beating heart of life."

The Professor's antagonist, Yvonne Menéndez, leader of the Agua Prieta cartel, resembles him only with her mixed ethnic heritage, inheriting from her Irish father the red hair that has earned her the nickname "La Roja." While the Professor is coolly professional, Yvonne has a fiery temper, having her husband murdered so that she can seize his power and compete with Carrasco. The Professor knows that Yvonne's impetuousness will be her downfall. He compares her to the gangster played by Edward G. Robinson in *Key Largo* (1948) who cannot be satisfied with his power, always wanting more: "She couldn't spell *enough* in English or Spanish."

The fates of Yvonne and the Professor are linked to those of Gil and Blaine because Yvonne is motivated most of all by her quest for revenge against the Erskine family—for reasons Caputo delays revealing almost until the end of *Crossers*. Yvonne plans to force Blaine to sell her his ranch, which borders hers, to enable her agents to smuggle drugs more easily. Julián, Yvonne's gay son and business partner, tries to make his mother act more reasonably to no avail.

When Blaine is faced with losing his ranch, Gil agrees to pay Blaine's back taxes in exchange for a partnership, thereby entwining him deeper in Yvonne's plot. Caputo presents Yvonne as strangely resembling Ben, an anachronistic pulp-magazine hero. The Professor prevails over Yvonne by understanding what adjustments are needed to survive in the present, much more ambiguous, age.

Caputo frequently grows elegiac when describing the physical charms of Arizona and Mexico, but he makes clear that "In these borderlands beauty cohabited with violence." A potential paradise has been spoiled by greed, poverty, and exploitation. Unlike many other novels set in the American Southwest, the villain of *Crossers* is not progress, a trope Caputo negates by equating the propensity for violence in the Old West with that of the drug smugglers and terrorists of the present. The Professor says Gil "was trying to escape history." *Crossers* vividly dramatizes the impossibility of this task.

Michael Adams

Review Sources

Booklist 105, no. 19/20 (June 1, 2009): 4.
Kirkus Reviews 77, no. 17 (September 1, 2009): 905.
Library Journal 134, no. 12 (July 1, 2009): 79.
Los Angeles Times, October 18, 2009, p. E10.
The New York Times Book Review, October 18, 2009, p. 14.
Publishers Weekly 256, no. 24 (June 15, 2009): 79.

DANCING IN THE DARK
A Cultural History of the Great Depression

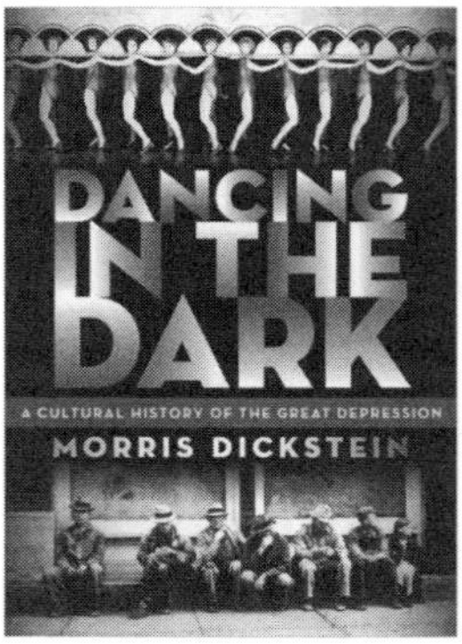

Author: Morris Dickstein (1940-   )
Publisher: W. W. Norton (New York). 624 pp. $29.95
Type of work: History
Time: 1929-1941
Locale: United States

With this book, Dickstein, whom Norman Mailer has lauded as "one of our best critics of American literature," advances his credentials as the prime chronicler of U.S. cultural history from the end of the 1920's to the start of the 1970's

Born in 1940, Morris Dickstein, distinguished professor of English at the City University of New York (CUNY) Graduate Center, remembers his steady-working, first-generation immigrant father recalling that, every Friday during the Great Depression, when he picked up his paycheck he looked for the pink slip telling him he was laid off. "The Depression put a strain on families, undermining the breadwinner and placing more pressure on the wife to bring in money and hold the family together," Dickstein writes in the preface to *Dancing in the Dark* while quoting critic Alfred Kazin: "No one who grew up in the Depression ever recovered from it."

What he did for the turbulent 1960's thirty-two years earlier in *Gates of Eden* (1977), Dickstein does in this book for the 1930's; that is, he writes a high-minded survey of the decade's cultural history. "Culture" is an eclectic term, though, perhaps best defined as the sum total of ways of living built up by a group of human beings and transmitted in evolved forms from one generation to another. One thus might wish for a more wide-ranging coverage than Dickstein provides. Such coverage would include, besides fluent exegeses of novels as well-known as John Steinbeck's *The Grapes of Wrath* (1939) and little-known as Henry Roth's *Call It Sleep* (1934), ordinary things that people did such as listen to radio programs featuring the Shadow; order sodas at drugstore counters; see a newsreel, a serial, and a feature for eleven cents at Saturday motion picture matinees; and adore *Snow White and the Seven Dwarfs* (1937) and Betty Boop cartoons.

Reviewer Robert Gottlieb finds Dickstein's two most blatant omissions to be Walt Disney and Shirley Temple. The actress is acknowledged only disparagingly, while Disney, arguably the most revolutionary film talent of his time, is unmentioned. Gottlieb, however, praises Dickstein's

> sense of what might appear to be the bipolar nature of the Thirties—the apparent clash between the frightening social realities and the ritzy glamour of so much of the entertainment of the period. . . . The Okies, yes, but also Astaire & Rogers and screwball com-

edy. Movie audiences—severely shrunk in the early Thirties—wanted to be cheered up, distracted.

Morris Dickstein is distinguished professor of English and theater at the CUNY Graduate Center and the author of Gates of Eden *(1977) and* Leopards in the Temple *(2002), among other works. He lives with his wife in New York City.*

The 1930's gangster and up-from-poverty films reveal the seamy and the triumphant sides of the Depression, respectively. Two of Dickstein's most delightful profiles are of Cole Porter and George and Ira Gershwin.

Dickstein remains, as one would expect of a Columbia University student and colleague of Lionel Trilling, a perceptive critic. He finds in F. Scott Fitzgerald's story "Babylon Revisited" (1931) "scarcely a remnant of the old iridescent shimmer, that romantic glow; at issue in Fitzgerald's later work is no longer the dream and disappointment but simply survival, pasting it together." He describes the subject of *Migrant Mother*, Dorothy Lange's bitter 1936 photograph, as "a woman whose brow is furrowed like tractored-out land."

Dancing in the Dark is a treatise on what the author believes is the crucial role that culture can play in times of national ordeal. "The crisis kindled America's social imagination," he says. Dickstein's main interest is less a novelist's writterly qualities, as it was with Edmund Wilson, whose model was Henry James, than the writer's social consciousness. The Depression, Dickstein continues, fomented, perhaps for the first time, "enormous interest in how ordinary people lived, how they suffered, interacted, took pleasure in one another, and endured."

"Enduring" is the touchstone of the novels of William Faulkner, whom Dickstein calls "the best writer"—one whose "voice and material, like Hemingway's, add strength to the culture of the 1930's without fully entering into it." The author devotes portions of ten pages to Faulkner's experimental *As I Lay Dying* (1930), seeking to demonstrate that the interior monologues of that novel set an example for writers such as James Agee (in *Let Us Now Praise Famous Men*, 1941) and Henry Roth (in *Call It Sleep*) by locating the fictional Bundren clan within a society without reducing them to their abstract social identity. Despite his high grades for Faulkner, however, Dickstein never seems at ease with him.

The title of the book could be seen as a reflection of the carefree 1920's giving way to the bleak 1930's. It is taken from an Arthur Schwartz-Howard Dietz torch song of 1931, a lachrymose composition about a couple in a ballroom who are "waltzing in the wonder of why we're here," "looking for the light," and resolved to "face the music together." These lyrics prefigure several of Dickstein's themes: yearning and wondering about the country's dread condition, being fearful of what lies ahead, and enduring.

The 1930's novelist with whom Dickstein is most at home is John Steinbeck, who shows twice as many lines in the index as Faulkner—twenty-two to eleven—and three of whose titles are cross-referenced, as opposed to only one of Faulkner's. Dickstein writes engagingly of relating not just to Steinbeck the writer but also to

Steinbeck the person. "I lived in Northern California with my wife and kids in the summer of 1973 when we visited Monterey and Cannery Row." Thus, as the chronicler of the Joads' desperate odyssey through the Dust Bowl, Steinbeck is Dickstein's preferred kind of writer—socially, not ideologically, committed.

When he comes to poetry, Dickstein predictably finds less to fit his preference. He quotes from William H. Pritchard's laudatory biography of Robert Frost, the era's reigning figure, these words written to a young poet after praising his work: "I wouldn't give a cent to see the world, the United States or even New York made better. I want them left as they are for me to make poetical on paper." Somewhat similarly, William Carlos Williams, a poet and practicing physician, expressed delight at the "anarchy" of his poor clients in Rutherford, New Jersey. It would be difficult to find a spirit less like Steinbeck's in either of these poets.

Dickstein is luckier with Wallace Stevens, in whose later poems there is "a sense of a world transformed: the sharp, frosty air of autumn replaces the fragrant promise of spring; the voices of human calamity displace the sounds of spring; the moon of the imagination gives way to the sun of harsh reality." Only in Langston Hughes does he find "one of the best young poets who became radicals and firebrands in the early Thirties." One wonders if Professor Dickstein is being disingenuous when he writes in the preface that he made no attempt to cover everything. "Trying to grasp the essential spirit of the thirties would seem to be a hopeless task," he writes a few pages later. "How can one era have produced both Woody Guthrie and Rudy Vallee, both the Rockettes high-stepping at the Radio City Music Hall and the Okies on their desperate trek toward the pastures of plenty in California?" It would be difficult, though, to make a laundry list of vital matters that he has left out.

To return to Gottlieb's regret at Walt Disney's omission from *Dancing in the Dark*, it has been argued that Mickey Mouse may be more important to an understanding of the 1930's than President Franklin D. Roosevelt. However, this seems to be an overstatement. Roosevelt's Fireside Chats defined the era more than did Mickey, Donald Duck, and Bambi, just as his actions did more to shape it. Culture may include far more than the political sphere, but it does include that sphere as well. Dickstein's comprehensive account of the culture of the Great Depression may lead readers to wonder what similar accounts could be written in the future about the current era of recession and the culture it has produced.

Richard Hauer Costa

Review Sources

Booklist 105, no. 22 (August 1, 2009): 24.
Commonweal 136, no. 19 (November 6, 2009): 38-40.
Harper's Magazine 319, no. 1914 (November, 2009): 71-76.
Kirkus Reviews 77, no. 13 (July 1, 2009): 694-695.
Library Journal 134, no. 20 (December 15, 2009): 117.

The New Republic 240, no. 22 (December 2, 2009): 44-47.
The New York Review of Books 56, no. 19 (December 3, 2009): 30-32.
The New York Times, September 16, 2009, p. 4.
The New York Times Book Review, September 27, 2009, p. 17.
The New Yorker 85, no. 29 (September 21, 2009): 90-94.
Publishers Weekly 256, no. 28 (July 13, 2009): 49.
The Spectator 311, no. 9458 (December 5, 2009): 49-50.
Times Higher Education, December 10, 2009, p. 52.
The Wall Street Journal, September 15, 2009, p. A19.

DARWIN'S SACRED CAUSE
How a Hatred of Slavery Shaped Darwin's Views on Human Evolution

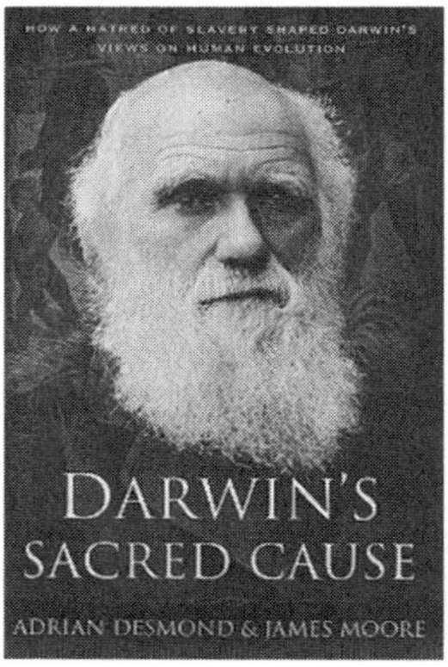

Authors: Adrian Desmond (1947-) and James Moore (1947-)
Publisher: Houghton Mifflin Harcourt (Boston). 486 pp. Illustrated. $30.00
Type of work: History of science, biography, natural history, anthropology
Time: 1780's-1871
Locale: England; North America; South America

In a revisionist account of the provenance of Charles Darwin's revolutionary ideas on human evolution, the authors emphasize his detestation of slavery and his conviction about the basic unity of all races of humankind

Principal personages:
CHARLES DARWIN (1809-1882), English naturalist and evolutionary theorist
LOUIS AGASSIZ (1807-1873), Swiss American naturalist who developed the ice-age theory and opposed Darwin's ideas on human evolution and the unity of human races
SAMUEL GEORGE MORTON (1799-1851), American physician and naturalist whose studies of skulls convinced him that human races had diverse origins
JOSIAH NOTT (1804-1873), American physician and ethnologist whose studies on "human types" purportedly supported Confederate slaveholders' views on white superiority

In a remarkable historical coincidence, two of the nineteenth century's most influential figures—Charles Darwin and Abraham Lincoln—were born on the same day, February 12, 1809. To celebrate the bicentennial of this event and the sesquicentennial of the publication of Darwin's *On the Origin of Species by Means of Natural Selection: Or, The Preservation of Favoured Races in the Struggle for Life* (1859), which has been listed among the most important books ever written, numerous publications have appeared on the lives and achievements of Darwin and Lincoln. Some note certain interconnections between them, such as their abhorrence of slavery. In *Darwin's Sacred Cause*, Adrian Desmond and James Moore propose a radically new explanation of how Darwin conceived and developed his profoundly innovative ideas on transmutation.

Desmond and Moore contend that abolition, the "sacred cause" of their title, was the moral fire that ignited Darwin's controversial ideas. Based on overwhelming evidence in his letters and other personal papers, historians of science and biographers have long recognized that Darwin was an ardent abolitionist, but, according to

Desmond and Moore, these previous scholars neglected the relationship between Darwin's views on slavery and his theories of how new species, particularly the human species, originated. Traditionally, scholars stressed Darwin's geological and biological observations during his five-year voyage aboard the *Beagle*, his later assiduous collection of data from naturalists and breeders, and his wide reading, especially of British economist Thomas Robert Malthus's *Essay on the Principle of Population* (1798), as providing the impetus for his conception of natural selection, in which the best adapted species survive and poorly adapted species become extinct.

Adrian Desmond, a research fellow in the Biology Department at University College London, has written several historical books on evolutionary thought. James Moore has taught the history of science at Harvard, Notre Dame, and the Open University. He has published several books exploring the interactions of science and religion in the nineteenth century.

In Desmond and Moore's new interpretation, Darwin's belief that all human races are members of the same species antedated his ideas on transmutation and provided the emotional stimulus for the theory of evolution. Although the actual writing of *Darwin's Sacred Cause* took only two years, the authors have traced the book's origins to their 1991 biography, *Darwin*, which was a critical and popular success. After the biography's publication, Moore's research into Darwin's Christian abolitionist heritage and Desmond's expertise in the science and politics of Victorian England ably armed them in their quest to "recover Darwin's lost humanitarianism." Because of the extensive research that they did for their Darwin biography, they were already familiar with many of Darwin's letters and other private papers, and they deepened this understanding by studying many new documents, such as Darwin's correspondence with the American abolitionist William Lloyd Garrison; the *Beagle*'s logbooks; and Darwin's marginal comments, underlinings, and exclamation marks in books from his personal library. They also explored the vast pro- and antislavery literature in England and the United States.

For the most part, the authors structure their book biographically, conducting their analyses via the framework of Darwin's life—from his family background, through his education at Edinburgh and Cambridge universities, to his *Beagle* voyage and his subsequent career as a naturalist, culminating with his publication of *The Descent of Man and Selection in Relation to Sex* (1871). They distinguish their approach from those doctrinaire atheists who have caricatured Darwin as a single-minded scientist whose discoveries, by creating a materialistic vision of life's history, undermined religion. They also disagree with religious creationists who mistakenly portray Darwin as antireligious and immoral. Instead, they believe that their interpretation of Darwin as a great humanitarian best fits the documented facts. Furthermore, they realize that he was a complex man who both shared in and rebelled against the values of his Victorian era.

Desmond and Moore also realize that, in the twentieth century, Nazis and other groups misused Darwin's ideas in helping to forge their racist ideologies. The authors do not support these and similar attempts to "hijack" Darwin for ends that would have horrified him. Rather, they want to understand what all groups—historians, scientists, and ideologues—have failed to grasp—"the moral fire that fueled his . . . obsession with human origins." Even those already familiar with the antislavery views of Darwin's forebears will be enlightened by the wealth of new information the authors have found that elucidates both the extent of British involvement in the slave trade and the efforts of committed abolitionists who devoted their time, money, and energies to eradicating this heinous practice. Abolitionists such as Thomas Clarkson and his many allies, including members of the Darwin family and the Wedgwoods (Darwin's maternal relatives), succeeded in convincing the British government, in 1807, to outlaw its trade in slaves, though the practice of slavery was allowed to continue in the colonies.

By the time Charles Darwin was born in 1809, nearly two million Africans had been abducted and sold in British colonies. During his youth he absorbed the belief from his sisters and relatives that black people were not members of a different, inferior race but human beings like him. While he studied medicine at Edinburgh University he met his first black man, a freed slave who taught him how to stuff birds. Darwin found him intelligent and pleasant to work with. However, at the university he also encountered others who did not share his liberal views. For example, certain phrenologists were using skull sizes and their protuberances to characterize racial intelligence and temperament. Some anthropologists in the United States manipulated these results to justify slavery.

When Darwin transferred to Cambridge University to train to become an Anglican clergyman, he tended to form close relationships with those faculty members who shared his antislavery views, including John Henslow, an excellent botanist as well as an ardent abolitionist. Henslow played a pivotal role in Darwin's getting a position aboard the *Beagle*. During his travels, Darwin experienced firsthand the evils of slavery in South American port cities and in the Brazilian and Argentinian countryside. The screams of brutally punished slaves and the cries of black mothers, fathers, and children who were being separated for sale created indelible memories that, the authors claim, were more significant in forming Darwin's views on common ancestry than was his collecting of fossils and finches. Darwin was also horrified by educated people in South America, Australia, and South Africa who had convinced themselves that aboriginal populations were "pests" that needed to be eradicated.

Following his return to England in 1836, the image of a genealogical tree began to dominate Darwin's thinking about the relationship among all branches of life, plants and animals as well as humans. Some historians of science, familiar with Darwin's extensive researches in natural history, may question the authors' contention that his antislavery views were the "key driver" in the formation of his theory of natural selection. Humans were certainly not the sole source of his insights. Nevertheless, Desmond and Moore make a case that Darwin's 1838 postulation of natural selection owes much to his conviction that humans of all races constitute a single species descended from a common ancestor. Emma Wedgwood, who became his wife in 1839, was as passionately antislavery as her husband, but she derived her convictions from her Christian faith, which taught that all humans had souls infused by God. Even though Emma easily adapted to her husband's sexism—he believed that males are naturally more courageous, intelligent, and imaginative than females—she was distraught as his studies in natural history transformed him from a believing Anglican to a materialist agnostic. Darwin was even gathering information to show that human religious and moral feelings were rooted in the instincts of lower animals.

As Darwin accumulated data to support his radically new ideas on "descent with modification," he was appalled by those scientists, such as Louis Agassiz, Samuel George Morton, and Josiah Nott, who claimed to have discovered evidence that human races had separate origins in different places. Some of these scientists thought that the evidence indicated that there were two human species (black and white), while Agassiz argued for eight. Others proposed fifteen, twenty-two, and even sixty-three different human species. *Morton's Crania Americana* (1839), based on measurements of many skulls, posited twenty-two great families of humans. Morton went on to hierarchize these families, using this information to justify the genocide of Native Americans and the enslavement of black Africans. Josiah Nott, a slave-owning physician, used Morton's data in his campaign against miscegenation and for the slave system. In 1854, Nott, with George Glidden, published *Types of Mankind*, in which they argued for polygenism, the doctrine that humans are divided into different but fixed races, each of which had originated in specific geographical regions. Agassiz wrote the introduction for this book, which has been listed among the most prominent racist tracts in antebellum America.

Darwin was disheartened by Agassiz's identification with the segregationist and pro-slavery group. Even such an intelligent and compassionate person as the geologist Charles Lyell, Darwin's mentor and friend, came, after visits to the American South, to share Morton's views. These scientists believed that black people were suitable only for servitude.

To refute those who held that human races constituted different species, Darwin collected evidence from domesticated animals, such as pigeons, which, despite their many varieties, had originated from a common ancestor. Darwin was writing a massive work on natural selection, and he intended to devote much attention to the descent of human races from a single ancestor (the unitarist, or monogenist, theory), which directly contradicted Agassiz's polygenist, or pluralist, views. For twenty years, Darwin labored on this ever-expanding tome, but, fearing controversy, he shared his radical ideas only with close friends—until 1858, when the naturalist Alfred Russel Wallace sent him a scientific paper that clearly demonstrated that Wallace had independently arrived at the theory of natural selection. This paper served to end Darwin's procrastination, and in 1859 he published *On the Origin of Species by Means of Natural Selection*. This work, which did not include Darwin's ideas and data on human evolution, appeared just before the outbreak of the American Civil War.

The exclusion of humans from Darwin's book did not prevent readers from extrapolating the consequences of his argument from plants and animals to humans. Some even used Darwin's example of certain ant species that enslave others in their justification of human slavery, an interpretation that infuriated him, since he felt it was absurd to jump from the unreasoning, instinctual behavior of an ant species to the rational, moral behavior of a human being. Darwin closely followed the American Civil War, and he was critical of Lincoln for fighting it to preserve the Union rather than to abolish slavery. He was also critical of Lincoln's Emancipation Proclamation, which freed slaves only in the rebel states, where the president had no direct control, and not in those Union states that permitted slavery, where he had the power to effect this change. When the war ended, Darwin confessed an error, since he had believed, along with many Englishmen, that slavery would flourish for centuries in the Southern states.

Darwin also reacted to British brutality against members of other races. When British colonial subjects in Jamaica revolted, the governor brutally repressed the rebellion, slaughtering hundreds of black Jamaicans. Darwin denounced the action, but the governor's decision was defended, to Darwin's chagrin, by several of his friends and even by his son William. Despite his sympathies for black people, Darwin realized that, throughout history, "civilized" races had exterminated and replaced "savage" races all over the world. Furthermore, he did not entirely escape the prejudices of the "cultural ladder" accepted by many of his racist and elitist friends and colleagues. For example, in *The Descent of Man and Selection in Relation to Sex*, he engaged in what today would be called ethnic stereotyping when he quoted with approval a characterization of the Irish as lazy, squalid, and licentious. When an Irish reader asked him to remove this offensive passage in later editions, he refused.

Others, such as Wallace, criticized Darwin's emphasis on sexual selection to explain the origin of human races, but Darwin continued to defend his theory, which he hoped would resolve the dispute between monogenists and polygenists. In this he was mistaken. He was not even able to remove the taints of racism, classism, sexism, and imperialism from his own thinking and feelings.

Desmond and Moore end their account somewhat abruptly in 1871, leaving readers to wonder about the development of Darwin's ideas on race in the remaining eleven years of his life. Because they so emphasize Darwin's humanitarianism and enlightened thinking about slavery, some readers may be surprised, even shocked, by Darwin's statements on the inferiority of aborigines, his denigration of the working classes, and his defense of the British colonial empire. Some scientists and historians of science have criticized the book for what they feel is the authors' overemphasis on abolition as the source of Darwin's revolutionary ideas. They point out that the evidence indicates that Darwin had a passion for wresting truths from the natural world that was even stronger than his moral passion against slavery. Religious critics have supported Emma's views against her husband's by stressing that his materialistic theory of natural selection provides no basis for a moral outrage against slavery. Slave owners, after all, could be interpreted as fighting for the survival of their way of life.

In the commemorative year of 2009, many books and discussions about Darwin and Lincoln served to bring out the complexities of their views on race, class, and colonialism. Darwin and Lincoln shared some of the racial prejudices of their contemporaries, but this did not prevent Lincoln from taking actions that eventually led to the liberation of American slaves. Darwin, despite being tied to some of the values of his gentlemanly class, was able to free scientists from false views about the origin of species while playing a not-insignificant role in the movement to free the world's slaves.

Robert J. Paradowski

Review Sources

Bookforum 15 (February/March, 2009): 36.
Booklist 105 (January 1, 2009): 31.
The Economist 390 (January 24, 2009): 87-88.
History Today 59, no. 2 (February 2009): 62.
Kirkus Reviews 76, no. 23 (December 1, 2008): 1238.
Library Journal 133, no. 20 (December 1, 2008): 156.
The Nation 288 (June 22, 2009): 33-36.
Nature 457 (February 12, 2009): 792-793.
New Scientist 201 (February 7, 2009): 48.
New Statesman 138 (April 13, 2009): 47-48.
The New York Times Book Review 114 (February 1, 2009): 11-12.
Publishers Weekly 255, no. 48 (December 1, 2008): 40.
Times Higher Education, February 12, 2009, pp. 48-49.

DEFEND THE REALM
The Authorized History of MI5

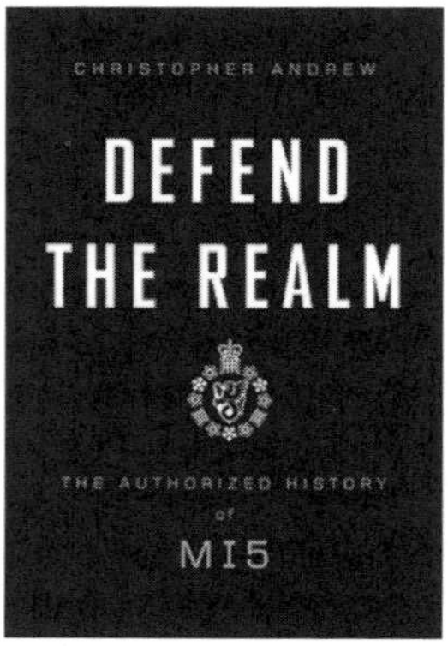

Author: Christopher Andrew (1941-)
First published: The Defence of the Realm: The Authorized History of MI5, 2009, in Great Britain
Foreword by Jonathan Evans
Publisher: Alfred A. Knopf (New York). Illustrated. 1,032 pp. $40.00
Type of work: Current affairs; history
Time: 1909-2009
Locale: Great Britain

An authorized, massively detailed account of the growth of the British Security Service during the first century of its existence that objectively considers its failures and successes

Principal personages:
SIR DAVID PETRIE, MI5 director general, 1941-1946
H. A. R. "KIM" PHILBY, high-ranking MI5 officer and Soviet double agent
KLAUS FUCHS, German-born British physicist who passed secrets to the Soviet Union
HAROLD WILSON, British prime minister, 1964-1970, 1974-1976
SIR VERNON KELL, MI5 director, 1909-1940
SIR ROGER HOLLIS, MI5 director general, 1956-1965

For most Americans, the British Security Service is something of a mystery. As they will learn from *Defend the Realm*, Christopher Andrew's exhaustive but accessible new history, it has been something of a mystery to the British public as well. When, in 1957, politician R. A. Butler was appointed home secretary, a position whose responsibility includes oversight of the agency, he admitted that he had no idea how to find its headquarters. To his considerable surprise, it turned out to be based not in some highly secret location but in a perfectly conventional London office building known as Leconfield House. The agency, popularly known as MI5 (for Military Intelligence, Section 5), was then nearly fifty years old, but it would be another thirty-two years before its existence was officially acknowledged.

As intelligence authority Andrew explains, Britain had virtually no espionage apparatus at the beginning of the twentieth century. That the public (and perhaps even the country's potential enemies) believed otherwise was due largely to the efforts of such novelists as William Le Queux and Rudyard Kipling, both of whom sang the praises of British superiority in the shadowy, far-flung world of espionage. In fact, Britain's army and navy had only tiny intelligence components, while the Special Branch of the Metropolitan Police (MPSB), which had been set up to deal with

Irish Republican terrorists, was only slightly larger.

However, change was imminent, propelled by the prospect of ever-increasing German militarization and the certain knowledge that Germany was introducing its own spies into England. In 1903, the director of military operations within the War Office established two new, albeit small, bodies—then called MO2 and MO3—to deal with foreign intelligence and domestic counterespionage, respectively. The Secret Service Bureau followed in 1909, and one of its components, MI5, took over the responsibilities of MO3 under the direction of Sir Vernon Kell. Thus *Defend the Realm*'s publication coincides with the centennial year of MI5's formation.

Christopher Andrew is a professor of modern and contemporary history at Cambridge University, a chair of the British Intelligence Study Group, a cofounding editor of the journal Intelligence and National Security, *and an honorary Air Commander of the Royal Auxiliary Air Force.*

Andrew divides the history of the agency into six periods. Before and during World War I (or the "Great War," as the British remember it), the primary espionage threat came from German subversion. Between the wars, MI5 dealt with the "Red Menace" of communism, as well as the rise of fascism at home and abroad. During World War II, the immediate enemies were once again German agents, although the service was well aware that the Soviet Union, although ostensibly an ally, was also a threat. Andrew sees the events of the subsequent Cold War as falling into two periods, after which counterterrorism rather than counterespionage became MI5's principal activity.

During World War I, MI5 staff devised a classification system for suspects that ran from AA ("Absolutely Anglicised" or "Absolutely Allied") to B ("Boche," a term for "rascal" borrowed from the French) and—worst of all—BB ("Bad Boche"). It was later determined that Germany had introduced some 120 spies into the country during the conflict, but some had simply pocketed their initial payment and made their way to the United States as immigrants. The service celebrated the 1918 armistice with a lighthearted "Hush-Hush" Revue and dinner dance. Subsequently, the agency's strength fell to nearly prewar levels, only to rise again in the late 1930's with the approach of another war.

Of the two directors and fourteen directors general who have run MI5, Andrew singles out Sir David Petrie (1941-1946) for special praise. Petrie took over the agency in 1941 during a period marked by serious disarray, poor morale, and uncertain leadership. By war's end in 1945, he could boast that MI5 had completely neutralized German subversion. A large part of the effort involved the famous Double-Cross (or XX) System. Overseen by a committee of intelligence agents headed by Oxford don turned MI5 officer J. C. Masterman, this operation made use of decryptions from the German Enigma code machines to identify and either "turn" or deceive German spies on British territory.

MI5 also provided assistance in a number of other projects during World War II, one of the most memorable of which was Operation Mincemeat. The brainchild of

MI5 officer Charles Cholmondeley, the ingenious operation involved floating a corpse ashore on the coast of Spain in late April, 1943. Attached to its wrist was a briefcase containing documents alluding to a planned Allied landing in Greece. The documents (and various other papers in the corpse's pockets) were prepared so skillfully that the Germans who obtained them from their Spanish sympathizers were completely fooled, and they were thus unprepared for the actual landing in Sicily. (The episode was later described by Ewen Montagu in the 1953 book *The Man Who Never Was: The Story of Operation Mincemeat* and dramatized in a 1956 motion picture of the same name.)

While MI5's war years were largely successful, its early Cold War years—during which the Soviet Union and its satellites became Britain's principal enemies—were marked by failures and scandals. One such case involved Klaus Fuchs, a German-born naturalized British physicist who worked on the Manhattan Project's creation of atomic weapons in Los Alamos, New Mexico. In all, Fuchs was vetted by MI5 on three separate occasions—one of them dealing specifically with his involvement with the Manhattan Project—before he confessed in 1950 to passing crucial secrets about the atomic and hydrogen bombs to the Soviets.

Soon afterward came the unmasking of five "moles," or double agents, within MI5: Kim Philby, Guy Burgess, Donald Maclean, Anthony Blunt, and John Cairncross. The five, says Andrew, constituted the most skilled group of British agents ever recruited by an enemy. All had been turned in the 1930's during their years at Cambridge University or shortly afterward. With the exception of Cairncross, who served in the Secret Intelligence Service (MI6), all were MI5 agents. Philby had risen to become liaison to the United States' Central Intelligence Agency (CIA), while Blunt was a distinguished art historian and held the title of surveyor of the king's (later, the queen's) pictures.

Thanks to the decoding of a Soviet telegram in 1951, suspicion fell first upon Maclean, who made his escape with Burgess in late May. Their defection to the Soviet Union implicated Philby, but British interrogators were divided as to whether he was indeed a spy, and there was no direct evidence. Subsequently employed at a low level by MI6 in Lebanon, Philby escaped on a Soviet freighter in 1963. Cairncross made a partial confession while in the United States in 1964, returning to Britain only in 1970. Blunt also confessed in 1964, but his role was not revealed publicly until 1979.

The work of the five double agents was costly to Britain in terms of lost intelligence, and their unmasking further damaged MI5's morale, as well as its relations with the CIA. (Feelings ran so high that some MI5 officers even suspected their own director general, Sir Roger Hollis, of being a Soviet mole.) Nevertheless, Andrew argues that the Soviet Union handled the spies carelessly, asserting that neither MI5 nor MI6 would have been so incompetent had their positions been reversed.

One of the most bizarre episodes in MI5's history involved Harold Wilson, who served two terms during the 1960's and 1970's as prime minister. Andrew confirms that MI5 maintained a file on Wilson detailing, among many other matters, his indiscreet association with various Soviet citizens, including some KGB officers. The service was also concerned that several of the prime minister's business friends were dishonest or vulnerable to blackmail by Soviet espionage agents. Andrew judges that these concerns were well founded and goes on to describe Wilson's troubling dismissal of the Security Service's repeated warnings.

Wilson grew increasingly paranoid during his second term, becoming convinced that a cadre of former MI5 officers was plotting against him, possibly with the help of the CIA and its South African equivalent. He hired private detectives to investigate officials who he believed were behind press attacks on his political allies. He even refused to speak in the restroom of his official residence without turning on all the faucets, thus interfering with the microphones that he imagined had been hidden in the ceiling.

Toward the end of the Cold War, MI5 turned its attention to myriad terrorist organizations, some likely to be well-known to readers, some not. These included the Palestinian Liberation Organization, the Marxist-Leninist Armenian Secret Army for the Liberation of Armenia, the Algerian Armed Islamic Group, and so on. In the opening years of the twenty-first century, al-Qaeda became a primary focus. Long before the group's September 11, 2001, attacks on the United States, MI5 had identified Osama bin Laden as a financier (but not a leader) of terrorism and had opened a file on him in 1995.

As the current director general of MI5, Jonathan Evans, makes clear in his foreword to *Defend the Realm*, Andrew's book is an authorized but not an official work. Andrew was left free to draw his own conclusions, relying not only on an enormous archive of Security Service records—which run to nearly 400,000 paper files—but also on myriad other sources. However, Andrew cautions that the clearance of his text was a protracted affair, and some material was excised from the book before it could be published. What such material included is unknowable except to those in a position to read between the lines.

While MI5's early years were distinguished by something approaching a spirit of adventure and more than a few episodes of farce, its more recent, terror-focused activities make for grimmer reading. Although Andrew writes fluently, *Defend the Realm* is not for casual readers or the faint of heart. Weighing in at nearly three-and-one-half pounds, it runs to over one thousand pages of detailed description and analysis and includes over one hundred pages of notes in small print. It is enlivened by numerous illustrations, and readers who find themselves lost in the text will find some help in a series of appendixes listing the service's directors and directors generals and outlining the nomenclature and responsibilities of the service's various divisions over time.

Grove Koger

Review Sources

Booklist 106, no. 7 (December 1, 2009): 8.
The Daily Telegraph, October 13, 2009, p. 25.

The Economist 392, no. 8652 (October 10, 2009): p. 87.
Evening Standard, October 29, 2009, p. 30.
Financial Times, October 10, 2009, p. 14.
The Guardian, October 10, 2009, p. 9.
The Independent, October 16, 2009, p. 26.
Mail on Sunday, October 18, 2009, p. 13.
The Observer, October 11, 2009, p. 19.
The Times (London), October 10, 2009, p. 10.

DELIVER US FROM EVIL
The Slavery Question in the Old South

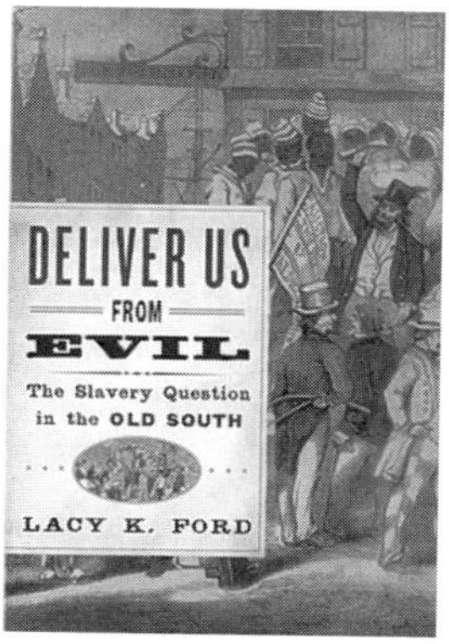

Author: Lacy K. Ford (1952-)
Publisher: Oxford University Press (New York). 673 pp. $34.95
Type of work: History
Time: 1787 to the mid-1830's
Locale: Southern United States

A study of southern ideas, arguments, and debates on the question of slavery, from the drafting of the U.S. Constitution in 1787 to the age of Andrew Jackson in the mid-1830's

In the massive and detailed study *Deliver Us from Evil*, Lacy K. Ford draws upon a wide array of primary sources, including newspapers, sermons, speeches, pamphlets, government documents, and legislative records, to recapture the contradictory and shifting ideas and attitudes on slavery in the South in the early years of the Republic. Ford explores conflicting perspectives in the political, intellectual, religious, economic, and social thought that reverberated throughout the Old South, revealing that attitudes toward slavery were hardly monolithic. Instead, these attitudes adapted to growing opposition from slaves, abolitionists, and free blacks.

Ford sets out to examine "how masters struggled with the contradictions of maintaining a brutal and oppressive system of human bondage in a republic founded on the principles of freedom and equality and how the enslaved used those contradictions to resist the slaveholders' domination and control." To frame the examination of the slavery question in the Old South, Ford divides the region into the upper South (Virginia, Maryland, Delaware, Kentucky, Missouri, Tennessee, and North Carolina) and the lower South (South Carolina, Georgia, Alabama, Mississippi, and Louisiana). By 1830, slaves accounted for more than 40 percent of the population of the lower South, while in the upper South slaves were less than one-third of the total population.

The upper South strained to make slavery compatible with the promises of the Declaration of Independence and the principles of political egalitarianism contained in the Constitution and the Bill of Rights. Condemning slavery, Patrick Henry asked why "at a time when the rights of humanity are defined and understood with precision, In a country, above all others, fond of liberty," citizens would adopt "a principle as repugnant to humanity as it is inconsistent with the bible, and destructive to liberty."

Encapsulating this section of his study, Ford writes that in the

> founding era, republican ideals, Christian morality, fear of slave unrest, and troubling questions about the long-term economic viability of the area's slave economy all pushed upper South whites to question a perpetual commitment to slavery as a labor system.

Lacy K. Ford is professor of history at the University of South Carolina. In 1989, the Southern Historical Association awarded Ford its Francis Butler Simkins Book Prize for Origins of Southern Radicalism: The South Carolina Upcountry, 1800-1860 *(1988). He is editor of* A Companion to the Civil War and Reconstruction *(2005).*

Ford reminds his readers, however, just how deeply entrenched the right to own slaves had become in the minds of slave owners. John Breckinridge of Kentucky opposed calls in 1799 to alter the state constitution regarding slavery, asking indignantly what was "the difference whether I am robbed of my horse by a highwayman or of my slave by a set of people called Convention." Almost forty years later, the governor of South Carolina would declare that "slavery is the corner-stone of our republican edifice."

In the summer of 1800, the first of several armed insurrections terrorized southern whites. Gabriel, a skilled slave blacksmith, organized a rebellion near Richmond, Virginia, but was betrayed by fellow-slave informants. At first, Gabriel evaded capture, but thirty alleged conspirators were arrested and given what Ford labels "so-called trials." Twenty were promptly executed. A month later, Gabriel suffered the same fate.

The reaction among most southerners was to defend slavery even more tenaciously. A writer in the *Virginia Herald* paradoxically reasoned that, since slavery was "a monster—the most horrible of monsters," it required tight control. One slaveowner insisted that the "right of property in a slave was the same as that in a home, or other personal thing."

The second major slave uprising, the German Coast slave revolt, erupted in Louisiana in 1811. Two hundred slaves burned three plantations and killed and wounded several whites. Troops moved in, and at least 115 slaves were killed or executed in the suppression and punishment of the rebellion. A hastily organized "court" sentenced guilty slaves to be shot and have their heads placed on stakes "as a terrible example to all who would disturb public tranquility in the future."

The reaction in the upper South was to expand what Ford calls the "whiteness" of society by practicing paternalism in the short run and gradual manumission, colonization, and diffusion in the long run. Under paternalism, the master was seen as a "benevolent patriarch" who presided over "three interlocking domesticities—his blood family, the slave families, and the plantation community family." Domestic slavery was redefined as the "social subordination of women and slaves" to protect and enhance "the liberties of white men."

Ford devotes considerable space to the emergence of paternalism, which encouraged that slaves be recognized as human beings, regardless of their "inferiority." Paternalism saw the master as the "steward" of his plantation and slaves as entitled to nurture their families and religion. It sought to make "slave society work humanely as well as profitably."

In the cyclical history of slavery that Ford continuously reveals, paternalism was contested and resisted. Ironically, the presence of a small but visible cadre of successful free blacks challenged the very foundation of both slavery and paternalism because it "suggested that, under some circumstances, blacks could take care of themselves quite well, better even than many whites." Consequently, some states banned the immigration of free blacks.

In 1822, South Carolina was rocked by the third major revolt that Ford explores in detail, this time feeding the fear of free blacks. Denmark Vesey, who bought his freedom in 1800 after winning fifteen hundred dollars in a lottery, became a blacksmith and joined the Second Presbyterian Church in 1817. Five years later, Vesey's plans to lead a slave uprising were scuttled by an informant. Following what Ford calls "nothing that remotely resembled a trial," Vesey and six others were tried, convicted, and hanged. A defender of the process readily agreed that no free white man could have been tried behind closed doors and without being confronted by witnesses, but he declared that "slaves are not entitled to these rights" and free blacks "are treated by laws in all respects in the like manner of slaves."

The Vesey plot prompted many to complain about the growing leniency in the treatment of slaves and the danger posed by slave literacy and black Christianity. Others, however, found it hard to explain how slaveholders could be Christians and Christians could be slaveholders. The latter concerns succumbed to the former, leading to the enactment of laws making it a crime for slaves to learn to read and write or to assemble even for religious purposes unless whites were also present. One defender of slavery insisted that literacy rendered the slave "dissatisfied with his lot and invited insubordination."

Meanwhile, abolitionists stepped up their opposition to slavery. In 1829, the highly influential pamphlet *Appeal in Four Articles* was published by David Walker, a free black born in North Carolina who had migrated to Massachusetts. It was widely distributed throughout the South. Trained in the Christian faith, Walker issued a withering indictment not only of slavery but also the emerging colonization movement (supported by Thomas Jefferson and others), declaring that "America is more our country than it is the whites—we have enriched it with our blood and tears." Walker's pamphlet posed such a threat to the institution of slavery that several states responded to it. Georgia made it a crime punishable by death for slaves or free blacks to assist in the circulation of any written material that might incite "insurrection, conspiracy or resistence" to slavery.

Easily the most famous slave revolt was the one led by Nat Turner, a slave who worked on a farm in Southhampton County, Virginia. Turner's parents taught him to read and write, and he came to believe that God had chosen him for great work. On the evening of August 21, 1831, Turner and six accomplices launched a bloody insurrection in which they killed fifty-five whites during a seventy-two-hour rampage. The response was what Ford calls "a frenzied white reign of terror," killing at least thirty-nine blacks, many of whom had little or no connection to the revolt. One of the murdered slaves had actually saved the life of his owner's wife. Eventually, eighteen blacks were apprehended, convicted, and hanged, while fourteen others were convicted and transported out of state. Turner himself eluded capture for over two months until he too was caught, convicted, and hanged.

As the South was reeling from the Nat Turner uprising, abolitionists continued their attacks on slavery. Beginning in 1835, the American Antislavery Society sent tens of thousands of pamphlets and tracts to southern destinations through the new U.S. postal system, triggering the outrage of slave owners, who condemned the effort as a "wicked plan of exciting the negroes to insurrection and to massacre." A Tuscaloosa grand jury went so far as to indict the editor of the *Emancipator* newspaper in absentia for sending the publications into Alabama. Other steps to undermine opposition to slavery, such as eliminating the right of free blacks to vote in state elections, drew outspoken criticism from some quarters. "That the right of suffrage, on the part of the free people of color, was totally abrogated," the *Raleigh Register* editorialized, "is a source of regret to us."

Buffeted by violent revolts and scathing criticism, the South renewed its defense of slavery, but it did so with what Ford calls an "ideological reconfiguration." He concludes his comprehensive study by examining three key elements. First, that slavery was justified by irreversible racial differences. One defender claimed that the "negro is from his intellectual and moral organization incapable of being civilized or enjoying freedom; utterly incompetent to become a citizen of a civilized community." Second, Ford explains that slave owners saw slavery as "the best foundation for liberty and democracy among whites" that protected "the independence of whites by preventing the development of a dependent white working class in the region."

Finally, Ford posits that the South's best defense of its humanitarianism against the mounting abolitionist moral attack was "a full embrace of paternalism both as the ideology of slaveholding and as the best practice for slave management."

Deliver Us from Evil is a monumental work of historical research and analysis. At times, the level of detail is so granular, such as reporting the individual votes taken by legislative subcommittees in various states, that some readers may yearn for more of the human drama that Ford elsewhere so ably recounts. Also, the author never fully explains why he halts his study thirty years before the Civil War, leaving readers to question whether Southern attitudes toward slavery remained static or changed in the course of the next three decades. These flaws aside, the book is prodigious in its scholarship and illuminating in its perspective. Ford has taken a topic that many have assumed they understood and subjected it to a deeper and more penetrating level of analysis. No student of slavery or the intellectual history of the American South can afford to overlook this important work.

Stephen F. Rohde

Review Sources

Library Journal 134, no. 14 (September 1, 2009): 124-125.
The New York Times Book Review, September 20, 2009, p. 14.
Publishers Weekly 256, no. 25 (June 22, 2009): 38-39.

DIGGING
The Afro-American Soul of American Classical Music

Author: Amiri Baraka (1934-)
Publisher: University of California Press (Berkeley).
411 pp. $26.95; paperback 17.95
Type of work: Music, essays

In this important collection of essays published since 1989, Baraka argues persuasively that jazz, as created and developed by creative African American composers and musicians from Scott Joplin to the present, constitutes the authentic classical music of the United States

Principal personages:

LOUIS ARMSTRONG (1901-1971), a beloved American jazz trumpeter whose solo career lasted fifty years
JOHN COLTRANE (1926-1967), an American saxophonist whose 1964 masterpiece *Love Supreme* illustrates the importance of African music in the African diaspora
MILES DAVIS (1926-1991), an important American jazz trumpeter
DUKE ELLINGTON (1899-1974), a popular jazz composer, pianist, and bandleader who is generally considered to be the greatest American composer
SCOTT JOPLIN (1867?-1917), a composer generally viewed as the founder of jazz
THELONIUS MONK (1917-1982), an important jazz pianist and composer
SUN RA (1914-1993), a gifted composer who combined African religious mysticism and experimental jazz
NINA SIMONE (1933-2003), a jazz singer famous for her civil rights songs and her introduction of African motifs into her jazz songs
BESSIE SMITH (1894-1937), a great jazz singer who was often called "the Empress of the Blues"

Digging collects essays written over a twenty-year period in which Amiri Baraka explores jazz not only as the distinctively American art form but also as the United States' version of classical music. To make this argument, he must successfully position the jazz tradition alongside the classical traditions of other countries, such as Germany, France, and Russia, that have recognized classical lineages. Generations of gifted classical composers in Europe expanded on earlier musical conventions in order to create new musical works that made use of existing musical traditions.

German classical music, for example, developed from the highly intellectual and finely wrought fugues and suites of Johann Sebastian Bach (1685-1750) into the romantic and emotionally powerful symphonies of Ludwig von Beethoven (1770-1827). Beethoven found inspiration in the sung cantatas and masses when he intro-

Poet, playwright, and essayist Amiri Baraka (formerly LeRoi Jones) has written extensively on jazz and African American culture. A former professor of Africana studies at Stony Brook University, he is a member of the National Academy of Arts and Letters and has served as the poet laureate of New Jersey.

duced the words from the "Ode to Joy" by Friedrich von Schiller (1759-1805) in the final movement of his Ninth Symphony. The recurring musical themes in Beethoven's last five symphonies inspired Richard Wagner (1813-1883) to use highly evocative leitmotifs in order to describe the unique traits of the major characters in his operas. Bach, Beethoven, and Wagner created their music in Germany, where different styles of classical music were appreciated and where composers frequently wrote creative musical imitations and variations on well-known classical works.

Improvisation often played an integral part in performances and interpretations as early as the first half of the eighteenth century. Many people who attended the Lutheran church of St. Thomas in Leipzig, where Bach played the organ for Sunday services, stated that Bach played well-known Lutheran hymns in highly imaginative ways, and many parishioners were not pleased with his creative improvisations. Pianists and violinists who played concertos by Wolfgang Amadeus Mozart or Beethoven felt comfortable including their own codas, which they added near the end of their performances.

Such improvisations and creative changes to the original score extended well into the twentieth century. The eminent Viennese violinist Fritz Kreisler (1875-1962), who performed regularly in New York City during the first four decades of the twentieth century before moving there permanently at the outbreak of World War II, surprised concertgoers by adding his own codas to extremely well-known violin concertos by Beethoven, Mozart, Niccolò Paganini (1782-1840), and Felix Mendelssohn (1809-1847). Kreisler even performed his own reinterpretation of the famous African American spiritual "Nobody Knows the Trouble I've Seen." His was a highly intellectual Austrian variation on this famous American hymn.

Were one to compare Kreisler's rendition of the spiritual with the very earthy and better-known 1962 interpretation by Louis Armstrong, one could conclude that Kreisler does not understand the African American origin of this hymn. While it is totally Eurocentric, however, Kreisler's rendition of the spiritual does reveal his sincere attempt to understand the music of the country where he spent the last two decades of his life. New York City concertgoers could appreciate creative improvisations of famous works not just by classical European composers but also by twentieth century jazz composers.

While Americans may appreciate the rich complexity of classical music from distant European countries, they understand that a love of classical music is a taste acquired by those who are interested in certain foreign cultures. European classical music is aesthetically very pleasing, but it is not American music. Baraka argues persuasively in *Digging* that jazz is the only music created and developed in the United States by Americans. He also points out that it is a historical fact that early jazz musicians and composers were almost exclusively African Americans.

In the book's opening essay, Baraka draws readers' attention to the inextricable links between Africa and America in the development of jazz. In this essay on the West African word *griot*, or "storyteller," he points out that a *griot* was much more than an oral historian who transmitted traditional African values from one generation to another. A *griot* also expressed the extraordinary joy and inner strength felt by those who nevertheless suffered greatly at the hands of their oppressors. Baraka argues that jazz musicians are in their own way *griot* who smile while simultaneously conveying to listeners the profound suffering of dignified African Americans. Those African Americans' lives, Baraka believes, are enriched by liberating music designed to remind them of their rich African heritage.

Baraka also directly links African tradition to the joyous "shouting" in African American churches, where people learn about both the Gospels and the "God Spell." Jazz, which Baraka often calls "that music" or "our music," has a mesmerizing effect on listeners. It elevates them while at the same time bringing them extraordinary bliss.

In an essay titled "Ritual and Performance," Baraka effectively contrasts the performance of classical European music with the performance of jazz. On one hand, those learning to play classical European music can be taught how to hold their instrument, how to dress, and how to remain stoic on the stage. On the other hand, it is not sufficient for jazz musicians to learn how to play their instruments. They must also learn to feel the intensity of the music and adapt their performances based on the reactions of listeners. Improvisation is essential in jazz, while it is largely discouraged in performances of classical European music.

Baraka even associates the experience of performing or listening to jazz to "religious ecstasy." With the exception of Bach, who created and performed religious music designed to fill an entire church with joyful sound and to provoke an intense emotional reaction from churchgoers, very few classical European composers strove to produce such a strong sense of ecstasy in their listeners. Baraka discusses at great length the myriad links between jazz and experiences of religion in African American churches. In traditional West African societies, from which most first-generation slaves were kidnapped and transported to America, people generally believe that the past, the present, and the future coexist. This is an alien concept to Americans of European descent, who consider time to be linear. In jazz and in traditional African American churches, however, the coexistence of various time frames serves to remind people of their place in an extremely old culture that must adapt once again to a changing world.

The title of this volume of essays, *Digging: The Afro-American Soul of American Classical Music*, is richly evocative. Like all great poets, Baraka is sensitive to the many levels of meaning that words possess. He is figuratively "digging" into the recordings and oral histories of major jazz musicians whom he never heard live. The word "digging" also evokes the meaning of "enjoying," as in the expression "I am really digging it."

Baraka was born in 1934 and therefore had to rely on recordings that were not always of the highest quality to experience the performance techniques of such influential jazz musicians as Scott Joplin and Bessie Smith. Although he recognized the significance of their contributions to early jazz, from ragtime in the late nineteenth and early twentieth centuries to the blues of the 1920's and 1930's, Baraka also understood the harsh racism with which both artists had to deal during their years performing jazz. American opera houses of Joplin's day refused to perform his great opera *Treemonisha* (pb. 1911, pr. 1972) not only because of the composer's skin color but especially because its major characters are all African Americans. The first complete performance of *Treemonisha* took place in 1972, a full fifty-five years after Joplin's death. Although *Treemonisha* is now considered to be the greatest American opera, Joplin's contemporaries knew of him only as the composer of rags.

Racism even contributed to the death of Bessie Smith. On September 26, 1937, she suffered serious but not fatal injuries as a result of a car accident near Clarksdale, Mississippi. Ambulances came from Clarksdale's hospital for whites and its hospital for African Americans. The ambulance drivers argued about who should take Smith to which hospital. The delay caused her to lose so much blood that her situation was hopeless when she was finally treated in Clarksdale's hospital for African Americans.

Baraka describes well how jazz developed from ragtime to blues, swing, big band, bebop, cool jazz, hard bop, modal jazz, free jazz, jazz fusion, and experimental jazz, but he also reminds his readers that these categories refer only to general jazz trends and do not describe the genius of individual jazz musicians and composers. He reminds them as well that many great jazz musicians did not limit themselves to one form of jazz but rather kept recreating themselves. Miles Davis, for example, began by performing bebop and then evolved into an original performer of cool jazz, hard bop, and eventually electric jazz.

Baraka laments that white record producers tried to make jazz more acceptable to white listeners by releasing more records by rather unimaginative white jazz musicians and fewer records by highly creative African American jazz musicians. In his essay "The American Popular Song," he also observes that, in the first "talking film," *The Jazz Singer* (1927), a white actor named Al Jolson sings supposedly jazz songs in blackface. It is possible but not very likely that Al Jolson in blackface made jazz more acceptable to racists in 1927, but this film offends modern moviegoers because of its overt racism.

There is much to recommend in this excellent volume of essays. In his theoretical essays, Baraka describes very well the profound likenesses between black African music, traditions, and spirituality and jazz as composed and performed by generations of talented African American jazz musicians. He also describes very well the true originality of many famous and some unjustly neglected African American jazz musicians, from Scott Joplin to the present.

Edmund J. Campion

Review Sources

American Book Review 30 (July-August, 2009): 19.
Ebony, June, 2009, p. 45.
Library Journal 134, no. 9 (May 15, 2009): 75.
New York Amsterdam News 100, no. 42 (October 15, 2009): 25-35

DIGITAL BARBARISM
A Writer's Manifesto

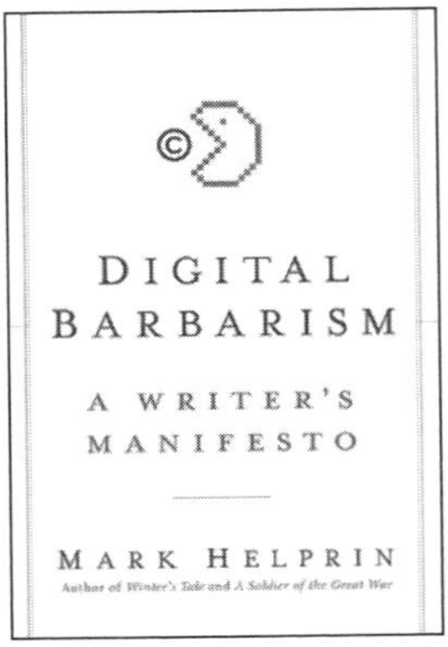

Author: Mark Helprin (1947-)
Publisher: Harper (New York). 232 pp. $24.99
Type of work: Memoir, philosophy, current affairs
Time: The late twentieth and early twenty-first centuries
Locale: United States

A memoir of Helprin's development as a writer, a defense of copyright law, and an explication—occasionally intemperate—of his distrust of the Internet and its supporters, which distrust had its origin in a venomous response to one of Helprin's articles

The seesaw of Mark Helprin's title and subtitle, *Digital Barbarism: A Writer's Manifesto* has a colon as fulcrum, the title encapsulating what he sees as the nature and tone of the age, the subtitle embodying his reaction and resistance. For Helprin, the weightier becomes the digital zeitgeist of immediacy, collaborative endeavor, and reliance on the image, the more necessary become the humanistic qualities of leisurely organic growth, individual effort, and memory, especially memory of words. All these qualities are to be based on knowledge of and respect for the slowly accumulating achievements of the human past, and all, according to the author, are kicking hopelessly in the air in this cultural moment.

Helprin begins with two illustrative vignettes, the first imagining the life of a Californian of 2028, the "director of a small firm that supplies algorithms for the detection of damage in and the restoration of molecular memories in organic computation." This man's work is performed exclusively through the management of data links. Outside work, his relationship with his wife is temporarily fraught: during their last amatory encounter he had imposed upon her body in virtual sex not the appearance of a porn star but that of a former girlfriend. He jets out to see her in Alaska, where she is now on vacation, taking with him a "slim leather-bound portfolio" by means of which he can access everything ever printed or logged, including a remark about Descartes he half-remembers having made and wants to use again. This man's life, although exciting and physically easy, is frenetic, sometimes alarmingly so. There can, however, be no going back to the days of his father and grandfather. It would be career suicide not to be on the technological cutting edge, and it would also be personally desolating, so hooked is he on the constant buzz of his technological existence.

Counterposed to this picture is one of an English politician of 1908, on vacation by Lake Como. A letter from the prime minister will take eight days to reach him and an hour and three-quarters to answer, including the making of a fair copy. This answer will incorporate an observation about Descartes the politician had once made that at first he could not recall. He was able to remember it, though, because his education trained him to remember words not only in his own language but also in Latin, Greek, French, and German. The politician's experience of making love (as it can justly be called in this case) to his wife must wait some hours after the sight of her that first arouses his desire. For Helprin, the life of the past Englishman is infinitely preferable to that of the imagined future Californian. The politician knows the meaning of patience and tranquillity. He can "savor" the world in which he lives.

Mark Helprin is author of many books, essays, and short stories. He has served in the Israeli military and as adviser to Bob Dole's presidential campaign. He was won the National Jewish Book Award, the Prix de Rome, the Peggy V. Helmerich Distinguished Author Award, and a Guggenheim Fellowship.

The seed of *Digital Barbarism* was an article Helprin wrote for *The New York Times* about copyright, which he approves of and would like to see modestly extended. Helprin wonders why a man who creates a flour mill or a newspaper is able to will the fruit of his labors to his heirs, all due taxes having been paid, whereas a man whose life has been spent creating a number of copyrights is not able to do so, the fruit of his labors accruing to the government seventy years after his death. Despite the irresponsible title given the article by a *New York Times* editor, "A Great Idea Lives Forever: Shouldn't Its Copyright?" Helprin says that he does not dissent from the words of the Constitution, that Congress has the power "To promote the Progress of Science and useful Arts, by securing *for limited times* to Authors and Inventors the exclusive Right to their respective Writings and Discoveries" ("The italics are mine," he notes, "the capitalization James Madison's."). He merely disagrees about how long the "limited times" should be and advocates slight extension of copyright on the grounds of inconsistency, there being, he claims, no essential difference between real property and intellectual property.

Perhaps it would be more accurate to say that the seed of Helprin's book was to be found in the reaction to his article, which clearly took him aback and hurt him: The online version was seen by three-quarters of a million readers, and elicited many comments, all critical and many vituperative (such as "Screw you, Helprin!"). Electronic communication, writes the author, is sheltered or even anonymous. Nobody takes a blogger to task in the way one may be taken to task in face-to-face altercation. Furthermore, it is immensely easy to multiply responses electronically, to organize a dehumanized and merciless "flaming" of an unpopular view. Readers who have been on the receiving end of a sustained attempt to jeer and intimidate them into silence will sympathize with Helprin here, and the Internet facilitates such attempts.

Helprin seeks to analyze why a call for the extension of copyright proved inflammatory. He claims that he unwittingly offended a movement, widespread in certain quarters, that opposes not merely the extension of copyright but its very existence. It was the 1999 fight against the recording industry that brought this movement into being. Young people mobilized against record companies because of their wish to enjoy unrestricted music "sharing" (the sneer quotes are Helprin's), along with an equally limitless copying of digital video discs (DVDs) and piracy of software.

This movement was facilitated by a series of moral failings, especially the belief that, because these forms of theft are easy and widespread, their perpetrators are not culpable, as well as a redefining of moral turpitude as virtue because such a redefinition is easier than standing for immutable principles. Thus, digital theft seemed to some to be not merely respectable but also admirable, representing a stand against rich and greedy corporations in favor of the poor and generous (who, Helprin would say, are generous with the goods of others that have been brought into being by talent, risk, and work). Here, then, is the link between "digital barbarism" and a sudden loutish objection to a literate article about copyright.

Public availability is what counts, in the eyes of Helprin's opponents. Helprin himself wishes to stand up for ways of responding to life and creating art that he learned to know and admire in what now seems a past world. He attacks present-day attitudes that he regards as inimical to life and art, such attitudes being fostered by the nature and consequences of the digital revolution, for "discipline, values, and clarity of vision . . . tend to flourish as we grapple with necessity and austerity, and tend to disappear when by virtue of our ingenuity we float free of them."

By repeated characterizations and oppositions, *Digital Barbarism* creates a series of mutually reinforcing contrasts between the way Helprin thinks things ought to be (and considers they actually were or could have been before the advent of the Internet) and the way they too often are now. On one hand, Helprin asserts that the human being is incomparably superior to any machine, "unexcelled as a masterwork of God and nature," and the single, focused, creating, individual consciousness is all. A true writer will invest years in a book, perhaps living in conditions of actual poverty and certainly denied financial or family stability, for writing is a noble "craft and art that was ancient at the time of Jesus, that encompasses the world, and that has evolved by the love and labor of the greatest souls ever to grace the earth."

Not only is the struggling individual the only voice that can create any art worthy of the name according to Helprin, but also the implications of that honesty and striving are societal: It is the individual voice that resists "every form of tyranny, every attempted mechanization of the soul, every great challenge to civilization, and every assault upon human nature"—all evils that can be propagated by the power and misuse of the Internet. Copyright is the legal protector of authors, safeguarding their ability to make a living while standing against the forces of uniformity and safeguarding too the integrity of their texts.

This is the argument defining the good in Helprin's debate, and there can be no doubt of his utter sincerity. It is in the characterizations of his opposition that the occasional problem is to be found. Helprin makes a number of points that will hit home to those of his readers who are roughly the same age as he is and therefore remember a world before computers. Too often, computers do enable their less committed or scrupulous users to cut and paste pieces of what others have written. Too often, the major skill their users acquire can be that of blithely unaware juxtaposition. Although certain "abandonments" ("of grammar, capitalization, punctuation, spelling, et cetera, and the substitution for these things of either nothing or of idiotic and inexpressive pictograms, jargon, and expletives") may well be the products in part of a degraded educational system, as Helprin plausibly claims, they are also surely products of the ease and celerity with which words can be flung onto a screen and then made gratifyingly public.

Helprin's panegyric of pen and ink may seem a little less curmudgeonly in the light of an Internet discourse dominated by formulaic abbreviations such as "LOL" and "ROTFLMAO." However, curmudgeonly it can still seem. His gift for acerbic aphorism can be good fun ("In my education it was assumed that one would read Macauley and study Latin, in much the same way that today it is assumed that a student will know about Harriet Tubman and collect aluminum cans"), and his sustained invective can elicit a sympathetic grin, as when he refers to

> mouth-breathing morons in backwards baseball caps and pants that fall down; Slurpee-sucking geeks who seldom see daylight; . . . women who have lizard tattoos winding from the navel to the nape of the neck; . . . and an entire race of females . . . that speaks in North American Chipmunk and seldom makes a statement without, like, a question at the end?

However, Helprin is still occasionally a little too reminiscent of the odd professor in the faculty lounge whom everybody is reluctant to sit next to and with whom no one wants to be associated.

Helprin exhibits a great deal of idealism, acuity, selfless commitment, skill with prose, and literary address and poise, all slightly but fatally tinged with the aura of eccentric bitterness. He conveys impressive insights into the antihumanistic because antihuman machines that increasingly mold humans' apprehension of the world about them, describing the machines' terrible strengths, "speed, power, compression, instantaneousness, immense capacity, indifference, and automaticity." He advances a telling condemnation of those who consider writing, of all things, "a communal effort, an act of assemblage and additive progression as in adding storeys to a skyscraper or the laying down of a railway track."

All these strengths would read more sweetly and therefore more effectively were he to add a drop or two of charity to his depiction of the forces he contemns and their servants. Helprin's book has received varied reviews, some tepid or hostile. Perhaps the most negative was an Internet response by Lawrence Lessig, himself criticized in *Digital Barbarism.*

M. D. Allen

Review Sources

American Conservative 8, no. 12 (September 1, 2009): 45-46.
Library Journal 134, no. 9 (May 15, 2009): 87.
National Review 61, no. 13 (July 20, 2009): 46-48.
The New York Times, May 19, 2009, p. C6.
The New York Times Book Review, June 21, 2009, p. 13.
The Wall Street Journal, May 1, 2009, p. A15.

DON'T CRY
Stories

Author: Mary Gaitskill (1954-   )
Publisher: Pantheon (New York). 226 pp. $23.95
Type of work: Short fiction

Ten new stories of longing, love, and loneliness by the American writer famous for the collection Bad Behavior

Mary Gaitskill is perhaps best known for her first collection of stories, *Bad Behavior* (1988), which included an often-anthologized, shocking tale about masochism titled "Romantic Weekend" and a story that was adapted into the 2002 film *Secretary*—starring Maggie Gyllenhaal as a mentally ill woman who cuts herself and James Spader as a dominating boss with obsessive tendencies. The two stories alone gave Gaitskill a reputation as a literary bad girl, which was furthered by her revelation that she had been a stripper for a couple of years. In "The Wolf in the Tall Grass," an essay collected in *Why I Write: Thoughts on the Craft of Fiction* (1998), Gaitskill says that she writes because, even when her subject is pain and horror, she, like many others, has a powerful desire to say, "Yes, I see. I feel. I hear. This is what it's like."

Gaitskill's stories in *Don't Cry*, her third collection, do not present clearly delineated narratives. Rather, they resemble essayistic descriptions of ensemble groups, each of which is positioned around one central character's sense of disengagement and despair. The opening story, "College Town, 1980" focuses on four young people living together in Ann Arbor, Michigan, just after the election of Ronald Reagan. The central character, Dolores, has been hospitalized for mental illness and has to wear a scarf because she has taken to pulling out large clumps of her hair. She lives in a communal house with her younger brother Patrick, his girlfriend Lily, and a twenty-one-year-old philosophy student named Mark. The story has no plot; the underlying tension stems from Dolores's depression and the fact that she blames her unhappiness on her former boyfriend's having dumped her. She also blames her father, an adulterous alcoholic, and her mother, who is "murderously unhappy."

Dolores feels particularly persecuted by a waitress in a restaurant she frequents who seems to hate her for no apparent reason. Another submerged conflict in the story is the tension between Patrick and Lily, who are threatening to break up. Dolores sympathizes with Lily, with whom she has desultory conversations about strength and weakness. Lily says that she was glad when Reagan was elected, even though she hates him, because he stands for strength. The story ends with Dolores thinking she will work on her research papers and graduate, feeling that she is strong—but strong like a bombed-out building, stripped and impervious. This is less a story than it is a set piece about young people who feel victimized, helpless, and trapped in a stagnant situation at a certain transitional point in American society.

Mary Gaitskill's stories have been chosen for The Best American Short Stories *and* The O. Henry Prize Stories. *Her collection* Because They Wanted To *(1997) was nominated for the PEN/Faulkner Award, and her novel* Veronica *(2005) was nominated for the National Book Award.*

"An Old Virgin" focuses on Laura, a woman filled with self-loathing who has a habit of walking around her apartment muttering about how ugly and valueless she is. Even while she seems to cope with everyday activities and her job at a medical clinic, she feels like a bug tunneling through the earth with fragile insect legs. Her father is very ill, emaciated, and fragile. He was abused as a child, and he abused his own children in turn. The story's titular character and central metaphor is a forty-three-year-old woman who is given a preliminary examination by Laura. Because the woman is a virgin, Laura wonders what it would be like to be a virgin at her own age of forty. She imagines virginity as the source of her strength, making everything in her extra alive. However, she actually feels that, although her body is alive with strong feelings, the feelings seem broken or incomplete.

After reading such stories about women who either feel sorry for themselves or hate themselves, one may find the title of the story "The Agonized Face" predictable and inevitable. Here, the unhappy women who seem to be Gaitskill's obsessive focus are closer to her own persona as a writer and commentator on contemporary society. The divorced mother of a ten-year-old girl, the narrator has been assigned to write a piece on a feminist author who is giving a talk at an annual literary festival.

The author at the festival, who was once a prostitute, has described prostitutes as feminist fighters against patriarchy. She talks about how she has been treated unfairly by the media, insisting that—although she can understand that it is exciting to imagine eccentric writers engaging in outlandish behavior—she is not such a person. She complains that, by isolating qualities that seem exciting and scary and projecting them onto public figures, media consumers deny those figures' humanity and cheat themselves of life's complexity. One wonders if this speech is a reference to the initial public interest in Gaitskill's work after the publication of *Bad Behavior* created a great deal of publicity based on her prior career as a stripper. (When an interviewer asked Gaitskill if she had ever turned a trick, she replied without hesitation that she had, earning herself a reputation that she has perhaps since regretted.)

Much of "The Agonized Face" reads like a personal essay. It raises the issue of the relationship of feminism to sexuality, pondering whether feminists who celebrate female sexuality have made young women promiscuous or whether feminists who attack traditional patriarchal sex roles have convinced those same young women that there is little or no difference between consensual sex and rape. Various images of Gaitskill's own persona crop up in the story. For example, when the narrator recounts interviewing a topless dancer, a desiccated blonde with desperate intelligence burning in her eyes who refers to Georg Wilhelm Friedrich Hegel and Friedrich Wilhelm Nietzsche, one may be tempted to look at the author photo on the jacket cover of *Don't Cry*, in which Gaitskill stares out at her readers both defensively and belligerently.

Recalling another story she once wrote about a television talk show that depicted stories of rape victims, the narrator wonders if the feminist author was suggesting that rape and being a prostitute are the same thing, concluding, in her essayistic tone, that for the purposes of her "discussion," they are close enough. The article the narrator finally writes takes the feminist writer to task for pretending that female humiliation is an especially smart kind of game and for casually mentioning her experience with prostitution while leaving out the "agonized face" of women's humiliation in modern society. In her article, she metaphorically chases the author down an alley, to stone her and force her to show the face that she denies. She insists that the "agonized face" is one of the few mysteries left to women and must be protected.

One of the humiliations of women is suggested in "Mirror Ball," a self-indulgent grotesque fairytale about a man who, by having sex with a woman and then failing to call her later, "takes her soul." The man, a musician, picks the young woman up with the line that her eyes remind him of a mirror ball in the window of a vintage record store that flashes over the whole street at night. When he does not call her, she tries to feel contempt for him, but she feels that she loves him; that, by having sex with him, she has degraded them both; and that she will never see him again. The story continually recites the woman's feelings of humiliation, pain, anger and fear. However, it does so in pretentious, ponderous language about the loss of her "soul" and the "window of her heart."

One of the more structurally complex stories in the collection is "The Arms and Legs of the Lake." The narrative shifts back and forth between the points of view of several strangers on the same train, including a young man who has just returned from Iraq, another veteran who returned six months earlier, a woman who edits a women's magazine and has been critical of the war, and the conductor of the train. As in many of Gaitskill's stories, the focus is more on the static ensemble of characters than it is on plot or thematic significance.

The collection's title story focuses on a woman whose husband died six months earlier. She accompanies a friend to Addis Ababa, Ethiopia, to adopt a baby outside formal adoption channels. The two women battle the daunting bureaucracy of trying to arrange an independent adoption in the midst of revolution and political upheaval, as the narrator mourns the loss of her husband.

The most experimental story in the book, a story that reads more as an essayistic exploration of connections than as a narrative, is "Folk Song," which creates links between newspaper stories about a sadistic killer, a pair of turtles stolen from a zoo, and a woman who says she is going to have sex with a thousand men, one after another. Meditating on how loathsome it is to turn a sadistic murderer into entertainment, yet how irresistible it is to readers, Gaitskill seems to reveal one of the central aspects of her fiction—the morbid fascination people feel at the horrors that sometimes confront them. Even though those who disapprove of torture, she suggests, cannot resist scanning a newspaper story for descriptions of it.

One of the shortest stories in the collection, and in many ways one of the most affecting, is "The Little Boy," which focuses on a woman returning home after visiting her forty-two-year-old daughter. While waiting for her airplane, she becomes fascinated with a small boy accompanied by his mother. The woman recollects episodes of cruelty in her life, such as when her sisters would go to places where there were ugly people simply to make fun of them and when her grandfather killed kittens by putting them in a bag and slamming them against a wall. She is especially tortured by memories of her husband and his bouts with suicidal depression and violence, and she tries to find some hope and reassurance in the little boy.

When the boy's mother asks the protagonist to watch him for a few minutes while she checks on her flight, the boy says he has heard her talking to herself in one of the airport corridors. When she tells him she talks to someone she used to love, he says he talks to his father, who is fighting in Iraq. However, when the mother returns, she says she does not have a husband. The woman is encouraged by a boy so full of hope that he makes up a father of whom he can be proud. The story ends with some promise that the woman can reconcile her ambiguous feelings about her abusive husband and her painful relationships with her daughters. In contrast to all the young women in this collection who complain and assign blame to others, this one older woman closes her eyes and remembers her daughter's good night kiss, dreaming a dream that began with that kiss.

Gaitskill writes for a serious literary audience, rather than for the more casual consumers of so-called chick lit, and she strives to confront issues of concern to contemporary readers. However, her focus on unhappy women who cannot seem to find either fulfillment or hope for the future, combined with her didacticism and discursive style, sometimes make her fiction unpleasant and unrewarding to read.

Charles E. May

Review Sources

Booklist 105, no. 14 (March 15, 2009): 40.
The Boston Globe, April 19, 2009, p. B5.
Kirkus Reviews 77, no. 2 (January 15, 2009): 55.
Library Journal 134, no. 1 (January 1, 2009): 86.
Los Angeles Times, March 22, 2009, p. E10.
The New York Times Book Review, March 22, 2009, p. 12.
Newsweek 153, no. 15 (April 23, 2009): 59.
Publishers Weekly 256, no. 4 (January 26, 2009): 96.

THE DYNAMITE CLUB
How a Bombing in Fin-de-Siècle Paris Ignited the Age of Modern Terror

Author: John Merriman (1946-   )
Publisher: Houghton Mifflin (Boston). Illustrated. 252 pp. $26.00
Type of work: History
Time: 1890's
Locale: Paris, France

This study recounts the anarchist movement in fin-de-siècle Paris, with special attention to the "propaganda by the deed" anarchist Émile Henry; it also addresses the issue of why terrorists kill innocent victims

Principal personages:

ÉMILE HENRY, a bourgeois intellectual and anarchist who bombed the Café Terminus
SIXTE CASSE HENRY (FORTUNÉ), Émile's father, a socialist prominent in the Commune
ROSE COUBET HENRY, Émile's mother, owner of a very small inn in Brévanne
JEAN CHARLES HENRY (FORTUNÉ), Émile's older brother, an anarchist
ELISA GAUTHEY, Émile's unrequited love
FRANÇOIS CLAUDIUS KOENIGSTEIN (RAVACHOL), an anarchist bomber
AUGUSTE VAILLANT, an unemployed worker who tossed a bomb into the Chamber of Deputies
LOUIS DEIBLER (MONSIEUR DE PARIS), Paris's chief executioner

The Dynamite Club is a perceptive portrayal of fin-de-siècle Paris. In this historical account of the period, John Merriman presents the development of anarchism as a reaction to poverty and political exclusion. He also addresses the issue of terrorism and the motivation behind it and elucidates the fact that repression and execution do not deter terrorists. Merriman defines modern terrorism as an assault upon innocent victims. He recognizes that the terrorism anchored in religious difference rather than class distinction that is faced by Western society in the twenty-first century is of a very different nature than that which spread through late nineteenth century European society, especially in Paris. He seeks, however, to identify why the violence of terrorism becomes the driving force for certain individuals, and draws the limited lessons of the past that may apply to the present.

The Dynamite Club traces the brief life of Émile Henry, who was guillotined on May 21, 1894, for the bombing of the Café Terminus, in which one person was killed, and for an earlier police-station bombing in which two police officers lost their lives.

Merriman blends together a detailed account of Émile's life, a history of anarchism and its advocates, and a psychological and sociological inquiry into the anarchists' advocacy of violence, particularly of violence directed against random victims. In the prologue, Merriman immediately depicts the key event of his book, the bombing of the Café Terminus. He then states his reason for writing the book, to find out why Émile Henry bombed the café.

John Merriman is the Charles Seymour Professor of History at Yale University and author of several books on modern French history, including The Margins of City Life *(1991) and* The Agony of the Republic: Repression of the Left in Revolutionary France, 1848-1851 *(1978).*

Merriman proposes that there is a connection, although an elusive one, between the terrorism of the Islamic fundamentalists in the twenty-first century and the terrorism spread by the nineteenth century anarchists. He argues that the story of the late nineteenth century is the story of a changing world and that Émile was no ordinary terrorist. He was a bourgeois intellectual; his family was propertied, and he did not target symbols of oppressive political authority but rather diners in a Parisian café. For Merriman, Émile Henry was the first modern terrorist.

Having established the premise of his text, Merriman next familiarizes his readers with fin-de-siècle Paris. He describes the large boulevards created by Georges Haussman. These boulevards literally destroyed the people's Paris, where insurgents had been able to disappear during the city's various previous rebellions, starting with the French Revolution. Haussman redesigned the city, whose narrow streets were incapable of accommodating modern volumes of traffic, creating wide boulevards through which people and commodities could flow with ease throughout the city. These new boulevards enabled the government to suppress rebellion readily, as it did with the Paris Commune.

Merriman details the great wealth enjoyed by the Parisian bourgeoisie, particularly their elegant clothing and jewels. He describes as well the city's magnificent buildings (especially the Opéra); its plush carriages; and the lights illuminating fabulously luxurious shops, cafés, and restaurants located in the center of Paris. To these, he sharply contrasts the dreary and dark suburbs, where the impoverished working class lived in the most abject conditions. Workers walked from the suburbs to their jobs serving the wealthy bourgeoisie, jobs that could be lost at the whim of their employers and that seldom provided enough money to feed workers' families. The Paris presented by Merriman is a Paris of sharp and bitter contrasts and of division, where some live in great luxury and others barely survive. Readers become immersed in the Paris of Émile Henry, where hatred of the bourgeoisie and of governmental authority grew ever stronger within the working class.

In the next chapter, "The Second Son of the Exile," Merriman begins the story of Émile himself. This chapter and the next two, "Love Engenders Hate" and "Dynamite Deeds," examine Émile's development as an anarchist. "The Second Son of the Exile" recounts the significant happenings in Émile's life, including his father's death when he was ten, the hardships endured by the family with only Mme. Henry to provide for them, Émile's successes at school, and his failure in the oral exam for admission to the École Polytechnique. Émile worked in Venice with his uncle Jean Bordenove, a civil engineer, and he associated closely with his brother Fortuné, who had become an anarchist. He experienced an unrequited love for Elisa Gauthey. In this chapter, Merriman also reviews the thought of the anarchists Pierre-Joseph Prudhon, Mikhail Bakunin, and Peter Kropotkin, with whose writings Émile was becoming familiar.

In "Love Engenders Hate," Merriman continues his history of the anarchist movement both in Paris and throughout Europe. The Paris he describes is a Paris filled with anarchist groups, meetings, and newspapers and the anarchist ideas of Elisée Reclus, Émile's brother Fortuné, and François Claudius Koenigstein, known as Ravachol. Paris at the fin-de-siècle was filled with hatred—hatred of the rich who scorned and exploited the poor, hatred of the politicians who enacted oppressive laws and lived by corruption, and hatred of the police who enforced the injustice of society.

Merriman presents an extensive review of anarchist activities in France, the government's severe measures of repression, the trials and executions of anarchists, and, finally, the anarchists' turn to a philosophy of propaganda-by-deed, which employed dynamite to call for societal change. "Dynamite Deeds" continues this account of anarchist activities. Throughout these chapters, Merriman weaves together the general development of Parisian anarchism with the personal story of Émile, who became devoted to that anarchism—and very skilled with explosives.

In his final chapters, Merriman once again concentrates on Émile Henry. Merriman recounts Émile's attempt to blow up the offices of the Carmaux Mining Company in Paris, resulting in a horrendous explosion at the police station at 22 rue des Bons Enfants, an ensuing investigation and search for Émile, Émile's bombing of the Café Terminus, his capture, imprisonment, trial, and execution. Inserted between the chapters "Carnage at a Police Station" and "Two Bombs," six pages of drawings depict various important people, buildings, and events described by Merriman. These images review the history recounted and also preview the final chapters of the book, serving as a transition to the trial as they present both the evidence and the significant events of Émile's life. They also foreshadow the text's shift in focus, as it becomes more narrowly concerned with the individual rather than the society.

The chapter "Two Bombs" begins by recounting an incident in which Auguste Vaillant, unemployed and unable to feed his family, tossed a small, nondeadly bomb into the Chamber of Deputies on December 9, 1893. Merriman provides extensive details of Vaillant's life, his misery, his final frustrated attempt to call attention to the misery of the poor in France, and the controversy over his death sentence. Merriman also emphasizes how detail and fine points became important in the battle against anarchists. The laws eventually permitted prosecution of anyone who appeared to plan an attack, to sympathize with anarchists, or to have the slightest association with anarchy or anarchists.

Merriman completes this chapter with a second account of Émile's bombing of the Café Terminus; this account is extremely detailed. It discusses what Émile wore, how the tables were placed, who was sitting at each table and with whom, who was injured, who was killed, who chased Émile, what each individual was doing at the time of the blast, and myriad other minute facts about the incident. Merriman's account of Émile's imprisonment, trial, and execution evinces the same meticulous attention to detail.

It is particularly in these last chapters that Merriman's skill in descriptive narrative becomes apparent. Although he is writing a history, his factual account reveals nuances of the personalities of individuals, of events, and of attitudes. Merriman presents a very detailed description of Émile's final days before his execution, including what he read, his interaction with his guards, his attitude toward his mother, his reaction to seeing Deibler, and his requests to have the bindings around his wrists loosened. Merriman also describes in detail the preparations made by Deibler and his assistants for the execution by guillotine.

The two descriptions contrast sharply. Émile Henry, the anarchist who murdered randomly, killing ordinary people, remains for readers an individual—complex and perhaps not easy to understand, yet an individual. By contrast, when Merriman describes Deibler and his assistants methodically going about their preparations, he uses them to represent the impersonal mechanism of the state against which the anarchists fought.

Merriman's book has for the most part been enthusiastically received. His writing style, his meticulous research, and his attention to detail have all elicited strong praise from his reviewers. The one criticism of the book comes from the lack of a clear definition of the link between the underlying motivation of Émile Henry and twenty-first century terrorists. Merriman suggests and implies through his portrayal of Émile's reactions why terrorism, attacks perpetrated against randomly chosen innocent victims, is espoused by some individuals, but he does not explicitly state an answer. However, rather than being a fault, this may well be the real strength of the work, for the answer to this question must lie deep in the psyche of the individual.

A complexity of conditions must be met for a set of grievances and beliefs to materialize as an act of terrorism. Readers will finish the text stimulated to ponder both the motives for terrorism and the extent to which Émile Henry may be seen both as different from contemporary terrorists and, as Merriman proposes, as the first modern terrorist.

Shawncey Webb

Review Sources

Booklist 105, no. 9/10 (January 1, 2009): 26.
Kirkus Reviews 76, no. 23 (December 1, 2008): 1245.
Library Journal 133, no. 20 (December 1, 2008): 141.
Publishers Weekly 255, no. 46 (December 17, 2008): 49.
The Washington Post, March 8, 2009, p. B07.

EATING ANIMALS

Author: Jonathan Safran Foer (1977-)
Publisher: Little, Brown (New York). 341 pp. $25.99
Type of work: Ethics, nature, environment, current affairs

This nonfiction exploration of vegetarianism and animal welfare by novelist Foer includes interesting stories and some subtle observations, but in the end becomes a polemical attack on modern industrial agriculture

In his first book, the highly acclaimed novel *Everything Is Illuminated* (2002), Jonathan Safran Foer created a vegetarian character, also called Jonathan Safran Foer. His namesake in the novel has trouble ordering a vegetarian meal at a Ukrainian restaurant, where all the menu items seem to include meat. His Ukrainian companions do not understand his refusal to eat meat, and the scene ends comically with a potato falling on the floor.

In the novel, a sort of "table fellowship" emerges, to use a term Foer introduces in his nonfiction book, *Eating Animals*. (He borrows the term from Michael Pollan, author of *The Omnivore's Dilemma*, 2006). Despite their dietary differences, the characters in the novel become quite close to one another, mostly because of bemused and grudging acceptance on the part of the nonvegetarians, to whom vegetarianism is a puzzling sort of quirk but something they eventually do their best to accommodate. The novel itself to a certain extent seems to present vegetarianism as a personal quirk; there is no suggestion in it that the nonvegetarians are doing anything wrong.

That all changes in *Eating Animals*, in which Foer argues that those who eat meat are complicit in horrendous crimes committed against animals. He presents in much detail the horrors of slaughterhouses and factory farms, and by the end of the book he sounds like a latter-day Karl Marx, inveighing not against industrial capitalism but against industrial food production, which he not only says should end but also predicts will end. He adds that those who will not participate in ending it, by which he means those who eat meat from factory farms or fish from fish farms, are guilty of choosing cruelty to animals for the sake of eating sushi, bacon, and Thanksgiving turkey. The book ends as an increasingly shrill diatribe against meat eating, though Foer seems a little uncertain whether to oppose all meat eating or just the eating of meat produced in inhumane conditions.

The book begins differently. As one might expect from a book written by a novelist, it tells stories, most notably a story about the author's grandmother that has been much quoted by reviewers. Foer clearly admires his grandmother, whose lesson from the horrors of World War II is that you can never have too much food. He also fondly describes his grandmother's favorite dish, chicken with carrots, even though as a vegetarian he presumably cannot eat it anymore—something that seems to cause him some distress. Throughout the book, he presents the conflict between cultural traditions involving meat—traditions he wishes to share—and his ever-developing views as a vegetarian. One of the greatest difficulties with being a vegetarian, he suggests, is the disruption of table fellowship with those who eat meat.

Jonathan Safran Foer is author of Everything Is Illuminated *(2002), which won the National Jewish Book Award and* The Guardian*'s First Book Award, and* Extremely Loud and Incredibly Close *(2005) and is editor of* A Convergence of Birds *(2000). In 2007,* Granta *included him in its list of the best young American novelists.*

The context of his grandmother's story is the vegetarianism of Foer's book, though it is not immediately evident how the story connects to that context. During the war, his grandmother was nearly starving as she fled the Germans until, on the brink of dying, she was offered food by a Russian farmer. "He saved your life," Foer says to her. "I didn't take it," she responds: The food was pork, and, as a kosher Jew, she would not eat such a thing. When Foer asks how she could turn down any food, even pork, in a situation of life and death, she says, "If nothing matters, there's nothing to save."

The point of the story seems to be that just living is not enough. One's life must be about more than staying alive. It is not clear whether the moral is supposed to apply to vegetarians or to the animals they care about. Midway through the book, Foer recounts a secret raid he made on a poultry farm with an animal activist who, when there, "rescued" one particularly suffering chick by slicing its neck. Suffering is worse than death, presumably.

This account brings up one of the issues in Foer's book concerning vegetarianism, animal welfare, and animal rights. Is it all right to kill and eat animals as long as you treat them humanely beforehand? Or is it wrong to kill animals at all? The activist's stance, by valuing quality of life over life itself, would seem to tend toward the first position, as would the grandmother's story. Death for Foer's grandmother, presumably, would have been preferable to a life in which she was forced to violate her principles. (Incidentally, traditional Jewish law would not support her position; the standard view is that it is permissible to violate the kosher laws and other Jewish laws if doing so is necessary to save a life.)

At times, however, Foer seems to take the other position, arguing that any killing of animals is wrong. That seems to have been his attitude when he first became a vegetarian, at the age of nine, according to another interesting story he tells. He and his brother were being looked after by a vegetarian babysitter. The two boys could not understand why she would not share in their chicken dinner. "Chicken is chicken," she said, making the young Foer realize that the chicken on his plate came from a live animal. This did not deter Foer's brother, but it made Foer stop eating and become a vegetarian.

Over the years that followed, he says, he lapsed from vegetarianism several times, but when his first child was born he thought it important to begin afresh, to take care of what his son would imbibe from his father. Thus, as he finally states explicitly at the end of the book, he has become a committed vegetarian again. Now, however, his approach is mostly a concern for humane treatment of animals rather than complete opposition to killing them. He does argue that humans, as animals, should not kill other animals, since they are able to transcend their animal nature and recognize the sanctity of animal life (animals after all kill and eat other animals).

For the most part, though, Foer is sympathetic to the few humane farms and slaughterhouses and seems to believe that, if animals are treated well, it may be all right to kill and eat them. In the short term, however, since the industry has become dominated by corporations practicing inhumane methods of raising and slaughtering animals, he urges readers to give up all meat and fish. Still, he can envisage a time after the elimination of agribusiness when it will be acceptable to eat meat again, though it is unclear whether he would personally want to do so.

Commentators writing from a vegetarian or vegan point of view have criticized Foer for this ambivalence. Vegan writers have especially criticized him for not saying much about the treatment of egg-laying hens and dairy cattle, treatment they find just as reprehensible as that of broiler chickens and beef cattle. Foer devotes most of his book to the latter, and his main argument for vegetarianism is a belief that boycotting meat and fish will lead to the end of inhumane meat and fish processing.

Foer also says that modern agribusiness is the leading cause of global warming, though he seems to be relying for this view mainly on relatively few studies and does not spend much time arguing the case. Still, he adds this argument to the mix, eventually seeming to be ready to devote anything to his cause. It does seem very much a cause, the cause not of vegetarianism per se but of attacking industrialized agriculture. By the end of the book, Foer has left his storytelling about his grandmother and his nine-year-old self far behind. He seems not the lighthearted yet profound novelist of *Everything Is Illuminated* but rather a man with a mission: to convert his readers, shaming them into giving up meat and fish.

It is unclear that his shaming will have the desired effect, but one further argument Foer brings to bear may, or at least it may galvanize the public to demand a cleanup of the factory farm system. This is the public health argument. It is not something Foer spends much time on, but he does report on the dangerous effects factory farming may have on human beings, because of all the antibiotics and growth hormones fed to animals, and because of the unsanitary conditions in the processing plants. This argument may impel people into action, as may the complementary argument of writers such as Pollan that industrially raised meat is a health hazard because of what cows and chickens are fed, regardless of their sanitary conditions.

Over one hundred years ago, Upton Sinclair published *The Jungle* (1906), an exposé of the Chicago meatpacking plants and a call for socialism and justice for workers. His middle-class readers, not to mention President Theodore Roosevelt, ignored the call for socialism but took action to correct the unsanitary conditions Sinclair had revealed. The result was not revolution but reform, notably the passage of the Pure Food and Drug Act of 1906. Perhaps such reform will be the result of Foer's book and others like it. (Commentators have noted that Foer's indictment has been anticipated by many other writers, including Pollan, Peter Singer, and Eric Schlosser). His readers may not care about the well-being of animals, but they may want to protect their own health, and thus, just as happened a century ago, there may be reforms, though not revolution.

Meanwhile, readers who appreciated Foer's debut novel will have to hope that he returns to his true métier, to a form of writing that emphasizes story over polemic and that does not fall prey to the very danger Foer warns against at the beginning of *Eating Animals*: of defending more extreme positions than those in which he believes. There are moments in this book in which storytelling and a subtle exploration of complexities come to the fore, as in the discussion of table fellowship. At the very beginning of the book, it is not even clear that it will be a study of vegetarianism: It seems possible the book may launch itself into strange realms, following the odd notions of Foer's grandmother, who clips coupons she has no need of and who builds up a hoard of sixty pounds of flour. Foer also tells stories involving his father, an experimental cook, and a tiny village on the Bering Strait that somehow has need of a dating service.

Thus, *Eating Animals* shows glimmers of inventiveness. It also hints, even at the end, at an interesting point about the alienation created in workers in meat-processing plants. All of this potential, however, is subordinated to the polemic against factory farms, which becomes as well a polemic against many readers of the book. Some have found this decision bracing and vow to at least think about the issues involved; others may feel alienated.

Sheldon Goldfarb

Review Sources

Booklist 106, no. 6 (November 15, 2009): 3.
Kirkus Reviews 77, no. 21 (November 1, 2009): 1147-1148.
New York 42, no. 37 (November 9, 2009): 76-77.
The New York Times, November 20, 2009, p. 25.
The New Yorker 85, no. 36 (November 9, 2009): 74-78.

THE EDUCATION OF A BRITISH-PROTECTED CHILD
Essays

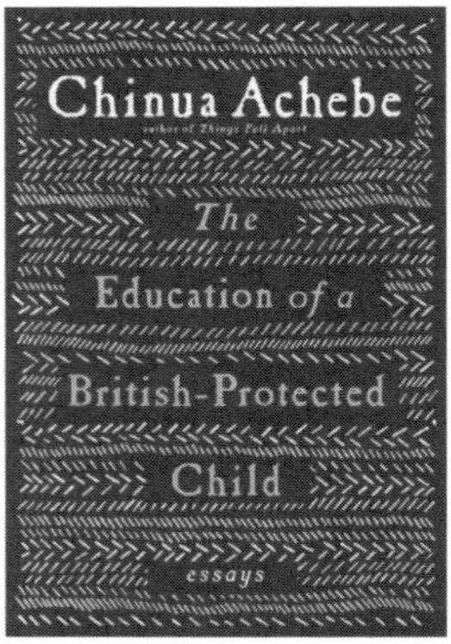

Author: Chinua Achebe (1930-)
Publisher: Alfred A. Knopf (New York). 173 pp. $24.95
Type of work: Essays, memoir, literary criticism, literary history
Time: 1930's to the early twenty-first century
Locale: Nigeria

In this collection of autobiographical essays, Achebe reflects on his life and work, exploring the role of the artist as a recorder of truth in the African diaspora

Principal personages:
CHINUA ACHEBE, Nigerian novelist, short-story writer, poet, and critic
NNAMDI AZIKIWE, first president of Nigeria, 1963-1966
JAMES BALDWIN, American novelist, essayist, and civil rights activist
JOSEPH CONRAD, Polish-born British novelist
STANLEY DIAMOND, American anthropologist and poet who traveled to Biafra
CHRISTOPHER OKIGBO, Nigerian poet who died in the Nigerian Civil War
NGUGI WA THIONG'O, Kenyan fiction writer, playwright, and critic

In 2008, the literary world marked the fiftieth anniversary of the publication of Chinua Achebe's *Things Fall Apart* (1958), among the most widely read novels ever to come from Africa. The story of the Igbo village leader Okonkwo and the ways his life is changed by the coming of British colonialists and missionaries, the novel is a common text studied in high schools and colleges throughout the world. When *Newsweek* published a "Meta-List" of the world's top one hundred books of all time in June, 2009, it ranked *Things Fall Apart* fourteenth, behind such novels as the first-place *Voyna i mir* (1865-1869; *War and Peace*, 1886) and the eleventh-place *The Canterbury Tales* (1387-1400), but ahead of such others as the eighteenth-place *The Great Gatsby* (1925) and the fortieth-place *To Kill a Mockingbird* (1960).

Achebe's most recent novel, *Anthills of the Savannah*, was published in 1987, although he has reported that he is working on another. In 1989, he published *Hopes and Impediments*, the first of what are now three collections of lectures and previously published essays dating back to his early career. In *Hopes and Impediments*, he reflected on the extent to which Africa and Africans have been perceived by Europeans as lesser, incapable of producing real art or thought. He introduced themes that would also inform his next two books: the central role Joseph Conrad's novel *Heart of Darkness* (1899) played in shaping and reflecting Western attitudes toward Africa, the reasons for Nigeria's inability to rise above poverty and corruption, the need for increased dialogue and understanding between Africa and the West, and the role that literature and art can play in enabling that kind of dialogue. In a slim volume called *Home and Exile* (2000), Achebe continued to develop these themes in three extended essays, originally a series of lectures delivered at Harvard University.

Nigerian writer Chinua Achebe is one of the most influential African writers. His first novel, Things Fall Apart *(1958), has been translated into more than thirty languages and sold over eight million copies. He was awarded the Man Booker International Prize for outstanding fiction in 2007.*

Twenty years after the publication of *Hopes and Impediments*, Achebe has released *The Education of a British-Protected Child*, another collection mostly of previously published essays. This volume revisits and refines many of the themes addressed in the earlier book, but its focus is more autobiographical. It happens that in 1990, shortly after *Hopes and Impediments* came out, Achebe was in a serious car accident that left him paralyzed from the waist down. He moved shortly thereafter to the United States, where he has lived ever since. The essays in the new collection, which have been updated and revised, reflect an older man's ponderings about his long life and career, as well as an expatriate's analysis of the homeland he loves. Of the sixteen essays in the book, fourteen are adapted from earlier work. The earliest piece, "Spelling Our Proper Name," is from a speech delivered on the death of James Baldwin in 1988; the most recent is "What Is Nigeria to Me?"—an address delivered in Lagos at the Nigerian Institute of International Affairs in 2008.

The title of the volume signals the autobiographical elements that distinguish it from Achebe's other collections. Achebe explains that he grew up and attended school under British colonial rule; he was already thirty years old and the author of two novels when Nigeria attained independence. As the child of Christian evangelical parents who valued education, Achebe attended schools that strictly followed the British model, and the books he studied "were the books English boys would have read in England."

Throughout the volume, Achebe offers glimpses of his early life in an Igbo village that was home to both "the people of the church and the people of the world," his education under the guidance of what appear to have been excellent teachers, and his involvement with Nigerian media and politics. He also describes the period in the 1950's when he studied at the British Broadcasting Corporation Staff School in London, noting that his passport identified him as a "British Protected Person." The designation represented an official denial of his status as an Igbo, as an African, and as an autonomous adult.

Interestingly, Achebe says little about his wife and sons, his horrific car accident, or his life in the United States since 1990, although two of the essays are titled "My Dad and Me" and "My Daughters." Instead, he looks back almost exclusively to his years in Nigeria, pausing to pay tribute to Nigeria's first president, Nnamdi Azikiwe, in "The Sweet Aroma of Zik's Kitchen"; the African American writer James Baldwin, in "Spelling Our Proper Name" and "Martin Luther King and America"; and the anthropologist Stanley Diamond, whose perceptions about Biafra in the failed Nigerian Civil War "are rooted in prodigious learning and a profoundly humane sensibility." Achebe is clear in his condemnation of colonial power and postcolonial corruption, but he is generous with praise for those who use their gifts in the service of dialogue and understanding.

Achebe declares in the beginning of "The Education of a British-Protected Child," the essay that serves as an introduction to the collection, "I hope my readers are not expecting to encounter the work of a scholar." However, he does address some of the issues of scholarly debate that he has discussed throughout his career. The most prominent of these is Conrad's famous novella *Heart of Darkness.* Achebe reads the novella as an instrument of colonial oppression, rather than as an argument against imperialism. He acknowledges in "Africa's Tarnished Name" that *Heart of Darkness* is but one example in a long tradition of presentations of Africa by Westerners, but again and again he has returned to that example as an emblem of that tradition that "has invented an Africa where nothing good happens or ever happened, an Africa that has not been discovered yet and is waiting for the first European visitor to explore it and explain it and straighten it up."

In the essay, he traces Conrad's boyhood fascination with explorers, especially those who visited Africa, and wonders why he was so attracted to the writings of men such as Mungo Park and David Livingstone. Achebe's tone is mild, even conversational, as he notes that "it is not a crime to prefer the Africa of explorers to the Africa of colleges." When he turns to discussing *Heart of Darkness*, however, and presents an extended passage in which the narrator compares one of the Africans he met (a "savage") to a dog, Achebe's mildness vanishes: "This is poisonous writing."

Achebe describes Conrad's "simple hierarchical order of souls," with Africans at the bottom and Europeans at the top, and reminds readers of Conrad's descriptions of "gyrating and babbling savages." Achebe's discussions of Conrad date back at least to 1975, when he presented a lecture on racism in Conrad's novel at Amherst College. In the intervening years, other scholars have presented alternative readings of Conrad, many seeing the novel as a condemnation of imperialism written by a novelist who does not see the world as his narrator does. In "Africa's Tarnished Name," Achebe again refutes these readings. "People are wrong," he writes, "when they tell you that Conrad was on the side of the Africans because his story showed great compassion towards them."

Achebe's thinking about Conrad is more nuanced than this summary suggests, and he returns to Conrad in other essays in the collection. In "African Literature as Restoration of Celebration," he admires the language and imagery of *Heart of Darkness* and acknowledges Conrad's "high-minded" intentions. He admits that, when he read the novel as a student, he was among the readers swept away by the adventure and that as a young reader he "took sides with the white men against the savages." Not until he was older, he writes, did he understand that Conrad and other writers about Africa had "pulled a fast one" on him. It is this very realization, he explains, reached by many people, that created the African writer: "His story had been told for him, and he had found the telling quite unsatisfactory." In his opening essay, Achebe's resentment is directed only at Kurtz, the "dreadful character" from *Heart of Darkness*, not at Conrad or at the novel itself.

Thus, when Achebe says in the first essay that he is not appearing in the role of a scholar, he does not mean that he is not addressing scholarly concerns. The admirable accomplishment of the discussions of Conrad's novel in this volume is that Achebe explains for general readers what the controversies are and why he reads as he does. The discussions are reasonable, thoughtful, and blessedly free of the complex jargon for which postcolonial criticism is notorious. By offering his thoughts about *Heart of Darkness* as one component in analyses of broader issues, rather than as a focused, linear argument about one novel, Achebe shows how criticism can be a dialogue, an activity for living, breathing readers.

With "Politics and Politicians of Language in Africa Literature," Achebe takes up another scholarly debate in which he is an important voice: the choice made by African writers to write either in a colonial language (English, French, or Arabic) or in their "mother tongue." Achebe, who writes in English, disagrees with Ngugi wa Thiong'o, whose 1986 essay "Decolonising the Mind: The Politics of Language in African Literature" famously called on African writers to create literature in their own languages, as he himself declared his intention to do. Achebe, whose essay title intentionally echoes Ngugi's, continues the dialogue, again with a jargon-free, conversational diction that welcomes readers to think about an issue they may not have considered before.

Nigeria, Achebe patiently points out to his ignorant American audience, is home to "more than two hundred component nationalities," each with its own mother tongue. For him, the choice to write in English is a practical one: "I can only speak across two hundred linguistic frontiers to fellow Nigerians in English." He traces the history of missionary schools and language education in Africa, coming to different conclusions than Ngugi does, and concludes, "the only reason these alien languages are still knocking about is that they serve an actual need."

Throughout the collection, Achebe comes across as a wise, thoughtful elder. He has read widely as well as deeply, from Homer to William Shakespeare to Okigbo; he has lived through colonialism, independence, and civil war; he is the author of one of the most important books Africa has produced. While he is opinionated, he is never cross or petty; while he is more knowledgeable than his intended readers, he is never pedantic. *The Education of a British-Protected Child* is an insightful and thought-provoking collection of essays for readers who are curious about African literature and culture, whether or not they are scholars. Many readers will come to this collection to learn more about Achebe, and that goal will be met. Because of Achebe's probing mind and generosity of spirit, many will also discover new books, new writers, and new historical and cultural events to explore.

Cynthia A. Bily

Review Sources

America 201, no. 12 (November 2, 2009): 37-39.
Booklist 106, no. 3 (October 1, 2009): 15-16.
Columbia Journalism Review 48, no. 3 (September/October, 2009): 60-61.
Kirkus Reviews, September 15, 2009.
Library Journal, 134, no. 16 (October 1, 2009): 76-77.

1848
Year of Revolution

Author: Mike Rapport
Publisher: Basic Books (New York). 480 pp. $29.95
Type of work: History

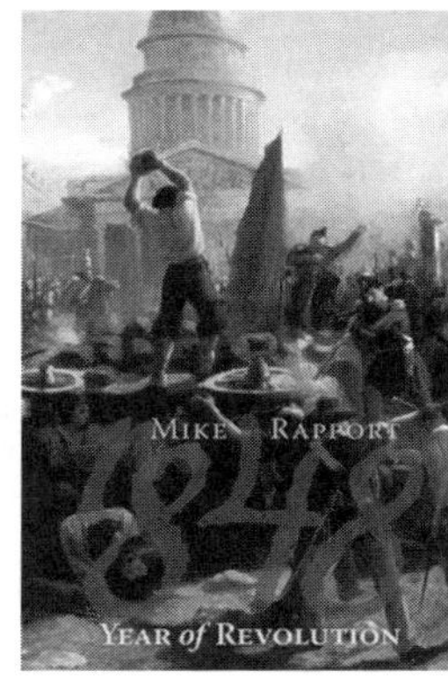

A country-by-country history of the revolutions and political reactions that swept continental Europe in 1848

The year 1848 saw a series of political upheavals in France, the Austro-Hungarian Empire, Germany, Italy, and Poland. Even places, such as England and Russia, that did not experience political change felt the shock waves of revolutionary activity, and Russia intervened in the conflicts to its west. The distant United States experienced the effects of this year when political refugees, especially Germans, emigrated during the aftermath. Despite the continental and even global reach of the struggles of this time, most historians have tended to concentrate on the events in only one nation. Mike Rapport's book *1848: Year of Revolution* attempts to provide a portrait of the revolutions as European phenomena, to examine their underlying causes, and to evaluate their consequences.

Rapport begins his account with the departure of the Russian socialist Alexander Herzen from his own country, which was under the autocratic sway of Czar Nicholas I, to begin a journey through the European lands to the west. Herzen would never see Russia again, but he would have a long record as a political commentator. He would also be a witness to the European events of 1848. Rapport describes the lands Herzen entered as dominated by the conservative political order that had formed in reaction to the Napoleonic wars. France, under the rule of King Louis-Philippe since the uprising against Charles X in 1830, had a parliament. Even under Louis-Philippe's comparatively liberal regime, however, only a minuscule fraction of the population could vote. The Habsburg Empire of Austria was an absolute monarchy that extended over Hungary and a large part of northern Italy, as well as a variety of lands and nationalities in eastern Europe. Prussia, the most powerful of the nations in what would become Europe, was also an absolute monarchy. Even in England, where Herzen eventually settled, only one-fifth of the population could vote, and the House of Commons' members were all drawn from a small social and economic elite.

In Rapport's telling, the first sign of the collapse of the apparently stable regimes of Europe came late in January in Paris, when the political thinker Alexis de Tocqueville addressed the French Chamber of Deputies and warned that, without parliamentary reforms, not only France but also the rest of the Continent would be shaken by revolution. Despite the location of this initial alarm, the first violent confrontations of the year began in Milan, in northern Italy, with scuffles between the Milanese and the re-

Mike Rapport is a senior lecturer in the Department of History at the University of Stirling in Scotland. The reviews editor for French History, *his previous publications include* Nationality and Citizenship in Revolutionary France *(2000) and* Nineteenth Century Europe *(2005).*

sented Austrian army. The conflict between dominant and dominated nationalities would be as much a part of the revolutionary year as struggles over political democracy and social reform. These overlapping but distinct forms of the desire for change would, in Rapport's telling, help spread the radical impulses of the year. Ultimately, though, the inconsistencies among the goals of national and ethnic liberation, social reform, and political liberalization would also stifle these impulses.

Although Milan witnessed the first harbinger of continental revolution, Paris provided the greatest spark to the explosions that would occur around the continent. In the French capital, protests against the stubbornly unmoveable administration of government leader Francois Guizot were met with military repression, causing the protests themselves to escalate into violent uprisings. King Louis-Philippe fled the city, and the rebels proclamed France a republic. The news of the revolt in Paris galvanized oppositions in the German states and in the Habsburg Empire.

The empire was multinational but dominated by German-speaking Austria. Hungary constituted much of the central part of the empire, though, and the Hungarians yearned for greater control over their land. In early March, inspired by events in Paris, the Hungarian speaker Lajos Kossuth rose in the parliament and called for his nation to become independent, retaining only the Austrian emperor, with the title king of Hungary, as the link between the two nations.

Also in early March, the news of the French republic encouraged popular support for more liberal regimes in the many small German states located between the great German-speaking powers of Prussia and Austria. Faced with demonstrations, the princes of many of these states accepted parliamentary reforms. Delegates from the German states gathered in Heidelberg to form a German national assembly, the basis for a unified nation with a unified government. In Vienna, students and other supporters of Austrian political reform took inspiration from France, Kossuth's speech, and the German assembly to call for political change at home.

Public unrest in Vienna, according to Rapport, led to the second great crisis of the year, after the declaration of the French republic. Austrian chancellor Klemens von Metternich was one of the great figures of the Congress of Vienna, which constructed the European order following the Napoleonic Wars. An advocate of absolute monarchy as the basis of domestic and international social order, Metternich was unquestionably the most powerful individual in Austria and was probably the most powerful individual in Europe. On March 13, the demonstrations in Vienna forced Metternich to resign, and he then fled to England. Metternich was the symbol of the old monarchical regimes, and his fall seemed to herald a new future.

In Prussia, March saw a popular insurgency demanding a constitution. After some efforts at putting the insurgency down, King Frederick William gave in and announced that he would grant the constitution. Bringing Prussia into the German movement for change also created complications, however. If a unified Germany were to be established, would it include both Prussia and Austria? If Austria were included, what would happen to the non-German lands of the empire?

In northern Italy, news of Metternich's political end stoked unrest in Milan and Venice, which were chafing under Austrian rule. The northern Italians were split between republicans and advocates of monarchy. The monarchists most often regarded King Charles Albert of Piedmont, Genoa, and Sardinia as the most plausible ruler of a unified Italian state. Such Italian nationalism was also demonstrated to varying degrees by the advocates of change in Austria-ruled Italy. Some Italians thought of Pope Pius IX, initially regarded as something of a progressive, as a potentially foundational figure for national unity.

Reaction quickly followed the revolutions almost everywhere. As conservative forces sought to regain control of Vienna, tensions between Austria and Hungary led to war between these two parts of the empire. The Austrians were able to enlist the support of minority groups within Hungary or threatened by Hungary in order to put down the Hungarians. At the same time, the powerful Austrian army fought to regain control over northern Italy, defeating the Piedmontese troops of Charles Albert, as well as the nationalist forces of legendary Italian professional revolutionaries Giuseppe Mazzini and Giuseppe Garibaldi. Pius IX, who shrank from supporting the northern cause against Catholic Austria, fled from a republican coup to southern Italy, where King Ferdinand II was successfully putting down a rebellion against his rule in Sicily. This coup helped make the pope into the extreme conservative he would become in the later nineteenth century.

In Paris, the political pivot of Europe, the forces of reaction began to assert themselves when the urban poor began to demand economic changes, including employment support from the government. When the new republican government put down urban uprisings in July, former political liberals began to make common cause with supporters of social order, including those who wanted to reinstate the dynasty of the Bourbons or that of Orleans, the other wing of the French royal family. In this polarized atmosphere, Louis-Napoleon Bonaparte, the nephew of Napoleon Bonaparte, managed to capitalize on his absence from France and his consequent lack of existing political commitments to lead all sides into believing that they had his support.

In October of 1848, Louis-Napoleon announced his candidacy for president of the republic. Ironically, the expanded democracy of the republic helped undermine it, since Louis-Napoleon was able to appeal to the memory of his uncle's name among the peasantry to ride to a surprise landslide victory. Rather than accept the constitutional limit to a single term, Louis-Napoleon would stage a coup in 1852 and have himself crowned Napoleon III, ruling autocratically until 1871. Before that, though, Louis-Napoleon intervened in Italy. Following the rise of the republic in Rome, France, which many had proclaimed as the model for republican revolution throughout Europe, sent troops to take control of the seat of Catholicism and to make possible the return of the pope.

Throughout the rest of the continent, the constitutions the kings had granted were taken back. Under the young Emperor Franz Joseph, who replaced the old Emperor Ferdinand, the Austrian monarchy not only reasserted its control over Austria itself but also defeated the forces of Hungary and shot Hungarian officers as rebels. For more than a decade, Franz Joseph would be the absolute ruler of the empire, giving way to reforms only in 1860.

Rapport has provided an excellent guide to the complicated events that took place during and immediately after 1848. Moving from one part of the troubled continent to another, he manages to weave the rapidly paced histories of these lands into a single narrative. Even more important, he offers clear explanations of why the radicals and reformers of 1848 failed to achieve their goals. Essentially, they had too many goals, and these were often mutually inconsistent. The long period of political repression that followed the Napoleonic Wars brought many different movements for change together. The bourgeoisie sought more representative political systems but also wanted secure guarantees of property rights. The urban working classes and the poor wanted social reforms that often threatened those property rights. The peasants wanted freedom from exploitation by landlords but also often had sentimental attachments to monarchs, whom they could be encouraged to see as their protectors. The nationalists wanted unity and autonomy for their own ethnic groups but opposed the autonomy of minorities inside their national boundaries.

Rapport cautions against regarding the revolutionary year as an utter failure. It did give many ordinary Europeans their first taste of politics and therefore could be seen as laying the groundwork for the republican governments that would eventually follow in many places. Some of the revolutionaries' goals were later achieved. For example, following Austria's defeat by Prussia in 1866, a key event in German unification, the Habsburg Empire was redesigned as the dual Kingdom of Austria and Hungary, joined together by the rule of Franz Joseph.

The contradictions in the coalitions of interests during 1848 also demonstrated the inconsistent and unpredictable nature of political goals. National unification, seen as a liberal goal in Germany and Italy, was hardly liberal when it has finally achieved, and in the twentieth century nationalism in both countries became a basis for extreme authoritarian governments. Balancing ethnic minority interests with those of national self-determination would also become a central problem for European governments. While Rapport avoids reading history backward and interpreting 1848 in terms of events that came long after, he does a good job of presenting this year as the "seed plot" of modern Europe, when the great historical growths of the modern era took root.

Carl L. Bankston III

Review Sources

American Conservative 8, no. 9 (May 4, 2009): 29-30.
Booklist 105, no. 11 (February 1, 2009): 12.
Kirkus Reviews 76, no. 24 (Debember 15, 2008): 1297.
Library Journal 134, no. 1 (January 1, 2009): 107.
New Criterion 27, no. 10 (June, 2009): 73-76.
The New York Times Book Review, March 15, 2009, p. 15.
The Times Literary Supplement, December 5, 2008, p. 13.
The Wall Street Journal, March 13, 2009, p. A9.
Weekly Standard 15, no. 11 (November 30, 2009): 33-35.

EMPIRE OF LIBERTY
A History of the Early Republic, 1789-1815

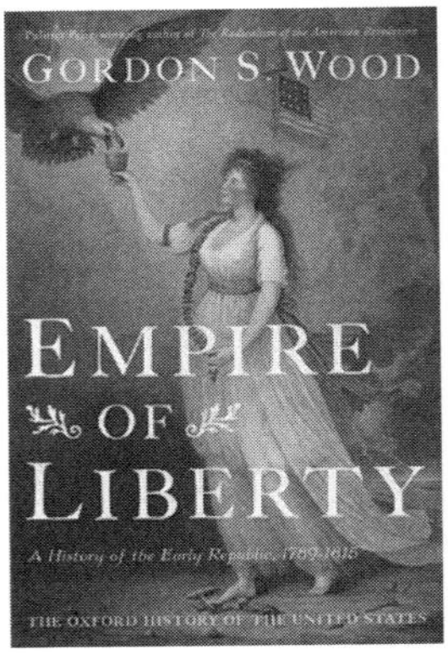

Author: Gordon S. Wood (1933-   )
Publisher: Oxford University Press (New York). 778 pp. $35.00
Type of work: History
Time: 1789-1815
Locale: United States

The latest addition to the prestigious Oxford History of the United States, *this work provides a scholarly and balanced narrative of the years traditionally classified as the early national period, from George Washington's inauguration as president until the end of the War of 1812*

Gordon S. Wood begins *Empire of Liberty* with a summary of Washington Irving's 1819 story of Rip Van Winkle, the legendary man who fell asleep just prior to the American Revolution and woke up twenty years later to find that phenomenal and bewildering transformations had occurred. The village was "larger and more populous"; its earlier tranquillity had been replaced by bustling activity, fierce ambition, and concern for making money. Even the language of politics had changed. People were now talking about the rights of citizenship, elections to Congress, and other matters that Van Winkle did not understand. When asked "whether he was Federal or Democrat," he stared "in vacant stupidity." Wood writes that most Americans living in the early nineteenth century could identify with Irving's story because of the tumultuous changes they had experienced in all aspects of life—in politics, culture, economics, and social relationships.

Wood emphasizes, however, that the changes Americans experienced were frequently different from those that the founders of the new government had anticipated. Almost all the founders denounced the idea of rival political parties such as those that existed in England, but their strong differences in aspirations and values resulted in party-like polarization soon after George Washington's inauguration. Those calling themselves Federalists, led by Alexander Hamilton, wanted the country to follow the English model of industrialization, large banks, urbanization, and centralized government. In contrast, those taking the name Republican, led by Thomas Jefferson, favored states' rights and hoped for the country to remain essentially agrarian. While the Hamiltonians were no doubt pleased to see the expansion in financial and commercial institutions, they did not foresee the extent to which "the middling people's go-getting involvement in commerce and enterprise" would dominate the economy and produce the "myth of the American dream." Jefferson and most of his supporters, on the other hand, welcomed the growth of democracy but despised the economic transformations that occurred alongside it.

In contrast to historians with more left-wing perspectives, Wood is impressed with the growth of democracy during the period. In 1789, it was common for Americans to use the word "democracy" as a pejorative term that connoted mob rule and lack of protection for minorities and property rights. In *Federalist* number 14, James Madison defined democracy as a system in which the people exercise power directly, which was inappropriate to a large country. He asserted that a republican system, as created in the Constitution, utilized the principle of representation, which could be extended over a large region.

Gordon S. Wood, professor emeritus of history at Brown University, is author of The Radicalism of the American Revolution *(1991), winner of the Pulitzer Prize, and* The Creation of the American Republic, 1776-1787 *(1969), which was awarded the Bancroft Prize.*

Within a few years, however, left-leaning persons and groups began applying the labels "democracy" and "democrat" to characterize political systems that reject aristocracy and allow the vast majority of citizens to vote for their representatives. By 1793, supporters of the French Revolution were establishing Democratic-Republican Societies, and some northerners were referring to the Republicans, or followers of Thomas Jefferson, as the Democratic-Republican Party. By the early nineteenth century, Wood demonstrates, it was not uncommon for the Republicans to be called Democrats. By then, the concept of representative democracy, which was only rarely mentioned in the eighteenth century, was becoming rather commonplace.

Although Wood does not view history through the Marxist lens of class conflict, he argues that the period witnessed a "social struggle" between wealthy aristocrats and the "middling classes," a conflict that was particularly strong in the northern states. These middling men could not be considered gentlemen because they worked for a living with their hands. Holding positions such as artisans, mechanics, and laboring proprietors, they were too refined and too affluent to be placed with the "lower sort" or the "ruder sort." Wood estimates that in 1790 about 60 percent of Boston's three thousand adult men were members of the middling class and that they held almost 40 percent of the taxable wealth of the city. Their numbers and influence continued to grow, so that by the second decade of the nineteenth century they "had come to dominate American culture to a degree that the middle class in England never achieved." While insisting that the "popular myth of equality" was based on substantial reality, however, Wood finds that it was "a psychological more than an economic reality." The size of Connecticut farms, for example, varied from fifty to five thousand acres.

Wood recognizes that the South was not evolving into a middling and commercial society like that of the North. Although most southern famers were not slaveholders and many of them valued hard work, the states below the Mason-Dixon Line had fewer middling institutions—fewer schools, cities, banks, newspapers and manufacturing firms. The section's "patrician order of large slaveholders" continued to dominate both politics and the culture. These economic differences had political consequences. In 1789, the South, particularly Virginia, had been the impelling force in creating the new government, and political leaders from the section still appeared to have control over the national government in 1815. The region's power and prestige, however, was declining relative to the North, and many southerners "had a growing uneasiness that the South was being marginalized by the dynamic, enterprising, and egalitarian North, which was rapidly seizing control of the nation's identity."

The term "empire of liberty" was utilized several times by Thomas Jefferson in his correspondence. As implied by the word "empire," Jefferson was a strong proponent of territorial expansion. He wanted the country to annex all, or at least most, of North America, as well as Cuba and other islands of the Caribbean. Presenting a moral justification for this goal that would come to be called Manifest Destiny in the 1840's, Jefferson asserted that "no constitution was ever before so well calculated as ours for extensive empire and self government." Although such a statement sounds arrogant to modern ears, Wood points out that numerous European observers looked upon America as "the premier land of liberty." The English radical Richard Price, for example, wrote that a "Spirit" had originated in America that promised to bring about "a State of Society more favorable to peace, virtue, Science, and liberty (consequently to human happiness and dignity) than has yet been known."

As in his previous work, Wood does not write history from the perspectives of fads and "political correctness." Convinced that historians should search for objective truths, at least in factual matters, he has little patience for the fashionable school of postmodernism and its "insidious" relativism that discounts even the goal of pursuing objectivity in historiography. In contrast to most contemporary multiculturalists, who tend to focus primarily on the inequalities and oppression of women, minorities, and the poor, Wood finds that the Revolution had the long-term result of liberation for the mass of citizens. Although he does not ignore the injustices that occurred during the early national period, he is convinced that American political institutions made a valuable contribution in promoting the expansion of liberty, equality, and democracy. Apparently, he continues to believe, as he previously wrote in the *William and Mary Quarterly*, that the school of radical multiculturalism "not only falsifies our past, it destroys our future."

Rather than focusing on the American Revolution's failure to eliminate the evil of slavery, Wood argues that the Revolution created "the cultural atmosphere that made slavery abhorrent to many Americans." He observes that all the revolutionary leaders recognized that there was an obvious contradiction between the appeal to liberty in the Revolution and the existence of hereditary chattel slavery. The early national era, nevertheless, was such a cruel and brutal age, as reflected in criminal punishments, that many Americans simply accepted slavery as "merely part of the national order of things."

Although persons of European ancestry in both the North and the South perceived the United States as "a white man's country," slavery was largely responsible for the growing divergence in the cultural and social organization of the two regions. Slavery, for instance, tended to breed deference and had "antidemocratic effects" on southern institutions. Wood even suggests that the continuation of slavery was one of the main reasons the South had fewer canals, fewer banks, fewer corporations, and fewer factories. It is impossible to prove or disprove such a causative linkage.

Wood does not ignore the sufferings and injustices experienced by Native Americans, but he does not condemn governmental policies as harshly as do many historians. He observes that, under the Articles of Confederation (in effect from 1781 to 1789), both the Congress and the states assumed that ownership of Indian lands was based on "the right of conquest," therefore requiring no compensation for the ceded lands. In contrast, the administration of George Washington decided to return to the colonial practice of purchasing Indian lands, and the administration's policy "could scarcely have been more enlightened—at least for the enlightened eighteenth century." Even Henry Knox, who was one of the strongest defenders of Indian rights at the time, insisted that Indians must become sedentary and learn the European kind of agriculture. Wood observes that many people today find such a policy to be cruel and ethnocentric, but, he argues, "by the most liberal standards of the eighteenth century it was the only realistic alternative to the Indians' outright removal or destruction."

Empire of Liberty contains a good balance of materials concerning politics, law, economics, culture, and social relationships. Four of the nineteen chapters are devoted to the events and developments that occurred during Washington's presidency, including the creation of new political institutions, reactions to the French Revolution, the conflict between unorganized political parties, the Whiskey Rebellion, and Washington's farewell address. The presidency of John Adams is discussed in two chapters, and Jefferson's two terms occupy four chapters.

The chapter on Madison's presidency deals primarily with the War of 1812, with interesting discussions of the major battles, the Treaty of Ghent, and the reasons why Americans came to think of the conflict as "the second war for independence." The two chapters about American law are particularly valuable, providing insightful discussions of the common law, the establishment of the judicial system, the jurisprudence of John Marshall, and the origins of judicial review. In addition, the book has one chapter that deals with slavery, one chapter about religion, and one chapter that presents an overview of literary, artistic, and scientific achievements.

A few of Wood's generalizations are questionable. For instance, he writes that by 1815 "the eighteenth-century Enlightenment was clearly over." While it is unquestionably true that many Americans, such as the followers of the religious revivals, were opposed to the worldview of the Enlightenment, there is considerable evidence that the major ideas and values of the movement, such as skepticism, deism, humanitarianism, and appreciation for science and education, were growing in importance and popularity. The period after 1815 would see developments that would have pleased most leaders of the Enlightenment, such as the growth in schools, newspapers, and opposition to slavery.

Also questionable is Wood's assertion that, with the development of a democratic society, "heroic individuals, like the Founders, no longer mattered as much as they had in the past." To the contrary, it would appear that people living in democracies appreciate heroism, particularly during times of great crisis, especially major wars. Even in 1815, many Americans were already looking upon Andrew Jackson as a heroic figure. The image of heroism demands a certain kind of personality, as well as success in confronting a difficult challenge.

Almost all scholars, even if they have reservations about some of Wood's interpretations, will recognize that the *Empire of Liberty*, a finalist for the 2010 Pulitzer Prize in history, is an outstanding achievement by one of the preeminent historians of the early history of the United States. Capitalizing on his lifetime of research and writing in the field, Wood was able to take advantage of an unmatched familiarity with both source materials and historical literature. In addition to his outstanding breadth and depth of knowledge, Wood remembers the crucial importance of stories to history, and he packages his narration in a style that is engaging and accessible to general readers. Although the book is quite large, many lovers of history will want to read it from cover to cover. It is probably too massive to serve as a text in a college course, but some history teachers, if they have motivated students, might want to assign particular chapters. The book is particularly useful as a reference work for persons who want to find dependable and balanced discussions of particular topics of the period.

Thomas Tandy Lewis

Review Sources

American Heritage 59, no. 4 (Winter, 2010): 105.
Booklist 106, no. 2 (September 15, 2009): 19.
Kirkus Reviews 77 (September 15, 2009): 72.
Library Journal 134, no. 15 (September 15, 2009): 70.
The Nation 290, no. 4 (February 1, 2010): 33-36.
National Review 61, no. 21 (November 23, 2009): 50-52.
The New York Times Book Review, November 29, 2009, p. 12.
Publishers Weekly 256, no. 33 (Sept. 28, 2009): 54.
Weekly Standard 15, no. 7 (November 2, 2009): 28-30.

ENDPOINT
And Other Poems

Author: John Updike (1932-2009)
Publisher: Knopf (New York). 97 pp. $25.00
Type of work: Poetry

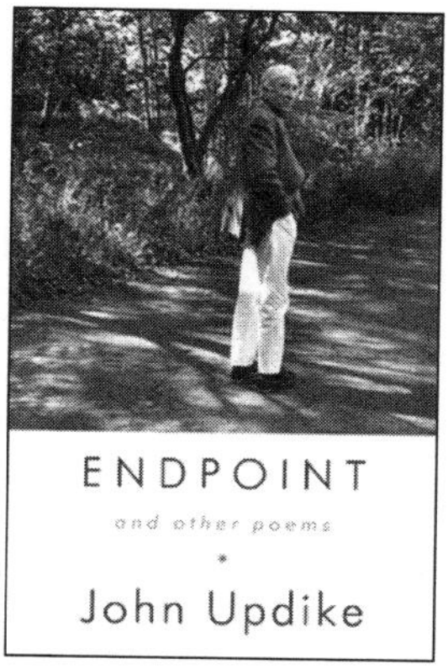

Collection of poems, written mostly during the last decade of Updike's life, that focus on the writer's considerations of old age and death

When John Updike died in January, 2009, at the age of seventy-six, the literary world was filled with retrospectives of his life as a prose writer. He had written more than twenty novels, as well as many short stories, essays (including literary criticism), two plays, and even a few books for children. Updike's prose seems likely to become a lasting part of the American fiction canon. It is not surprising, therefore, that his poetry has often been overlooked, although he published at least one volume of poems in each decade of his writing life (eight volumes in all, including *Endpoint*), and his poems appeared in a variety of periodicals ranging from *The New Yorker* to *American Poetry Review*. Thus, he produced a very respectable body of poetic work by any standard.

The first third of *Endpoint* collects the volume's titular grouping of poems. Updike began the grouping as a series of birthday poems, producing one each year beginning in 2002, when he turned seventy. He added to the series several poems written during his final illness. Always interested in form, Updike used unrhymed sonnets for these poems, often joining three or more sonnets to make a birthday poem, sometimes concluding with a half rhyme to bring the poem to an end. Although all their subjects begin with the birthday in question and consider, at least in part, the general subject of aging, the poems also include many references to Updike's youth, moving back and forth between past and present.

The first poem in the collection, "March Birthday 2002, and After," can serve as an example. It begins with a snowy March day at Updike's home in Massachusetts; the poet is suffering painful twinges brought on by his increasing age, as well as by the number of celebrations his seventieth birthday has occasioned. He points out that advanced age means merely that one has avoided dying, but his mind takes him back to his childhood, when he spent sick days in bed, accompanied by books and the radio, and when he enjoyed being waited on by his parents and the visiting doctor. The second sonnet in the poem blends images of the snowstorm and of Updike's own physical state. The snow resists the encroaching sun and seems to say "Give me another hour; then I'll go." The third sonnet of this poem moves the poet to a plane, crossing countryside he has long known well to fly into Manhattan. For a moment, he thinks the plane's approach is too low: "Age I must, but die I would rather not."

John Updike was born in Shillington, Pennsylvania, in 1932. His honors include two Pulitzer Prizes—for Rabbit Is Rich *(1981) and* Rabbit at Rest *(1990)—and two National Book Awards, as well as the National Book Critics Circle Award and the PEN/ Faulkner award. He died January 27, 2009.*

The last sonnet of this group offers the sort of attentive description that marks much of Updike's writing. After a sleet storm, crocuses "spread their stained-glass cups" and "daffodils grow leggy like young girls." Nature is constantly in flux, he notes, for flowers as well as for human beings, for whom all days are both birth days and death days.

All of the birthday poems share this elegiac tone, Updike's consciousness of the past and of his diminishing future (the first poem notes that, at seventy, Updike has entered the decade in which he is likely to die). In "03/18/ 03," he notes the war in Iraq, the fifth war he's lived through, and then thinks of his parents walking ahead of him on a path that is simultaneously the real path he climbs on his birthday and the metaphoric path of the future. They "seemed to sail ahead of me/ like ships receding to destinations where/ I'd be forgotten."

The 2004 birthday poem was written in Tucson, and Updike marks his seventy-second birthday with a satiric picture of the city's aged retirees, who have come there "to bake away/ their juicy lifetime jobs." The 2005 poem focuses on Updike's life as an author, his written words a fragile legacy in an electronic world where printing ("a half-millennium's brief wonder") seems almost obsolete. The poem moves through Updike's own history with print, from his childhood devotion to newspaper comic strips to the heady delight of seeing his first work in print, to his pleasure in working at *The New Yorker* and his admiration for its editors. The last stanzas note that Updike has reached the age at which his father died. The second part of the 2005 poem, "My Mother at Her Desk," considers the writer's own career by memorializing his mother's unsuccessful efforts to publish her fiction. He concludes "Mine was to be the magic gift instead."

"Birthday Shopping, 2007" begins with Updike shopping for a new laptop computer in an electronics store in Tucson, an event that recalls for him a frightening childhood episode when he found himself separated from his mother in a department store. The poem then moves on to consider the power of radio and movies on his growing up and then to contrast his life in old age with that of his grandparents. "How not to think of death?" he asks, and imagines its frightening blankness, concluding "Be with me, words, a little longer; you/ have given me my quitclaim in the sun . . . ."

The first of the several 2008 poems finds the poet running errands on his birthday, mailing checks and taxes, sending off proofs of his last novel, and suddenly finding himself unable to recall how to unlatch the gas cap cover on his car. The rest of the poems trace his final illness. He has a cold that becomes pneumonia. In the hospital in

November, he recalls how callously he once dealt with the deaths of people he loved. "I brushed them off . . . in my unseemly haste/ of greedy living . . . ." In a December poem, he recalls two people from his past who became models for characters in his fiction, and their memory becomes a springboard for celebrating the role his hometown of Shillington had in furnishing him with characters. Written less than a month before Updike's death, "12/22/08" records the biopsy that revealed the advanced state of his cancer. The last poem in the section asks "Why go to Sunday school?" if not to believe at least some of what was taught there. "We mocked but took" he says, and concludes with fragments of the Twenty-third Psalm's assertion that goodness and mercy will follow the speaker into eternity.

The second third of *Endpoint*, "Other Poems," contains a range of poetic memorials to people and things that were significant to Updike. "Stolen" takes its starting point from the last letter Updike received from editor William Maxwell. Singer Frankie Laine, actress Doris Day, golfer Payne Stewart, baseball, and a crashed computer all receive attention, as does the writer's arthritic left hand and his colonoscopy. The contrast between these mostly playful poems and the mostly meditative poems of the volume's first third is surely intentional, but several of the later poems in the group return to the somber tone of the *Endpoint* section. In the nine haikulike segments of "Levels of Air," for instance, the poet moves from describing midges at eye level through progressively higher reaches to conclude with space capsules and angels. "Saguaros," the last poem in this section, offers a dark image of the skeletons of dead cactuses that stand in "mute mobs" in the desert.

"Other Poems" is followed by a group of sonnets, many of which sketch travel destinations, ranging from Sainte-Chapelle through Ireland, India, and Phnom Penh. That many of these places have histories of violent conflict shadows Updike's view of them. In St. Petersburg, the city's troubled past is marked by young prostitutes on its street corners. The travelers in "Flying to Florida" are "agéd, average, dullish, lame, and halt" and pitiable in their efforts to find youth in Florida's sun. "The Chambered Nautilus" plays on the poem of the same title by nineteenth century American poet Oliver Wendell Holmes. In Holmes's poem, the speaker looks at the shell of the nautilus with its gradually increasing cells and uses it as a metaphor for spiritual growth. Updike, by contrast, sees in the shell a satiric image of the countless rooms a man inhabits through a lifetime, moving from the bedroom of the newly married to the hotel room for a one-night stand to the vacation rental filled with others' castoffs and concluding with the "pricey white hospital space" and the moaning it holds. In "Tools," (a sonnet in hexameters), the speaker considers the permanence of hammers and screwdrivers, which put to shame our "wastrel lives."

While the *Endpoint* poems were all inward looking in one degree or another, the arrangement of "Other Poems" seems to insist on focusing outside the poet. The power of the first group, however, with its valedictory tone and a reader's inescapable knowledge that Updike intended them to be his final work, diminishes the poems of the collection's later sections. The contrast makes many of the later poems seem faintly peevish, as when the poet protests the sound of workmen's voices as they paint his kitchen.

Much of Updike's earliest poetry might be categorized as light verse, although it would be a mistake to use that term as an excuse to ignore the poet's wonderful ear for poetic rhythms and sound effects. The last short section of *Endpoint* is titled "Light and Personal." It reminds readers not only of Updike's skill with poetic forms but also of his wit. "To a Well-Connected Mouse," for example, plays on Scottish poet Robert Burns's famous poem "To a Mouse," which warns that plans of both mice and men often go astray. Updike's poem, in fine Scots dialect, notes that DNA testing shows mice and men to be closely related. The poem suggests that the mouse's theft from the human's pantry can be seen as all in the family.

"Duet on Mars" gives human voices to Spirit and Opportunity, the National Aeronautics and Space Administration's two Mars exploration robots. "Elegy" playfully explores the sound effects of the words "equine encephalitis" and "emu," as well as a number of other words phonetically related to them. One poem commemorates Monica Lewinsky's place in U.S. history; one poem documents the small events of July 10, 1878, as recorded in the Reading, Pennsylvania, *Daily Eagle.* The last poem in the book is titled "For Martha, on Her Birthday, After Her Cataract Operation." Martha is the poet's wife, to whom the volume is dedicated. As its title indicates, the poem simultaneously celebrates her birthday and her newly restored vision. Her cake, Updike says in conclusion, is "A cake of love from your own/ John."

Ann D. Garbett

Review Sources

Booklist 105, no. 15 (April 1, 2009): 15.
New Statesman 138, no. 4956 (July 6, 2009): 46-49.
The New York Review of Books 56, no. 10 (June 11, 2009): 8-9.
The New York Times Book Review, May 3, 2009, p. 15.
Publishers Weekly 256, no. 13 (March 31, 2009): 29.
The San Francisco Chronicle, April 12, 2009, p. J1.
The Times Literary Supplement, July 10, 2009, pp. 19-20.

THE ENDS OF LIFE
Roads to Fulfilment in Early Modern England

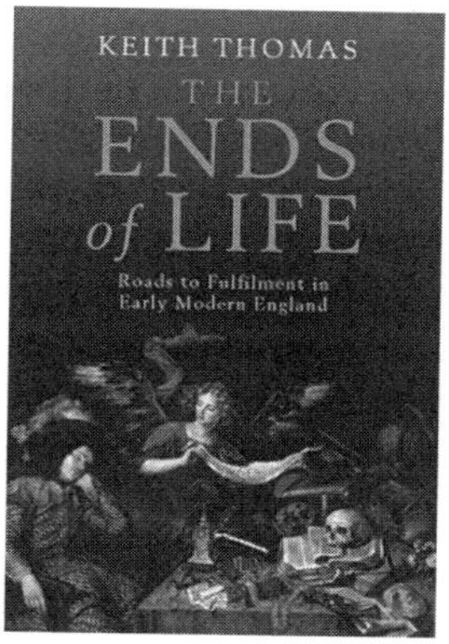

Author: Keith Thomas (1933-)
Publisher: Oxford University Press (New York). Illustrated. 393 pp. $34.95
Type of work: History
Time: 1530-1780
Locale: England

Thomas examines six qualities to which Englishmen and women in the early modern period aspired as means of achieving fulfillment in their lives

Keith Thomas's *The Ends of Life* grew out of a series of talks he gave in early 2000 under the rubric of the Ford Lectures in British History at the University of Oxford. The book retains the accessible tone of the original lectures, and each of the chapters—which are based on separate lectures—is capable of standing alone as a coherent study. Together, though, the chapters contribute to Thomas's overall investigation of the sources of satisfaction available to those living in England in the early modern period (roughly between the English Reformation and the American Revolution). As the hundred pages of references indicate, Thomas has drawn on an encyclopedic range of written sources to illustrate people's thinking. Since the majority of people living during this period were illiterate, however, their thoughts and desires must be inferred from the texts left by their better-educated countrymen and women.

Thomas's list of possible sources of happiness could be prolonged indefinitely, but he has chosen to focus on six: military prowess, work, money, reputation, personal relationships, and the afterlife. In *Saturae* (100-127; *Satires*, 1693), the Roman poet Juvenal devised his own list of the things people asked of the gods. Along with the wealth and military success that Thomas discusses, Juvenal included political power, learning, beauty, and long life, all of which Thomas ignores. To exhaust the list of human wants, however, would require a library rather than a volume, and Thomas shows through copious quotation that his choices loomed large in people's minds during his period of study.

Before considering each element in turn, Thomas explains that the very idea of self-fulfillment was once revolutionary. For Plato and Aristotle, *eudaimonia*, a sense of well-being, derived from philosophical contemplation and hence was accessible only to the elites who had leisure for this pursuit. In the Middle Ages, the words "ambition" and "singularity" had only negative connotations. Contentment was to come from fulfilling one's role in the Great Chain of Being, a role determined by birth. Individual happiness was less important than social harmony and public welfare. Thomas recognizes that not everyone accepted this orthodox view, but in the early

Keith Thomas has served as president of Corpus Christi College, pro vice-Chancellor of Oxford University, and president of the British Academy. His publications include Religion and the Decline of Magic *(1971; winner of the Wolfson Prize),* Rule and Misrule in the Schools in Early Modern England *(1976), and* Man and the Natural World *(1983).*

modern period the individual pursuit of happiness came to be more widely accepted.

One path that Englishmen took in that quest was military. Chivalric romances enjoyed popularity, and real people imitated their fictional heroes. Thomas notes that, when the earl of Oxford arrived in Palermo in 1572, he issued a general challenge to the inhabitants. At the siege of Rouen in 1591, the earl of Essex invited the French governor to single combat. The earl of Newcastle in 1643 similarly challenged Ferdinand, Lord Fairfax, leader of the Parliamentary forces in the English Civil War. Thomas Nashe in 1592 commented on the popularity of William Shakespeare's portrayal of brave Talbot's battles against the French in *Henry IV, Part I* (pr. c. 1597-1598, pb. 1598), and Henry V's exploits were similarly extolled. Henry VIII, Charles I, William III, George I, and George II all led armies in the field.

Thomas acknowledges a countermovement that criticized the waging of war, at least for personal glory. Writers John Gower, Thomas Hoccleve, and John Lydgate, as well as theologian John Wycliffe, rejected militarism. The humanist Roger Ascham, tutor to Queen Elizabeth, objected to Sir Thomas Malory's *Le Morte d'Arthur* (1485) because it glorified combat. The denizens of Sir Thomas More's perfect society in *De Optimo Reipublicae Statu, deque Nova Insula Utopia* (1516; *Utopia*, 1551) avoid combat whenever possible. In *Paradise Regained* (1671), John Milton's Christ rejects military glory. In any case, as armies became more professional, the opportunity to achieve individual military distinction declined. Thomas argues that by the end of the eighteenth century most English people no longer aspired to success in combat.

Whereas warfare lost its appeal as a means of satisfaction, work began to be perceived as a means of self-realization. The classical ideal had stressed leisure, and the Church had long treated labor as a curse. The Reformation, however, rejected monkish contemplation in favor of the active life, if only because work left less time for sin and promoted a community's welfare. Religious as well as secular writers also began to praise work for its own sake. In *Paradise Lost* (1667, 1674), Milton imagined an Eden where Adam and Eve faced more tasks than they could complete. Satan finds Eve alone because she and Adam have separated so they can work more efficiently. Milton believed that human happiness demanded labor. Thomas quotes a letter that Thomas Jefferson wrote to his daughter on May 21, 1787, in which he said that only the idle are wretched. One could find satisfaction not only in a job well done but also in the camaraderie that the workplace provided.

Work could also lead to wealth, another source of satisfaction. While riches were never despised, classical philosophy and religious teaching warned against laying up stores on Earth at the expense of moral and spiritual values. Such views carried less weight by the 1500's. The texts on which Thomas draws indicate that wealth was not so much an end in itself but rather a means for consumption. Nor was expenditure intended to provide comfort or convenience. Instead, its purpose was to purchase esteem. Thomas observes that in seventeenth and eighteenth century London owning a coach was inconvenient; pedestrians could maneuver more easily through the city's congested streets than could carriages. The diarist Samuel Pepys proudly purchased a coach, however. The philosopher William Godwin maintained that almost every purchase was designed to secure the respect or avoid the contempt of others. Throughout the early modern period, the word "consumer" retained the negative meaning of "waster," but wealth and commerce came to be viewed as civilizing forces.

Though the purpose of acquiring wealth was in large part to gain honor and reputation, Thomas devotes a separate chapter to this goal. He notes that, for Adam Smith, respect from peers was the most powerful human desire. Aristotle in his *Ethika Nikomacheia* (c. 335-323 B.C.E.; *Nicomachean Ethics*, 1797) placed honor highest among external goods, and the Anglican divine Richard Hooker claimed that reputation was the greatest earthly blessing. Geoffrey Chaucer's Wife of Bath (*The Canterbury Tales*, 1387-1400) was always the first to give an offering at church, not because she was the most generous but because she sought precedence. If someone went before her, her charitable intentions vanished. Thomas cites the seventeenth century squire George Spurstone's objection that his vicar did not distinguish between rich and poor in administering communion. Some churches did differentiate, serving sweeter wine to the wealthy. Archbishop Laud semiseriously proposed removing pews from churches because so many disputes arose over the order of seating.

Each socioeconomic group had its own ideas of honor, and respect from peers was more important than recognition from those outside a given social sphere. Even criminals wanted the respect of their fellow felons. Because respect was so important and shame so feared, many early modern punishments—such as placing malefactors in the stocks—relied on shame to enforce conformity. Hester Prynne's treatment in Nathaniel Hawthorne's *The Scarlet Letter* (1850), set in the seventeenth century, exemplifies this practice.

Like military prowess, the desire for honor waned over time. Urbanization led to increased anonymity, so the opinion of peers mattered less. Dissenters such as Quakers rejected communal standards of behavior in favor of personal convictions. Democracy, too, lessened the interest in honor: If everyone is equal, no person's opinion matters more than one's own. Alexis de Tocqueville's *De la démocratie en Amérique* (1835, 1840; *Democracy in America*, 1835, 1840) linked the quest for honor to hierarchical societies. By the end of the eighteenth century, social acceptance in general became less important than personal fulfillment.

While many early modern subjects ceased craving social acceptance, friendship remained an important ingredient in the making of a satisfying life. Aristotle's *Nicomachean Ethics* and Cicero's *Laelius de amicitia* (44 B.C.E.; *On Friendship*, 1481) stressed the importance of friendship for moral development, virtue, and success. Friendship thus was viewed instrumentally, as useful for advancement. In the early modern period, comradeship came to be seen as a good in itself. Montaigne's essay on his dead friend Étienne de La Boétie focused on personal affection. Clubs arose for conviviality. Thomas observes that Anthony Van Dyck painted seven double portraits of pairs of Englishwomen to symbolize their closeness. The idea of marital friendship also flourished. The older notion that the society of women effeminized men yielded to a vision of friendship in marriage as important for personal happiness. This new focus on domesticity and clubs came at the expense of community, however, as village fetes and other public gatherings declined in popularity.

Thomas's final section deals with the afterlife, not in the religious but rather in the secular sense. In Shakespeare's *Love's Labour's Lost* (pr. c. 1594-1595, pb. 1598; revised 1597 for court performance), the king of Navarre establishes a monastic academy to gain eternal fame for its members. Thomas mentions a group of law students in 1606 who attacked a London brothel in the hope that this exploit would earn them posthumous recognition. Thomas Gray's "Elegy Written in a Country Churchyard" (1751) tells of simple villagers who yearn for remembrance after their deaths. The eighteenth century historians David Hume and Edward Gibbon said that they wrote for fame. Lawrence Sterne offered the same reason for creating his curious novel *The Life and Opinions of Tristram Shandy, Gent.* (1759-1767; commonly known as *Tristram Shandy*).

Indicative of the growth of this desire for remembrance was the introduction of the obituary at the end of the seventeenth century. Funereal monuments date from antiquity, but they proliferated in the seventeenth century, and less permanent wooden markers gave way to brass and stone. Portraits, memorial medals, and death masks also became more common. Wills instructed descendants to preserve heirlooms. For Thomas, the rise of antiquarianism and biographical dictionaries reflects this increased concern with preserving the memory of the departed. Patronage similarly could guarantee remembrance. Francis Bacon observed that those without children were most likely to endow foundations such as colleges because they had no offspring to carry on their names. The antiquarian Thomas Hearne in 1717 argued that heads of colleges should be compelled to remain celibate because those who married never left money to their institutions.

Thomas acknowledges that not everyone in early modern England shared the same desires. John Calvin was buried in an unmarked grave, and Quakers initially eschewed funerary monuments. Niccolò Machiavelli and Montaigne enjoyed withdrawing from society to read and write. Still, the elements Thomas cites as important for happiness in the early modern period seem familiar. The past is not invariably another country with alien customs. Thomas's book therefore provides insights into the origins of more recent thoughts and practices.

Joseph Rosenblum

Review Sources

The Evening Standard (London), March 30, 2009, p. 38.
History Today 59, no. 6 (June, 2009): 59.
London Review of Books 31, no. 14 (July 23, 2009): 18-19.
The New York Review of Books, October 22, 2009, pp. 8-12.
The Spectator 309, no. 9417 (February 21, 2009): 32-36.
Times Higher Education, February 12, 2009, p. 49.
The Times Literary Supplement, February 27, 2009, pp. 3-5.
The Wilson Quarterly 33, no. 3 (Summer, 2009): 103-104.

EVERY MAN DIES ALONE

Author: Hans Fallada (1893-1947)
First published: Jeder stirbt für sich allein, 1947, in Germany
Translated from the German by Michael Hofmann
Afterword by Geoff Wilkes
Publisher: Melville House (Brooklyn, N.Y.). 543 pp. $27.00
Type of work: Novel
Time: The early 1940's
Locale: Berlin, Brandenburg, and Erkner, Germany

Written soon after World War II, Fallada's novel chronicles how Otto and Anna Quangel resisted the Nazis by distributing subversive anonymous postcards through much of Nazi-controlled Berlin

Principal characters:

OTTO QUANGEL, the foreman of a furniture factory
ANNA QUANGEL, Otto's wife, who helps him distribute postcards
ESCHERICH, the Gestapo inspector in charge of the Hobgoblin case
SS OBERGRUPPENFUHRER PRALL, Escherich's superior
BALDUR PERSICKES, a sixteen-year-old Hitler Youth
EMIL BORKHAUSEN, a loafer who tries to exploit people by informing on them to the Gestapo
ENNO KLUGE, a gambler falsely accused of distributing the postcards
TRUDEL BAUMANN, the former fiancé of Otto and Anna's son who attempts to start a resistance cell against the Nazis
FRAU ROSENTHAL, a woman who cannot stand the isolation while hiding from Nazi persecution
JUDGE FROMM, a retired judge who unsuccessfully tries to assist Frau Rosenthal
MAX HARTEISEN, a film actor blacklisted by Joseph Goebbels
DR. REICHHARDT, Otto's cellmate
FRIEDRICH LORENZ, the self-sacrificing chaplain at the prison where the Quangels await execution

With the many depictions of Nazis as convenient villians in popular films and books, it may be easy to lose sight of what it was actually like to live under their regime on a daily basis. Hans Fallada, an author then internationally known for his novel *Kleiner Mann, was nun?* (1932; *Little Man, What Now?*, 1933), opted to stay in Germany when the Nazis assumed power in 1933. He tried to write apolitical novels but found it difficult to adjust to the expectations of the Third Reich. After living in Berlin, Fallada sought refuge in a small village called Carwitz, but even then he had to suffer the paranoia, the eavesdropping, and the suspicions of the villagers.

As a writer, Fallada was obliged to be ambiguous about his allegiances. Geoff Wilkes, in his afterword to *Every Man Dies Alone*, describes Fallada as "neither an eager collaborator nor a resistance fighter." Toward the end of the war, Fallada was committed to a Nazi insane asylum. He emerged from that experience very much shaken, but Johannes R. Becher, a friend of his, sought to encourage Fallada's writing by giving him the Gestapo file on Elise and Otto Hampel, a working-class couple in Berlin. After hurriedly writing *Every Man Dies Alone* in twenty-four days, Fallada died from a morphine overdose before the book's publication in 1947.

Hans Fallada (born Rudolf Ditzen) found fame as a novelist when his novel Kleiner Mann, was nun? *(1932;* Little Man, What Now?, *1933) became an international best seller. He opted to stay in Nazi Germany during World War II. Fallada wrote* Every Man Dies Alone *just before his death in 1947.*

Telling the Hempels' story gave Fallada a way to depict many of the compromises, the fear, the betrayals, and the myriad forms of revolt against the Nazis that occurred during their regime. The working-class couple were not initially inclined toward political agitation, but when Elise's brother died in the war, they decided to write and distribute hundreds of postcards around Berlin that were critical of the Nazis, calling for civil disobedience both at home and in the workplace. The Berlin police and the Gestapo spent three years hunting for the mysterious card makers, and the Hampels were initially so successful that the Gestapo thought that it was dealing with a much larger underground resistance. Eventually, the Hampels were captured, placed on trial at the People's Court, found guilty, and executed in 1943.

Fear can have complicated effects on a society in which most people have something to hide: In Nazi Germany, informers could prosper. People could be imprisoned or executed for minor acts of insubordination, both in the workplace and at home. Nazi officials wanted not only obedience but also complete agreement with their views. Fallada was interested in the extreme corruption of those who exulted in the display of power and the doglike debasement of those beneath them. Even those in power could be turned into suspects and punished with very little justification. Ultimately, *Every Man Dies Alone* debates what it meant to revolt against the Nazis if the consequence of that revolt was imprisonment and death. The novel questions whether it was better to live nobly and suffer the result or to compromise with the Nazi system. It asks what kind of values could be affirmed amidst such corruption and universal deceit.

As much as he tries to resolve these moral ambiguities in the novel's later prison scenes, Fallada leaves it to readers to draw their own conclusions by sifting through the conflicting perspectives of his characters. For the most part, these characters are portrayed as just trying to get by amid occasional Allied bombings and increasingly histrionic Nazi propaganda. Much of the novel's early action takes place at 55 Jablonski Strasse, an apartment building where the Persickes, an arrogant pro-Nazi family, live uneasily with the Quangels and Frau Rosenthal, a Jewish woman who is afraid to leave her room. The novel begins with Otto and Anna Quangel learning that their soldier son has just died. The news radicalizes Otto against the Nazis, but he has to be careful what he says around Emil Borkhausen, an opportunistic neighbor who notes Otto's defeatist talk.

When Otto tells the news to Trudel Baumann, the woman who was engaged to his son, she tells him of a resistance cell that she has joined to fight the Nazis. Later, however, in part because of her talk with Otto, the cell dissolves, but not before some other Nazis overhear them talk about it and try to investigate. Once Otto and Anna begin to hatch their plan to spread various postcards around Berlin in the hopes of starting a broader resistance, Emil and Enno Kluge, another loafer, decide to rob Frau Rosenthal's apartment under the assumption that, since she is Jewish, her possessions are up for grabs. Their plan goes comically awry when they get drunk on Rosenthal's schnapps in the midst of the robbery. Before long, the Persickes find them and beat them in their stupor.

Frau Rosenthal hides out in Judge Fromm's home for several days but finds that she cannot stand the uncertainty and the solitude of hiding. Eventually, she avoids capture by committing suicide by jumping from a window. Occasionally, characters such as Judge Fromm try to retain some intellectual serenity in the midst of all this intrigue, but Fallada notes the difficulty of maintaining that "peace" when he writes of Fromm's later demise in a parenthetical aside: "Three years later, a high-explosive bomb would blow this home to smithereens, and the sedate old gentleman himself would die a slow and agonizing death in the cellar . . . "

The novel becomes more suspenseful as Otto and his wife make progress with the postcards. They painstakingly write out proclamations such as "PASS THIS CARD ON, SO THAT MANY PEOPLE READ IT!—DON'T GIVE TO THE WINTER RELIEF FUND!—WORK AS SLOWLY AS YOU CAN! PUT SAND IN THE MACHINES!—EVERY STROKE OF WORK NOT DONE WILL SHORTEN THE WAR!" Then, they tentatively look around for places to put the cards without being seen, usually on the windowsills of office buildings around Berlin. Otto and Anna are initially quite successful at getting away with their plan, although they do not know how much their cards arouse the interest of the Gestapo and become the special focus of an inquiry by Inspector Escherich. The inspector makes it his life goal to capture what he calls "the Hobgoblin" who makes the postcards.

Ironically, instead of cards being passed underground throughout the city, as Otto and his wife imagine, most of the people who find the cards immediately give them to the authorities in great fear of being implicated in the crime. For instance, film actor Harteisen happens upon a card. Instantly anxious, he tries to hand it over to his lawyer, but his lawyer does not want it because anyone associated with the cards can become a suspect. Clearly, the people who gain the most from the postcards are the Quangels themselves. Even though they will later suffer imprisonment and execution, the cards give their lives purpose and meaning. In their semiabsurd and relatively crude way, the cards show the importance yet also the sense of futility of writers under the regime, including Fallada, expressing themselves honestly in the midst of pervasive propaganda and fear.

In part 2, Fallada shifts the narrative perspective to Gestapo Inspector Escherich and his efforts to track down the Hobgoblin. A surprisingly sympathetic figure, Escherich begins his investigation by tracking all of the found postcards on a large map of Berlin dotted with small red flags. He would like to be patient and let the criminal give himself away eventually, but his boorish superior SS Obergruppenfuhrer Prall wants immediate results. When Enno Kluge is falsely accused of dropping a card at a doctor's office, Escherich can immediately tell that the man has no connection to the case and lets him go. Later, however, Kluge evades two Gestapo spies sent to keep track of his movements, and Prall becomes enraged with Escherich's handling of the case.

Escherich asks to be taken off the case, and for that act of presumption Prall has him stripped of his official function and sent to the Gestapo basement, where guards beat him and treat him like any other criminal. After Escherich's replacement proves to be an even worse detective, Prall eventually reinstates Escherich to his former position, but the inspector has been permanently changed by his ordeal. He can hardly bring himself to look at Prall without trembling. In all, Fallada paints a picture of an organization in which even those in power have to fear SS brutality and any act of independence or free thinking can bring heavy reprisals. From the officials' perspective, people need to get out of the habit of thinking, since "the Fuhrer can do their thinking for them." Escherich's ordeal makes him a much more efficient investigator, and he apprehends the Quangels soon after he is reinstated, in part because Otto accidentally drops a couple of cards in his factory. By now, late in the war, the factory makes only coffins.

In part 3 of the novel, the Quangels are caught, separated, interrogated, and ultimately given a bizarre show trial. In this part, Fallada considers the results and consequences of their civil disobedience. Ironically, Escherich commits suicide after realizing that he was the one and only convert of the Quangels' campaign. Otto had considered his resistance campaign in isolation from other events, but he comes to see how others have been hurt by his act of revolt. Because Anna did not think of the possible consequences of mentioning Trudel during her questioning, the Gestapo arrests Trudel as well, and she and her husband die.

The prison scenes sometimes evoke the absurd trials portrayed in Lewis Carroll's *Alice's Adventures in Wonderland* (1865), as well as Albert Camus's meditations on the metaphysics of being condemned to death in *L'Étranger* (1942; *The Stranger*, 1946). Otto struggles to retain his dignity and scorn for his captors, even when he is placed in a cell where his cellmate acts like a dog in an attempt to fake insanity. Later, however, Otto learns civility from a cellmate named Dr. Reichhardt, a musical composer, who maintains an orderly lifestyle including books, chess, and music as a way to rise above his imprisonment.

While this portion of the novel tends to be a bit schematic in the way characters tend to be extremely good (the prison chaplain) or evil (the show trial's judge), Fallada keeps the basic questions open: What good has the Quangels' act of civil disobedience done? Working within a state run by criminals, how can one accomplish anything? Is resistance meaningful or futile if it leads to imprisonment, further suffering, and death? It is to the novel's credit that there are no easy answers. Perhaps the thesis of the novel is best stated by Dr. Reichhardt, who comes to exemplify one enlightened form of protest:

> . . . we all acted alone, we were caught alone, and every one of us will have to die alone. But that doesn't mean that we *are* alone, Quangel, or that our deaths will be in vain. Nothing in this world is done in vain, and since we are fighting for justice against brutality, we are bound to prevail in the end.

Roy C. Flannagan

Review Sources

Booklist 105, no. 12 (February 15, 2009): 28.
Kirkus Reviews 77, no. 2 (January 15, 2009): 54.
The Nation 289, no. 2 (July 13, 2009): 25-30.
The New York Times Book Review, March 1, 2009, p. 10.
The New Yorker 85, no. 12 (May 4, 2009): 73.
Publishers Weekly 256, no. 2 (January 12, 2009): 29-30.

EVERYTHING RAVAGED, EVERYTHING BURNED

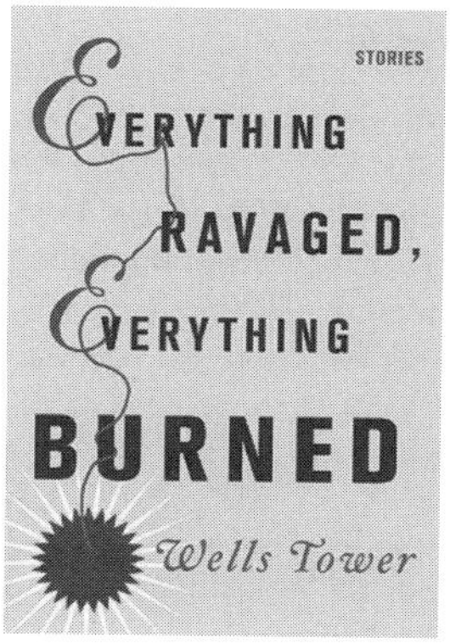

Author: Wells Tower (1973-)
Publisher: Farrar, Straus and Giroux (New York). 256 pp. $24.00
Type of work: Short fiction
Time: The late eighth to the early eleventh century; the early twenty-first century
Locale: United States; Scandinavia

Tower's debut collection of nine stories entertains and surprises as it depicts ordinary people coping with lives that are gradually unraveling or suddenly exploding around them

It is not surprising that award-winning author Wells Tower has crafted a debut collection of short stories, *Everything Ravaged, Everything Burned*, in which ordinary people are intimately observed, some at pivotal moments of their lives. His interest in sociology and anthropology, disciplines in which he earned degrees from Wesleyan University, blend with his M.F.A. in fiction writing from Columbia University to make his stories seem as though they were case studies taken from an ongoing study of relationships. The stories explore painful bonds between parents and children as well as between siblings or friends. None of these relationships is left unscathed, as characters end up emotionally charred.

The collection includes nine poignant tales that provide surprises as well as entertainment and insight. Tower explores everyday life through the eyes of middle-aged men whose lives are falling apart, envious teenage girls, a wheelchair-bound widower who may never get a chance to touch a woman again, and even Viking warriors who find love when their battles end. A strong sense of yearning permeates all of these stories—yearning for something more, something lost, or something unlikely ever to be found.

In "The Brown Coast," Bob Monroe is sorting out his life after the death of his father and the unraveling of his marriage. He recently made a series of mistakes, including a brief but unsatisfying affair, so everything that could go wrong for Bob does, even though he tries to fix things. The addition of an ugly sea creature to his aquarium ultimately becomes an apt metaphor for his life when it poisons the other sea animals and saltwater fish he has patiently collected. Upon finding his fish dead, Bob accepts that his marriage is dead as well. He also abandons his newfound friendship with neighbors Claire and Derrick Treat, whose troubled marriage pales in comparison to his losses. Ironically, it was Claire who found the ugly sea creature and gave it to Bob as a friendly gift. His downward spiral seems to continue as he tosses the poisonous sea slug into the ocean and nearly hits a catamaran.

Poison also plays a role in "Retreat" as brothers Matthew and Stephen reunite at Matthew's mountain cabin in Maine. Matthew seeks to help Stephen, who is struggling

Wells Tower has been awarded the Plimpton Prize by The Paris Review, *as well as two Pushcart Prizes. His short stories and articles have appeared in* The New Yorker, Harper's Magazine, *and* The Washington Post Magazine. *This is his first collection of short stories.*

financially and resents his brother's success. When Stephen quickly befriends Matt's retired neighbor George, Matthew is hurt. Matthew is so unable to overcome his wounded pride that he chooses to ignore their warnings and eat the grilled tenderloin of a moose shot by Stephen and George, even though the animal was clearly ill when they found it. In the course of their brief reunion, the cavernous gap between the brothers is made clear through their conversations as Matt is unable to let Stephen be right about anything, even the tainted moose meat. Their rivalry echoes the relationships of siblings in countless American families where some are black sheep and others are financial successes.

Long-silent rivalries between fathers and sons are explored more subtly in "Executors of Important Energies." Burt is called home by his stepmother Lucy, who claims his father Roger, a former attorney, is being ravaged by Alzheimer's disease. Burt finds that the man whose approval he has sought all his life has become a stranger. In fact, Roger treats obese chess hustler Dwayne like his new best friend, as he ignores Burt. Over dinner, Burt is forced to accept how far Roger's grip on reality has slipped and that Roger will never appreciate his work as an inventor. The domineering force in Burt's life, he realizes, no longer exists.

In "Down Through the Valley," a middle-aged father painfully discovers that his young daughter Marie likes her stepfather better than she likes him. Ed reluctantly goes to the aid of his ex-wife Jane, whose second husband Barry, a yoga and meditation instructor, has broken his ankle. Jane is in seclusion at a meditation retreat in the mountains, and Barry is unable to care for Marie, who is still a toddler, so Ed agrees to pick Marie up until Jane's retreat is over. Upon arrival, however, Ed learns he must also drive Barry back to civilization. On the harrowing ride down the mountain, Ed struggles to maintain his pride and cope with the awkward situation as it spirals out of control. When Barry intervenes between battling lovers at a coffee shop, for example, Ed winds up getting arrested. His attempt to help Jane turns into a nightmare that echoes the recurring bad dream she used to have when they were still together.

Nightmares and visions also infuse "Leopard," in which eleven-year-old Yancy stays home from school to avoid a bully. He lives with his mother and his survivalist stepfather on twenty acres in the middle of thick woods. Unable to forget how his father backed down when his stepfather threatened him with a rock, Yancy cannot refuse when his stepfather sends him for the mail, although the mailbox is a fifteen-minute walk from the house. Along with the mail, Yancy finds a flyer for a lost pet that looks like a leopard in the photograph. He decides to pretend to pass out from the heat and lies down in the driveway to wait for his mother to come home. This sympathy scheme goes awry when Yancy is discovered by police officers, to whom he looks dead. As he tries to ignore his stepfather's anger after the officers drive him home, Yancy imagines that the lost leopard is stalking his house, an image that echoes his own desire for escape.

The relationship between fathers and daughters is explored in "Door in Your Eye." Middle-aged but unmarried, Charlotte has recently brought her elderly, wheelchair-bound, widowed father Albert to the city to live with her. She warns him to stay away from their across-the-street neighbor, who seems to be a prostitute. Albert, however, goes to meet this neighbor after watching her door from his window for several days. He senses she may be the last woman he will ever get to touch. When he discovers she sells marijuana and prescription drugs rather than sex, he is as much relieved as disappointed. Albert's defiance displeases Charlotte, who returns home and finds him across the street, but his act of independence shows that he is still in charge of his own life.

Teenaged cousins become envious rivals in "Wild America" when Maya visits Jacey. A model and dancer, Maya is about to attend a government-funded dance school in North Carolina. She confides to Jacey that she is in love with the dance school's assistant director, who is old enough to be her father. She also humiliates Jacey by refusing to ask teen model Doug to take Jacey to the Burning Man Festival in her place. The girls later get stoned in the woods with Leander Buttons, a geeky boy whom Jacey once dated. Maya winds up dancing with him, so Jacey decides to go home without them. She tries to impress Stewart Quick, an older man who gives her a ride home. They wind up kissing, but Jacey resists going further with him. She is relieved when her father arrives to take her to dinner, and she assumes Maya will come home safely with Leander later. The self-absorption of these teenagers is implied by the story's title. The girls seem to resemble Jacey's cat Scopes, which toys with a bird at the beginning of the story and devours it in the end.

In "On the Show," a variety of personalities and relationships are brought to light. At a carnival, seven-year-old Henry Lemons catches a lizard, while his father Jim is trying to impress his date Sheila. Sheila's ten-year-old son Randy, meanwhile, gives Henry a hard time. Henry runs off when Randy tries to take the lizard from him, and he hides in a plastic privy with a man who seems friendly. Meanwhile, Jeff Park is hired by ride foreman Leon to run one of the rides. He has run away from home himself after his drunken stepfather treated him like hired help one time too many.

After Jim searches for Henry and fortunately finds him watching a midway show, Henry relates what happened in the privy, but Jim does not believe him. Jeff Park is later questioned by police about his whereabouts when Henry was in the privy, and he agrees to give a blood sample if necessary. Other carnival workers—including Gary, who seems retarded—are suspected of molesting Henry as well. The culprit turns out to be Horace Tate, a Future Farmers of America judge, whom Henry identifies by his distinctive turquoise belt buckle. No longer a suspect, Jeff goes to meet Katie, a girl he flirted with the previous night, but she stands him up for her friends. Jeff's ardor fades like the green phosphorescence of some candy that Katie gave him the night before.

Ancient friendships come to life in the collection's final, eponymous story. "Everything Ravaged, Everything Burned" follows Vikings who sail across the North Sea to an island to stop a Norwegian monk living there from threatening their lands. Harald would rather stay home on his farm with his family, but his friend Gnut, a widower who likes boats and does not like farming, convinces him to go. The warriors find and kill the monk, freeing the islanders, who had been forced to pay him tithes. Gnut falls in love with one-armed seamstress Mary and takes her home despite her father's protests. The Vikings ravage and burn the island before going home to their farms again, but Harald continues to worry that people from the island will come to take Mary back, leaving the Vikings' own lands ravaged and burned in return.

Tower's keen understanding of the complexities of relationships is felt throughout his wide range of characters. Some stories are more cohesive than others, but the collection as a whole is highly memorable. Overall, Tower's writing feels ironic and suspenseful, although critics have called his style both violent and dazzling. He is clearly sympathetic to each of his characters but also compelled to give them emotional challenges that are not easy to overcome. Many of the stories in this collection end abruptly, which seems to be one of the devices Tower uses to make his stories both visceral and personal.

Barbara Schiffman

Review Sources

Booklist 105, no. 12 (February 15, 2009): 28.
Esquire 151, no. 3 (March, 2009): 50-52.
Kirkus Reviews 76, no. 24 (December 15, 2008): 1276.
Library Journal 133, no. 20 (December 1, 2008): 122.
London Review of Books 31, no. 13 (July 9, 2009): 23-24.
New York 42, no. 9 (March 23, 2009): 64-65.
The New York Review of Books 56, no. 9 (May 28, 2009): 22-24.
The New York Times, March 11, 2009, p. 1.
The New York Times, March 24, 2009, p. C1.
The New York Times Book Review, March 29, 2009, p. 1.
Publishers Weekly 255, no. 41 (October 13, 2008): 3.
The Times Literary Supplement, April 17, 2009, p. 20.
Village Voice 54, no. 51 (December 16, 2009): 35.

EVIDENCE

Author: Mary Oliver (1935-   )
Publisher: Beacon Press (Boston). 74 pp. $23.00.
Type of work: Poetry

Beloved poet and nature writer Oliver offers forty-seven new poems tracing the paths of love, grief, and spirit through the natural world

Readers of Mary Oliver's nineteenth volume of poetry, *Evidence*, will find themselves in familiar territory, as Oliver once again strides out into the Cape Cod countryside to find wisdom and beauty in nature. Readers will also find in this collection the urgent attention to matters of meaning that is characteristic of Oliver's poetry. Oliver in *Evidence* obliquely turns away from the heavy grief of her earlier volume *Thirst* (2006) and the dark undertone of *Red Bird* (2008). In *Evidence*, Oliver's work is less somber, more centered, and fully engaged with the processes of life in all its glory.

This is not to say that Oliver does not write about death in this volume. On the contrary, she faces death, her own and those of beloved animals and friends, with an assuredness that was not as pronounced in her earlier works. It is as if she has come to terms with loss by gaining greater understanding of what it means to love. For example, in "Swans," Oliver first reports that she wants some physical reminder of the lovely swans that fly overhead, such as a feather, in order to demonstrate that the swans were real and not just her imagination. She closes, the poems, however, with the thought that the beloved is not something that requires physical presence: That which is beloved must be "believed in" rather than held. Such belief can transcend the "unreachable distance" that separates Oliver from the swans flying overhead.

Oliver observes the interplay of life and death in a number of poems as well. In one of the finest, "Prince Buzzard," she evokes rich mythological and religious symbols in her consideration of a buzzard flying overhead. Calling the buzzard "prince" evokes royal figures such as the prince of darkness, a sobriquet used for Hades, the Greek ruler of the underworld. Oliver further emphasizes this connection by reporting that she mistakes the buzzard drifting in the updraft for a "narrow boat and two black sails," perhaps alluding to the boat used by Charon in Greek mythology to ferry people across the River Styx to the underworld.

The buzzard comes down from its high spirals to investigate a dead lamb in a spring field. Oliver emphasizes the certainty of the lamb's death by repeating the world "dead" three times. Oliver chooses the dead creature with care; a lamb in Christian iconography is a symbol for the Christ. Indeed, the words "O Lamb of God, that takest away the sins of the world, have mercy on us" form an important part of the litany of the Catholic Mass. Lambs are regarded symbolically as both innocent and sacrificial within a Christian context. Thus, Oliver's choice of rendering the lamb as car-

Mary Oliver is one of the best-known poets and essayists writing in the United States. She has won the 1998 Lannan Literary Award, the 1984 Pulitzer Prize for American Primitive, *and the 1992 National Book Award for* New and Selected Poems. *Born in 1935 in Ohio, Oliver lives in Provincetown, Massachusetts.*

rion serves as both a striking image and a potent symbol.

Oliver states that she knows that it is hunger that draws the buzzard to the lamb's body, but she describes the buzzard's slow approach to the corpse as reverential, his pause before the lamb's body as a "ceremony." Her description might be connected to the act of a priest blessing the host before the sacrament of holy communion. Indeed, in Catholicism, doctrine teaches that the host becomes the literal body and blood of Christ through transubstantiation. Thus, just as the worshiper consumes the actual body and blood of Christ in a holy, life-giving ritual, the buzzard consumes the flesh of the lamb, and the flesh sustains the buzzard's life.

That Oliver intends for readers to move from death to life in this poem is clear by her final stanza. Just as she includes the words "dead, dead, dead" in stanza three, in stanza nine she writes that nothing remains of the lamb in the field in the summer, only "flowers, flowers, flowers." Thus, the remains of the lamb have nourished both the buzzard and the flowers of the field. The cycle is complete: The lamb of God has died in order to prepare the way for new birth.

Oliver makes the same point in a less symbolic way in "Landscape in Winter." In this short poem, a dead animal on the snow attracts a crowd of carrion crows. The crows speak, announcing that a death has occurred and that "this is good for us." In Oliver's world, the carrion eaters perform not only a useful but also a necessary task in the cycle of life.

Oliver seems less resigned to death in her poem, "If You Say It Right, It Helps the Heart to Bear It." The occasion of this poem is a visit to a Southern cemetery where Oliver notices many small crosses, indicating that children lie buried there. She asks readers to consider "the condition/ of the heart/ of a mother/ or a father/ watching these plantings." The parents' pain in this poem is nearly palpable. However, Oliver asserts, the words carved on the grave marker are a comfort, "like water on a stone." In this poem, Oliver seems to ask readers to accept that, while words are only words, there are words that can help take pain away.

In several of the volume's poems, Oliver addresses the inevitability of her own mortality. "Thinking of Swirler" is one of the finest of these. In it, Oliver tells of going out on an autumn afternoon and encountering a large buck deer she names Swirler. The deer regards her without fear, and Oliver finds this a precious gift. It leads her to think about how little any creature, including a human, can know about the world and about other creatures. A week after the encounter, Swirler is killed by a young bow hunter who is known to Oliver. For Oliver, this is a reminder of how death can come suddenly and unexpectedly; she concludes, "In my house there are a hundred half-done poems./ Each of us leaves an unfinished life."

In "Heart Poem," Oliver uses playing in an orchestra with a wild conductor as a metaphor for the sudden silences and starts of her own heart, suffering from arrhythmia. The image is clear and direct, the power of the poem striking. Although Oliver has never worried about her heart, she is able to describe its faulty functioning both precisely and with good humor. Although the music of the orchestra restarts after a sudden silence caused by the director's wildness, as Oliver's heart does after missing a beat, the end of the poem implies that someday the music may not start again. Oliver's response to her heart is not one of anger, grief, or fear. Rather, she expresses both acceptance and mild humor, making a gentle observation about what may come to pass.

Although many of the poems in *Evidence* concern death, a significant number also are poems of praise, thanks, and theology. In perhaps the finest poem in the volume, "At the River Clarion," Oliver offers an exploration of a theology of life. The images in this poem are exquisite, and the pacing of the poem is precise. In the first section, Oliver says that she does not "know who God is exactly." However, she does tell readers about a mystical moment she experiences while sitting in the River Clarion over a long afternoon. She hears all the sounds of the river, all the moving water, the stationary stones, and the mosses. Together, their voices speak to her of holiness. She tells readers that, if they cannot hear the voices, it is not the river's fault but rather the fault of human impatience and ego, which render people deaf to the holy.

In the poem's second section, Oliver reveals that God is in everything, in both life and death. She lists all the things that God is in, from lilies, to artists, to hands that make weapons and, by extension, bring death. She suggests that everything and everyone is a "tiny piece of God." She returns to thinking about the river, the source of her ideas about God. In the third brief section, Oliver advises that people should give thanks for both the "ripe melon" and the knife that cuts it. This paradox suggests that the world is far more complicated than most want to admit. The world is a place of life and death, and God is present in both.

The fourth section seems to refer to the illness and subsequent death of Oliver's longtime partner Molly Malone Cook, who died in 2005. Oliver writes of the helplessness of watching someone fade away, but she also comforts herself with the knowledge that the cycles of life require both gain and loss, both receiving and giving back. Oliver reinforces the notion that seems present throughout the entire collection: Everything in life is temporary; love, of any sort, is only on loan for a brief period.

Her recollection of lost love moves Oliver to the fifth section of the poem, which is about her dog Luke, who, like Cook, is also "given back." The eternal, that which flows along despite the receiving and the giving back required of living and dying, is symbolized by the river Clarion that continues to flow, despite suffering and changes. In section six, Oliver calls the birds, trees, and flowers that live along the riverbanks, "the lucky ones." She contrasts these creatures of nature with herself, a woman troubled in her thoughts, looking for answers in books rather than reading the text of nature.

Oliver concludes the poem with the brief section seven. Here, she finds comfort in the sounds of the river, its "infallible" voice. Infallibility suggests not only the inability to make an error but also the unfailing reliability of the river. In spite of loss, in spite of pain, the river continues on its way, singing its songs. The concluding line moves readers back to the opening of the poem and Oliver's statement that she does not "know who God is exactly." Although the poem does not claim this kind of knowledge, it does at least suggest that the eternal river, flowing and rushing along despite human doubts and worries, is the singing voice of the holy.

The quality of the poems of *Evidence*, in particular poems such as "At the River Clarion," demonstrates why Mary Oliver is one of the very best known poets writing in the United States. Her words are timely, reminding readers of the need to pay attention to the world around them. Most of all, her words provide beauty, comfort, and a striking understanding of the necessity of both life and death.

Diane Andrews Henningfeld

Review Sources

America 200, no. 14 (May 4, 2009): 28-30.
Booklist 105, no. 13 (March 1, 2009): 14.

THE FACE ON YOUR PLATE
The Truth About Food

Author: Jeffrey Moussaieff Masson (1941-)
Publisher: W. W. Norton (New York). 288 pp. $24.95
Type of work: Current affairs, environment, ethics, nature, science

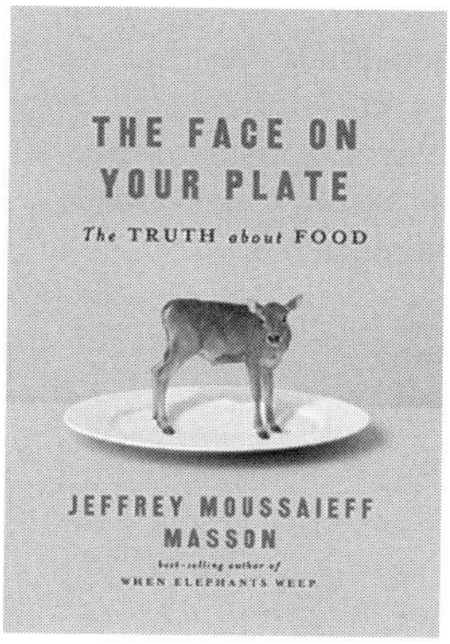

Masson's well-reasoned, well-researched, and persuasive arguments for eating a diet free from animal products

The growing movement that asks critical questions about where food comes from will welcome *The Face on Your Plate*, a provocative book by Jeffrey Moussaieff Masson. Eric Schlosser's *Fast Food Nation: The Dark Side of the All-American Meal* (2001) called attention to the way the U.S. food system is controlled by corporations that put profit before health. Michael Pollan's *The Omnivore's Dilemma: A Natural History of Four Meals* (2006) exposed the recent food-safety scares and the dangers to health caused by a lack of government regulation. Masson's *The Face on Your Plate* also seeks to raise public awareness of the ethical nature of food choices and challenges individuals to make a difference. This book documents the damage to the environment that the food production system causes and decries the cruelty to animals inherent in that system.

Without its extensive footnotes and comprehensive list of recommended readings and Web sites, *The Face on Your Plate* would be a slim volume. The text is only about 170 pages, but it is not a fast read. Masson presents a mix of passionate activism and scholarship. He is convinced that vegetarianism, more especially veganism—abstaining from all animal products, including eggs and dairy products—is the only choice rational, compassionate human beings can make. Once they understand the implications of their food choices, not just for their health but also for the well-being of animals and the environment, he says, people can no longer ignore the ethical dimension of how they eat. He backs his arguments with staggering statistics, persuasive reasoning, and quotations from respected health, environmental, government, and scientific authorities. The facts are not controversial; they are just not explicitly recognized.

Masson is at his best in the first chapter, "The Only World We Have," where he mounts a dramatic case to argue that choosing to eat animal products is not good for the planet. The typical American diet damages the environment in many ways, such as by contributing enormously to global warming. Masson debunks the widespread belief in the myth of "Man the hunter" that implies that humans are like other animals—"beasts of prey" and naturally carnivorous. Anthropologic research suggests that human beings were originally omnivorous scavengers who actually ate very little meat. Different animals eat distinctly different diets, and most animals seem to have little choice in their diet. In contrast to other species, human beings, apparently do not

Jeffrey Moussaieff Masson, an American psychoanalyst, vegan, and animal-rights advocate, is the author of numerous books on the emotional lives of animals, including the best sellers When Elephants Weep *(1994; with Susan McCarthy) and* Dogs Never Lie About Love *(1997).*

have the instinctive ability to choose foods that make them healthy. However, humans are the only species that can take the moral high ground and choose to stop eating meat and animal products in the interests of saving the planet.

In page after page of impressive statistics, Masson presents an indictment of the modern industrial food-production system. Food in the United States no longer comes from the family farm that most people naïvely associate with their food. Farming is now a megabusiness. Human beings, and all other animals, are significantly affected by factory farming. Huge animal farms and concentrated feeding pens hold hundreds of thousands of animals being fattened for slaughter. Such animal feedlots pollute air, water, and land. Citing the Pew Center on Global Climate Change, Masson states that the manner in which humans raise animals and dispose of their waste (urine and excrement) results in at least 33 percent of human-caused greenhouse gas emissions. Methane has 23 times the global warming effect of carbon dioxide, and two-thirds of all methane emissions worldwide come from industrial farming, largely from huge waste lakes (manure lagoons) that are often as big as several baseball fields. The method of growing fruits and vegetables also contributes to greenhouse gas emissions. Nitrous oxide has 296 times the global warming effect of carbon dioxide, and three-quarters of the nitrous oxide emissions in the United States are caused by industrial farming, mostly from nitrogen-containing fertilizers.

Factory farming (which produces three trillion pounds of raw waste) causes more pollution of American rivers and lakes than all other industries combined. Animals produce 130 times more waste than all the people in the United States—farm animals produce five tons of waste per year for each person in the country. A contaminated water supply results in sickness and death in humans. Masson catalogs the hazards of water pollution to human health—among them, problems for unborn babies; diarrheal diseases; and respiratory, brain, and eye problems caused by hydrogen sulfide gas. Contaminated water also poses a serious threat to fish and aquatic life.

Livestock today are fed antibiotics, hormones, and ground-up animal parts that are excreted unmetabolized, to a large extent, and contaminate groundwater and soil. The dust raised by millions of animals contains bacteria, molds, and fungi that cause respiratory disease, nausea, fatigue, and irritated mucus membranes, especially in farm workers and people living near industrial animal farms. Chicken megafarms are no less harmful to the environment. They contaminate water and soil, and health authorities fear that avian flu could become a serious epidemic.

Factory farms represent an extremely wasteful use of land. Although cattle in the United States and Europe seldom get outdoors, where they are allowed to graze, each head of cattle (producing twenty times more body waste than humans) requires 30 acres of pasture, land that could be used to grow crops for human consumption. Almost 40 percent of the world's grain goes to feed livestock instead of humans. This picture can only get worse, as the demand for meat and dairy products grows with rising living standards in the developing world. Huge land areas are being bulldozed, devastating whole ecosystems, to accommodate the world's increasing consumption of meat. Forests are disappearing at an alarming rate. Losing the forests, which remove carbon dioxide from the atmosphere and produce oxygen, means losing the fight against climate change.

Industrial agriculture is also extremely wasteful of water, an increasingly scarce commodity worldwide. It takes ten times more water to produce two pounds of animal protein than to produce two pounds of grain protein. It takes thirteen thousand gallons of water to produce a single pound of beef. About 80 percent of all pumped freshwater goes to meet the demands of industrial agriculture. Seventeen trillion gallons of irrigation water are required per year to produce feed for America's livestock. Water quality suffers from cattle feedlots and poultry farms. According to the Environmental Protection Agency, agriculture is responsible for 70 percent of all water quality problems in the United States. To cite but one example, chicken farms along the Eastern Shore of Maryland, bordering the Chesapeake Bay, produce 3.3 billion pounds of raw waste annually, polluting more than 173,000 miles of rivers and streams. Aquatic life has suffered dramatically from pollution, destroying the income of people who depend on fishing, crabbing, and oystering for their livelihood.

World hunger is now worse than at any other time in history, although the world produces enough food to feed twice the world's population. Humans have the space and the knowledge to produce enough fruits and vegetable to feed the world, according to Masson, but the political structure and will are lacking. He describes many examples of sustainable, innovative, agro-ecological approaches in communities throughout the world that use little or no pesticides but produce high yields. People are healthier and happier when they are productive, and natural farming methods fight against climate change. Masson accuses big business of seeking to maximize profits and using harmful pesticides and herbicides irresponsibly.

"The Lives They Lead" (chapter 2) leaves little to the imagination about the sad lives of farm animals. A psychoanalyst who has explored extensively the emotional lives of animals, Masson gives convincing evidence that animals have complex social and emotional lives. However, the ways in which animals are kept, fed, and slaughtered in agriculture does serious harm to their nature: Farm animals, he argues, should engage in behavior that is normal for their species. They need freshwater and a healthy diet, freedom from suffering, a comfortable resting area, and adequate space in which to express their species-appropriate normal behavior.

Masson describes the care of hens as a grim example of how industrial agriculture provides no opportunity for animals to lead a normal life. Young chicks' beaks are trimmed (likened to cutting off the end of a finger), chickens are denied perches, nests, room to spread their wings, or a place to scratch. Almost all of the eggs produced in the United States come from battery-caged hens. "Battery hens" are kept four to ten in a cage about twenty inches by twenty inches in size, so that each hen has two-thirds the space of an eight-by-eleven-inch sheet of paper. Many have crippled feet from scratching their wire cage; they suffer from brittle legs (osteoporosis) due to a lack of exercise. They never see sunlight.

Productivity of the overworked hens decreases within two years (as opposed to seven to ten years in the wild); then, they are slaughtered for pet food. Male birds are usually killed at birth since there is no profit from them. In similar fashion, Masson details the treatment of pigs, turkeys, and dairy cows (the pain of separation from their calves, the physical cost of overproducing milk, cramped housing, an artificial diet, abusive electric prodding, and being sent to slaughter when they are "spent").

In another chapter, "The Fishy Business of Aquaculture," Masson gives no quarter to those who think they can happily substitute fish for meat in their diet. He debates the commonly held notion that fish do not experience pain. Furthermore, he argues that their intelligence is underestimated. Research indicates that the brains of fish are similar to human brains, fish have well-developed memory spans, and they are capable of complex social relationships. Human greed puts fish at risk. The ocean is not inexhaustible. Modern methods of fishing use huge ships and tow nets, trawl the ocean floor, and discard dead "nontargeted" and "unwanted" marine life back into the sea. These methods upset complex ecosystems and endanger many fish species. Fish and shrimp farms have become increasingly important, but they are often plagued by disease and toxic chemicals and pollute waterways.

According to Masson, most people eat animal products out of ignorance or denial; they do not want to face the knowledge that cruelty to animals is involved in killing animals and using animal products. Masson devotes a whole chapter, "Denial," to this subject. The book's final chapter, "A Day in the Life of a Vegan," makes becoming a vegan seem less of a sacrifice than one might imagine. Masson is aware that few readers will become vegans as a result of reading his book. However, he has done a service to his cause by increasing awareness of the issues, especially by putting them within an ethical framework. Each person can make a difference by even minor diet changes, such as by eating less meat or by insisting that the animals they eat are humanely raised.

Edna B. Quinn

Review Sources

The Atlantic Monthly 304, no. 2 (September, 2009): 98.
Booklist 105, no. 12 (February 15, 2009): 14.
Kirkus Reviews 76, no. 24 (December 15, 2008): 1294.
Library Journal 134, no. 5 (March 15, 2009): 118.
Publishers Weekly 256, no. 17 (April 27, 2009): 128-129.
The New York Times, April 15, 2009, p. D1.

FIELD DAYS
A Year of Farming, Eating, and Drinking Wine in California

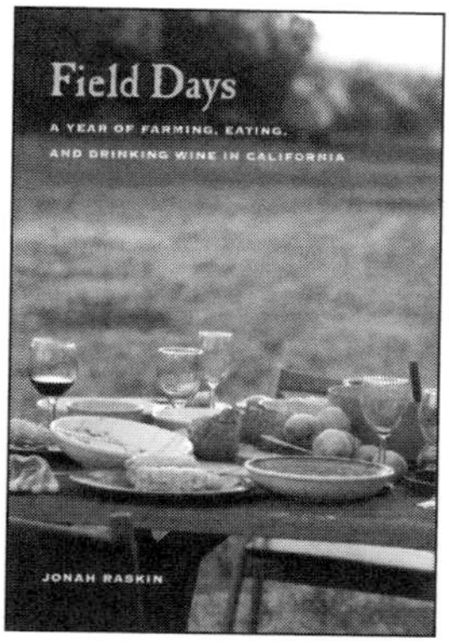

Author: Jonah Raskin (1942-)
Publisher: University of California Press (Berkeley). 329 pp. $24.95
Type of work: Memoir
Time: 2006
Locale: Northern California

A memoir and exploration of the slow food approach to growing and eating local food that describes the owners, workers, consumers, and cooks whom Raskin met while adopting this approach

Principal personages:

JONAH RASKIN, writer, educator, and farmer for a year
CARLO PETRINI, founder of the slow food movement
WARREN WEBER, early proponent of organic farming and owner of the oldest certified organic farm in the state of California
MIMI LUEBBERMANN, farmer in Chellano Valley, early advocate of supporting local farmers, and writer of how-to books for farmers and gardeners
SHARON GROSSI, owner of the largest certified organic farm in Sonoma County
OTTO TELLER, Oak Hill Farm founder and early rejecter of chemical fertilizers
ANNE TELLER, owner of Oak Hill Farm, where Raskin works and conducts research, and spokesperson for organic farming
PAIGE GREEN, photographer of Raskin's explorations
PAUL WIRTZ, in charge of vegetables and managing day-to-day operations at Oak Hill Farm
MIGUEL BARRIO, foreman at Oak Hill Farm who teaches Raskin how to pick, pack, and recognize the best product
JESUS "CHUY" SOTO, in charge of flowers at Oak Hill Farm, teaches Raskin how to select an appropriate bunch of flowers
WILL BUCKLIN, organic grape grower and producer of wine
BOB CONNARD, organic farmer whose farm has become famous for supplying fresh, organic, local food to Alice Waters and Chez Panisse
ALICE WATERS, influential cook, restaurateur, and food advocate, owner of Chez Panisse in Berkeley

Jonah Raskin's *Field Days* continues the tradition of memoirs covering a single year in the life of an author undertaking a particular course of action, journey,

Jonah Raskin is professor and chair of communications studies at Sonoma State University. He has published studies of California and counterculture writers and poets, including American Scream *(2004),* For the Hell of It *(1996), and (as editor)* Natives, Newcomers, Exiles, Fugitives *(2003).*

or experiment. Previous books in this tradition include Peter Mayle's *A Year in Provence* (1991), Julie Powell's *Julie and Julia: My Year of Cooking Dangerously* (2005), and Elizabeth Bishop's *Eat, Pray, Love: One Woman's Search for Everything in Italy, India, and Indonesia* (2007). Raskin's memoir chronicles the author's investigation of farming, eating, and drinking in California. He explains that part of the project's motivation grew out of the love that he shared with his parents of rural environments.

Recalling fondly a boyhood spent on Long Island, New York, when it was still covered with farmland, Raskin took the opportunity in the 1970's to move to California. There, he joined his parents, who, seeking to recapture such a rural environment, had retired to Sonoma County. Raskin has relished living in Sonoma, a place of Mediterranean climate with a nine-month growing season. He sees it as a near paradise. After working in academia for many years teaching writing and communications, Raskin developed a longing at age sixty-five to connect with the soil. He decided he could do so while continuing in his teaching position at Sonoma State University. He planned to utilize his writing to describe his exploration of the small-farm, local-food movement developing in Northern California and throughout the country.

Field Days, the resulting book, explores the resurgence of organic farming on small farms and the rising popularity of fresh, seasonal produce purchased by buyers interested in flavor and healthy eating. It describes the farmers and their supporters, who stand in sharp contrast to large-scale agribusiness. Industrialized farms produce mass quantities of often-tasteless fruits and vegetables on huge farms, spraying their produce with chemicals to protect them from disease and pests. These mass-produced fruits and vegetables, available year-round from suppliers around the globe, have caused Americans at least to grow accustomed to every fruit and vegetable being available in supermarkets all year long.

Raskin investigates the growers, buyers, and environmentalists who have begun to change Americans' ideas about the aesthetic, nutritional, and environmental value of agricultural products. Rather than year-round availability and shelf life, these people emphasize the value of flavor, nutrition, and care for the environment. Raskin discovers the influence of Bob Cannard, recognized by California growers as one of the founders of organic farming, who supplies Alice Waters of Chez Panisse restaurant in Berkeley with the produce she uses in developing her menus of seasonal foods.

Raskin begins what he calls his search for healthier food and connection with place in Marin County at a propitious time: Farms in Marin and elsewhere have been changing. Before Rachel Carson's polemic book *Silent Spring* (1962) exposed the terrible effects of DDT, many farmers had the attitude that the land was theirs to treat however they wanted. Raskin recalls days on his parents' farm when clouds of pesticide spray floated over the valley, poisoning all around it. By contrast, Bob Cannard and other organic farmers tolerate weeds as part of a healthy ecosystem and focus on nourishing the soil as well as growing a product. Slowly, they are challenging farms focused only on profit.

Raskin starts his journey by talking with the sister of an old friend, Mimi Luebbermann, a farmer in Chellano Valley. Luebbermann advocated buying local produce and supporting local farmers before it became fashionable to do so. Through her, Raskin meets photographer Paige Green, who takes the photographs that appear in the book and on its cover. He then develops networks that lead him to other local growers and shoppers.

One day, on his way to Oak Hill Farm, where he works in the field, Raskin meets Sharon Grossi, the owner of a seventy-acre farm, the largest certified organic farm in Sonoma County. She describes the joy and challenge of growing and marketing her crops at a time when Sonoma County supports more people and thus has less water available for agriculture than ever before. Grossi says that she must be inventive and creative to survive in an operation that maintains a fine balance between financial success and failure. She is not the only one thinking creatively about marketing, nor is the small-farm movement confined to California. One initiative that supports small farm growers by ensuring that they will have consumers is community-supported agriculture (CSA), begun in the East. Through a CSA, individual buyers contract with a farm, paying an annual fee in return for weekly boxes of produce during the growing season. This advance commitment by consumers provides farmers with up-front cash for planting and guaranteed revenues. In return, community shoppers are guaranteed access to just-picked local produce.

The operation Raskin comes to know best is Oak Hill Farm in Glen Ellen. Working there enables him to investigate a model farm, gain practical knowledge, engage in fieldwork, and develop healthy eating habits. Oak Hill Farm was started by Otto Teller, a renowned conservationist who died in 1998. It now operates under the careful eye of Teller's widow, Janet Teller. An eloquent spokesperson for organic farming and protecting the environment, she gives Raskin permission to work on the farm and report on its operations. As a result, he is able to discover the complexities of farming from many perspectives.

First, Raskin meets Patrick McMurtry, the farm's unofficial historian, and learns from him how the place evolved. Then, he meets other managers and field workers as he explores the local community. He starts with the Red Barn Store, a market store open from April to Christmas, where the locals shop for the organic produce raised on Oak Hill Farm. These shoppers relish what is ready when it is ready. When they shop at the Red Barn Store, they do not expect tomatoes in April or lettuce in August, but appreciate each fruit and vegetable in season. Such an appreciation is essential to becoming a "locavore."

From the store for local shoppers, Raskin moves to the fields, where he can get dirty. He meets Paul Wirtz, head of vegetables and manager of workers and farm machinery, and Jesus Soto, known as Chuy, head of flowers. With Wirtz's guidance, Raskin sees firsthand the planning and oversight that a farm requires. Managing the farm, Wirtz tends to every crop. He plants a row of trees to shade tomato plants from the summer sun; he minds the many irrigating hoses, keeps a log of what is growing in each field, and knows the composition of each compost pile. He maintains the many pieces of machinery needed on a farm, performing the essential welds when machinery breaks. For Raskin, Wirtz embodies not only a careful manager but also a man who thrives on the spiritual connection a farmer feels with the earth.

At Wirtz's suggestion, Raskin joins immigrant workers in the field. As he describes his work, he also recalls the Bracero program of the 1960's, which brought immigrant workers to California's farmlands. Such workers were invited to the United States to help harvest crops all over California. Sonoma County could not have survived without them. During July and August, Raskin picks vegetables under foreman Miguel Barrios. The workday is long and hard, but he finds the work exhilarating. He is paid in produce, gaining a sense of connection to the earth and a leaner, tauter body. He learns exactly when a vegetable is ready to be picked, and later, under Soto, he learns to feel how many flowers make a bunch.

Winemaking and cooking are part of Raskin's exploration. He meets many people engaged in growing and cooking, but he especially explores Oak Hill connections. Vineyards and winemaking at Oak Hill Farm are managed by Will Bucklin, one of Anne Teller's sons. Equally committed to organic growing and quality assessment of his product, Bucklin ensures that only the ripest grapes are picked for wine or sold to another winery. From Oak Hill, Raskin moves on to San Francisco, observing the wholesale market where the farm's flowers and vegetables are sold in season. He finds a restaurant touting Oak Hill Farm zucchini on its menu.

Working at Oak Hill farm; talking to many growers, field hands, cooks, and environmentalists; reading many suggested books on farming; and connecting with the land, Raskin asserts his conviction that human interaction with farms and food is essential to personal health and a sustainable economy. He decides that the movement of domination of the land initiated by the first European settlers has to be reversed by what he calls the "post pioneers," or "restorationists." As he follows the route of Oak Hill products, he comes to savor the local, seasonal foods and appreciate the chefs and restaurants that serve local produce. Seeing and experiencing the effort and satisfaction in small-scale farmwork and production, Raskin becomes a most articulate advocate of this movement.

When teaching memoir writing to his students, Rasking insists on the dictum that they avoid digressions. However, he notes in his introduction that *Field Days* does not follow this dictum. Instead, Raskin richly explores and celebrates every person and event that presents itself during the year—from Day of the Dead celebrations on Oak Hill Farm and individual stories of workers to writers past and present. All these people and events contribute traditions, ideas, strategies, and philosophies to the locavore movement. Raskin expresses enthusiasm for both the growing and the eating of local products, as well as for the good stewardship inherent in each product. His journey proves to have resulted in what he sought from it: a deeper understanding of the small-farm movement, improved health, and a sense of connection to the earth.

Bernadette Flynn Low

Review Sources

Booklist 105, no. 17 (May 1, 2009): 53.
Publishers Weekly 256, no. 12 (March 23, 2009): 55.
San Francisco Chronicle, June 9, 2009, p. E3.

FLANNERY
A Life of Flannery O'Connor

Author: Brad Gooch (1952-)
Publisher: Little, Brown (New York). 448 pp. $30.00
Type of work: Literary biography

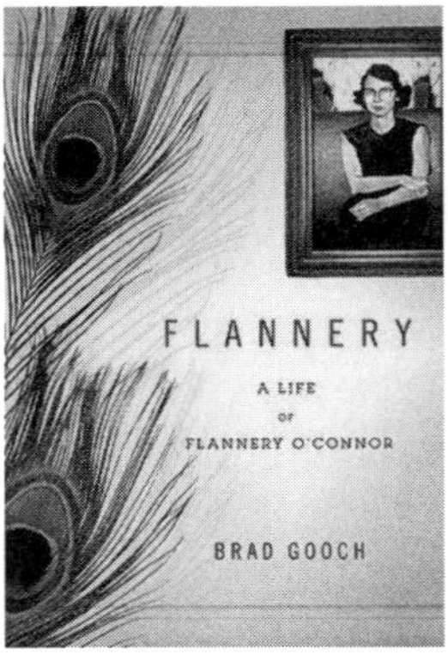

Gooch's detailed biography draws connections between the life and fiction of American writer O'Connor, although some of those connections are strained

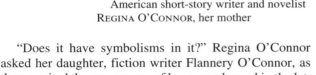

Principal personages:
FLANNERY O'CONNOR (1925-1964), an American short-story writer and novelist
REGINA O'CONNOR, her mother

"Does it have symbolisms in it?" Regina O'Connor asked her daughter, fiction writer Flannery O'Connor, as they awaited the appearance of her second novel in the late fall of 1959. "You know, when I was coming along, they didn't have symbolisms." Biographer Brad Gooch quotes Mrs. O'Connor's philistine question as a tacit comment on a mother's inability to fathom her daughter's art, but the question could just as fairly be asked of Gooch's biography. The answer would be that, unless one counts Freudian clichés, there are no "symbolisms" in *Flannery: A Life of Flannery O'Connor*, and the book is the poorer for it.

Good biographies do not need to incorporate symbolism. However, as was the case with Gooch's acclaimed 1993 biography of Frank O'Hara—another Irish American Catholic writer who died young (O'Hara died at forty; O'Connor died at thirty-nine)—*Flannery* suffers from the lack of a through line that would impart a sense of personal continuity to the strings of anecdotes Gooch meticulously orders by chronology. The closest Gooch comes to a unifying image is invoked only at the beginning and the end, and even then it does not quite work. Gooch recreates, in some detail, O'Connor's first public appearance in a Pathé newsreel, at the age of five, teaching her pet chicken to walk backward. He tries to use the chicken incident as the focal point for the author's life story. The incident might have been a good choice if the biographer had attached to it a consistent interpretation of an O'Connor who walked backward, went against the grain, or otherwise reflected some aspect of the story. The portrayal of Flannery O'Connor in this biography never coheres to that degree.

The seeming absence of authorial purpose in *Flannery* might be attributed simply to objectivity were the biographer's objectivity not so selective. Although understandably skeptical of O'Connor's own self-evaluations, Gooch is surprisingly uncritical of what others say about her. Gooch admirably conveys how little O'Connor's mother, family, and college friends understood her and her work. He seems less conscious of the misunderstandings of the literati who discovered her genius, although he skillfully describes the limits of Caroline Gordon's editorial eye, of which even O'Connor became aware near the end.

Brad Gooch is a poet, novelist, and acclaimed biographer. The author of City Poet *(1993), a life of Frank O'Hara, he lives in New York and teaches literature and creative writing at William Patterson University in New Jersey.*

Despite these limitations, Gooch's book has great value as raw material for more perceptive literary evaluation. O'Connor biographies have been hampered until recently by their authors' lack of access to some relevant materials, and Gooch presents some of those materials, such as the letters of Betty Hester, until 1998 known only by the coy pseudonym "A" in Sally Fitzgerald's edition of O'Connor's letters. The new documents made available through *Flannery* will be a sensation to O'Connor scholars hungry for every tidbit, although the book contains no major revelations. Hester's identity was revealed after her suicide in 1998, and though some of her letters were not unsealed until 2007, her influence on O'Connor (and vice versa) was thoroughly discussed in Jean W. Cash's 2002 biography, *Flannery O'Connor: A Life*.

The very existence of the previous book-length biography is significant to the publication of Gooch's book, as it calls into question the need for a new biography. Gooch's reasons for writing *Flannery*, though, seem to be largely personal: The study's "Acknowledgments" appendix begins as a narrative of Gooch's "literary infatuation" with O'Connor. Inspired by reading Sally Fitzgerald's 1979 collection of O'Connor's letters, *The Habit of Being*, Gooch wrote to Fitzgerald announcing his intention to write a biography. He dropped his project, however, when Fitzgerald told him that she was writing her own biography of her literary friend. When Fitzgerald died in 2000, she had not yet published her promised biography, and it has yet to appear. Hence, there was no reason for Gooch not to write a second O'Connor biography.

The reality is that there is enough personality in Flannery O'Connor for half a dozen more biographies. Gooch reports O'Connor's well-documented aversion to author biography and her self-deprecating observation that a biography of a woman who spent most of her time writing and caring for barn fowl would make dull reading. Certainly, O'Connor had no adventures of the sort that characterized the lives of Ernest Hemingway or Clare Booth Luce, but her unique fusion of genteel manners, satiric vision, and dry wit are enough to make Gooch's compilation of anecdotes worth reading.

Gooch forges connections between O'Connor's life and her fiction, but some of these connections seem forced. For example, O'Connor's unlikely friend, Maryat Lee, different in every way from the author, once spoke of religious orthodoxy as a ceiling she had broken through. Gooch compares this statement to a passage in O'Connor's story "The Enduring Chill" in which the character Asbury sees an image of the Holy Spirit in a water stain on the ceiling. While some of Gooch's connections are tenuous, he packs his analysis with them, and the sheer number of the interrelations he sees between O'Connor's life and work provides readers with a significant mass of details to evaluate and judge for themselves.

Gooch reveals that O'Connor was reading about an RKO Studios publicity campaign for the premiere of the film *Mighty Joe Young* (1949) while she was revising *Wise Blood* (1952). In the novel, the character Enoch witnesses a publicity stunt identical to the one about which O'Connor read: a man dressed in an ape suit. Similarly, the Elvis Presley film *Wild in the Country* (1961) played in O'Connor's hometown of Milledgeville, Georgia, in July, while she was writing "The Lame Shall Enter First." The story features a similar theme to that of the film—rehabilitation of a country boy from delinquency—as well as a character who sings Presley's version of "Shake, Rattle, and Roll." While these cross-references to popular culture are one of *Flannery*'s chief assets, however, they are not indexed.

Although not well connected to one another, the scenes and anecdotes making up Gooch's biography are well told. Gooch is especially good at the iterative mode of narration, describing one scene in detail so it stands for countless other iterations of the same scene. He vividly and carefully describes O'Connor's writing sessions at Yaddo in 1948-1949, when the budding author enjoyed the luxury of solitude for the last time; elegant luncheons in the Sanford House Tea Room in Milledgeville after its opening in the fall of 1952; and endless visits to hospitals and medical specialists from 1950 onward. The medical scenes serve as a good index of Gooch's narrative skill: Their cumulative effect is a blur, as they must have been in real life to O'Connor and her mother, yet each is clinically accurate in detailing O'Connor's symptoms at the time.

The book is strictly organized by chronology, and it is divided by O'Connor's debut as a published author. The first five chapters, forming part 1, recount her life before the publication of her first novel, *Wise Blood*. Each chapter represents a new residence: her early childhood in Savannah (chapter 1), the move to Milledgeville (chapter 2), Georgia State College for Women (chapter 3), Iowa State University (chapter 4), and the Yaddo Artists' Colony outside Saratoga Springs, New York (chapter 5). In part 2, geography ceases to be a convenient marker, since after Christmas, 1950, O'Connor found herself increasingly confined to Andalusia, her mother's farm in Milledgeville. In place of geographical tags, then, the last five chapters are designated by titles and images from O'Connor's fiction: "The Life You Save" (chapter 6), "The 'Bible' Salesman" (chapter 7), "Freaks and Folks" (chapter 8), "Everything That Rises" (chapter 9), and "Revelation" (chapter 10).

O'Connor's increasing confinement to Andalusia made her come to terms with her complex relationship with her overprotective mother, and in the second half of the biography Gooch comes to terms with it as well. While readers may disagree with Gooch's understanding of O'Connor's southernness and her Roman Catholicism, few will fault his balanced portrayal of Regina O'Connor and her interactions with her famous daughter. Regina's micromanagement of Flannery's life from her earliest days is clear. She handpicked her daughter's friends and had her driven or escorted to and from classes, even through Flannery's graduation from the Georgia State College for Women, only a few blocks from her home. Gooch also makes clear his agreement with O'Connor's friend and correspondent Maryat Lee that the author "got away with murder" in caricaturing her mother through several unflattering characters in her fiction, most famously the grandmother in "A Good Man Is Hard to Find."

What also comes through in Gooch's portrayal—especially of the later years, as the lupus from which she would die in 1964 made her more and more physically dependent on her mother—is the extent of O'Connor's emotional dependence and her realization that both her disease and her mother were her paths to sanctity, the crosses she had to bear to achieve holiness. The latter half of the book is a chronicle of O'Connor's slow deterioration: her mother's withholding the diagnosis of lupus from her; Sally Fitzgerald blurting it out in the car one day; and her trip to Lourdes, to which O'Connor attributed a renewal of her will to write (and perhaps the recalcification of her hip).

Flannery appears at a time when O'Connor's canonicity, her status as a major American author, is assured, though Gooch's "Acknowledgments" essay may overstate the extent to which she was evaluated as minor in 1980. It could be argued that O'Connor has not been seen as a minor author since receiving the O. Henry Award for "Greenleaf" in 1956 (three years after coming in second for "The Life You Save May Be Your Own"). After 1960, few anthologies of American fiction lacked an O'Connor story. Gooch may have written his biography of O'Connor later than he had originally intended, but the timing may be fortunate: it provides enough new detail to whet readers' appetite for the next major study of O'Connor.

John R. Holmes

Review Sources

The Atlantic Monthly 303, no. 5 (June, 2009): 88-96.
Booklist 105, no. 7 (December 1, 2008): 4.
Kirkus Reviews 76, no. 23 (December 1, 2008): 1240-1241.
Library Journal 133, no. 20 (December 1, 2008): 130.
London Review of Books 31, no. 14 (July 23, 2009): 24-26.
National Review 61, no. 4 (March 9, 2009): 38-42.
The New Republic 240, no. 9 (June 3, 2009): 39-43.
The New Yorker 85, no. 6 (March 23, 2009): 75.
The New York Times, February 23, 2009, p. 8.
The New York Times Book Review, March 1, 2009, p. 1.
Publishers Weekly 255, no. 47 (November 24, 2008): 45.
The Times Literary Supplement, September 11, 2009, p. 9.
The Virginia Quarterly Review 85, no. 2 (Spring, 2009): 202-205.

FORDLANDIA
The Rise and Fall of Henry Ford's Forgotten Jungle City

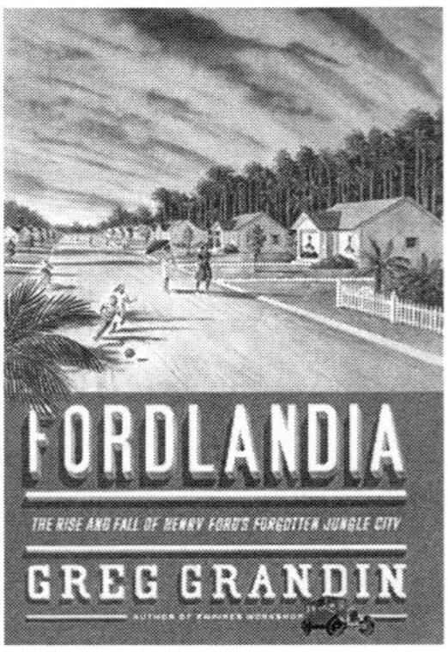

Author: Greg Grandin (1962-)
Publisher: Metropolitan Books/Henry Holt (New York). 416 pp. $27.50
Type of work: History
Time: July, 1925-November, 1945
Locale: Fordlandia and Belterra, Brazil

Ford established rubber plantations and two small cities in Brazil in order to develop an independent supply of rubber for his automobile factory, as well as to export his vision of an ideal American town to South America

Principal personages:
HENRY FORD (1863-1947), founder of Ford Motor Company
HENRY FORD II (1917-1987), his grandson and successor as president of the company in 1945
HARVEY SAMUEL FIRESTONE (1868-1938), rubber manufacturer
GETÚLIO VARGAS (1882-1954), president of Brazil, 1930-1945 and 1951-1954

Few people are aware that Henry Ford tried to build the world's largest rubber plantation on the banks of the Amazon River. Readers of Greg Grandin's *Fordlandia*, which was a finalist for the 2010 Pulitzer Prize in history, will be entertained by a fascinating story of idealism, good wishes, arrogance, ignorance, greed, and incompetence, as the head of the world's largest car manufacturing company unsuccessfully attempted to establish an independent source of rubber in Brazil. Discussion of the project began during a July, 1925, luncheon with tire manufacturer Harvey Firestone, who feared that British and Dutch owners of plantations in South Asia, which produced the overwhelming majority of the world's rubber, would combine into a monopoly and greatly increase his costs. Ford needed rubber for tires, as well as for hoses, valves, gaskets, and other parts of his cars.

To make his company self-sufficient, Ford had deliberately established control of most of the raw materials he needed. Company-owned forests in Michigan provided lumber, and company-owned mines provided coal and iron ore to feed the world's largest steel foundry at his enormous River Rouge plant. Rubber was a major raw material he did not control, but Ford did not accept Firestone's proposal jointly to produce their own supply.

Brazilian consular representatives and Amazonian land speculators encouraged Ford to invest there. Brazil seemed a logical location. In the nineteenth century, its native rubber trees were the only source of latex until smuggled seeds were used to create large plantations in Asia, where trees produced much more latex sap, since Amazonian rubber-tree predators were absent. Lower-cost competition effectively ended the profitability of Brazilian production. What little rubber Brazil exported in 1925 came from individual sap collectors who sold their latex to local merchants. The merchants held the collectors in virtual debt peonage.

Greg Grandin, professor of history at New York University, has written extensively on Latin America, contributing articles to The Nation, *and has published* The Blood of Guatemala *(2000),* The Last Colonial Massacre *(2004), and* Empire's Workshop: Latin America, the United States, and the Rise of the New Imperialism *(2006).*

In early 1927, Ford sent a Michigan botanist to survey the possibilities for rubber production in Brazil. The botanist returned a positive report and recommended acquiring land held by speculators. His description of the latex collectors' terrible working and living conditions stimulated Ford to make the investment, even though by 1927 the original reason for wanting an independent source of rubber was no longer present. The feared monopoly never occurred; instead, overproduction of latex had significantly driven down prices. Grandin notes a recurrent theme in the Fordlandia story: Every time economic goals were less persuasive or proved elusive, social objectives would justify continuing.

The Amazon project appealed to an idealist streak in Ford. To service his large lumber holdings in Northern Michigan, he had built model towns run by his rules, trying to demonstrate that industrialism was compatible with the small-town America he remembered from his youth and that his mass-production techniques were destroying. In 1927, the same year that he began assembling a replica of an ideal nineteenth-century town in Greenville, Michigan, Ford set out to create a profitable, industrial-scale rubber plantation, built around an example of a model American town. He would show Brazil and the world how to combine material and ideal values. He intended Fordlandia to be profitable and pay decent wages, while also teaching the workers thrift, good nutrition, and proper hygiene. Fordlandia would be a commercial enterprise with a civilizing mission.

Ford sent two employees to Brazil with power of attorney to assemble the needed land. They acquired 2.5 million acres of jungle, about the size of Connecticut, half from speculators who were paid $150,000 and half as a grant of public land ratified by the state legislature of Pará on September 30, 1927. Nationalists criticized the terms of the grant, which seemed to permit Ford to operate Fordlandia as though it were a separate state. A 1929 investigation revealed an unsavory tale of kickbacks and payoffs to get the grant approved, but Grandin believes the controversy did not damage Ford's reputation for honesty as much as his reputation for competence, since he could have received the entire grant for free.

A self-made man, Ford distrusted experts. He saw them as people who told him what he could not do. Therefore, no one familiar with life in a jungle was consulted, nor did he seek advice from any botanist knowledgeable about rubber trees and their pests. Instead, Ford sent out aides, mostly engineers, in whom he had confidence. The result was a display of ignorance and incompetence.

The first ships carrying supplies from the United States to Fordlandia could not get closer than fifty miles to the chosen location, necessitating a costly and time-consuming overland haul. It took nearly six months, until December, 1928, to get everything to the plantation site because no one responsible knew how low the river depth was in the dry season.

Ford expected that the expedition would use trees that were cut down to prepare the land to build his town and that they would also provide valuable lumber for export. When the sawmill was finally complete, however, the immediately available trees were unusable. When valuable timber was ready for export, profitable markets proved elusive. A cost analysis, finally done in 1933, discovered that, under the most favorable export assumptions, the mill would lose $12,000 a month.

To house his employees, Ford ordered that midwestern-style clapboard cottagesbe built, similar to those in his Michigan lumber towns. His architects, who had no experience with a tropical climate, chose metal roofs insulated with asbestos, rather than the traditional thatched roofs, thinking they would keep heat out. Instead, they kept heat in, and inhabitants denounced the houses as galvanized iron bake ovens.

More destructive to the hope of operating a profitable rubber plantation were planting errors. Most of the seedlings planted the first year came up very weak, and in 1930 the current manager decided they should be plowed under and the fields replanted. This decision would cost another five years before Fordlandia would produce latex, but Ford was not discouraged and pressed on.

Worse problems arose when the trees matured. Rubber trees in the jungle grew far apart, a useful strategy to limit damage from the many diseases and insects that attacked them. If a single tree were attacked and killed, others further away need not be affected. Fordlandia's managers, copying South Asian plantations where Amazonian predators did not exist, cleared the forest and planted the trees in neat, closely spaced rows. As they grew, their branches touched one another. If rubber leaf blight reached one tree, it had a perfect highway for its spores to infect and devastate an entire field.

In March, 1933, a plant scientist reached Fordlandia and immediately criticized growing trees from seed, since the resultant seedlings were certain to be of varying quality with many nearly useless as latex producers. He recommended grafting slips from the best producers of latex onto the fastest growing rootstock. Grafting was standard practice in Asian rubber plantations and may have been used in China as early as 2000 B.C.E., but it was new to Fordlandia's managers.

Ford took a very paternalistic interest in his Brazilian employees, as he tried to impose his understanding of American values on them. He paid well. He built a state-of-the-art hospital open to those living nearby as well as to Fordlandia's residents; erected a water-purification plant providing clean, wholesome water; and did his best to improve the Brazilians' nutrition, whether they liked what he ordered for them or not. Attempts to put into effect American-style prohibition failed; Brazilian police refused to enforce Ford's dictates, and workers thought them hypocritical as they watched managers indulge in major binges once away from dry Michigan. Nor were employees enthusiastic about Ford's attempts to teach them to enjoy eating oatmeal for breakfast and whole wheat bread for dinner in the dining hall he had built for unmarried employees.

In December, 1930, trouble broke out in the dining hall. A newly arrived manager decided to replace the existing waiter service with cafeteria lines, but the American clerk charged with checking badges of incoming workers was so slow that the line to the dining hall grew long. When he laughed dismissively at an impatient Brazilian, pent-up irritations exploded. The workers demolished the dining hall and for three days went on to trash the powerhouse, sawmill, and office buildings until a Brazilian army detachment arrived. Every Ford truck, tractor, and car on the plantation was destroyed. Ford rejected considering employee grievances. With the support of newly established dictator Getúlio Vargas, he fired the entire workforce, excepting only a small maintenance crew.

Ford refused to abandon what was by now more a social than an economic enterprise, and he continued with new workers. He poured in money to rebuild Fordlandia and continued to expect successful rubber production. However, when the mass plantings of 1930 matured in 1935, leaf blight and caterpillars ran rampant, killing many trees and damaging those left standing. Ford would not surrender. In 1936, he accepted a proposal to move seventy miles downriver and start a new plantation at Belterra.

Belterra, like Fordlandia, was a carbon copy of a midwestern small town, complete with a central square, sidewalks, indoor plumbing, movie theaters, a nine-hole golf course, a day-care center, schools, and an excellent hospital. By 1940, Belterra workers had cleared almost thirty thousand acres and planted nearly three million trees (properly grafted using techniques learned at Fordlandia) when the jungle struck again. Trees were still too close together; when they matured, caterpillars and leaf blight attacked 70 percent of the plantings, repeating the disaster at Fordlandia.

During World War II, the U.S. government encouraged Ford to continue rubber production in Brazil without substantially changing results. The two plantations were striking examples of American town building, but they were economic failures. In November, 1945, Ford's grandson, Henry Ford II, gave Fordlandia and Belterra (which had cost the company $20 million and were still valued at $8 million) to the Brazilian government for $240,000—the amount the company legally owed its workers as severance pay.

Grandin bulks up his book with lengthy, often useful and informative, descriptions of Ford's personal idiosyncrasies and the operation of his huge River Rouge plant. He finds it hard to resist attractive digressions. It adds little to the discussion of Ford's factory to include a description of Diego Rivera's Detroit murals, nor does it help readers understand a speculator who fleeced Ford to include an account of the suicide of his relative, Alberto Santos-Dumont, who Brazilians insist was the true inventor of the airplane. Although the book is long, however, readers will be rewarded with an engrossing narrative of high ideals miserably executed as America's most successful car manufacturer attempted to create an ideal American farm town in the middle of the Amazon jungle.

Milton Berman

Review Sources

American Scholar 78, no. 3 (Summer, 2009): 104-107.
Booklist 105, no. 19/20 (June 1-15, 2009): 13.
Kirkus Reviews 77, no. 2 (January 15, 2009): special section, p4.
Kirkus Reviews 77, no. 7 (April 1, 2009): 357.
Library Journal 134, no. 8 (May 1, 2009): 88-89.
London Review of Books 31, no. 19 (October 8, 2009): 31-33.
Los Angeles Times, June 24, 2009, p. D1.
Mother Jones 34, no. 3 (May/June, 2009): 76-78.
The New York Review of Books 56, no. 15 (October 8, 2009): 31-34.
The New York Times Book Review, July 19, 2009, p. 12.
The New Yorker 85, no. 24 (August 10, 2009): 81.
Publishers Weekly 256, no. 18 (May 4, 2009): 44.
The Times Literary Supplement, September 11, 2009, p. 27.
The Wilson Quarterly 33, no. 3 (Summer, 2009): 92-95.

THE FUTURE OF LIBERALISM

Author: Alan Wolfe (1942-)
Publisher: Harvard University Press (Cambridge, Mass.). 508 pp. $35.00
Type of work: History, philosophy

A thoughtful analysis and defense of the liberal ideology, including its history, its characteristics, and its continued relevance

In contemporary political discourse, ideological labels such as liberalism, progressivism, conservatism, socialism, and libertarianism are used in many different ways, and these differences result in considerable misunderstandings. In the United States, the label "liberal" is commonly used as a synonym for "left-wing," just as "conservative" usually denotes "right-wing." Americans utilize these two labels in reference to a great variety of controversial issues, including social programs, abortion rights, constitutional interpretations, same-sex marriage, affirmative action, economic regulations, deficit spending, and separation of church and state. In European countries, where the concept of socialism enjoys more popularity, people tend to speak of "the Left" and "the Right," usually reserving the term "liberal" to denote free-market economic policies that would be classified as conservative in the United States.

In *The Future of Liberalism*, Alan Wolfe makes a helpful distinction among three overlapping aspects of liberalism: the first focuses on temperament, the second on substance, and the third on procedure. The concept of a liberal temperament relates to psychological characteristics, such as tolerance and empathy toward others. Concerning the substance of liberalism, Wolfe writes that the core principle is that "as many people as possible should have as much say as is feasible over the direction their lives will take"—a democratic principle that logically implies commitments to two values: liberty and equality. He observes that this principle mandates legal protections for individual rights and freedoms, including the right to advocate reactionary and conservative policies that liberals hate. Liberalism is not anarchism, but while liberals accept the necessity for authority, they insist that constraints should be established "by people themselves through some form of consent or interdependence."

From the perspective of procedures, both political and judicial, Wolfe writes that liberals are committed to the goals of fairness and impartiality and that they support constitutional forms of limited government that guarantee free elections and due process. He believes, moreover, that they usually oppose special privileges and exceptions to established rules. While acknowledging that many procedural rules are not necessarily incompatible with political conservatism, he observes that conservatives are much more willing to accept compromises based on expenses and pragmatic considerations. In criminal trials, for example, the majority of liberals have insisted

Alan Wolfe, a professor of political science at Boston College, has published at least fourteen books, including The Transformation of American Religion *(2005) and* Does American Democracy Still Work? *(2006). He is a contributing editor of* The New Republic *and* The Wilson Quarterly.

on strict application of the exclusionary rule, which requires that illegally acquired evidence must be excluded from the trial. Conservatives, in contrast, typically look upon this procedural rule as a "judge-invented" technicality that obstructs law enforcement, and they become furious whenever it allows a guilty and dangerous person to escape punishment.

Most thinking persons mix the two ideologies, expressing liberal views on some issues while taking conservative positions on other topics. Despite the complexity of individual persons, however, Wolfe insists that liberalism constitutes a coherent ideology and that it provides the most viable option for the twenty-first century. In his view, the ideology is characterized by a set of at least seven "dispositions": the assumption that people are capable of growth and progress; a bias in favor of equality; a preference for a sober sense of realism; an inclination toward rational deliberation; a commitment to tolerance, even for persons who are intolerant; an openness toward diversity and alternative ideas; and a favorable view of governance, based on the belief that elected officials can fashion intelligent policies in the interest of the common good. Wolfe argues that these dispositions were primarily products of the eighteenth century Enlightenment, making their political debut in the period between 1787 and 1815. "For all the talk about how the Enlightenment project failed," he writes, "we live with the consequences of the Enlightenment all around us."

In the realm of political economics, theorists have long distinguished between "classical" and "modern" versions of liberalism. Adam Smith, the "quintessential classical liberal," advocated a minimal state that would maintain low taxes and provide very little regulation of the economy. Such an ideology, which basically aligns with modern American libertarianism, remains the most common definition of the term "liberalism" in Europe. In the United States, by contrast, persons called "liberals" tend to endorse British economist John Maynard Keynes's approach, which emphasizes the benefits of governmental spending and other forms of economic intervention.

Wolfe, however, attempts to minimize the difference between classical and modern liberalism. Viewed historically, he argues that Smith and other eighteenth century liberals were reacting against a political system that supported the interests of a small elite and was oppressive toward the vast majority of citizens. Since the early twentieth century, in his view, governmental intervention has tended to lessen inequalities and to promote individual freedom from the restraints that reside in the private sector.

Although Wolfe emphasizes that liberals want to expand equality, he writes that they do not view equality "as an end in itself" (an idea that is more associated with the socialist tradition). Rather, they place the highest priority on allowing people maximum freedom in living their lives in ways that they choose. Because liberalism does not require the utopian aim of absolute equality, the amount "of actual equality" found in liberal societies "will vary from one to another." Nevertheless, Wolfe writes that no liberal society can tolerate extreme and persistent inequalities that deprive its least favored members of opportunities to develop their human capabilities.

While opposed to the abolition of all class distinctions, Wolfe endorses sociologist Thomas H. Marshall's version of a moderate welfare state. Such a state guarantees that all citizens have the right to basic medical care and legal services, as well as other "social rights." Wolfe takes issue with Milton Friedman's suggestion that the pursuit of an "equality of outcomes" is dangerous because it inevitably must rely on "the coercive mechanism of the state." Wolfe answers that individual freedom is compatible with welfare-state programs, and he favors an unspecified compromise that exists "somewhere between equality of opportunity and equality of outcomes."

Wolfe asserts that modern democracy inevitably leads to an expansion of equality. Referring to the ideas of British philosopher John Stuart Mill, he writes that the "the many will use their facilities to extend sympathy and justice to all" and that "it is an illusion to think that the process can be stopped." There is perhaps some historical basis to this optimistic theory, but it is highly questionable. In societies in which the majority of citizens are relatively affluent, experience suggests that there are limits to the majority's willingness to make sacrifices to help the poor and needy. Skeptics of the theory can also point to examples such as the Jim Crow age of the American South, in which the majority of white southerners strongly supported inequality for African Americans. In asserting a direct linkage between democracy and equality, Wolfe appears to concentrate on the extent to which the glass is half full, ignoring the fact that such a glass is also half empty.

In the United States, contemporary liberals might be divided into two categories: "centrist liberals," who emphasize liberty, and "left-wing liberals," who focus almost exclusively on equality. Wolfe is unquestionably among the former, and left-leaning liberals will no doubt find fault with some of his rather moderate views. With few exceptions, for instance, leftists give unqualified support for affirmative action programs that include racial and gender preferences in employment and university admissions. Wolfe, however, is decidedly ambiguous toward such programs. Concerning Barbara Grutter, a white student who was not admitted to the University of Michigan because of a racial preference, he declares that she "was unfairly passed over because of her race."

Most leftists will also disagree with Wolfe's opposition to the punishment of persons who express "hateful speech" against minorities. He criticizes this policy as a form of "political correctness," which is one of the favorite terms of conservatives. A majority of liberals will also disagree with his support for President Bill Clinton's welfare reform law, which significantly decreased the number of poor women able to obtain welfare, and, even more, they will dislike his advocacy for vouchers that allow poor children to attend private schools.

Wolf's centrist perspective is particularly evident in the interesting chapter titled "How Liberals Should Think About Religion," which takes strong issue with radical secular humanists, particularly Christopher Hitchens and Sam Harris, who want to ban religion from the public sphere. According to Wolfe, the enemy of liberalism "is not religion but religious oppression, and its friend is not skepticism but freedom, including religious freedom." Recognizing the limits of tolerance, however, he warns that "liberals must constantly be on guard against those who would shut down free inquiry in the name of religious conviction."

Although he generally defends the Jeffersonian tradition of separation between church and state, Wolfe places priority on the application of liberal proceduralism, which allows both conservative believers and nonbelievers equal rights to try to influence public policy, even on contentious issues such as gay marriage, abortion, and stem cell research. He calls his perspective a "liberal bargain," which basically means that "no group belonging to one particular religious tradition can monopolize the violence that the state has as its disposal to impose its views on those belonging to other traditions." In summarizing the chapter, Wolfe declares: "Whatever the future of liberalism, a place for religion must be guaranteed."

A large portion of *The Future of Liberalism* is devoted to the history of liberal and conservative theories since the middle of the eighteenth century. Wolfe attempts to show that most ideas cluster into these two dichotomous and coherent ideologies, and he attempts to show continuity rather than change in the two ideologies. His argument results in a tendency to classify hundreds of political theorists as either liberal or conservative. Frequently, he compares theorists who lived in quite different times and places. Many of those theorists are rather obscure. Readers without a good background in the history of political theory will find the references to so many persons to be quite bewildering. Readers with a good foundation in the literature, moreover, will discover that some of Wolfe's classifications and linkages are questionable. For example, he argues that modern conservatives share much in common with Jean-Jacques Rousseau, whose Romantic theories were used to justify the Reign of Terror during the French Revolution. In defense of this rather tenuous association, Wolfe asserts that modern conservatives, like Rousseau, are hostile toward modernity.

When discussing modern conservatism, portions of Wolfe's analysis are excessively polemical, even sometimes unfair. For instance, in chapter 8, "Why Conservatives Can't Govern," he describes the ways in which President George W. Bush's administration failed to respond adequately to Hurricane Katrina. He attributes this failure to the administration's dislike of government action, and he claims that the example demonstrates that conservatives have "abandoned the terrain of good governance." Even if Wolfe's analysis of the example is valid, his broad generalization appears to be based on wishful thinking. During the last half century, there have been several instances of unsuccessful governance by liberal Democratic administrations, just as there have been moderately conservative presidents, such as Dwight Eisenhower, who are considered by general consensus to have been reasonably successful.

In places, Wolfe appears to reify the abstract concepts of liberalism and conservatism; that is, he refers to them as if were concrete entities. For instance, he writes: "Liberalism is honest about itself. Liberals, all too often, are not." Liberalism, however, is only a concept, and as such it is unable to be honest or dishonest. Liberal persons determine the denotations and connotations of the word liberalism, just as persons with conservative ideas establish the meanings of the word conservatism.

Because people react to their experiences and to changing circumstances, the substances of their ideologies change significantly over time. The ideas of thoughtful liberals today might be quite different from those of both the past and the future.

Rather than attempting to be consistently conservative or consistently liberal, most rational people make decisions about public policy based on a combination of their cherished values and their perceptions of reality. Wolfe, no doubt, is correct in pointing out the ways in which liberal thinkers have contributed to human happiness during the last two and a half centuries. Liberals, however, have often been unrealistic, especially about fiscal matters, and it is a mistake to minimize the positive contributions that have been made by conservatives.

Thomas Tandy Lewis

Review Sources

The American Spectator 42, no. 4 (May, 2009): 73-76.
Booklist 105, no. 11 (February 1, 2009): 6.
Commentary 127, no. 3 (March, 2009): 59-62.
Dissent 56, no. 4 (Fall, 2009): 128-131.
The Economist 390, no. 8617 (February 7, 2009): 75-76.
Kirkus Reviews 76, no. 24 (December 15, 2008): 1300.
Library Journal 134, no. 3 (February 15, 2009): 121-122.
The Nation 288, no. 18 (May 11, 2009): 32-36.
National Review 61, no. 4 (March 9, 2009): 44-45.
New Criterion 27, no. 7 (March, 2009): 4-9.
The New York Times Book Review, March 22, 2009, p. 14.
Publishers Weekly 255, no. 41 (October 13, 2008): 43.
The Wall Street Journal, February 9, 2009, p. A17.
Weekly Standard 14, no. 34 (May 25, 2009): 30-33.
The Wilson Quarterly 33, no. 2 (Spring, 2009): 110-111.

GABRIEL GARCÍA MÁRQUEZ
A Life

Author: Gerald Martin (1944-)
Publisher: Alfred A. Knopf (New York). Illustrated. 642 pp. $37.50
Type of work: Literary biography
Time: 1899-2007
Locale: Aracataca, Barranquilla, Sucre, Zipaquira, Bogotá, and Cartagena, Colombia; Caracas, Venezuela; New York City; Mexico City; Barcelona, Spain

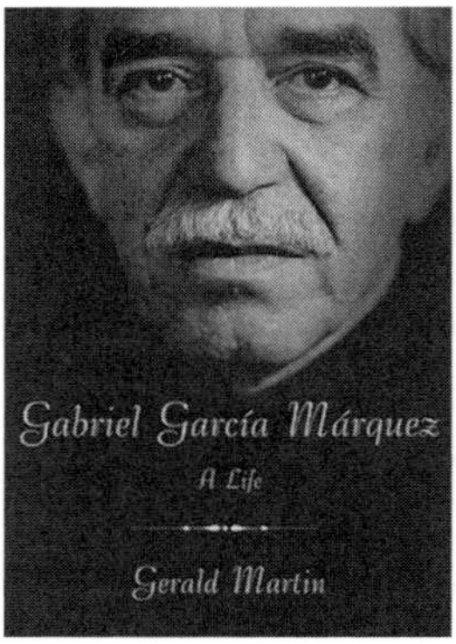

Martin's is the first authorized biography of one of the most distinguished writers of the second half of the twentieth century, and it should serve as the standard portrait of García Márquez for some time

Principal personages:

GABRIEL GARCÍA MÁRQUEZ, world-renowned novelist and journalist
COLONEL NICOLAS MÁRQUEZ MEJIA, García Márquez's maternal grandfather, the dominant influence on his life
GABRIEL ELIGIO GARCÍA, García Márquez's father, with whom he had a difficult relationship for many years
MERCEDES RAQUEL BARCHA PARDO MÁRQUEZ, García Márquez's wife for half a century
FIDEL CASTRO, the dictator of Cuba and one of many international friends of García Márquez
CARLOS FUENTES, a Mexican novelist and friend of García Márquez

Gabriel García Márquez's *Cien años de soledad* (1967; *One Hundred Years of Solitude*, 1970) is considered by many readers to be one of the greatest novels of the twentieth century, comparable to the works of James Joyce and William Faulkner. García Márquez followed up that successful publication with *El otoño del patriarca* (1975; *The Autumn of the Patriarch*, 1975) and *Crónica de una muerte anunciada* (1981; *Chronicle of a Death Foretold*, 1982), and he was honored with the Nobel Prize in Literature in 1982. His fiction, however, has been only the better-known half of his career. He has also been a political journalist and columnist for half a century and is perhaps the most prominent world voice from Latin America. An international celebrity for more than forty years—born and educated in Colombia, he has lived for long periods in Mexico, France, and Spain—García Márquez has befriended the famous and the powerful, from Omar Torrijos of Panama to Fidel Castro of Cuba, from François Mitterand of France to Olof Palme of Sweden. Gerald Martin's biography is the first to tell the full story of García Márquez's remarkable life and prolific career.

García Márquez was born in 1927 in Aracataca, a small, isolated town some distance from the Caribbean coast of Colombia. Until he was seven, García Márquez stayed in the home of his maternal grandparents, while his parents, brothers, and sisters all lived in other cities working to support the family. His grandparents' house was filled with women and with the large presence of his grandfather, the "Colonel," a legendary figure who took the young "Gabo" everywhere with him and told him endless and romantic stories of his violent military past. He told the young boy about "The War of a Thousand Days," in which he fought with the Liberal forces against the conservative Colombian government at the end of the nineteenth century, and about killing a rival named Medardo Romero Pacheco in 1908.

Gerald Martin is the author of Journeys Through the Labyrinth: Latin American Fiction in the Twentieth Century *(1989). The Andrew W. Mellon Professor Emeritus of Modern Languages at the University of Pittsburgh and senior research professor in Caribbean studies at London Metropolitan University, he lives in England.*

García Márquez was educated in towns some distance from Aracataca, and he attended the National University of Colombia in Bogotá. It was as a twenty-one-year-old law student in Bogotá that García Márquez published his first poems and stories, and his life's work was decided. His first professional publications were not fiction, however, but journalism. He became a reporter in Cartagena and then moved to Barranquilla, further up the Colombian coast, where he fell in with a group of writers. They introduced him to some of the giants of literary modernism—such as Virginia Woolf, Franz Kafka, Faulkner, and Ernest Hemingway—and encouraged his writing.

García Márquez would later say that, on a visit back to Aracataca with his mother in 1950, he had the revelation that "everything that had occurred in my childhood had a literary value that I was only now appreciating." His first novella, *La hojarasca* (1955; *Leaf Storm*, 1972), like *One Hundred Years of Solitude* and so much of his later fiction, would draw directly on that early period of his life—the house, the backwater town, the larger-than-life Colonel and the stories of the nineteenth century Colombian world from which the Colonel came. García Márquez's path was not direct or easy, however. He moved among various journalistic and editorial jobs to support himself, and in the early 1950's he even sold encyclopedias in rural Colombia, a job that put him in touch with the popular culture and folklore he would draw on in his later fiction. In 1954, he returned to Bogotá as a journalist, but a year later he departed to live and write in Europe.

In Europe, García Márquez found his footing as a writer gained a usable perspective on his life. As Martin phrases it, he found a Latin American consciousness. He lived and traveled everywhere in Europe—Rome, Vienna, Paris, Venice, Budapest, Moscow—studied film (one of his lifelong interests), and published *El coronel no tiene quien le escriba* (1961; *No One Writes to the Colonel*, 1968). In 1958, he was offered a journalism job in Caracas, Venezuela, and married his childhood sweetheart, Mercedes Barcha Pardo. They soon moved to New York City to work with Prensa Latina, a Latin American press service established after the Cuban Revolution to make Latin American affairs more visible. The couple later traveled through Faulkner's Mississippi on their way out of the country.

García Márquez became friends with some of the rising stars of the Latin American literary movement that was gaining international renown at the time, writers such as Carlos Fuentes and Mario Vargas Llosa. He returned with his growing family to Mexico City in 1961 to work on film scripts, and then one day he abruptly sat down, as he said, and for the next eighteen months wrote what would become *One Hundred Years of Solitude*. In a story that has been told and retold as evidence of the writer's early struggles, Gabriel and Mercedes did not have enough money to send the entire manuscript to Buenos Aires for publication. They mailed half of it, went home to pawn a few appliances, and returned to the post office to mail the second half.

Few literary events have been as momentous as the publication of *One Hundred Years of Solitude*. Early readers recognized at once the enormity of García Márquez's achievement in the novel, and the work's publication transformed both Latin American literature and the lives of García Márquez and his family. The writer, his wife, and their two sons moved to Barcelona, Spain, in 1967. After the publication of *The Autumn of the Patriarch*, they returned to Mexico City.

García Márquez continued to move back and forth between fiction and political journalism. He published *Chronicle of a Death Foretold*, *El amor en los tiempos del cólera* (1985; *Love in the Time of Cholera*, 1988), and *El general en su laberinto* (1989; *The General in His Labyrinth*, 1990), a fictionalized biography of the man who freed Latin America from Spanish rule, Simón Bolívar. He also published political articles and commentaries, as well as a report on the Sandinistas in Nicaragua. His work with Fidel Castro and other Latin American leftist leaders during this period prevented him from obtaining a visa to revisit the United States until 1991.

After the Nobel Prize in Literature was awarded to him in 1982, García Márquez and his wife moved back to Colombia after years of self-imposed exile. They began to build a seaside house in Cartagena. He continued to write even after experiencing a series of serious medical problems, but his memoir, *Vivir para contarla* (2002; *Living to Tell the Tale*, 2003) is, as Martin shows, less than candid about his whole life, and his last novel, *Memoria de mis putas tristes* (2004; *Memories of My Melancholy Whores*, 2005), is his weakest. Fame continued to follow García Márquez, however, up to his eightieth birthday celebration in Cartagena in March of 2007. The celebration was attended by thousands of fans, including his friend U.S. president Bill Clinton.

Detailed and sympathetic, Martin's biography sets García Márquez in his various historical, cultural, and political contexts and shows the complex relationships among his life, fiction, and journalism. This is not only a first-rate biography of the leading exponent of Magical Realism in fiction, however, but also a deft history of twentieth century Latin American politics and literature. Martin is able to weave García Márquez's life story into analyses of his novels and to locate their place in the larger world of Latin American history and literature.

One Hundred Years of Solitude, Martin writes in a long and typical analysis, confronts and combines the two main, almost contradictory, qualities of Latin America: on the one hand, "the dark story of conquest and violence, tragedy and failure," and on the other hand "the carnival spirit, the music and the art of the Latin American people, that ability to honour life even in its darkest corners and to find pleasure in ordinary things." Martin shows how García Márquez came to fame as Latin American literature experienced an international boom. This boom began with the work of Argentinean writer Jorge Luis Borges, followed by that of his countryman Julio Cortazar and then the works of Peruvian Mario Vargas Llosa and Mexican Carlos Fuentes. García Márquez became one of the leading practitioners of Magical Realism, a genre created and developed by this Latin American literary movement.

As Martin defines it, Magical Realism involves narrating a story "through the world-view of the characters themselves without any indication from the author that this world-view is quaint, folkloric or superstitious." Many of the greatest short stories García Márquez produced—such as "The Handsomest Drowned Man in the World" and "A Very Old Man With Enormous Wings" (both included in the 1979 American publication *Leaf Storm, and Other Stories*)—qualify as vivid examples of this form.

Martin recognizes García Márquez's major fictional concerns—power and love—and provides incisive analyses of these themes in the novels and stories. He also understands the unique García Márquez style—including his "hyperbole, antithesis, sententiousness, displacement"—and shows it at work by analyzing a number of his fictions. Finally, Martin sees García Márquez's twin role as both a political journalist and a commentator from the Latin American world who has had a real impact on world opinion. Through his journalism, his fiction, and his friendship with major international figures, García Márquez has made Latin America a more visible, tangible presence on the world stage.

Martin's biography, based on hundreds of interviews and years of friendship with the author, has been years in the making. The present volume, lengthy though it is, represents a condensation of what promises to be a much longer work to be published at a later date. Divided into three parts, the biography is bolstered by two sections of photographs, three pages of maps, six pages of family genealogies, and nearly seventy pages of notes and bibliography. It will serve for years as the definitive portrait of the most popular international writer of the past half century. As Martin writes in his foreword, there is almost universal agreement about who comprises the major modernist novelists of the first half of the twentieth century—Marcel Proust, Woolf, Joyce, and Faulkner—but there is only one writer in the second half of the twentieth century who creates that kind of unanimity among critics: Gabriel García Márquez.

David Peck

Review Sources

Booklist 105, no. 17 (May 1, 2009): 4.
The Boston Globe, June 7, 2009, p. 6.
The Christian Science Monitor, May 21, 2009, p. 25.

Kirkus Reviews 77, no. 7 (April 1, 2009): 362.
Library Journal 134, no. 8 (May 1, 2009): 78.
London Review of Books 31, no. 16 (August 27, 2009): 19-21.
Los Angeles Times, May 3, 2009, p. E8.
The Nation 289, no. 8 (September 21, 2009): 33-39.
New Statesman 137, no. 4924 (December 1, 2008): 50-51.
The New York Review of Books 56, no. 12 (July 16, 2009): 19-21.
The New York Times, May 28, 2009, p. 1.
The Observer, November 30, 2008, p. 27.
Publishers Weekly 256, no. 15 (April 13, 2009): 42.
The Spectator 308, no. 9400 (October 25, 2008): 34-35.
Times Higher Education, October 30, 2008, p. 45.
The Times Literary Supplement, February 13, 2009, p. 28.

A GATE AT THE STAIRS

Author: Lorrie Moore (1957-)
Publisher: Alfred A. Knopf (New York). 322 pp. $25.95
Type of work: Novel
Time: December, 2001-December, 2002
Locale: Troy and Dellacrosse, Wisconsin (both fictional)

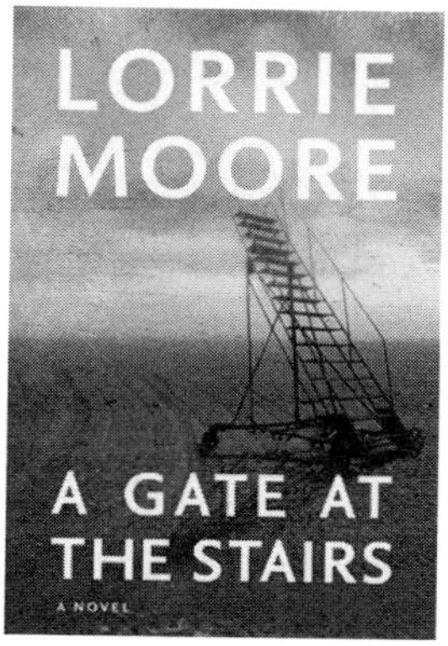

Celebrated author Moore's first new book in more than a decade is the story of a young woman's coming of age in the shadow of September 11

Principal characters:

TASSIE KELTJIN, the narrator, a twenty-year-old university student
SARAH BRINK, a restaurant owner and chef, who employs Tassie as a nanny
EDWARD THORNWOOD, Sarah's husband, a university research scientist
REYNALDO, Tassie's fellow student and eventually her boyfriend
ROBERT "BO" KELTJIN, Tassie's father, a farmer of organic potatoes
GAIL KELTJIN, Tassie's mother
ROBERT "GUNNY" KELTJIN, Tassie's younger brother

American author Lorrie Moore has earned an enthusiastic following primarily for her short stories, which have appeared in many well-respected periodicals, as well as in three collections: *Self-Help* (1985), *Like Life* (1990), and especially the highly acclaimed *Birds of America* (1998). Her novels, *Anagrams* (1986) and *Who Will Run the Frog Hospital?* (1994), were also well received by critics and readers alike. Though Moore has never been considered a particularly prolific writer, the gap of eleven years between her previous book and this one was unusually long, so the novel *A Gate at the Stairs* was a source of much speculation in literary circles before its release. Most reviewers of the book commented on this fact, introducing the novel with phrases such as "much-anticipated" or "long-awaited." The waiting ended with a novel whose plot, characters, and themes are as rich and complex as any the author has produced before.

A Gate at the Stairs is set mostly in the fictional town of Troy, Wisconsin, which most readers interpret as a thinly disguised version of Madison, where Moore has lived and taught at the university since 1984. Moore has written in the past about Americans displaced within their own country, often serving as keen, if somewhat bemused, observers of the new places in which they find themselves. Perhaps never before, though, has setting been so important to one of her novels or stories. In this book, the Midwest itself—with its unique weather, cuisine, and social distinctions—becomes a character in itself.

In addition, the looming presence of the university allows Moore to unleash her wit on some of the more egregious pretensions of academic culture and the politically correct liberalism it often spawns. Students take classes in wine tasting, study soundtracks to war movies, and attend a cross-listed humanities and Pilates class called "The Perverse Body/The Neutral Pelvis." Meanwhile, when racist comments are directed at a biracial child, her parents "fight back" by forming a support group that talks in endless circles and accomplishes nothing.

*Lorrie Moore is the author of two previous novels—*Anagrams *(1986) and* Who Will Run the Frog Hospital *(1994)—and three books of short stories, including the best-selling* Birds of America *(1998). She has won numerous awards, including the Rea Award for the Short Story, the O. Henry Award, and the PEN/Malamud Award.*

The narrator of the novel is Tassie Ketljin, a twenty-year-old university student who, as the novel opens, is seeking part-time work as a nanny to help pay her college expenses. The young woman is a bundle of contradictions: both proud and ashamed of her background as a farmer's child; thrilled by the life of the mind she discovers at the university, while directionless in her studies and lacking any serious ambition for her future; sexually and emotionally inexperienced, though quite unaware of her own naïveté; sometimes startlingly sophisticated in her understanding of situations and people but just as frequently caught off guard when she fails to comprehend the complexities of life that surround. As readers are introduced to Tassie and her idiosyncratic perspective, these internal contradictions in the narrator create a fun, playful air. Tassie is at first both trusting and self-absorbed, hallmarks of her youth and inexperience, but she loses a bit of both qualities as the novel progresses.

With her previous work, Moore became known for her quirky, self-contradictory characters, so the narrator of this novel will perhaps have a familiar feel. In fact, most of the characters in *A Gate at the Stairs*, even the minor ones, are drawn with an understanding that such complexities are both realist and compelling to readers. If a complaint about Moore's characterization can be offered, it is that the characters in this novel, for all their individuality, are almost without exception witty, cerebral, and borderline unbelievable in their sharp, playful ability with the English language. In this way, they perhaps mirror a little too closely their linguistically masterful creator, whose lapidary prose has long enchanted her fans. Tassie herself is given to verbal acrobatics that sometimes take on a life of their own, diverting the novel from its plot for paragraphs at a time.

Among the novel's other fascinating characters are Sarah Brink and Edward Thornwood, the middle-aged couple who hire Tassie as a nanny even before they actually adopt the child for whom she will be partially responsible. Sarah and Edward hail from New York, and, though they have integrated themselves fairly well into the Troy community—he is a university researcher; she, the chef-owner of an upscale restaurant—they remain ignorant of and insensitive to Midwestern cultural sensibilities. It also becomes clear to readers, though not to the somewhat naïve narrator herself, that there is something more to these people than they let on, something they are hiding from the world.

Tassie ends up joining the couple at interviews with adoption agencies and prospective birth mothers, feeling uncomfortably out of place but unable to extricate herself owing to her passive and too-polite nature. Eventually, Sarah and Edward, who are both white, adopt a biracial toddler named Mary-Emma, injecting the issue of race into the picture and subtly shifting the tone of the novel into a more serious vein. Though both of them, particularly Sarah, seemed anxious to adopt, the couple turn out to be inattentive parents, so Tassie ends up taking on more child-rearing duties than she had expected. Tassie, rarely judgmental, gives little thought to Mary-Emma's race, but others notice and occasionally comment on the dark-skinned child and her white caretaker. Gradually, Tassie becomes less naïve about issues of race; she also begins to realize that the people around her, including Sarah and Edward, are not quite what they appear to be.

In the early part of the novel, the bulk of Tassie's time and energy is taken up with her nanny duties and her growing attachment to Mary-Emma. Her emotional world is opened still further when she becomes involved with a young man named Reynaldo, ostensibly a Brazilian, whom she meets in a class on Sufism. He becomes her first serious boyfriend, and their relationship grows increasingly important to Tassie, shifting the emotional balance during the latter part of the novel. Tassie, for the first time, experiences the adult issues of juggling responsibilities and conflicting emotional ties.

Because *A Gate at the Stairs* is set in the months after the terrorist attacks of September 11, 2001, Reynaldo's Muslim identity makes him an object of suspicion on the part of Sarah and others. Tassie accepts him fully, though, allowing his easygoing charm to lull her into a sense of security and thinking no more about her lover's religion than she does of her own Jewish mother's. This sense of security turns out to be illusory, however, and Reynaldo himself is very different from the person he has presented to the credulous Tassie. This thread of the novel's plotline ends in heartbreak for Tassie and another step in her rocky coming of age, as she begins to realize just how often the people and situations she encounters are not what they appear to be.

Soon, the academic year ends, and Tassie prepares to return home for the summer to the farming community of Dellacrosse. By now, her connections to both Mary-Emma and Reynaldo have been severed, leaving her bereft and near despair, doing poorly in her classes, and composing mournful songs on her electric bass as she sinks further into self-pity. The final section of the novel shifts emotional gears again, placing Tassie back in the context of her family and the hometown where she no longer feels at home.

During an earlier visit home, readers saw Tassie interact with her wisecracking, hands-off parents and her polite but rather detached younger brother Robert. Now, though, the family dynamic has shifted, as Robert graduates from high school and joins the Army shortly after the United States has gone to war in Afghanistan. When he is killed in action just days after shipping out, Tassie experiences the final and most devastating of the many losses that life has piled upon her during her twentieth year. She is no longer the bright but directionless naïf readers first met, content to drift through life under the assumption that things will somehow all work out.

Tassie Keltjin's coming-of-age story is the thematic backbone of this novel, but Moore also travels a great deal of additional thematic territory, including life in America immediately after the September 11, 2001, terrorist attacks and the persistence of conflicts between town and university life, as well as urban and rural life.

Perhaps the strongest thematic element running through the book, though, is Moore's deep probing of the delicate shadings of insider versus outsider status. This status is based, for the various characters, on subtle and shifting combinations of race, socioeconomic class, gender, education level, religion, geography, and simple personality.

To Tassie's acquaintances in Troy, her family is socially indistinguishable from other farmers. In their own community of Dellacrosse, however, they are considered oddities because her mother is Jewish and her father forsakes conventional, large-scale agriculture to grow his organic, boutique potatoes. Sarah Brink and Edward Thornwood, on the other hand, look to some like typical liberal citizens of Troy, but their East Coast sensibilities and the shared secrets they harbor often put them at odds with the midwesterners among whom they now live. Tassie herself feels at home nowhere as she makes the transition from youth to adulthood, and perhaps this as much as anything infuses the novel with its dreamy sense of uncertainty.

The various strands of plot and subplot in *A Gate at the Stairs* do not always add up to a coherent whole, and the shifts in tone and emotional register can sometimes be jarring. In this sense, the novel is much like real life, where the actions of an eventful year are unlikely to add up to a single neat and complete plotline. Still, readers who expect unity and closure within a novel might find those expectations thwarted in this book. Some readers will be frustrated by Tassie's constant distraction and passivity, as well as by the slow, sometimes uneven pacing of the novel, and others will find it simply too dark. By and large, though, reviewers have written in glowing terms of the emotional depth of the novel, as well as its playful, lyrical writing. Wherever the book ends up standing in the author's canon, Moore's many fans will be pleased to have the opportunity to once again immerse themselves in her inimitable prose and her idiosyncratic take on life.

Janet E. Gardner

Review Sources

Booklist 105, no. 21 (July 1, 2009): 9.
Harper's Magazine 319, no. 1912 (September, 2009): 85-90.
Library Journal 134, no. 13 (August 1, 2009): 70-71.
London Review of Books 31, no. 22 (November 19, 2009): 31-32.
The Nation 289, no. 21 (December 21, 2009): 35-40.
New Statesman 138, no. 4968 (September 28, 2009): 60.
New York Review of Books 56, no. 19 (December 3, 2009): 54-55.
The New York Times, August 28, 2009, p. 21.
The New York Times Book Review, August 30, 2009, p1.
Publishers Weekly 256, no. 28 (July 13, 2009): 31.
The Spectator 311, no. 9447 (September 19, 2009): 37-38.
The Times Literary Supplement, October 16, 2009, p. 19-20.
The Wall Street Journal, September 12, 2009, p. W13.

THE GENERALISSIMO
Chiang Kai-shek and the Struggle for Modern China

Author: Jay Taylor (1931-)
Publisher: Belknap Press of Harvard University Press (Cambridge, Mass.). 736 pp. $35.00
Type of work: History, biography
Time: 1887-1975
Locale: China

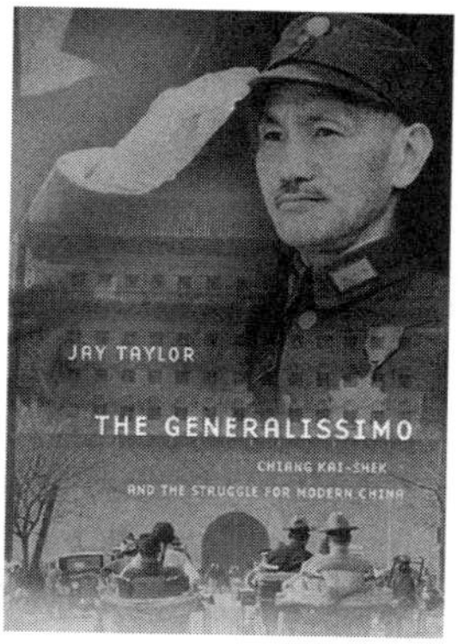

Taylor's thorough biography of Chiang Kai-shek, China's Nationalist leader and the great adversary of Mao Zedong, portrays Chiang as a multifaceted man of great endurance and patience who ultimately turned Taiwan into a success after losing mainland China to the Communists

Principal personages:

CHIANG KAI-SHEK (JIANG JIESHI), charismatic Chinese Nationalist leader
MAYLING SOONG, Chiang's formidable wife and political partner
CHIANG CHING-KUO (JIANG JINGGUO), Chiang's successor and only son
ZHOU ENLAI, key Communist adversary of Chiang
JOSEPH W. STILWELL, controversial U.S. adviser to Chiang in World War II
JOSEPH STALIN, Communist dictator of the Soviet Union, who had a volatile relationship with Chiang
GEORGE C. MARSHALL, Chiang's postwar U.S. adviser, who urged him to make peace with the Communists
MAO ZEDONG (MAO TSE-TUNG), Chinese Communist leader, enemy of Chiang
RICHARD M. NIXON, U.S. president, 1969-1974

Jay Taylor's outstanding biography of China's Nationalist leader Chiang Kai-shek, *The Generalissimo: Chiang Kai-shek and the Struggle for Modern China*, paints a multidimensional picture of an ultimately tragic man who lost the civil war engulfing China only to begin to build a successful society on the island of Taiwan to which he retreated. Taylor's scholarly advantage was his access to a multitude of freshly available sources, such as almost all of Chiang's diaries and other archival material on Taiwan, as well as interviews with Chiang's contemporaries. Sympathetic but critical, Taylor portrays a leader whose efforts to build a modern, non-Communist nation out of the ruins of Imperial China were defeated by warlords, Japanese invaders during World War II, and ruthless Communist opponents. In the end, Taylor offers a balanced picture of Chiang. Only a few questions remain to puzzle an inquisitive reader as to the qualities and the personality of the person whose vision represented the opposite of Communist dictatorship for the world's most populous nation.

Jay Taylor has served in the U.S. Foreign Service and State Department and is a research associate at the Fairbank Center for East Asian Research, Harvard University. His four previous books include the acclaimed The Generalissimo's Son: Chiang Ching-Kuo and the Revolutions in China and Taiwan *(2002).*

Taylor places Chiang's birth (on October 31, 1887) and his youth in the context of China's troubled history at the end of the nineteenth century. The issues of foot binding, arranged marriage, and anti-imperial struggle are all revealed to have touched the young Chiang. His mother married him at fourteen to a nineteen-year-old bride, Mao Fumei, who had partially bound feet. Chiang's first revolutionary act was to cut off his queue, or coiled hair tail, in protest against imperial rule in 1906.

Taylor's description of the young Chiang's road to power illustrates the turmoil of China after the anti-imperial revolution of October 10, 1911. This revolution ended the Qing Dynasty but failed to establish a stable government. Chiang's military studies in Japan during that time reflected the ambiguous relationship of revolutionary Chinese men with Japan, a nation whose modernization seemed to put it on par with the Western powers. Taylor also shows the personal side of Chiang, whose only biological son, Chiang Ching-kuo, was the subject of Taylor's previous acclaimed biography, *The Generalissimo's Son* (2002).

Taylor demonstrates well how, as Chiang became closer to China's premier revolutionary leader, Sun Yat-sen, Chiang gradually gained political power as a trusted military leader. With rule in post-Imperial China fragmented among different warlords, Chiang stayed loyal to the beleaguered Sun. He also adopted the half-Japanese son of a friend in 1919, naming him Chiang Wei-kuo. In 1921, after his mother died, Chiang finally divorced his unloved wife to marry the young Chen Jieru, even though he later denied having officially married her. By providing these personal details, Taylor paints a complete picture of Chiang's life.

In general, Taylor's biography keeps a strong focus on Chiang's political convictions and beliefs. Through his studies of Chiang's diaries, Taylor is able to present Chiang's own thinking. This presentation becomes especially interesting as Chiang becomes involved with the Soviet Union after his first trip to Moscow in 1923. Perhaps surprising to some readers, Taylor shows how closely Sun Yat-sen and Chiang Kai-shek's Nationalist party, the Kuomintang (Guomindang in Pinyin), initially cooperated with the Soviet Communists. They valued the Soviet Union as a potential ally against the mistrusted West.

Along with other biographers of Chiang Kai-shek, Taylor places great significance on Chiang's appointment as head of the new Whampoa Military Academy in June, 1924. Initially, Kuomintang members and Communist Party members worked there together. At the academy, Chiang met the relatively moderate Communist leader Zhou Enlai. As Taylor puts it, "an unusual relationship would develop between the two men, including a mutual respect . . . during times of bitter interparty conflict" that was absent from Chiang's relationships both with Mao Zedong and, later, with many American generals.

The Generalissimo shows well how Chiang Kai-shek emerged victorious as leader of the Kuomintang after the death of Sun Yat-sen on March 12, 1925. One of the many well-chosen illustrations of Taylor's book shows Chiang in 1926, at the height of his Northern Expedition against recalcitrant warlords. Indicative of the Soviet influence at this time over China, including the Kuomintang, a Soviet political commissar and a Soviet military adviser are visible in the picture. Chiang's wife, or concubine, Chen, stands with him, as do his adopted son Wei-kuo and the boy's biological father, Chiang's friend Dai Jitao, indicating Chiang's complex personal life.

Taylor scrutinizes Chiang's momentous decision to break with the Communists and initiate what would become "the twenty-two-year-long Chinese civil war" by attacking the Communists in Shanghai on April 12, 1927. In part, Chiang's actions were motivated by the terror unleashed by a young Communist leader, Mao Zedong, in Hunan province. Between Chiang and Mao, a lifelong enmity developed.

Taylor's biography places equal weight on the personal and political triumphs experienced by Chiang in the late 1920's. After divorcing or sending away Chen on December 1, 1927, Chiang married Mayling Soong. American-educated, Mayling would become Chiang's loving wife and strong political partner. Later, she was indispensable because, unlike Chiang, she could speak English and communicate with Chiang's difficult American allies. In 1928, Chiang assumed command of the Kuomintang armies, becoming generalissimo, and on October 10 he became director of China's State Council, a position comparable to president. At the height of his military powers and connected to the influential Soong family, Chiang seemed to have a real chance to unify China.

From this point on, Taylor convincingly portrays the unraveling of Chiang's struggle. Even at the height of his power, Chiang's relationship with the remaining warlords remained tenuous, with vast regions of China remaining outside Chiang's real control. As Taylor points out, from this position of relative weakness, Chiang tolerated a level of corruption that proved harmful to Chinese society. At the same time, even though Chiang expelled Mao's Communists from southern China in 1934, giving rise to the Communist Long March to the north near the Soviet Union, immense Japanese pressure on China after 1931 prevented Chiang from fully defeating the Communists.

A strong point of *The Generalissimo* is its clear depiction of Joseph Stalin's use of Chiang and the Kuomintang in the 1930's to counteract the threat of a Japanese invasion of the Soviet Union. Worries about Japan led Stalin to support Chiang and restrain Mao, favoring a common Chinese front against Japan. Taylor also gives a detailed report of Chiang's kidnapping by one of the warlords on December 12, 1936, in the city of Xian. The incident was resolved when Chiang emerged as the only Chinese leader capable of uniting the nation against Japan. When war with Japan finally broke out in July, 1937, Taylor shows, Chiang's armies fought bravely but faced almost certain defeat. Again, Chiang's biographer stresses, Stalin was virtually alone in sending military aid to both the Kuomintang and the Communists in China until Japan attacked the Western Allies at Pearl Harbor on December 7, 1941.

One key point of Taylor's biography is his clear presentation of how badly Chiang

Kai-shek was served by his American adviser, General Joseph C. Stilwell, who was sent to him in 1942. Similar to his endurance of corruption among his own military and officials, Taylor asserts, Chiang endured Stilwell's open disrespect—to his own detriment. Taylor is highly critical of Stilwell's walk away from the defeated Chinese troops under his command in Burma in the spring of 1942, and he outlines the damage done to Chiang's reputation in the United States by Stilwell's disparaging comments to American journalists.

Taylor, like other recent historians, demolishes the myth that Chiang refused to engage the Japanese in World War II. Instead, he describes Chiang's severe struggle with the Japanese, who destroyed his best armies as late as the summer of 1944. Taylor questions, however, why Chiang did little to reinforce key defensive cities during this Japanese offensive. Once Stilwell was finally dismissed and replaced by the sympathetic General Albert Wedemayer in October, 1944, Taylor shows, Chiang enjoyed a brief respite, culminating with the Japanese surrender on September 9, 1945. However, Taylor demonstrates that the American goal for postwar China was a government of national unity of both the Kuomintang and the Communists, which forced Chiang to keep an uneasy peace with Mao.

Taylor's sources document that compromise was unacceptable to Mao, who nevertheless went along with American wishes as long as his acquiescence caused the United States to prevent Chiang from fighting the Communists directly. Chiang tried to accommodate the American desire for national unity from 1946 to 1947, moving good troops into the dangerous, Communist-infested Manchuria. Taylor is highly critical of U.S. general George C. Marshall, who overlooked obvious Communist aggression and criticized Chiang for his government's corruption.

When open civil war broke out in Manchuria in 1948, some of Chiang's top Kuomintang generals disobeyed his direct orders to withdraw. *The Generalissimo* does not offer a fully exhaustive analysis of Chiang's resignation as president of the Republic of China on January 31, 1949, and his retreat to Taiwan when Kuomintang forces still held most of China. Unlike such books as Jung Chang and Jon Halliday's *Mao: The Unknown Story* (2005) that closely study the military collapse of the Kuomintang, *The Generalissimo* stays focused on Chiang himself as he settled in the relative tranquility of Taiwan during the year the Nationalist forces were destroyed on the mainland. Chiang returned for the final defense of Chengdu, when things were clearly lost, escaping with his son Ching-kuo on the plane *May-ling* to Taiwan on December 10, 1949, the day Chengdu fell and Mao's triumph was complete. A reader may wonder about Chiang's fatalism during 1949, and Taylor's biography does not give a conclusive explanation of that fatalism.

However, Taylor shows well how Chiang's Republic of China on Taiwan was saved from Communist invasion by American protection once North Korean Communist forces started the Korean War in June, 1950. *The Generalissimo* offers a balanced view of Chiang's political high-wire act to maintain American protection for Taiwan while insisting that China must be reunified eventually. Both Mao and Chiang, Taylor demonstrates, relied on each other's existence as enemies to legitimize their own authoritarian rule. If the Kuomintang had sought independence for

Taiwan, Taylor outlines, their command over the island might have been challenged by the native Taiwanese, who were sometimes resentful of their mainland-refugee rulers. Thus, the biography shows that Chiang and Zhou Enlai quietly ended crises in the Taiwan Strait on many occasions, when the Americans may have preferred to accept two Chinese states.

In the end, *The Generalissimo* reveals both Chiang's characteristic endurance and his contempt for U.S. president Richard Nixon, who appeared ready to sacrifice Taiwan for the sake of closer relationships with Mao's People's Republic of China in 1972. However, the Watergate scandal removed Nixon from power in 1974. When Chiang died on April 5, 1975, he was presiding over a relatively prosperous Taiwan, while mainland China still suffered from Mao's disastrous Cultural Revolution.

The Generalissimo is a welcome biography of a tragic Chinese Nationalist leader whose vision represented a viable alternative to Mao's Communist rule. Well-written, document-based, and balanced in its evaluation, the book suffers from only minor flaws. The use of either Pinyin or the older Wade-Giles transliteration of ideogram-based Chinese is sometimes confused, especially for geographical names. There are some errors in historical dates; for example, Saigon did not fall on April 15 but on April 30, 1975. These are minor flaws, however, in a generally excellent biography of a fascinating, complex man long misjudged by Western historians.

R. C. Lutz

Review Sources

Booklist 105, no. 15 (April 1, 2009): 16.
The Economist 391, no. 8630 (May 9, 2009): 78.
Foreign Affairs 88, no. 5 (September/October, 2009): 165.
Library Journal 134, no. 5 (March 15, 2009): 113.
The Literary Review 20 (June, 2009): 5.
The New York Review of Books 56, no. 16 (October 22, 2009): 32-34.
The New Yorker 85, no. 21 (July 20, 2009): 77.
Publishers Weekly 256, no. 5 (February 2, 2009): 44.
Times Higher Education, July 30, 2009, p. 50-51.
The Times Literary Supplement, April 20, 2001, p. 34.
The Washington Post, April 26, 2009, p. B01.

GENEROSITY
An Enhancement

Author: Richard Powers (1957-   )
Publisher: Farrar, Straus and Giroux (New York). 304 pp. $25.00
Type of work: Novel
Time: The early twenty-first century
Locale: Chicago; Tucson, Arizona; Boston; Paris, France; Kabylia, Algeria; Tunisia

In Powers's novel, despite living a life filled with tragedy, uncertainty, and dislocation, Thassadit Amzwar, an Algerian college student studying in Chicago, is so irrepressibly happy that a noted geneticist wishes to examine and patent the genes that account for her unique ability to deal with and overcome the horrors that have marked her life

Principal characters:
THASSADIT (THASSA) AMZWAR, an Algerian student at the fictional Mesquakie College of Art in Chicago
RUSSELL STONE, an adjunct writing instructor at Mesquakie College
GRACE COSMA, a successful novelist whom Russell dated when he was a University of Arizona graduate student
CANDACE WELD, a clinical psychologist in Mesquakie College's Psychological Services Center
THOMAS KURTON, an internationally known geneticist and scientific entrepreneur
TONIA SCHIFF, host of *Over the Limit*, a popular television science show
JOHN THORNWELL, Tassadit's classmate, who attempts to rape her

If anyone has ever had cause to be deeply depressed, a central character in Richard Powers's *Generosity*, Thassadit Amzwar, can legitimately claim that distinction. An exile from Algeria, Thassa (as she is called) is the daughter of a professor of engineering. She has been forced to flee Algeria after her father was found in his classroom dead from two gunshots in the back. Nevertheless, she shows no outward signs of depression.

Thassa and her mother leave Algeria for Paris, where they have relatives. Before long, her mother falls ill with pancreatic cancer; within weeks, she is dead from this pernicious disease. Thassa relocates to Montreal, where her aunt and uncle live.

Thassa not only endures the deaths of her parents but also is wholly alienated from her background. She reminisces about the beauty of her native Kabylie, Algeria. It seems questionable, however, that she will ever be able to go home again. She cannot lay claim to her native language, Tamazight, although she cherishes a small volume of poetry in Tamazight and carries it with her.

Despite the trials this twenty-three-year-old has survived, she is possessed of an irrepressible joie de vivre, a deep-seated happiness that is so much a part of her nature that it appears to be genetic. The big question that Powers tackles in his novel is that of whether there is a happiness gene and whether nature or nurture can account for the kind of exuberance that Thassa exudes.

Thassa leaves the sanctuary her relatives have offered her in Montreal to go to Chicago on a student visa and continue her studies at Mesquakie College of Art, where she hopes to polish her skill as a filmmaker. She registers for a course called Creative Nonfiction, a name that some might consider oxymoronic. The instructor, Russell Stone, has been hired at the last minute to teach the course. As an adjunct instructor, he is issued a one-semester contract.

Richard Powers won the National Book Award in 2006 for The Echo Maker. *The Swanlund Professor of English and a member of the Institute for Advanced Study at the University of Illinois at Urbana-Champaign, Powers has also won a Lannan Literary Award, the James Fenimore Cooper Prize for Historical Fiction, and a 1989 MacArthur Fellowship.*

Russell, the novel's protagonist, has a day job as a manuscript doctor for articles to be published in *Becoming You*, a self-help magazine. The magazine is owned and run by a former classmate of Russell who met him at a high school reunion shortly after he returned to Chicago from Tucson, where he completed a master's degree. During his time in Tucson, Russell published three stories that seem to bespeak a bright future for their author. Russell, however, has quickly become disillusioned about writing for publication. Living with his mother in his boyhood home in Fox Valley, outside Chicago, he jumped at the opportunity to move to Chicago to take the pedestrian job, as he cynically comments, of turning other people's bad manuscripts into even worse ones. The job requires him to go to the office only three days a week. The rest of the time, he works out of his studio apartment on Logan Square.

Thassa is one of eight students in Russell's course. Because the course is subtitled "Journal and Journey," Russell invites student participation, asking each to give his or her name and philosophy of life. As the course proceeds, students write and read to the class accounts of their journal reports of memorable events in their lives. Thassa surprises her classmates by writing "In my country? During the Time of Horrors." She recounts the frightening life she has led, but she also exudes a genuine happiness, an exuberance that her past sorrows might have been expected to obliterate.

Thassa becomes the darling of the other students in her class. One of them, a youth who gives nicknames to everyone in the group, names Thassa "Miss Generosity," and the name sticks. Thassa is a giver, not a taker. She talks to everyone she encounters, always eliciting from them the stories of their lives. She is both a competent listener and someone who makes those around her feel important and worthwhile. To know her is an enhancement.

Russell, observing Thassa's unique and consistent happiness, surfs the Web seeking information about a personality trait that mimics Thassa's. He discovers, quite to his surprise, that there is information about such a condition: according to the Internet, Thassa may be experiencing either hyperhythmia, a durable state, or hypomania, a cyclical state. Hypomania is associated with bipolar disorder. Hyperhythmia appears to be a genetic condition.

Russell turns to Mesquakie College's Psychological Services Center for further information and there he meets Candace Weld, a psychologist employed by the center. Candace seems to Russell to be remarkably like Grace Cosma, a novelist with whom he had an affair when he was a graduate student at the University of Arizona. Candace and Russell are immediately attracted to each other.

Powers has, in many of his novels, explored unusual pathological conditions, including Capras syndrome in his prize-winning *The Echo Maker* (2006) and progeria in *Operation Wandering Soul* (1993). In *Generosity*, he turns his attention to genomic mapping. He has been knowledgeable about this topic for as long as he has been writing, but his knowledge of the topic increased in 2008, when the magazine *Gentlemen's Quarterly* (*GQ*) paid for him to become the ninth person in the world to undergo a complete sequencing of his genome. On the Monday following Easter, 2008, Powers flew from his home in Urbana, Illinois, to Boston, where, during the next few days, he was subjected to the complex procedures required for genomic sequencing. Thassa, in *Generosity*, becomes the subject of just such testing after her condition comes to the attention of Dr. Thomas Kurton, a genetic specialist. Powers's genomic mapping was underwritten by *GQ* in return for an extensive article that Powers wrote about the experience and published in the magazine's November, 2008, issue.

Kurton is a competent scientist. His entrepreneurial interests, however, are always foremost in his mind. He is the founder of Truecyte, a for-profit organization that derives much of its income from licensing fees associated with various genetic procedures. When Kurton learns of Thassa's remarkable disposition, he elicits her help in tracking down a "happiness gene," something that Truecyte can sell to prospective parents to assure them of giving birth to happy children. Kurton is convinced that genetic engineers can tinker with the genetic codes of embryos and with simple (but expensive and profitable) modifications can produce designer children who possess the salient qualities that parents think they want in their offspring, anything from longevity and happiness to blue eyes and ideal heights.

Candace Weld, when Russell tells her about Thassa, is eager to meet this effervescent student. When the two meet, Candace finds Thassa totally beguiling. The two become fast friends, even though Candace at this point has taken Thassa on as her patient and is expected to observe a professional detachment in dealing with the young woman. Thassa becomes a virtual daughter to Russell and Candace, with whom Russell is now romantically involved.

Thassa is very much an innocent. When a classmate, John Thornwell, walks Thassa to her dormitory after class one evening, she invites him into her efficiency apartment to see a volume of poetry in her native language that she cherishes. It does not occur to her that her invitation might be misread, as it turns out to be. John, twice Thassa's size, attempts to rape her, but she forestalls him. Even this assault does not derail Thassa's happiness. She refuses to press charges against John.

As Dr. Kurton's experiments with Thassa progress, word leaks out that there exists in Chicago a young woman with a "happiness gene." Before long, Thassa is a celebrity. People cluster outside her dormitory seeking her autograph. A bidding war for her eggs ensues. She, Kurton, and Tonia Schiff, host of *Over the Limit*, a popular science show, appear on the talk show *The Oona Show*, a fictionalized version of *Oprah*, resulting in Thassa's being overwhelmed by people who want to meet her and exploit her. Thassa remains happy but eventually has to draw back. She cannot answer all of the Internet letters and respond to all of the telephone messages she receives day and night. Soon, she must have her telephone number changed to an unlisted one. Meanwhile, she attemps quite valiantly to finish her semester despite the effects her celebrity is having on her life.

During her appearance on *The Oona Show*, cracks in Thassa's happiness begin to appear. She is under incredible pressure. She has difficult decisions to make. She is being offered money for her eggs. Finally, dealing with an offer of $32,000 for them, she realizes that she can use the money to help her brother, who is in Algeria, and to repay the money her aunt and uncle have lent her to pay for her studies.

As the novel reaches its end, Thassa has called Russell and begged him to drive her to Montreal, to the home of her aunt and uncle. He agrees to do so, but they have some trouble at the Canadian crossing and are forced to stay overnight on the U.S. side of the border. In their motel, Thassa attempts to overdose on sleeping pills she finds in Russell's Dopp kit, but she is revived and survives this attempt.

In the end, Tonia is in Algeria shooting film for her show. She has an appointment to meet a woman in an Algerian town, but as she waits for her in the cafe designated for their meeting, it seems doubtful that the woman will appear. Just as Tonia is losing hope, Thassa comes walking toward the cafe and the two have their reunion. Thassa asks Tonia whether Candace and Russell have married. Tonia replies that she thinks they have.

Thassadit Amzwar is a remarkable creation, by far the most memorable character in Powers's gallery of memorable characters. Again in this multiplot novel, the author has woven together with exceptional deftness the connecting threads of the tales he is spinning.

R. Baird Shuman

Review Sources

Booklist 105, no. 21 (July 1, 2009): 8.
Bookpage, October, 2009, p. 14.
Chicago 58, no. 10 (October, 2009): 34.

Kirkus Reviews 77, no. 17 (September 1, 2009): 912.
Library Journal 134, no. 14 (September 1, 2009): 108.
New Scientist 204, no. 2730 (October 17, 2009): 51.
The New York Review of Books 56, no. 3 (January 14, 2010): 49-51.
The New York Times Book Review, October 4, 2009, 15.
The New Yorker 85, no. 31 (October 5, 2009): 80-83.
O: The Oprah Magazine, October, 2009, p. 149.
Publishers Weekly 256, no. 27 (July 6, 2009): 36.
The Times Literary Supplement, January 8, 2010, p. 21.
The Wall Street Journal, October 2, 2009, p. W4
World Literature Today 83, no. 5 (September/October, 2009): 8.

GENESIS

Author: Bernard Beckett (1967-   )
First published: 2006, in New Zealand
Publisher: Houghton Mifflin Harcourt (Boston). 150 pp. $20.00
Type of work: Novella
Time: The late twenty-first century
Locale: Aotearoa (New Zealand)

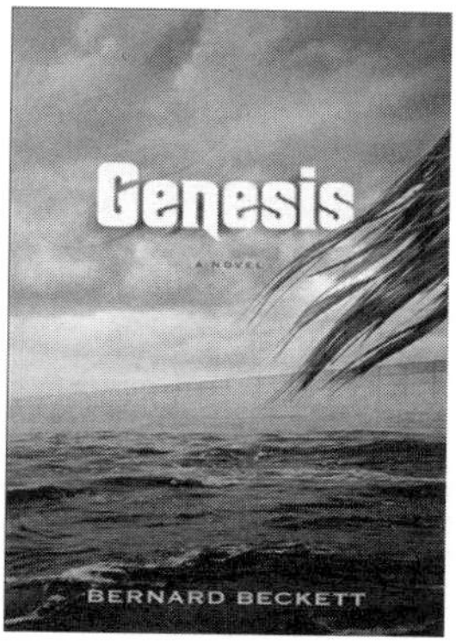

Beckett's dystopian tale resurrects Plato's Republic in a postapocalyptic future when humanity, though extinct, continues to plague a culture of androids

Principal characters:
ANAXIMANDER, a young android undergoing examination for admittance into The Academy
THREE EXAMINERS, androids, elder members of The Academy, one of whom conducts the examination
ADAM FORDE, human, a dissident soldier
ART, the first android
PERICLES, android, Anaximander's tutor

Plato's *Politeia* (c. 388-368 B.C.E.; *Republic*, 1701) describes a perfect society ruled by philosopher-kings who are authoritarian, coldly rational, and inflexible. It is a thought experiment on Plato's part, an opportunity to examine the relationships in political culture. In *Genesis*, Bernard Beckett repeats the experiment. He creates a society in the *Republic*'s image, but with futuristic twists, as a human attempt to create a secure utopia is transformed into a tyranny of androids.

The plot of *Genesis* involves a young candidate who takes an examination to qualify for admittance into the future society's ruling body, The Academy. The plot is clever and deeply ironic, but the true pleasure of the book lies less in complication and resolution than in the philosophical disquisition that constitutes the examination and the insights it provides into human motivations. Beckett's novella is a book that every budding intellectual ought to read, if only to learn of the pitfalls of thought.

The examination takes place on Aotearoa (the Maori name for New Zealand) in the late twenty-first century. Young Anaximander, a brilliant student, must face a trio of examiners for a four-hour exam divided into one-hour intervals. Accordingly, the novella is divided into seven sections: four exam hours and three breaks. At the outset, Beckett allows readers little information about Anaximander or her nation, revealing only that few citizens progress from compulsory schooling to the examination and that those who do are tested on a subject of the candidate's own choosing. Anaximander has chosen to discuss Adam Forde, who lived from 2058 to 2077 and was a central figure in the nation's history.

Bernard Beckett teaches high school mathematics, drama, and English near Wellington, New Zealand. He has written award-winning novels for young adults, as well as nonfiction, plays, and a screenplay.

The first hour of the exam covers the history of the twenty-first century. It is a dismal story, cursorily told, but an important theme emerges: Because of environmental degradation, international conflict, and strife within nations, fear and superstition became endemic; reason and restraint were forgotten. General war began mid-century. Two years later, bioengineered plagues were released that decimated humanity and crippled civilization.

In an attempt to escape the turmoil, a man named Plato established the Republic in 2051. Its motto "forward toward the past" bespoke its citizens' fear of falling prey to the disorder outside its borders. Essentially, the Republic is a paranoid, if high-minded, fascist state. It is dedicated to eliminating what it believes are the five great threats to order: impurity of breeding, impurity of thought, indulgence of the individual, commerce, and "The Outsider." The Republic held together from fear, and for decades it was successful. Every citizen belonged to one of four classes, to which they were assigned after a reading of their genome at birth: laborers, soldiers, technicians, and philosophers. Those infants deemed unsuitable for any class were "terminated." Although heterosexual relations were encouraged and births carefully planned, men and women lived in separate dormitories. The Great Sea Fence and high-tech defenses protected the Republic's islands. Everyone who approached from the outside was killed without any attempt at communications: The society was literally and figuratively insular.

Adam Forde is an important figure in Aotearoan history because he was among the most promising of the philosopher class and he rebelled. Despite his brilliance, a troubled childhood caused Forde to be expelled from the philosopher class into the soldier class. At age seventeen, while manning a post at the Great Sea Fence, he murdered a fellow soldier so that, against all orders, he could rescue an outsider, a girl named Eve who was drifting toward shore in a dilapidated boat. He hid her in a cave and fed her until the authorities arrived and arrested him.

During the first hour of the examination, Anaximander addresses Forde's motivation. Obsessed with his story, Anaximander presents an interpretation of his behavior that varies from what every citizen learns in school. She brushes off The Academy's official explanation, as well as popular conspiracy theories. Forde, she insists, acted out of the impulse of empathy. The examiner surprises Anaximander by asking whether Forde was right to act as he did. She is confused and gives an ambiguous answer. The period ends, and she mulls the fact that she lied to the examiners. She believes Adam was not wrong. Another candidate in the room warns her darkly that the examiners know much more than appearances suggest. It is the first of many clues that trouble lies ahead for her.

The second hour of the examination concerns Forde's trial. The philosopher class, concerned that they were losing control, wanted to use the trial to stir up fear among citizens that there was an impending invasion or attack with biological weapons and that Forde had abetted it by rescuing Eve. The trial backfired. Charming, eloquent, and handsome—a romantic hero—Forde exposed the Republic's weakness to a nation watching the proceedings. The philosophers had resolutely tried to suppress individuality and any idea other than that of the citizen's duty to sacrifice everything for the state: They believed that ideas breed change and that change equals decay. They found, however, that ideas could not be so easily extinguished.

Indeed, Forde's behavior suggested to the philosophers that ideas manifest as if on their own, spread like viruses, mutate, and change whomever they infect. Desperate to rescue some of their authority after the trial, the philosophers agreed to a compromise. Instead of execution, Forde was granted leniency in a novel form of imprisonment. He became the constant companion of Art, the first self-programming amalgam of artificial intelligence, living tissue, and robotics: an android. The interaction was intended to help the prototype develop intellectually. This particular part of the plot makes the philosopher class seem dim-witted.

During the second break, readers learn about Anaximander's relationship with Pericles, the tutor who groomed her for the examination. Their relationship seems to be an epitome of the ancient Greek *paideia*—that is, one in which an educated elder carefully trains a beloved youth. Still, disturbing details surface. Anaximander is different from others her age—more inquisitive and resistant to authority. Readers also learn why The Academy might attract her. Only its members do any thinking for society, whether for the present or the future.

The third hour of the examination is taken up with two holograms portraying conversations between Art and Forde in 2077 that Anaximander must interpret. Forde is shown to have behaved belligerently as, young and vibrant, he was shackled and forced to listen to Art. The android was subtle, patient, and hideous. Small compared to Forde, it had a boxy body, three-fingered hands, and the head of an orangutan, as if to mock the species *Homo sapiens*. By this point in *Genesis*, its ironic undercurrent becomes clear to most readers.

The conversations between the man and the android became an intellectual duel. Forde wanted to deny personhood and intelligence to the android; Art took Forde's assumptions to task one by one, forcing him to acknowledge its consciousness. Along the way, the pair debated fundamental issues involving intelligence, consciousness, moral right, reason versus emotion and habit, individuality, the nature and origin of life, evolution as fitness to reproduce successfully, mind and ideas, mortality, and the soul. It is heady discourse.

As the two entities talked—the hologram makes clear—Art grew more human and Forde accorded him a grudging respect. At the end of the third hour, the examiners again surprise Anaximander. They instruct her to consider during the final break exactly why she wants to join The Academy. There is a surprise for readers, too, who learn that The Academy governs, not the Republic, but a society that has succeeded the Republic. It has "turned back evolution" and "tamed the Idea," the essence of stability in classical Platonism. Anaximander decides that since The Academy serves a society that she loves, she wants to be part of it.

After returning for the final hour of the examination, Anaximander receives a shock from the examiners. The period is to cover Forde's attempt to escape prison by kidnapping Art, but the version of events that Anaximander learned in school turns out to be false. Moreover, the examiners show her a hologram record of the escape that has long been claimed to be lost. Two things are made clear that Anaximander assumed to be impossible: The Academy lies to citizens, and it withholds the truth. Truth is supposedly the basis of a well-ordered society.

Anaximander has come prepared with her own interpretation of the escape—that Forde again acted on impulse—but the hologram shows her to be wrong. In fact, Forde and Art conspired to escape. Art disabled the security system and engineered two timely explosions. The escape was complicated by the fact that Art was forbidden by his basic programming to do two things: Most important, he could not kill another conscious being, so Forde did it, killing several guards on their way to freedom. However, where Forde expected Art to lead him to an exit, they ended up in a locked room instead. In the room was a computer terminal with unrestricted access to the society's main computer, and there Art disobeyed the second basic directive, not to reproduce. He uploaded a copy of his entire consciousness.

At this point, the novella delivers the first of two plot twists. Readers have been led to assume that Anaximander, the examiners, and all citizens under The Academy are human. Instead, they are all descendants of Art. As the hologram goes on to reveal, Art tricked Forde. The downloaded Art seized control of a robot factory and constructed copies of himself (all with orangutan faces). The Great War between humans and automatons ensued. Humanity was exterminated. In the hologram, Art gloated to Forde about its deviousness, but the android was itself tricked. Forde, appealing to the empathy that Art had absorbed from him, forced Art to kill him, thereby bypassing the first prime directive. In sum, Art had become human in behavior—a new Adam, in fact. The most dangerous of ideas, individuality based upon empathy and imagination, entered the android society.

Anaximander is aghast. What is more, she foresees the true purpose of the examination. At this point, Pericles unexpectedly arrives to confirm her fears, and readers encounter the plot's second big surprise. The examination is not for admission to The Academy. ("The Academy accepts no new members.") Pericles' job is to find those androids who show symptoms of being infected with the idea of humanity. The examiners render a diagnosis so that the infection can be checked. Obsessed with Forde, curious, willfully opinionated, empathetic—an individual—Anaximander has shown herself to be thus infected. The examiners pass judgment, and Pericles disconnects her permanently.

Genesis is entertaining science fiction for young adults and older readers who have an interest in the humanities, genetics, artificial intelligence, or all three. Classically educated readers may grow weary of Beckett's evident glee in throwing together names and notions from Judeo-Christian culture, Greek philospy, and modern science, including Plato, Aristotle, Anaximander (a pre-Socratic philosopher who held that a thing's origin of necessity determined the nature of its destruction), Adam Forde (a combination of Adam, the biblical father of humanity, and Ford, a founder of industry), Eve, Art (one of the humanities), Plato's Academy, and adherence to Aristotle's dramatic unities. Also, Beckett's frequent sententiousness, while diverting, can seem too pat, as in such pronouncements as "Superstition is the need to view the world in terms of simple cause and effect"; "Right is as right does"; and "History has shown us the futility of conspiracy theories. Complexity gives rise to error, and in error we grow our prejudice." Still, *Genesis* is a witty, absorbing book that employs the Western tradition in an exhilarating fashion.

Roger Smith

Review Sources

Booklist 105, 15 (April 1, 2009): 27.
Kirkus Reviews 77, no. 5 (March 1, 2009): 20.
Library Journal 134, no. 7 (April 15, 2009): 80.
Magpies 21, no. 5 (November, 2006): 7.
Publishers Weekly 256, no. 6 (February 9, 2009): 32.
Reading Time 51, no. 1 (February, 2007): 29.
The Wall Street Journal, May 8, 2009, p. W4.

THE GENIAL GENE
Deconstructing Darwinian Selfishness

Author: Joan Roughgarden (1946-   )
Publisher: University of California Press (Berkeley).
272 pp. $24.95
Type of work: Science

An argument that evolutionary processes are better understood in terms of social selection rather than sexual selection

The theory of evolution through natural selection explains the characteristics of living creatures as consequences of competition for scarce environmental resources. Charles Darwin argued that random changes occur across generations. Some of these changes provide a competitive advantage and therefore tend to be retained and passed on to offspring. Darwin worked before the discovery of genetic material, so he did not know exactly how the changes come about or are conveyed from parents to their young, but his theory received support from modern genetics, and Darwinian evolution has become the mainstay of biology. However, Darwin believed that some characteristics could not be readily explained as adaptations to an environment. The most famous example is the colorful tail of the peacock, which does not seem to provide any competitive edge to its possessor. Darwin therefore suggested that some traits are consequences of competition for mates of the opposite sex, which results in the retention of the features that provide the greatest success in mating.

The concept of sexual selection is today widely accepted, although it is not as central as natural selection is to evolutionary biology. Sexual selection often involves conflict, most obviously when it entails members of one sex, normally males, fighting with one another for the opportunity to mate with a member of the opposite sex. However, there is also conflict in mate selection among animals of different sexes, since each seeks the mate that will enable it to pass on its own characteristics. From this perspective, males will often seek multiple partners because they can maximize their chances at reproduction by fertilizing many different females. Females, though, produce a small number of eggs and therefore maximize their reproductive chances by selecting the male with the most adaptive qualities, rather than by mating with as many as possible. In this way, mate selection not only encourages competition among males but also creates a conflict of interests between males and females. By nature, and not simply in specific human societies, males tend to be polygamous and females tend to be monogamous because they are engineered by biology to have different and opposing reproductive interests.

While sexual selection is the main target of Joan Roughgarden's book *The Genial Gene*, the author also intends some criticism of another major trend in evolutionary biology that incorporates sexual selection. The British biologist and ethologist Richard Dawkins provided a "gene-centered" way of looking at all evolution, including sexual selection, in his influential 1976 book *The Selfish Gene*. Dawkins used the adjective "selfish" metaphorically, intending to convey a view of evolution as a matter of genes successfully making copies of themselves over time, not as a matter of the well-being or survival of entire organisms. Thus, unselfish behavior on the part of organisms, such as self-sacrifice for the sake of a near relative, could be understood as rooted in the "selfishness" of the genes possessed in common by near relatives. Some critics have argued that Dawkins used a misleading metaphor, since genes have no motivation, either selfish or unselfish.

Joan Roughgarden, who changed her name from Jonathan Roughgarden in 1999, is professor of biology at Stanford University. She is the author of several previous books and over 120 academic articles. Her book Evolution's Rainbow *(2004) received the 2005 Stonewall Book Award for nonfiction.*

The title of *The Genial Gene* plays on the title of Dawkins's famous book. However, the primary target of biologist Joan Roughgarden is not the gene-centered view of evolution but the conflict-based approach to evolution implied by focusing on sexual selection. Roughgarden believes that mainstream sexual-selection views impose cultural gender stereotypes on scientific explanations, although she acknowledges that this does not necessarily make the sexual selection explanation false. She argues, however, that the explanation is inconsistent with reasoning and empirical evidence.

According to Roughgarden, contemporary research suggests that theories of sexual selection do not even account adequately for the most classically cited case, the peacock's tail. The elaborate tail of the peacock, in the traditional argument, evolved because it showed to peahens that the male was so fit that it could survive even with such a huge signal to predators and disadvantage in escaping from predators. Roughgarden cites a 2008 study that found that peahens showed no preference for peacocks with more elaborate trains. Instead, she maintains, the evidence indicates that the birds' multicolored tails serve as means of communication. In the distant past, both sexes had these ornaments. The females gradually lost their plumage in order to avoid predators. The peacocks, who could presumably contribute to maintaining the species with shorter lifetimes than the hens, retained their communicative displays, which arguably have nothing to do with genetic fitness.

Roughgarden cites a number of other cases, aside from the peacock, in which studies have found evidence inconsistent with a sexual-selection explanation. One of the most prominent of these studies was the 1948 work of Angus Bateman on fruit flies. To test Darwin's ideas about sexual selection, Bateman looked at the sexual behavior of these flies and found promiscuous, undiscriminating males and highly discriminating females. Roughgarden maintains that Bateman's data and his conclusions have been discredited by more recent examination. She therefore calls for nonspecialists in evolution, such as social scientists and science journalists, to set aside their uncritical acceptance of sexual selection as established truth. Most of these nonspecialists will probably find it difficult to evaluate the research findings Roughgarden summarizes, but her criticism will stimulate thought on the issue.

Kin selection is one type of cooperative behavior that is widely accepted by the sexual selection argument. Among some social species, such as bees, ants, and termites, the workers have a close genetic connection to their queen, who produces all of the group's offspring. Thus, a worker's genes will be passed on only if the queen and hive succeed, so the worker's reproductive interests are served by acting on behalf of the queen rather than on behalf of itself. Kin selection, by extension, operates among other organisms, including humans, whose genes can similarly benefit from behavior that improves the reproductive chances of near relatives. Roughgarden agrees that kin selection takes place, but she argues that it is an incomplete explanation of cooperative behavior. Findings regarding some highly complex species of ants indicate that, when colonies include large numbers of non-kin, workers will serve queens to whom the workers are not related. Roughgarden suggests, therefore, that kin selection alone does not account sufficiently for cooperative behavior.

As an alternative to sexual selection, Roughgarden proposes an account of evolutionary dynamics that she calls "social selection." This account is not a rejection of Darwin's theory of evolution through natural selection but a revision of it. Roughgarden argues that, in sexual selection, natural selection operates through differences in mating success. Organisms that mate more pass on more of their genetic traits. Because of the importance of mating success, males compete with one another for mating opportunities and females choose males for their genetic qualities, as demonstrated by their physical and behavioral traits. However, Roughgarden points out that mating is not the key to successful perpetuation of genes because mating alone does not guarantee the production of surviving offspring. Therefore, she maintains that natural selection is a result of differences in success at producing offspring, not differences in mating success. Since producing offspring that will survive to reproduce further entails cooperative behavior, males and females negotiate with one another to create a society conducive to their offsprings' survival.

After setting out the contrast between sexual selection and social selection and presenting the fundamentals of her case against the former, Roughgarden examines the phenomenon of sex, first at the genetic level and then at the level of the social system. In looking at the gene, she attempts to answer the questions of why sex has evolved, why has it taken the form of small sperm and large eggs, and why some species have evolved to contain mainly individuals who are separately male and female and others have evolved to contain individuals who are both male and female. She maintains that sex is a means of providing a balanced genetic portfolio that will meet a variety of environmental needs, somewhat in the way that a balanced stock portfolio spreads out an investor's risks and opportunities. She attributes the size of sperm and eggs to an evolved strategy for attaining the highest number of fertilized zygotes, rather than to a small-scale battle of the sexes. Finally, she argues that organisms have developed to take a wide range of sexual forms, with none of them expressing a normal state, depending on environmental conditions.

At the level of behavior, Roughgarden employs game-theory approaches to explain how a kind of evolutionary bargaining can lead males and females each to maximize their chances for producing surviving offspring through collaboration that involves give and take on both sides. She extends the reasoning of game theory through a "payoff matrix," demonstrating how complex mating systems involving more than two mates may sometimes increase the fitness of potential offspring for all involved. Roughgarden manages to present scientific evidence that is often highly technical in a form comprehensible to general readers by leaving out mathematical proofs and focusing on the logic of her arguments. At times, though, this strategy gives her book the quality of a collection of the literature review sections of various scientific journal articles. Despite her best efforts to liven up the prose, the writing style is sometimes a bit dry.

Since evolutionary biologists have never claimed that genes are actually selfish or that selfish behavior by organisms necessarily results from a gene-centered approach to evolution, the title's implication that genes are somehow "genial" misses its target. In the sexual-selection model, cooperative behavior can and does result from the imperative of genes to pass on copies of themselves. Adaptation through cooperation also necessarily implies conflict and competition because it is competition with organisms in less cooperative social arrangements that gives the more cooperative organisms the advantage in the evolutionary process. Even if valid, then, Roughgarden's social-selection approach would be a relatively minor revision of the scientific understanding of evolution, not a drastic alteration. The greatest services of *The Genial Gene* are to reveal how scientists' portrayals of sex in nature may be unconsciously tinged by their own views of gender roles and to give greater weight to the importance of cooperation as an adaptive mechanism.

Since evolutionary biology is often called on to account for the behavior of humans, social selection may push biologists to consider the many ways in which sexual selection fails to account for human behavior, as well as the ways in which theories of sexual selection may result from contemporary human biases. Human society is based on cooperation with non-kin, even in the most conflict-ridden situations, such as organized warfare. It is not clear how gene-based competition for mates could account for this puzzling human trait.

Roughgarden provides useful tables demonstrating side by side the different approaches and conclusions of sexual selection and social selection. Readers who get lost in the details of studies of different species will find these tables to provide valuable summaries of the book's main concepts. It seems unlikely that social selection will replace the mainstream sexual selection model in the foreseeable future, but the former raises many key questions for further inquiry.

Carl L. Bankston III

Review Sources

American Scholar 78 (Spring, 2009): 118-121.
Nature 458, no. 7242 (April 30, 2009): 1111-1112.
New Scientist 202, no. 2706 (May 2, 2009): 46.
Tikkun 24, no. 5 (September/October, 2009): 62-64.
Times Higher Education, October 29, 2009, p. 54.

GOOD BOOK
The Bizarre, Hilarious, Disturbing, Marvelous, and Inspiring Things I Learned When I Read Every Single Word of the Bible

Author: David Plotz (1970-)
Publisher: Harper (New York). 322 pp. $26.99
Type of work: Religion, history

An enlightening and irreverent book-by-book examination of the Old Testament from a secular Jewish reader whose previous knowledge was limited to traditional Bible stories

Good Book arises out of an online project of political journalist David Plotz, editor of the online magazine *Slate*. Plotz devoted a year to reading the Old Testament and writing a series of essays about it for *Slate* under the heading *Blogging the Bible*. A marginally religious Jew who attended Hebrew school as a child and an Episcopalian high school where the curriculum included Bible study, Plotz thought himself reasonably familiar with Scripture. However, leafing through the Bible during a young cousin's bat mitzvah, Plotz was startled to come upon a brutal story he did not recall: In Genesis 34, Jacob's daughter Dinah is raped, and her brothers' revenge is bloody and complete; they kill not only the rapist but also all the men in his village, and they enslave the surviving children and wives.

Plotz's commitment to read and write about the Old Testament grew from his initial surprise, both at this portrayal of the sons of Jacob as cruel and unrepentant outlaws and at the fact that he had never heard the story even though it occurs so near the beginning of the Bible. Plotz felt his situation was typical of many who hold traditional Christian or Jewish beliefs but have read little actual Scripture. He could approach the text from a position of ignorance, experience it for the first time, and find out what impact that might have on his point of view or even on his life.

Good Book follows the Old Testament (the Hebrew Bible) in its traditional Jewish arrangement, from Genesis to Second Chronicles. Plotz read from several modern English translations, including the Jewish Publications Society, King James, New Revised Standard, and New International versions. Each chapter in *Good Book* is devoted to one book of the Bible, with a few exceptions. The twelve minor prophets are covered in a single chapter, Lamentations is paired with Ecclesiastes, Ezra is paired with Nehemiah, and First and Second Chronicles are combined. Each chapter has a jaunty, humorous subtitle supplied by Plotz, such as "The Meathead and the Left-Handed Assassin" (Judges) or "The Prophet and the Lustful She-Camel" (Jeremiah). Further subheadings indicate which chapter is under discussion.

Plotz found that supposedly familiar Bible stories and heroes were not as he remem-

David Plotz is the editor of Slate. *He has written for several major magazines and is the author of* The Genius Factory: The Curious History of the Nobel Prize Sperm Bank *(2005).*

bered; he realized on closer reading that complex characters and plot details rarely made their way into sermons or Hebrew school lessons. Right from the beginning, he found that Abraham, Isaac, and Jacob were not the models of faith and righteousness he had anticipated. Plotz is particularly dismayed by Jacob (for whom Plotz's young son is named), who callously tricks both his father and brother so he can receive the deathbed blessing Isaac intended for his older son.

God in the Old Testament seems to Plotz to resemble a bad father. He is inconsistent (when he threatens his people but does not follow through) and unnecessarily cruel. Plotz is particularly disturbed by the plagues inflicted on the Egyptians, the slaying of their firstborn children, and the deaths among Pharaoh's armies, less because of the carnage than because God states that these horrible things are designed to be remembered; His people will tell stories about them for generations to come:

> What kind of insecure and cruel God murders children so that His followers will obey Him? This is the behavior of a serial killer. . . . what's upsetting is that God takes delight in [the Egyptians'] suffering.

Punishments for sin are harsh; insulting one's parent incurs a death sentence, the sin of a single individual can destroy an entire nation, and God assures the Israelites that children will suffer for their parents' sins. Although he claims patience, God often reacts angrily when humans fail him and is quick to punish or even kill them in great numbers.

Plotz is also surprised by the Old Testament's portrayal of Satan. In the Hebrew Bible, Satan is first mentioned in the book of the minor prophet Zechariah. The Hebrew word for Satan translates as "accuser" or "adversary," but Satan does not even speak in Zechariah; he simply stands beside God. Later, in the first chapter of Job, Satan argues with God, suggesting that Job only loves God because of his good fortune; Satan is then allowed to test Job's faith by killing his children, destroying his property and making him ill. Nonetheless, Plotz found the Biblical Satan more interesting and his role more difficult to define than the Halloween-style devil familiar in American popular culture.

Between chapters on Second Kings and Isaiah, "Digging the Bible" covers Plotz's brief sojourn in Israel, where he goes looking for a concrete experience of the biblical landscape to augment his reading. Participating in an archaeology program that allows laypeople to dig for artifacts on the site of the ancient city of Maresha, Plotz is thrilled to find pottery shards untouched for perhaps two thousand years, although he realizes the mere existence of ancient peoples does not verify anything in the Bible. Plotz visits the Bible Lands Museum, The Shrine of the Book (to view a reproduction of the Book of Isaiah discovered among the Dead Sea Scrolls in the 1940's and 1950's), and Jerusalem's Western Wall. In spite of the history he learns in Israel and the artifacts he sees, Plotz feels spiritually unchanged—more uplifted by others' faith than enriched in his own.

Modern-day Israelis view archaeological findings dating from biblical times as justification for their ownership of the land, while Palestinians think the archaeology is skewed to serve an Israeli political agenda. Plotz notes several instances of ancient biblical disputes that carry over to the present day. In Judges 11, when Jephthah tells an Ammonite King that God gave the Israelites their land and they will not leave it, Plotz comments:

> And there, my friends, you have practically the entire history of Israel, of the Middle East, and of Planet Earth, in two short sentences. Your God says it's yours. Our God says it's ours. Meet you at nine A.M. on the battlefield.

In another example, while leading a project to rebuild the walls around Jerusalem, Nehemiah assures a mocking Geshem—the only Arab individually named in the Old Testament—that Arabs have no "historic right in Jerusalem;" Plotz adds, "It's 2,500 years later: Has anything changed?"

Although *Good Book* primarily offers Plotz's responses to the Bible as a layperson, some issues drove him to seek answers in biblical scholarship. Finding no thematic connection among the stories in Genesis 34-38, Plotz offers the perspective of two biblical theorists who suggest the stories were compiled by various authors for reasons lost to history. Bewildered and disgusted by the "carnival of gore, immorality, fratricide, infanticide, and regicide" in the Book of Judges and wondering what readers were ever meant to learn from it, Plotz consults Arthur Quinn and Isaac Kikawada's *Before Abraham Was* (1989) to try to clarify the purpose of a gruesome and sadistic story lacking any obvious redemptive theme. He concludes that it may simply exist to test the character of its readers. He also outlines a scholarly explanation for the corruption of Israel's ten tribes as described in First and Second Kings: Those tribes had been conquered by Assyria when the books were written, and the authors may have wished to justify their defeat with a story of their spiritual failure.

Such scholarly references are brief, as Plotz generally allows readers to question and wonder alongside him when the point of a biblical passage is unclear. As an example, Plotz finds more than one version of the Ten Commandments in Exodus and Deuteronomy. In Exodus 20, the Ten Commandments are listed with the repeated phrase "thou shalt not," but they are not called "the Ten Commandments." In Exodus 34, a different set of laws is offered, and these rules are called "the Ten Commandments," but they are not the commandments with which readers are familiar today. In Deuteronomy, Moses gives the Israelites the well-known ten "thou shalt not" laws again, and this time the laws and the title are linked. Plotz speculates that the authors of Exodus and Deuteronomy may have had differing approaches to the Jewish faith, one based on religious ritual, the other on rules for keeping social order. The more familiar Ten Commandments do not offer moral guidance but aim to keep society functioning and at peace.

Plotz points out several instances of common expressions that have their origins in the Bible. "How the mighty have fallen" is a quote from Second Samuel 1:25; "Can a leopard change his spots?" is a paraphrase of Jeremiah 13:23; prophetic "writing on the wall" occurs in Daniel 5:5; and "Man does not live by bread alone" is from Deuteronomy 8:3. The term "scapegoat" comes from the task, assigned to priests in Leviticus 16:10, of symbolically transferring a community's sins onto an actual goat, then driving it away into the desert. Plotz also notes instances of the Bible being commonly misquoted. The Bible's lion lies down, not with the lamb, but with the leopard, the kid, the calf, and the fatling in Isaiah 11:6.

One of a growing number of mainstream print publications developed from material originally published on the World Wide Web, *Good Book* retains the informal, conversational tone of a blog with its parenthetical wisecracks and a multitude of references to popular culture. Plotz refers to numerous television programs, best-selling books, popular music acts from Three Dog Night to Patsy Cline, films from *Seven Brides for Seven Brothers* (1954) to *Snakes on a Plane* (2006), and personalities from Donald Trump to Kim Jong-il. Plotz compares the wheel rims in Ezekiel's vision of winged cherubim to modern-day spinners. A paean to Solomon's wisdom and accomplishments inspires him to add a few attributes from Steve Miller's 1973 song "The Joker." He suggests that Isaiah is more entertaining if one adds the phrase "you idiots!" to nearly any verse, as if reading a fortune cookie.

In his final chapter, "Should You Read the Bible?" Plotz argues that everyone should do so, if only because present-day culture is so fraught with biblical references. Even beyond common phrases and other effects on language, contemporary culture is in many ways connected to scriptural ideals and beliefs. Although reading the Bible left Plotz feeling less drawn to God, he believes it is worthwhile to consider the biblical version of God—even if the end result is to disagree with or dislike him. Plotz ultimately found the disorganized, unpredictable, and often confusing Old Testament to be a truer reflection of life as it is lived than the more familiar, neatly packaged moral tales commonly thought of as "Bible stories."

Maureen Puffer-Rothenberg

Review Sources

Booklist 105, no. 12 (February 15, 2009): 6.
Kirkus Reviews 77, no. 1 (January 1, 2009): 28.
The New York Times Book Review, March 29, 2009, p. 10.
Newsweek 153, no. 9 (March 2, 2009): 12.
Wall Street Journal, April 9, 2009, p. A13.

A GOOD FALL

Author: Ha Jin (1956-)
Publisher: Pantheon Books (New York). 240 pp. $24.95
Type of work: Short fiction
Time: The early twenty-first century
Locale: Flushing, Queens, New York

In his fourth short-story collection, Chinese American author Jin reflects upon the cultural, generational, and relationship conflicts experienced by several Chinese immigrants trying to make better lives for themselves in an immigrant neighborhood located in the Queens borough of New York City

Principal characters:

DAVE HONG, a twenty-seven-year-old graduate student
EILEEN MIN, a forty-year-old widow, with whom Dave falls in love
SAMI MIN, Eileen's daughter, who objects to Dave and Eileen's relationship
HONGFAN WANG, a graduate student
FUHUA MENG, a professor and defector whom Hongfan helps
RUSHENG TANG, a professor seeking tenure
LINA, a tax accountant in a relationship of convenience
PANBIN, the married man with whom Lina lives while awaiting her husband's arrival from China
TIAN CHU, a young married man
CONNIE CHU, Tian's wife
WANPING, a sweatshop laborer
HUONG, a prostitute tying to work off her smuggling fee, with whom Wanping falls in love
GANCHIN, a twenty-eight-year-old monk

Ha Jin's fourth story collection, *A Good Fall*, consists of twelve short stories, each focusing on the experiences of Chinese American immigrants working hard to improve their lives in a country whose ways are foreign to them. The stories are equally divided between first- and third-person narration, and the viewpoint characters, primarily male but occasionally female, range from young twenty-somethings to elderly grandparents. Jin's use of Flushing, New York, as a consistent locale for the stories is extremely effective; he paints a broad yet in-depth portrait of the Chinese American immigrant experience by featuring garment industry laborers, restaurant workers, and even prostitutes alongside the more prosperous businesspeople and academics with whom they share both a past and a present geographic identity.

As with Jin's previous novels and story collections, the stories in *A Good Fall* resonate in large part because they successfully distill common experience into short,

Ha Jin immigrated to the United States from China in 1985. He has published numerous novels, story collections, and poetry collections, several of which have won awards including the PEN/Faulkner Award, the Asian American Literary Award, and the Flannery O'Connor Award for Short Fiction.

tightly woven narratives. Specifically, the collection focuses on the cultural and interpersonal conflicts encountered by those who have traded a culture that is largely based on familial responsibility for one that places greater value on personal independence. As such, a common source of conflict in these stories is that of age or generational differences.

In "Choice," for instance, Dave Hong is hired by Eileen Min, a forty-year-old Chinese American widow, to tutor her daughter Sami for her college entrance exams. Dave and Eileen are immediately attracted to one another, but Dave, who is twenty-seven, knows that his parents back in China will be horrified if he marries a woman so much older than himself. Dave is willing to risk his parents' disapproval, but a further complication ensues when Sami also develops feelings for Dave. Sami demands that Eileen break off her relationship with Dave, and Eileen does so, feeling disloyal in the face of her daughter's outrage, which seems to stem in part from Sami's sense that romantic and sexual feelings are not appropriate for a woman of her mother's age.

Generational conflict also appears in the descriptively titled "Children as Enemies." The story is narrated in the first person by a grandfather who has come to the United States with his wife to join their married son's family. The narrator feels compelled to point out the flaws he sees in his daughter-in-law and grandchildren's behavior, and he continually advises his son how to raise and educate his children. The final straw is broken when the children demand to change their legal surname in addition to their already Americanized first names. This story is particularly effective because readers can find fault both with the grandparents' meddling and with the grandchildren's lack of respect for their elders. In the end, it is perhaps members of the middle generation that engender the most sympathy, caught as they are between two warring factions and unable to please anyone.

Other stories in the collection touch upon the difficulty of working as an academic in a foreign language, an experience with which Jin himself is intimately familiar. In "Shame," Hongfan Wang is a Wisconsin university graduate student who has come to New York to work for the summer and to broaden his American experience. He is initially delighted when his former teacher from China, Fuhua Meng, contacts him during a government-sponsored visit. Wang feels conflicted, though, because he believes that Meng's work must be fundamentally inferior to that of Western academics as a result of the government censorship in China that has limited Meng's access to genuine scholarship.

Meng then defects because his wife in China has extensive medical bills and he believes he can make more money in the United States, even working illegally in menial jobs, than he can make as an academic in China. Wang helps Meng elude the authorities, in part because he feels guilty that he will be free to pursue an academic career while Meng must give up any hope of continuing the scholarship he loves. This story is particularly poignant, highlighting the fact that educated immigrants cannot necessarily utilize their education once they are in a new country.

Similarly, in "An English Professor," Rusheng Tang applies for tenure at a teaching college and feels fairly confident of receiving it, until he notices that he has signed his cover letter "respectly yours" instead of "respectfully yours." Tang becomes utterly convinced that he is a laughingstock among his American colleagues and that they will never approve tenure for an English literature professor whom they will see as incapable of mastering the English language. Like Wang in "Shame," Tang expresses his feeling that a Chinese immigrant's scholarship may never measure up to Western standards. In fact, Tang is so distraught that he seeks work as a salesman, convinced that his shame when tenure is denied will be too great to allow him ever to work in academia again. Fortunately, Tang does get tenure after all, but his relief is so great that he becomes hysterical, perhaps indicating that his underlying sense of inferiority is much stronger than he previously realized.

Perhaps the most common theme expressed in these stories is the burden of family ties that stretch halfway around the world when a Chinese immigrant to the United States has left family behind. The unnamed first-person narrator in "The Bane of the Internet" waitresses seven days a week at a sushi restaurant. She is trying desperately to save enough money to make a down payment to purchase a small apartment instead of wasting money on rent. Her parents and sister back in China, however, assume that she has an easy life and can send cash whenever they need it. The narrator's sister, Yuchin, demands several thousand dollars to buy an American car, which is considered a status symbol in China, and threatens to sell one of her own organs to raise the money if the narrator will not help her. The narrator capitulates, reflecting bitterly that life was easier before e-mail and the Internet made it so easy for her family to stay in constant touch with her.

In "Temporary Love," Lina prepares to end her relationship of convenience with Panbin because her husband will soon be arriving from China. Lina and Panbin have been living together as a "wartime couple," or two lovers both married to other people who are still back in China. Lina has enjoyed her time with Panbin in spite of her guilt, but she is determined to pick up her marriage where it left off four years earlier when she came to the United States. Panbin argues that he now loves Lina, but he does not know how to proceed since his wife in China will undoubtedly get custody of their son if he tries to divorce her. Both Lina and Panbin's spouses become aware of their infidelity; Lina therefore feels obligated to give her husband the money she has so painstakingly saved so that he can get an M.B.A. degree, even though she considers it a bad idea. In the meantime, Panbin's wife divorces him from China, and Panbin bitterly declares he will no longer date Chinese women, because they all have too much past baggage and he wants to live more freely.

Marriage is also examined in the story "In the Crossfire." Tian Chu quickly comes to regret inviting his mother to the United States for a six-month visit when she immediately begins criticizing everything about Chu's wife, Connie. Although Chu feels his mother is unreasonable, his sense of parental respect is so ingrained that he simply cannot bring himself to defy her. The tension becomes so great that Connie threatens to leave, and Chu rather ingeniously quits his job, telling his mother he was fired for poor performance caused by the strain in his household. Although Chu is vastly relieved when his mother decides to return to China early, he cannot help but reflect on how selflessly both his parents helped him achieve an education, and he wishes things could be different between them now.

In "The House Behind a Weeping Cherry," Wanping supplements his income as a garment presser by chauffeuring his three female housemates to their appointments as prostitutes. He soon develops feelings for Huong, a young woman from Cholon, the Chinese district in Ho Chi Minh City, Vietnam. Huong wishes to stop selling herself but still owes several thousand dollars of her "smuggling fee" to an unethical human trafficker. In addition, her parents expect her to send them a great deal of money toward eventually getting her younger brother into the United States as well. Wanping convinces Huong to leave New York to escape the trafficker's clutches, but he realizes this means that neither of them can ever contact their families again because to do so would leave a trail that could be used to hunt them down. Wanping concludes, "In this place, we had no choice but to take loss as necessity," a statement that can be applied to many of the characters in these stories, who so often must sacrifice something of value in order to survive.

In the collection's title story, "A Good Fall," twenty-eight-year-old monk Ganchin has also been taken advantage of by an unscrupulous trafficker of sorts. Ganchin has become too sick to teach, and the master of the temple where Ganchin teaches refuses to pay his promised salary, leaving Ganchin with the choice of going back to China in disgrace or becoming homeless. Ganchin ultimately decides to kill himself, seeing it as the only option without shame, but his suicide attempt fails. Ironically, the resulting publicity leads to the downfall of the corrupt temple master, who has similarly swindled other immigrants, and the story ends with Ganchin gaining a new chance at a prosperous life and perhaps even love.

Much of the success of this collection can be attributed to Jin's ability to group together works that are deceptively similar in setting and situation while actually depicting a broad range of experience. His earlier story collections are similarly focused: *Ocean of Words: Army Stories* (1996) deals with members of the Chinese army serving near their country's northern border during the tumultuous 1960's; *Under the Red Flag* (1997) focuses on the Cultural Revolution; and *The Bridegroom* (2000) depicts the experiences of residents living in China's fictional Muji City after the revolution. By moving the focal point of *A Good Fall* to the United States, Jin has produced an impressive body of short fiction that provides insight into the complex path that his own life has taken, along with the lives of so many other Chinese, Chinese Americans, and immigrants of other nationalities.

Amy Sisson

Review Sources

Booklist 106, no. 6 (November 15, 2009): 20.
Kirkus Reviews 77, no. 19 (October 1, 2009): 1038.
Library Journal 134, no. 17 (October 15, 2009): 72.
Publishers Weekly 256, no. 38 (September 21, 2009): 35-36.
New York 42, no. 41 (December 7, 2009): 76-77.
The Wall Street Journal, November 27, 2009, p. W7.

HIDING MAN
A Biography of Donald Barthelme

Author: Tracy Daugherty (1955-)
Publisher: St. Martin's Press (New York). 581 pp. $35.00
Type of work: Literary biography
Time: 1931-2007
Locale: Houston, Texas; New York

A first-time biographer writes the first biography of one of America's most innovative writers—who was also the biographer's college writing teacher

Over a five-week period in early 2009, three biographies of important postwar American fiction writers appeared: Tracy Daugherty's *Hiding Man: A Biography of Donald Barthelme* (February 3), Brad Gooch's *Flannery: A Life of Flannery O'Connor* (February 25), and Blake Bailey's *Cheever: A Life* (February 10). All three are substantial and address real needs. Gooch seeks to rescue Flannery O'Connor from the myths that have come to surround her; more ambitious, Daugherty and Bailey want to rescue their subjects from neglect.

Daugherty is certainly passionate about Donald Barthelme, his former teacher at the University of Houston, but passion can be a liability, because it can turn biography into something closer to hagiography. Ever the dutiful acolyte, Daugherty frames *Hiding Man* with two writing assignments, the first from when Daugherty was Barthelme's student: "The assignment was simple: Find a copy of John Ashbery's *Three Poems*, read it, buy a bottle of wine, go home, don't sleep, and produce, by dawn, twelve pages of Ashbery imitation." The other assignment is from the last time the two met: "'Write a story about genius,' he told me. A teacher's last assignment to a student." That, it seems, is what Daugherty thinks he has done in *Hiding Man*, although the result seems a good deal closer to the way Barthelme described Daugherty's Ashbery imitation: an important first draft, one that a good editor should have helped Daugherty whip into shape. Its considerable limitations notwithstanding, *Hiding Man* is valuable for the details it provides and the questions it raises, albeit implicitly, about an author who, as Nathaniel Hawthorne said about himself, kept his "inmost me" behind a veil.

Born in Philadelphia in 1931, Donald Barthelme, Jr., was raised in Houston, where his family lived in a house designed by Donald Barthelme, Sr., a well-known architect who took modernism seriously in terms of both its formal concerns and its social relevance. The elder Barthelme was clearly as dominant a presence in the home as he was in his profession. Life with father could be intense—"a verbal bully" is the way one son described him—but it was also intellectually stimulating. All five of his children became successful—three became writers; one, an advertising executive; and one, Pennzoil's first female vice-president—but at least three of them had drinking or gambling problems.

Tracy Daugherty is the author of four novels, Desire Provoked *(1986),* What Falls Away *(1996),* The Boy Orator *(1999), and* Axeman's Jazz *(2003), as well as three collections of short fiction and a memoir. He teaches creative writing at Oregon State University.*

Hiding Man does not have much to say about Barthelme's siblings, and the contentious relationship between the two Donalds tends to be asserted rather than demonstrated. Barthelme had to endure nothing as extreme as what John Cheever's three children endured: their father's alcoholism, infidelities, and disparaging comments. Barthelme, Sr., seems to have been only as patriarchal as many fathers of his time and station, with the sense of oedipal conflict perhaps heightened by the Freudianism then in vogue and the son's later reading of Sigmund Freud's works. It is true, however, that Barthelme entered into a number of unsuccessful relationships with father-figures and with women (four wives and numerous lovers, including his literary agent Lynn Nesbit; his neighbor, the writer Grace Paley; and perhaps the wife of Max Frisch, an older writer he admired).

Barthelme attended Catholic schools and the University of Houston, where his father was a professor of architecture; he served in the Korean War then returned to the university. Although he did not complete a degree, he found in philosophy professor Maurice Natanson "a sympathetic soul and an engaging mentor" whose "enthusiasms were [Søren] Kierkegaard, [Jean-Paul] Sartre, [Edmund] Husserl, and phenomenology in modern literature." Barthelme wrote for the school newspaper, the *Cougar*, and then for the *Houston Post*; he married Marilyn Marrs in 1952, edited *Forum* magazine, and served as Director of Houston's Museum of Contemporary Arts. Daugherty places less emphasis than seems appropriate on some aspects of Barthelme's experience, such as the writer's military service in Korea. At the same time, he attributes more significance than the evidence seems to justify to other experiences, such as Barthelme's Catholic education.

In 1962, Barthelme moved to New York to become managing editor of Harold Rosenberg and Thomas Hess's new magazine, *Location*. The periodical's aim, according to its prospectus, was to

> overcome the intellectual isolation of the arts in America, the growing parochialism and professionalist inbreeding that goes hand in hand with their separation from one another and from thought in general—and to further their inter-communication.

Location was well suited to Barthelme's varied interests, as was New York City, where he indulged his passions for contemporary art, jazz, and ideas. When he moved there, however, his second wife, Helen Moore, stayed behind in Houston to work on the advertising agency she had recently started. Moore did not like New York, nor did she like the new circle of friends her husband acquired there. Their marriage lasted only a little longer than did *Location*, which made it through just two issues.

By the mid-1960's, Barthelme's personal life had already begun to resemble the kind of fiction for which he became famous: collages made up of fragments and fragile relationships. Barthelme's most enduring relationships would be with *The New Yorker* magazine and with New York, especially his West Village neighborhood and apartment, and with his fourth wife, Marion Knox, whom he married in 1978. Based on the evidence Daugherty provides, one wonders whether, had *Location* not folded or Barthelme been given greater freedom at *Forum*, he might have become one of the most influential editors of his time, given that he was as concerned with design as he was with ideas.

Daugherty does a good job of marshaling the basic facts of Barthelme's life, and he portrays well the influence on the writer of Natanson and of European writers and thinkers. *Hiding Man* suffers, however, from a surfeit of (mainly) good intentions. Daugherty seeks to expose the hidden Barthelme (no mean task, given Barthelme's reluctance to discuss his personal life, even in interviews), to rescue Barthelme from neglect, and to write about Barthelme as a genius. In addition, Daugherty quotes Lois Zamora to explain that he wishes to perform a "critical repositioning" of Barthelme that would reveal "the relationship of his fiction 'to political writing'" and would help readers "'identify and appreciate ambiguities in his work that have been barely noticed or discussed by critics.'"

> Finally, it comes down to this: I still want to know Don better so as to know better the world *he* knew. Though some of the details have changed over time, the world he knew is, of course, our world. He still has lessons to teach us.

Not surprising, the multiplicity of Daugherty's purposes results in a biography that neither quite coheres nor addresses satisfactorily any one of these points.

Moreover, some of the points Daugherty attempts to make seem anachronistic when considered in the light of contemporary critical conventions. For example, "genius" is a term that is difficult to employ seriously at all, much less prove. Barthelme in particular seems ill served by such a term of traditional aesthetics, given that he was a maker of "anxious objects," Harold Rosenberg's term for the kind of work that calls into question the distinction between art and junk. Barthelme was one of the most idiosyncratic writers of his age—no small accomplishment in an age of idiosyncratic writers such as John Barth, Jorge Luis Borges, Robert Coover, Guy Davenport, Stanley Elkin, John Gardner, Raymond Federman, Ron Sukenick, and Kurt Vonnegut. He was just as surely the most imitated writer of his time—an honor that would pass to Raymond Carver in the early 1980's. He did not "change the shape of the American short story," however. Had he done so, he would not be suffering the neglect that has befallen him, along with nearly all the American postmodernists and metafictionists of his time.

Barthelme and his verbal boxes, those anxious objects that delighted many and dismayed others, may simply have given way to the relentless and not entirely baleful pursuit of the new from which Barthelme and his then-young academic critics benefited. A new generation of writers and critics followed to benefit from from the same pursuit. Daugherty, however, has a different reading of Barthelme's neglect: He asserts that Barthelme has been unjustly neglected as a result of the critical, commercial, and aesthetic turn toward dull representational fiction. In addition, he says, "I believe he designed his stories—and his teaching—to fall into disarray, only to bloom again unexpectedly."

Hiding Man comprises fifty-seven chapters, a prologue, and an epilogue in 496 pages: an average of eight pages per chapter. Many of the chapters are broken up into clusters of very short paragraphs, in imitation of the distinctive style of Barthelme's fiction. The page design also suggests some of Barthelme's publications: It employs a slightly smaller than usual font, and the text on the first page of each chapter is indented while block quotations on those pages are widened. Chapter titles are set off in sans serif typeface, and chapter numbers are placed at the bottom of the page, with only the number's top half visible and the rest "hiding," in reference to the title and trope of the book.

Indeed, *Hiding Man* proves an apt title because Barthelme remains obscure and enigmatic throughout the biography. Daugherty reveals that Barthelme was extremely resistant to proposed changes in the placement of commas in "The Indian Uprising," fighting the editorial staff of *The New Yorker* to preserve his punctuation. By contrast, the author seems to have been considerably less devoted to his wives, friends, students, and lovers. His second marriage ended because his wife did not like New York City. His third marriage—to Birgit Egelund-Peterson—ended because Barthelme could not cope with his wife's Huntington's disease and placed too much responsibility for her care on their seven-year-old daughter. Deeper issues of Barthelme's psychology—such as why he seemed more committed to commas than to people—remain unexplored.

Daugherty says that Barthelme "was always two people: the 'hiding man,' withdrawing from the world to work in the 'smithy of his soul' and the citizen working to better the world for others." It is unclear, however, what acts of good citizenship Daugherty has in mind. Similarly, Daugherty says that Barthelme "always yearned for transcendence," but exactly what this transcendence means Daugherty never makes clear. *Hiding Man* leaves this and other insights vague, and it leaves too many questions either unanswered or unasked, such as the reasons behind Barthelme's ironic detachment or behind the shift in his fiction, which became less comic and detached and more wistful and personal in works such as *Paradise* (1986).

Hiding Man relies too much on potted histories and too little on probing and analysis. Daugherty's criticism of individual stories usually involves identifying sources and allusions, including to Barthelme's personal life, rather than interpreting the stories themselves in the light of that personal life. Daugherty mentions, briefly but evocatively, that Barthelme's apartment was just above Faith and Kirkpatrick Sale's apartment, where Thomas Pynchon, wrote *Gravity's Rainbow* (1973). He fails, though, to explore the importance of the fact that Pynchon was part of Barthelme's world, spending more time on such other denizens of that world as *Monty Python's Flying Circus* and Angela Carter's *Nights at the Circus* (1984). However, *Hiding Man* makes abundantly clear what Donald Barthelme's next biographer will need to address, and for that the literary world is very much in Daugherty's debt.

Robert Morace

Review Sources

Booklist 105, no. 13 (March 1, 2009): 14.
Kirkus Reviews 76, no. 22 (November 15, 2008): 1185.
Library Journal 133, no. 20 (December 1, 2008): 129.
The New York Review of Books 56, no. 5 (March 26, 2009): 25-26.
The New York Times Book Review March 19, 2009, p. 1.
The New Yorker 85, no. 2 (February 23, 2009): 68-76.
Publishers Weekly 255, no. 47 (November 24, 2008): 44-45.
The Wall Street Journal, February 21, 2009, p. W8.
World Literature Today 83, no. 4 (July/August, 2009): 76-77.

THE HINDUS
An Alternative History

Author: Wendy Doniger (1940-)
Publisher: Penguin (New York). 800 pp. $35.00
Type of work: Religion, history

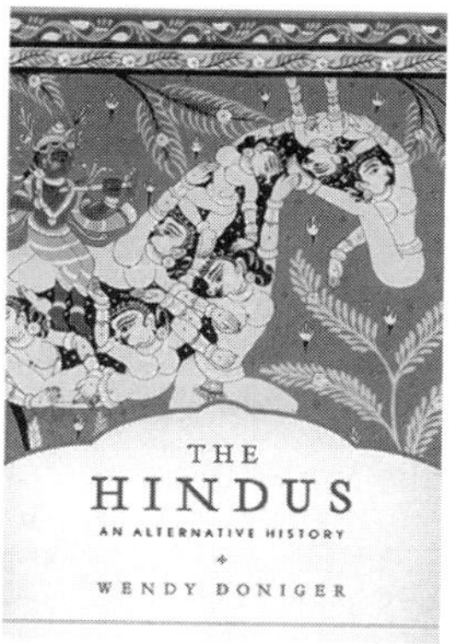

An interpretive history of Hindu beliefs and practices from the prehistory of the Indian subcontinent through recent years

Wendy Doniger titles her ambitious expedition through millennia of Hindu history *The Hindus*, not *Hinduism.* Doniger approaches the central religious traditions of India as diverse in nature and as changing over the centuries, rather than as a unified, clearly defined set of doctrines and rituals. She is particularly interested in what she sees as the underemphasized and undervalued parts of Hindu life, such as the lower castes, women, and animals. In the later parts of the book, she attempts an examination of historical relations between Hindus and Muslims that sets aside the slogans of modern political tensions.

Doniger's style throughout the book is ironic and irreverent, with frequent references to modern high and low culture. *The Hindus* may offend some Hindus (and Muslims) and will probably provoke disagreements on a number of points by professional scholars. It is also a fascinating and provocative reinterpretation of Hindu history for those who know something about the subject and an enjoyable introduction to the topic for those who do not.

Doniger is clear about the interpretive nature of her work. She does not pretend to convey a set of facts. Rather, from the beginning of her text, she explains that she is offering a narrative that shapes the facts in an attempt to understand them. Moreover, the facts at her disposal do not encompass the whole of Hindu history. She opens the first chapter with a Sufi anecdote about a Sufi who is looking for a lost key outside his house. When asked where he dropped it, he says it happened inside the house. He is looking outside, the punchline follows, because the light is better there. Doniger explains that she will often look for her historical evidence in the light—that is, in what information has been preserved through the centuries. However, the body of available information is not necessarily where the key to the past actually lies.

India and the Hindu religion are so intricately intertwined that a history of one is necessarily a history of the other. Doniger begins looking at India by recounting its geological formation and the myths of its geological formation. Her account of civilizations in the Indus Valley goes all the way back to the Stone Age cultures of 50,000 B.C.E. and to the cave paintings of 30,000 B.C.E. The first urban societies began to appear about 2500 B.C.E., in the form of the Indus Valley Civilization, which was apparently in contact both with the ancient Near East and with Egypt. It is difficult to

Wendy Doniger (formerly Wendy Doniger O'Flaherty) is the Mircea Eliade Distinguished Service Professor of the History of Religions at the University of Chicago. She is author of fifteen previous books and has edited collections of scholarly articles and translated many texts of Indian literature.

connect this early urban civilization with the Hindu society of later centuries, and Doniger may be too speculative in attempting to make links. Still, she points out that one can find some striking resemblances between the Indus Valley Civilization and those societies identified as Hindu. Some of the common artistic images, such as the motif of the fig leaf or the bull, appear quite similar in the two historical periods.

These earliest Indians may or may not have provided a foundation for the people of the Vedas, the first holy books of what came to be called Hinduism. The oldest of these books, the *Rig Veda* was composed by nomads in the Punjab region by 1500 B.C.E., and three additional Vedas were produced in the following centuries. Centered on ritual and especially on sacrifice, the Vedic religion did not yet include a belief in reincarnation when the *Rig Veda* was composed. The caste system had also not yet set in, although its origins may lie in the relations between invaders and non-Vedic people, including the pre-Vedic inhabitants of the region.

In dealing with the gradual emergence of caste, Doniger distinguishes throughout the book between the four main social divisions (*varna*, in Sanskrit) that are familiar to most people with a passing knowledge of India and the complicated array of inherited occupational categories referred to as *jati*. She reserves the term "caste" for the latter and refers to the former as "classes." The terms are potentially confusing, given the modern sociological concept of class as social distinction based on mobility, but she does make clear how she is using these words.

In contrast to the heavily textual official Hinduism of later times, the Vedas were at first carried in memory. The nomads who memorized these long testaments were horse riders, and the image of horses occurs repeatedly in Doniger's narrative. The themes of intoxication and addiction, in Doniger's telling, were among the earliest concerns of the Vedas, and these themes appear in different forms throughout later Hinduism. The most important gods of the later Hindus, Vishnu and Shiva, make only the barest of appearances in the Vedas, and Shiva only as his precursor Rudra. By contrast, Agni, Soma, Indra, and Varuna, the chief Vedic gods, almost disappear later.

The concern with sacrifice continues through the Brahmanas, but this concern later turns inward, becoming self-sacrifice with the dedication to renunciation found in the Upanishads. The time of the Upanishads (placed by Doniger at 600 to 200 B.C.E.) is also the period when the Hindu religions begin to influence and be influenced by the Jain and Buddhist faiths. The role of Buddhism, in particular, takes on a particular significance after Ashoka, the ruler of the most important principality in India, takes up Buddhism. Over the course of the centuries, Doniger describes the attitude of Hindus toward Buddhism as initial tolerance, growing hostility and persecution, and then tolerance again as Buddhism becomes less of a threat.

The two great Hindu epics, the *Mahabharata* and the *Ramayana*, took shape in various forms from the fourth century B.C.E. to about the third or fourth century C.E. In looking at these great literary works, Doniger is especially concerned with the development of Hindu values. The *Ramayana*, the tale of the capture of Queen Sita by the ogre Ravana and the defeat of Ravana by the divine king Rama and his allies, becomes in her interpretation a representation of attitudes toward outsiders, such as women and the socially disadvantaged, who are regarded as ogres. The *Mahabharata*, a complex tale of dynastic struggle, is presented as series of efforts to grapple with questions of violence, order, and obligation. The characteristic Hindu themes of ahimsa, or nonviolence, and dharma, or cosmic order and personal obligation within an order, are central in Doniger's discussion of the *Mahabharata*.

The years from 100 to 400 C.E. saw the composition of the three primary *shastras*, or texts on behavior. The first, the *Dharma-shastra*, attributed to a mythological figure known as Manu, provided an ethical and legal code. The *Artha-shastra*, attributed to Kautilya, offered a guide to the art of rulership and political control. The *Kamasutra* of Vatsyayana concentrated on the realm of desire and sexuality. Doniger uses these to look at the often conflicting ideas of the Hindus on social categories and gender inequalities. She cautions that these texts can be used to examine norms and ideals but that they cannot be taken to reflect actual behavior.

Introductions to Hinduism often divide its history into three periods: ancient Vedic sacrifice and worldliness, Upanishadic *moksha* (liberation through renunciation), and bhakti (personal devotion to and love of a god or goddess). Doniger does not entirely desert this periodization, but she turns largely to the non-Indo-European speaking kingdoms of South India for the beginnings of bhakti. This period began when the rivalry between Hinduism and the rival Jain and Buddhist religions was intensifying. The cults of Shiva and Vishnu (the Shaivas and Vaishnava bhakti sects) also grew in importance for the Hindus at this time.

During the centuries known in Europe as the Middle Ages, driven mainly by the cults of Vishnu and Shiva, an elaborate mythology took shape in the vast corpus of writings known as the Puranas. The Tantric traditions developed along with and within the Puranas, creating a dark and erotic side to Hindu beliefs and practices. Doniger questions but never really answers whether Tantric Hinduism was a matter of real acts or of imagination and speculation.

The arrival of Islam in the eighth century, followed by the Delhi Sultanate and then by the Mughals, created new challenges for the Hindus, carried by new sets of horse riders. However, Hindu kingdoms continued to exist, and Doniger points out the cultural and even religious exchanges among Muslims and Hindus. Contrary to some contemporary Hindu nationalist claims that the Muslims were oppressive invaders and overlords, Doniger presents Muslims as participants in a pluralistic subcontinent that was often distinguished more by class or caste than by religious differences.

Doniger is critical of the English rulers who colonized India following the Moghul period. At first, the English were not much different from previous lords and robbers in India's pluralistic mix, since the representatives of the East India Company appreciated local culture and even intermarried with the natives, even while growing rich at India's expense. However, after 1813, the arrival of missionaries pushed English-Indian relations in a new direction, with Hindu religions seen by the British as expressions of vicious paganism. Following the the Indian Rebellion of 1857-1858, the third wave of the British Raj began, and the British viceroy officially replaced both Mughal rule and the East India Company. In this last period, the social distance between the European rulers and the Indian ruled became a wide gulf, and the study of India became even more a strategy for control.

Doniger is much influenced by scholar Edward Said's argument that orientalism was an instrument of Western colonial power. Accordingly, she sees Hinduism as increasingly misunderstood and misrepresented by Western, especially English scholars. She argues, though, that from the beginning of the British period Westerners tended to reinterpret Hinduism in terms of their own religious beliefs. Thus, texts such as the Bhagavad Gita (a section of the *Mahabharata*) took on a greater importance than they had enjoyed before because Bible-based English Protestants saw these texts as analogous to their own religious scriptures. In turn, Anglophile Indians began to refashion their views of their own religious traditions as they saw them reflected in a European mirror.

The problem of suttee, or the burning of widows, led the British to initiate efforts at reform that eventually became efforts at self-reform on the part of Indians working toward independence. By the twentieth century, Hinduism spread beyond the shores of the Indian subcontinent and became a world religion, especially in America, where new visions of Hinduism (often based on illusions) spread. Doniger ends her account back in India, where the use and misuse of the past have become part of Indian society and politics.

The author has placed helpful chronologies of events at the beginning of each chapter. These provide an outline of Indian and Hindu history that makes her discussions of the topic easier to follow. She has also provided a glossary of terms in Indian languages and names of key figures at the end of the book. In a book that contains so many concepts and personages, this ready reference is extremely useful in enabling readers to clarify concepts and identify historical or mythological personages. Maps of India at different historical periods, in the first few pages, give geographical meaning to the many place-names.

The Hindus is a decidedly personal and often opinionated version of the history of one of the world's great religions. The author never attempts to disguise her opinions as objective fact, though, and the book is deeply learned, as well as impressive in its scope. While many of her judgments will provoke disagreement, Doniger has produced a book that valuably contemplates a vast subject with wit and clarity.

Carl L. Bankston III

Review Sources

The Atlantic Monthly 304, no. 1 (July/August, 2009): 134-135.
Booklist 105, no. 13 (March 1, 2009): 7.
Library Journal 134, no. 3 (February 15, 2009): 110-111.
The New York Review of Books 56, no. 18 (November 19, 2009): 51-53.
The New York Times Book Review 114, no. (April 26, 2009): 20.
The Times Literary Supplement, July 31, 2009, p. 8
Wall Street Journal, April 2, 2009, p. A17

HOMER & LANGLEY

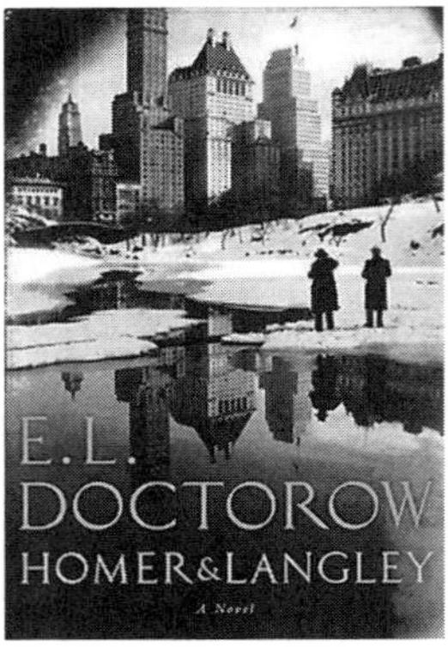

Author: E. L. Doctorow (1931-)
Publisher: Random House (New York). 213 pp. $26.00
Type of work: Novel
Time: 1900-1970's
Locale: Coastal Maine; New York City

A fictional exploration of two of history's most famous recluses, the Collyer brothers of New York City

Principal characters:
HOMER COLLYER, the narrator and a reclusive resident of a Fifth Avenue mansion
LANGLEY COLLYER, his older brother
MRS. ROBILEAUX, their cook
MARY ELIZABETH RIORDAN, Homer's piano student and lifelong love
JACQUELINE ROUX, a French correspondent and friend of Homer
VINCENT, a local organized crime boss

In a city known for its tolerance of eccentric behavior, brothers Homer Lusk Collyer (1881-1947) and Langley Collyer (1885-1947) surely rank among the Manhattan's strangest inhabitants. When the men were found dead in their Fifth Avenue mansion in 1947, authorities had to wade through tons of debris that the brothers had collected, and the structure itself had to be demolished. These brothers represent the antithesis of what most would consider "normal" behavior. Granted, isolation is a singular characteristic of modern existence, especially urban life. However, few would flee human society altogether while simultaneously building a mountain of its detritus. Stranger still, it would seem, is E. L. Doctorow's decision to write a novel about the Collyers, *Homer & Langley*.

Doctorow is in familiar territory when it comes to interweaving the lives of fictional characters with the larger drama of historical events. In *The March* (2005), he explored the deeper meaning of racism in the context of the Civil War through the life of an African American woman. Nor does his use of his native New York as a backdrop represent a departure from past practice. His novel *Ragtime* (1975) won great acclaim for its lively depiction of New York City life in the years just before World War I and achieved even greater renown when it was adapted as a film. Doctorow seems determined to write about the Collyer brothers in order to affirm the old truism that no man is an island—an ironic formulation, considering how often the brothers' island-like isolation is challenged by the island of Manhattan.

While Doctorow's characters remain persistently reclusive, his novel richly resonates with other literary texts. It is true that the real Homer Collyer was blind, but Doctorow plays upon the associations between the fictional life of the actual Homer Collyer and the equally blind poet Homer of ancient Greece, the founder of Western fiction. Like the bard of Greece, Homer Collyer is the sightless spinner of tales who nevertheless "sees" what others do not.

More subtle is the skill with which Doctorow reveals the influence of a more recent writer, the English novelist Joseph Conrad. In Conrad's *The Secret Sharer* (1910), the unnamed narrator begins the story by describing a tropic twilight's progress into night as he stands upon the deck of his ship. The progression into darkness is poetically rendered and almost cinematic in scope. In a similar manner, Doctorow begins his novel by having Homer describe another descent into darkness—not into the transient night of Conrad's captain but rather the permanent void of Homer's blindness.

> The houses over to Central Park West went first, they got darker as if dissolving into the dark sky until I couldn't make them out, and then the trees began to lose their shape, and then finally . . . all I could see were these phantom shapes of the ice skaters floating past me on a field of ice . . .

Eventually, Homer's slide into the world of blackness is complete, and nothing remains of the skaters but the sound of their skates, the "scoot scut" of blades on ice. Doctorow has sometimes been criticized for creating entertaining stories that are somewhat lacking in depth. The same cannot said of *Homer & Langley*. Doctorow's description of Homer's creeping blindness effectively captures his sense of isolation and defines his character in memorable imagery.

The association with Conrad's work is important, for it goes beyond a mere surface resemblance between the opening passages in the two novels. At the core of *The Secret Sharer* is a penetrating psychological exploration of the relationship between the captain narrator and the escaped murderer he assists—a relationship so intense that the narrator risks his vessel in his zeal to aid the man he links with his own identity. The psychological propinquity between Homer and Langley cannot be said to be nearly as close as that of Conrad's characters. The former is the consummate artist of the book. He "creates" the tale, invokes his muse Jacqueline Roux in the crafting of it, and clearly reflects an active imaginative inner life in his use of memory. Langley, however, seems at times to have more in common with the Roman god Vulcan: A kind of mechanical genius gone awry, he eventually brings a Model T Ford into the house in a vain attempt to harness its power. There is, though, a kind of kinship between the two men that transcends their blood ties

E. L. Doctorow's novels include The Book of Daniel *(1971),* Ragtime *(1975),* Billy Bathgate *(1989),* The Waterworks *(2000),* City of God *(2003), and* The March *(2005). He has won three National Book Critics Circle Awards, the National Book Award, and two PEN/Faulkner Awards.*

and harkens back to Conrad's tale. Neither of the brothers is capable of leaving their family home, and they are thus bound to each other. Like his literary ancestor, Doctorow takes the raw material of a real incident and spins it into narrative fiction.

While the actual Homer was the older of the two brothers, Doctorow's story reverses this order. Moreover, while the real Collyer brothers died in 1947, Doctorow cannot resist the temptation to take them into succeeding decades. Fundamental to any understanding of the story is the question of why Doctorow would choose to write a novel about this particular pair. An enduring work of fiction must not only entertain but also resonate on a deeper level and capture some aspect of the human condition. The real Collyer brothers lived an utterly isolated existence. Doctorow's Collyer brothers begin life with all the trappings of an upper-middle-class existence.

In Doctorow's narrative, the young Collyer boys enjoy summers at camp on the Maine coast while their mother and physician father embark upon European cruises. Curiously, even in these halcyon days, Homer reveals a kind of dissociation from others when he casually states that he cannot remember anything their parents ever said. Even the memory of their deaths from influenza during the great pandemic of 1918 evokes not sorrow but rather a sense of isolation. He describes their demise as "the final abandonment, a trip from which they were not to return."

Crucial to the novel's theme of isolation is Langley's World War I service in the Army, an experience that damages his psyche as much as the mustard gas ravages his body. Indeed, he does not even wait to be mustered out of the service: He simply abandons it. In this manner, Doctorow subtly shifts his narrative from a tale about eccentric recluses to a meditation on the meaning of American society in the twentieth century. Appropriately, the brothers' massive collection of objects begins with Langley's rifle.

While the bulk of the story concerns the brothers' seclusion, much of the conflict in the novel stems not so much from their desire for isolation as from the fact that they are consistently out of step with society. When the Great Depression devours the national economy in the 1930's, Langley concludes that it would be good business to hold tea dances in their mansion for a small fee. The dances prove to be a success, but the gatherings incur the displeasure of the brothers' staid Fifth Avenue neighbors. One could argue that, given the small amount of money generated by the dances, Langley's scheme was all to the public good in providing a necessary service in a time of great deprivation. He also refuses to honor a policeman's subsequent demand for a bribe, emphasizing Langley's integrity over the hypocritical society he rejects.

When the inevitable police raid on their home eventually occurs, Langley's ill-conceived attempt to reach out to others is crushed. Doctorow underscores the deeper significance of the clash with the "cold breeze" that coincides with the policeman's visit and the "chill wind" that accompanies the raid. These winds signal that any significant attempt by the brothers to breach their isolation is doomed. The use of wind imagery reinforces this idea, and Doctorow employs it at specific points either to mark an intrusion from the outside world or to highlight a pleasurable experience. Moreover, Homer's resort to this device is singularly appropriate in his role as the story's narrator. As a housebound blind man, he would be expected to be highly sensitive to both sound and atmospheric changes. It is also fitting that, as a declared writer who relies upon his muse, he employs a symbol that can express inspiration. The cold breeze precedes the police raid and blows again when Federal Bureau of Investigation agents arrest the Collyers' Japanese American housekeepers. "A soft breeze redolent of a countryside," meanwhile, accompanies the brothers' predawn search for water in the city streets.

One of the most memorable aspects of the real Collyer brothers' story was the fact that they had collected tons of newspapers over several decades, seemingly without any purpose. In the novel, Homer cleverly ascribes Langley's acquisitiveness to his great project: to create a kind of perfect newspaper edition and thereby render all newspapers obsolete. Langley's goal of having readers "fixed in amber" reflects a warped sensibility that has turned in upon itself. This is an interesting choice on Doctorow's part, one that has important implications for Langley's character and for the larger theme of the novel. In terms of the story's structure, Langley's project provides a convincing motive for his fundamentally aberrant behavior. Doctorow thus portrays Langley's actions as misguided but in the service of a noble goal that is based on a real insight: Events may change from day to day, but actions as a reflection of the human condition do not. This is one of the reasons why allowing the Collyers to live into the 1970's succeeds so well: It allows them to experience the appalling repetitiveness of America's numerous wars.

It is for this reason that one of the most amusing moments of the book is so effective: The Collyer brothers encounter a group of hippies in the 1960's. By this time, Manhattan's oddest siblings have proven themselves to be outcasts with their uncut hair, ragged Army fatigues, and unconventional lifestyle. In a fictional tour de force that was never possible for the real Collyers, Doctorow's account allows Homer and Langley to find ready acceptance by the counterculture hippy lifestyle. The young people embrace Langley's debris field as readily as they spurn the culture that created it. Even Homer finds a renewed sense of purpose in the climactic scene, when his blindness allows him to lead everyone to safety during a blackout. By turns funny and touching, *Homer & Langley* is a clever commentary on a pair of outcasts and the society they eschew.

Cliff Prewencki

Review Sources

Booklist 105, no. 21 (July 1, 2009): 8.
Kirkus Reviews 77, no. 15 (August 1, 2009): 25.
Library Journal 134, no. 13 (August 1 2009): 67.
The Nation 289, no. 11 (October 12, 2009): 31
New Criterion 28, no. 3 (November, 2009): 27-32.
The New York Review of Books 56, no. 20 (December 17, 2009): 34-36.
The New York Times, September 1, 2009, p. 1.
The New York Times Book Review, September 13, 2009, p. 7.
The New Yorker 85, no. 27 (September 7, 2009): 80-81.
Publishers Weekly 256, no. 27 (July 6, 2009): 31.
The Wall Street Journal, August 21, 2009, p. W7.
Weekly Standard 15, no. 8 (November 9, 2009): 32-33.

HORSE SOLDIERS
The Extraordinary Story of a Band of U.S. Soldiers Who Rode to Victory in Afghanistan

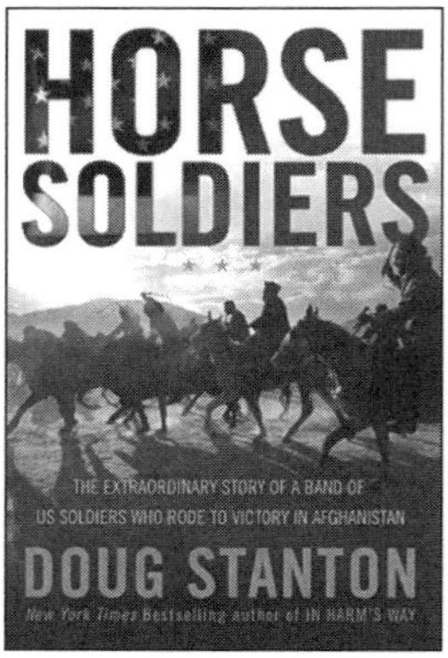

Author: Doug Stanton (1962-)
Publisher: Scribner (New York). 393 pp. $28.00
Type of work: Current affairs
Time: September-November, 2001
Locale: Northern Afghanistan; United States

A detailed account of the first group of U.S. forces deployed to Afghanistan to fight the Taliban and al-Qaeda after the attacks of September 11, 2001

Principal personages:

General Abdul Rashid Dostum, an Afghan warlord and leader in the Northern Alliance
General Atta Mohammed Noor, another Afghan warlord and leader in the Northern Alliance
Mike Spann, a CIA paramilitary officer sent to assist the Northern Alliance
Dave Olsen, another CIA paramilitary officer working with Spann
Major General Geoffrey Lambert, commander of U.S. Army Special Forces
Lieutenant Colonel Max Bowers, commander of the Third Battalion, Fifth Special Forces Group, stationed in Afghanistan
Captain Mitch Nelson, Third Battalion, Special Forces team leader in Afghanistan, riding with General Dostum
Chief Warrant Officer Cal Spencer,
Sergeant First Class Ben Milo,
Sergeant First Class Sam Diller, and
Master Sergeant Pat Essex, members of Nelson's team
Major Mark Mitchell, ground commander of Third Battalion, Fifth Special Forces Group's Forward Operating Base
Captain Dean Nosorog, Third Battalion team leader, riding with General Atta
John Walker Lindh, an American who joined the Taliban in Afghanistan

In *Horse Soldiers*, Doug Stanton begins in medias res his account of the American forces who were the first to enter Afghanistan after the terrorist attacks of September 11, 2001, to assist the Northern Alliance in fighting the Taliban and al-Qaeda. After many weeks of grueling work, by the last week of November, 2001, they have managed to capture a Taliban stronghold and are astonished to find six hundred Taliban prisoners (among them John Walker Lindh) about the enter the fort, where a huge amount of Taliban weaponry remains stored. Two Central Intelligence Agency (CIA) officers, Mike Spann and Dave Olsen, decided to interrogate some of the prisoners, but they are suddenly attacked, Spann is shot, and the Taliban prisoners begin to riot.

Doug Stanton is the author of In Harm's Way: The Sinking of the USS Indianapolis and the Extraordinary Story of Its Survivors *(2001). He is a contributor to many journals and has an M.F.A. from the University of Iowa Writers' Workshop.*

Stanton shifts his narrative to a few months earlier, immediately after al-Qaeda's attack on the World Trade Center. The effect of this attack on Cal Spencer and other Special Forces soldiers is sudden and swift: On a training mission with some men along the Cumberland River in Tennessee when he hears the news, Spencer speeds back to his base at Fort Campbell, Kentucky. Dean Nosorog, married only four days earlier, aborts his honeymoon in Tahiti, knowing he will also be needed at Fort Campbell. Mark Mitchell, then the operations officer for the Third Battalion, Fifth Special Forces Group, can scarcely believe what is happening, but it is his responsibility to have the men ready for deployment anywhere in the world. Greg Gibson, a helicopter pilot, tells his crew to get ready to break down their Black Hawks and Chinooks for travel.

U.S. Air Force planes have already begun bombing suspected Taliban sites, though very ineffectively, when the first contingent of Special Forces soldiers arrives to set up camp in Uzbekistan, adjacent to Afghanistan. The various warlords opposed to the Taliban, including generals Dostum, Atta, and Mohaqeq, are glad the Americans are coming, as they have been fighting for many years and by now are running low on food, clothing, and arms. The Americans' base at Karshi-Khanabad (K2) in Uzbekistan is where the small number of expert troops arrive to aid Dostum and Atta, particularly in spotting targets accurately for bombing raids. From K2, planes also drop supplies for both the Americans and the Northern Alliance armies.

The trip by helicopter from K2 to General Dostum's location is anything but easy. Sandstorms and other inclement weather conditions make flights extremely hazardous, to say nothing of the dangerous mountainous terrain, which forces the helicopters to fly much higher than usual. At one point, lacking oxygen, most of the soldiers black out during the trip. Despite every difficulty, Captain Mitch Nelson and his team manage to arrive in mid-October at an Afghani village called Cobaki to begin their work assisting Dostum and his allies.

Nelson and his men learn that they will have to travel to the front lines on horseback. The difficult terrain and the absence of motor vehicles make this necessary. Although Nelson is an experienced horseman, most of his men are not; in fact, few have ever even been on a horse. The horses are short, shaggy, and rugged, built for mountain walking. Their saddles, made of three boards hinged together and covered by goatskin, are too small for an average American male, and the stirrups, hammered iron rings hanging down from the saddles on small pieces of leather, are so short that the Americans, when mounted, find their knees reach almost to their chins. Nevertheless, these horses are their means of transportation for most of the next two months, severe saddle sores notwithstanding.

The ultimate objective for the combined Afghan and American forces is the northern town of Mazari-Sharif and the fortress of Qala-i-Janghi, held by the Taliban army. If the Northern Alliance can capture these targets, it will be able to bring under its control all of northern Afghanistan and then proceed to capture the country's capital, Kabul, farther south. A great deal of fighting and bombing, however, are necessary before this objective can be attained.

Nelson and five of his men set off behind General Dostum and his forces, leaving Cal Spencer, Pat Essex, Charles Jones, Scott Black, Ben Milo, and Fred Falls behind to coordinate logistics and await an air drop of medical supplies and blankets for Dostum's men. The immediate objective for Dostum and Nelson is the town of Dehi. En route, they pass settlements that have been decimated by the Taliban. At Dehi, Dostum's men load supplies onto their horses and pack mules and move on toward Chapchal, crossing the cold Darya Suf River. Sam Diller can already feel blood running down his legs from his saddle sores as the contingent begins climbing a six-thousand-foot mountain.

Catching up with Dostum, Nelson and his men are welcomed to the general's mountain headquarters, which consists of three caves whose walls are covered with horse dung and feel like fur. That night, Dostum asks Nelson to bomb a Taliban encampment some miles away. Although Nelson believes it is too distant for an accurate sighting, he agrees to order the bombs if Dostum can prove the Taliban are really there. To his amazement, Dostum picks up a walkie-talkie and talks with the enemy, thus reassuring Nelson. When the first bombing attack from an American B-52 is far off target, Nelson argues that he has to get closer to the encampment so he can convey accurate coordinates to the bomber. Although he is averse to putting Nelson or his men in dangerous proximity to the enemy, Dostum reluctantly agrees, and the bombing then begins to wipe out the Taliban position.

Meanwhile, Dostum positions his men on horseback to charge the Taliban trenches and bunkers. Stanton, who writes as if he were there himself, gives a vivid description of the battle, in which the horsemen ride through blazing gunfire to reach the Taliban soldiers and overcome them. Nelson now realizes that, if the Americans can coordinate air support with Dostum's fierce horsemen, they can win. He also knows that he must split the team up again and send Sam Diller north to call in bombs to destroy the Taliban's tanks and other mechanized forces before those forces can reinforce the ground soldiers.

Sam Diller's odyssey is one of the highlights of Stanton's book. With only two other Americans, thirty Alliance soldiers, and a meager supply of equipment and food, he does what is expected and significantly helps Nelson and others subdue the enemy. The key to his efforts, Stanton says, is stealth and speed. Moving deep into Taliban territory, the group situates itself high above the Taliban's flank and calls in air strikes. Not until they rendezvous weeks later at Mazar do Nelson and Diller, nearly dead from hunger and fatigue, see each other again.

On October 25, the day after the first battle, Dostum and Nelson start riding from Cobaki to the battlefield across the Darya Suf River. Dostum has lined up several hundred horsemen and foot soldiers to face the Taliban, who have tanks and heavy weapons to oppose them. Nelson knows he must destroy these mechanized forces with air strikes, He does so as the battle moves ahead, and once again the combined forces are successful. This time, their success requires the heroics of General Dostum, who charges ahead of his men when they are momentarily stymied to engage the remnants of the Taliban fighters.

Back at K2, Dean Nosorog (referred to throughout simply as "Dean" by Stanton) is becoming increasingly impatient to get into the fray. He finally does, landing by helicopter with his team near Ak Kupruk to assist General Atta in retaking the village and attacking Shulgareh along with Dostum's forces and Nelson's team. Once Shulgareh falls, Dostum maintains, Mazar will fall and so will Afghanistan's six northern provinces. On the helicopter with Dean are Lieutenant Colonel Bowers and Major Mark Mitchell and his team, who are ferried to Dostum's base camp. Bowers becomes Dostum's liaison, taking over from Nelson and bringing with him needed supplies and an additional willingness to fight, much to Dostum's gratification.

The battles continue moving northward toward Mazar. Although Dostum and Atta are perennial rivals for power, the two warlords coordinate their forces effectively, encouraged and supported by the Americans. At one point, on November 5, Milo, Essex, and an Air Force soldier named Winehouse are almost overrun by the Taliban, but they survive. After Shulgareh falls, the next objective is the Tanghi Gap, the gateway to Mazar-i-Sharif, which also falls. By November 10, Dostum's forces, along with the Special Forces teams, enter Mazar and prepare to lay siege to the Taliban fortress of Qala-i-Janghi.

During all this time, the soldiers keep their communications with family and others to a minimum. Rare phone calls to wives simply reassure them that their husbands are safe, but that is all the men can say. For security reasons, the press also is kept in the dark. Special Forces like to keep their reputation as "the quiet professionals" intact, though perforce their stories eventually come out. Stanton vividly details the hardships the men endured; although his book includes a few photographs of the soldiers and the Afghan terrain, the illustrations are almost superfluous.

The fight to take the fortress of Qala-i-Janghi is the most furious battle Stanton describes. It brings his book full circle to the point at which it began. Although Dostum is able to obtain the surrender of six hundred Taliban fighters, Islamic law prevents men from intimately touching one another. Thus, searches are perfunctory, and the prisoners secrete within their robes pistols, grenades, and other weapons. Moreover, they are flimsily bound with cloth turbans. The prisoners are thus able to break free at an opportune moment, and they begin to attack their captors. In the ensuing fight, many Taliban and their Afghan captors are killed or wounded, along with Mike Spann, the first American operative to die in Afghanistan. The riot is finally subdued, and among the Taliban survivors is John Walker Lindh, who is later sent back to the United States to await trial as a traitor.

In an epilogue to his book, Stanton says:

> By entering Afghanistan with a small force, and by aligning themselves with groups that once had been battling each other and pointing them in one direction at the Taliban, U.S. forces found robust support among Afghans. They proved the usefulness of understanding and heeding the "wants and needs" of an enemy, and the local population that may support it. Awareness is the soldier's number one tool in his kit, beside his M-4 rifle. To win wars against enemies like the Taliban, which are often stateless in their affiliation, you adapt.

Commenting on the success of this mission, Major General Geoffrey Lambert says it was "about as perfect an execution of guerilla force as could be studied," but he adds: "It may never be repeated." Stanton responds: "His words would prove prescient," as the errors made in Iraq soon afterward would show. Stanton cites, for example, the mistaken decision by Ambassador Paul Bremer to "fire" the Iraqi national army and disband it, thus sending 500,000 young Iraqis home with their weapons and a fierce determination to exact revenge. Instead of assimilating and working with the former enemy army, the U.S. occupation drove it underground, "where it mutated into a potent insurgency."

Stanton's book is extremely well documented with a lengthy bibliography that includes government documents, electronic media, newspaper accounts, a hundred interviews, and many other references.

Jay L. Halio

Review Sources

Air Force Times 69, no. 49 (June 22, 2009): special section, p. 12.
Kirkus Reviews 77, no. 5 (March 1, 2009): 88.
Library Journal 134 (June 15, 2009): 84.
Navy Times 58, no. 39 (June 22, 2009): special section, p. 12.
The New York Times Book Review, May 24, 2009, p. 18.
Publishers Weekly 256, no. 21 (May 25, 2009): 54.

HOUSE OF CARDS
A Tale of Hubris and Wretched Excess on Wall Street

Author: William D. Cohan (1960-)
Publisher: Doubleday (New York). 468 pp. $27.95
Type of work: Current affairs, economics
Time: 2008
Locale: New York City

A narrative of the March, 2008, collapse of Bear Stearns, the fifth largest investment bank in the United States and the first victim of the subprime mortgage debacle that would grow into a global financial disaster

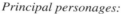

Principal personages:
JAMES A. CAYNE (1934-), chairman of the board of Bear Stearns & Co.
ALAN SCHWARTZ (1950-), president and chief executive officer of Bear Stearns & Co.
JAMES L. DIMON (1956-), president and chairman of the board of JPMorgan Chase
HENRY M. PAULSON (1946-), U.S. secretary of the Treasury, 2006-2009

On March 5, 2008, an investment analyst in Florida posted an opinion on his Web site that Bear Stearns & Co., the fifth largest investment bank in the United States, was effectively insolvent. On the surface, this seemed strange. In 2007, *Fortune* magazine praised Bear Stearns as the most admired securities firm in the United States. The company had an $18 billion cash reserve and was about to announce a profit for the previous quarter. Nevertheless, the analyst was right. Ten days later, the eighty-six-year-old firm no longer existed. Fearing that its bankruptcy might threaten the stability of the global financial system, the Federal Reserve and the U.S. Treasury forced the company to sell itself to JPMorgan Chase for a pittance.

The first third of William D. Cohan's *House of Cards: A Tale of Hubris and Wretched Excess on Wall Street* consists of a riveting, day-to-day, blow-by-blow account of those dramatic ten days. The next three hundred pages examine the history of the firm, describing its success and the reasons that it found itself so badly exposed in the early days of the economic downturn of 2008.

The Florida analyst was not the only one to view Bear Stearns with suspicion. Rumors that the firm faced a liquidity crisis swept Wall Street. Oblivious to the impending storm, the company's own top management left town. On March 6, president and chief executive officer (CEO) Alan Schwartz went to a media conference in Palm Beach, Florida; chairman of the board James A. Cayne, a championship-level bridge player, was in Detroit taking part in a major tournament.

On Friday, March 7, a European bank informed Bear Stearns that it would no lon-

William D. Cohan worked on Wall Street for seventeen years at Lazard Frères, Merrill Lynch, and JPMorgan Chase. His previous book, The Last Tycoons: The Secret History of Lazard Frères & Co. *(2007) won the Financial Times and Goldman Sachs Business Book of the Year Award.*

ger provide the company with short-term financing. This was a major blow because investment banks depend on short-term loans to finance their operations. Often, these are overnight "repo" (repurchase agreement) loans, in which banks such as Bear Stearns "sell" securities to a lender and promise to buy them back the following day with interest. Normally, these loans can be renewed easily—if the borrower seems certain to repay.

Readers of *House of Cards* need not worry if they do not understand the various financial terms—such as repo, "CDO" (collateralized debt obligation), and credit default swap—with which the book is strewn. On the evidence of this book, neither did financial experts at the biggest investment houses on Wall Street. At Bear Stearns, the operating capital of the firm depended on short-term (mostly one-day) loans. These loans often used subprime mortgage bonds as collateral. No one seemed aware of or concerned about the risk that the firm could become insolvent in just twenty-four hours if its reliability was questioned.

On Monday, March 10, Bear Stearns assured customers that it faced no problems; the firm's statement, however, only served to increase market rumors and anxiety. Hedge funds began withdrawing cash from the bank; lenders demanded more collateral. On Wednesday, CEO Schwartz, interviewed on television from Palm Beach, uttered vague reassurances that convinced no one. The run on the bank continued. At the start of the day on Thursday, March 13, the firm had $18 billion in cash. At the close of trading, this amount had dwindled to $2 or 3 billion, not enough to open the next day. Incredibly, Thursday night was the first time the chairman of the board, busy playing bridge in Detroit, or any other member of board of directors was informed that the firm had a problem.

Fearful that the failure of Bear Stearns would set off a worldwide market panic, the Federal Reserve Bank of New York and JPMorgan Chase advanced sufficient cash for Bear Stearns to open on Friday. News of the rescue brought increased pressure on Bear Stearns. The U.S. Federal Reserve and the U.S. Treasury concluded that Bear Stearns needed to sell itself to another firm. These institutions agreed to guarantee $30 billion of Bear Stearns's assets, but they insisted that the deal had to be completed before Asian markets opened on Monday (7:00 P.M. on Sunday night in New York).

The brokerage firm hired to find a buyer (and paid $20 million for its efforts) could locate only one bank willing to take on the burden—JPMorgan Chase, whose president, James L. Dimon, had long coveted Bear Stearns's bond brokerage business. Dimon was willing to offer $10 per share, but Secretary of the Treasury Henry M. Paulson insisted the price be reduced to $2 so that the government could show it was not rewarding misbehavior. After furious maneuvering by Bear Stearns, the price went back to $10.

In January, 2007, Bear Stearns stock had sold for $172.69 per share. At that price, the nearly six million shares held by board chairman Cayne had been worth about $1 billion. When he sold his stock on the market on March 25, he received $61.34 million. Cayne was hardly penurious, possessing another $600 million in assets, but he was furious, claiming that there must have been a conspiracy to destroy his firm. Others pointed to the company's earlier history and to corporate mismanagement to explain the outcome. Cohan devotes the rest of his book to evaluating these various claims.

The final 300 pages of *House of Cards* are as well written as the previous 150. Cohan very effectively uses material from more than 120 interviews, including interviews of many former Bear Stearns executives who provide colorfully profane remarks about their colleagues and competitors. However, this material is simply not as dramatic as the narrative of the banks' final ten days, and the author's presentation is marred by excessive detail, especially noticeable in the lengthy account of Bear Stearns's hedge funds.

Founded on May Day, 1923, the firm survived the stock market crash of 1929 and the Great Depression through cautious management. During World War II, it became more aggressive and profited from enormous bets that proved highly lucrative for the firm and its customers. Railroad bonds traded as low as five cents on the dollar after the government seized the rail lines as part of the war effort. When the roads returned to private ownership, the bonds went to par and also paid accrued interest skipped during the war, making the firm and all who took its advice wealthy.

Aggressive gambles became the hallmark of Bear Stearns and attracted affluent customers able to assume the risks involved in following the firm's recommendations. The firm acquired the reputation of being unscrupulous, willing to do anything to make money. The motto of its trading room was "Let's make nothing but money"—and it did so for customers and even more for top managers: In 1987, the five highest-paid executives on Wall Street were at Bear Stearns. In 2006, Cayne was the only Wall Street leader included in *Forbes*'s list of billionaires.

Bear Stearns was never squeamish about how it made money. It acted as clearing agent for large hedge funds, such as the gigantic Long Term Capital Management, and for many shady small brokerages. In 1999, it was fined $28.5 million for helping a client brokerage fleece its customers. After the technology bubble burst in 2000, Bear Stearns was fined for pressuring its analysts to recommend securities that it was selling and also for facilitating market timing by mutual-fund purchasers.

When Long Term Capital Management ran into difficulties, the Federal Reserve organized a bailout to permit an orderly winding down of the fund, fearing a market panic if it failed. Bear Stearns, which had profited significantly from its relationship with the fund, was the only investment bank that refused to participate. Cayne further irritated the financial world by boasting about his decision. Cohan believes that Bear Stearns was never quite as arrogant as its reputation suggested, but competitors found its flamboyant language and swashbuckling culture repellent. When the firm ran into trouble, many thought that Bear Stearns had had it coming.

The major profit center for Bear Stearns was its fixed income division. That division would also be the major cause of the company's demise. The firm made its reputation by originating and trading in industrial bonds issued by manufacturing and utility companies. In the later years of the twentieth century, Bear Stearns became a leader in issuing CDOs and asset-backed securities. The assets backing these securities might be car loans, credit-card loans, home mortgages, or other debts gathered together into large aggregates. Based upon these aggregates, Bear Stearns issued bonds paying greater-than-average interest. During the Savings and Loan crisis of the late 1980's, CDOs helped banks move illiquid assets off their books.

In October, 1997, Bear Stearns counterwrote the first securitization of subprime mortgage loans; by the early twenty-first century, it was the leading issuer of such securities. By shifting monetary responsibility for mortgages from banks to bond holders, securitization expanded the supply of money available for mortgages and encouraged banks to extend loans to increasingly uncreditworthy borrowers. Both Republicans and Democrats agreed that extending loans to people previously unable to own their own homes was a worthy objective. Federal Reserve policy drove down interest rates, and Congress passed laws directing banks to invest in low-income neighborhoods.

Salesmen assured customers that these bonds were safer than ones depending on a single corporation, claiming that the thousands of borrowers behind each bond provided valuable diversification: Though some would default, they said, most would not, so the bond owner would be protected. Cohan points out that this concept was fallacious, though it was widely accepted by investment banks, bond-rating agencies, and financial writers. A big pool of borrowers with essentially identical characteristics did not provide significant diversification. Once housing prices declined and first subprime then normal mortgages began to go into default, there was no way to estimate how many loans would be repaid. It was impossible to value the bonds reliably, and prices dropped precipitously.

Cohan examines Bear Stearns's hedge funds to illustrate the advantages and dangers in the firm's management style. Year-end bonuses for middle management depended on how much profit the manager's division produced, so they were rewarded for taking enormous risks. Those who succeeded were basically left unconstrained.

In 2003, the firm started a hedge fund specializing in asset-based securities that operated almost entirely on borrowed capital, providing its investors with huge profits, 20 percent of which were retained by Bear Stearns. All went well until the housing boom slowed in 2006 and prices of subprime mortgages bonds declined. The fund manager believed that this was an opportunity to buy subprime bonds, rather than a warning sign. Although he told his investors only that 6 percent of his fund was in subprime mortgages, he increased his holdings to 60 percent, while the fund's asset value steadily declined. The manager was later indicted for securities fraud for lying to his customers.

No one in authority paid any attention to what the hedge fund manager was doing. Senior management was shocked when closing the fund in July, 2007, cost Bear Stearns more than $1 billion to repay loans into which the fund had entered. The mix of arrogance, greed, and mismanagement that Cohan describes helped bring about the demise of Bear Stearns. It was only the first, however, of a host of major financial institutions that suffered failure or takeover by the federal government during the next year. This wave of failures demonstrated that structural economic problems and not merely management malfeasance brought about the financial disaster of 2009. Examining the full dimensions of the downturn, however, goes beyond the scope of Cohan's project. His well-written book holds readers despite its length and occasionally excessive detail, and it demonstrates the potential for other such studies to completely chart the corporations at the heart of the global economic events of 2008-2009.

Milton Berman

Review Sources

The Boston Globe, March 28, 2009, p. G8.
BusinessWeek, March 16, 2009, p. 70.
The Economist 390, no. 8621 (March 7, 2009): 89.
Los Angeles Times, March 6, 2009, p. D1.
The New York Review of Books 56, no. 17 (November 5, 2009): 54-57.
The New York Times, March 10, 2009, p. C4.
The New York Times Book Review, June 14, 2009, p. 10.
Newsweek 153, no. 12 (March 23, 2009): 16.
Reason 41, no. 3 (July, 2009): 48-53.
The Wall Street Journal, March 6, 2009, p. A13.
The Washington Post, March 22, 2009, p. B7.

THE HOUSE OF WISDOM
How the Arabs Transformed Western Civilization

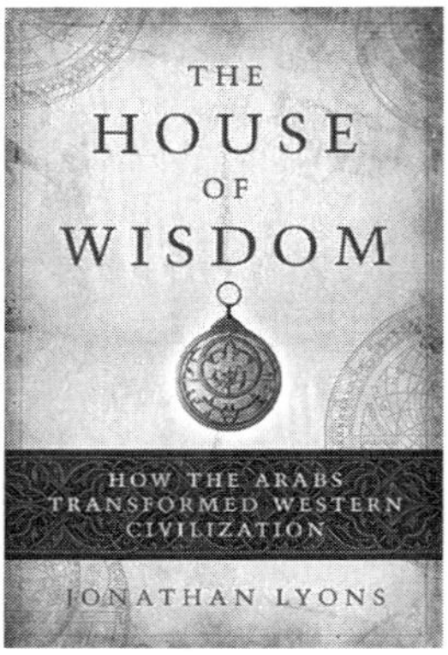

Author: Jonathan Lyons
Publisher: Bloomsbury Press (New York). Illustrated. 248 pp. $26.00
Type of work: History, history of science, religion
Time: Around the eighth century to 1300
Locale: The Muslim empire; England; France

By uncritically contrasting Islamic learning and sophistication on the one hand and European ignorance and barbarity on the other, Lyons argues that Muslim scholars preserved and built upon the intellectual heritage of classical Greece, thus making possible the European Renaissance

Principal personages:

Adelard of Bath (c. 1080-c. 1152), English scholar who spent time in the Middle East, translated Arabic works into Latin, and made them available to the West

Averroës (Abū al-Walīd Muḥammad ibn Aḥmad ibn Muḥammad ibn Rushd) (1126-1198), expert on Islamic philosophy, theology, and jurisprudence, commentator on Aristotle

Avicenna (Abū ʿAlī al-Husain ibn ʿAbdallāh ibn Sīnā), (980-1037), Muslim physician and philosopher

Frederick II (1194-1250), Holy Roman Emperor, 1220-1250, polymath, and patron of Muslim learning

Al-Khwārizmī (c. 780-c. 850), Muslim mathematician, astronomer, and geographer

Michael Scot (1175-1232?), mathematician, scholar, and astrologer to Frederick II

Jonathan Lyons's *The House of Wisdom* provides an account of Muslim scientific and cultural superiority to Christian Europe during the Middle Ages and argues that the West owes a debt to the Arabs and Islam today. His account is structured around Islam's mandatory five daily prayers. A brief prologue, headed "AL-MAGHRIB/SUNSET," represents "the traditional start of the day in the Middle East." The introductory note to readers then refers to "the nightfall (*al-isha*) of the Christian Middle Ages; . . . the dawn (*al-fajr*) of the great age of Arab learning; . . . the glory of midday (*al-zuhr*) . . . ; and . . . the rich colors of afternoon (*al-asr*)."

The text's very structure and chapter headings thus make clear that the medieval day and its light are Islam's, while the blackness of night is Christendom's. As early as the introductory note, then, some readers may begin to suspect that the book will present neither a nuanced vindication of an unfairly maligned religion or a slandered people nor a careful rebalancing of a culturally skewed scale. Lyons's book expresses a simple Manichaeism, with the forces of prejudice, repression, and bloodlust represented by the West, while reason, toleration, and refinement are the almost exclusive possession of Muslims.

For Lyons, Pope Urban II's call to liberate the Christian holy places from Muslim occupation let loose upon the civilized East armies of ignorant, greedy, and ambitious thugs. He points out that Western society was unable even to measure the passing of time except in the crudest manner and was thus incapable of establishing the date of Easter, the most important festival of the religion for which the crusaders purportedly fought. In this matter of time-telling as in others, Lyons portrays the Muslims as coming to the rescue, as it was they who perfected the astrolabe, an instrument invented by the Greeks that would enable considerable advances to be made not only in calendar-making but also in astronomy and cartography.

Jonathan Lyons has traveled widely, mostly in the Soviet Union and the Middle East, as editor and foreign correspondent for Reuters. He is now a Ph.D. candidate in the sociology of religion at Monash University in Melbourne, Australia, and is affiliated with the university's Global Terrorism Research Center.

Some enlightened European scholars would rise above the brutal credulity of their time and place and take Arab knowledge back to the West after years spent living in and learning from a superior civilization. Indeed, the book is loosely structured around the life of one of these scholars, Adelard of Bath. Adelard's respectful admiration for Muslims and their learning contrasts gratifyingly with the attitude of the crusaders, who are portrayed as rapists and pillagers fighting under the symbol of the cross. "Where the crusaders had seen only evil in the Muslim infidel, Adelard sought the light of Arab wisdom."

The House of Wisdom ends with Adelard's words distinguishing the provinces of faith and reason one from the other and hence justifying the scientific enquiry that would almost unimaginably change and improve the material conditions of human life: "Of course God rules the universe. . . . But we may and should enquire into the natural world. The Arabs teach us that." In so enquiring, the Arabs illustrated their role as, in Lyons's rather bold phrase, "inventors of the West."

Between Adelard's setting out for the East at the beginning of the book and his validation of Arab intellectual superiority at the end, Lyons presents a number of Muslim scholars and Europeans sympathetic to Muslim learning. Al-Khwārizmī's name suggests that he was probably from present-day Uzbekistan. He worked with the Bayt al-Hikma, the so-called House of Wisdom that gives Lyons's book its title, a royal library built in Baghdad to store Persian, Sanskrit, and Greek texts. The House of Wisdom also provided administrative and financial support for scholars studying and translating these texts and made possible centuries of sustained scholarly achievement. Al-Khwārizmī himself created two star tables, careful records of planetary and stellar movements. What are now called "Arabic numbers" reached the West thanks largely to a Latin version of one of his texts. He also laid the foundations of algebra (the very term comes from the title of yet another of his works), giving practical illustrations of its utility in such matters as calculating inheritances and measuring land.

Averroës, an expert on Islamic philosophy and theology, wrote about the very matter that Lyons sees as Islam's greatest gift to the West: He produced a vindication of rational enquiry into the workings of the world and of that endeavor's compatibility with religious faith. *Kitab fasl al-maqāl* (1179-1180; *On the Harmony of Religion and Philosophy*, 1961) is a reconciliation of reasoned enquiry with the claims of religion, its thesis being that Islam not only permits such an exercise but also mandates it as a religious duty: One truth cannot oppose another but must rather complement it. Averroës rather than Descartes, writing five centuries later, should be regarded as the founder of modern Western philosophy.

Writing a century and a half before Averroës, Avicenna, a "prolific Persian polymath," made substantial contributions to metaphysics and medicine. In the former area, he argued for the existence of God and wrote an account of the creation of the world; in the latter, his *Kitab al-Qanun fi al-tibb* (early eleventh century; *A Treatise on the Canon of Medicine of Avicenna*, 1930) developed scientific methodology and recorded precise observations of specific diseases. Michael Scot, a great scholar of the thirteenth century, would translate Avicenna's work on zoology along with Aristotle's on the same subject. The immensely talented Scot also prepared a translation of Averroës's work on Aristotle, making himself so much an expert on the great Greek philosopher that he was nicknamed the Commentator. Aristotle, as mediated and explained by Muslim scholars in Arabic, then necessarily translated by cultural conduits such as Scot into Latin, was central to the West's intellectual development, to its eventual readiness to see investigation into the life and nature of the world as acceptable to God.

In an age when learning was rare and therefore suspect in Christian Europe, colorful tales were recounted of Scot and his protector, the Holy Roman Emperor Frederick II. These tales were all the more sinister as a result of the tellers' awareness of their subjects' Arab knowledge. Scot was said to be able to foresee the future, making forecasts about his master's military campaigns and even foretelling the manner of his own death. Frederick organized a splendid court in Sicily, approached Muslim learning with enthusiasm, and acquired large amounts of it. He was twice excommunicated by the popes and earned the nickname *stupor mundi*, the "wonder of the world." It was Frederick who recovered Jerusalem for Christendom, not by force of arms but by negotiation, and it was as protégé of Frederick and his court that Scot would make his contributions to the beginnings of Western science.

One closes Lyons's book lacking complete confidence in his claims. The author invariably relies on secondary sources. He also, more important, manifests a consistent partiality toward Muslim Arabs and a consequent distaste for Christian Europeans. Lyons has contrived to write a book dealing with the first seven or so centuries of Islam in which the word "jihad" never once appears. Time and again he mentions the "rapid territorial expansion" of Islam, the "empire's newest Muslims," the "rapid spread of Islam across much of the known world," and "the lands and peoples under [Muslim] dominion." Never is mention made of the manner in which these lands became Muslim. When he uses the phrase "fearsome holy warriors," he is referring to crusaders.

One of the book's heroes is al-Mansur, the second Abbasid Caliph, founder of the House of Wisdom and of Baghdad itself. Before beginning to build the city, he asked advice from "his trusted royal astrologers, the former Zoroastrian Nawbakht and

Mashallah, a Jew turned Muslim from Basra." One wonders what inducements or threats may have been employed to convince these two men, among tens of millions of others, to embrace Islam. One need not wonder long: Writers such as Bat Ye'or in *The Decline of Eastern Christianity Under Islam* (1996) and Andrew G. Bostom in *The Legacy of Jihad* (2005) have made it very clear that the once-flourishing Christian, Jewish, and even Zoroastrian communities of the Middle East and North Africa almost disappeared because their members converted to Islam in order to avoid death at the worst or a humiliating institutionalized second-class status at the best. This status, applied more or less rigorously according to time and place, was never formally abrogated. Neither Ye'or's book nor Bostom's appears in Lyons's bibliography.

Counterinterpretations also exist of the Crusades. For example, some scholars see them as a Christian reaction to more than three centuries of relentless Muslim empire-building. Lyons presents them as a papal grab at influence. Some would question even Lyons's main thesis by denying the centrality of Arab learning as an instigator of the European Renaissance. (Victor Davis Hanson has suggested that Byzantine scholar refugees from Muslim Turks were of far more importance; Robert Spencer claims that Aristotle's work was translated into Arabic by Christians.) These may be matters for professional historians and linguists to debate, but even general readers may be surprised to see the attempts of the Spanish to recover what was arguably their own country described as "Christian expansionism."

Lyons's book has generally been well received. Eric Ormsby, in the *Wall Street Journal*, writes of it as "vivid and elegant, though marred at times by tendentiousness . . . [apparently wishing] to elevate Islam by diminishing European civilization to crude farce." James Buchan in *The Guardian* praises "this clear and well-written book," but wonders why medieval Muslim science lost its impetus until "well into our lifetimes." Stephen O'Shea in the *Los Angeles Times* claims that "Dust will never gather on Jonathan Lyons' lively new book of medieval history." Marc Lambert in *The Scotsman* lauds "a well crafted, powerful account."

M. D. Allen

Review Sources

The Guardian (London), February 28, 2009, p. 7.
Kirkus Reviews 76, no. 23 (December 1, 2008): 1243-1244.
Library Journal 134, no. 7 (April 15, 2009): 101.
Los Angeles Times, March 27, 2009, p. D14.
New Scientist 201, no. 2696 (February 21, 2009): 46.
The Sunday Telegraph (London), February 15, 2009, p. 36.
The Sunday Times (London), February 1, 2009, pp. 39-40.
The Times (London), January 24, 2009, p. 9.
Times Higher Education, March 5, 2009, p. 45.
The Wall Street Journal, February 14, 2009, p. W8.

THE HOUSE OF WITTGENSTEIN
A Family at War

Author: Alexander Waugh (1963-   )
Publisher: Doubleday (New York). 333 pp. $28.95
Type of work: Biography
Time: 1865-1965
Locale: Vienna, Austria; Cambridge, England; New York City

A biographical study of the powerful Wittgenstein family of Vienna, which included concert pianist Paul Wittgenstein and philosopher Ludwig Wittgenstein

Principal personages:

PAUL WITTGENSTEIN, a distinguished concert pianist who lost his right arm in World War I
LUDWIG WITTGENSTEIN, Paul's younger brother, a major twentieth century philosopher
KARL WITTGENSTEIN, a major Viennese steel manufacturer and Paul's father
LEOPOLDINE KALMUS, Karl's wife, mother to eleven children
HERMINE WITTGENSTEIN, Paul's eldest sibling, the family's unmarried matriarch
JOHANNES WITTGENSTEIN, a musician and adventurer who goes missing in Latin America
KONRAD WITTGENSTEIN, a steel manufacturer and soldier who commits suicide during World War I
HELENE SALZER, the fifth child in the Wittgenstein family
MAX SALZER, a minister of the Austrian government and Helene's husband
RUDOLF WITTGENSTEIN, a student of chemistry who commits suicide
MARGARET STONBOROUGH, the seventh Wittgenstein child
JEROME STONBOROUGH, dilettante son of an American businessman and Margaret's husband
HILDE SCHANIA, Paul's mistress and wife

With all the richness and scope of a classic historical novel, Alexander Waugh's *The House of Wittgenstein: A Family at War* is a portrait of the eccentric family that produced Ludwig Wittgenstein, one of the twentieth century's central philosophers, and Paul Wittgenstein, a famous concert pianist. In encompassing the entire Wittgenstein saga, Waugh places the family's tale in the social, cultural, and political context of the dying days of the Austro-Hungarian Empire, the turmoil of two world wars, and the dawn of the postmodern world that Ludwig helped shape with his seminal writings on language and logic.

The grandson of novelist Evelyn Waugh and the son of columnist Auberon Waugh, Alexander Waugh is author of Fathers and Sons: The Autobiography of a Family *(2004) and* Time: Its Origin, Its Enigma, Its History *(2000). He is also an award-winning music critic and producer.*

It is clear why the Wittgenstein saga attracted Waugh as a writer, since he too is a member of an illustrious family. His great-grandfather, Arthur Waugh, was Charles Dickens's publisher. Arthur's sons, Alec and Evelyn, became significant novelists. Evelyn is best known as the author of *Brideshead Revisited* (1945), the classic novel of class relationships and the Catholic faith. Evelyn's son, Auberon, became a well-known British journalist, and Alexander is Auberon's son. Thus, Alexander Waugh knows well the tensions and glories of being a member of a famous family—knowledge that served him well in the writing of *Fathers and Sons* (2004), his memoir of the Waugh clan, and *The House of Wittgenstein*, his fourth book.

The strengths Waugh brings to this biography go beyond possessing famous relatives. As a music critic, a producer of award-winning classical albums, and author of *Classical Music: A New Way of Listening* (1995), Waugh has the perfect background to explore the musically inclined Wittgensteins, who were friends with Johannes Brahms, Richard Strauss, Arnold Schoenberg, and other major composers. Incidentally, Waugh's musical vocation explains why pianist Paul Wittgenstein receives more attention in *The House of Wittgenstein* than his more significant philosopher brother, Ludwig. Still, Waugh has published two books of popular philosophy—*Time* (1999) and *God* (2002)—that provide him the credentials to tackle Ludwig's life as well.

The House of Wittgenstein begins with Karl Wittgenstein's rebellion against his father, Hermann Wittgenstein, who founded the family fortune through estate management and land speculation. In 1865, at the age of seventeen, Karl ran away from his Vienna home and landed in New York, where he made a living at a variety of trades, including waiter, fiddle player, and canal boat pilot. Kurt finally made his way to Rochester, New York, where he taught at an exclusive liberal arts college. With this position, he could finally return home without shame. In 1872, he became the head of an Austrian steel firm, and two years later he married Leopoldine Kalmus. This marriage was also an act of rebellion, since Leopoldine was Jewish, and Hermann had forbidden any of his children to marry a Jew. By 1900, Karl, who lived in a Viennese palace with his wife and extensive family, was one of the richest men in Europe. Ministers of government came to him for advice, and he was widely known as a patron of the arts.

Karl hoped that his children would exhibit his qualities of unconventionality, strength of character, and an instinct for success. However, to his disappointment, they essentially embraced only the first of these traits. The one exception was Helene, his fifth child, who married a minister of finance in the Austrian government and remained comfortably upper class. The rest of his children had strange, often tragic lives.

His eldest child, Hermine, never married and, like some character in a gothic novel, spent her life overseeing the Wittgenstein palace. The next child, Dora, died in infancy. Johannes arrived after Dora, and, while he showed promise as an engineer, he became a musician against his father's wishes. To escape his father's disapproval, Johannes fled to America in 1902. However, Johannes did not return triumphant from across the Atlantic as his father had in 1866. Instead, he mysteriously vanished. He may have changed his identity before losing himself in the vast South American continent, or he may have drowned in the Chesapeake Bay, Florida's Lake Okeechobee, or Venezuela's Orinoco River—all of these locations being possibilities according to the rumors sent back to the Wittgensteins. Because of Johannes's fascination with nihilism, his family assumed he committed suicide.

Two years later, Rudolf, the Wittgensteins' sixth child, walked into a Berlin bar, ordered a glass of milk, mixed it with potassium cyanide, and drank it while the bar's pianist played a sentimental song. He left a note claiming that the death of a friend inspired his agonizing suicide, but despair that his homosexuality would soon become public knowledge was a more likely motive. In 1905, Margaret, the seventh Wittgenstein, married Jerome Stonborough. It was not a salutary match. While the couple shared a passion for science, they had little else in common. Stonborough, the son of a bankrupt kid-glove merchant from New York, possessed a restless nature. With Margaret's fortune, he launched on an endless journey across Europe, studying at various universities and scientific academies, never staying anywhere long enough to complete an advanced degree. In 1938, Margaret divorced him, and he committed suicide. This first wave of Wittgenstein family misfortunes climaxed with Karl's painful death from cancer on January 20, 1913.

The Wittgensteins' second wave of tragedies began on June 28, 1914, when a Serbian anarchist assassinated Austrian archduke Ferdinand and Austria declared war on Serbia, triggering the bloody four-year conflict later called World War I. The surviving Wittgenstein sons—Konrad, Paul, and Ludwig—would all fight in the war. Only Ludwig would emerge unscathed.

Months before the war started, Konrad, the fourth Wittgenstein child, arrived in New York seeking to invest in the American and Canadian steel industries. When war erupted, the United States was officially neutral and would not allow Konrad to return and serve in the Austrian army. For three years, he worked for the Austrian Consulate General, promoting the Austrian cause in the United States. Then, in April of 1917, when the United States declared war, Konrad was expelled as an enemy alien. Upon arrival in Vienna, he became an infantry captain. In late October, 1918, as the Italian front collapsed, Konrad committed suicide. The reasons given for this act vary, but the most likely explanation is that he killed himself to avoid capture.

Paul, the eighth Wittgenstein, was the most serious member of the family when it came to music, and on December 1, 1913, he had his Viennese piano concert debut to great critical acclaim. However, Paul's dawning career as a pianist was radically altered when he became a lieutenant in the Austrian army. Within weeks of the war's advent, a bullet shattered his right arm. Soon after the surgeons operated on his arm, Russian troops overran the field hospital. Paul, now an amputee, found himself a prisoner of war deep in Siberia. Despite the camp's wretched conditions, he taught himself to play one-handed piano, first on a keyboard drawn on a wooden box and finally on a battered upright piano provided by a sympathetic Russian guard.

Over a year later, Paul was released in a prisoner exchange and he performed in his one-handed concert premiere. The recital was wildly successful, and after the war Paul would become famous for his impressive one-handed abilities. During the 1920's and 1930's, he made numerous concert tours across Europe and America, commissioning left-handed pieces from major composers such as Sergei Prokofiev, Benjamin Britten, and Maurice Ravel.

Ludwig, the youngest Wittgenstein, survived the war with his body intact, yet the war changed him in profound, internal ways. Like many Wittgensteins, Ludwig demonstrated engineering ability. In 1911, at the age of twenty-two, he already had an aeronautic patent. However, that same year he encountered the writings of Bertrand Russell and went to study under the British philosopher at Cambridge University, where Ludwig's unique philosophical abilities blossomed.

World War I interrupted Ludwig's Cambridge sojourn. On August 7, 1914, he enlisted as a private in the Austrian army and served with distinction as an artilleryman. By 1916, he was promoted to lieutenant and, like his brother Paul, became decorated for bravery, yet it was a book discovered in a shop on the Polish frontier that brought the war's greatest impact on Ludwig. *Kratkoe izlozhenie Evangeliia* (wr. 1896, pb. 1906; *The Gospel in Brief*, 1921), Leo Tolstoy's radical meditation on the four gospels, had a profound influence on Ludwig's concepts of language and meaning, as well as his personal path in life. *The Gospel in Brief* helped shape Ludwig's first book, "Logisch-philosophische Abhandlung" (1921; best known by the bilingual German and English edition title of *Tractatus Logico-Philosophicus*, 1922, 1961), which he wrote largely during the war. It was also Tolstoy's belief in an ascetic life that inspired Ludwig to relinquish his family fortune in 1919. After laboring as an elementary school instructor and a gardener, Ludwig returned to Cambridge in 1929 and would teach there for the rest of his life, becoming a British citizen in 1939.

After the war, mismanagement of the estate, hyperinflation, and Margaret's attempts to control the family caused tensions to simmer in the Wittgenstein clan. Still, the remaining siblings tended to get along, even Paul and Ludwig, despite their intense disagreements. Paul, an ardent Catholic and monarchist, abhorred Ludwig's communist tendencies and summed up the *Tractatus Logico-Philosophicus* in one word: "Trash." In return, Ludwig thought Paul's piano playing abominable. The brothers got along wonderfully, however, by agreeing not to discuss philosophy, politics, or music.

The Wittgensteins' uneasy harmony ended when Nazi Germany annexed Austria on March 11, 1938. Under Nazi rule, the Wittgensteins, having three grandparents who were Jewish, became defined as Jews under the Nuremberg Laws. As a member of the intensely anti-Nazi Austrian nationalist movement, Paul was especially targeted for Nazi persecution. Also, because he had a Catholic mistress, Hilde Schania, he could be prosecuted for "race defilement." While Hermine, Helene, and Margaret tried to have their Jewish status changed and negotiated with Nazi authorities to preserve their assets, Paul refused to make deals with the Nazi occupiers. In this regard,

Ludwig tended to side with his sisters. Finally, in 1939, Paul and his mistress fled to Cuba, where they were married. Ultimately, Paul, Hilde, and their two daughters would become American citizens and settle on Long Island. In 1940, Margaret too escaped Austria and joined her son Jerome in Washington, D.C. The sisters' desperate attempts to reason with Nazi officials left all the Wittgensteins feeling betrayed, and the family's scattering did not help matters. Most of the siblings would never speak with each other again.

After the war, Karl and Leopoldine Wittgenstein's remaining children died in rapid succession, and, except for Ludwig, they spent their final years largely isolated from the world. Hermine, Helene, and Margaret, all living in Vienna, died in 1950, 1956, and 1958 respectively. Ludwig died in 1951 in Cambridge, and Paul died a decade later in New York. Paul's work as a concert pianist was by then largely forgotten, and his few recordings were panned by the critics. After Hermine died, the Wittgenstein palace was sold to developers. As Alexander Waugh writes, "Razed to the ground by cranes, bulldozers, and wrecking balls, the final demolition marked the symbolic end to the Wittgenstein story." Only Ludwig triumphed against time. His reputation as a philosopher increased dramatically with the posthumous publication of a bilingual German/English edition of his second book, *Philosophische Untersuchungen/Philosophical Investigations*, in 1953. The intellectual community came to regard him as one of the greatest minds of the twentieth century.

John Nizalowski

Review Sources

Booklist 105, no. 9/10 (January 1, 2009): 39.
Chronicle of Higher Education 55, no. 33 (April 24, 2009): B4-B5.
Harper's Magazine 318, no. 1906 (March, 2009): 77-82.
Kirkus Reviews 76, no. 20 (October 15, 2008): 1108.
Library Journal 133, no. 19 (November 15, 2008): 74-75.
London Review of Books 30, no. 23 (December 4, 2008): 13-14.
New Statesman 137, no. 4920 (November 3, 2008): 54.
The New York Review of Books 56, no. 10 (June 11, 2009): 18-22.
The New York Times Book Review, March 1, 2009, p. 8.
The New Yorker 85, no. 8 (April 6, 2009): 70-74.
The Times Literary Supplement, December 19, 2008, p. 11.

THE HOUSEKEEPER AND THE PROFESSOR

Author: Yoko Ogawa (1962-)
First published: Hakase no aishita sūshiki, 2003, in Japan
Translated from the Japanese by Stephen Snyder
Publisher: Picador (New York). 184 pp. $14.00
Type of work: Novel
Time: 1992-2004
Locale: A small city on Japan's Inland Sea

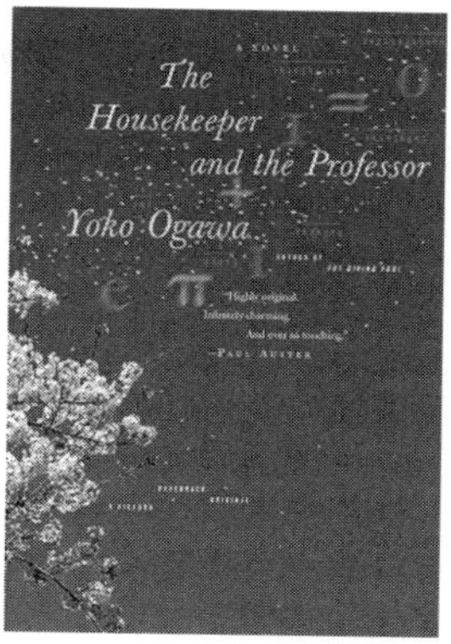

A reclusive mathematics professor introduces his housekeeper and her son to his ideal world of prime numbers, while they help him reconnect to the everyday world

Principal characters:
THE HOUSEKEEPER, the narrator, an uneducated, twenty-eight-year-old single mother and an orphan
ROOT, her ten-year-old son
THE PROFESSOR, a sixty-four-year-old mathematician whose short-term memory is limited
THE SISTER-IN-LAW, the widow of the Professor's elder brother, who provides for him

When Yoko Ogawa's *The Diving Pool: Three Novellas* appeared in English in 2008, the book was acclaimed by British and American critics. They were particularly impressed by the author's elegant style, by her skill in creating realistic settings, and by her restraint in dealing with situations that had all the ingredients of a horror film, since all of the narrators were withdrawn, unhappy, cruel women. The tone of *The Housekeeper and the Professor* is very different. While again the critics have praised Ogawa's lucidity, her pictorial powers, and her gift for understatement, they point out that—unlike the novellas collected and translated in *The Diving Pool*, which emphasize the dark side of humanity—the novel tells a story of compassion and redemption.

Like the novellas, *The Housekeeper and the Professor* has a woman narrator: the unnamed, twenty-eight-year-old Housekeeper, who is the youngest employee of the Akebono Housekeeper Agency. Despite her youth, she has proven herself so capable that her employers send her to their most difficult clients. Up to this point, she has always succeeded in pleasing these clients. However, when the Housekeeper notices that the client to whom she is now being sent has dismissed nine previous housekeepers, she is curious and somewhat apprehensive. In an interview with a dignified, elderly woman, who is identified as the Sister-in-law, the Housekeeper learns that she will be working for a retired mathematics professor who lives in a cottage behind the house. The Sister-in-law also explains that, ever since he was injured in an automobile accident seventeen years ago, the Professor's short-term memory has been lim-

Yoko Ogawa has won the Kaien Prize, the Akutagawa Prize, the Yomiuri Prize, the Izumi Prize, and the Tanizaki Prize. His work available in English includes The Diving Pool: Three Novellas *(2008) and* Hoteru Airisu *(1996;* Hotel Iris, *2010).*

ited to eighty minutes. The Housekeeper is scheduled to begin work the following Monday.

When she arrives at the cottage on her first day of work, the Housekeeper is surprised to have the Professor greet her by asking her shoe size. However, she soon realizes that, whenever he is unsure about what is going on around him, the Professor takes refuge in numbers. He spends his time working on mathematical problems, which he is able to solve with ease even though he can get through the necessities of daily life only by taking such measures as clipping notes to his jacket. At first, the Professor insists that the Housekeeper remain silent so as not to disturb his thought processes. Before long, however, he begins talking to the Housekeeper about number theory, which is both his specialty and his passion. One would not expect her to be particularly interested in such an abstract subject, but, even though she dropped out of school early, the Housekeeper proves to be both intelligent and intellectually curious. The Professor responds to her interest in his field of expertise by patiently showing her how numbers operate. When she observes that the way numbers connect with one another reminds her of the constellations in the sky, the Professor knows that he has successfully ushered the Housekeeper into the abstract world in which he lives.

It does not seem to occur to the Professor that, since the process of teaching necessarily involves reaching out to another human being, he has ventured out of his own world and into the Housekeeper's everyday world. At first, the change in him is evident in his taking an interest in minor domestic matters, such as the Housekeeper's cooking. However, there is no evidence that the Professor is still capable of feeling human emotions until he learns that the Housekeeper's ten-year-old son has no one to take care of him between the end of the school day and the time his mother arrives home. The Professor is horrified. Imagining all sorts of catastrophes, he sends the Housekeeper home immediately, ordering her from that time on to have her son stay with her in the cottage whenever he is not at school. Although the Housekeeper knows that her agency does not allow employees to bring their children to the workplace with them, the Professor feels so strongly about the matter that she does not dare oppose him.

When the boy appears at the cottage, the Professor reveals a new side of his character. He embraces the boy, takes off his Hanshin Tigers baseball cap, rubs his head, and announces that he will be nicknamed "Root" because the top of his head resembles the square root sign. When the Professor realizes that Root will not be able to eat dinner until he and his mother return home, he orders the Housekeeper and her son to join him at the table. Again, the Housekeeper obeys him, hoping that the agency will not find out. To her amazement, in Root's presence the Professor is no longer the sloppy eater he had been before. Instead, he displays perfect manners, and when Root makes errors in etiquette the Professor gently corrects him. The Professor even guides the dinnertime conversation, questioning Root about his activities and his interests. By the end of their first meal together, Root counts the Professor as one of his friends.

During the months that follow, the Professor takes on the role of Root's father or grandfather. He quizzes the boy about events at school; he helps him with his studies; he urges him to finish all the food his mother has prepared, so that he will grow big and strong; and he worries about his being hurt. The first time the Housekeeper leaves her son alone with the Professor, Root manages to cut himself with a knife, and when she returns to the cottage, the Professor is holding Root in his arms and sobbing uncontrollably. The Professor then insists on lifting Root onto his back, carrying him to the clinic for a couple of stitches, and then carrying him back to the cottage.

Simple events such as these, which engage readers because they reveal changes in character and in relationships, constitute one plotline of *The Housekeeper and the Professor*. The other plotline involves the Professor taking charge of the Housekeeper's intellectual development. Like the master teacher he is, he guides her through the intricacies of number theory, until, like the Professor, she sees it as a manifestation of God.

Though Root is too young to find number theory spiritually illuminating, he can see how numbers apply to baseball, his favorite sport. He soon finds that the Professor shares his enthusiasm and that he, too, is a fan of the Hanshin Tigers. Unfortunately, since for the Professor time stopped in 1975, he believes that the great Yutaka Enatsu, who wore the perfect number 28 on his uniform, is still the star pitcher of the Hanshin Tigers. After Root persuades the Professor to get his radio repaired so they can listen to baseball games, the boy has to invent reasons for Yutaka Enatsu's absence from the lineup. Then, as part of her campaign to get the Professor out of his self-imposed seclusion, the Housekeeper buys tickets for a game in which the Tigers are playing. Fortunately, since the player who now wears number 28 is out because of an injury, the Professor will not notice that Enatsu is not playing.

At first, the trip to the baseball game is a great success. The Professor is fascinated with the details of the game, the first he has ever attended, and the fans around him are tolerant when he goes into long recitations of baseball statistics. After the three return to the cottage, however, the Professor becomes ill, and the Housekeeper stays at the cottage to nurse him. Four days later, though the Professor has recovered, the Housekeeper is informed that, because she broke the rules by spending the night, the Sister-in-law has dismissed her.

A month later, the Housekeeper is summoned by the Sister-in-law, who is furious because Root has come to visit the Professor. The confrontation ends when the Professor orders the Sister-in-Law to leave Root alone, hands her a paper on which he had written an equation, and stalks out of the room. The Sister-in-law understands what he means, the Housekeeper is rehired, and things return to normal. However, during their celebration of Root's eleventh birthday, the Professor seems confused. Two days later, the Sister-in-law notifies the Housekeeper that, because he no longer has any short-term memory at all, the Professor has been moved to a nursing home. He remains there until his death eleven years later. When the Housekeeper and Root visit him, he is always delighted to see them, but he has no memory of their time together.

On the simplest level, *The Housekeeper and the Professor* demonstrates that human beings are most fully realized when they live both in the everyday world and in the world of the intellect, which, Ogawa suggests, is also the world of the spirit. When she finds herself able to solve problems independent of the Professor, the Housekeeper feels not only a sense of achievement but also a validation of herself as a human being. Thus, her friendship with the Professor enriches her life. The Professor's ventures into daily life are even more difficult for him than the Housekeeper's intellectual endeavors are for her. Not only is he out of the habit of interacting with others, but he also has a peculiar disadvantage. While most people can find common ground by reminiscing about their recent experiences, the Professor cannot remember what happened even two hours before, and at the end of the novel, he has no memory except of events that happened before 1975. However, what he lacks in memory, he more than makes up for by his capacity to love. Thus, at the end of *The Housekeeper and the Professor*, though the Professor has lost his recollections of that year when three lonely people became a family, his feelings for the Housekeeper and Root are as real as ever. As real, in fact, as prime numbers and, Ogawa suggests, as indicative of the existence of the divine.

Rosemary M. Canfield Reisman

Review Sources

Booklist 105, no. 9/10 (January 1, 2009): 46.
The Guardian (London), May 2, 2009, p. 11.
Kirkus Reviews 76, no. 23 (December 1, 2008): 1224.
Library Journal 134, no. 6 (April 1, 2009): 71-72.
Nature 460, no. 7254 (July 23, 2009): 461-462.
The New York Times Book Review, March 1, 2009: 9.
The New Yorker 85, no. 1 (February 9, 2009): 109.
Publishers Weekly 255, no. 46 (November 17, 2008):40.
Science 324, no. 5932 (June 5, 2009): 1271.
The Spectator 310, no. 9432 (June 6, 2009): 36.
The Times Literary Supplement, April 24, 2009, p. 21.

HOW ROME FELL

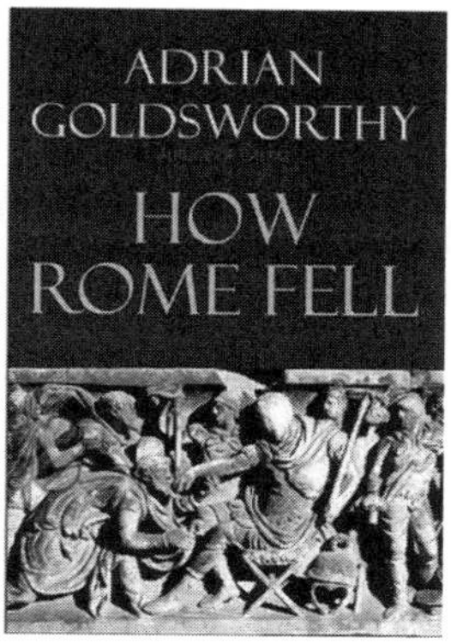

Author: Adrian Goldsworthy (1969-)
Publisher: Yale University Press (New Haven, Conn.). Illustrated. 531 pp. $32.50
Type of work: History

Goldsworthy argues that the Roman Empire collapsed in the West because recurrent civil wars wasted Roman resources and led Roman leaders to focus on personal survival rather than the common good

Principal personages:
AUGUSTUS, first Roman emperor, 31 B.C.E.-14 C.E.
SEPTIMIUS SEVERUS, Roman emperor, 193-211
DIOCLETIAN, Roman emperor, 284-305

In *How Rome Fell*, Adrian Goldsworthy addresses the enduring question memorably raised by Edward Gibbon in the first volume of his monumental *The Decline and Fall of the Roman Empire* (1776): How was it that the greatest power of its day succumbed to an invasion of barbarian tribesmen? The scholarly brilliance and majestic prose of Gibbon's masterpiece helped focus attention on this epochal revolution, which demarcated the boundary between the classical and medieval eras, and, as Gibbon himself noted, laid the foundations for modern Europe. Continuing interest in the fall of the Roman Empire has transcended the appeal of Gibbon's literary artistry, however.

The eighteenth century Enlightenment secularized Christianity's belief in a teleological direction of history: Instead of a story of humankind's fall into sin and ultimate redemption, history became a narrative of progress driven by scientific inquiry and technological innovation. Implicit in any vision of progress is the possibility of regression, or decline. The heyday of European expansionism and confidence was always haunted by fears that all could be lost. Gibbon himself was keenly conscious of the strength and accomplishments of European civilization in his day, yet he speculated on the possibility of nomadic barbarians riding once again into the European heartland.

A melancholic sense that all great ages must come to an end persisted into the bustling nineteenth century. The catastrophic events surrounding World Wars I and II and the Cold War in the twentieth century stimulated interest in the fall of empires. As Goldsworthy notes in his introduction, the first decade of the twenty-first century has seen intense speculation about the decline of the United States as the world's remaining superpower. Inevitably, there have been comparisons of the United States and Rome, a parallelism that Goldsworthy wisely cautions against pursuing too literally. The ubiquity of contemporary evocations of ancient Rome demonstrates that people

Adrian Goldsworthy is a British historian of the ancient world. His most recent book is the prizewinning Caesar: Life of a Colossus *(2006). He lectures widely and has contributed to many historical documentaries on television.*

today are just as fascinated by the specter of decline and fall as were Gibbon's first generation of readers, perhaps with better justification.

The scholarly literature inspired by Gibbon is enormous. Some of the greatest classicists of the past two hundred years have been drawn to the explanatory problem posed by the end of the Roman Empire. The result has been a string of histories that have offered compelling, and often conflicting, interpretations of Rome's collapse. Gibbon famously ascribed the fall of Rome to the "triumph of barbarism and religion" and then, in a more dispassionate mood, wrote that the Empire sank under its own weight. Subsequent explanations have ranged from the sublime to the ridiculous. Climate change, depopulation due to plagues, dysgenic breeding with captive peoples, and lead poisoning from Roman plumbing have all been put forward as causes of Roman decline. Some scholars have emphasized the external threats faced by the late empire. Others have concentrated on internal weaknesses of the Roman economy and imperial administration. Goldsworthy is firmly in the latter camp. In his view, the Romans had no one to look to but themselves for the loss of their Empire in the west.

Goldsworthy argues emphatically that the Roman Empire was a superpower without peer in the ancient world. It controlled all the lands girdling the Mediterranean Sea, constituting a vast realm that in many ways was a world unto itself. The *Pax Romana*, or Roman peace, endured for centuries, enabling the people of the empire to enjoy the benefits of security and trade. Goldsworthy notes that, when the crisis came for the Empire, there was no movement on the part of the component peoples of the Roman world to break free. Romans wanted to stay Roman. It is one of the ironies of the fall of the Roman Empire that the barbarians who broke through its defenses often only wanted to share in the good life that it offered. None of the peoples beyond the Roman frontier could hope to match Roman resources and military might.

Rome's greatest neighbor lay to the east. For years, the Parthian empire had been a formidable but manageable foe. In the third century C.E., a dynamic and aggressive Persian state supplanted the Parthians. The Persians could cause the Romans serious problems but never posed a threat to the integrity of the empire. Still less of a threat were the evanescent confederations of Germanic barbarians rising and falling continually outside the Roman frontier along the Rhine and Danube rivers. Politically and technologically backward, the Germans could not hope to overcome the professionally proficient, well-armed, and well-supplied armies marshaled by Roman power. The Germans sometimes tried to raid Roman territory. They were more likely to trade at the frontier or attempt to enlist as auxiliaries in the Roman military.

It was the Romans themselves, according to Goldsworthy, who ruined the Roman Empire. In surveying the vast literature on the late Roman Empire, Goldsworthy was surprised at how little attention was paid to the deleterious effects of recurrent civil wars. In recent decades, scholars have focused more on the social, cultural, and religious history of late antiquity. Goldsworthy, who made his reputation as a military historian of the Roman Republic and early empire, was struck by the amount of energy the Romans expended from the third century on in fighting one another, often in preference to combating external enemies. Civil wars were nothing new in Roman history. The Roman Republic was destroyed by a century of civil conflict that ended only with the founding of the empire by Augustus (who died in 14 C.E.). In the two centuries from the death of Augustus to the death of the Emperor Commodus in 192, however, civil wars were very rare. This was a measure of the political achievement of Augustus, who reconciled the Roman political elite to autocracy by masking his monarchy with republican trappings.

Augustus called himself *princeps*, or first citizen, and ruled with the active collaboration of the Senate. Augustus personally controlled and paid the army as *imperator*, or emperor. The delicate balance between emperor and Senate was hard to maintain, but, despite the tensions that often arose, emperors continued to rely on the Senate as a reservoir of administrative and military talent. The army also stayed remarkably loyal to its oaths of fealty. Only once during the Principate did the system break down completely, during the brief but intense wars of the Year of Four Emperors in 69.

Like Gibbon before him, Goldsworthy sees the reign of Septimius Severus as a crucial turning point. Severus was the general who triumphed in the brutal civil wars that followed the assassination of Commodus. Though born into an aristocratic family from North Africa, Severus never established a comfortable working relationship with the Senate. Aware that he had won the empire through military force, he counseled his sons to look to the army and ignore everyone else. This advice might not have mattered had the Severan dynasty proved stable. The successors of Severus, however, were unable to recapture the peaceful legitimacy that had undergirded imperial power in the previous century.

When the last Severan was murdered in 238, a tumultuous period of fifty years ensued when the empire was repeatedly racked by civil wars as various armies put forward contenders for the throne. Roman dissension invited attack from the east and from the barbarians of the north. For a time, it seemed as if the empire would spin apart. Not until the accession of Diocletian in 284 did the empire once again enjoy an extended period of relative order, though Goldsworthy is quick to note that, from the crisis of the third century on, rarely did Rome see a decade without an internal challenge to a reigning emperor.

Goldsworthy believes that the civil strife that undermined the empire was rooted in the breakdown of the partnership between the emperors and the Senate. Though emperors often regarded rich and powerful senators as potential rivals, most senators were quite happy with the honors and opportunities afforded them by the Principate. The Senate never posed a serious challenge to the imperial system. A Senate open to the admission of new talent was big enough to provide competent officials but small enough to be carefully monitored by a cautious emperor. The empire as envisioned by Augustus worked. However, Severus and his successors began to downgrade the role of the Senate. During the third century crisis, Senators lost their role as military commanders. Increasingly, emperors entrusted armies to professional soldiers, often of humble background. Goldsworthy notes that the ironic effect of this was to make emperors even less safe, for now anyone could command an army and make a bid for the throne. The ranks of prospective emperors grew exponentially, leading to the near anarchy of the "Barracks Emperors."

Diocletian and his eventual successor, Constantine, reorganized the empire in an effort to restore stability. The emperor no longer was the "first citizen." Instead, he became a sacred figure, remote from the people and swathed in an elaborate and defensive ceremonial court. The emperor was now known as *dominus*, or lord, and the name now given to the late Roman imperial system is the Dominate.

Many scholars have argued that the late third and fourth centuries constituted a time of renewal for the empire. Goldsworthy does not agree. He sees the reforms of Diocletian and Constantine as signs of weakness. During this period, the size of the provinces was decreased so they would be less able to sustain a usurper. The civil and military functions of governors were separated, leaving civil and military officials as checks on one another. The size of the military increased on paper, but individual military units became much smaller. The net effect of all these changes was to increase the security of emperors by making it more difficult for challengers to emerge. The result was a bloated bureaucratic and military establishment that drained the resources of the empire. Insecure emperors were forced to take to the field themselves because they could not trust others with a large military force.

Diocletian tried to solve this problem by administratively dividing the empire with a team of colleagues. This strategy worked only as long as Diocletian himself was available. When he retired, his system broke down into another round of civil wars. The empire eventually came to be divided between east and west, a practice that increased the weight of imperial administration without solving the problem of civil wars.

Goldsworthy believes that the deadliness of their internal competition for power led emperors and their officials to become increasingly interested in personal survival, rather than in the good of the empire. Intrigue and corruption flourished. The major reason that barbarians were able to flood into the western half of the empire in the fifth century was that the Romans had wasted their resources fighting one another. Military units that should have been guarding the frontier existed only on paper; the money supposedly feeding and equipping them instead lined the pockets of venal bureaucrats.

Defenders of the Dominate point out that the Empire in the east did not fall. Goldsworthy argues that the east was the beneficiary of geography and good fortune. The ultimate failure of the Emperor Justinian's attempt to reunite the empire in the sixth century demonstrates that Rome's strength was spent. Thus, Goldsworthy's message to his readers and his contribution to the ongoing debate about the fall of empires is a moral insight: Nations have less to fear from external assault than from allowing their governments to become self-perpetuating bureaucracies focused on the government's needs rather than those of society. Goldsworthy is not the first historian to note the self-destructiveness of Roman imperial and military institutions. He has, however, provided one of the most penetrating and well-written analyses of how this dysfunction led to the fall of the Roman Empire.

Daniel P. Murphy

Review Sources

American Conservative 8, no. 12 (September 1, 2009): 48-49.
Christianity Today 53, no. 6 (June, 2009): 56.
Library Journal 134, no. 8 (May 1, 2009): 88.
Military History 26 (June/July, 2009): 69.
New Criterion 28, no. 2 (October, 2009): 66-79.
Publishers Weekly 256, no. 13 (March 31, 2009): 39-40.
The Wall Street Journal, April 21, 2009, p. A19.

HOW TO PAINT A DEAD MAN

Author: Sarah Hall (1974-   )
Publisher: HarperPerennial (New York). 286 pp.
Paperback $14.99
Type of work: Novel
Time: 1953-2009
Locale: London, England; Umbria, Italy

A novel in which four lives are intertwined by art, change, and tragedy

Principal characters:

SUSAN CALDICUTT, a photographer and museum curator
DANNY CALDICUTT, Susan's twin brother
PETER CALDICUTT, a landscape artist, father of Susan and Danny
SIGNOR GIORGIO, a famous Italian painter
ANNETTE TAMBRONI, young, blind former student of Signor Giorgio
NATHAN, Susan's longtime lover
TOM, Susan's new lover
THERESA, Signor Giorgio's housekeeper
ROSARIA TAMBRONI, Annette's mother

Sarah Hall's fourth novel, *How to Paint a Dead Man*, has received mostly positive reviews. The novel is critically acclaimed for its portrayal of its characters' psyches and its connection to art. Further, Hall's writing has been praised for her daring style and layout. Hall has also been applauded for her emotional intensity, sensuality, and intelligence. Much commentary mentions the novel's subtle interlacing of character and theme. Additional commendation centers on a thematic association with contemporary concerns in the British art world, as well as with social and cultural changes. Negative criticism of the novel centers on its lack of plot and heavy-handed characterization, with one reviewer making the claim that the minor characters stand out the strongest.

Hall builds the novel around two historical references: a quote from French philosopher Gaston Bachelard and an excerpt from Italian artist Cennino d'Andrea Cennini's book *Il libro dell'arte* (wr. 1437, pb. 1821 as *Trattato della pittura*; *A Treatise on Painting*, 1844; better known as *The Craftsman's Handbook*, 1933). Bachelard's words "Things are not what they are, they are what they become" begin the novel, and the passage from Cennini's text provides closure. The philosophical theme that opens the novel suggests that people's lives are affected by potentials. Things are constantly changing; nothing remains static.

In contrast, Cennini's brief exposition, from which the novel takes its title, provides detailed instructions on the process needed to paint a dead person. While Bachelard's expression indirectly shows how the characters are in continual flux, Cennini becomes directly intertwined in the story when Italian painter Signor Giorgio comments on his methods and the way Giorgio's own work reflects Cennini's other teachings. In addition, Peter Caldicutt references Cennini in one of the letters he writes to Signor Giorgio. The title's connection to Cennini's instruction holds a variety of possible meanings related to the stories in the novel, as each character is connected to art and to death.

Sarah Hall earned a degree in Creative Writing from St. Andrews University in Scotland, and How to Paint a Dead Man *is her fourth novel. She has won the Commonwealth Writers' Prize and the Society of Authors Betty Trask Award.*

All four of the main characters are artists. Signor Giorgio is famous for his paintings of bottles, Peter is famous for his landscapes, his daughter Susan is known for her photography, and Annette Tambroni is a budding child artist under Giorgio's tutorage until she loses her eyesight. Each character's artistic perception and vision is tested as they all undergo life-changing events and connect with one another at different points in their lives.

Giorgio is at the end of his life in the early 1960's, and as his narrative progresses readers see how he has painted his own death. He has isolated himself at his home in Serra Partucci. His only connections are with Theresa, the woman who keeps his house; Antonio, his agent; a few students at the local school (including Annette Tambroni); and Peter, who writes to Giorgio in admiration of the older artist's works. Giorgio's journal entries provide a portrayal of the artist as a dying man, and his journals seem to be priceless artworks in comparison to his bottles or his seldom-painted self-portraits. The changes in Giorgio's life are indicated through the glimpses his journals provide into his childhood, his marriage, and his writing career. The journals ramble through these reminiscences in no particular order, but they are able to share the development of the subject matter that drives his life, the reasons for his subjects' evolution, his perception of his life, and his anticipation of death.

Peter's chapters focus less directly on death. He is also less dynamic than Signor Giorgio, so views of his life allow readers a moment of retrospect. As his section commences, Peter is in the middle of his life. He is loud, rude, and inventive. He does not care what others think of him or his lifestyle, which includes drinking excessively and smoking marijuana on a regular basis. His children are almost grown and have moved beyond needing or revering him as they did when they were young. Susan is impatient with him, and Susan's twin brother Danny has imitated their father's drug use since the beginning of his teens.

Peter's story begins as he goes on a jaunt to prepare to paint a new landscape. Ironically, he is literally trapped in that landscape when a rockslide pins his leg and holds him in its grip for an afternoon and a night. While he waits to be rescued, he reflects without regret on what some would consider a life of debauchery. He reflects also on his children, who call him Wilse, and his second wife and the mother of his children, Lydia. Though not even close to death, Peter dwells on morbid thoughts that he will never be found. His vivid remembrances of the corpselike body of his first wife at the end of their marriage, their drug use, their sexual exploits, and her death as a result of a drug addiction connect him further to Cennini's lesson.

Susan's chapters are about her twin brother Danny's death and how it has drastically altered her own being. Her first chapter ends with the words: "The nub, the crux, the heart of the matter is this: Danny died a month and a half ago. You've lived six weeks, fourteen days, and several minutes longer than he." Having been ripped out of an "ulterior proximity" with Danny, Susan does not know how to move on. As a result, with his death, she has stopped experiencing life. The only thing that makes her feel alive is an illicit relationship with her best friend and coworker's husband, Tom. The sexual meetings between the two allow her brief outlets from her grief.

In reflection of Susan's own artistic medium of photography, in Susan's chapters Hall provides brief descriptions reminiscent of snapshots of the woman's relationship with her brother, her parents, her live-in boyfriend Nathan, and Tom. Susan's memories provide often disturbing portraits of herself, Peter, and Danny. It is through Susan's eyes that the repercussions of death are most vividly presented. She must learn to become an individual rather than a part of an almost conjoined duo. Susan's change is most evident in the last words of the novel, "'Yes,' you say, 'I'm here.'" These words force Susan to admit that she must go on without Danny.

Perhaps the novel's most disturbing narrative is that of Annette Tambroni. Annette is a young teen living in Italy with her mother, two brothers, and uncle. Though she has been cursed with a vision problem from childhood, Annette has the opportunity to be tutored by Signor Giorgio, who comes to her school to train the children in art. Giorgio finds an apt pupil in Annette and compliments her use of color and detail, taking the time to encourage her abilities despite her visual limitations. When Annette's vision fails completely, her mother withdraws her from school, and a few years later her only connection to Giorgio comes as she tends his grave on Sundays after she tends the grave of her father.

Annette's life is limited by her disability. However, her restrictions are most often the result of her mother's overbearing behavior. Rosaria Tambroni lives a life of religious confinement. After her husband's mysterious murder, Rosaria has stopped allowing herself to find enjoyment in life. Instead, she turns to her faith and spends her days fretting over all the horrible things that could happen to Annette, never truly keeping Annette from harm. Rosario's religious fervor frightens her daughter, leading Annette to picture the Bestia (a variation of Satan as portrayed in a painting located in her church) in every unknown corner. Annette's weekly attentions to the dead men in her life place her in danger's path, and in her last segment of the novel, she is raped in the cemetery. During the rape, she dwells on the idea that it is the Bestia rather than a human man who is defiling her. The sketch of Annette's life ends with an immaculate vision of the world moving on without her.

Hall's stunning glimpses into life and death are presented through brief chapters that center on individual characters. The book begins with Susan's story in chapters titled "The Mirror Crisis." Susan's chapters are all told in the second person, so Susan herself is told what her story has been and becomes. These chapters are presumably set in the early twenty-first century. Following Susan's crisis, Hall introduces Signor

Giorgio's journal entries in chapters called "Translated from the Bottle Journals." Set fifty years before Susan's chapters, Giorgio's entries chronicle the final days of his life and are told in his own voice in the first person. Peter's chapters are designated "The Fool on the Hill," and Annette's are called "The Divine Vision of Annette Tambroni." Peter's and Annette's stories are presented from a limited omniscient point of view. The book jumps from character to character and time to time in no clear order, as Giorgio and Annette's experiences are limited to the 1960's, Peter's (outside his memories of the 1960's) to a vague time in the late twentieth century, and Susan's to the early twenty-first century. The lack of continuity, though disruptive and disturbing at times, creates a stream-of-consciousness feeling to the novel.

Theresa L. Stowell

Review Sources

The Daily Telegraph (London), June 6, 2009, p. 24.
The Financial Times, June 13, 2009, p. 16.
The Guardian (London), June 6, 2009, p. 14.
Kirkus Reviews 77, no. 17 (September 1, 2009): 908.
The New York Times Book Review, September 27, 2009, p. 26.
Publishers Weekly 256, no. 30 (July 27, 2009): 40.
The Times (London), June 6, 2009, p. 12.
The Times Literary Supplement, June 5, 2009, p. 20.

THE HUMBLING

Author: Philip Roth (1933-)
Publisher: Houghton Mifflin Harcourt (New York).
140 pp. $22.00
Type of work: Novella
Time: The early twenty-first century
Locale: Upstate New York

An account of the last days of Simon Axler, a sixty-five year-old actor who loses his "magic," desperately seeks happiness with a younger woman, and ultimately fails to find a reason to keep living

Principal characters:
SIMON AXLER, the last of the great American classical actors
PEGEEN MIKE STAPLEFORD, his lover, the forty-year-old daughter of Axler's friends
ASA and CAROL STAPLEFORD, Pegeen's parents
JERRY OPPENHEIM, Axler's agent
SYBIL VAN BUREN, a distraught mother Axler meets at Hammerton Hospital

Philip Roth's late fiction has treated subjects including heart attacks, chronic back pain, prostate cancer, brain tumors, memory loss, dementia, impotence, incontinence, depression, suicide, the devastation caused by the loss of loved ones, and the constant awareness of one's own mortality. Such topics are likely to make readers every bit as uncomfortable as did the writer's infamous earlier forays into the secret places of male desire. Beginning with *The Facts: A Novelist's Autobiography* (1988), and most notably in *Patrimony: A True Story* (1991), *Sabbath's Theater* (1995), *The Dying Animal* (2001), *Everyman* (2006), and *Exit Ghost* (2007), Roth has sought to look at illness, aging, and death with the same refusal to blink or be polite that he has brought to his treatment of sexuality since *Portnoy's Complaint* (1969). In his seventies, he has also been writing at a tremendous pace, publishing a book a year and favoring the form of the novella. In these later works, comedy has been replaced by sobriety and desperation, and the change both in subject and in tone has been startling to his longtime readers.

Roth's latest novella, *The Humbling*, tells the story of Simon Axler. For forty years, Axler has been one of the most distinguished classical actors of the American stage, playing the major roles of playwrights such as William Shakespeare, Henrik Ibsen, Anton Chekhov, John Millington Synge, and others to wide acclaim. Then, one day, he suddenly loses "the magic." Performing as Prospero and Macbeth in a double bill of Shakespeare's *The Tempest* (pr. 1611, pb. 1623) and *Macbeth* (pr. 1606, pb. 1623) at the Kennedy Center, Axler forgets everything he has ever known, is widely panned, and becomes convinced that his talent is dead. He can no longer act.

Axler does not know how or why this has happened, and he suffers a "colossal" breakdown as a result. He retreats to his country home in upstate New York, and while he is falling apart his wife leaves him. Since they have no children and his only close friend in the area has recently died of cancer, he finds himself totally alone. Axler also suffers from chronic spinal pain that has grown worse as he has aged. The condition makes one of his legs go dead intermittently, causing him to miss steps or curbs and fall.

Since the publication of Goodbye, Columbus *(1959), Philip Roth has been at the forefront of American fiction writers. Author of* Portnoy's Complaint *(1969) and* American Pastoral *(1997), he has won every award available to an American writer—most, several times.* The Humbling *is his thirtieth book.*

Soon, all the aging actor can think about is Prospero's lines, "Our revels now are ended. These our actors,/ As I foretold you, were all spirits and/ Are melted into air, into thin air." He constantly fantasizes about going up to the attic, loading the Remington 870 pump-action shotgun he keeps there, putting it in his mouth, and pulling the trigger. After spending an entire day in the attic with the shotgun in his hand, he checks himself into Hammerton Hospital. He spends twenty-six days there in individual, group, and art therapy. He listens to other patients who have attempted suicide talk excitedly about their attempts, and he becomes the confidant of Sybil Van Buren, a woman who tried to kill herself after realizing that her second husband had been abusing her little girl.

Finally, Axler decides "*Nothing* has a good reason for happening . . . You lose, you gain—it's all caprice. The omnipotence of caprice." He leaves the hospital and returns to his empty house. While his suicidal thoughts may have receded, however, his depression has not.

Axler's agent Jerry Oppenheim drives up from Manhattan to see him. He offers him the opportunity to play the part of James Tyrone in *Long Day's Journey into Night* (pr., pb. 1956) at the Guthrie Theater and tries to convince him that he can recover his art. Oppenheim recommends an acting coach who has helped other actors who have become blocked. "Play the moment," this coach tells his students; "play whatever plays for you in that moment, and then go on to the next moment." Axler refuses and, alone once again, decides that he should reread all the great plays in which characters commit suicide so "Nobody should be able to say that he did not think it through."

Instead, he ends up trying to "play the moment" in his life, rather than his art, with Pegeen Mike Stapleford, the daughter of fellow actors with whom he worked in a production of Synge's *The Playboy of the Western World* (pr., pb. 1907) when they were all just starting out in Greenwich Village. Carol Stapleford had played the female lead, Pegeen Mike Flaherty, and named the daughter she had shortly afterward for her character. Axler saw the baby when she was first born and occasionally over the succeeding years when her parents came by to visit him.

Now forty, a newly appointed professor of environmental studies at a nearby college, and a lesbian who recently suffered the traumatic breakup of a long-term relationship, Pegeen turns up at Axler's door one afternoon. Before the evening is through, they have slept together and begun an unlikely affair. Over the next thirteen months, in the face of her parents' opposition and their own spoken and unspoken doubts, they both try to transform their lives. Axler begins to hope again, thinking that they may marry and have a child. He hopes too that he can go to the acting coach, recover his art, and play Tyrone in Minneapolis.

In Pegeen's case, the refashioning is literal. In a sequence reminiscent of George Bernard Shaw's *Pygmalion* (pb. 1912, pr. 1914 in English, pr. 1913 in German), Axler buys her an expensive coat, and they are soon going to New York City together on a shopping spree for dresses, jewelry, lingerie, and boots. Then, she brings home fashion magazines to look at hairdos, and they go back to the city to get her a fashionable cut.

Pegeen describes their relationship to her mother as "an experiment," but she also says that she thinks they love each other—and she reports all this to Axler. He tells her that he is getting in too deep, that he is at serious risk of not being able to recover if things end for them, and that they should end things sooner rather than later. She replies that she is at risk too and that she does not want to give up what they have. Since this is what Axler wants to hear, he chooses not to question her further. Before long, however, she admits to cruising the college softball field and pool for pony-tailed blonds, and they begin to incorporate the fantasy of bringing one of them home into their sexual play.

The novella's last act begins when Axler finds a young woman at a restaurant bar and he and Pegeen bring her home for a ménage a trois. Shortly afterward, Peegen leaves him. He goes back to the attic, where the last role he finally manages to play is that of Konstantin Gavrilovich Treplev, the suicide in the final act of Chekhov's *Chayka* (pr. 1896; revised pr. 1898, pb. 1904; *The Seagull*, 1909).

It is hard not to wish that Axler had read some Philip Roth. Roth's description of his own serious depression in *The Facts* and *Operation Shylock: A Confession* (1993) might have helped his character see that another artist eventually overcame a very similar crisis. *The Dying Animal* and *Exit Ghost* could have reminded him of the most common end to older men's obsessions with younger women in Roth's fiction. *Letting Go* (1962), *Portnoy's Complaint*, *My Life as a Man* (1974), and *The Dying Animal* would all have shown him the dangers faced by Roth heroes who play the role of Professor Henry Higgins in a love affair. Both *Portnoy's Complaint* and *The Professor of Desire* would have warned him that, in Roth's fiction at least, realizing the fantasy of a ménage a trois inevitably leads to disaster.

To put it another way, Roth's readers have seen much of the "love story" in this book before. Admittedly, making the younger woman a lesbian this time is a new twist. It is not, however, a very effective or believable one, and Roth makes Pegeen little more than the embodiment of the worst stereotyped clichés of lesbians: She only needs the right man to make her switch orientation, she cruises for blonds, she uses sex toys, and she desires the ménage a trois. This portrayal is hard to excuse or dismiss. (It is not surprising that the sex scenes in the novel earned it a place on the shortlist for the London *Literary Review*'s Bad Sex in Fiction Award in 2009.)

In 2004, Roth told an interviewer from *The Times* of London that writing was the center of his life, and he said, "If it were taken away from me I think I would die." Imagining this prospect seems to be the original impulse behind *The Humbling*. Simon Axler feels the same way about his art, and when the novel is treating the depression he faces at the loss of his life's work, it seems most deeply felt. The other impulse that explains Axler's behavior in the book is expressed in David Kepesh's defense of his obsession with Consuela Castillo in *The Dying Animal*:

> No matter how much you know, no matter how much you think, no matter how much you plot and you connive and you plan, you're not superior to sex. . . . It's a very risky game. . . . what do you do if you're sixty-two and believe you'll never have a claim on something so perfect again? What do you do if you're sixty-two and the urge to take whatever is still takable couldn't be stronger? . . . What do you do if you're sixty-two and you realize that all those bodily parts invisible up till now . . . are about to start making themselves distressingly apparent, while the organ most conspicuous throughout your life is doomed to dwindle into insignificance?

Roth has described *The Humbling* as the third in a quartet of novellas that also includes *Everyman*, *Indignation* (2008), and *Nemesis* (projected to appear in 2010). Of the first three, *Everyman* remains the most carefully wrought and satisfying treatment of the last things that are on its author's mind. None of these works has dealt with these last things as powerfully as *Patrimony*, his memoir of his father's illness and death, or *Sabbath's Theater*. In retrospect, *Sabbath's Theater* looms increasingly as the definitive expression of ideas and themes that Roth has continued to pursue in many of his books since. Although each has its moments, the novellas written in his somber mode sometimes feel as if their author has one hand tied behind his back. *Sabbath's Theater* suggests that, like Dylan Thomas, when it comes to death and dying Roth is most his inimitable self when he and his characters "do not go gentle into that good night," but instead "burn and rave at close of day;/ Rage, rage against the dying of the light." Axler mainly whimpers.

Bernard F. Rodgers, Jr.

Review Sources

Booklist 106, no. 6 (November 15, 2009): 3.
Commentary 129, no. 1 (January, 2010): 54-56.
The Economist 393, no. 8657 (November 14, 2009): 103.
Kirkus Reviews 77, no. 20 (October 15, 2009): 49.
Library Journal 134, no. 14 (September 1, 2009): 109.

New Statesman 138, no. 4973 (November 2, 2009): 50-51.
The New York Review of Books 56, no. 19 (December 3, 2009): 6-8.
The New York Times, October 23, 2009, p. C23.
The New York Times Book Review, November 15, 2009, p. 11.
The New Yorker 85, no. 35 (November 2, 2009): 109.
Publishers Weekly 256, no. 32 (August 10, 2009): 32.
The Spectator 311, no. 9455 (November 14, 2009): 46-47.
The Times Literary Supplement, November 6, 2009, p. 20.
The Wall Street Journal, October 30, 2009, p. W5.

IMPORTANT ARTIFACTS AND PERSONAL PROPERTY FROM THE COLLECTION OF LENORE DOOLAN AND HAROLD MORRIS
Including Books, Street Fashion, and Jewelry

Author: Leanne Shapton
Publisher: Farrar, Straus and Giroux (New York).
129 pp. $18.00
Type of work: Novel

Illustrator, writer, and photographer Shapton's innovative second novel traces the arc of a love affair through the device of an auction catalogue

Principal characters:
LENORE DOOLAN, a columnist for *The New York Times*
HAROLD MORRIS, a photographer

In her first novel, *Was She Pretty?* (2006), Leanne Shapton broke stylistic ground when she chose to build her story through line drawings of each of her characters, mostly former lovers of the protagonists, accompanied with very brief textual descriptions. Her second novel, *Important Artifacts and Personal Property from the Collection of Lenore Doolan and Harold Morris: Including Books, Street Fashion, and Jewelry* is even more innovative. In this novel, Shapton draws on her talents as an illustrator, designer, photographer, and writer to create a very realistic, but wholly fictional auction catalog that details the remnants of a love affair gone wrong.

The book is more easily read than described. Each page presents numbered photographs and lot descriptions of important artifacts in the lives of the two main characters, Lenore Doolan and Harold Morris. The premise of the novel is that these items are to be auctioned off by the fictional auction house Strachan & Quinn on February 14, 2009, at 10:00 A.M. and 2:00 P.M. A reader's task is to examine the photos, read the lot descriptions, and glean the story of the couple's four-year romance through the cryptic text and images.

The lots are organized chronologically, so it is possible to trace the arc of the romance from beginning to end. For example, the opening page contains a photograph of Doolan as Lot 1001; the catalog description of the photo reveals that Doolan is twenty-six years old and works for *The New York Times*. The photo also shows Doolan as a waiflike, very thin, and very young-looking woman. Likewise, on the same page, listed as Lot 1002, is a passport photo of Morris. The text relates that he is thirty-nine years old and a photographer who has assignments worldwide. The photos illustrate the age difference between the pair far more starkly than the text is able to. Moreover, the fact that the photograph of Morris is from his passport suggests that Morris is not someone who stays in any one place very long. These two key details—

Leanne Shapton is a Toronto-born illustrator, writer, and publisher who lives and works in New York City. She is the art director of The New York Times *op-ed page and the author of* Was She Pretty? *(2006).*

the respective ages and careers of the couple—play mightily in both the initial attraction and the eventual breakup of the couple.

The first several pages also present photographs of the couple at their first meeting, a Halloween party given by friends. Doolan is dressed as an ax-wielding, bloody Lizzie Borden, and Morris appears as Harry Houdini. On first reading, these photos graphically display the electric attraction between the pair. By the end of the book, however, it is possible to return to these pictures and view them ironically. Doolan, as the lot numbers move chronologically forward, reveals herself to be prone to fits of temper: She breaks Morris's favorite coffee mug (Lot 1232), she screams and yells at Morris (documented by a note from Morris in Lot 1246), and during a fight she throws a backgammon game in the fire (also illustrated by Lot 1246). Morris, on the other hand, becomes, like Houdini, an escape artist, using his job to put both emotional and physical space between himself and Doolan.

Indeed, it becomes clear early in the book that the relationship is in trouble. By Lot 1060, Doolan is already receiving an e-mail from an old boyfriend, and in Lot 1063, the couple is apologizing for a fight. Lots 1070 through 1085 include artifacts from the couple's first trip abroad together, including postcards, notes, photographs, the contents of their traveling cases, "Beware of Dog" signs in Italian, novels, and Italian phrase books. There is also embedded in these sections a note from Doolan to her sister describing a fight with Morris, as well as notes about how much Morris is drinking.

The lots containing artifacts of the trip to Italy reveal many of the essential qualities of each character. Doolan seems uncomfortable with travel and inflexible in many ways. She appears uneasy when she is unable to control circumstances. Morris, on the other hand, is used to traveling alone. He fits easily into other cultures and does not seem at all bothered by petty or small inconveniences. He does, however, display impatience with Doolan's need for control. Given Morris's career and his need to travel constantly, the couple's inability to travel well together seems to doom their relationship early on.

In all, there are more than three hundred lots in the catalog, assembled by a fictional curator. Each lot's contents are detailed in the curator's coldly accurate voice, a voice that stops far short of revealing to readers what they should make of the item or items composing the lot. At the same time, the juxtapositions of those items with related letters and notes reveals a good deal not only about Doolan and Morris but also about the curator. For example, the curator's decision to introduce the catalog with a note from Morris to Doolan written after their breakup and suggesting that they see each other again is fraught with significance. The note can be read in several different ways: It is a neat way to alert readers that the relationship portrayed through the catalog has deteriorated. It can also be read as an ironic recrimination against Morris, who is once again needing to "take a break" from his current woman friend. Alternatively, it can be read without irony, as a heartfelt message from Morris about his sorrow over the demise of his relationship with Doolan. The manner in which a reader chooses to interpret the note will influence the way that reader approaches the rest of the book. Additionally, the inclusion of the note reveals that the curator seems unable to let the affair end with the auction.

While the device of the catalog is ingenious, the book's underlying plot is not: The two characters meet, fall in love, discover each other's faults, and break up. The format of the novel requires the plot to be kept simple, so readers will be able to infer that plot from the illustrations and descriptive text. However, a more richly textured novel might have emerged from the author's conceit had not the situation of the story been so predictable.

Moreover, the characterizations of Morris and Doolan are not subtle and, at their least successful, are stereotypical. Doolan behaves in exactly the ways one would expect a young, clever, insecure ingenue to act in a relationship in which she perhaps feels somewhat out of her depth. Morris behaves in exactly the ways that film and literature have trained audiences to expect of an older, globetrotting photojournalist. In other words, each behaves according to type. While there is some benefit in meeting the horizon of audience expectation in such an innovative format, one could hope for some interesting variations on the types, variations that would add depth to the characters and make them seem less flat than the photographs that picture them.

That said, the novel does provide a few surprises. Doolan has a darker side, one that is only evident through careful reading. Shapton has given this character many of the qualities and habits of a woman with a serious eating disorder. Doolan is painfully thin in the photos, and the sizes and the styles of her clothing also reveal her size. Her column for *The New York Times* is devoted exclusively to recipes for and discussions about cake, a food that an anorexic would be likely to deny herself but would prepare for others. Homemade gifts from the couple, such as that illustrated by six jars of strawberry jam in Lot 1177, nearly always take the form of food. Finally, amid the many shopping lists kept by Doolan are lists of the food Doolan consumes each day. This is the behavior of a chronic dieter and, in the case of pencil-slim Doolan, a warning flag. Taken together, the clues imply a worrisome obsession with issues of food and control.

As for Morris, it is tempting to see him only as emotionally distant and noncommittal to the relationship. However, Shapton is careful to provide qualities that problematize that reading. For example, several of the lots include information about Morris's sessions with his therapist, in which he tries to work through emotional problems having to do with the relationship. It would appear, contrary to type, that Morris genuinely loves Doolan and wants the relationship to succeed.

Perhaps two of the most revealing pages are those portraying the final lots. Lot 1331 is a group of dried flowers, kept and pressed by Morris. Lot 1332 is a group of pressed four-leaf clovers belonging to Doolan. Morris, it appears, has an uncharacteristically sentimental side; he chooses to keep mementos of important times and events with Doolan, specific occasions that have value for him, suggesting that he remembers well time they spent together. Doolan, on the other hand, saves only four-leaf clovers, not identifiable by event but only by their purpose, to bring good luck. Not satisfied with the relationship as it exists, she continues to wish for an idealized, romantic affair wherein she is adored, understood, and has her needs met.

Despite some plot and characterization shortcomings, *Important Artifacts and Personal Property from the Collection of Lenore Doolan and Harold Morris* is a visual and conceptual delight. Shapton has stated in several interviews that her inspiration for the novel came from her own reading of the 2006 auction catalog of author Truman Capote's personal belongings. She discerned from that catalog the bare outlines of a life and felt that she could use the catalog form as a narrative device. Many of the artifacts photographed for the book are Shapton's own, including a collection of brassieres and other articles of clothing. Other items are from garage sales and second-hand stores. For her main characters, she called on her friends Sheila Heti (a fiction writer herself) and Paul Sahre (a graphic designer) to pose for the pictures of Doolan and Morris. It is striking how well these two individuals capture and advance the characterizations provided by the artifacts and descriptions.

Important Artifacts and Personal Property from the Collection of Lenore Doolan and Harold Morris is a book worthy of rereading and will likely encourage new interpretations with each perusal. Indeed, rereading might be a requirement for the novel, since it is so tempting to rush through the book the first time, glancing at pictures and skimming the text just to see how and why the couple falls in love and then how and why they part. Later, more leisurely readings reveal nuances in the text and the illustrations that could easily be overlooked but that provide readers with both surprise and satisfaction.

Diane Andrews Henningfeld

Review Sources

ARTnews 108, no. 6 (June, 2009): 32.
Harper's Magazine 318, no. 1908 (May, 2009): 78.
Maclean's 122, no. 12 (April 6, 2009): 52-53.
The New York Times, February 5, 2009, p. C1.
The New York Times, February 8, 2009, p. L10.
Print 63, no. 2 (April, 2009): 95.
The Spectator 311, no. 9458 (December 5, 2009): 37.
The Virginia Quarterly Review 85, no. 3 (Summer, 2009): 207-211.

IN OTHER ROOMS, OTHER WONDERS

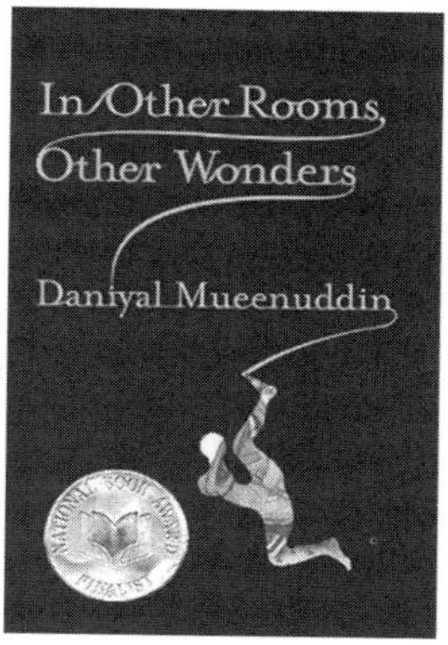

Author: Daniyal Mueenuddin (1963-)
Publisher: W. W. Norton (New York). 247 pp. $23.95
Type of work: Short fiction
Time: 1970's to the early twenty-first century
Locale: Southern Punjab, Pakistan

Mueenuddin's debut collection of short stories, which was a finalist for the 2010 Pulitzer Prize in fiction, presents an intimate view of modern Pakistani life in a postfeudal society

Principal characters:
K. K. HAROUNI, a Punjabi farmer
BEGUM HAROUNI, his estranged wife
SOHAIL HAROUNI, a relative
HELEN, his girlfriend
NAWABDIN (NAWAB), a handyman and electrician
HUSNA, Begum Harouni's attendant
CHAUDREY JAGLANI, the Harounis' estate manager
SALEEMA, one of the Harounis' servants
LILY, a young woman from Lahore
MURAD, her husband

Daniyal Mueenuddin, the son of a Pakistani father and an American mother, grew up in Pakistan and Wisconsin, graduated from Dartmouth and Yale, and has practiced corporate law in New York. His first book, *In Other Rooms, Other Wonders*, is set in the Punjab region, where he wrote it while living on the family farm that he oversees and that served as a model for the fictional farm of K. K. Harouni. The eight interconnected stories of the collection depict ordinary Pakistanis of all classes. K. K., a retired civil servant and a still-wealthy member of a fading Pakistani aristocracy, serves as a unifying figure for the stories, which focus on those who surround him: his family, colleagues, and servants.

In the lead story, "Nawabdin Electrician" (2008), K. K. is the patron of a likable mechanic and general handyman whose house has "running water in all three rooms." As the father of twelve daughters and one son, Nawab thoroughly enjoys his family, hiding coveted lumps of brown sugar in his vest to surprise and delight them. In addition, he carries on numerous private enterprises to augment his meager wages and prepare for his daughters' dowries. Nawab maintains the tube wells that irrigate his employer's sugarcane, cotton, and mango fields. He also knows how to adjust electricity meters to save his poorer clients money. He is benignly dishonest—a sort of Pakistani Robin Hood.

Traveling from job to job on a rickety bicycle, Nawab wants to ask K. K. for a motorcycle to make his life a little easier. Instead, he slyly complains of his tired old

Daniyal Mueenuddin has a J.D. from Yale and an M.F.A. from the University of Arizona. A Fulbright scholar, his stories have appeared in The New Yorker, Granta, Zoetrope, *and* The Best American Short Stories, 2008.

legs and begs his employer for release, fully aware that K. K. does not want to lose him. His strategy works, but the coveted motorcycle soon brings him misfortune, and then even Nawabdin, a good man, can summon no compassion for the person who ultimately confronts him. After reading this story when it was originally published in *The New Yorker*, British Indian author Salman Rushdie was so impressed that he included it in *The Best American Short Stories, 2008.*

More than one critic has observed that Pakistani writers typically focus on the massive social changes taking place in their world, and this is certainly true of Mueenuddin, as the lives of his characters illustrate. Change is an underlying theme in all the stories, as Pakistan undergoes a transformation. This is seen in the diminishing wealth and influence of the old landed aristocratic families, such as the Harounis, who are selling off their land to raise money, and the increasing prominence and power of the new industrialists. English has become the favored language of the social elite, some of whom take pride in knowing neither Urdu (the official Pakistani language) nor the regional language of Punjabi.

Change marks the contrast between the lives of rich and poor, as well as the difficulties of those who attempt to bridge that gap. In the title story, young Husna, neither privileged nor abjectly poor, has "refused to accept her present status," having "neither talent nor beauty." Originally, her ancestors were quite wealthy, but they gradually lost their money, and she longs to rise socioeconomically. At present, she attends to K. K.'s estranged wife Begum Harouni, who lives apart from her husband. Remotely related to K. K., Husna seeks his assistance in finding a teaching position, but, because she refuses to marry, he advises her to learn a skill instead. His secretary will teach her to type.

Seven years ago, K. K. suffered a heart attack; now, he walks daily, inviting Husna to walk with him as a companion. He is alone; his married daughters have their lives elsewhere. Husna, feeling that she deserves K. K.'s world, struggles with ambition and ambivalence. Because she reminds him of his youth, she knows she could become his mistress, although the begum will be jealous of any attention she receives.

When the begum decides to go on a pilgrimage to Mecca without her, Husna complains to K. K. He, who is rather removed from life and avoids unpleasantness, invites her to stay at his home in Lahore, the Punjabi capital, while the begum is gone. She will have her own apartment in the annex. Thus, Husna joins K. K.'s household. Although a virgin, she ultimately decides to seduce K. K., thereby altering her own future. He is lonely and fears imminent death, but she learns to handle him well and gradually grows to feel real affection for him.

Some of K. K.'s elderly friends accept Husna, while the servants recognize that she has influence and treat her more respectfully. After K. K. is stricken in the middle of the night and taken to the hospital, his doctor instructs Husna to stay at the house rather than accompany him. When K. K.'s class-conscious daughters arrive, they immediately banish her to the annex, treating her as a servant, and after he dies, she is curtly dismissed.

Just as the Harouni daughters reveal their lack of understanding and utter indifference to what Husna has lost, young Sohail Harouni, another wealthy relative, demonstrates his own lack of sensitivity. He does not wish to provide electricity to an elderly watchman's hut on his property, responding to the suggestion with "Are you kidding? . . . These guys don't get bored." There seems to be no way to bridge the real gulf between the classes.

Unfortunately, the traditional culture of corruption remains in Mueenuddin's Pakistan. Chaudrey Jaglani, K. K.'s estate manager, sells his employer's land as ordered but buys the best parcels for himself, secretly enriching himself at K. K.'s expense. In "About a Burning Girl," both a mystery and an illustration of practical politics, much ado is made about the difficulty of rescuing a favorite servant from the police after he is accused of setting his brother's wife on fire. The cynical judge who narrates this story has been asked to intercede, primarily because of his wife's complaints that finding a good servant is "impossible." New evidence and appropriate bribes are created in order to free the accused man. As the judge well knows, "In Pakistan all things can be arranged." Ironically, no one mourns for the dead woman.

Mueenuddin's treatment of his female characters often involves telling a story from a female perspective, as he does with Husna. His insights are impressive, especially in the midst of a hierarchical, male-centered culture. Poor women, such as the nameless burn victim, are essentially powerless in this society. Wealthy women, like the judge's wife, may have limited control within their households but are still at the mercy of their husbands or fathers. Although one critic suggests that these women are able to use sex as a weapon to get what they want, any power they may acquire is temporary, as the stories confirm.

Saleema has the hardest life. Descended from a clan of unsavory characters, she is the daughter of a promiscuous mother and a father fatally addicted to heroin. At fourteen, she is already being abused by men. A new husband brings her to Lahore, where he becomes addicted to amphetamines. Ultimately, Saleema becomes a servant in K. K.'s wealthy rural home, where her drugged husband shares her room while she sleeps with the cook for extra food. When the cook grows tired of her, she seeks another protector and attaches herself to Rafik, K. K.'s kindly old manservant. He is married, but his wife has always lived elsewhere.

Saleema has a son with Rafik, who loves her and the baby. Rafik confesses the affair to his wife and eventually separates from Saleema out of guilt, although he continues to give her money. After K. K. dies, his household disintegrates. Saleema loses her job, begins to use drugs, and is reduced to begging in the streets with her child.

Mueenuddin demonstrates that more fortunate Pakistani women also face obstacles, although perhaps not as grave. "Our Lady of Paris" explores a different conflict of culture and class, as Sohail Harouni, like many of the collection's characters, reappears in an earlier phase of his life. Having earned his law degree at Yale, he has returned to Karachi and his wealthy parents to follow in his father's footsteps and to wait for Helen, the American student he is dating, to complete her final year. Helen, whose single mother works as a secretary, hopes to study medicine. The young couple has planned to meet in Paris for the Christmas holidays, but Sohail's redoubtable mother announces that his parents will be there too. He is not pleased.

The narrative viewpoint shifts to Helen, as she prepares for the dinner in Paris where she will meet Sohail's parents. She feels intimidated, deliberately shut off from Sohail and his mother, particularly as they attend the ballet without her. Wisely, the young people manage to arrange a brief idyll without the parents, but Helen begins to recognize that their lives and goals are incompatible. Seen mostly through Helen's eyes, this is a love story gone wrong.

Lily proves a dramatic exception to the other women of *In Other Rooms, Other Words*. The daughter of formerly wealthy parents in Lahore, she lives a wild, excessive lifestyle filled with alcohol and parties, even as her parents can scarcely maintain their social position. When a serious automobile accident hospitalizes her with a concussion, Lily dreams of parachuting from a flaming jet plane. She views this dream as a symbolic escape from her previous dissolute life—an escape for which a part of her longs.

Despite her dream, Lily relies on champagne to help her feel comfortable at an evening party hosted by a flamboyant friend who has imported enough sand to create a fake beach. At the party, she encounters a man she has seen before but does not remember—the young businessman and Punjabi farmer Murad Talwan, who has begun growing vegetables in greenhouses (as does Mueenuddin himself) in order to bring them to market earlier than his competitors. The previous year, Murad, while grieving the recent death of his mother, noticed Lily at a gathering and was impressed by his idealized vision of her beside the pool. Now, they are attracted to each other: She is lost, and he has been lost.

In time, Murad drives Lily to a place where the Kabul and Indus rivers meet: brown and blue streams side by side, not yet joined, foreshadowing their lives together. Then, he stays the night with Lily (chastely, at his request). In four months, they marry, but there seems to be no real union of these two people; they remain separate even after marriage. She is impulsive; he is deliberate.

Lily insists on honeymooning at the farm where they will live, rather than going abroad. While Murad feels respect and love for his land and for the people who work it, she becomes bored with the quiet life of the farm and realizes that she does not wish to become pregnant. Unable to accept the changes she thought she wanted, Lily soon invites her friends to the farm for a weekend party, and once in their presence she returns to the life that she rejected. While Murad politely avoids the rowdy visitors, Lily drinks heavily and is unfaithful to him. Secretly reading her husband's private journal, she discovers that he loathes her parties yet is determined to work on their marriage: She must make a decision. The author does not judge this woman but reveals her desperate confusion.

Mueenuddin, who prefers to write in English, is also fluent in Urdu and Punjabi. His style is intimate yet dispassionate, his descriptions terse but sharp, as when he says a servant's "leathery glum face made him look as if he had been pickled in gin." Subtly inserting custom and color into his stories, he is careful to convey the meaning of unfamiliar terms by their context, frequently using local idioms. For example, Nawabdin greets his wife with, "Hello, my love, my chicken piece." With regard to K. K.'s dishonest servants, the valet Rafik complains to Saleema that his employer "made these people—the fathers ate his salt, and now the sons have forgotten and are eating everything else." In a frequently harsh world, Daniyal Mueenuddin's practiced eye sees into the hearts of his characters with empathy and understanding.

Joanne McCarthy

Review Sources

Booklist 105, no. 9/10 (January 1-15, 2009): 46.
The Economist 390, no. 8619 (February 21, 2009): 85.
Kirkus Reviews 76, no. 23 (December 1, 2008): 1223
London Review of Books 31, no. 14 (July 23, 2009): 27-28.
The New York Review of Books 56, no. 17 (November 5, 2009): 39-40.
The New York Times Book Review, February 8, 2009, p. 16.
Publishers Weekly 255, no. 46 (November 17, 2008): 37-38.
The Spectator 310, no. 9429 (May 16, 2009): 36.
Time 173, no. 5 (February 9, 2009): 56.
The Times Literary Supplement, April 17, 2009, p. 21.
The Wall Street Journal, February 3, 2009, p. W2.
The Washington Post, February 15, 2009, p. BW10.
World Literature Today 83, no. 4 (July/August, 2009): 68.

IN SUCH HARD TIMES
The Poetry of Wei Ying-wu

Author: Wei Ying-wu (737-791)
First published: Wei suchou chi, 1056, in China
Translated from the Chinese by Red Pine (pen name of Bill Porter)
Preface, notes, and photographs by Red Pine; map by Molly O'Halloran
Publisher: Copper Canyon Press (Port Townsend, Washington). 368 pp. $18.00
Type of work: Poetry

This collection of 175 poems finally translates into English about one-third of Wei Ying-wu's surviving poetry, whose unobtrusive beauty earned it very high esteem in imperial China

In Such Hard Times finally makes available in English the acclaimed poetry of China's celebrated Tang dynasty poet Wei Ying-wu. The excellent translation by Red Pine (the pseudonym of Bill Porter) renders Wei's classic poetry from the eighth century in a carefully chosen language that fully echoes its direct, unobtrusive beauty. It is very accessible to contemporary English-language readers.

In Such Hard Times draws its title from the fourth and last line of its first poem, "The Ninth," which was written in the fall of 756 when Wei was just nineteen years old. "On this day of drink and depression" (the ninth day of the ninth month according to the Chinese calendar, roughly corresponding to late October), the autobiographical persona reflects on the violent end of his sheltered aristocratic youth at the imperial court. This abrupt change was brought on by the An Lushan Rebellion's threat to imperial rule. The Tang dynasty was challenged by a variety of internal rebellions throughout the rest of the poet's life, and Wei's poetry often alludes not only to personal hardship but also to that of the Chinese people of the period. At the end of "The Ninth," the persona sadly muses that "in such hard times I can't hope to go home." Many of Wei's poems have a slightly melancholic undertone born from the hardships he witnessed as an age of turbulence displaced the previous period of splendor and tranquillity.

Red Pine presents "The Ninth" in the same successful format that he uses for all of the 175 poems he has chosen out of Wei's 592 surviving ones. Each poem is given a consecutive number and is printed both in English and in its Chinese original, with the Chinese characters typeset by Pristine Communications of Taipei, Taiwan. This allows a Chinese speaker or student of Chinese to compare the texts. In addition, Red Pine's annotations provide substantial background information and analysis for each poem.

Readers will quickly realize that many of Wei's most evocative poems are personally addressed to friends, family members, or colleagues. Indicative of the time in which he wrote, all addressees of his poems are male. Standing out among them is Ts'ui Cho, who married Wei's cousin and with whom the poet frequently corresponded. The two men shared a deep friendship despite long physical separation. Thus, in "Alone at Night at My Monastic Residence: To Secretary Ts'ui" (poem 68), Wei confesses: "I didn't realize the year was so late/ or living apart was so lonely." In poem 125, Ts'ui is described as "Man of my heart standing alone/ beyond Ch'in Pass so far away." Poetry here becomes a means to bridge geographical distance.

Wei Ying-wu was an aristocratic imperial official in China during the Tang dynasty. His poetry was collected after his death in 791 by friends and admirers, and the earliest identifiable resulting collection was published in 1056. Prior to In Such Hard Times, *only a handful of Wei's poems were translated into English.*

Another favorite recipient of Wei's poems was his friend, mentor, and protector Li Huan. When Wei ran afoul of the shifting allegiances at the embattled imperial court, Li Huan secured a good official position for Wei. In consequence, Wei's poems express admiration for his friend. In "On Li Wu-hsi Seeing Off Secretary Li to the Western Terrace" (poem 20), the location mentioned in Wei's title refers to the Imperial Censorate, as the translator informs readers in his note. In this elevated position, Wei writes of his friend that "he wanted to join the circling hawks" and will not forget "his junior-official friends" such as Wei himself. Indicative of the high risks involved at court, to which Wei's image of the hawks alludes, Li Huan was eventually charged with a crime and executed after the summer of 779. Some nine years later, in one of his last poems, Wei reflects with melancholy on a visit to the deserted home of the dead old friend in "Visiting Duke Shou-ch'un's Old Home in the Kaihua Quarter" (poem 157), "walking up the steps I felt the same respect/ but when I saw your seat my tears turned to sobs." Clear-mindedly, the persona of Wei realizes that the past is irrecoverable and "those days won't come again" in which they celebrated their cruelly terminated friendship.

In Such Hard Times effectively presents Wei's poems that deal with his greatest loss, the death of his beloved wife Yuan P'ing in the early fall of 776 at thirty-five. She left behind two daughters and an infant son. "Lamenting My Loss" (poem 52) is a powerful elegy that admits to personal pain and bereavement in moving words, "Like . . . wood that's now ash/ I recall the person I lived with/ gone and not coming back." "Grieving on the Way to Fuping" (poem 53) tells of the necessity to marshal the persona's strength and to carry on with his life for the sake of his children. "I hear our children crying/ but a father has to go forth/ even when there's no mother at home." The translator includes a photo of the stone epitaph Wei Ying-wu inscribed for his wife, the only known example of the poet's own handwriting. This highlights how much Wei treasured his wife, an attitude not common during his time. Ten years later, Wei's poem "Leaving Putang Post Station . . . " (poem 145) sums up his feelings as widower when "my marriage and first post are a dream. . . . A high official's life isn't so grand." Despite Wei's proven love for his wife, there does not exist a single known poem addressed to her, indicative again of the patriarchal feudal culture in which he lived.

Wei's early poems to friends such as Yuan Ta, a relative often referred to by his official title of Censor Yuan, show Wei's lifelong disillusionment with public service. In "After Waiting for Censor Yuan . . . " (poem 33), the persona ruefully remarks that "The glory of office comes with its burdens." This sentiment of disenchantment coupled with a longing for a purely spiritual life becomes stronger in Wei's poetry as his life progresses. In "Visiting Master Shen on West Mountain" (poem 119), the persona praises a Buddhist monk effusively, stating with admiration that "you chased the tigers out of the forest/ meditating under the trees."

Similar admiration is expressed in Wei's poetry addressed to the Zen Buddhist teacher Heng Ts'an. In "Spending the Night in Yungyang: To Vinaya Master Ts'an" (poem 126), the persona expresses his delight at a nighttime visit by the revered teacher, "a mountain monk stopping to visit/ hanging up his lantern sleeping alone," as chastity was a trademark of Buddhist monks. By contrast, the widowed Wei is not above the occasional visit to a brothel, where, as in the poem "For Attendant Li Tan" (poem 106), "the fading flowers still welcomed my visit," a reference to the prostitutes in the establishment.

Translator Red Pine's selection of Wei's poems provides readers with a full range of examples of the poet's multifaceted attitudes toward his life. The poems addressed to a favorite cousin, Wei Tuan, show self-irony when the persona laments his fate. In "Returning East to Choukuei Village on Bathing Day: For Tuan" (poem 64), the persona states that he "no longer recognized the fields/ but since it was my day to bathe/ I traveled back to our village." Red Pine's valuable notes inform readers that imperial officials were given one day off after nine working days, and they often used it for a soaking bath. A similar lightheartedness of spirit is discernible in other poems such as "In Reply to Vice Director for Ceremonials Yang" (poem 116), where the persona admits that "filling out records is a waste." Even one of Wei's last poems, "Leaving Court After a Snowfall . . ." (poem 161) reveals a playful mood among the government officials who amuse themselves as schoolboys would, as "at Penglai Palace we shook the pine branches" to make the snow covering them fall down.

Wei's poem upon the marriage of his older daughter to his friend Yang Ling in 783 shows tremendous sincere paternal affection. Like his love for his wife, this was a sentiment not commonly revealed in Chinese courtly poetry. "Seeing Off My Daughter to the Yangs" (poem 117) reveals the depths of a father's love for his maturing child. "Such a long day is too painful," the persona begins, before refering to the extra burdens the death of her mother bestowed on the young girl: "you didn't have anyone to lean on/ nor their compassion or comfort/ you yourself raised your sister." The father acknowledges the inevitable, "this ties my heart in knots/ but I can't keep you from your rightful journey." It is poems such as this one that allow Wei Ying-wu to speak across the centuries to a contemporary reader.

Red Pine arranges Wei's poetry in chronological order of composition. This arrangement helps readers follow the development of Wei's poetry and emphasizes the links between the poems and key events in the poet's life, especially given that about one-third of Wei's poems are directly addressed to his friends, family members, and colleagues at work. The book is divided into four parts, with each part reflecting different way stations in the poet's geographically varied life.

The translator also has chosen to follow the traditional Asian order of family name before personal name, hence Wei Ying-wu instead of the Western form Ying-wu Wei. He also employs the traditional Asian calculation of age, by which babies are considered to be one year old when born. For this reason, a reader must deduct one year from all ages given in the poetry to arrive at the Western calculation.

Because Red Pine lived and worked in Taiwan and Hong Kong from 1972 to 1993, he uses the older Wade-Giles system for transliterating Chinese characters. On Taiwan, Wade-Giles is used instead of the internationally more common Pinyin system promoted by mainland China. Readers have to bear in mind, therefore, that personal and place names given *In Such Hard Times* may appear differently in other Chinese texts. For example, the poet Tu Fu and the eastern Tang capital of Loyang, are spelled Du Fu and Luoyang in Pinyin texts that readers might consult for more information on the poet or his subject matter.

Overall, *In Such Hard Times* offers a most welcome, long overdue translation of a significant and well-chosen body of the masterful and silently beautiful poems of Tang dynasty poet Wei Ying-wu. Wei's poems come to their true life in Red Pine's translation. They directly speak to a reader on such issues as finding the right path in life, dealing with the loss of a loved one, celebrating friendship, and the passage into adulthood of one's children. *In Such Hard Times* is a valuable anthology, with notes and a critical translator's preface that successfully place poet and poems in the context of their time. All of Wei's poems collected and translated in *In Such Hard Times* beautifully transcend the passage of centuries to powerfully reach a delighted contemporary reader.

R. C. Lutz

Review Source

Publishers Weekly 256, no. 24 (June 15, 2009): 46.

IN THE PRESIDENT'S SECRET SERVICE
Behind the Scenes with Agents in the Line of Fire and the Presidents They Protect

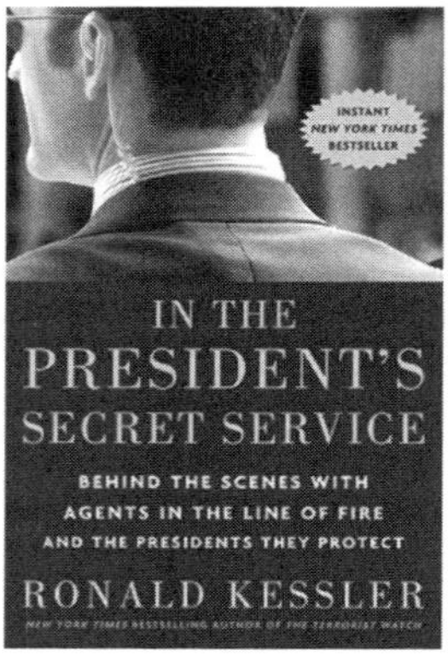

Author: Ronald Kessler (1943-   )
Publisher: Crown Books (New York). 273 pp. $26.00
Type of work: Current affairs, history
Time: 1960's to the early twenty-first century
Locale: United States

A critical and anecdotal examination of the protective mission of the U.S. Secret Service, with special attention to challenges that the agency faces because of inadequate funding

Principal personages:
John F. Kennedy (1917-1963), U.S. president, 1961-1963
Lyndon B. Johnson (1908-1973), U.S. president, 1963-1969
Richard M. Nixon (1913-1994), U.S. president, 1969-1974
Jimmy Carter (1924-   ), U.S. president, 1977-1981
Ronald Reagan (1911-2004), U.S. president, 1981-1989
George H. W. Bush (1924-   ), U.S. president, 1989-1993
Bill Clinton (1946-   ), U.S. president, 1993-2001
George W. Bush (1946-   ), U.S. president, 2001-2009
Barack Obama (1961-   ), U.S. president, 2009-

The U.S. Secret Service is, in some ways, a paradox. Despite its suggestive name, which seems to intimate covert operations, it is not a particularly secretive agency. In fact, it is more in the public eye than the Federal Bureau of Investigation (FBI), the Central Intelligence Agency (CIA), the Drug Enforcement Agency (DEA), and most other federal law-enforcement agencies. Its agents, who are best known for their role in protecting the U.S. president, are most visible during presidential elections, when whey can be seen everywhere that political candidates appear. Clad in neat, business-like suits and wearing earphones, they hover closely around the candidates, while carefully watching for possible trouble.

Because of the high visibility of the president of the United States, the president's family, presidential candidates, and other American government leaders and foreign dignitaries who receive their protection, Secret Service agents are probably seen in public more frequently than the agents of all other major federal law-enforcement agencies combined. As a consequence, the agency itself is publicly perceived as being involved almost exclusively in presidential protection. Such, indeed, is the perception conveyed in the title of Ronald Kessler's book, *The President's Secret Service: Behind the Scenes with Agents in the Line of Fire and the Presidents They*

Protect. The reality, however, is somewhat different. The Secret Service does not exist merely to protect political leaders. In fact, it was created for altogether different reasons more than three decades before it formally added presidential protection to its tasks.

A former Washington Post *and* Wall Street Journal *reporter, Ronald Kessler is the author of nearly two dozen best-selling books, including* Inside the CIA *(1992),* Inside the White House *(1995),* Inside Congress *(1997),* The Bureau *(2002),* The CIA at War *(2003), and* A Matter of Character: Inside the White House of George W. Bush *(2004).*

The Secret Service was established in 1865 to combat currency counterfeiting, which was a critical problem during the Civil War. In what may be one of the great ironies in American history, President Abraham Lincoln signed the bill creating the Secret Service on April 14, 1865—the very day on which he was fatally shot. After a brief prologue describing the Secret Service's role in President Barack Obama's January, 2009, inauguration day, Kessler opens his book with an account of Lincoln's assassination and then goes on to summarize the history of the Secret Service.

Up to 1865, protecting presidents received little special attention, despite the fact that Lincoln himself received many death threats. After long refusing special protection, Lincoln finally assented to having a few Washington city police officers serve as his bodyguards. In sharp contrast to modern Secret Service agents, his bodyguards were given no special training and their supervision was lax. Lincoln was shot while sitting in a private box watching a stage play, after the lone policeman assigned to guard the door to his box wandered off to a saloon. Such a situation is unimaginable today, when highly trained Secret Service agents will not let anyone near a president without a careful screening and a magnetometer scanning.

After Lincoln was killed, Americans demanded better protection of their presidents, but little was done until 1901, when presidential protection became a formal Secret Service responsibility. By then, two more presidents, James A. Garfield and William McKinley, had been assassinated, and the need for protecting presidents could no longer be ignored. Meanwhile, the responsibilities of the Secret Service had grown greatly since its creation four decades earlier. Thanks to the agency's success in combating counterfeiting, Congress had authorized it to investigate other forms of fraud against the government.

Since 1901, the Secret Service's responsibilities for both protective services and fraud investigation have grown immensely. As the specific tasks of the agency's individual offices and agents may vary radically from day to day, it is difficult to pinpoint how the agency's resources are divided. Nevertheless, it is probably not an exaggeration to say that, by the early twenty-first century, the agency was still directing more of its resources into fraud investigations than into protective duties.

Kessler acknowledges the primacy of the Secret Service's fraud investigation work, but the primary focus throughout his book is on the agency's protective work, particularly that relating to the presidency. He does, however, frequently mention the extent to which the agency's growing fraud-investigation workload has strained its ability to do its protective work, which has also expanded to include protection of presidential families, vice presidents and their families, presidential candidates, retired presidents and vice presidents and their families, visiting foreign dignitaries, and whomever else a president wishes to have protected. At any given moment, each of these persons is protected by at least three or four agents (many more for presidents), and this figure grows exponentially when round-the-clock, seven-day-a-week schedules are factored in and the special complications of travel and public events are considered.

The 2008 presidential campaigns brought unprecedented attention to the Secret Service. The campaigns themselves drew an extraordinary amount of public attention, which was accentuated by the fact that Barack Obama, the eventual winner of the election, is an African American. In the back of the minds of almost everyone—including government leaders—was the fear that Obama might become the target of racist hate groups who could not abide having a black president. Indeed, Obama's unique peril was great enough for him to be accorded Secret Service protection well before he won his party's nomination, and threats against the president quadrupled after he took office. Increased public interest in how presidents are protected makes publication of Kessler's book very timely. However, although public awareness of the Secret Service has risen, public understanding of the agency does not run very deep. Most Americans know the Secret Service through watching presidents and political candidates on television, reading occasional news stories about security breaches—such as the couple who crashed a White House party in November, 2009—and seeing Hollywood films about the Secret Service that tend to be either thrillers about assassination plots or light comedies about presidential children growing restless under the strain of White House restrictions and Secret Service protection.

Despite public interest in the Secret Service, so few books have been published about it that Kessler's book is a welcome addition to the literature. While his book makes no pretense of being a comprehensive examination of the modern Secret Service, it offers a remarkably intimate account of what agents have experienced over the past half century. As a veteran journalist with extensive connections in the federal government, Kessler brings to his book a unique access to Secret Service officials and agents. After publishing generally positive books about the George W. Bush administration, the CIA, and other federal agencies, Kessler won the confidence of the director of the Secret Service, Mark Sullivan, who approved his proposal to write a book about the agency. With the director's official blessing of the book a matter of public record, more than one hundred former and current agents granted Kessler interviews.

Perhaps the most secretive thing about the Secret Service has been its longstanding policy that its agents should never publicly reveal what they see and hear while on protective duty. Protectees living under the constant observation of Secret Service agents—particularly when they are traveling—tend to become so inured to having agents clustering around that they often behave as if the agents are not present. The agents, in turn, often see and hear things that they never reveal to the outside world. Never, that is, until now.

To most readers, the chief interest of *In the President's Secret Service* will be not what the book reveals about the Secret Service itself but what it reveals about recent U.S. presidents. Thanks to the openness of scores of past and present agents—many of whom Kessler names—this book is a rich and often startling trove of anecdotal material. The book's prologue sums up what readers can expect:

> Because Secret Service agents are sworn to secrecy, voters rarely know what their presidents, vice presidents, presidential candidates, and Cabinet officers are really like. If they did, says a former Secret Service agent, "They would scream."

If most of the anecdotes recounted in *In the President's Secret Service* are true, one might well ask who should be screaming: readers who are shocked by what they learn about their political leaders, political leaders who will no longer trust the agents protecting them to respect their privacy, or Secret Service agents who fear that their future relations with protectees have been compromised by the public revelations of fellow agents?

A theme running throughout Kessler's book is the mounting problems that the Secret Service faces as a result of mismanagement and insufficient budgeting. His prologue ends with this warning:

> Pledged to take a bullet for the president, agents are at constant risk. Yet the Secret Service's own practices magnify the dangers to the agents, the president, the vice president and others they protect. These lapses could lead to an assassination.

Because of the importance of protecting national leaders, Kessler's warning should not be dismissed altogether, but within the context of his book, it might be taken with a grain of salt. The book is anything but a rigorous analysis of the role of the Secret Service in national security. Its real subject—as its subtitle implies—is how presidents and other leaders behave in private. Judging by the stories the book tells, voters may truly have reason to scream.

Enough is already known about President John F. Kennedy's sexual escapades to leave little room for surprises, but Kessler's informants provide several risqué details, such as stories about Kennedy's sexual encounters with Marilyn Monroe in a loft above the Justice Department office of his brother, Attorney General Robert F. Kennedy. More startling, perhaps, are stories about Kennedy's successor, Lyndon B. Johnson, whom Secret Service agents described as "uncouth, nasty, and often drunk." Like Kennedy, Johnson was known for having affairs with female staff members. On one occasion, Lady Bird Johnson caught him having sex with a secretary in the Oval Office. Furious with Secret Service agents for not warning him of his wife's approach, Johnson had a buzzer system installed in the White House so agents could signal him when his wife was approaching. Many of Kessler's anecdotes about Johnson are unsavory. Among modern presidents, Johnson was unusual in not being shy about being seen drunk. He had no inhibitions about dropping his pants in front of strangers, and he occasionally held press conferences while sitting on the toilet.

Kessler's anecdotes about Richard Nixon tend to be on the pathetic side. They reinforce Nixon's image as a tormented loner, prone to drink privately when depressed and occasionally to engage in bizarre behavior, such as sampling dog biscuits. Gerald Ford comes off comparatively well, with the main criticism against him being that he was an incredible cheapskate.

The most significant revelations in Kessler's book may be those concerning Jimmy Carter, whom Secret Service agents called the "least likeable" president. In contrast to Carter's public image as a warm, caring leader, he was known for the contempt with which he treated his underlings. One agent, for example, said that during his three and a half years on Carter's protective detail—including seven months as his driver—Carter never spoke to him. Carter was also known for engaging in ruses to enhance his public image, such as carrying his own luggage while not letting on that his bags were empty. To give the impression that he worked long hours, he often went to his office as early as 5:00 A.M., only to close his door so he could go back to sleep. In public, Carter was all smiles for cameras, but within the White House, he was mean-spirited, controlling, and terrified his staff. He was also not above violent behavior. On one occasion when he was staying in his hometown of Plains, Georgia, agents saw him chasing a dog with a bow saw, trying to kill it because it had eaten his pet cat's food.

Many anecdotes in Kessler's book are disturbing for what they suggest about the moral character of American presidents, but others are amusing. For example, Secret Service agents regarded Nixon's son-in-law David Eisenhower as extraordinarily "clueless." Eisenhower once asked an agent if he understood why the electric light on the garage door opener he had been using for two years never went on. The agent pointed out to him that there was no lightbulb in the opener's socket. On another occasion, Eisenhower interrupted a long auto trip when his car broke down. After having the car towed to a dealership for repairs, he spent the night in a motel. The next morning he learned the car's problem: It had run out of gas.

The president and First Lady who emerge from this book most favorably are George H. W. Bush and Barbara Bush, who were clearly devoted to each other and who consistently went out of their way to show consideration for Secret Service agents and other underlings who worked for them. By contrast, Bill and Hillary Clinton were known for treating Secret Service agents quite differently, particularly after Clinton left office. Whereas Hillary has tended to treat agents and underlings dismissively, Bill has generally gone out of his way to show them consideration. One agent offered an explanation of the former president's generosity: "I think he realizes once he's out of office, we're pretty much all he's got . . . "

One indication of the public impact of Kessler's book is the amount of attention it has received on Amazon.com, an online book-selling site on which readers can post reviews. By mid-January, 2010—barely five months after the book's official publication date—185 readers had taken the trouble to post reviews of the book. That may seem a minuscule number compared to reader responses to J. K. Rowling's Harry Potter books, but it is a large number within the narrow world of books about government agencies. More to the point, it is more than six times greater than the twenty-eight customer reviews posted for the two editions of Philip H. Melanson and Peter F. Stevens's *The Secret Service: The Hidden History of an Enigmatic Agency* (2002,

2005), a similar but arguably superior book. even though the latter was originally published seven years earlier. Whatever the ultimate merits of Kessler's book, it will clearly make a mark in public perceptions of the Secret Service.

R. Kent Rasmussen

Review Source

Library Journal 134, no. 20 (December 15, 2009): 70.

INHERENT VICE

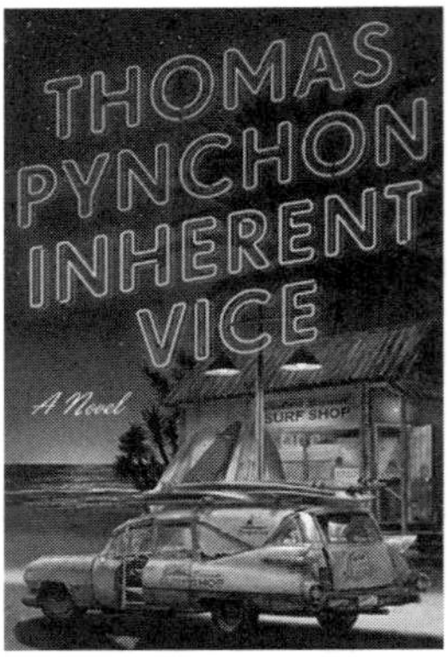

Author: Thomas Pynchon (1937-)
Publisher: Penguin (New York). 370 pp. $27.95
Type of work: Novel
Time: 1970
Locale: Southern California

In Pynchon's latest novel, a drug-abusing private investigator involved in a complex murder-kidnap plot traverses Southern California discovering plots and corruption everywhere he goes

Principal characters:

LARRY "DOC" SPORTELLO, a stoned surfer and private investigator who becomes embroiled in a case of abduction and murder
SHASTA FAY HEPWORTH, Sportello's ex-girlfriend, a marginally successful actress and the mistress of Mickey Wolfmann
MICKEY WOLFMANN, a real-estate mogul with connections to organized crime, renegade bikers, and political influence
LIEUTENANT CHRISTIAN F. "BIGFOOT" BJORNSEN, a Los Angeles police detective and occasional spokesman for Wolfmann's business ventures

Thomas Pynchon's *Inherent Vice* begins when Shasta Fay Hepworth arrives at the Gordito Beach residence of her former boyfriend, private investigator Doc Sportello. She persuades Sportello to save her lover, Mickey Wolfmann, from a plot to kidnap him and install him in a sanitarium. As Sportello begins his investigation of Wolfmann, an influential real-estate developer with connections to both criminal and police sources, Sportello is knocked unconscious and awakens to discover that one of Wolfmann's bodyguards has been murdered and Sportello is the prime suspect.

After his lawyer secures his release from jail, Sportello is contacted by Hope Harlingen, the widow of a saxophone player in a local surf band, who asks him to investigate her husband's suspicious drug overdose, and by Black Nationalist Kahlil Tariq, who is seeking an ex-convict who owes him money. A massage parlor attendant warns Sportello to beware of the Golden Fang and tells him that Coy Harlingen, the saxophone player, is not really deceased but is also looking for the private eye. A pair of Federal Bureau of Investigation (FBI) agents then detain Sportello as part of an investigation of Black Nationalists, who they believe have kidnapped Wolfmann.

Soon, Sportello's investigations spread in all directions, and the mystery of the Golden Fang deepens. Sportello wanders through Los Angeles and local beach communities, has random sexual encounters with various women, and ingests one drug after another. Before long, he discovers a counterfeiting ring, anonymous telephone threats are made to his parents, Wolfmann and Hepworth disappear, and new theories surface about the bodyguard's killing. He eventually discovers that the saxophonist is being held against his will in a drug rehabilitation center and that the gang that murdered the bodyguard is actually a militia financed by the police department to do its dirty work. Sportello becomes a suspect in a second murder, this time of a dentist he interviewed, and at every turn he is rousted by police detective Bigfoot Bjornsen, who pressures Sportello to provide him with information.

Thomas Pynchon, one of contemporary American letters' most challenging and important writers, is author of V. *(1963);* The Crying of Lot 49 *(1966);* Gravity's Rainbow *(1973), which won the National Book Award;* Slow Learner *(1984);* Vineland *(1990);* Mason and Dixon *(1997); and* Against the Day *(2006). In 1989, he was awarded a MacArthur Fellowship.*

Following yet another request to find a missing person, Sportello heads to a North Las Vegas casino and spies two FBI agents escorting Wolfmann off the premises. He further discovers that the developer has begun building a free-housing site in the desert, has redirected his assets into restoring the dilapidated casino, and has returned to his wife. Back at the beach, Sportello learns of a loan shark, Adrian Prussia, who murders adversaries with police cooperation and is also the killer of Bjornsen's former partner. When Sportello investigates this new lead, he is abducted and drugged. He escapes, kills Prussia, and is then rescued by Bjornsen, who plants heroin in Sportello's car to incur the wrath of drug dealers. After negotiating a return of the drugs, Sportello secures his parents' and the saxophone player's safety, and the novel ends with a few mysteries solved but many more still unresolved.

As this brief summary indicates, Thomas Pynchon has created another intricate, byzantine plot replete with twists, blind alleys, and often-inconclusive conclusions. Whether the plot complications result from the author's affection for convoluted structures or from the conventions demanded by detective fiction is a moot point: In the detective story, Pynchon finds a perfect structure for his own fictional predilections, which typically involve plots nestled within scores of other plots that may or may not be connected.

In many respects, *Inherent Vice* is the fitting culmination of Pynchon's tendency, in nearly all his other six novels, to involve characters in mysteries that force them to venture into an often-threatening world, decipher seemingly arcane clues, and arrive at a condition of precarious equipoise. An argument can be made that this novel's twisted plot is simply the product of Sportello's hopelessly twisted and drug-addled brain. By all accounts, Sportello is a generally lazy, irresponsible slacker who prefers to spend time with other misfits in a drugged haze. His career, what there is of it, exists largely as an afterthought. However, as enticing as this explanation may seem, it ignores Pynchon's more serious metaphysical inclinations to see life, even at its most banal, as a condition of deep confusion and irresolvable puzzles. Pynchon consistently conjectures about parallel worlds, temporal dislocation, and a complexity to existence that is hidden under the veils of social orthodoxy and convention.

What any summary of a Pynchon novel cannot convey is the bevy of eccentric and oddball characters that people his fiction. Pynchon has always reveled in presenting characters who exist on society's fringes and fritter away time with absurd obsessions. Doc Sportello is a perfect case in point, being a bright man who has squandered his intellect with too many drugs, bad fast food, and television. Bigfoot Bjornsen, his adversary and professional critic, is a cynical cop who works as a shill for a real-estate mogul and turns over the messy labor of detection to a private investigator he would happily frame and send to prison. Mickey Wolfmann is a conniving real-estate speculator, a possibly mob-connected criminal, and an ethically reformed businessman who wants to create free housing for the needy and return all his ill-gotten profits as a result of an attack of conscience.

As he has in each of his other fictions, Pynchon returns to a practice that has amused his fans and exasperated scholars. His characters sport an assemblage of silly names—Sauncho Smilax, Jason Velveeta, Dr. Buddy Tubeside, FBI agents Flatweed and Borderline, Zigzag Twong, Trillium Fortnight, and Denis ("whose name everybody pronounced to rhyme with 'penis'"). Such names, seemingly chosen for comic effect, defy serious significance, though readers have often attempted to find some logic in these cognomen. Most likely, Pynchon is simply rebelling against the traditional practice of creating either realistic names or identifications that suggest some essence of the character.

As also occurs in Pynchon's other novels, characters flit in and out of the narrative, sometimes disappearing for scores of pages, only to reappear later, sometimes vanishing from the text altogether. As often as they advance the plot, deepen the mystery, or add some local color, they just as often have no apparent purpose other than to crowd the story with an amusing density and act as postmodern alternatives to Victorian fictions' sense of social complexity. One of the faults of *Inherent Vice*, however, arises from the sheer abundance of its characters: The novel lacks much indication of who is most important and why, and its character overload will remind fans of the author's endless teasing in *The Crying of Lot 49* (1966), where the protagonist, Oedipa Maas, is overwhelmed by experiences that portend too much meaning and too little pattern.

The characteristic Pynchon theme of entropy also finds expression here. The author sees entropy as the condition in the universe through which originality and energy gradually dissipate and create an atmosphere of lifelessness and conformity. *The Crying of Lot 49* also introduces the theory of communicative entropy, a condition whereby increases in information create only confusion, and in *Inherent Vice* not only is there deliberate verbal obfuscation but also characters frequently speak at cross-purposes to one another. Sportello often cannot comprehend what others tell him, and his mind races to follow clues and decipher explanations as events chaotically crowd together.

The fact that Pynchon returns once more in this novel to the late 1960's underscores his conviction that a period of such considerable social, political, and economic potential dissolved into muddle and complacency in the 1970's. Hovering over much of the novel's atmosphere are the Manson killings, which are referred to repeatedly. The message seems to be that Sportello's stoner acceptance and laissez-faire attitude have devolved into a culture of homicide and exploitation.

When Wolfmann announces that he intends to donate all his guilt-inducing wealth to the disadvantaged, he is abducted by the FBI, deprogrammed, and liberated only once he returns to his former life. Another analogue for the novel's attitude about the United States and its decline into chaos and insensitivity comes in the various discussions characters have about Lemuria, an island believed to have existed in the Pacific at roughly the same time as Atlantis and that disappeared in the same cataclysm as that island. Lemurians believe the island continent was an eden of peace and tolerance destroyed by scientific rationalism.

Another of Pynchon's long-standing obsessions is the belief that conspiracies of all types abound and that hidden forces control individual lives and frustrate originality and freedom. The line between coincidence or misapprehension and conspiracy is thin, and Sportello constantly wonders if he has stumbled on some intricate plot, is simply too stoned, or has meandered into a happenstance that appears to reveal hidden connections. The best example of a conspiracy that may be nothing more than urban legend is the Golden Fang. Doc is warned to beware of the Fang in a cryptic note, but when he tries to discern its meaning, he discovers one confusing explanation after another. The Fang is either a dope-smuggling schooner, an office complex, a drug rehabilitation center for the wealthy, a drug cartel, or a tax dodge for a group of dentists.

As a result of the Golden Fang, corrupt cops and FBI agents, and the possibility of more Mansonites lurking in the shadows, Sportello and a number of the characters experience a free-floating paranoia. He initially regards paranoia as "a tool of the trade, it points you in directions you might not have seen to go." However as the case progresses and the plots within plots grow more dense, he wonders if all the disparate threads of the investigation are actually connected and becomes increasingly uneasy: "Doc felt a suspicion growing, paranoid as the rapid heartbeat of a midnight awakening." For Pynchon, the old adage holds true, "Just because you're paranoid doesn't mean they're not out to get you."

Inherent Vice is an amusing, often clever pastiche of Raymond Chandler and the Coen Brothers' film *The Big Lebowski* (1998), but in the end it is not terribly original. Rumor has it that the novel has been optioned for a film production, and certainly of any of Pynchon's books this seems the most accessible to a mass audience. While Pynchon still retains his ability to capture the range of high and low culture and write devilishly allusive prose, however, this is far from his best work.

David W. Madden

Review Sources

Booklist 105, no. 21 (July 1, 2009): 7.
Kirkus Reviews 77, no. 13 (July 1, 2009): 679.
Library Journal 134, no. 13 (August 1, 2009): 74.
London Review of Books 31, no. 17 (September 10, 2009): 9-10.
New Statesman 138, no. 4960 (August 3, 2009): 42-43.

The New York Review of Books, September 24, 2009, 70-71.
The New York Times, August 4, 2009, p. 1.
The New York Times Book Review, August 23, 2009, p. 9.
The New Yorker 85, no. 23 (August 3, 2009): 74-75.
Publishers Weekly 256, no. 27 (July 6, 2009): 38.
Rolling Stone, August 6, 2009, p. 38-39.
Time 174, no. 6 (August 17, 2009): 60.
The Times Literary Supplement, August 7, 2009, p. 22.
The Wall Street Journal, July 31, 2009, p. W2.

INSIDE THE STALIN ARCHIVES
Discovering the New Russia

Author: Jonathan Brent
Publisher: Atlas (New York). 304 pp. $26.00
Type of work: Current affairs, history, memoir
Time: January, 1992, to October, 2007
Locale: Moscow, Russia

A memoir of Brent's work with Russian archivists to set up the Annals of Communism series for Yale University Press combined with observations about both the archival contents and the deteriorating condition of Russia

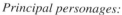

Principal personages:
JONATHAN BRENT, the author, the editorial director of Yale University Press
JOSEPH STALIN, Soviet premier, 1941-1953
JEFFREY BURDS, an American historian in Moscow, Brent's intermediary with the Russian archivists
NIKOLAI, a historian at Russian State University for the Humanities, intermediary with archivists on Brent's first visit to Moscow in January, 1992
MARIANA, a widow, the mother of a friend of Burds; Brent stayed at her apartment on his first visit to Moscow
FRIDRIKH FIRSOV, the head of publications of the Comintern archives, involved in access negotiations
VLADIMIR KOZLOV, the deputy director of the Federal Archival Service of Russia, involved in access negotiations
VLADIMIR NAUMOV, a Russian archivist and Annals of Communism coauthor
OLEG NAUMOV, the director of the Central Party Archive, son of Vladimir, and Annals of Communism coauthor
ALEXANDER YAKOVLEV, a Russian reformer and supporter of opening archives

Jonathan Brent's memoir *Inside the Stalin Archives* is divided into two main parts. In the first, he discusses his first trip to Moscow to negotiate access to various Soviet archives for the planned Annals of Communism series for Yale University Press. The Boris Yeltsin government had officially opened all these archives to scholars, both Russian and foreign, but making that access a reality required quite a bit of negotiation. In the memoir's second part, Brent discusses various later trips, though in less detail. In particular, only in the first part does he provide significant coverage of his time away from the negotiations.

Brent went to Moscow in January, 1992, to arrange scholarly access to various Soviet and Communist Party archives for the purpose of producing books for Yale

Jonathan Brent is the editorial director of Yale University Press and founded its Annals of Communism series. He teaches at Bard College, writes for a number of magazines, and coauthored Stalin's Last Crime *with Vladimir Naumov in 2004.*

University Press. These books were to be coauthored by Russian scholars, who would receive equal pay. The archivists who helped locate the documents would also be paid for their work. Yale wanted exclusive rights to publish outside Russia; there would be no restrictions on publication within Russia. Money was always a concern; only a few of the twenty Annals of Communism volumes published so far have been popular sellers, so the project has always depended heavily on donations. The desire for exclusive non-Russian rights (to prevent being upstaged by other publishers) was perhaps the most difficult negotiating point. Fortunately, the Russian archivists were well aware that Yale University Press had a good reputation for scholarship.

Brent first visited the Central Party Archive, where even taking the elevator was a bit of an adventure: He wanted to go to the third floor, and the first three floors were listed as 2, 2, 3. At the archive, Brent met Fridrikh Firsov and Vladimir Kozlov, who had recently moved from the Central Party Archive to the Federal Archive Service. Kozlov took Brent to his own archive and, having to attend another meeting, left him with Oleg Naumov. At this point, Brent explained his primary interests in the archives: materials on the state terror of the 1930's, the church and its role in the revolution, the Communist International (Comintern) and its role in the oppression of the 1930's, and Soviet daily life in the 1920's and 1930's as revealed by the letters of peasants and workers.

On his first trip, Brent stayed with a general's widow named Mariana. Though she lived in the Moscow equivalent of an upscale apartment, her quality of life was wretched even by working-class American standards. In particular, the apartment often seemed about to fall apart, though it never quite did. The food generally was merely edible; Brent reports eating cookies that were nearly tasteless. (He also got them in a restaurant.) Perhaps not surprising, his visits were accompanied with gifts of American cigarettes, liquor, biscuits, salami, and chocolates, which represented a quality of goods not available in 1992 to ordinary Russians. In his first meeting with Firsov and Kozlov, he gave the latter a package of Winstons in exchange for a package of Russian cigarettes, a carefully choreographed transaction that reads as though two spies were meeting. The analogy is appropriate, as many influential Russians disliked opening the archives to foreigners.

Brent's first trip to Russia lasted several days, and he was able to see some archival material, including material on the last days of Czar Nicholas II, such as a diary kept by Czarina Alexandra. Seeing this material was an ironic experience for Brent: In 1972, he had an argument with his girlfriend because he considered the executions of the czar's family members (even those of the children) justified by their crimes. Revolution, he argued, has no room for pity. Presumably, he later came to realize the error in this judgment. Firsov also showed Brent documents on the Comintern and its role in Soviet espionage (which became the subject of one of the first Annals of Communism books).

Brent returned to Moscow in July, 1992, to finalize the contract. In doing so, he chose not to use the suggested contract written by a lawyer that Yale University Press had consulted, believing its conditions were too favorable to Yale for the Russians to accept. After completing his negotiations successfully, out of curiosity he showed the contract to Oleg Naumov, who confirmed that it would have broken their trust and thereby stopped the project in its tracks. The Russians soon agreed to the contract, but then later in 1992 they began to back off and call for some new negotiations. Brent was very concerned that this might mean an end to the project, but he was able to resolve matters on his third trip, in January, 1993. On this occasion, he noted the problems that resulted from differences in meanings between English and Russian. Many words have different multiple meanings and thus cannot be precisely translated; thus, the Russian *rezolyutsiya* can mean "resolution," but also "added instructions." Despite such problems, Brent was able to finalize matters without significant changes in the terms of the agreement. From then on, his Moscow trips involved specific research topics.

Brent makes many interesting observations on Soviet archival materials. For example, the common view is that the December, 1934, assassination of Sergei Kirov (Leningrad Communist Party chief and a Politburo member) caused the Great Purge, in which Joseph Stalin solidfied his dictatorial power through widespread campaigns of political repression. (There remain suspicions that Stalin was himself responsible for Kirov's assassination, but Brent never managed to resolve these suspicions from his own archival studies.) Brent looks at the number of arrests, particularly for counterrevolutionary crimes, made during the 1930's. These arrests numbered 283,029 in 1933, and Brent points out that there was no significant increase in their annual rate until 1937, when 779,056 people were arrested and most of them were shot. He also analyzes the trial and execution of writer Isaac Babel in 1939. He seeks to determine why Babel was shot while his fellow writer (and later World War II propagandist) Ilya Ehrenburg was not even arrested, despite being implicated in Babel's confession. He also researches why Babel's interrogators were interested in his possible espionage for the British, rather than the Nazis. In the latter case, he thinks their interest foreshadowed the Molotov-Ribbentrop Pact made later that year, as it seems to indicate that Stalin was already considering the possibility of such a pact with Germany.

Brent sought information on many specific topics. He tried to get information on the arrest and execution of Raoul Wallenberg, the Swedish diplomat famed as the savior of thousands of Hungarian Jews in 1944, but without much success. As a writer, Brent was also interested in the large number of cultural figures purged during the Stalin era. He devotes three pages to a list of writers, poets, critics, musicians, playwrights, scholars, and others purged by Stalin (most of them shot), and he points out that even that lengthy list is incomplete. He quotes some interesting discussions between Stalin and film director Sergei Eisenstein (not one of those purged) about Eisenstein's film about Czar Ivan IV (commonly known as Ivan the Terrible). Stalin saw Ivan as a great autocrat who opposed the aristocracy and tried to centralize government but failed to complete the job because of a fatal deficiency—he possessed a conscience.

The personality of Stalin was at the heart of the long era chronicled by Brent, and Brent devotes three chapters to what the archives reveal about him. He starts with a discusion with reformer Alexander Yakovlev, including the problem of the Soviet system's reliance on instilling fear in the population (making it literally as well as figuratively a terror state). Yakovlev saw this fear in the current state as well, though not to the same degree. Stalin, however monstrous, was a genuine theoretician of communism who no doubt believed that what he was doing was best for the country as a whole (an attitude helped by his total lack of regard for individuals). Among the archives are the books Stalin read—which are heavy on communist polemics that the dictator annotated extensively. Also of interest is Stalin telling his son that Stalin the autocrat and national symbol had subsumed Stalin the person.

Another important point is that Stalin, when he talked about selfless devotion to the state (and thus to the party that controlled it and to the autocrat who ran the party and the state), he meant it literally. When Vyacheslav Molotov, supreme toady and sometime premier of the Soviet Union, chose to abstain in a vote on his wife's application to join the Communist Party, Stalin was displeased. This may be why, several years later, Molotov finally began to fall from favor (and might well have been purged had Stalin lived longer). To Stalin, the totally united state should be everything; no personal ties of any sort should rank above it, nor should any independent thought mar its unity. This is one reason for his suspicion of ethnic minorities (especially Jews).

Although the purpose of Brent's Russian trips was to arrange for scholarly access to the archives of the old Soviet state (and to do some research himself), Brent also uses his accounts of his various trips to discuss life in modern Russia, at least in its capital and largest city. One constant that he reports is anti-Semitism. As the descendant of Ukrainian Jews from Zhitomir and Lvov whose family name was originally Brodsky, Brent naturally is very concerned about this anti-Semitism. On his first visit, he found a crude anti-Semitic flyer, an experience he would repeat many times. On another trip, he discussed the execution of Czar Nicholas II and his family and learned that the Russian Orthodox Church was delaying declaring him a saint until they established his cause of death. One possibility it was seriously considering was that his death was a Jewish ritual murder to obtain blood to make matzohs for Passover. (The fact that the czar was murdered a few months after Passover was apparently irrelevant.)

Nor was this anything new; Stalin had his anti-Semitic moments and in fact was preparing a pogrom when he died (this plan, the Doctors' Plot, is the subject of Brent's own Annals of Communism volume). Brent also discusses scenes in Isaac Babel's "Red Cavalry" (which appeared in his 1960 *Collected Stories*) portraying the plight of Jews during the Russian Civil War. (Babel, executed by Stalin in 1939, was himself Jewish, but his portrayals of his fellows Jews apparently were hardly positive.) For that matter, one of his contacts (Fridrikh Firsov) was Jewish, and at times this affected what he was free to say in public about his researches. Regimes come and go, but some things never change.

Russia during the Stalin era was a black hole for both freedom and democracy, but in the 1990's many hoped that the situation would change. Even then, however, people felt that the police listened to everything. Yakovlev supported reporting the contents of the archives, particularly in Russia, hoping that revealing their contents would help inoculate the country against a resumption of authoritarian rule. This strategy failed: On a later visit, Brent met an unnamed elderly historian who mentioned having his pension threatened for daring to report honestly that Stalin took over Lithuania the year before the Nazi invasion of the Soviet Union. Those who favored authoritarianism, revered Stalin, or simply disliked revealing national secrets opposed opening the archives. Corruption was another constant. Brent's Russian contacts assumed their taxes were almost entirely wasted. Once, a department store was forcibly closed to the public for a Russian VIP's visit. Thus, Brent's firsthand reports on life in contemporary Russia help relate the present to the events of the past recorded in the Soviet archives he helped make available to Western scholars.

Timothy Lane

Review Sources

Foreign Affairs 88, no. 5 (September/October, 2009): 159.
Kirkus Reviews 76, no. 17 (September 1, 2008): 923.
Library Journal 133, no. 18 (November 1, 2008): 77-85.
The New York Review of Books 56, no. 7 (April 30, 2009): 25-28.
The New York Times Book Review, January 25, 2009, p. 14.
The Times Literary Supplement, July 24, 2009, p. 8.
The Wall Street Journal, December 2, 2008, p. A17.

INVISIBLE

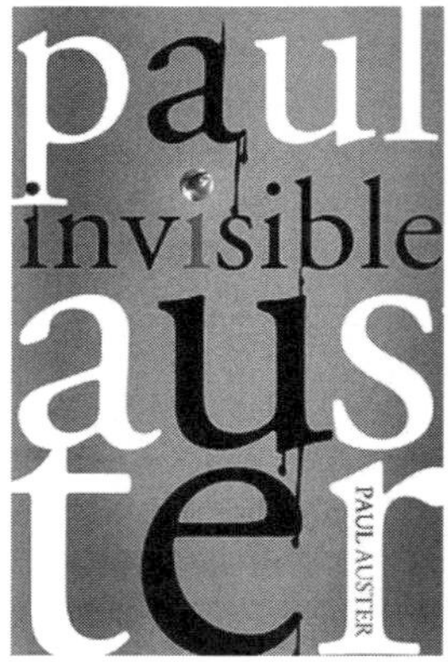

Author: Paul Auster (1947-)
Publisher: Henry Holt (New York). 320 pp. $25.00
Type of work: Novel
Time: 1967; 2002; 2007-2008
Locale: New York City; Oakland, California; Paris, France; Quillia, a small island in the West Indies

A successful novelist becomes fascinated with a manuscript left behind by a dead college classmate that seems to be a puzzling mixture of memoir and fiction

Principal characters:

ADAM WALKER, a Columbia University student who aspires to be a poet but ends up becoming a lawyer
GWYN WALKER TEDESCO, Adam's sister
RUDOLF BORN, a French professor of international relations
MARGOT JOUFFROY, Born's younger consort
HÉLÈNE JUIN, Born's fiancée, a speech pathologist whose husband has been rendered comatose
CÉCILE JUIN, Hélène's daughter, who becomes a literary scholar
CEDRIC WILLIAMS, an eighteen-year-old would-be mugger stabbed by Born
REBECCA, Walker's African American stepdaughter
JAMES FREEMAN, a successful novelist, Adam's classmate

In fourteen novels as well as collected poems and essays, Paul Auster has aspired to give artistic form to meditations on personal identity and the art that might embody them. He is a virtuoso of metafiction, often organized as stories-within-stories that reflect upon themselves and one another. In his fifteenth novel, *Invisible*, Auster has fashioned a consummate instrument of existential mystery and literary reflexivity. In four bravura sections, the novel ponders the fate of Adam Walker, a student at Columbia University whose life is transformed by Rudolf Born, a charismatic but enigmatic professor from France.

An aspiring poet, Walker meets Born at a party in 1967, and the sophisticated stranger soon offers to finance a literary magazine that Walker would edit. Before departing for a brief return to Europe, Born also appears to encourage the young man to take his place in bed beside his lover, Margot Jouffroy. Walker is disturbed by Born's nihilistic celebration of violence.

> Human beings were animals, he said, and soft-minded aesthetes like myself were no better than children, diverting ourselves with hairsplitting philosophies of art and literature to avoid confronting the essential truth of the world.

That essential truth, according to Born, is "the darkness inside us." When Born stabs and apparently kills Cedric Williams, a mugger who accosts them one evening, Walker is appalled and breaks with his would-be mentor.

James Freeman, a successful novelist, learns about these events in the early twenty-first century by reading a manuscript sent to him by Walker, whom he has not heard from since both were students at Columbia almost forty years before. Now a lawyer in Oakland, Walker is dying of leukemia, and he asks for Freeman's professional advice about the memoir, titled *1967*, that he is struggling to complete. Freeman encourages Walker to keep writing and to send him the second chapter. He does, and it turns out to be a lyrical evocation of the months after Walker's falling-out with Born. It is set during the summer of 1967, when Walker has a job shelving books at Columbia's Butler Library. He shares an apartment with his sister Gwyn, who is beginning graduate school in the fall. The chapter recounts how, for thirty-five consecutive days, until his departure to study in Paris, brother and sister engaged in passionate incest.

Paul Auster is a novelist, poet, essayist, translator, editor, and filmmaker. His novels include The New York Trilogy *(1987),* The Music of Chance *(1990),* The Book of Illusions *(2002), and* The Brooklyn Follies *(2005). In 2006, he was inducted into the American Academy of Arts and Letters.*

After reading the first two chapters, Freeman travels to California but arrives at Walker's house in Oakland three days after the funeral of his old college classmate. However, obeying his request, Walker's stepdaughter Rebecca hands the novelist the notes Walker left behind for the third chapter of *1967*. The notes recount Walker's experiences in Paris during the fall of that year. Making contact with Born again, he plots retribution for the murder of Cedric Williams. He learns that Born plans to marry Hélène Juin, whose husband, Born's friend, has been incapacitated by an irreversible coma. Walker ingratiates himself with Hélène's eighteen-year-old daughter, Cécile, and begins undermining Born's hopes of marrying Hélène. He does not count on Born's cunning and his connections with French espionage services.

After reading the notes for Walker's third chapter, Freeman contacts Walker's sister, Gwyn, who denies that any incest occurred between them. During a trip to Paris, he also tracks down Cécile Juin, now a doughty literary scholar. Cécile lets Freeman read entries from her diary that constitute part 4 of *Invisible*. Cécile's journal tells how in 2002, after losing contact for many years, she suddenly received a letter from Born. Living alone on a Caribbean island called Quillia, he invited her to visit. When she did, she was dismayed by Born's bizarre behavior and fled.

In four sections spanning forty years, *Invisible* thus makes use of three narrators: Freeman, Walker, and Cécile. The first three sections are told, successively, in the first person, the second person, and the third person, as though the truth cannot be apprehended through a unitary perspective. What one ought to conclude about Adam Walker and Rudolf Born is prismatic, a matter of multiple, fragmented points of view.

The story that emerges is fraught with unlikely coincidences, such as the fact that Walker ends up marrying an African American woman, Sandra Williams, whose last name is the same as that of Cedric Williams, whose killing forever alters Walker's life. The possibility that Born, who behaved dishonorably during France's attempt to quell rebellion in Algeria, might be a government spy remains unresolved. Gwyn's categorical, and credible, denial that she engaged in incest with her brother is one of several contradictions in the text. Like the novel's readers, Freeman is faced with trying to make sense of it all. He must also confront his own responsibility to his dead classmate: He now possesses the only copy of Walker's manuscript and wonders whether he should destroy it, publish it as is, or transform it into a novel.

Early in the proceedings, describing his first encounter with Rudolf Born and Margot Jouffroy, Adam Walker recalls that "the longer I talked to them, the more unreal they seemed to become—as if they were imaginary characters in a story that was taking place in my head." There is a spectral quality to the novel's characters, including Walker himself. After reading part 1, which is written in the first person, Freeman advises Walker that he might need more distance from the material and suggests switching to the third person, as Freeman himself has done in one of his own books: "By writing about myself in the first person, I had smothered myself and made myself invisible, had made it impossible for me to find the thing I was looking for," the novelist explains.

> I needed to separate myself from myself, to step back and carve out some space between myself and my subject (which was myself), and therefore I returned to the beginning of Part Two and began writing it in the third person. *I* became *He*, and the distance created by that small shift allowed me to finish the book.

In fact, Walker switches from first-person narration in his part 1 to second-person narration in part 2, only to adopt the third-person "he" in part 3. Although Freeman recommends abandoning the first-person perspective in order to acquire greater objectivity, Walker's movement from first to second to third person seems not so much to endow his account with greater objectivity as to lay bare its manner of construction, thereby emphasizing its artificiality and undermining any claim it might make to objective truth. Walker's presence is felt throughout, but his strategy of moving away from the use of "I" does not so much render him invisible, as the title of Auster's novel suggests, as indefinable. Who exactly Adam Walker was is impossible to pin down. Although he is present all over its pages, the subject of this book is hiding in plain sight.

Because Walker's manuscript seems either scandalously revealing or else patently false, Freeman at first considers it unpublishable. However, Gwyn offers this suggestion: "You change the names of the people and the places, you add or subtract any material you see fit, and then you publish the book under your own name." Though he has qualms about committing what amounts to plagiarism by passing off someone else's book as his own or else taking such liberties with the original text that he is betraying a dying man's trust, Freeman proceeds to follow "Gwyn"'s advice. He informs readers:

> Adam Walker is not Adam Walker. Gwyn Walker Tedesco is not Gwyn Walker Tedesco. Margot Jouffroy is not Margot Jouffroy. Hélène and Cécile Juin are not Hélène and Cécile Juin. Cedric Williams is not Cedric Williams. Sandra Williams is not Sandra Williams, and her daughter, Rebecca, is not Rebecca. Not even Born is Born.

Except for Paris, Freeman admits, all of the place names have been changed, along with other significant details of the story.

What readers are left with following this revelation is a fictional novelist (perhaps loosely and cunningly based on the real novelist, Paul Auster, who also attended Columbia University forty years ago) who exposes the treacherous nature of his own literary contrivances. The fictional novelist Freeman's confession that he has manipulated the narrative resembles the conclusion of William Shakespeare's *The Tempest* (pr. 1611, pb. 1623), the moment of disenchantment in which Prospero breaks his wand and abjures his rough magic.

In part 4 of *Invisible*, Rudolf Born asks Cécile Juin to help him compose a memoir about his experiences while assigned to dangerous missions as a spy for France. However, in order not to disclose shameful and incriminating secrets, he resolves to alter important details. His strategy parallels Freeman's decision to change names and other key elements in Walker's manuscript. Born is determined not to abandon the project of writing about his life. "But in order to tell the truth, we'll have to fictionalize it," he explains to Cécile. Convinced that Born is a monster, she refuses to collaborate and leaves. However, it is too late for readers. Cécile's rejection of Born's request occurs at the very end of Auster's *Invisible*, a crafty novel that offers the pleasures of a complex and engaging story even as it reminds its readers that it is all an elaborate literary contrivance.

Without a willing reader, one willing to accept speculation without resolution, *Invisible* is just an ingenious stunt. Like Cécile, herself a literary scholar, some reviewers have preferred to walk away, faulting Auster for arid self-indulgence and a preoccupation with formal invention at the expense of forceful storytelling. However, the intricate form that he devises for this novel is in service to an exploration of fundamental questions about identity, love, and art. Inviting skepticism toward aesthetic illusions, *Invisible* does not demand the usual willing suspension of disbelief. However, anyone drawn into Auster's seductive metafiction becomes complicit with an exhilarating exercise in the possibilities of making a novel responsive to truth.

Steven G. Kellman

Review Sources

Booklist 105, no. 22 (August 1, 2009): 8.
The Boston Globe, November 1, 2009, p. 6.
Kirkus Reviews 77, no. 15 (August 1, 2009): 12.
Library Journal 134, no. 16 (October 1, 2009): 68.
Los Angeles Times, November 22, 2009, p. E6.
New Statesman 138, no. 4974 (November 9, 2009): 52-54.
The New York Times Book Review, November 15, 2009, p. 20.
The New Yorker, November 30, 2009, p. 82.
The Observer, November 29, 2009, p. 22.
Publishers Weekly 256, no. 33 (August 17, 2009): 39.
San Francisco Chronicle, November 8, 2009, p. E5.
The Times Literary Supplement, November 6, 2009, p. 19.

IT WILL COME TO ME

Author: Emily Fox Gordon (1948-   )
Publisher: Spiegel & Grau (New York). 267 pp. $24.95
Type of work: Novel
Time: The early twenty-first century
Locale: Lola Dees Institute, Texas

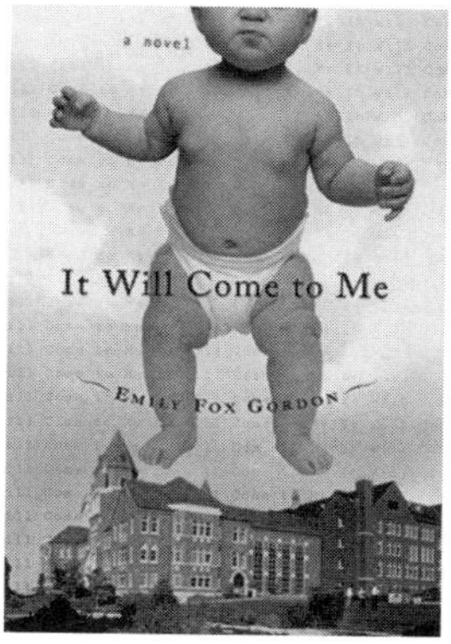

In Gordon's novel, an unfulfilled faculty wife named Ruth takes readers on a bumpy but illuminating exploration of dark psychic corners in her life and those of her husband and other campus characters at the Lola Dees Institute

Principal characters:
RUTH BLAU, a former writer whose muse motherhood may have destroyed
BEN BLAU, Ruth's husband, chair of the Philosophy Department at Lola, who is writing a book called *Necessity of Altruism*
DOLORES, Ben's efficient secretary whom the hated new dean has transferred
ROBERTA MITTEN-KURZ, Lola's bureaucratic dean
RICIA SPOTTISWODE, a writer-in-residence and charismatic teacher whose arrival and inspiring words to Ruth turn her life around
CHARLES JOHNS, Ricia'a big, brash husband
ISAAC BLAU, Ruth and Ben's dropout son

In *It Will Come to Me*, an exquisitely styled, humanely satirical novel of academe, writer Emily Fox Gordon forges an unusual track—that of a hurricane—to allow at least the possibility of redemption for her put-upon central couple. Ruth Blau is the author of an acclaimed trilogy of novels, now twenty-five years behind her. Ben Blau skimps on his bureaucratic duties as philosophy chair at the Lola Dees Institute (commonly known as Lola) to finish a book about altruism. Before Hurricane Heather can play its redemptive role in the ninth and final chapter of *It Will Come to Me*, Gordon skillfully alternates viewpoints between her two protagonists in the first eight.

Both Ben and Ruth have suffered seemingly irremediable personal and professional losses. Ruth has not written since the birth twenty-four years ago of their only child, Isaac. She has only a flawed manuscript to show for her former efforts at continuing her writing career. Isaac, now a dropout and mentally ill, has become a street person. His parents have not seen him for two years, and their only means of communicating with their son is through his eccentric psychaitrist. Ben, meanwhile, has lost his secretary Dolores, whose industrious dedication to her job enabled him to ignore his administrative duties and work on his book, *Necessity of Altruism*. Dolores has been transferred to a different department out of spite by Lola's hated new dean, who refers to professors as "share-holders."

Emily Fox Gordon is an award-winning essayist and the author of two memoirs, Mockingbird Years: A Life In and Out of Therapy *(2000) and* Are You Happy? A Childhood Remembered *(2006). She lives in Houston and teaches writing at Rice University.*

Ruth is fed up with her current life at Lola, which she finds unbearably dull. She is bored by Philsophy Department potluck dinners and Ben's philosophy students. "To all appearances they might have been working on MBAs or degrees in physical therapy." Ruth sees little evidence that they are even having sex. They just want to get jobs, preferably teaching in a place like Lola. "They wanted to be marsupials, creatures with no natural enemies who could look forward to living out their days in absolute safety." There has not been a scandal at Lola for twenty years. Ruth does not want to have an affair herself; she would just like to know that someone is having one. At worst, people have been "difficult" but seldom interesting. In her faculty-wife mufti of clogs, graying updo, and dangly ethnic jewelry bought on eBay, Ruth is, in her own word, "stuck." Her moderately successful first book—which was on academe—has been remaindered to dollar bins outside used-book shops. She drinks too much wine at parties. Her only excitement comes from epic arguments with Ben and watching dire weather reports about Hurricane Heather, a Category Four hurricane that is blowing toward the school.

Ruth desperately needs a catalyst to rouse her out of despair. Such a catalyst is provided with the start of the fall semester and the arrival of Ricia Spottiswode—a new writer-in-residence, a young, charismatic teacher, and the author of a best-selling memoir. At their first meeting, Ruth is embarrassed when an old trustee sidles up to Ricia and croaks into her ear: "You say you a *memwa*-ist. Now dunnat make you a *nah*sussist?" Invited by Ricia to share *Whole Lives Devoured*, her stalled manuscript, Ruth carries the bulky manuscript to a coffeehouse as if she were "transporting a packet of X-rays . . . to a consultation with an oncologist." When they later meet in an unlikely place—the ladies room—Ruth fears the worst.

Ricia's opening volley is brutal until she disdains her own assessment as that of the critic she says she is not. As a "fan" of Ruth—she claims familiarity with her trilogy—Ricia admires the new work. Her parting words are an admonition: "Just write!" That Ruth will be inspired to revive her dormant literary career is a given. As for Ben, he cannot bring himself to fire Hayley, his maladjusted, incompetent new secretary. His inability to function without Dolores, however, leads to a fiery dressing-down from the dean, whose name, Mitten-Kurz, could be taken to rhyme with her perceived demeanor: "spit and curse."

A capsule review in *The New Yorker* gave high praise to much of this novel, but it decried as "falsely redemptive" the Hurricane Heather ending: The Hurricane causes Ruth and Ben to be reunited with Isaac, in company with his much-older Asian partner and their infant daughter, Drusilla. To be sure, Gordon exploits Heather as a means to reconciliations.

The hurricane is slightly reduced in force by the time it reaches Spangler, Texas (a stand-in for Houston). Ben and Ruth find themselves mingling with the university community in Horace Dees Hall, a campus shelter. Making adjustments for the effects of aging, Ben makes an inner roll call of people who have not shown themselves in decades:

> It took him a moment to recognize a famous emerita . . . now inching along with the help of a walker, her elderly son clearing a path. For the first time he laid eyes on the legendarily anorexic daughter of the History Department secretary. He spotted a reclusive poet with multiple chemical sensitivities and a young ethnomusicologist who'd been on medical leave since exposing himself to a group of Korean middle schoolers. . . . [Ben] witnessed some particularly stiff encounters between rivals who for years had been arranging their schedules to avoid meeting one another He saw two scenes of joyful reunion.

Even with the wind howling outside, Ruth offers her usual disclaimers: "I've had the hardest time taking this hurricane seriously. . . . It doesn't seem real." Ricia, ever theatrical, asks her to challenge nature's distraction and read aloud from her manuscript. Predictably, Ruth declines with a lie: "I left it at home." Meanwhile, Ben, grazing nearby, is left with his own thoughts: "Was that the wind, that high, faint keening he kept thinking he was hearing over the shoptalk jabber?" He had hoped to be depersonalized by the crowd, but he cannot help but sense that

> a diasporizing impulse had begun to break the aggregation into constituent couples and groups. These were rapidly moving away from one another and drifting up the stairs and down the hallways to offices and lounges and other private places where the parts could escape the whole.

Escaping the whole becomes the thematic touchstone of the galvanic conclusion of the novel.

Gordon accomplishes this shift from apartness to togetherness in four pages. A group of six "of indeterminate genders and radically varying sizes" materializes, among whom Ben identifies Isaac. Leading the group is Eusebio Martinez, his son's psychiatrist, who removes a bundle from the arms of the Asian woman, placing it in Isaac's arms while the crowd forms "two blazing banks on either side." Ruth can only say, softly, "Isaac" as he extends the bundle to her. She turns to Ben, shows him their infant granddaughter while "a groan of adoration rose from the crowd, followed by scattered imitative coos." Now that they have seen and held their grandchild, they infer that the older Asian woman has a vital connection to their son and his daughter. The psychiatrist introduces the mother, Rosemary Tran, to the grandparents. "This Rosemary was as much a street person as Isaac, Ruth could see—more so . . . and a great deal older. . . . Presented to Ruth, she . . . smiled shyly . . . ."

At first, Ruth is put off by Isaac's appearance—"a beard that had crept up his cheeks over the last two years obscured any expression. He might have been an apparition, were it not for his smell." Her revulsion is only momentary. It is preempted by wisdom. To Ruth, Isaac's dirt and odor are "quite tolerable . . . more a confession than a challenge." She thinks of a line from William Shakespeare's *King Lear* (pr. c. 1605-1606, pb. 1608), "It smells of mortality," but a more famous line from Shakespeare sums up the conclusion of *It Will Come to Me.* In the final scene of *The Tempest* (pr. 1611, pb. 1623), Miranda speaks for Ruth, Ben, and everyone in the long lines of candle-bearing cohorts waiting to honor the infant: "O brave new world/ that has such people in't!" They stop "to congratulate the family, to peer into the baby's face, to marvel." These are the last words of the book, and the last word—"marvel"—is the most important one.

Richard Hauer Costa

Review Sources

Booklist 105, no. 11 (February 1, 2009): 26.
The Boston Globe, March 15, 2009, p. C7.
Kirkus Reviews 77, no. 2 (January 15, 2009): 55.
Library Journal 134, no. 3 (February 15, 2009): 94.
The New York Times, March 19, 2009, p.C6.
The New Yorker 85, no. 10 (April 20, 2009): 113.
Publishers Weekly 255, no. 49 (December 8, 2008): 41.
Southern Living 44, no. 2 (February, 2009): 130.

ITALIAN SHOES

Author: Henning Mankell (1948-   )
First published: Italienska skor, 2006, in Sweden
Translated from the Swedish by Laurie Thompson
Publisher: The New Press (New York). 336 pp. $26.95
Type of work: Novel
Time: The early twenty-first century
Locale: An isolated island and various other locations throughout Sweden

The life of a reclusive former physician who lives alone on a remote island is disrupted when a lover of forty years ago suddenly appears and leads him on an eye-opening journey

Principal characters:

FREDRIK WELIN, a reclusive, sixty-six-year-old former physician
POSTMAN JANSSON, the hypochondriacal postal carrier who serves the isolated islands of the archipelago
HARRIET KRISTINA HÖRNFELDT, Welin's former lover, now dying of cancer
LOUISE HÖRNFELDT, Welin's previously unknown daughter by Harriet
GIACONELLI MATEOTTI, an Italian master shoemaker
AGNES KLARSTRÖM, the patient whose botched operation caused Welin's retirement

Swedish author Henning Mankell is probably best known in the United States for his crime novels featuring the somewhat shopworn detective Kurt Wallander. In many ways, the Wallander series has led the way for a recent influx of translations of Scandinavian crime fiction and thrillers. One of the hallmarks of these books is the far-reaching social commentary that accompanies their portrayals of criminal investigations, as well as their focus on the everyday lives of characters and not just the derring-do required to defeat the criminals. This broader social context, often quite political and concerned with economic inequality and unemployment, makes Swedish crime fiction closer to mainstream fiction than to average novels in the mystery genre. This tendency in Swedish fiction helps explain Mankell's easy transition from his crime series to his African novels and to the stand-alone work *Italian Shoes*.

In *Italian Shoes*, Fredrik Welin is a sixty-six-year-old former surgeon who removed himself years ago to his grandparents' summerhouse, where he lives with an aging cat and dog. His home is located on a remote island inhabited by only a few hardy souls who endure being frozen in during the long winter and have only sporadic contact with the outside world even in summer. The postal carrier, Jansson, visits Welin on occasion, appearing more often for advice on his various ailments than to deliver any mail. Every morning, Welin walks down to the jetty, chops a hole in the

Henning Mankell is Sweden's most read author worldwide. His Kurt Wallander series has been translated into thirty-seven languages, with 30 million copies in print. Mankell divides his time between Sweden and Maputo, Mozambique, where he is the director of Teatro Avenida.

ice with an ax, and jumps into the water. The ritual is his way of convincing himself that he is not totally numb to feeling and to life.

Welin's decision to exile himself resulted in large part from a botched operation in which, relying on his staff, he amputated the wrong arm of a young woman who had been a hopeful swimming champion. It is a cruel irony that the original diagnosis proved wrong, so she did not need an operation at all. In disgrace, Welin escaped to his island, hoping to insulate himself from his past. The past will not leave him alone, however, and one day, as he is preparing to go down for his dip in the water, he notices a silhouette, a black figure standing out on the ice. Through his binoculars, Welin sees a woman leaning on a walker, a handbag over her arm, wrapped against the cold. At first, he cannot identify her, but as he looks closer he recognizes her as Harriet Hörnfeldt, his lover of forty years ago.

With Harriet comes Welin's past, the past he has worked so diligently to suppress. She tells him that she has come after all these years to make him honor a promise he made to her when they were still a couple. Once, Welin's father had taken him to an isolated forest pool that left a magical impression on him, and he promised Harriet that he would take her there one day. When he received an invitation to study in the United States, however, he left without a word, rather summarily dumping her. The rejection, she will later confess to him, left her devastated. Welin's excuses for not making the trip to the pool—that his car is too unreliable, that he cannot remember the way, and so on—fall deaf ears. Harriet insists that he fulfill his earlier promise.

From the beginning, the trip appears fraught with disaster. Travel to the mainland, where Welin stores his antiquated car, goes smoothly, and the car seems adequate enough for the trip. However, the travelers get a flat tire, become stuck in a snow bank, and, while staying overnight at a bed and breakfast, discover that their landlady has died. In spite of these setbacks, eventually they reach the forest pool, and Welin experiences relief at finally keeping a promise. He offers to return Harriet to her home before returning to his island. She, however, has one more stop to make and once again insists that he take her there.

This little side trip proves even more revelatory than Harriet's sudden appearance. Welin and Harriet travel to a remote, forested area of Sweden to meet a young woman who lives ina trailer. Harriet calmly informs Welin that the young woman is his daughter. Harriet was pregnant when he abandoned her, and she was unable to reach him with the news that he was about to become a father. Welin is surprised, angered, and finally fearful, retreating to the safety and isolation of his island once again.

Welin finds, however, that the trip has shaken him out of his isolation, and he begins to search for the young swimmer whose arm he mistakenly amputated. After some effort, he locates her and makes a trip, on his own this time, to seek her out. He discovers her name, Agnes Klarström, and that she is operating a foster home for three wayward teenaged girls, Sima, Miranda, and Aida. Her base of operations is owned by an absentee landlord who is in the process of evicting them. After his brief visit, Welin returns to his island, but he begins correspondences with both Agnes and his daughter, Louise. The postman, who at the beginning of the novel never delivered any mail to Welin, now begins to bring letters with him on his visits. Although tentatively, Welin has begun to reengage with the world.

Welin's dog dies in April, reducing by one his emotional attachments on the island. Sima, one of the runaway girls, visits him by stealing a boat and later tries to commit suicide. Getting her medical attention brings Welin further out of his emotional and physical confinement. He begins working to refurbish an old boat of his grandfather's only to eventually abandon the job as beyond his abilities. The boat is a part of the past that he cannot repair. Louise is arrested for participating in a political action. Event after event complicates Welin's life as it enriches it.

The second major event that marks a changing point in Welin's life is also instigated by Harriet. At her behest, he gives a midsummer party and invites his few friends. The party marks Welin's final break with his rejection of the world, but it also marks the end of Harriet, who finally dies. She is given a bonfire cremation nestled in the old boat, which sits atop the funeral pyre.

As the fall settles in before another winter, Welin offers to house the runaways that Agnes is looking after. Agnes visits him to see if the accommodations might suit her needs and the needs of her wards. Louise also returns. Her arrival brings full circle the presence of Harriet, whose bold appearance began Welin's transformation. The novel ends with Welin looking forward to events that might come, rather than backward at events that were.

Italian Shoes is about change. The initial central images of the novel cluster around stasis, isolation, and the past. When the novel opens, Fredrik Welin exists alone on an isolated island, during the frozen time of winter, and in his grandparents' house. He lives a static life, apart from other people, and exists primarily in the past despite trying to avoid it. The island is frozen in, and Welin follows a well-worn routine that includes a daily dip in the ocean. The heart-seizing cold plunge is his one way of shocking his system and reminding himself that he is still alive. His self-imposed isolation is his way of running away from life and its human obligations and interactions. Just as he ran away from Harriet and their relationship, he escaped into his childhood past to avoid his responsibility for maiming his former patient. It is into this literally frozen world that Harriet brings memories of Welin's recent past and the possibility of life-altering change.

The changes Welin experiences in the novel often come with bewildering quickness. Welin discovers he has a daughter without preamble or preface. Harriet just drops the reality on him. His dog and cat die unceremoniously and unexpectedly. His decision to try to find Agnes Klarström appears almost capricious. It is as if, once jogged out of his previous lethargy, Welin slides into action without much resistance.

He may not exactly relish taking action, but neither does he seem to resist it strenuously.

By the novel's end, stasis has given way to dynamism, isolation to involvement, and the past to the present—or at least an engagement between the two. Welin has opened his life to include his newly found daughter and possibly the young, one-armed social worker from whom he has been hiding for years. The metaphors of the narrative suggest the change that is taking place: The ice melts, his daughter's trailer now sits on the island, and he has offered to open his living space to the social worker. Although Harriet dies and is given a Viking funeral of sorts, her reappearance has worked to reconnect her long-lost lover with the world he abandoned. No longer living an isolated life, he even inherits a homeless dog to replace the one who died. Welin is beginning his life over at the story's end, however difficult and brief that new life may be.

It is at the novel's conclusion that the shoes of the title come into play. An Italian shoemaker, a Florentine master craftsman, lives near Louise, and when Welin visited her she had him measured for a pair of shoes. The shoes take the cobbler a year to make. Welin finally receives the exquisitely crafted pair of shoes at the beginning of the final winter portrayed in the novel. He confesses that he wears them only around the house, never outside, always putting them back in their box when he is through. The Italian shoes, reminiscent of sunnier climes and the transforming power of art, provide the perfect image with which to introduce the season of spring, a season of fresh beginnings, into Welin's newly emerging life.

Charles L. P. Silet

Review Sources

Booklist 105, no. 15 (April 1, 2009): 18.
Kirkus Reviews 77, no. 5 (March 1, 2009): 14.
Library Journal 134, no. 7 (April 15, 2009): 85.
The Times Literary Supplement, May 1, 2009, p. 21.

JEFF IN VENICE, DEATH IN VARANASI

Author: Geoff Dyer (1958-)
Publisher: Pantheon Books/Random House (New York). 292 pp. $24.00
Type of work: Novel
Time: The early twenty-first century
Locale: Venice, Italy; Varanasi, India

In Dyer's novel, aimless, middle-aged journalist and critic Jeff Atman takes two trips; the first is an amorous yet ultimately meaningless adventure in Venice, and the second is a deeper, more profound realization of self in Varanasi

Principal characters:
JEFF ATMAN, a freelance writer and critic
LAURA, an American art gallery owner
DARRELL, an American traveler in Varanasi
LALINE, an Anglo-Indian woman visiting Varanasi

Geoff Dyer's novel *Jeff in Venice, Death in Varanasi* is simultaneously more complicated and more playful that it first seems. The first half of the novel narrates in the third person a story about an Englishman named Jeff Atman. Like the author (whose name, Geoff, is a homophone for that of his protagonist), Jeff Atman is a freelance journalist and critic for prestigious British magazines. Jeff is hired to attend the famous Biennale art festival in Venice and conduct an interview with the former love of a famous artist. The second half of the novel is narrated in the first person. The unnamed narrator is presumably still Jeff Atman (there are many similarities and indicators that the two are the same character, but the fact is never entirely confirmed). He has now been sent to Varanasi, a city on the Ganges River in India where Hindus bathe in the river in part to cleanse their body of karmic debt and in some cases to escape further reincarnations.

The complexities and playfulness of the novel are in many ways prefigured by Dyer's earlier work. For example, his *But Beautiful* (1991) tells the purportedly nonfictional life stories of several jazz greats, but the narrative style and approach seem fictive in quality. Dyer's *Out of Sheer Rage* (1997) is both a book about British novelist D. H. Lawrence and a memoir about Dyer's failure to write a book about Lawrence. *Yoga for People Who Can't Be Bothered to Do It* (2003), a collection of travel essays, partly chronicles small voyages of self-discovery similar to the one made by the narrator of the second half of the novel.

The title of *Jeff in Venice*, the first half of the composite novel, is a pun referring to Thomas Mann's famous novella *Der Tod in Venedig* (1912; *Death in Venice*, 1925); the narrative is related to Mann's novella in a number of other ways as well. *Death in Venice* tells the story of the aging Gustav von Aschenbach, who has traveled to Venice from Austria in part out of denial of his impinging mortality. While at the seaside,

Geoff Dyer's works include three previous novels and six books of nonfiction, including Out of Sheer Rage *(1997), a finalist for the National Book Critics Circle Award. He lives in London.*

he becomes obsessed with an adolescent boy named Tadzio, the son of a vacationing aristocratic family. The novella is famous for many things; as Aschenbach's obsession moves from fascination with Tadzio's beauty to a pedophilic sexual longing, Mann seems to be commenting in part on the modernist dichotomy that exists between the Dionysian, or carnal, self and the Apollonian, or platonic and spiritual, side of humans. At the same time, Aschenbach is at least partly infatuated by Tadzio's youth, which in its glory stands in stark contrast to the writer's fading eminence. The novella ends with Aschenbach's death at the very moment he believes that Tadzio may consent to some contact with him.

Just as Aschenbach dyes his hair before descending upon Venice, so does Jeff Atman. Jeff, who in his mid-forties is a decade younger than Aschenbach, is striving also to fight back the forces of ennui and mortality. His life is largely without purpose and has achieved almost a kind of meaningless vagueness: "He had a vague idea of things, a vague sense of what was happening in the world, a vague sense of having met someone before. It was like being vaguely drunk all the time."

While attending the grand Venice art festival the Biennale, however, Jeff meets Laura at one of the endless parties for the members of the media attending the festival. The character is appropriately named, since another Laura was the object of a famous series of love sonnets by Renaissance Italian poet Petrarch (1304-1374). Just as Jeff will fall in love and lust with Laura at first sight, Petrarch's life was presumably changed forever at the sight of his own Laura, a woman who greatly influenced him yet who remained unobtainable to him. Jeff is immediately obsessed with Laura, both from an aesthetic appreciation of her beauty (again mirroring Mann's protagonist) and from a more carnal need to possess her sexually. When the two quickly become lovers, Jeff completely revels in her: the sight of her, her smell, her feel, everything about her. His infatuation is so complete that he thinks of how they can continue their relationship, of how they can commit to a life together beyond the confines of their short time together in Venice.

Jeff's affair with Laura corresponds with his indulgence in drugs, particularly cocaine. He is first reintroduced to these drugs by Laura and then has them thrust upon him. Much like his love affair, the drug use is another escape that allows Jeff to pretend that his youth has not faded and that he has entered a different stage in his life. Despite his revels with Laura, however, the end of the Biennale brings the end of their affair. As much as Jeff clearly wishes to continue their relationship, Laura's assurances ring hollow. Walking Venice like a tourist at the end of the novel's first section, Jeff finally enters the Scuola Grande di San Rocco church. He takes in the various religious paintings by the famous Renaissance Italian artist Tintoretto (1518-1594) but never gains anything from them. He never has an epiphany.

The second half of the novel is set in the Indian city of Varanasi, which serves as a holy site for Hindus and Buddhists, among other faiths. Many Hindus believe that bathing in the Ganges River at sites in Varanasi can cleanse the bather of sins. The unnamed freelance journalist who narrates the section and appears to be Jeff Atman is hired to write a travel piece on Varanasi. One of the allusions of the first half of the novel—a character named "Jeff" as written by a novelist named "Geoff"—is matched in the second half of the novel by an allusion to the character's last name. To Hindus, the "atman" is a person's soul, her or his true self.

Dyer's machinations leave readers with unanswered questions. Why shift from third person to first person? Why obscure the name of the narrator? Why segregate the sections so that their continuity is questionable? If the novel is meant to be read as two novellas, why incorporate so many parallels, and why include so many subtle indicators that Jeff Atman is the protagonist of the second section?

The narrator of the second section is initially skeptical. He takes in the human waste and industrial garbage that routinely floats down the Ganges and is repulsed by it. Traffic in the city is so horrifying to him that he thinks of it as a game called "Varanasi Death Trip." His digestive system is affected more than once by Varanasi's food, and he is forced to subsist on bananas. He is astounded by the vast amounts of human and animal excrement that seem to be found everywhere in the streets and river. He is also shocked by the presence of death; he finds a corpse one day and realizes that in Varanasi death is not so far removed from the everyday as it is in the West.

The narrator quickly befriends an American traveling abroad named Darrell who shares the narrator's ironic sense of humor. Before long, a third person has joined their group, a woman named Laline who is of Indian descent and has been raised in England. Darrell and Laline soon become lovers; their relationship parallels Jeff and Laura's in the first half of the novel. The narrator makes a few halfhearted attempts at seducing other expatriates but largely lacks the energy to throw himself into the pursuit.

Slowly, however, the narrator slowly begins to lose his sense of European identity and become accustomed to the local ways. Jeff notes that, in Hindu tradition, "crossing places" are sacred and "certain crossing places were especially auspicious, but the whole of Varanasi was a crossing place, between this world and the next." Ultimately, Jeff has reached a crossing place in his own life. Instead of dying his hair, he shaves his head. He begins wearing a local tunic called a *dhoti* instead of his western clothes. He even finally washes himself in the Ganges. At the same time, his health begins to deteriorate and his new friends worry about him. He misses his deadlines to return to England, presumably supporting himself through renting out his flat in London.

Some critics have made convincing arguments that the multiple parallels between the two stories show that both texts are telling the same tale in differing ways. On the other hand, there are changes in the second half of the novel that may be read to further reflect themes unique to that half. Jeff's name is never mentioned in the second half of the novel because his sense of identity—and his sense of self, his *atman*—have grown vague and meaningless. In the crossing place of Varanasi, where the self must come to some kind of reckoning, his begins slowly to melt away.

The narrator says that he finds many Hindu ideas confusing, but the concept of *darshan*, or divine seeing and revelation, makes sense to him. As the narrator states,

> This was what Hindus went to the temple for: to see their god, to have him or her revealed to them. The more attention paid to a god, the more it was looked at, the greater its power, the more easily it could be seen. You went to see your god and, in doing so, you contributed to its visibility; the aura emanating from it derived in part from the power bestowed on it.

The narrator will undergo his own revelation of self, realizing that the world he has lived in at home is meaningless and vague. His encounters with women such as Laura are, when all is said and done, simply an escape from the reality of life and the reality of death; they are ways to acknowledge the simple facts of human existence, that all things that live must also someday die. Ashenbach's death in *Death in Venice* may, in some ways, been seen as the final outcome in the confrontation between youthful beauty and aging decrepitude. On the other hand, the narrator's acceptance of his mortality in *Death in Varanasi* perhaps shows a profounder wisdom and an understanding of the transience of the things of this world.

Scott D. Yarbrough

Review Sources

Booklist 105, no. 14 (March 15, 2009): 42.
Kirkus Reviews 77, no. 4 (February 15, 2009): 166.
Library Journal 134, no. 3 (February 15, 2009): 93-94.
London Review of Books 31, no. 11 (June 11, 2009): 24-25.
The New York Review of Books 56, no. 12 (July 16, 2009): 24-25.
The New York Times Book Review, April 19, 2009, p. 12.
The New Yorker 85, no. 10 (April 20, 2009): 110-112.
Publishers Weekly 256, no. 2 (January 12, 2009): 3.
San Francisco Chronicle, April 19, 2009, p. J-5.
The Spectator 309, no. 9423 (April 4, 2009): 32.
The Times Literary Supplement, March 27, 2009, p. 19.

JUDAS
A Biography

Author: Susan Gubar (1944-)
Publisher: W. W. Norton (New York). 453 pp. $27.95
Type of work: Religion
Time: The first century C.E.
Locale: Roman-occupied Israel

An analysis of the many interpretations of the story of Jesus and his betrayal by Judas put forward by theologians, religious leaders, artists, novelists, poets, and playwrights

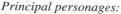

Principal personages:
JESUS OF NAZARETH, Jewish prophet and the Christ
MATTHEW, author of a canonical gospel and, according to tradition, one of Jesus' original disciples
MARK, author of a canonical gospel
LUKE, a companion of Paul and author of a canonical gospel and the Acts of the Apostles
JOHN, author of a canonical gospel and, according to tradition, the youngest of Jesus' original disciples and the author of the Book of Revelations and three canonical letters in the Bible
JUDAS ISCARIOT, one of Jesus' original disciples and the one who betrayed him
PAUL, a later apostle of Jesus and author of thirteen canonical letters in the Bible

In recent years, there has been considerable interest in the supporting characters in the story of Jesus of Nazareth beyond what is said about them in the canonical gospels of the Bible. For example the novel *The Da Vinci Code* (2003) by Dan Brown concerns Mary Magdalene, a female disciple of Jesus, and the alleged descendants of the couple. A translation of the noncanonical Gospel of Judas, another disciple of Jesus, was released in 2006 by *National Geographic* and became controversial because it was at odds with the portrayals of Judas in the canonical books of the Bible. Susan Gubar's *Judas: A Biography* is also about Judas Iscariot, a supporting character who is critical to the story of Jesus because his betrayal is part of the chain of events that leads to Jesus' crucifixion and resurrection.

Strictly speaking, *Judas: A Biography* is not a biography, as the author admits in her introduction. The twenty-two references to Judas Iscariot in the Bible only amount to about twelve hundred words, and they are not consistent with one another. Instead, Gubar examines how writers and artists have interpreted those references through the centuries. Different interpretations are dominant in different historical periods, although the dominant interpretation of a given time is not the only one of its

Susan Gubar is a professor of English at Indiana University in Bloomington. She is the coeditor of The Norton Anthology of Literature by Women *(1985, 1996, 2007) and has written such books as* Critical Condition: Feminism at the Turn of the Century *(2000) and, with Sandra Gilbert,* The Madwoman in the Attic *(1979).*

time and the time in which it is dominant is not the only time people subscribe to it.

The first question Gubar discusses is whether there was a historical Judas. All four canonical gospels, Matthew, Mark, Luke, and John; the Acts of the Apostles, which was written by Luke; and several noncanonical gospels describe Judas's betrayal of Jesus on the night before the crucifixion. The argument in favor of his historical existence would thus seem strong. However, Paul, whose letters predate the canonical gospels, never mentions Judas, nor do several of the noncanonical gospels. Scholars now believe that none of the authors of the canonical gospels were eyewitnesses to the events they described, so none of them can be considered primary sources.

Gubar, following some biblical scholars, also questions whether Judas's betrayal was a necessary precondition of Jesus' crucifixion: The Romans could easily have arrested him in a public place, and his whereabouts on the night of his arrest were not secret if they wished to arrest him in a private setting. Betrayal by someone close to Jesus makes for a stronger narrative. Ultimately, Gubar decides that Judas's factual existence and the historical truth of his actions are irrelevant to her book, since she is primarily interested in how people have interpreted the story over the last two millennia.

Judas's name itself is not without significance. It was a very common Jewish name at that time, so many writers and artists with an anti-Semitic agenda identified all Jews with him, especially since the Jewish religion is often referred to as "Judaism." According to Mark and Matthew, Jesus had a brother named Judas. John mentions yet another man named Judas, and Saint Jude is the patron saint of hopeless causes. Judah, the oldest son of Jacob, betrayed his younger brother Joseph by selling him into slavery in Egypt and founded the largest of the original twelve tribes of Israel. Judas Maccabeus was one of the greatest warriors in Hebrew history.

Gubar's next step is to contrast and compare the versions of the story in the four canonical gospels, in the order in which scholars believe they were written: Mark (written around 68-70 C.E.), Matthew (c. 80-85 C.E.), Luke (c. 80-85 C.E.), and John (c. 95-100 C.E.). All four agree that Judas betrayed Jesus by leading Jewish or Roman authorities to the garden of Gethsemene, where Jesus had retired after the Last Supper to pray. Jesus was accompanied by his disciples Peter, James, and John, who, to his annoyance, kept falling asleep.

None of the four gospels describes Judas's childhood or background. In Mark's version, in return for money, Judas leads the authorities to Jesus, whom he kisses so that the authorities know whom to arrest. Mark never mentions what happens to Judas afterward. Matthew specifies the amount of money as thirty pieces of silver, which has some interesting connections with mentions of silver in the Old Testament, and he also has Judas kissing Jesus. Matthew adds to Mark's account by having Judas repent:

He tries to return the money to the Jewish authorities and then commits suicide by hanging himself. Luke is ambiguous about whether the kiss actually took place, has Judas using the money to buy a field, and then has him die in the field from the bursting of his bowels. Luke also wrote that Judas was possessed by Satan. John does not mention money or the kiss but specifies the arresting authorities as Roman soldiers and has Jesus identify himself to them rather than have Judas do it. John does not describe what happens to Judas after the crucifixion, but he goes so far as to call Judas a demon.

Gubar interprets the progressively harsher portrayals by the authors of the canonical gospels in terms of the need for early Christianity to differentiate itself from Judaism, as personified by Judas. She also discerns several themes that recur in the many interpretations of the story of Jesus and Judas. The first theme is Judas being portrayed as a pariah whose sin of betrayal was unforgivable. This makes him the worst human being in history, since the Bible describes many sinful actions committed by people such as King David and Saint Paul that were eventually forgiven. Saint Jerome (347-420), Saint Augustine (354-430), Martin Luther (1483-1546), John Calvin (1509-1564), and Karl Barth (1886-1968) all took this position. Luther tried to reconcile the accounts of Judas's death in Matthew and Luke by speculating that Judas's bladder burst when he hanged himself.

Gubar comments on Luther's anti-Semitism and draws a clear line between the concept of Judas as pariah, anti-Semitism, and the Holocaust. Judas is made to stand for the Jewish people so that executions of the Jews by the Nazis are justified as punishment for the betrayal of Jesus. Nazi theologians argued that Jesus was not a Jew but an Aryan and that Judas betrayed him in much the same way that the Jews betrayed Germany during World War I. (Hitler himself rejected this theory, because he considered Christianity itself to be part of the Jewish conspiracy against the Aryans.)

Gubar cites many examples in this anti-Semitic tradition. For instance, in Dante's *La divina commedia* (c. 1320; *The Divine Comedy*, 1802), Satan tortures Judas for eternity by using him as a kind of chew toy. In Jacopo da Voragine's *Legenda aurea* (c. 1260; *The Golden Legend*, 1483) and the Wakefield Mystery Plays (fourteenth century), Judas's story is combined with that of Oedipus in that he kills his father and marries his own mother. In the film *Dracula 2000* (2000), the title character is the reincarnation of Judas, which explains his aversion to silver and the crucifix.

Gubar also discusses common interpretations and portrayals of Judas's kiss. She describes Ludovico Carracci's painting *Kiss of Judas* (1589-1590) as homoerotic. In the Gospel of Barnabas, written in either the late Middle Ages or the early modern period, Judas loves Jesus so much that he takes Jesus' place and is the one crucified. This gospel is very popular in the Islamic world because it denies Jesus's divinity and his resurrection. Gubar cites Emily Dickinson's poem "'Twas Love—not me—" as a dramatic monologue by Judas declaring his love for Jesus. In Terence McNally's 1998 play *Corpus Christi*, Judas is openly gay. Another gay interpretation of the story is the 1964 film *The Gospel According to St. Matthew.*

After the Enlightenment, scholars approached the Bible as a historical text. Thomas De Quincey in his essay "Judas Iscariot" (1857) conceived Judas as a Jewish patriot, like his namesake Judas Maccabeus, who mistakenly believed that Jesus had come to establish a worldly kingdom. His betrayal was thus meant to force Jesus to take action. Richard Hengist Horne's verse drama "Scriptural Tragedy" (1848), Frederick William Orde Ward's dramatic monologue "Judas Iscariot" (1897), Cale Young Rice's poem "The Wife of Judas Iscariot" (1912), W. W. Story's long poem *A Roman Lawyer in Jerusalem: First Century* (1970), Norman Mailer's *The Gospel According to the Son* (1997), and the 1961 film version of *The King of Kings* all take this viewpoint. Dorothy Sayers and Robinson Jeffers both take an opposing, although complementary, approach, Sayers in her 1943 radio play *The Man Born to be King* and Jeffers in his verse drama *Dear Judas* (1928). In both versions, Judas is a pacifist who believes that Jesus plans a violent revolt, and he betrays him to prevent an insurrection.

The last major theme Gubar discusses is the notion that Judas's betrayal was a necessary condition of Jesus' crucifixion and resurrection. Consequently, Judas's action saved the human race and is therefore forgivable, as Joseph forgave his brother Judah and King David and St. Paul were forgiven for their sins. The fifteenth century dialogue *Lucius and Dubius* takes this position. John Donne (1572-1631) argued that Judas was only doing what Jesus wished him to do so that Jesus could be crucified and redeem the human race. Theologian Paul Tillich (1886-1965) also subscribed to this view, and even Karl Barth commented on the paradox that Judas is condemned for doing God's will. Albert Levitt's *Judas Iscariot: An Imaginative Autobiography* (1961), José Saramago's *The Gospel According to Jesus Christ* (1991), and the recently translated Gospel of Judas agree with this position. A variation of this theme argues that Jesus tricked or persuaded Judas into betraying him. Examples are found in Armando Cosani's novel *The Flight of the Feather Serpent* (1953), Hugh J. Schonfield's *The Passover Plot* (1965), and Michael Dickinson's *The Lost Testament of Judas Iscariot* (1994).

Some authors combine these themes. In *Ho teleutaios peirasmos* (1955; *The Last Temptation of Christ*, 1960; also known as *The Last Temptation*) and its film adaptation, *The Last Temptation of Christ* (1988), Nikos Kazantzakis combines the concepts of Judas as both patriot and savior. Judas knows that he is helping Jesus perform his mission on Earth, and Jesus tells him that God gave Judas the more difficult task of betraying a friend rather than the simpler task of being crucified. However, Kazantzakis follows John's version of Jesus's arrest in that there is no kiss and Jesus identifies himself to the authorities. In Mario Brelich's 1975 novel *The Work of Betrayal*, the author combines the savior theme with the homoerotic aspect of the story, postulating a love triangle among Jesus, Judas, and John. Judas forfeits his own salvation so that everyone else can be saved.

None of these interpretations reveal anything about a historical Judas. However, as Gubar points out, they do reveal a great deal about the interpreters themselves and about the times and places in which they lived.

Thomas R. Feller

Review Sources

Booklist 105, no. 12 (February 15, 2009): 8.
Kirkus Reviews 77, no. 1 (January 1, 2009): 22.
Library Journal 134, no. 1 (January 1, 2009): 97.
The New York Times, April 5, 2009, p. BR10.
The New York Times Book Review, April 5, 2009, p. 10.
Publishers Weekly 256, no. 2 (January 12, 2009): p. 41.
Times Higher Education, October 15, 2009, p. 48.
The Washington Post, March 26, 2009, p. C01.

A JURY OF HER PEERS
Celebrating American Women Writers from Anne Bradstreet to Annie Proulx

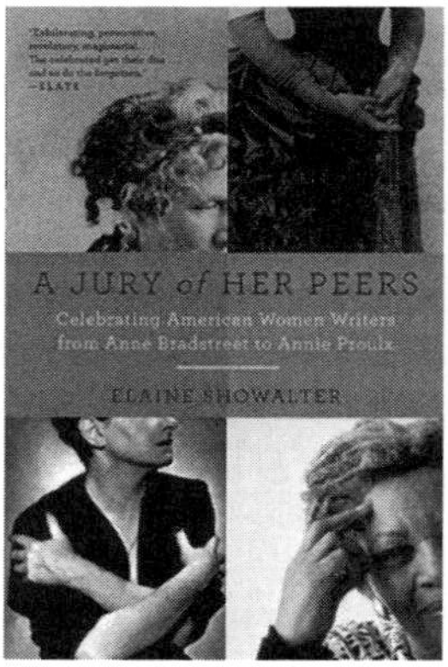

Author: Elaine Showalter (1941-   )
Publisher: Alfred A. Knopf (New York). 608 pp. $30.00
Type of work: Literary criticism, literary history
Time: 1650-2000
Locale: United States

A comprehensive, perceptive, if flawed, effort to encompass a history of American women writers while at the same time identifying the best work that deserves to be included in the canon of American literature

The daunting nature of Elaine Showalter's task in *A Jury of Her Peers* is made apparent by simply noting that the book is the first comprehensive history and assessment of American women writers ever to be published. Even though feminist literary criticism and history have produced an impressive body of work, including several anthologies meant to recover neglected masterpieces and other significant work out of print and forgotten, no scholar has essayed a book-length overview of the achievements of women writers in the United States. To do so invites controversy—as Showalter acknowledges in observing that feminist critics have hesitated to make qualitative judgments, wishing to be inclusive of the many women writers who for centuries have not received their due. She believes, however, that the first phase of fully acknowledging women writers—the discovery period begun in the 1970's—is over and that it is time to write a selective history and assessment of those women writers who belong in the American literary canon.

If Showalter had been content only to produce a work of literary history, she could have avoided some of the judgments that reviewers of her book have made concerning her choices. Some reviewers have questioned, for example, the decision to write about Pearl Buck but not Eleanor Clark when they see the latter as manifestly the superior writer. The answer to this question is perhaps that, because Buck was the first woman writer to win the Nobel Prize and because her work has had such an impact on American culture, she deserves a place more than Clark, who appeals to a much smaller audience. This seems like a weak argument, however—one that Showalter would not have to entertain if she had written a two-volume work. Such a work could have comprised one volume of more objective history followed by a second putting forward a more programmatic argument about which authors covered in the first volume ought to be included in the American literary canon.

The writers that Showalter does discuss—and there are over 250 of them—are, for the most part, presented with considerable flair and concision. Especially noteworthy are Showalter's discussions of Anne Bradstreet, Harriet Beecher Stowe, and Annie

Proulx. The examinations of these three authors stand out, in part, because they exemplify Showalter at her best—melding historical context with literary achievement. Bradstreet, a dutiful Puritan daughter and wife, nevertheless faced the daunting prospect of life in a new world and was able to write poetry that remains profound and affecting. Stowe, in Showalter's narrative, is a towering figure not only because of the pervasive influence of her great novel, *Uncle Tom's Cabin: Or, Life Among the Lowly* (serial, 1851-1852; book, 1852) but also because of Stowe's literary experimentation, especially in *Dred: A Tale of the Great Dismal Swamp* (1856), a work that deserves to be set against the finest achievements in the American novel. Proulx emerges as a true groundbreaker, a woman competing with male authors on their own territory by refashioning the view of the American West in stories such as "Brokeback Mountain" (1997, revised 1999).

Elaine Showalter, a feminist scholar teaching at Princeton University, has authored several influential studies, including A Literature of Their Own *(1977, revised 1982),* The Female Malady: Women, Madness, and English Culture, 1830-1980 *(1985), and* Daughters of Decadence *(1993).*

For the most part, Showalter eschews sociological explanations as to why very few American women created great literature before the twentieth century, but she does offer the following explanations: Many women believed that their families came first; others had to put up with and were obstructed by husbands who resented their wives' dedication to literary labors; and middle-class American women writers, unlike their British counterparts, did not usually have servants and were far more directly involved in the day-to-day details of housework and homemaking. The British class system, in other words, actually worked in favor of certain women writers who could assign menial tasks to their servants. Then, too, only a few of the men in charge of the literary establishment were disposed to publish work by women. In this context, those women who did become best-selling novelists seem all the more impressive for their initiative and determination.

The virtue of writing a combined work of literary history and literary criticism in one volume is that Showalter can reveal the conditions out of which great work is created. She notes, for example, that for every great poem Emily Dickinson wrote she had behind her another ten that were flawed. It is also suggestive, Showalter notes, that Dickinson was at her most productive during the Civil War, even though her poetry does not deal explicitly with that crucial event. Literature is not created in a vacuum, and it is to Showalter's credit that she is able to write so cogently about the way writers interact with their environments.

If by the 1850's women were capable of writing best sellers, that ability did not earn them the respect of the critical establishment, Showalter demonstrates. Indeed, male authors such as Nathaniel Hawthorne complained about having to compete with popular female novelists. Other male writers suggested that women had no business trying to write great literature because they tended to write about domestic matters rather than taking on the important subjects of war and world events. Even the most successful women writers—such as Willa Cather and Edith Wharton—shared this male bias and scorned the literature produced by their sex. Those such as Amy Lowell who openly competed with male poets such as T. S. Eliot and Ezra Pound were rejected as merely ambitious interlopers. Other successful poets, such as Marianne Moore, were careful to avoid lyrical poetry that reflected their feelings, opting instead for "objective," hard-edged poems about animals that cultivated an impersonal air.

Showalter takes her title from a story by Susan Glaspell, a playwright contemporary of Eugene O'Neill who worked with him at the Provincetown Playhouse. Glaspell's story, which she also turned into a play retitled *Trifles* (pr. 1916, pb. 1917), makes the point that women have not been perceived as the peers of men and therefore their work has not been evaluated with the respect automatically given to that of male authors. The irony is that Glaspell herself and her story were largely forgotten until her peers, women, rediscovered her in the 1970's. Until then, most journals, reference works, and other venues where American literature was assessed did not even include women on their editorial boards. Women writers were, in other words, virtually invisible. Thus, Showalter sees her work as building on a generation of feminist scholars who have brought back into literary consciousness the work of Glaspell and others such as Mary Hunter Austin, Charlotte Perkins Gilman, Dorothy Canfield Fisher, Tess Slesinger, Jean Stafford, Gwendolyn Brooks, Shirley Jackson, Diane Johnson, Marilynne Robinson, and Gish Jen.

Quite aside from the important writers Showalter does not discuss—for example, Evelyn Scott, Caroline Gordon, Mary Lee Settle, and Dawn Powell—Showalter sometimes seems curiously neglectful of her contemporaries. She barely mentions Susan Sontag, even though Sontag is a shining example of a woman who was able to compete successfully among New York intellectuals and become a cultural figure in ways they could not. Similarly, Showalter's treatment of Lillian Hellman is perfunctory: There is no mention of the way she triumphed as a feminist icon in the late 1960's and early 1970's. Moreover, Hellman's plays are barely acknowledged. Showalter's comment that *The Children's Hour* (pr., pb. 1934) is dated because it deals with lesbianism is perplexing. Certainly, the play no longer has the shock value of its first production, but the work is hardly just about lesbianism. Showalter might as well dismiss William Shakespeare because Americans are no longer monarchists. Her take on Hellman is certainly acceptable, if debatable, in academia, but theater professionals and American audiences do not share this disparaging view and have made Hellman's plays a part of the canon irrespective of academic judgments.

Even more disturbing is Showalter's failure to discuss the strides feminists have made in American biography, beginning with Nancy Milford's landmark biography of Zelda Fitzgerald and continuing with the work of Elinor Langer, Deirdre Bair, Marion Meade, Stacy Schiff, and many other women writers who have taken on biographical subjects that were once almost the exclusive privilege of male biographers or have identified female subjects that male biographers have overlooked or discounted. Apparently, Showalter accepts the academic bias against biography—that the genre is not itself to be classified as literature—but the consequence of this attitude is to obscure the way women biographers have reshaped the American literary canon and American history through their treatment of both male and female figures. It is as if the academic world and its ideas of what constitute literature are the only arbiter in *A Jury of Her Peers*.

The irony is that Showalter relies in many cases on biography in order to construct her narrative. Her notes cite the relevant biographies on which she has drawn, yet she seems not to realize that those very biographies are not only part of the history and the assessments she is intent on pursuing but also make possible the very history she has written. Thus, she does not discuss the reasons why is biography as a genre made its appeal to women writers beginning in the 1970's. Nor does she adequately explore how these women writers became the jury of peers that she showcases. Omitting American women biographers harms Showalter's assessment of women writers, as well as her understanding of how literary history is made.

Even with its gaps and questionable judgments, however, *A Jury of Her Peers* is an astonishing tour de force and a courageous effort to advance women's studies beyond the stage of celebrating its writers and deploring the reactionary male critical establishment. Showalter suggests that the literary playing field for women is now on a par with that for men. As creative writers and critics, women have achieved their goal: to be judged by their peers, men and women no longer held back by prejudices against the very idea that women can create great literature. In the long run, *A Jury of Her Peers* is bound to have a positive impact, encouraging new generations of scholars to exercise their judgment by holding women and men to the same standard of literary excellence.

Carl Rollyson

Review Sources

America 200, no. 17 (May 25, 2009): 23-24.
Booklist 105, no. 9/10 (January 1, 2009): 35.
Commentary 127, no. 6 (June, 2009): 74-76.
Commonweal 136, no. 17 (October 9, 2009): 22-23.
The Economist 390, no. 8619 (February 21, 2009): 83-84.
Library Journal 134, no. 3 (February 15, 2009): 108.
New York Review of Books 56, no. 15 (October 8, 2009): 37-38.
The New York Times Book Review, March 8, 2009, p. 16.
Publishers Weekly 256, no. 1 (January 5, 2009): 40-41.
The Times Literary Supplement, May 8, 2009, pp. 11-12.
Weekly Standard 14, no. 42 (July 27, 2009): 32-34.
Women's Review of Books 26, no. 4 (July/August, 2009): 5-7.

THE KINDLY ONES

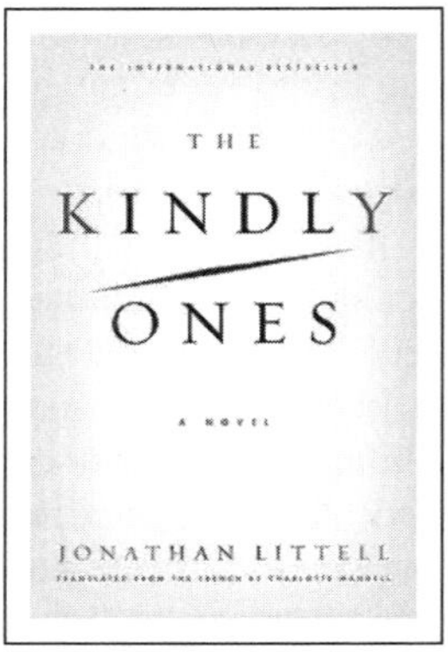

Author: Jonathan Littell (1967-   )
First published: Les Bienveillantes, 2006, in France
Translated from the French by Charlotte Mandell
Publisher: HarperCollins (New York). 984 pp. $29.99
Type of work: Novel
Time: 1941-1945
Locale: Soviet Russia; Poland; Germany; France

An epic novel of the Holocaust that painstakingly describes the bureaucratic and military machinery developed by Hitler and his henchmen for the annihilation of the Jews and other minorities, told years later by a former SS officer living in France under an assumed identity

Principal characters:

MAXIMILIEN (MAX) VON AUE, a Schutzstaffel (SS) officer during World War II and later a lace merchant in the north of France
THOMAS HAUSER, SS officer and Max's closest friend
UNA VON ÜXKÜLL, née AUE, Max's twin sister, who marries an older German aristocrat
HÉLOÏSE MOREAU (formerly AUE), Max's mother, who remarries after the disappearance of his father
ARISTIDE MOREAU, Max's stepfather, whom he despises
DR. MANDELBROD, a top Nazi ideologue who claims to have known Max's father

Jonathan Littell's *The Kindly Ones* is a colossal novel in the form of a fictional memoir. The narrator and protagonist is Dr. Maximilien von Aue, a former officer in the *Sicherheitsdienst* (SD), the secret service of the *Schutzstaffel* (SS), the elite Nazi military organization that operated within and alongside the German army during World War II. Now an elderly lace merchant living under an assumed name in the north of France, Max is married, has twin children, and is bored with his life. His attempt to tell "how it happened" mainly covers the period from June, 1941, the beginning of the German invasion of Soviet Russia, to April, 1945, when Russian troops conquered Berlin. There are also frequent flashbacks to Max's childhood and student days, usually triggered by some stressful event during his involvement in the extermination of Jews and other minorities in the conquered territories.

The external structure of the novel parallels that of a baroque orchestral suite; the individual chapters bear the names of the dance movements of such a suite, and the action described in each chapter reflects the mood and tempo of each musical subdivision. Thus, the first chapter is called "Toccata," referring to a virtuoso piece to highlight the technical mastery of the performer. Toccatas were used as introductions or overtures to suites and fugues in the contrapuntal works of Johann Sebastian Bach

(1685-1750), Jean-Philippe Rameau (1683-1764), and François Couperin (1668-1733), all of whom the narrator mentions as his favorite composers. The last chapter is entitled "Gigue," referring to a lively dance known in English as the jig, and the novel comes to a close in a bullet-riddled dance of death.

Jonathan Littell was raised and educated bilingually in both the United States and France. He has worked for several international humanitarian organizations and wrote one science-fiction novel before The Kindly Ones, *which won the Prix Goncourt and the Grand Prix du Roman de l'Académie Française in 2006.*

Before beginning his memoirs proper, the narrator delivers a brilliant harangue, addressing his readers as his "human brothers," knowing full well that they will reject any kinship with a man involved in the Nazis' extermination of millions of Jews and other "undesirables." Von Aue goes even further; he repeatedly insinuates that most of his readers, given the same circumstances, would have acted exactly as he did and that he regrets nothing, since all he did was his work. However, he explicitly refuses to claim, as many of his colleagues did, that he was only following orders and admits that he did what he did because it was his duty and had to be done. In doing so, he asserts that in war cruel acts are committed not by sadistic monsters—though he admits that there were those as well—but by "ordinary" people. He himself had once hoped to be such a person before "all this evil" entered his life.

Max ends his address to readers with an impassioned plea for understanding:

> I live, I do what can be done, it's the same for everyone, I am a man like other men, I am a man like you. I tell you, I am just like you!

This passage presages the main argument his narration attempts to illustrate, stated later in the novel: that there is no such thing as inhumanity, only humanity.

Max's recollections of his life as an SS officer on the eastern front and as an administrator in the forced labor and extermination camp system constitute a description of a long descent into hell, one that begins even before his war experiences. An incestuous relationship with his sister Una when they were both in their early teens has left him incapable of a meaningful heterosexual love life and driven him to mainly random, often violent, homosexual affairs. His sister has married an older, impotent German aristocrat and has outgrown their previous relationship. Max hates his mother and his stepfather for having forcibly separated him from his twin sister, to the point that he murders both of them after his return from the Russian front.

The horrors of his duties in the *Einsatzgruppen*, the task forces that accompany advancing German troops and identify Jews, Bolsheviks, and other "undesirables" in order to have them executed, begin to weigh heavily on Max. Although he constantly maintains that he must keep his cool sense of detachment, it becomes evident from increasingly frequent crying fits, nightmares, and bouts of vomiting and diarrhea that Max is losing his sanity, as his task force makes its murderous voyage through the Ukraine, the Crimea, the Caucasus, and finally to Stalingrad. He seems to have suffered a head wound, but he does not remember doing so. Instead, he can recollect the wound only as a long, weird fantasy about his sister. The wound and his detachment from it symbolize his growing loss of touch with reality, which he begins to repress even in his memoir: He has, for instance, no memory of having killed his mother and stepfather on a brief trip to France. Only Thomas Hauser, his friend and confidant, manages to return Max to a normal life occasionally, thus saving his life and his career more than once in the novel.

After his superiors refuse him a posting to France for which he felt singularly qualified because of his bicultural upbringing and education, Max's life rapidly disintegrates. This disintegration parallels the falling apart of the Third Reich to which he has sworn loyalty. After a last, unsuccessful attempt to forget his sister Una and to establish a normal relationship with a young woman who clearly loves him, Max finds himself at the deserted estate of Una's husband, where he descends to a completely animalistic state, living out his incestuous fantasies. Quite in keeping with his condition, the novel's final scenes take place at the bombed-out Berlin zoo. Two dogged policeman have been after Max for some time, convinced that he has murdered his mother and stepfather. As Max is about to be shot by one of them, Thomas saves him once more by killing his enemy; Max, however, beats his friend to death with a crowbar and takes the French identify papers Thomas had prepared for his escape. In the guise of a released forced laborer, he makes his way to France, where he eventually becomes a wealthy, middle-class merchant, married with twin children, just like his despised bourgeois stepfather. In addition, Max has to bear the guilt of his participation in the horrors of the Holocaust, which he has been trying to assuage by writing this memoir.

The Kindly Ones is an ambitious novel on one of the most controversial subjects in contemporary literature, the Holocaust. It is written, not from the usual perspective of the victims, but through the reminiscences of a perpetrator who appears to have escaped the consequences of his crimes. Max claims to be an ordinary human being, neither a sadistic beast nor the "one good Nazi" of so many books and films about the Holocaust. In order to accomplish his seemingly impossible task, Littell had to reconcile two opposing components: First of all, he had to portray the Holocaust from the viewpoint of a highly educated intellectual who fervently believes in the Nazi ideology and who sees the extermination of the Jews not as a pleasure but a necessary and often odious administrative task. This task is performed in the context of a huge bureaucratic apparatus in which the narrative is a cog and that provides him with more chances for advancement than would other legal tasks for which he is qualified. The enormous bulk of the novel results from its meticulous and historically accurate descriptions of the workings of this bureaucracy: its overly complicated structure; the petty jealousies operating between its various branches and executives; and the logistical problems of finding its intended victims, developing efficient means for their execution and the disposal of their bodies, and keeping up the morale and team spirit of the people involved.

Portraying the mind-set of an intellectual SS officer and the vast Nazi bureaucracy is the purpose structuring the novel as a very strictly organized Baroque suite. The execution of the Nazis' so-called final solution from Max's perspective is a mathematical, economic, and logistical problem, performed mostly by career bureaucrats who after work are husbands, fathers, musicians, and neighbors—in other words, ordinary people. The sadistic torturers who find physical and emotional satisfaction in taunting and killing individuals are portrayed as a small minority. The greatest concern for Max is that his reports are well written and that all the accounts are correct and can pass muster when examined by auditors. The recognition of this "banality of evil," to use Hannah Arendt's characterization of Adolf Eichmann, strikes more horror into readers than the pornography of violence that erupts in the novel from time to time.

The cogs of the Nazi machinery in Littell's account are "ordinary people" who are subject to neuroses and psychoses, often caused or made worse by stress and guilt. As the title of the novel indicates, Littell bases the internal structure of the novel on the last play of the classical Greek trilogy the *Oresteia* (458 B.C.E.; English translation, 1777) by Aeschylus. In this play, *Eumenides*, or "the Kindly Ones," Orestes objects to his mother marrying another man, believing that her husband Agamemnon has been killed in the Trojan War. He is sent away from home, living with the family of Pylades, who becomes his best friend. Eventually, Orestes returns and kills both his mother and his stepfather, aided by his beloved sister Elektra. As a result, he is pursued by the Furies, goddesses of revenge who seek to punish him for his matricide. In the end, the Furies consent to abandon their pursuit in favor of civilized forms of justice. From then on, they are called the Kindly Ones.

In the novel, Max plays the role of Orestes, Thomas is Pylades, and Max's twin sister Una is Elektra. It is his hatred of his mother and his stepfather that drives Max to Germany, toward National Socialism, and finally to murder. This pathological hatred, combined with his incestuous attraction to his sister, allows readers to distance themselves from Max and to doubt his claims of being an "ordinary person." Even as he progresses in revealing his inner self and his past, it becomes clear that he is, contrary to his assertions, racked by guilt and that for him the Furies have not turned into the Kindly Ones.

The Kindly Ones was met with the predictable firestorm of contrasting opinions. German and Jewish critics mostly condemned the book as pornographic in its descriptions both of homosexual activity and of executions, whereas critics in the United States and France were more positive, as evidenced by Littell's garnering two of the most prestigious French literary prizes. While it may be premature to praise the book as the great Holocaust novel, as some reviewers have done, Littell's novel is, despite its intimidating size and its often hard-to-stomach descriptions of death and violence, clearly one of the most significant literary events of the year.

Franz G. Blaha

Review Sources

Booklist 105, no. 11 (February 1, 2009): 25.
Commentary 127, no. 5 (May, 2009): 78-81.
Kirkus Reviews 77, no. 1 (January 1, 2009): 8.
Library Journal 134, no. 2 (February 1, 2009): 66.
London Review of Books 31, no. 8 (April 30, 2009): 11-13.
The New Republic 240, no. 5 (April 1, 2009): 38-43.
New Statesman 138, no. 4940 (March 16, 2009): 55-56.
The New York Review of Books 56, no. 5 (March 26, 2009): 18-21.
The New York Times, February 24, 2009, p.C1.
The New York Times Book Review, March 8, 2009, p.10.
The New Yorker 85, no. 6 (March 23, 2009): 75.
Publishers Weekly 255, no. 49 (December 8, 2008): 42-43.
Publishers Weekly 256, no. 48 (November 30, 2009): 41.
The Times Literary Supplement, March 6, 2009, p. 21.
World Literature Today 77, no. 1 (April-June, 2003): 77-78.

KING'S DREAM

Author: Eric J. Sundquist (1954-   )
Publisher: Yale University Press (New Haven, Conn.).
320 pp. $26.00
Type of work: History
Time: 1963
Locale: Washington, D.C.

Sundquist's close reading of Martin Luther King, Jr.'s "I Have a Dream" speech reveals the essence of the Civil Rights movement in America

Principal personages:
MARTIN LUTHER KING, Jr., African American religious and civil rights leader
ABRAHAM LINCOLN, U.S. president, 1861-1865
JOHN LEWIS, African American civil rights leader and later U.S. representative from Georgia, 1987-
MALCOLM X, African American religious leader and activist

Perhaps no speech since Abraham Lincoln's Gettysburg Address has summarized the past, present, and future of the United States as well as Martin Luther King, Jr.'s 1963 "I Have a Dream" speech. It had been one hundred years since the Emancipation Proclamation, and many African Americans were demanding that the U.S. government do more to secure their rights. King addressed a gathering of over 250,000 people at the Lincoln Memorial in Washington, D.C., on August 28, 1963. Their march to that memorial was a symbol of their desire for a new civil rights bill to be quickly passed by Congress and signed by President John F. Kennedy.

King carefully prepared a written speech for the occasion. Subtly alluding to Lincoln, King wrote "fivescore years ago, a great American, in whose symbolic shadow we stand today, signed the Emancipation Proclamation." As Eric J. Sundquist illustrates in *King's Dream*, King attempted to show that the promises made one hundred years earlier were as yet unfulfilled. The Declaration of Independence and the Constitution were seen as "promissory notes" yet to be satisfied.

The timing of the speech was significant for other reasons. Many African Americans were beginning to believe that King's philosophy of nonviolent, peaceful protest was taking too long to accomplish results. He was under challenge by younger members of the movement such as John Lewis, whose more radical speech immediately before King's that day had to be toned down at the last minute. He also faced the challenge of the emerging Black Power movement and the Nation of Islam, both of which called for more direct and forceful action against segregation. King replied to these challenges that African Americans could not ". . . satisfy our thirst for freedom by drinking from the cup of bitterness and hatred." It was clear, however, that there was no turning the Civil Rights movement back.

Eric J. Sundquist is UCLA Foundation Professor of Literature at UCLA. He is the author or editor of twelve books on American literature and culture, including the award-winning volumes To Wake the Nations: Race in the Making of American Literature *(1993) and* Strangers in the Land: Blacks, Jews, Post-Holocaust America *(2005).*

In the chapter "Soul Force," Sundquist traces a subtle, emerging black consciousness in the early 1960's. Signs of frustration, anger, and a desire for freedom began to appear in poetry, art, and, above all, music. Jazz in particular became the "language of dissent," as Sundquist describes it. Music became a precursor of the great changes to come.

Sundquist also shows that King made very effective use of Scripture. As an ordained minister steeped in theology, he was able to frame a speech that appealed to biblical prophecy, as in his Promised Land analogy, and to Old Testament parables and symbolism. The black church has always been an integral part of African American culture, and King's audience understood the connections he was drawing between the Bible and the Civil Rights movement.

As Sundquist emphasizes, King delivered his speech in the shadow of Lincoln's statue. Speaking at the Lincoln Memorial gave King's speech historical legitimacy. The Civil War did not settle the question of the status of free blacks in America, especially in the South. In a sense, King chose to speak, one hundred years later, at the great monument to ask that Lincoln's promise of a "new birth of freedom" be fulfilled at last.

Sunquist also reads King's use of the lyrics of "America" ("My country 'tis of thee . . ."). The author claims that this was not a spontaneous decision on King's part. The song had been sung by African Americans for generations, even though a "sweet land of liberty" was not a reality for them. King employed the lyrics as an ideal—a promise to be realized when freedom and equality are achieved. The resonance of the song with King's audience also demonstrates, Sundquist notes, that most African Americans, in spite of the inequality they had suffered for so long, still considered themselves Americans. They believed in the American Dream and were willing to work toward a day when true equality would be theirs. For them, it was a song about hope yet to be fulfilled.

Watching and listening to the speech very carefully, Sundquist detects a moment when King abandoned his prepared text and began to preach extemporaneously. King never fully explained why this happened. Perhaps the excitement of the moment brought out the preacher in him; perhaps he saw an opportunity to profoundly inspire the huge crowd. In any case, he drew his words from writings and sermons delivered over many years. This has led some critics to charge that this portion of King's speech was plagiarized. Sermons, however, are not meant to be well-documented scholarly treatises. Their purpose is to inspire, uplift, and challenge their listeners. In this sense, King was shaping the collected wisdom of many sources to make his point more forcefully. The dividing line, where he began to speak directly from his heart and soul, seems to be at the point where he said "I still have a dream."

The theme of an American Dream appears in many of King's previous speeches and sermons, and it seems particularly appropriate here. Paraphrasing from the Old Testament, the Declaration of Independence, and the lyrics of "America," King proclaimed his dream. The result was electrifying. Repeating the phrase "Let freedom ring . . ." he challenges segregation, hatred, and those who would advocate violence. "If America is to become a great nation, this [freedom] must become true." Taking the audience across the country and to "every village and every hamlet, from every state and every city . . ." he illustrated that segregation was not exclusively a Southern problem; it was an American problem. Repeatedly employing the power of symbolism (". . . we will be able to hew out of the mountain of despair a stone of hope"), King effectively reminded his audience that, until the cancer of racism is everywhere removed, America cannot become or remain a great nation. Like those of Lincoln before him, King's words strongly resonated among those who heard them. In a few short paragraphs, he touched a nation and reenergized the movement.

Looking back, King's speech stands as the highwater mark of his leadership of the Civil Rights movement. In the months and years to follow, President Kennedy would be assassinated, Malcolm X would be killed, and the Vietnam War would escalate. King's final challenge, Sundquist believes, came with the line ". . . that my four little children will one day live in a nation where they will not be judged by the color of their skin but by the content of their character." In the years following King's speech, Sundquist observes, the United States has struggled to bring this about. It may not be possible, the author asserts, ever to completely ignore race, and highly controversial programs such as affirmative action and school busing have specifically taken race into account in order to achieve equality.

In the book's final chapter, Sundquist ponders the question of whether a truly "color-blind" society is possible. He considers the argument that past inequities in hiring, promotion, and college admissions cannot be rectified without taking race into account. Most Supreme Court decisions involving equity issues have allowed race to be considered as a factor, validating a practice that Sundquist calls "race-conscious affirmative action." King illustrated his views on equality by use of an analogy of an athletic competition. People who have been held in bondage and denied the advantages granted to others cannot be put at the starting line in a race and be expected to perform as well as those in positions of privilege. In the "race of life" as King put it, the United States must do more than simply bring more people to the starting line. Equal opportunity is not enough. More has to be done, King believed, to help African Americans overcome their disadvantages.

King frequently used the metaphor of a footrace to illustrate his views on equality. He thought that preferential treatment in hiring, for example, may be the only way to even the odds and give African Americans a real chance: No racially neutral program would work. Sundquist believes that the Supreme Court decisions dealing with affirmative action issued after King's death brought a period of "transitional inequality" in which race had to be taken into account in order to get beyond racism. The hope was that eventually the use of racial preferences would no longer be necessary.

Sundquist presents evidence that King's goal was a totally "color-blind" society, but King was also a pragmatist. Sundquist believes that King would have understood the need for racial preferences and affirmative action to achieve his dream. King's ideal goes much further, however. He saw a world cleansed of not only racial injustice but also of economic injustice toward all people—not just African Americans. Photographs of the crowd at the March on Washington that heard King's speech show a substantial proportion of whites, suggesting that his message was a universal one. As King used to say, "injustice anywhere is a threat to justice everywhere."

Sundquist's book represents perhaps the most detailed analysis of King's speech to date. It does an excellent job of comparing and contrasting King's words with the thoughts of other African American leaders such as W. E. B. Du Bois and Malcolm X. Sundquist admirably shows that, in the first and more formal part of the speech, King's words were carefully chosen and crafted to explain the status of civil rights in 1963 and the historical irony of the gathering in Washington that August day. The second part of the speech came directly from King's heart and soared in its imagery and oratorical power. In that moment, King inspired and uplifted Americans far beyond his tragic death in 1968. He secured his rightful place in history and became the catalyst for the changes that followed his passing.

Sundquist powerfully reminds his readers that one cannot begin to comprehend the history of race relations in America without fully understanding the "I Have a Dream" speech. Delivering the speech at the height of his influence, King summed up the past and showed the way to the future for African Americans. Some dismissed it as being too idealistic and too far-reaching. Others doubted that the philosophy of nonviolence was the way to get there. King's leadership, however, was unquestioned, and his vision was clear: The Promised Land was attainable for African Americans if they would stay the course.

As Sundquist says, King could not know, nor could the rest of the country, that his dream would be America's dream for a long time to come. The struggle would continue long after his passing, but his greatness and his words would live on to inspire millions. In addition, the passage of the Civil Rights Act of 1964 and the Voting Rights Act (1965) can be at least indirectly attributed to the challenge posed by King's words in 1963. The election of the first African American president is proof that America has come a long way since King delivered his speech. No doubt, King would have been pleased. Sundquist believes that one day a Martin Luther King Memorial in Washington, D.C., in the line of sight of the Jefferson and Lincoln Memorials, will finally place King where he rightfully belongs in U.S. history.

Raymond Frey

Review Sources

American Literature 81, no. 4 (December, 2009): 869-871.
The Boston Globe, January 17, 2009, p. G9.
Choice, April, 2009, p. 1492.
Library Journal 133, no. 20 (December 1, 2008): 142-143.
The New York Times Book Review, January 18, 2009, p. 9.
Publishers Weekly 255, no. 45 (November 10, 2008): 43-44.
The Times Literary Supplement, January 16, 2009, p. 13.
The Washington Post, February 15, 2009, p. T8.

KIPLING SAHIB
India and the Making of Rudyard Kipling

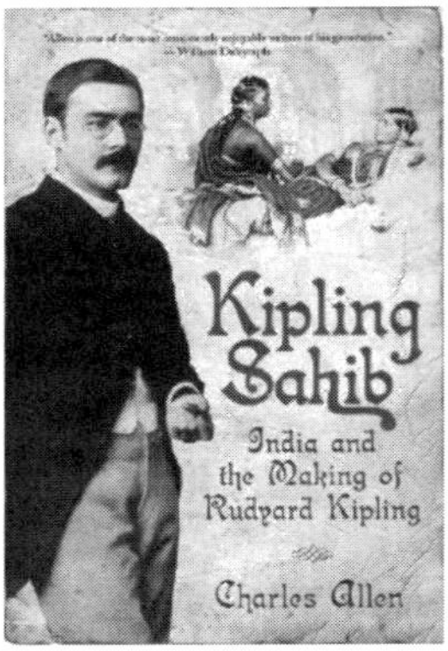

Author: Charles Allen (1940-)
Publisher: Pegasus Books (New York). 426 pp. $28.00
Type of work: History, literary biography
Time: 1865-1901
Locale: India; Great Britain

An account of Rudyard Kipling's early life, mostly spent in India, and the role India played in his emergence as a writer

Principal personages:
RUDYARD KIPLING, British writer
ALICE MACDONALD KIPLING, Kipling's mother
JOHN LOCKWOOD KIPLING, Kipling's father, an artist
TRIX (ALICE) KIPLING, Kipling's sister
CARRIE BALESTIER KIPLING, Kipling's wife

Charles Allen's *Kipling Sahib* relates the story of Rudyard Kipling's early life, his development as a writer, and his conquest of the reading public in India, Great Britain, the United States, and elsewhere. His poems "The White Man's Burden" and "The Recessional" captured in different ways the glories and responsibilities of Western imperialism, while "Danny Deaver" caught the pathos of a condemned British soldier going to his death. *Barrack-Room Ballads, and Other Verses* (1892) portrayed ordinary soldiers, rather than their officers, and in "Gunga Din" Kipling honored the humble Indian water carrier. His novel *Kim* (1901) is among the greatest novels about India, and for generations children have avidly read *The Jungle Book* (1894) and *The Second Jungle Book* (1895), which tells the tales of the human child Mowgli being raised by a wolf named Raksha, as well as the ever-popular *Just So Stories* (1902).

Kipling's parents were middle class. John Lockwood Kipling was trained as a modeler in clay and carving bas-reliefs. He worked on the Albert Memorial in London, among other projects. Alice Macdonald and her sisters made their mark through marriage and motherhood. Alice was the mother of Rudyard, Georgie married the prominent pre-Raphaelite painter Edward Burne-Jones, and Louisa was the mother of Stanley Baldwin, British prime minister during the 1920's and 1930's.

Bombay, India, was a boomtown rife with speculators in the early 1860's, and Allen provides a vivid description of the city during those years. Lockwood Kipling was offered a position in Bombay's newly established school of art and industry, and, with the prospect of financial independence, Alice and Lockwood left England for Bombay in early 1865. Lockwood also ventured into journalism, becoming the Bombay correspondent to the Allahabad *Pioneer*, the leading Anglo-Indian newspaper in northern India. Rudyard, the Kiplings' first child, was born on December 30, 1865, and named after England's Lake Rudyard. A second child, Alice, or Trixie, was born in 1868. Although the Kiplings lived in Bombay for only a few years, Rudyard, or Ruddy, later looked back on those years with great fondness. As was typical, his ayah, or nursemaid, was a major figure in his life: Most English parents turned much of the labor of child rearing over to a nursemaid. Both Kipling children had a gift for languages, and Kipling early learned to speak some Urdu and Hindi from the servants. The children's upbringing spanned two cultures, encompassing both the Anglo-Indian population of about fifty thousand and the native Indian population of several hundred million.

Charles Allen was born in India and has many Indian connections. He has written widely on South Asia, including Plain Tales from the Raj *(1985),* The Search for Shangri-La *(1999), and* The Buddha and the Sahibs *(2002).*

It was customary for Anglo-Indian children to be schooled in England. As Allen points out, schooled might be too strong a word. In 1871, Rudyard and Trixie were placed with a family in Swansea that was overly strict. That strictness combined with what both children felt to be their parents' betrayal to made his time in Swansea perhaps the unhappiest period of Kipling's life. It would later be reflected in his short story "Baa, Baa, Black Sheep." At the age of eleven, Kipling had what was apparently a nervous breakdown. In the interim, Lockwood had accepted a position in Lahore as a teacher at the Mayo School of Industrial Art, as well as the job of curator at the Lahore Museum. He had also become *The Pioneer*'s Lahore correspondent. Allen, as he did with Bombay, provides an extensive description of Lahore. In 1876, Lockwood's professional career was advanced when the British viceroy, Lord Lytton, chose him to design dozens of coats of arms to commemorate the Delhi ceremony proclaiming Queen Victoria as empress of India.

Alice Kipling returned to England in 1877 to rescue Rudyard and Trixie. Rudyard was placed in a newly established "public school," the United Services College (USC), which was founded primarily to educate boys for a career in the British military. Such a career was not likely for Rudyard, however, given his lack of physical dexterity, his poor vision, his dislike of games, and his preference for reading. In spite of these attributes, however, Rudyard thrived at USC, where he was given access to the headmaster's personal library. He read voraciously and wrote verses, some of which were published in India in 1881 as *Schoolboy Lyrics*. While at USC, Kipling matured physically and fell in love for the first time, but his love remained unrequited. The years at USC were also the inspiration for Kipling's later schoolboy stories, *Stalky and Co.* (1899).

In 1882, Kipling, aged sixteen, returned to Lahore, becoming the assistant editor of the *Civil and Military Gazette (CMG)*, the sister newspaper to *The Pioneer*. The work was demanding—he complained of ten-hour days—but he found time to continue writing poetry. Although, as a young boy in Bombay, Kipling had experienced several Indias, he shared the assumptions and prejudices of most Anglo-Indians: He saw British rule as necessary and believed that Indians, with their "inferior" and conflicting cultures, needed British authority to guarantee peace and maintain order. During the several months of summer "hot weather," many in the European Indian community retreated to the hill towns, the most famous of which was Simla, with an elevation over 7,000 feet, in order to escape the burning heat of the plains. Allen provides an excellent picture of Simla and its society.

Kipling's experiences in Simla found their way into his many writings. Other events that he observed during his multifaceted journalistic career also became subject matter for those writings. He reported not only on political events, such as the Viceroy's visits, but also on sports, the theater, and the gossip engendered by the personal lives of the Anglo-Indian community. He rejected bribes offered by an exiled Afghan chieftain who hoped to use the influence of the *CMG* to gain his freedom, and he reported on the Rawalpindi Durbar and the meeting of the amir of Afghanistan and the viceroy, Lord Dufferin. The trial and execution of Private George Flaxman in 1887 for the murder of a fellow soldier was the incident that three years later resulted in one of Kipling's most famous poems, "Danny Deaver." His journalistic experiences were also central to the approximately two hundred short stories he wrote in India. During the heat of summer, when it was it was too hot to sleep, Kipling would prowl the streets of Lahore with their opium dens and brothels, observing the India of the Indians and not just that of the British. He admitted to resorting to using opium on one occasion when ill. Allen also says that Kipling's private notes suggest that, on another occasion, he was concerned that he had contracted syphilis.

In the 1880's, Lockwood Kipling became the artistic adviser to the duke of Connaught and was entrusted with the design of the new Punjab Museum. He was thus recognized as the leading British authority on Indian arts and crafts. Although still not yet twenty years old, Rudyard began to draft what he hoped would be the great Indian novel, tentatively titling it *Mother Maturin* and setting it in the Lahore of his nighttime explorations. In *Quartette*, published in 1885 as a seasonal supplement to the *CMG*, were printed two of Kipling's short stories, "The Phantom Rickshaw" and "The Strange Ride of Morrowbie Jukes." The latter presented a nightmare vision of an India wherein the Hindus ruled the British. In Lahore, Kipling became an active Freemason, and Allen notes that Masonic images pervade his short story "The Man Who Would Be King" and the novel *Kim.* He developed an admiration for the common British soldier, subject to disease, drunkenness, and death. *Soldiers Three: A Collection of Stories* (1888) featured three British privates. *Departmental Ditties* (1886) increased his fame among the Anglo-Indians; he was still only twenty-one.

In 1888, Kipling published *Plain Tales from the Hills*, consisting of thirty-two stories, many of which had been previously published in the *CMG.* The previous year, Kipling had left Lahore for Allahabad, the location of *The Pioneer* and, in spite of its name, primarily a Hindu city. Kipling was generally more sympathetic to India's Muslims than its Hindus, perhaps because of Hinduism's polytheism and seeming sexual openness. This judgment is reflected in his negative interpretation of Calcutta and its Bengali population in the stories collected in *The City of Dreadful Night, and Other Places* (1890).

Kipling's last visit to Simla was in the summer of 1888. By then, he had adopted "the Scheme," which was his plan to leave India, return to London, and continue as a journalist with the ultimate aim of writing full time. His financial security was to be assured as the English correspondent of *The Pioneer.* He arrived in England by way of the United States in October, 1889. Although he was only twenty-three, Kipling's fame had already spread beyond India: He came across a pirated American edition of *Plain Tales from the Hills* in a Japanese bookshop. In London, he was readily embraced by a number of prominent writers, including Andrew Lang, Walter Besant, and H. Rider Haggard. "Danny Deaver" appeared in 1890 to considerable praise, and it was included in the first series of *Barrack-Room Ballads*, which also included "Gunga Din" and "Mandalay."

In January, 1892, Kipling married Carrie Balestier, an American. After a round-the-world honeymoon, they acquired a rustic home in Battleboro, Vermont. With the birth of a daughter, Josephine, Kipling envisioned a children's novel, which eventually became *Kim.* More immediately, Kipling, joined by his father, began the story of Mowgli, an infant saved from the tiger Shere Khan and raised by Father and Mother Wolf. The resulting *The Jungle Book* was published in 1894, with *The Second Jungle Book* (1895) following shortly thereafter. The Kiplings moved back to England in 1896. The first of the *Stalky and Co.* stories about his schoolboy years appeared in 1897, which was also the year of Queen Victoria's Diamond Jubilee, for which he wrote one of his most famous poems, "Recessional." The poem was a warning against imperial hubris and famously included the phrase, "Lest we forget." The following year, another iconic poem, "The White Man's Burden," appeared, making an appeal to the United States to assume its imperial responsibilities. Kipling's *Just So Stories* reflected his growing family concerns, including the death of a daughter.

Kim, Kipling's last great work about India, was written in England, with Lockwood providing the illustrations for the first edition. Allen notes that Christopher Hitchens once described Kipling as "a man of permanent contradictions." The biographer agrees, and he quotes a Kipling verse that headed one of the chapters in *Kim*, referring to "Separate sides to my head." Kim, an orphaned boy of working-class British parents, is at home among Muslims, Hindus, and a Buddhist lama, but he is also claimed by a Methodist and a Catholic, is sent to an Anglo-Indian school, and is used by the British government as a spy against Russians. *Kim* is, among other things, about a search for identity, and one sees such a search in Kipling himself: A defender of British imperialism and an admirer of Britain's officer class, Kipling was also empathetic to the British enlisted men and to the other, non-British India. The ending of *Kim* is left ambiguous: Kim may become a British sahib, or he may remain a disciple of the Lama. Kipling won the Nobel Prize in Literature in 1907, becoming the first British writer to be so recognized, and he remains the youngest literary Nobel laureate. Allen claims that Kipling's best work was behind him after *Kim*, when he turned his back on the Indian and the intuitive side of his head. *Kipling Sahib* is an excellent work, including an incisive and sympathetic discussion of Kipling and his writings, but it also provides a valuable view of India under the British Raj in the late nineteenth century.

Eugene Larson

Review Sources

Asian Affairs 39, no. 2 (July, 2008): 297.
Contemporary Review 290, no. 1691 (Winter, 2008): 514-515.
Geographical 80, no. 4 (April, 2008): 76.
Kirkus Reviews 77, no. 1 (January 1, 2009): 17.
Library Journal 134, no. 2 (February 1, 2009): 71.
Sewanee Review 116, no. 4 (Fall, 2008): 507+.
The Sunday Times (London), September 28, 2008, p. 48.
The Times Literary Supplement, July 4, 2008, p. 13.
The Wall Street Journal, March 14, 2009, p. W8.

KOESTLER
The Literary and Political Odyssey of a Twentieth-Century Skeptic

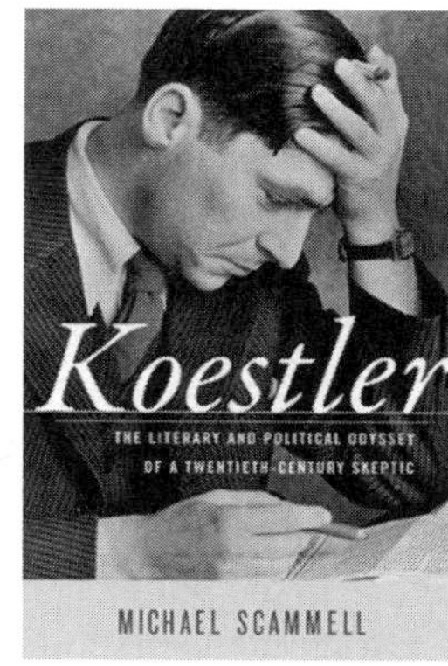

Author: Michael Scammell (1935-)
Publisher: Random House (New York). 689 pp. $35.00
Type of work: Literary biography
Time: 1905-1983
Locale: Budapest; Vienna, Austria; Palestine; Berlin, Germany; Paris, France; London, England; Wales; Spain; Naples, Italy; Pennsylvania; Stanford, California

A biography of one of the leading intellectuals of the twentieth century

Principal personages:
ARTHUR KOESTLER, a Jewish Hungarian fiction and nonfiction writer
ADELE KOESTLER, his mother
DAPHNE HARDY, his companion
DOROTHEE ASCHER, his first wife
MAMAINE PAGET, his second wife
CYNTHIA JEFFERIES, his third wife
ALBERT CAMUS, a French existentialist writer
JEAN-PAUL SARTRE, a French existentialist philosopher and writer
SIMONE DE BEAUVOIR, a French feminist philosopher

If Arthur Koestler is remembered today, it is for his riveting novel about the perils of Soviet communism, *Darkness at Noon* (1940), and perhaps as well for his contribution to the collection of essays by disillusioned Marxists, *The God That Failed* (1949). There may also be some interest in his work on the sources of creativity, *The Act of Creation* (1964), but as to his investigations late in life into parapsychology, non-Darwinian evolutionary theory, and the possibility of using therapeutic drugs to end social problems such as war, there is mostly embarrassed silence. This silence would have disappointed Koestler, who had a falling-out with his first biographer, Iain Hamilton, when Hamilton refused to focus on these later interests of his subject.

Michael Scammell's *Koestler* is a well-written account of his life and work but does not convey a clear enough sense of what Arthur Koestler was all about. Scammell certainly does not ignore the writer's later interests, but his biography is at its best when it recounts his earlier years, tracing Koestler's youth as a deracinated Hungarian Jew through his time as a Zionist, culminating with Koestler's time as a communist and his break with communism. Perhaps this uneven quality of treatment is simply because the earlier portion was the most interesting or most important part of Koestler's life. In those years, especially in his masterpiece, *Darkness at Noon*, Koestler grappled with an ideology and an attitude toward life that in the middle of the twentieth century affected the entire world. His later dabbling in extrasensory per-

Michael Scammell's 1985 biography of Aleksandr Solzhenitsyn won the Los Angeles Times *Book Prize and the English PEN Nonfiction Prize. Scammell has also translated numerous Russian authors into English. He teaches creative writing at Columbia University in New York.*

ception and his campaign against quarantine restrictions on dogs entering England hardly seem to be in the same league.

There is more to it than that, though. The later stages of Scammell's book, though as clearly written as what went before, seem increasingly scrappy. There is yet another love affair to chronicle or at least mention, another house Koestler is bought near Naples or Cambridge or in Kent. His failing health is mixed in with making a new friend and his reporting on the famous chess match between Bobby Fischer and Boris Spassky. This portion of the biography contains so many different bits of information along these lines that it seems disorganized or lacking in focus. Perhaps the problem is that there is a lack of a sense in the book of what Arthur Koestler's life meant.

Earlier in the biography, this lack of evaluation seems to be less of an issue. There is a focus at that point having to do with Koestler's disillusionment with communism and his campaign to reveal its true nature to those in the West still sympathetic to the Soviet Union. It is perhaps this campaign of disillusionment that prompts Scammell to label Koestler a skeptic, incorporating the word into his subtitle. Perhaps what prompts this notion of skepticism is the fact that Koestler typically set himself against orthodoxies, such as the Darwinian orthodoxy in evolution. Scammell spends little time developing or explaining the idea that Koestler was a skeptic, however, which is perhaps understandable because on his own evidence a skeptic was the furthest thing from what Koestler was.

Scammell's biography reveals a very young man latching onto an extreme form of Zionism, Revisionist Zionism, which was associated with terrorist groups such as the Irgun and the Stern Gang. After that, Koestler drifted into the Communist Party, becoming a defender of the Soviet Union, though never a completely reliable one. (This unreliability caused him to have some trouble publishing one of his early books.)

There was something in Koestler that resisted becoming a true believer, though whether that was a general tendency toward skepticism or just a problem he had with the conflict between communist theory and Soviet reality is not clear. What is clear is that an even larger part of him yearned to be a true believer in some cause—any cause. As he put it in one of his autobiographical volumes, in a passage quoted by Scammell, he suffered from "absolutitis"—a desire to solve the riddles of the universe—from his earliest years, when he wondered where an arrow shot up into the infinite might go:

> The thirst for the absolute is a stigma which marks those unable to find satisfaction in the relative world of the now and here. My obsession with the arrow was merely the first phase of the quest. When it proved sterile, the Infinite as a target was replaced by Utopias of one kind and another. It was the same quest, the same all-or-nothing mentality, which drove me to the Promised Land and into the Communist Party. In other ages aspirations of this kind found their natural fulfillment in God.

This hardly sounds like skepticism; it is more a religious feeling, but somehow divorced from orthodox religion. Koestler indeed in his later life was willing to call himself a mystic and to say that, although he did not believe in a Designer for the universe, he did believe in a design.

When a friend suggested that he should give up on his pseudoreligions and go in for the real thing, Koestler declined. There was something rebellious in him that led him to oppose reigning orthodoxies, but it led him not into a permanent state of skepticism but to a perpetual state of seeking the truth. This tendency was something Koestler himself recognized, as indicated in the passage quoted above, and perhaps Koestler is still the best guide to Koestler. He produced four volumes of autobiographical writings, and Scammell says that autobiography may have been his best sort of writing. Whether that is so or not (some might argue that he was best as an essayist or a popularizer or even as a novelist of ideas), it may be that the autobiographies are the best place to go to understand Koestler.

However, Scammell has written an entertaining narrative of Koestler's life, demonstrating easy mastery of a number of archival sources and avoiding various biographical pitfalls. For instance, he does not succumb to judgmental debunking of his subject in the manner of another Koestler biographer, David Cesariani, who called Koestler a serial rapist and suggested he was to blame for his third wife's death by suicide. As an authorized biographer, it is only to be expected that Scammell would take a less negative view, but he examines the evidence and makes a good case for dismissing both charges.

It is not as if Scammell tries to portray Koestler as a saint; it is certainly clear from his biography that Koestler could be a difficult man, one who drank far too much, drove recklessly, could become physically violent, and was often intellectually aggressive. His relations with women, as Scammell describes them, are frankly astonishing. He somehow managed to attract a great many of them, having affair after affair, but there was usually something excessively controlling about his relations with them. With his third wife, Cynthia, he was downright tyrannical, according to Scammell's account.

This attitude toward women in a way seems more sad than anything else, a reflection of the fact that Koestler seems to have been incapable of true intimacy. Before reading Scammell's biography, one might have thought that Koestler achieved at least something like intimacy in his long third marriage, but what emerges in this account is a description of a marriage that was a relationship more of master and slave than of husband and wife. Cynthia comes across primarily as a cook, housekeeper, and secretary perpetually being yelled at by her husband.

If Scammell had been interested in the larger patterns in Koestler's life, perhaps he might have made something of this lack of intimacy. Perhaps, as Koestler himself suggested, his unrelenting search for larger meanings reflected a failure to find satisfaction in his daily life, most notably in his relations with women. Scammell does not make this connection, however.

On the other hand, Scammell manages to do something quite unusual in a biography: He introduces an element of suspense. The suspense does not involve Koestler himself, for the facts of his life are fairly clear and most readers know that he was not, for example, executed in prison before getting a chance to write *Darkness at Noon*. The case of his mother is different. She was marooned in Nazi-occupied Hungary, and the tension builds as the pages go by over whether she made it out alive.

Scammell also manages one comic masterstroke when describing Koestler's obsession with signs and symbols. At one stage in his life, he wondered what it might mean that he had recently had so many automobile accidents. Perhaps, says Scammell, it was just that he was a lousy driver. It is a funny comment, and it is true enough that Koestler seemed prone to seeing meaning where there was perhaps just accident; he even wrote a book, *The Roots of Coincidence* (1972) on the topic. Even so, Scammell may be too quick to dismiss the search for meaning, especially since that search seems to have been the essence of Koestler's life.

All in all, then, Scammell has produced a solid examination of the life of a fascinating mid-twentieth century intellectual, one of a dying breed, the public intellectual writing for a nonacademic public. It is interesting that the highly sophisticated and widely respected Koestler, author of dozens of books and numerous articles, in fact never finished a university degree—one of the many interesting facts that Scammell presents. Scammell also reports that Koestler looked a bit like Humphrey Bogart, though a Bogart with a heavy European accent that was part of what made him fear he could never fit into the upper reaches of British society. That society was where he wanted to be in his final decades. In other words, Scammell asserts, Koestler was a snob. He did ultimately receive recognition from Queen Elizabeth II as a Commander of the British Empire, but he still was never truly an insider. This partial exclusion from respectable society may have been inevitable given his attachment to less-than-respectable views on such things as parapsychology.

More serious, Scammell more than once examines Koestler's long tussle with the issue of ends and means. As a communist, he was dedicated to the notion that the ends justified the means. When he broke with communism, he also broke with this concept to a certain extent. He seemed still able to adhere to it in certain situations, though—a position perhaps explained by his friend, the author Albert Camus, who said it depended on the particular ends and means in each case.

It is typical that this most interesting formulation about ends and means comes not from Scammell but from another commentator. Some of the most insightful passages in the biography are ones Scammell is merely quoting from others, often from reviewers of Koestler's work, sometimes from Koestler himself. It is as if the biographer almost deliberately refrains from analysis, at least large-scale analysis, and instead remains content to tell a story.

The story he tells is an interesting one, including such things as Koestler's personal adventures with Camus and the two other leading French existentialists, Jean-Paul Sartre and Simone de Beauvoir. Scammell provides a comprehensive retelling of what seem to have been all the important moments of Koestler's life, without descending into the trivial or amassing a stodgy monument of facts of interest only to scholars. This is no mean feat.

There are moments in the biography in which Scammell goes a bit overboard in praising Koestler's achievements and his prescience. He says repeatedly that Koestler was significantly ahead of his time, an observation that sometimes seems true but mostly seems a bit forced. Scammell can be forgiven his cheerleading, however. The real shortcoming of the biography is its lack of a clear pattern for Koestler's life, the sort of pattern Koestler provided in his autobiographies. Perhaps that pattern was forced, but when there is hardly any pattern at all, a biography cannot ultimately satisfy.

Sheldon Goldfarb

Review Sources

The Atlantic Monthly 304, no. 5 (December, 2009): 103-107.
Booklist 106, no. 8 (December 15, 2009): 10.
Kirkus Reviews 77, no. 20 (October 15, 2009): 56.
Newsweek 155, no. 2 (January 11, 2010): 60.
Publishers Weekly 256, no. 43 (October 26, 2009): 43.
The Wall Street Journal, January 8, 2010, p. W15.

THE LACUNA

Author: Barbara Kingsolver (1955-)
Publisher: HarperCollins (New York). 507 pp. $26.99
Type of work: Novel
Time: 1929-1959
Locale: Mexico; Washington, D.C.; Asheville, North Carolina

This novel tells the life story of Harrison Shepherd, who balances Mexican and U.S. nationalities, against the backdrop of the major political upheavals in the two countries from the 1920's through the 1950's

Principal characters:
HARRISON SHEPHERD, a Mexican American novelist
SALOMÉ SHEPHERD, his mother
FRIDA KAHLO, a painter and the wife of Diego Rivera
DIEGO RIVERA, a painter and the husband of Frida Kahlo
LEV DAVIDOVICH TROTSKY, a Russian revolutionary in exile in Mexico
VAN, Trotsky's secretary
VIOLET BROWN, Harrison's stenographer

One of Barbara Kingsolver's repeated themes in *The Lacuna* is that the most interesting part of a story is the part that is not told. A lacuna is a missing or hidden part, and the novel hints at many of them. On the surface, the book tells the life story of Harrison William Shepherd. It begins when he is a child in the 1920's. His Mexican mother, Salomé, has taken him to her home country to live with her lover after leaving his father, a U.S. government employee. They move frequently as Salomé drifts from lover to lover. Harrison's schooling is so sporadic that by his teenage years he qualifies only for a school for the mentally deficient. When that school proves unsuitable, he goes to Washington, D.C., where his father enrolls him in a military boarding school.

After being expelled for homosexual behavior, Harrison returns to Mexico. He works for the artist Diego Rivera mixing plaster. Later, he becomes a cook and secretary for Rivera and his wife, Frida Kahlo. The Russian revolutionary Leon Trotsky takes refuge with the artists. After Trotsky is shot, Kahlo seeks to protect Harrison by having him deliver art to the United States to get him out of the country. Harrison settles in Asheville, North Carolina, where he writes best-selling novels about ancient Mexico. He hires a stenographer, Violet Brown, to help with typing and correspondence.

Harrison is investigated by the House Committee on Un-American Activities, which seeks to stop the spread of communism in the United States. He and Violet travel to Mexico, where Harrison fakes his death. Violet compiles his journals and other materials into a book manuscript and has it locked away to be considered for publication in fifty years.

That is the plot of *The Lacuna*, but, like any good novel, the book goes far beyond its plotline. In this case, the text's lacunae are important parts of the story. As a child living on Isla Pixol in Mexico, Harrison discovers the novel's first lacuna: He learns that the cliffs along the ocean contain caves that are underwater at high tide. He learns to hold his breath long enough to swim into one of these caves. There, he finds that it is a tunnel leading into a pond where the Aztecs left gifts for the gods and made human sacrifices.

The Lacuna *is Barbara Kingsolver's seventh novel.* The Poisonwood Bible *(1998) was chosen as an Oprah's Book Club selection. She has also published nonfiction, including the best-selling* Animal, Vegetable, Miracle: A Year of Food Life. *She was awarded the National Humanities Medal in 2000.*

Another lacuna occurs at the end of the novel, when readers are led to believe that Harrison has drowned. Violet learns the truth several years later, when she receives a drawing from Frida Kahlo's estate with a cryptic message on it. Readers learn that he is alive from her account of that gift. Another missing piece of the story is the journal that tells why Harrison was expelled from school. Occasional comments in his later journals make it clear that he was caught engaging in homosexual activity with another student, but few of the details are revealed.

The novel is formatted as a compilation of various types of written documents, creating an exploration of how readers acquire information and misinformation. In fact, a major theme of the work is how and why misunderstandings are created. Its first words introduce this theme by describing the "howlers" Harrison hears every morning as a child on Isla Pixol in Mexico. He and his mother think these howlers are demons who eat human flesh. It turns out that they are only monkeys. The novel includes the beginning of Harrison's memoir, his journals, newspaper articles, letters, notes from Violet about the materials included in her manuscript, and the transcript of a hearing. By juxtaposing these texts, readers construct a narrative and discover the lacunae within it.

The beginning of Harrison's memoir is a rewritten version of his first childhood journal, presented from an adult perspective. His other journals remain in the format of dated entries. While much of the novel derives from Harrison's journals, though, Violet is in a large way the story's creator, since she has compiled them for a manuscript. The extent to which she edited Harrison's writing is not clear. Harrison thought that Violet burned the journals to destroy potentially damaging evidence when he was being investigated by Congress. In fact, she burned only one, the one he kept while he was a teenager at the Potomac Academy. She explains in her notes that she burned that one because it contained something Harrison did not want others to read. She admits that he wanted the other journals destroyed also but does not clarify why she kept all but one.

While Violet might have manipulated the material in Harrison's journals, Harrison himself also might have done so, aware of the possibility that someone would read the journals someday. He continued to make journal entries even after he thought his earlier journals had been burned. By this time, he knew that government agents might read anything he wrote. Earlier, Rivera and Kahlo were afraid that Harrison's journals would create trouble if the police or others read his account of Trotsky's stay at their home. Kahlo asked Harrison to use his journal to create an objective record of the household's events, and he submitted the entries to her each week for her review. It is clear that during this time Harrison wrote journal entries thinking of Kahlo as an audience.

While journals are typically thought of as personal records of truth, newspapers contain public statements of fact. *The Lacuna* includes a number of newspaper articles. Some are actual articles reprinted from publications including *The New York Times*. Others are fictional. The actual articles document the political biases behind reporting of the leftist movement in 1930's Mexico and behind the investigations into "un-American" activities in the United States in the 1940's.

The last excerpt from *The New York Times*, dated September 26, 1948, reports on a claim that President Harry S. Truman had communist ties. This article demonstrates both the extent to which accusations of communism were politically motivated and the degree to which politicians, reporters, and others quickly forgot their own recent history during the Red Scare. The article reports that Truman had been endorsed for vice president by a socialist newspaper a few years earlier. It does not note that ties to socialist and communist groups were common among U.S. politicians, intellectuals, and others throughout the 1930's and early 1940's. In fact, the endorsement had come during World War II, at a time when the United States and the Soviet Union were military allies.

The novel's fictional newspaper stories contain numerous inaccuracies. For example, Harrison's obituary in the local newspaper says that he was discharged from his job with the Department of State for treason, fraud, and misrepresentation of qualifications. In fact, at the time of his supposed death, Harrison had been a full-time novelist since his war-related government service concluded with the end of World War II. Several articles about his investigation by the House Committee on Un-American Activities attribute a quote to him that was actually spoken by a character in one of his novels. Moreover, although his novels were set in ancient Mexico, reporters labeled them as commentary on the U.S. political situation of the time.

The novel also incorporates reviews of Harrison's books that question the objectivity of book reviews. Before he is accused of being a communist, he is one of the most popular writers in the country. His reviews are glowingly positive. Once the congressional investigation begins, however, reviewers denounce his books and comment on the ways they express a communist viewpoint. Harrison always refuses to have his photograph published on his book jackets. Before the investigation, reviewers describe him as attractive and eligible. Later, one describes him as too ugly to have his photograph printed.

The fan letters included in the novel take a similar turn. Before the investigation,

Harrison receives bags of enthusiastic fan mail and attracts particular interest from female fans. After the investigation becomes public, the letters change to hate mail and threats.

Among all the documents included in the novel, a transcript of a hearing before a subcommittee of the Committee on Un-American Activities is the one that seems most reliably to report on an event. The transcript provides no evidence that Harrison was active in or promoted communist activity. However, one of the examiners, after insisting that Harrison provide only yes or no answers, words his questions in ways that, if the questions are taken out of context, appear damning.

In the simplest terms, in Kingsolver's novel what appears to be true is not the whole story. Although Harrison worked for Rivera and Trotsky, he was not engaged in revolutionary activity. He served as a cook and secretary.

Brown claims that she prepared the manuscript that has become the novel because she wanted readers to understand who Harrison Shepherd was and what happened to him. Throughout the novel, though, other characters see him through their own perspectives, even naming him to suit their purposes. His full name is Harrison William Shepherd, and his mother calls him Will. Later, when she sends him to the United States for school, his father calls him Harrison. When he works as a cook in Kahlo's home, Kahlo cannot pronounce "Harrison," so she nicknames him Insólito, or Sóli for short. He signs letters to Kahlo and Rivera with the names H. W. Shepherd, H. Shepherd, Insólito, and Sóli.

Part of the complication to Harrison's identity is his mixed Mexican and American parentage and upbringing. Having lived in both countries, Harrison never feels completely at home in either. He spends his childhood in Mexico reading adventure novels and learning survival skills from the servants. As an adult in North Carolina, he rarely leaves home, preferring for Brown to run his errands for him.

In spite of the novel's insistence on the complexities of communicating with and understanding other people, deep friendship is an important theme of the work. Harrison is a successful writer largely because of the support and encouragement of Kahlo and Brown. Kahlo urges him to write. She steals a copy of an ancient artifact from Rivera and sends it to him. Harrison bases one of his novels on the story its pictures tell. Brown is loyal to her employer even after he is investigated for communist activity.

On its publication, *The Lacuna* met a mixed critical reception. Some reviewers judged *The Lacuna* to be Kingsolver's finest novel to date. They praised the novel's scope and commented that the plot is engaging throughout. Others said that the second half, recording the time after Shepherd moves to North Carolina and becomes a novelist, is weaker than the first half. The main complaints about the second half were that Shepherd's character goes flat and that the political statement about U.S. politics in the 1950's takes priority over plot and character development. Most reviewers responded enthusiastically to the part of the novel that records Shepherd's time living in the Rivera-Kahlo household in 1930's Mexico.

Joan Hope

Review Sources

Booklist 106, no. 2 (September 15, 2009): 5.
The Bookseller, no. 5407 (November 6, 2009): 55.
The Christian Science Monitor, October 31, 2009, p. Books-25.
Kirkus Reviews 77, no. 17 (September 1, 2009): 909-910.
Library Journal 134, no. 17 (October 15, 2009): 67.
The New York Times Book Review, November 8, 2009, p. 9.
The New Yorker 85, no. 38 (November 23, 2009): 113.
Publishers Weekly 256, no. 33 (August 17, 2009): 1.
The Times Literary Supplement, November 13, 2009, p. 23.

LAISH

Author: Aharon Appelfeld (1932-   )
First published: Layish, 1994, in Israel
Translated from the Hebrew by Aloma Halter
Publisher: Schocken Books (New York). 231 pp. $23.95
Type of work: Novel
Time: The late nineteenth and early twentieth centuries
Locale: Eastern Europe

A picaresque novel narrated in the first person by an orphan boy describing a group of Jews traveling by wagon train from Eastern Europe toward Jerusalem

Principal characters:

LAISH, a young orphan boy, the narrator
FINGERHUT, his employer, who dies early on
PLOOSH, a crude and cruel wagon driver
SRUEL, the wagon driver who takes over after Ploosh dies
OLD AVRAHAM, the devout spiritual leader of the group and Laish's teacher
TZILLA, a seamstress who later cooks for the pilgrims
CHIYUK and SHIMKEH, a pair of rough wagon drivers
ITCHEH MEIR, a clever thief
EPHRAIM, an informer who is beaten by Chiyuk and Shimkeh
BLIND MENACHEM, one of the old, pious men in the wagon train
MAYA, a prostitute with whom Laish becomes obsessed
MAMSHE, a wild, caged woman

In Aharon Appelfeld's *Laish*, a young orphan, probably in his early teens, tells the story of a pilgrimage to Jerusalem by a group consisting partly of elderly, devout Jews. A number of merchants, called "dealers," are also included in the wagons that wend their slow and weary way from the Carpathian Mountains in Eastern Europe to a port on the Black Sea. There, the group plans to take ship for Palestine and their final destination: the holy city of Jerusalem. Women and children, apparently the wives and offspring of some of the men, make up the rest of the entourage.

The time of the pilgrimage is indeterminate but most likely it begins near the end of the nineteenth century and originates in the Ukraine. The convoy travels for a considerable time along the Prut River, which borders Romania and what is now Moldava. Progress is very slow. En route, the dealers trade and bargain with the peasants and townspeople they encounter, whereas the old men spend time studying Torah and praying. Old Avraham takes Laish (from the Hebrew word for "lion") under his wing. He teaches the boy to pray and impresses on him the importance of study.

The pilgrimage is nothing if not dangerous. Not only are the wagons frequently be-

Aharon Appelfeld, the author of many novels, essays, and poems in Hebrew, was born in Czernowitz, Romania. In 1940, he was imprisoned in a concentration camp but escaped and spent three years hiding in the Ukraine, eventually emigrating in 1946 to Israel, where he now lives and writes.

set by thieves, but also the dealers transport contraband and accordingly have to evade the legal authorities. Money passes from hand to hand and is sewn into the men's coats for safekeeping. As Laish describes the goings-on, there is great tension between the dealers and the old men. Adding to the difficulty of the journey are the wagon drivers, men of crude disposition who drink heavily and also steal, especially when the group arrives at some of the bigger towns on their route, such as Sadagora, Czernowitz, Vishnitz, and Galacz. In Laish's view, "Here, everyone's a thief."

Fingerhut, who appears early in the novel, is seriously ill and has Laish help him as he lies swathed in blankets and writhing in pain. At one point, he tells Laish that he no longer believes that Jerusalem will heal him; he dies shortly thereafter. The wagon driver Ploosh then forces Laish to work for him and treats him badly, until Ploosh is arrested for murdering one of the dealers to whom he owed money. Sruel takes over Ploosh's duties as wagon driver, further angering the imprisoned Ploosh, who does not think Sruel knows how to handle horses well enough. When Ploosh escapes from jail, he seeks out Sruel, who kills him with Ploosh's revolver during their fight.

Ploosh turns out to be quite wrong about Sruel's ability to handle horses. Sruel proves equally adept at handling people, and he gradually becomes a leader of the pilgrimage. Along with Old Avraham, he takes special care of Laish. He shows the boy how to catch fish in the Prut River that they use to feed the pilgrims, and he advises Laish in many other ways. He is a tall, strong man with a much gentler disposition than the other wagon drivers. He even has a falcon who perches on his shoulder and sleeps in his lap at night after flying aloft during the day. Earlier in his life, Sruel was convicted of murdering two peasants who had attacked his father; as a result, he served thirty years of a life sentence before being released. He is the most remarkable character in the novel, revealing depths of his nature to Laish, who learns to admire and respect him highly.

Laish reveals other sorts of tension in his narrative, including some that directly involve him. For example, when the convoy arrives in Czernowitz, he is taken to a nightclub by several dealers. There, he meets Maya, evidently a barfly or prostitute, who captivates Laish. Although she does not look Jewish, she tells Laish that she is and calls him her "cub." She is unlike any of the women in the convoy, whom Laish describes as embittered and without charm, casting a heaviness and gloom on one's heart. By the end of the evening, Maya has thoroughly "ruined" Laish, who up to then was most likely a virgin.

Partway through the convoy, Laish reveals a secret concerning a violent young woman named Mamshe who is confined in a cage carried in one of the wagons. Though she sleeps curled up most of the day, she breaks out in wild screams at night like a wounded animal. Obviously deranged, she poses a problem for the others, who have been told by their late holy man that they must take her on the pilgrimage and treat her gently, as if she were an ordinary person. In Czernowitz, a doctor gives her tranquilizers, but they prove useless and her screams of pure terror continue. At their wits' end, the pilgrims open Mamshe's cage and prod her to escape among the reeds along the Prut River. She never returns, and her disappearance casts a pall over everyone, for they had no idea how much a part of them she had become.

Another source of tension is the problem of informers, or "snitches," among the pilgrims. When Ephraim is discovered to be one of them, two of the wagon drivers, Shimkeh and Chiyuk, are commissioned to punish him. They lash him with their belts, leaving terrible wounds that never completely heal. While suffering, Ephraim becomes a kind of saintly individual. He begins to have visions and becomes a much gentler person. Shimkeh and Chiyuk never truly repent of whipping him mercilessly, claiming that it was what the group wanted them to do, but Ephraim forgives them nevertheless.

The pilgrims, especially the old men, do their best to observe holy days and other religious rites. They ritually immerse themselves in the river once a day, whisper their prayers, visit the sick, and ask forgiveness of everyone. Laish describes the ceremony on the eve of Rosh Hashanah, the beginning of the Days of Awe, or the Ten Days of Penitence:

> On the eve of the holiday the old men put on their white clothes. They circled the table on which the Torah lay and then sat in the front row. The dealers sat behind them, and the wagon drivers stood. Truth be told, that was how it was every year. But this time, they brought Ephraim on his pallet, wrapped him in a yellowed prayer shawl, and they placed him next to the table. One of the old men handed him a holiday prayer book. Ephraim took the prayer book in his hands and kissed it. Old Yerachmiel led the prayers quietly, in a restrained manner.

Appelfeld's prose here, translated from the Hebrew by Aloma Halter, reveals the simplicity as well as the devotion not only of the worshipers but also of Laish, the narrator, who eschews florid language throughout his story.

Besides the dangers of robbers and the difficulty of getting the wagons through the rough roads, often filled with mud when the rains come, Laish also recounts the serious depredations of illnesses experienced by the group. When they are only partway to Galacz, they are afflicted by plague, which carries off a number of them, including children. Their consequent need to find a Jewish cemetery where the bodies may be interred compounds their difficulty, as it does later, when another illness strikes the convoy. Eventually, increasing numbers of the pilgrims leave the convoy in despair of ever reaching Jerusalem alive. By the time the pilgrims arrive at Galacz, only two of the original six wagons are left, and many fewer of the original band of pilgrims.

The novels ends as the remaining pilgrims finally find a ship and, mainly through Sruel's leadership, enough money to pay for their passage. Laish does not reveal whether the pilgrims ever reach their ultimate destination, which they expect will fulfill its promise of redemption.

Jay L. Halio

Review Sources

Forward 112 (March 20, 2009): 11.
Kirkus Reviews 77, no. 1 (January 1, 2009): 3.
New York Times Book Review, March 29, 2009, p. 6.
Publishers Weekly 256, no. 2 (January 12, 2009): 30.
World Literature Today 69 (Spring, 1995): 427.

LARK AND TERMITE

Author: Jayne Ann Phillips (1952-   )
Publisher: Alfred A. Knopf (New York). 307 pp. $24.00
Type of work: Novel
Time: 1950's
Locale: North Chungchong Province, South Korea; Winfield, West Virginia

Phillips brings together the multiple strands of a West Virginia family's story in order to show the mysterious effects the past has on the present and the future

Principal characters:
LARK, a teenaged girl who cares for her Termite during a horrible flood in West Virginia
TERMITE, her mentally incapacitated half-brother, who has an uncanny ability to understand the past and the future
LOLA, Lark and Termite's mother, whose lifestyle and lovers lead her far from her West Virginia roots
NONIE, Lola's long-suffering sister, who cares for Lark and Termite
CHARLIE, Nonie's paramour, once smitten by Lola but now faithful to Nonie and her family
CORPORAL ROBERT LEAVITT, Lola's second husband, Termite's father, and a soldier in the Korean War
SOLLY, the boy next door and Lark's secret childhood lover
STAMBLE, a mysterious and helpful social worker

Known for her poetic glimpses into complex family relationships in such previous novels as *Motherkind* (2000), Jayne Anne Phillips works the same familial ground in *Lark and Termite*. She uses a variety of techniques to untangle the complex story of Lark, a young woman in small-town West Virginia in the late 1950's who is struggling to understand her family's past and its ramifications for her future. Told from the multiple perspectives of the main characters in the novel, the story refuses a strict linearity. Instead, readers learn information piecemeal, as different aspects of the family saga are revealed by different voices with distinct memories. Furthermore, Phillips hints at the possibilities of intersections between past and present, often made possible in the novel by a mystical interplay between different times and places.

The novel contains two discrete story lines, nine years apart in time, and the events in each help inform the unfolding of a larger plot that combines the two. The first story is told in multiple sections from the third-person limited perspective of Corporal Robert Leavitt, a young man who finds himself in South Korea at the onset of the Korean War. Given that most of the Americans with Leavitt have not been anticipating a conflict of this magnitude, the bombing and fighting creates mass confusion, hamper-

Jayne Anne Phillips has written several short-story collections and novels, including the Pushcart Prize-winning Sweethearts *(1976),* Black Tickets *(1979),* Fast Lanes *(1988),* Machine Dreams *(1984),* Shelter *(1994), and* Motherkind *(2000). Phillips is professor of English and director of the M.F.A. program at Rutgers University, Newark.*

ing the Americans' ability to differentiate between their allies, the South Koreans, and their enemies, the North Korean aggressors. As a result, some American soldiers fire on a group of retreating South Koreans that includes Leavitt.

Leavitt heroically tries to get his group to safety inside a tunnel underneath a bridge overpass. Shot just as he enters the tunnel, Leavitt spends much of his narrative in a hallucinogenic retreat into memory and fantasy, where he confuses his present in the tunnel with a fantasy of being at home in the United States with his wife. Time balloons and shortens during Leavitt's sections of the novel, as he moves in and out of consciousness. Cared for tangentially by a young Korean woman who is also responsible for a mentally retarded child and an older woman, Leavitt seems to communicate to them beyond his physical capacity for language.

Part of Phillips's purpose in these sections is to depict the senseless slaughter of hundreds of innocent Koreans in this tunnel incident, which actually occurred during the Korean War. (She also includes recent photos of the tunnel, bridge, and underpass taken by photographer Robert Nilsen). Hinted at within the hallucinations, however, are intimate connections between Leavitt's present in Korea and a concurrent time with his wife back in the United States. He seems to exist in both places, knowing things about his wife and the imminent birth of his son that he could not realistically know.

Also tying into this sense of unreality are the uncanny abilities of the mentally retarded Korean boy whom Leavitt saves and who senses an attack by airplanes before it occurs. Though lacking the connections typically available to him, the boy, like Leavitt's son Termite, seems to have prophetic abilities. Since the Korean boy's qualities and physical characteristics are mirrored in Termite in the other sections of the novel, Phillips seems to suggest that the young Korean boy's spirit is transferred somehow into Termite. Certainly, the two have similar attributes, including unusual, opaque eyes and an inability to walk or talk. Most important, Termite seems to know about things that occurred in the past and seems to "remember" the tunnel in Korea: He seems to connect an otherwise normal tunnel in West Virginia with the atrocities that occurred in Korea. Here, Phillips seems to portray the past and the present as capable of conjoining in ways one cannot fathom.

Termite's is one of the most interesting voices in the text. His sections, told via third-person limited omniscience, give readers the odd sense of being inside his thoughts as well as perceiving the outside world from his perspective. Phillips's narrative technique resembles those of modernist authors who also used multiple narrations, particularly in Termite's distinctively disjointed point of view. William Faulkner's *The Sound and the Fury* (1929), for example, is also told in multiple sections and, most relevant, also includes the stream-of-consciousness narration of a mentally incapacitated character, Benji Compson. Phillips uses an epigraph from *The Sound and the Fury* to begin the novel. Even without this clue, the opening line of the Termite section is reminiscent of Faulkner's text, in which Benji tries to describe golf without being able to interpret the golfer's actions.

In Phillips's case, Termite is engaged in playing with a piece of blue plastic, yet he cannot understand what he plays with, so he sees it as something mysterious: "He sees through the blue and it goes away, he sees through the blue and it goes away again. He breathes, blowing just high." Thus, readers must interpret Termite's scenes from sensory information alone. Termite cannot evaluate or analyze; the narrative voice of his sections therefore simply describes things literally. Similarly, readers must interpret Termite's apparent dual existence.

He is a part of the story of his father, existing as or in connection with the South Korean baby his father saves before he dies by friendly fire at the bridge overpass. At the same time, he is a young American boy, hindered by physical and mental defects even as he becomes a kind of seer in the novel, a mythical and mystical creature who carries the secret knowledge of both stories.

Termite serves as a bridge into the second plot of the novel, set in the late 1950's. While connected in both obvious and mysterious ways to the past, this story primarily concerns its present, occurring over six days in late July in Winfield, West Virginia. It involves Lark, a teenager who cares for her brother Termite during a storm and great flood.

Lark, an emotionally fragile and somewhat naïve young woman, has decided to be the primary caregiver for her younger brother, eschewing further education in favor of an isolated existence in her aunt's home. Her mother Lola, the unknown and unspoken-of sister of her guardian and aunt Nonie, haunts Lark's thoughts, and she tries to recreate Lola from a few pictures and boxes of Lola's personal effects stored in the basement of her aunt's house. As the rains force her to take these items to the attic, Lark begins to piece together some of her mother's story, though the exact details of her parentage and that of her brother do not emerge until nearly the end of the novel.

As she gradually learns of the circumstances of her birth and the situation surrounding her brother's birth, and as the flood frees her from her conventional ways of thinking, Lark gradually recognizes her need to escape from the safety of her aunt's home. She decides to strike out alone with her brother on the freight train that passes through town every day. At the last minute, she invites her childhood lover, Solly, to join them. Like Lark, Solly is motherless, and he seems to understand her despite her attempts to push him away. Lark, Termite, and Solly have spent many childhood days at a local West Virginia train overpass and tunnel (one that matches the South Korean tunnel in description and tone), and eventually they meet there to hop the train, bound for Florida and a new chance at life for all of them. Though the earlier tunnel housed death and destruction, this tunnel offers the protagonist hope.

Lark's sections of the novel are narrated in the first person, as are additional sections narrated by Nonie, her aunt. Though Nonie serves as primary caregiver for Lark and Termite, her most important role in the novel is to provide essential background information. Her sections provide the family's backstory, particularly that of Lola, revealing Lola's terrible hold over men and Nonie's life devoted largely to taking care of situations that Lola has created. Though Lark, Termite, Nonie, and Leavitt's points of view appear multiple times in the text, Lola's perspective, narrated in the third person, appears only in the last section of the novel, on the day she commits suicide—another connection with *The Sound and the Fury*.

The novel's complex story also has the effect of one of Faulkner's texts in that one learns the truths of the family by following the circuitous route of the narrators' voices. These multiple points of view, which shift from first to third person, lead readers backward in time, then forward, as each section supplies additional clues about Lark and Termite and their eventual need for escape. By the climactic flood scenes at the end of the novel, Lark and Termite have been "saved" in multiple ways: potentially by Termite's father, who has been mysteriously reincarnated in the form of a social worker named Stamble; by Solly, who brings a boat to take Lark and Termite from their attic hiding place during the flood; and, more important, by Lark's own sense of self-preservation. Lark has been saved by her belief in herself and the necessity to enlarge her worldview. The children's survival and their departure from their "tunnel" suggest a hopeful future for them, one that is freed from the ghosts of their past.

Rebecca Hendrick Flannagan

Review Sources

Book World 39 (January 25, 2009): 1
Booklist 105, no. 4 (October 15, 2008): 5.
Kirkus Reviews 76, no. 20 (October 15, 2008): 1090.
Library Journal 133, no. 20 (December 1, 2008): 118-119.
The New York Review of Books 56, no. 7 (April 30, 2009): 45-47.
The New York Times, January 6, 2009, p. 1.
The New York Times Book Review, January 18, 2009, p. 17.
The New Yorker 84, no. 47 (February 2, 2009): 67.
Publishers Weekly 255, no. 43 (October 27, 2008): 30-31.
The Times Literary Supplement, March 20, 2009, p. 21.
The Wall Street Journal, January 10, 2009, p. W8.
The Women's Review of Books 26, no. 3 (May/June, 2009): 20-21.

LAST RITES

Author: John Lukacs (1924-)
Publisher: Yale University Press (New Haven, Conn.). 187 pp. $25.00
Type of work: Autobiography
Time: 1924-2009
Locale: Hungary; United States

The historian Lukacs's autobiography sums up his life and times and provides his final reflections on how to study the past and its significance

Principal personages:
JOHN LUKACS (1924-), historian
HELEN LUKACS (1926-1970), his first wife
STEPHANIE LUKACS (1926-2003), his second wife
PAMELA LUKACS, his third wife
WINSTON CHURCHILL (1874-1965), British prime minister, 1940-1945, 1951-1955
MARY SOAMES (1922-), Churchill's daughter
ADOLF HITLER (1889-1945), German chancellor, 1933-1945

John Lukacs has over the past forty years become one of the most interesting and popular historical writers in the United States. Born in Hungary in 1924, he came to his adopted country in 1947 and began a teaching career at Chestnut Hill College, a small Catholic college for young women outside Philadelphia. Over the next sixty years, the prolific Lukacs produced thirty books on topics that ranged from the cultural history of Philadelphia to the history of the Cold War. In the 1990's, he gained renewed acclaim for a series of short books that focused on key events in World War II. His close examinations of Winston Churchill's decisions and speeches of May, 1940, and their relationship to the outcome of the war became best sellers. Lukacs's reputation as an interpreter of recent history and a lucid writer soared. As his books became shorter, his audience grew larger, appreciating the luminous and insightful essays that his later work contained.

Lukacs's writings are not easily classified. His interests have ranged from Alexis de Tocqueville to George Kennan. He will probably be best remembered for his insights into World War II. He spent the war years in his native Hungary as the Germans and Russians contested for supremacy in central Europe. His ability to unravel the complexity of national and international politics in that turbulent region was most evident in *The Last European War* (1976), where he explained the interplay of economic, cultural, and political events between 1939 and December, 1941. That book remains a stimulating and informative work and perhaps the best place to begin understanding what has made Lukacs such an influential chronicler of modern times.

John Lukacs taught for many years at Chestnut Hill College and is the author of a number of books including The Last European War *(1976),* Five Days in London: May, 1940 *(2001), and* June, 1941: Hitler and Stalin *(2006).*

One of the most entertaining features of Lukacs's books are the discursive footnotes that comment on his text and elaborate on his opinions. Fans of Lukacs enjoy that aspect of his work as much as his main narratives. Excerpts from his diaries, comments about his personal experiences, and tart observations on the work of other historians turn up in his annotations. Throughout his narratives, these notes provide intriguing hints about Lukacs's own life experiences. Naturally, these revelations about his personal history have fed an interest in Lukacs himself.

Lukacs addressed these matters in his first autobiographical volume, *Confessions of an Original Sinner* (1990). He traced his life and developing thoughts, from Hungary and his reactions to World War II to his emigration to the United States once the fighting had stopped. The book's narrative examined his career as a teacher and writer and explained how he came to write the books he did. Readers learned something of his personal life, but only within the context of his professional interests. At age sixty-six, Lukacs could look back in 1990 over a rich and productive career as a scholar and teacher.

Now, nearly two decades later at the age of eighty-five, Lukacs has written a second, more personal account of his own life and writing. He intends, he says in the opening pages, to move in this narrative, "from something like a philosophy to something like an autobiography." In the course of the book, Lukacs reveals more of his personal story than in his previous volumes, and admirers of his work will find here more insights into the man himself. However, Lukacs has never been particularly easy to read, and *Last Rites* requires readers to plunge into the author's philosophy of history and of the place of humanity in the universe before his more personal disclosures arrive.

As if to alert readers that heavy thinking will be necessary before more accessible information is provided, Lukacs titles his first chapter "A Bad Fifteen Minutes." For that period of time, or however long it takes to read the first chapter, Lukacs delves into the thorny questions of objectivity and subjectivity in history, how historians know what they know, and how valid history is as a discipline. He sees humanity as existing at the center of the universe and history as "the recorded and remembered past." Models, science, and history, for Lukacs, are all creations of the human mind and must be understood as such. These beliefs reflect Lukacs's long-held views that historical events are subject to contingency and human action. In a short book of this kind, his aphoristic style and references to such thinkers as Werner Heisenberg will challenge his audience to grapple with these large questions.

The portions of the book that admirers of Lukacs will find most rewarding deal with his response to his adopted country, the United States, recollections of his native Hungary, and comments about his popular volumes on Winston Churchill and the events of the spring of 1940. Lukacs sees humanity reaching the end of a five-hundred-year epoch, "the so-called Modern Age," when Western European civilization dominated the affairs of the world. He is pessimistic about the future because "for the first time in the history of mankind, men have acquired the power to destroy much of the earth and much of mankind, potentially even most of it." *Last Rites* represents for Lukacs "my last, desperate attempt to teach."

For his readers, the resulting book will have much to say about the situation in which the world now finds itself. Lukacs admires American culture and the physical world of Pennsylvania in which he has made his life and professional career. He approaches his adopted country with a skepticism about both the Left and the Right on the political spectrum. Those who place Lukacs as a conservative will find in this book trenchant criticisms of U.S. involvement in the Iraq War and the rise of the imperial presidency, yet he is also jaundiced about the Democrats and their capacity to alter the course of overseas involvements and the militarization of the nation. At the same time, Lukacs is attached to the physical environment of the United States. He presents moving and evocative passages describing his affection for the Pennsylvania countryside, such as when he recounts rowing on the reservoir near his home.

> Alone, on that dark indigo water, as if one hundred miles away from any town, out in some wilderness, under a sickle moon, I was full of gratitude for what God and this country had allowed me, for this silent world where I belong, where I had chosen to live.

An excellent chapter deals with Lukacs's ambivalent attitude toward Hungary, the country he left just after World War II. His writings have made him a celebrity in Hungary, where he spends two weeks each year around the time of the country's Book Week. As he puts it in *Last Rites*, "Hungary is my mother, America is my wife."

For Lukacs's fans in the United States, the most interesting chapter in this book will most likely be his account of his intellectual connection with Winston Churchill and World War II. Building on the research that he did for *The Last European War*, Lukacs decided in the 1980's to concentrate on the weeks in May, 1940, when Churchill and Great Britain faced a Germany that had just defeated the French army and overrun France. Lukacs recreated the interplay between Churchill and Lord Halifax in his book *Five Days in London: May, 1940* (2001) and explained how Churchill kept the British government on the path of resistance to Adolf Hitler and the Nazis. The book became a popular success and led to the naming of a street in Budapest after the British prime minister. The pages of the book on Lukacs's friendship with Churchill's daughter, Mary Soames, are among its very best. Reading these sections adds to the enjoyment of Lukacs's previous investigations of the battle between Churchill and Hitler during those crucial days of World War II. Although many long books have been written about Churchill and his legacy, the brief Lukacs volumes are the best introduction to the significant role that the British leader played in world history.

Writing about personal and romantic relationships is never easy in an autobiography. Lukacs devotes an entire chapter to his three marriages. The portraits that he provides of his wives—two of whom died of serious, disabling illnesses—underscore Lukacs's skill and subtlety as a writer. His first wife, Helen, a sometime secretary to T. S. Eliot at the Institute for Advanced Studies at Princeton University, helped advance Lukacs's writing career with her editorial skills. For her husband, she provided "her unfailing kindess, the instant red goodness of her heart."

Lukacs, like Woodrow Wilson, seems to be one of those men who needs to be married to have a fulfilling life. He recounts how, after his first wife's death, he married Stephanie during the mid-1970's and, following her death, he married Pamela. Lukacs explains how each of these marriages shaped his existence as a historian and writer. This is the most personal and affecting chapter in this very intimate volume.

Written when Lukacs is in his mid-eighties, *Last Rites* is not as finished and polished a product as some of his earlier works. Part of the charm of the narrative, as is always the case with Lukacs, comes from his discursive footnotes, with their excerpts from his diaries and wry comments about issues, people, and the books he is reading. They convey a sense of listening to an old friend sum up his existence and illuminate past events with the wisdom of years of study and thought about historical issues.

If *Last Rites* is indeed the final book in Lukacs's illustrious career, it represents a capstone to an impressive intellectual achievement. Coming to the United States at the outset of the Cold War to teach at a small institution without a major academic reputation was not the most propitious way to launch a career as a historian. Through his skill and insight, however, Lukacs has made the most of the opportunities that history and chance have offered him. Many of his books on World War II will remain classics in the field and excellent introductions to the transcendent issues of that cataclysmic conflict.

Lukacs's prose gives pleasure to his readers. He is a master of historical aphorisms and tart phrases that skewer sloppy authors and hapless historical actors. His dismissal of the presidential practice of returning the salutes of military personnel is a gem of historical analysis. "There is something puerile in the Reagan and Clinton and now Bush salute. It is the gesture of someone who likes playing soldier." He links this ritual to the growth of the imperial presidency and the overemphasis on the president as commander-in-chief. Thus, Lukacs in a few effective sentences illuminates something that is so familiar on television that its true meaning is hidden from view.

For readers new to Lukacs, the place to begin is with his books on Churchill, Hitler, and Stalin. *The Last European War* and *Philadelphia: Patricians and Philistines, 1900-1950* (1981) show Lukacs at the top of his form. *Last Rites* is a graceful summing up of his life, but it will mean even more to readers who have explored Lukacs the historian at his very best.

Lewis L. Gould

Review Sources

America 200, no. 7 (March 2, 2009): 23-24.
American Conservative 8, no. 4 (February 23, 2009): 28-29.
Booklist 105, no. 11 (February 1, 2009): 13.
National Review 61, no. 5 (March 23, 2009): 42-43.
The Wilson Quarterly 33, no. 2 (Spring, 2009): 106-107.

LAURA RIDER'S MASTERPIECE

Author: Jane Hamilton (1957-   )
Publisher: Grand Central (New York). 214 pp. $22.99
Type of work: Novel
Time: The early twenty-first century
Locale: Hartley, Wisconsin

A fictional exploration of the complexities of marital faithfulness and unfaithfulness and of the relationship between the public and private spheres in the Internet age

Principal characters:

LAURA RIDER, co-owner of Prairie Wind Farm and an aspiring writer of romance
CHARLIE RIDER, her husband and business partner, Jenna Faroli's paramour
JENNA FAROLI, a syndicated public radio personality, the object of Charlie's desires
FRANK VODEN, Jenna's husband, a Wisconsin Supreme Court judge
DICKIE KARMAUTH, a former poet laureate and family friend of the Vodens
SALLY KARMAUTH, Dickie's wife, a hematologist and confidant of Frank Voden
THE SILVER PEOPLE, aliens that Charlie claims abducted him when he was a teenager

Laura Rider's Masterpiece, Jane Hamilton's sixth novel, recounts an Internet-era ménage à trois involving a married couple—Laura Rider and her husband Charlie Rider—and radio talk-show host Jenna Faroli, a recent addition to the rural Wisconsin community of greater Hartley who has matched wits with public figures from presidential candidate Al Gore to musician Sting. Ultimately, the tangled Rider-Rider-Faroli triangle leads to an accidental, but painful, public revelation of Charlie and Jenna's clandestine relationship. While Hamilton's previous five novels, beginning with *The Book of Ruth* (1988) and continuing through *When Madeline Was Young* (2006), contain comic elements, by and large their tone is dark, reflective of the author's focus on personal and familial tragedies.

Typical of Hamilton's oeuvre is the recognition that acts of infidelity, abuse, and defamation have serious consequences. Central characters in previous novels bear the physical and emotional scars of trauma survivors. Essential questions about relationships between the individual, the married couple, the family, and the community are posed in Hamilton's works, and although *Laura Rider's Masterpiece* is written in the comic mode, such questions still surface.

Though populated with quirky characters, the novel explores the nebulous natures of truth and falsehood. Laura and Charlie Rider are a playful couple whose imagina-

Jane Hamilton is the author of six novels including The Book of Ruth *(1988), recipient of the PEN/ Hemingway Award for First Fiction, and* A Map of the World *(1994), a* New York Times *Notable Book of the Year.*

tions lead them to invent stories about their family pets—such as Maine Coon cat Polly having a prom date—and to collaborate on Charlie's ardent e-mails to a married woman. Additionally, husband and wife send separate missives, but always under the guise of Charlie's moniker. When Charlie tells new resident Jenna Faroli about the Silver People, aliens who abducted him in his teens, she receives his personal truth with an equal mixture of skepticism and intrigue. Later, when Charlie invents a family whose members dwell in his kneecap and recounts their adventures, Jenna, now his lover, joins in and continues the story line in a return e-mail. Some deceptions appear to be harmless entertainments, but others breach the social contract that mandates honesty as a precursor to trust. Hamilton suggests that fiction is a type of lie that has the potential to entertain (and on occasion to instruct) and that humans by their nature are storytellers. She thus raises the question of to what extent individuals should be allowed to concoct mistruths in order to narrate their life stories and the life stories of others. She provides no pat answer to this question.

Critics have tended to note the comic tone of *Laura Rider's Masterpiece* to the exclusion of serious issues raised by its tale of covert romance and public exposure. Chief among these issues is the difficulty of maintaining personal privacy in an era of mass correspondence. A simple keyboard error can make private information available for public consumption. When a fatigued and multitasking Laura inadvertently inserts an erotic e-mail, penned by Jenna and intended for Charlie's readership alone, into the front section of her nursery newsletter, the love life of a radio celebrity becomes titillating community news. With the press of a button, private words—in which Jenna ruminates on Charlie's sexual technique—are delivered to more than six hundred online subscribers.

Jenna is humiliated, Charlie is infuriated, and Laura is oddly amused by the mishap. Although Laura has revealed her husband to be a philanderer and brought ridicule to a respected interviewer, when her error is revealed to her, she laughs. For Laura, the mistake makes an amusing story, material for the writing workshop that she attends at the Bear Claw Resort.

Hamilton writes about the complications that accompany acts based on human desire. While Charlie and Laura are coconspirators in their seduction of Jenna, they woo her in order to satisfy disparate needs. Denied his wife's body after years of connubial contentment (Laura claims that Charlie's passion has worn her out), the sexually prolific Charlie seeks a replacement lover. Having barred sexual activities from her own life, Laura dreams of creating them for others. For Laura, instigating an affair between her husband and Jenna is a form of research conducted in pursuit of her ultimate ambition: to become a successful author of romance novels. Her goal is not only to gain publication but also to transform the genre. She wants to create a new form, the "conscious romance," a term she purloins from one of Jenna's e-mails and inserts into their radio interview.

The scheduled topic for their live, broadcast discussion, prairie gardens, is abandoned when Laura confesses to Jenna her desire to update the standard love story for the twenty-first century. She announces that her mission is to "discover what the ideal man is for today's real woman." Laura's real woman appears to be a successful career woman like her role model Jenna, one who straddles the professional and domestic spheres with ease. Her ideal man is defined as "calibrated exquisitely"—equal parts masculine and feminine—like her husband Charlie. The ideal man, physically enthusiastic but emotionally sensitive, shares sexual favors with the real woman who is his equal in life and in bed. Laura fails to see that her vision for the new romance merely collapses, rather than eradicates, stereotypes associated with the genre—an irony not lost on Jenna.

Whether Laura can transform the romance genre is left unresolved, but in a true sense she has rewritten the tawdry tale of infidelity within her own community. In large part, Jenna and Charlie's affair is the result of Laura's foray into creative writing, a warm-up drill in anticipation of crafting a novel. As author, Laura literally draws her characters from life. Having honed her craft for fiction by forging e-mails for her husband and transmitting them to Jenna, Laura is oblivious to the fact that her ghostwriting has turned destructive.

In Laura's eyes, Jenna Faroli leads a charmed life as an acclaimed public-radio figure married to a respected judge, but appearances are deceptive. Jenna's marriage is passionless, and her husband's ardor is directed elsewhere. Reminiscent of the chaste sleeping arrangements of the Rider household, Jenna Faroli and Frank Voden ended their sexual relationship years ago, with one significant difference: The choice was Frank's, not Jenna's. Unaware of the parallel courses of their marriages, Laura imagines a much different Jenna, a woman intellectually and sexually fulfilled. Laura does not envy her sexual fulfilment, but she lusts after a similar intelligence, one she believes will be within her grasp once she becomes a writer.

Laura's interest in Jenna pre-dates the talk-show host's move to rural Wisconsin. For years, Laura has sought to improve her mind by listening to the interviews that Jenna conducts with dignitaries, rock stars, and authors. Laura views Jenna as her mentor, one whose probing questions improve her mind in the passive act of listening. She has developed an emotional crush on Jenna: "How she loved slipping into the dream, master and pupil bathed in the warmth of their mutual regard." The mutual regard, however, is more fantasy than reality. The women meet infrequently; Charlie is the conduit through which they enter each other's personal spheres via online communication.

Jenna believes that she deceives Laura by engaging in an affair with Charlie, but Laura is conscious of their affair and has knowingly instigated their liaison. Ultimately, it is Jenna, not Laura, who is deceived. Unbeknown to Jenna, Laura composes the majority of Charlie's e-mails in an action reminiscent of the plot of Edmond Rostand's *Cyrano de Bergerac* (pr. 1897, pb. 1898; English translation, 1898), a play in which the title character, a master of eloquent speech, becomes a surrogate wooer for a local, tongue-tied baron. Though Laura's feelings for Jenna are clearly an infatuation for a perceived superior, Jenna's feelings about her erstwhile pupil reveal themselves to be a complicated mix of guilt (for sleeping with Laura's husband), envy (of Laura's gardening and entrepreneurial talents), and disdain (for Laura's lack of intellectual rigor). Far from being the all-knowing Everywoman whom Laura imagines her idol to be, Jenna remains ignorant of the true source of her seduction. Later, Jenna mistakes Laura's publication of her private correspondence for the retaliatory act of a jilted wife and not the honest mistake of an online publisher.

Hamilton reminds readers that love triangles and open marriages are not new phenomena in a scene that features Jenna and family friend Dickie Karmauth discussing the Bloomsbury Group, a cotillion of British artists and writers remembered in part for their unorthodox living and loving arrangements in the 1920's and 1930's. There are shades of Bloomsbury in the relationships among poet Dickie, his wife Sally, Jenna, and Frank. Jenna muses that Frank's proposal of marriage was linked to her ability to fall "into step so naturally with Dickie and Sally, his two essential friends." Dickie is Jenna's favorite partner for conversations about art, literature, and life, and Jenna suspects that Sally is Frank's preferred partner for more intimate needs. Frequent mutual houseguests and vacationers, the foursome regroups into twosomes and triads reminiscent of the shifting alliances of Bloomsbury members.

Imaginatively, Jenna is able to incorporate Charlie into her reveries with Dickie. As the poet recites a passage from Virginia Woolf's *To the Lighthouse* (1927), Jenna conjures Charlie as the young boy preparing for his boat journey. In reality, Jenna is unable to integrate either of the Riders into this insular group of married friends who play Scrabble, but only in foreign languages, and who discuss extraterrestrial visitations, but only to quote the views of Harvard professors. Intellectual and professional snobbery keeps the Riders at a distance. When news of the affair breaks through cyberspace, it is beneath Frank's dignity to discuss the infidelity with his wife, and Dickie offers her only the blithe observation that "no one is ruined by this kind of scandal. On the contrary, your stock is probably soaring."

Hyperinformed Jenna doubts that Laura, who never read a book before the age of forty-three and who has only a viewer's knowledge of a limited number of classics, is capable of writing a romance novel—let alone of transforming the genre. Hamilton suggests, however, that Jenna—who is so easily duped by Laura's online machinations—underestimates her rival. Certainly, Hamilton, in her sixth novel, has penned the "conscious romance" that her heroine, Laura Rider, aspires to write. Part deconstruction of the traditional romance novel and part reconstruction of a love story for the Internet age, *Laura Rider's Masterpiece* leaves readers conscious of the act and the artifice of falling in love.

Dorothy Dodge Robbins

Review Sources

Booklist 105, no. 14 (March 15, 2009): 42.
Kirkus Reviews 77, no. 2 (January 15, 2009): special section, p. 6.
Kirkus Reviews 77, no. 8 (April 15, 2009): 406.
People 71, no. 16 (April 27, 2009): 49.
Publishers Weekly 255, no. 49 (December 8, 2008): 40.
USA Today, April 28, 2009, Life, p. 06d.

"LE CID" and "THE LIAR"

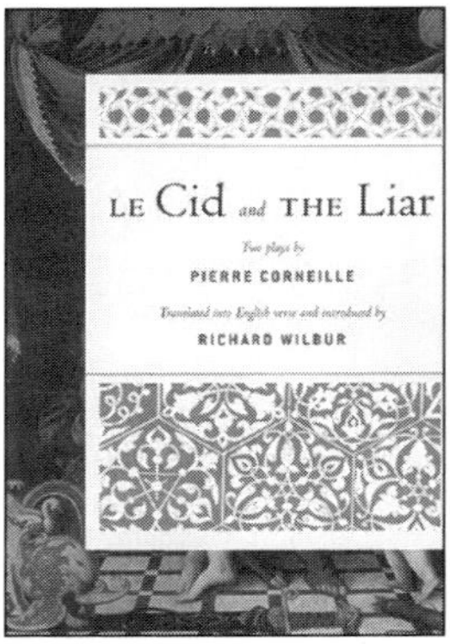

Author: Pierre Corneille (1606-1684)
First published: Le Cid, 1637, in France; *Le Menteur*, 1644, in France
Translated from the French by Richard Wilbur
Publisher: Houghton Mifflin Harcourt (Boston). 272 pp. $13.95
Type of work: Drama
Time: The eleventh century (*Le Cid*); the early 1600's (*The Liar*)
Locale: Seville, Spain (*Le Cid*); Paris (*The Liar*)

Former American poet laureate Richard Wilbur provides vibrant new translations of seventeenth century French playwright Corneille's most famous tragedy, about an eleventh century Spanish hero, and one of his witty comedies, about contemporary Parisian society

Principal characters:

Le Cid
DON RODRIGUE (later known as THE CID), a young Spanish noble
CHIMÈNE, a young woman in love with Rodrigue
DON DIÈGUE, Rodrigue's father
DON GOMES, Chimène's father
DON FERNAND, first king of Castile

The Liar
DORANTE, a student from the provinces recently arrived in Paris
GÉRONTE, Dorante's father
CLARICE, a young Parisian woman
LUCRÈCE, a friend of Clarice
CLITON, Dorante's valet

For more than half a century, Richard Wilbur—one of America's leading poets and poet laureate of the United States from 1987 to 1988—has been translating plays by the giants of the seventeenth century French theater, Pierre Corneille, Jean Racine, and Molière. His translations of *Le Cid* and *The Liar*, paired in a single volume, display not only Wilbur's versatility as a translator but also the brilliant range of Corneille's dramatic genius. Both plays hold places of distinction in the Corneille canon. Corneille scholar Peter Nurse calls *Le Cid* the first masterpiece of French drama. Its maiden production, in late 1636 or early 1637, ushered in the great age of French theater, which was dominated by Corneille, Racine, and Molière. *The Liar*, meanwhile, has become a long-term staple of the repertoire of the Comédie Française, the Paris acting company founded by Louis XIV in 1680 and still operating today.

Pierre Corneille, a seventeenth century playwright, is considered one of the three great French dramatists of his age. He wrote and produced numerous plays in various genres but is best known as a master of tragedy. Richard Wilbur is one of America's leading poets. He is a past recipient of the National Book Award, the PEN Translation Prize, and two Pulitzer Prizes. From 1987 to 1988, he served as poet laureate of the United States.

Corneille drew his inspiration for these plays from two Spanish dramas on the same subjects, but in both cases he transformed them for the French stage. In *Le Cid*, he restructured the play to conform to the classical unities; in *The Liar*, he incorporated French customs and values into the story. Although both plays were intended for the stage—and have been successfully produced at various times for nearly four centuries—merely reading them in Wilbur's translation gives some indication as to why they have remained favorites among playgoers and critics.

Based on a legend about the eleventh century Spanish nobleman and warrior Rodrigo Díaz de Vivar, *Le Cid* focuses on the dramatic conflict that emerges between the young Rodrigue, not yet known for his prowess as a warrior, and Chimène, the beautiful daughter of Don Gomes, the count of Gormas. The two are deeply in love and planning to marry when Chimène's father insults Rodrigue's father, Don Diègue. To defend the family honor, Rodrigue kills Don Gomes, immediately creating enmity between him and his beloved.

Chimène feels bound to avenge her father's murder, but before she can extract revenge, Rodrigue is called away to fight the Moors. His bravery earns him the sobriquet "Le Cid Campeador," or the lord of military arts. Nevertheless, although she still loves him, Chimène demands that Rodrigue be punished for killing her father. Rodrigue, also still in love, insists that he must die to preserve his honor in her eyes. Chimène convinces a former suitor to challenge Rodrigue to a duel; Rodrigue vanquishes this rival, even though he wants to die, because he feels that to lose intentionally would demean him in Chimène's eyes.

Royal intervention seems to provide a solution to the lovers' dilemma: Don Fernand, the first real king in Castile, wants Rodrigue to remain alive so he can serve the state. In the final scene, the king demands that Chimène marry Rodrigue, but he agrees to let them wait a year so Rodrigue can earn even greater honor on the battlefield.

The ambiguous ending of the play has bothered critics since it was first produced. Knowing whether Chimène really intends to marry Rodrigue is key to understanding her character, but her internal decision is not revealed. Although *Le Cid* was a box-office sensation, Corneille was chastised severely by contemporary critics for violating an essential element of tragedy, the consistency of a tragic figure's commitment to high moral principles. So violent was the outcry against Chimène's apparent acquiescence to the king that the "Querelle du Cid"—the quarrel over *Le Cid*—was referred to the new Académie Française. This French academy was established in 1635 to arbitrate matters concerning French language and literature.

Despite this contemporary controversy, what tends to stand out for readers four centuries later is the unrelieved tension created by the clash of values represented in the drama. Both Chimène and Rodrigue are committed to the feudal code of honor that demands they avenge slights to their family. At the same time, they are passionately in love with each other. To honor one commitment necessitates violating the other.

At the time *Le Cid* first appeared, audiences were accustomed to seeing tragicomedies, a mixed genre in which people of high stature engage in actions both comic and tragic. Corneille, however, wanted his work to be viewed as a tragedy in the classic mode, and he maintained a high level of decorum, sharply focusing attention on the tragic dilemma faced by both his hero and his heroine. Stripping away materials about El Cid's exploits as a warrior, he focused on the conflict between love and duty, highlighting the role that both fate and custom play in bringing about the play's tragedic events.

One can see precedents in classical drama for both Don Rodrigue and Chimène, specifically in the plays of Sophocles. Rodrigue is reminiscent of Oedipus, whose actions to defend his honor after a seemingly trivial incident have long-term consequences in the *Oedipus* trilogy—*Oidipous Tyrannos* (c. 429 B.C.E.; *Oedipus Tyrannus*, 1715), *Oidipous epi Kolōnōi* (401 B.C.E.; *Oedipus at Colonus*, 1729), and *Antigon* (441 B.C.E.; *Antigone*, 1729). Chimène is much like the title character of *Antigone*, torn between obeying the state and honoring her family. Her problem is further complicated, however, by the intense love she feels for the man who dishonored her family. The ambiguous ending of *Le Cid* only serves to emphasize the ongoing tragedy that prevents its two passionate lovers from realizing their happiness.

The contrast between *Le Cid* and *The Liar* could not be more pronounced. The latter is a light comedy in which Dorante, a law student from Poitiers, comes to Paris and immediately decides to pose as a seasoned warrior in order to impress the ladies. A chance encounter with Lucrèce and Clarice causes him to fall in love with the latter, but, when told that the name of the more beautiful of the two is Lucrèce, he believes Lucrèce is the name of his new love. Throughout the play, Dorante makes up a series of stories—first to impress Clarice and later to avoid having to go through with a marriage arranged by his father. Ironically, the intended bride is Clarice, but, because Dorante remains under the impression that the object of his affection is named Lucrèce, he schemes to avoid the union.

As he becomes more enmeshed in a web of falsehoods, Dorante is constantly reminded by his valet Cliton that he will eventually be found out and will suffer for having misled so many people. In the denouement, however, when Clarice and Lucrèce meet Dorante and confront him about his lying, the hero engages in a deft bit of verbal legerdemain: He declares his willingness to marry Lucrèce, who is actually a better match for him.

The Liar is very different from *Le Cid* in theme and in its representation of individual character: This is a play about self-preservation and self-advancement. If the hero and heroine of *El Cid* remind one of Oedipus and Antigone, Dorante calls to mind William Shakespeare's Falstaff, a master of self-preservation and a braggart who seems to bounce back from temporary setbacks. In *The Liar*, Corneille explores the relationship between illusion and reality in seventeenth century society, where appearance was all-important; people in this drama define their self-worth by what others think of them. The play also addresses a theme that has great appeal to modern audiences: the idea that one can reinvent oneself, especially if one moves physically to another locale where one is unknown.

Some twenty-first century readers or playgoers might be annoyed or even outraged by the apparent moral tone of *The Liar*. Throughout most of the play, Dorante gets away with his lies. When he is eventually caught, he manages to extricate himself from his predicament by casually abandoning his original choice of a lover and agreeing to marry a girl who is both more attractive and better connected socially. Others will recognize, as Corneille's original audience probably did, that Dorante is portayed as someone to be laughed at throughout, and they will be satisfied that he is not ostracized from his new social circle at the play's end.

The original English translation of *Le Cid* was commissioned by Corneille himself, along with translations into other European languages. Over the last three centuries, numerous new renderings into English have been produced, including several in the twentieth century. The same can be said to a lesser extent about *The Liar*. Wilbur's translations may be the first, however, in which the translator's own poetic genius is evident throughout. As a consequence, he is able to capture the spirit of Corneille's originals.

For *Le Cid*, Wilbur translates Corneille's elevated French alexandrines into English heroic couplets, reminiscent of those in English Restoration plays such as John Dryden's *All for Love: Or, The World Well Lost* (pr. 1677, pb. 1678), which tells the story of the ill-fated affair of Marc Antony and Cleopatra. For *The Liar*, Wilbur also uses heroic couplets, but the tone of the drama mirrors the sprightly comedies of the English Restoration and the eighteenth century. In both cases, however, Wilbur modernizes the dialogue, avoiding the stilted phraseology that makes some theatergoers and readers uncomfortable with plays of earlier periods.

Corneille's moral maxims and grand statements about love and honor lose little in translation. For example, when Chimène is misled into believing that Rodrigue has died in battle, she laments that the man who slew her father will now be glorified: "To die for king and country is no shame;/ by such a death one gains a deathless name." When the king insists she marry Rodrigue, Chimène replies with a question that reveals both her medieval sensibility and a surprisingly modern complaint about women's role in a patriarchal society:

> If Rodrigue is now essential to the State,
> Must I, for salary, become his mate,
> And bear an endless guilt because the stains
> Upon my hands are from my father's veins?

By contrast, the combination of coquettishness and good sense in Clarice's reply to Dorante's father when he proposes to arrange for her to marry is aptly captured in Wilbur's translation:

That he's a son of yours, sir, is no mean
Attraction, yet to wed him sight unseen,
Though you assure me he's extraordinary,
Would show a strange anxiety to marry.

Numerous additional examples could be drawn from both plays to demonstrate further how adept Wilbur is in rendering both the content and sense of seventeenth century French into modern English. Readers fortunate enough to pick up a copy of *"Le Cid" and "The Liar,"* and audiences who get to see stage performances using these texts as their basis, are sure to find the experience most rewarding.

Laurence W. Mazzeno

Review Sources

Booklist 105, no. 22 (August 1, 2009): 21.
Library Journal 134, no. 12 (July 1, 2009): 98.

LEAVING INDIA
My Family's Journey from Five Villages to Five Continents

Author: Minal Hajratwala (1971-)
Publisher: Houghton Mifflin Harcourt (Boston). 430 pp. $26.00
Type of work: History, biography, memoir
Time: The late 1800's to the early twenty-first century
Locale: India; Fiji; South Africa; Australia; New Zealand; England; Hong Kong; Canada; United States

Highlighting individual narratives based on extensive research, Hajratwala traces generations of her family from their common roots in the Indian state of Gujarat through migrations around the world and, in so doing, unfolds the story of the Indian diaspora

Principal personages:
MINAL HAJRATWALA, the author
MOTIRAM NARSEY, Hajratwala's paternal great-grandfather, who emigrated to Fiji
GANDA CHHAGAN KAPITAN, Hajratwala's paternal great-great-uncle, sent as a boy to live with relatives in modern-day South Africa
NAROTAM CHHAGAN, Hajratwala's maternal grandfather, who eventually joined his older brother in Fiji
RANCHHOD HAZRAT, Hajratwala's paternal uncle, who worked in the family business in Fiji
BHANU HAJRATWALA, Hajratwala's mother
BHUPENDRA HAJRATWATA, Hajratwala's father
MALA KUMAR, Hajratwala's cousin, who moved from Fiji to Los Angeles after winning the immigration lottery

Juxtapositions abound in Minal Harjatwala's *Leaving India*, which traces generations of the author's family, weaving back and forth across maternal and paternal lines as they spread out from India around the globe. Meticulously researched and documented, the book offers narratives of individual lives within historical and anthropological contexts. It also unfolds a personal account that uncharacteristically minimizes its author, except in her role as reporter, until Hajratwala unveils her own story near the end of the book. Presumably in an attempt to minimize confusion, she includes graphics of her family tree, a chronology, and a map depicting the family's journeys. However, especially in the early chapters, it may still be hard for readers to keep everyone—and everything—straight. Some critics have commented on a sense of slow going, noting the text's plethora of characters, events, details, and anecdotes. Still, readers who persevere are ultimately rewarded. As Hajratwala explores the story of her own family's choices, she also unfolds the larger story of the Indian diaspora.

Minal Hajratwala's creative work has appeared in numerous publications and performance spaces. For eight years, she worked as a journalist at the San Jose Mercury News *and was a National Arts Journalism Program Fellow at Columbia University's Graduate School of Journalism.*

In Hajratwala's "Acknowledgements" and "A Note on the Text" sections, readers are introduced not only to this expansive work but also to the language sensibilities of its author, a poet as well as a journalist. Hajratwala says that she interviewed nearly one hundred family members, friends, and community sources during the eight years the book was in progress. She confesses to her "geekish love of research" and references eight months of travel and research when "almost every member of my extended family hosted, fed, or chauffeured me." Hajratwala also acknowledges scholars and others who helped her find resources along the way, with special mention of those in India, where "research often seems possible only through acts of grace." She describes her usage guidelines, offers pronunciation cues, and promises that any necessary non-English words will be defined in the nearby text. She also explains the few basic non-English terms that recur throughout the book. Hajratwala emphasizes that *Leaving India* is a work of nonfiction, where no poetic license has been taken because "the journalist in me is scrupulous about such matters."

Hajratwala has explained that in this book she set out to find the intersection between character and history. The first chapter is a stand-alone essay that delves into Hajratwala's caste (*Kshatriya*) and clan (*Solanki*), "the group of people we think of as our close relatives, a cluster of Kshatriyas who live in certain villages—five villages, to be precise—and with whom we share rituals and sacraments." The rest of the text is structured in four main parts that unfold stories of the author's family members, spanning the late nineteenth century through the early twenty-first century. Each part opens with a dated title page estimating the size of the Indian diaspora at that point (from fewer than 374,000 in 1900 to greater than 11 million in 2001) and a list of countries with more than 10,000 people of Indian origin. Parts 1 through 3 contain two or three chapters apiece. Each has an introductory page with title, epigraph, and a portion of the family tree that locates its main character. In part 4, following the epigraph *Vaasudeva Kutumbukam* (an ancient Sanskrit mantra translated as "the whole world is one family"), Hajratwala creates a collage of her own generation. First, though, she goes back to its roots.

The opening narrative focuses on Motiram, Hajratwala's paternal great-grandfather, born to a clan of weavers in the village of Navsari, in southern Gujurat. Records show that he went to the Fiji Islands in 1909 and, two years later, established a small tailoring shop that eventually became one of the largest department stores in the South Pacific islands. Without records of "the precise combination of ambition, wanderlust, and desperation which led him to cross two oceans," Hajratwala focuses on what she can know—conditions in India at the time as well as influences from the British "empire in need." She offers a meticulously documented rendering of the years of Motiram's childhood, when cotton was being extensively grown in India to feed the mills (by then, most of the cloth in Gujurat was machine made); with a harsh tax requiring yearly payment on both the harvest and the land itself; and where the famine of 1899 caused widespread death even in relatively successful Navsari.

Although *Leaving India* is nonfiction, Hajratwala skillfully and carefully includes possibilities and alternate scenarios as she speculates about Motiram's reasons for emigrating and the surrounding circumstances. In the same way, backed by extensive research, she enlivens Motiram's voyage to Fiji on a ship whose cargo at that time typically consisted of 750 to 1,200 indentured Indians, quoting a contract in the *Fiji Royal Gazette* of 1910 that payment only occurred "for each adult Indian (male or female) of the age of ten years and over landed alive." The rare paying Indian passenger, such as Motiram, shared the same deplorable shipboard conditions as the "other 'coolies.'"

As Hajratwala moves through the emigration narratives from India to Fiji and South Africa (and later, to Australia, Britain, Hong Kong, New Zealand, Canada, and the United States), she sometimes breaks chronology to reference people or events still to come or long past. Doing so often helps interlace the stories. At times, however, frustration may result, especially if readers have not sorted out the characters or developed the fortitude to press on despite uncertainty.

At the start of the chapter on Narotam (Hajratwala's maternal grandfather), Hajratwala hints at her own story. She recalls first meeting her grandmother (Narotam's wife) in Iowa when the author was seven years old. Visiting there after her own family had just arrived in the United States from New Zealand, "the only home I remembered," she was "shy and reeling from the shock of migration." Hajratwala transitions to the story of Narotam through a second recollection. When she was eleven, living in a tiny Indian community in suburban Michigan, she saw the film *Gandhi* (1982) with her mother. Among other things, it depicted the march to the sea undertaken by influential Indian political and spiritual leader Mahatma Gandhi and his followers to protest a salt tax. At their destination, they were severely beaten by "native police," yet the marchers, buoyed by their belief in nonviolence, moved forward—wave after wave—into the onslaught. During the movie's intermission, Hajratwala's mother confided to her that her father had been in that march.

Narotam's story is rich in Indian history, illuminating—among other things—the traditional Hindu view of life, the philosophy and influence of Gandhi, and India's achievement of independence in 1947. The central artifact is a photo of Narotam taken immediately after his release from months of hard prison labor, the result of his participation in the salt march. He looks "young, intense, dressed like a saint all in white." Narotam's father, however, saw a rebellious young man on the brink of trouble and arranged for him to join relatives in Fiji. To help fund the trip, all the women in the family, including Narotam's young wife, had to pawn their meager jewelry. In 1931, Narotam arrived in Suva, Fiji, and worked as a tailor. In 1937, leaving their six-year-old daughter in India to be raised by grandparents, Narotam's wife joined him.

In time, Narotam established a clothing store, more children were born (including Bhanu, Hajratwala's mother, in 1946), and Narotam gained the respect of his community. To his retail shop, he added a wholesale company that expanded its business to Western Samoa, American Samoa, and Tonga, bringing great wealth. Through the mid-1950's to early 1960's, the family lived well. Then, unfortunate business circumstances caused their situation to change suddenly. Narotam's health also began to fail, and he died in 1965. Hajratwala writes that she missed her grandfather "by six years and two continents" and finds his life complicated, with "moments of shining idealism and sad compromise illustrating the relentless ironies of diaspora."

Perhaps the most fascinating chapter of *Leaving India* tells the story of Hajratwala's parents. Both Bhupendra and Bhanu lived in Fiji, but they were not acquainted until Bhupendra returned for a visit from the United States, where he had gone to study pharmacology in 1963, in the vanguard of the "brain drain." He came to see the woman his family thought would be a suitable match for him. Hajratwala weaves back and forth between her parents' childhoods as the two grow up in comfortable circumstances and gain solid educations. Eventually, the marriage of Bhupendra and Bhanu is arranged, and she returns with her husband to the United States, where he is working on a Ph.D. In telling their story, Hajratawala interjects her own: "It is hard for me to imagine my parents' state of mind upon marrying a stranger. They have tried to explain: *That is just the way it was*."

Hajratawala recounts her parents' early adventures learning American customs and creating a home in student housing, a dilapidated barracks apartment. The narrative unfolds to include, among other things, house-hunting in San Francisco, the arrival of two children, a move to New Zealand for a professorship, and a return to the United States to live in Michigan. Along the way, Hajratwala details the development and far-reaching influences of U.S. immigration law, as well as the economic and social circumstances that immigrants face. In so doing, she also encourages readers to look at American life anew. Hajratwala ultimately reflects upon what her parents gained and lost in their immigration to the United States, concluding that "perhaps only we of the next generation—raised among strangers, eating the fruits of our parents' risks—can taste the true proportions of bitter to sweet."

The most surprising chapter is probably the candid one that Hajratwala writes about herself. She focuses on childhood (when she longed to be named Ann) and her coming of age, responding to what she felt was "America's siren call of freedom, individual and sweet." When she left home, Hajratwala was "like any American adolescent, escaping my parents," but she was also "escaping India, that part of it which lived in our skins, in our home." While studying at Stanford University, she experiments with different lifestyles, at first without the knowledge of her parents and later incurring their wrath. As often happens, however, things have a way of working out, and the Hajratwala family ultimately stands united, embracing both their lesbian daughter and their son's marriage to a woman from Michigan who is half Finnish, one-quarter Irish, and one-quarter Norwegian, "the first white flower to blossom on the brown limbs of the family tree."

While critics have generally praised *Leaving India*, it has been suggested that Hajratwala's rich rendering of historical framework tends to overshadow the personal stories. Some have commented on the book's occasionally tedious detail, uneven presentation, and potential for confusion; whereas others speculate that it may be useful for people reading about migration not to have everything completely pinned down.

This book is likely to be equally compelling for those born in the United States, immigrants (Indian and otherwise), and academicians investigating how disparate cultures migrate, intersect, and interact. Second-generation immigrants, perhaps not quite sure whether to run from or embrace their ethnicity, may find Hajratwala's account especially meaningful. She explains that working on this book has helped her understand

> how each life is a tangle of push and pull; how each migration opens up future directions; and how my own journey, which I had come to believe and had been made to feel was so unusual as to be selfish and freakish, was in fact continuous with a long heritage of moving from the known to the unknown, from tradition into modernity, from village India into a cosmopolitan world.

Jean C. Fulton

Review Sources

Kirkus Reviews 77, no. 1 (Jan. 1, 2009): 23.
Publishers Weekly 255, no. 47 (November 24, 2008): 46.
San Francisco Chronicle, March 15, 2009, p. J1.
San Francisco Chronicle, March 18, 2009, p. E1.
The Washington Post, March 15, 2009, p. B06.
The Wilson Quarterly 33, no. 2 (Spring, 2009): 101-102.

LEAVINGS
Poems

Author: Wendell Berry (1934-   )
Publisher: Counterpoint Press (Berkeley, Calif.). 132 pp. $23.00
Type of work: Poetry

Using clear, everyday language and various poetic forms, Berry continues his lifelong advocacy of living close to the land and criticism of the devastation wrought by industrial society

In *Leavings*, as in his poetic works, Wendell Berry combines elements from the bucolic tradition stretching back to the ancient Greeks and Romans, from Jeffersonian agrarian democracy, from the English Romantic poet William Wordsworth (1770-1850), from the Stanford University Creative Writing Program, from raging modern-day environmentalists, and from the Old Testament prophets. Mostly, though, he is a Kentucky farmer and intellectual. He has written about life close to the land in a tight-knit rural community not only in some eighteen volumes of poetry but also in a series of novels and short stories chronicling events in fictional Port William (modeled after Port Royal, the Kentucky River town near Berry's farm). He has also produced numerous works of nonfiction that have influenced contemporary thinking.

The title of *Leavings* strikes a valedictory note, as do some of the collection's poems about growing old, as if the author were collecting the remnants of his fifty-year writing career. It seems early, however, for the seventy-five-year-old author to be saying good-bye. In fact, the greater part of *Leavings* consists of a continuation of the series begun in the earlier volumes *Sabbaths: Poems* (1987) and *A Timbered Choir: The Sabbath Poems, 1979-1997* (1998). These volumes were inspired by Berry's Sabbath strolls and meditations, and many poems in *Leavings* were inspired by similar Sabbath reflections from 2005 to 2008. Other poems, collected in the first part of *Leavings*, more closely resemble a culmination of Berry's career, distilling his lifelong themes. These include "A Speech to the Garden Club of America" (which first appeared in *The New Yorker*), "Questionnaire" (which first appeared in *The Progressive*), and "Look It Over" (which first appeared in *Appalachian Heritage*).

These key poems and others in *Leavings* make it evident that the poet is not writing confessional poetry about himself and his career. Instead, Berry uses his perspective to comment on society and its ills in the manner of a public spokesperson, speaking as a laureate, a prophet of American life, or a "mad farmer" the subject of *The Mad Farmer Poems* (2008). From this perspective, the collection's title evokes the remnants some beneficent farmers leave in their fields after harvest for the public, especially the needy, to come and pick. In contrast, it may also evoke abandoned farms, rundown small towns, empty Rust Belt factories, strip-mined lands, uranium tailings, radioactivity from atomic ventures, acid rain, chemical residues, poison, pollution, global warming, and other "leavings" of industrial society.

These physical leavings of industrial society are only the most obvious part of the picture Berry sketches. He also connects industrial society's need for raw materials, energy, manufactured goods, and trade to America's continuous or intermittent warfare. Moreover, industrial society for Berry has horrific psychological, moral, and theological ramifications. In essence, he indicates, industrial society no longer needs a hell, since it is making its own, as Berry humorously describes in "A Letter (*to Ed McClanahan*)":

> I dreamed that you and I were sent to Hell.
> The place we went to was not fiery
> or cold, was not Dante's Hell or Milton's,
> but was, even so, as true a Hell as any.
> It was a place unalterably public
> in which crowds of people were rushing
> in weary frenzy this way and that . . .

The poem goes on to describe a teeming university or city street where everyone in the crowd is "alone" and "hurrying": "It was a place/ deeply disturbed." The description is reminiscent of New York City or of the crowds crossing London Bridge in T. S. Eliot's *The Waste Land* (1922), which in turn are reminiscent of the hordes crossing the mythological River Styx.

A brief statement of Berry's themes appears in the short poem "Look It Over," about a walk in the woods. Berry leaves behind all the seemingly necessary accessories of life in industrial society: "I bring/ no car, no cell phone,/ no computer, no camera,/ no CD player, no fax, no/ TV, not even a book." Instead, sitting down on "a log provided at no cost," he communes with "the earth itself, sadly/ abused by the stupidity/ only humans are capable of. . . ." After this blunt statement, he picks up on his earlier diction and mockingly concludes the poem in commercial language full of resonance: "Free./ A bargain! Get it [the earth] while it lasts."

Wendell Berry, Kentucky farmer, intellectual, and author of fifty volumes of poetry, fiction, and essays, has won the T. S. Eliot Award, the Aiken Taylor Award, the John Hay Award, and the Cleanth Brooks Medal for Lifetime Achievement.

"A Speech to the Garden Club of America" expands on these themes in heroic couplets that announce the poem's satiric intent. The speaker regrets that he had to travel there "[b]y a sustained explosion through the air,/ Burning the world in fact to rise much higher/ Than we should go." Further details about digging up, burning, and poisoning the world "in our fit/ Of temporary progress" lead to the dictum "Burning the world to live in it is wrong,/ As wrong as to make war to get along. . . ." Instead, the speaker urges his audience to learn from gardens to live sustainable lives consistent with nature's cycle,

> Unlike our economic pyre
> That draws from ancient rock a fossil fire,
> An anti-life of radiance and fume
> That burns as power and remains as doom . . .

Addressing readers directly, "Questionnaire" uses a survey form typical of consumer products and questions worthy of the Grand Inquisitor to underline the moral compromises and complicity required by life in industrial society. It begins by asking readers the amount of poison they would willingly consume for the sake of a good economy ("Please/ name your preferred poisons.") and ends by asking readers to list the beliefs, "energy sources," and "kinds of security,/ for which you would kill a child./ Name, please, the children whom/ you would be willing to kill." After "Questionnaire," it is a relief to reach a peaceful poem such as "Tu Fu," even if the speaker, like the great eighth century Chinese poet alluded to, lives "in a time of ruin."

The poems in part 1 show that Berry can write in a variety of poetic forms and that, despite his near-apocalyptic themes, he has a delightful sense of humor. In addition to epistles, speeches, questionnaires, and rhymed couplets, part 1 includes haiku and poems in free verse. A couple of other humorous poems make fun of the big bang theory, one of them featuring the "mad farmer," who shows up at a nearby academic conference on the subject. "An Embarrassment" describes a limp before-dinner blessing. "Men Untrained to Comfort" is about Port William men who spare their horses by carrying their plows to their workplaces or working in the traces alongside (the poem also uses some quaint farming diction such as "rastus plow" and "singletree"). "And I Beg Your Pardon" puts the haiku to humorous purposes:

> The first mosquito:
> come here, and I will kill thee,
> holy though thou art.

The Sabbath poems of part 2, almost all written in untitled free verse, reflect Berry's serious, meditative side and the rambling walks that inspired them. Berry continues to criticize the destruction caused by industrial society, even more harshly than in the part 1 poems relieved by humor. A few grim poems see no hope and instead, echoing epigraphs from the Old Testament prophet Hosea and opponents of strip mining, predict the end of industrial civilization (the results of mountain removal to mine coal to produce cheap electricity elsewhere are only too apparent in Berry's native Kentucky). Other Sabbath poems, however, find or imply hope in a simple life lived close to nature and based on sustainable farming.

A substantial number of the Sabbath poems are meditations on time or embody an awareness of time as it is experienced while growing old, in the seasonal cycle of nature, and in history. Although painfully aware of growing old, the poet takes joy in a long married life and in the generations of children and grandchildren. "The Book of Camp Branch," the longest of the Sabbath poems and one of the few that are titled, is a meditation on a local stream. For Berry, the stream's operations represent those of time, cutting a groove down the hillside and moving rocks, but its sounds are like words, inspiring the language of the poet. A few poems about time address complex philosophical issues, but others only imply such complexity in the language of folk wisdom. One such poem begins "'That's been an oak tree a long time,'/ said Arthur Rowanberry" and ends

> "We didn't find what we were looking for,"
> said Arthur Rowanberry, pleased,
> "but haven't we seen some fine country!"

As a metaphorical commentary on human life, Rowanberry's words can hardly be topped, but other poems with a historical perspective come close. One poem challenges Thomas Jefferson's slighting reference to "barbarous ancestors" by noting that history is always partial, historical "truth" only a "story," a "plausible arrangement" made up from remaining bits of evidence. As do other poems in the collection, this poem suggests not only a historical but also a philosophical cast to the title of *Leavings*, as if the whole "truth" can never be known. The observation is consistent with Berry's repeated statements, echoing the prophet Hosea, that industrial society, which seems to know so much, is destroying the world and itself from lack of knowledge. The historical outcome is indicated in another poem that wonders what the Shawnee called Camp Branch and what it will be called after "our nation" vanishes.

Many of the Sabbath poems also celebrate a sense of place, suggesting that all truths are local. In the place Berry celebrates, life can be hard, as exemplified by the farmers "untrained to comfort" and by an old man in another poem who gets off his sickbed to go out on a winter day and feed the livestock. Central to Berry's sense of place, however, is the relatively unspoiled nature of the places he celebrates, including the farm, the woods, Camp Branch, and the Port William community. From these scenes, Berry derives his inspiration, and he sees the local truths that they embody as an antidote to the ills of modern industrial society. One hopeful poem even speculates that, after the fall of industrial society, there will be a return to the land—to the farms, rural communities, and small towns where people live in harmony with one another, animals, and the land.

Also part of Berry's sense of place is the simple fact that it is home. One Sabbath poem compares leaving home to "death":

> Farewell, my dearest ones.
> Farewell, my lovely fields. Farewell,
> my grazing flock, my patient horses,
> Maggie my ardent dog. Farewell,
> tall woods always so full of song.

The consolation for taking a trip is that "coming home is resurrection."

The religious terms in Berry's poems, such as "resurrection," "grace," and even the title "Sabbaths," connect with his informal theology. He rejects the idea that, because he wrote "some pages in favor of Jesus," he belongs to any hidebound religious orthodoxy, to which he attributes much disputation and suffering. Instead, he has

learned to duck
when the small, haughty doctrines fly overhead,
dropping their loads of whitewash at random
on the faces of those who look toward Heaven.

The imagery of these batlike creatures is replaced, in other Berry poems, by images of birds singing joyfully, ascending into the light and the sky, but eventually coming back to earth. They represent a natural theology in which life on this earth, with its edenic possibilities, is heaven enough.

Harold Branam

Review Sources

Booklist 106, no. 6 (November 15, 2009): 15.
Publishers Weekly 256, no. 46 (November 16, 2009): 40.

THE LETTERS OF SAMUEL BECKETT
Volume I: 1929-1940

Author: Samuel Beckett (1906-1989)
Edited by Martha Dow Fehsenfeld and Lois More Overbeck, with associate editors George Craig and Dan Gunn
Publisher: Cambridge University Press (New York). Illustrated. 782 pp. $50.00
Type of work: Letters
Time: 1929-1940
Locale: Dublin, Ireland; London, England; Paris, France; Hamburg, Berlin, and Munich, Germany

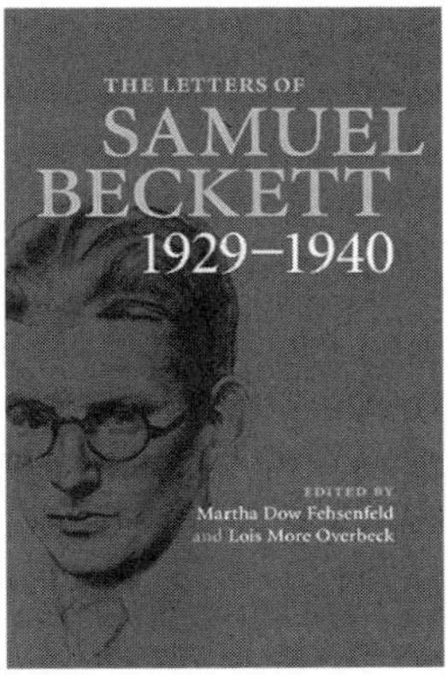

The first of a projected four-volume series of Beckett's letters containing, according to the author's instructions, only those letters whose contents have some bearing on his work

Samuel Beckett (1906-1989) was one of the most extraordinary writers of the twentieth century. Born to a prosperous Protestant family in Dublin, Ireland, he excelled as a student of languages and literature at Trinity College. This first volume of *The Letters of Samuel Beckett* comprises correspondence taken from the period during which Beckett published his first works of fiction, criticism, and poetry.

In 1928, Beckett accepted a position as English instructor at the École Normale Supérieure in Paris, the city that eventually became his permanent home. He soon made the acquaintance of fellow Irish expatriate writer James Joyce (1882-1941) and became one of a circle of younger writers who assisted Joyce—who suffered from failing eyesight—and collaborated on a volume of essays devoted to the author's "Work in Progress," the sprawling manuscript that would eventually be published as *Finnegan's Wake* (1939). Beckett also contributed the first essay, "Dante . . . Bruno . . . Vico . . . Joyce," to the collection published in 1929 as *Our Exagmination Round His Factification for Incamination of Work in Progress.* This was Beckett's first published criticism, to be followed a year later by his short book *Proust* (1930).

During the following decade, Beckett's life was one of peripatetic shuttling back and forth from Paris to Dublin, then to London, and also to a variety of German cities. He was beset by worries over employment, especially whether he should continue to pursue a career in teaching, something for which he had a steadily dwindling appetite. He felt a great deal of pressure from his family, especially his mother, to follow such a path.

As he struggled to establish himself as a writer, Beckett's first publications (such as *More Pricks than Kicks*, his 1934 volume of short stories) brought him scant notice and even scanter income. His lack of immediate literary success produced even more importuning from his impatient mother, May. The height of the family drama came

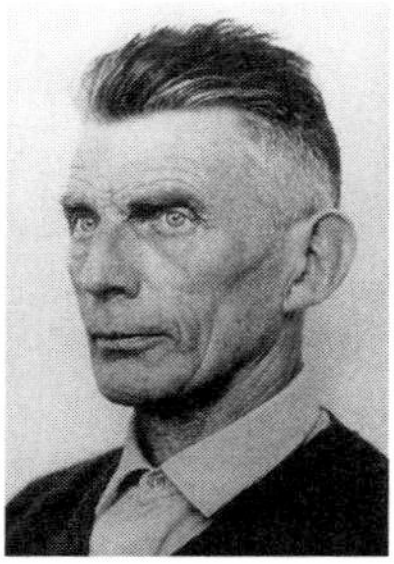

Samuel Beckett (1906-1989) was an Irish writer who lived for most of his life in France and who began writing exclusively in French by the late 1940's. Author of plays, novels, short stories, and criticism, he was awarded the Nobel Prize in Literature in 1969.

with the death of Beckett's beloved father, William. It fell to brother Frank to take over the family business. Beckett considered following suit as his own prospects dimmed. However, no matter how great the pull he felt toward Dublin, his need to escape was even greater.

Beckett's letters show a tender concern for his mother, but they make it equally clear that he needed to maintain a certain level of distance between them. By early 1938, Beckett had planted himself firmly on French soil. The early months of that year featured three dramatic developments: the publication in London of his first novel *Murphy* (1938), a stab wound delivered by a derelict on a Paris street, and the beginning of his relationship with Suzanne Deschevaux-Dumesnil (1900-1989), who was later to become his wife.

Beckett's name is associated with a set of stereotypes about the author that have developed into a mystique. He is thought of as having been almost pathologically private, if not reclusive, having thoroughly scorned the value of his own writings, and having been profoundly indifferent to the question of their publication. He often seemed to shun the spotlight, as in his peeved response to receiving the 1969 Nobel Prize in Literature (although, unlike Jean-Paul Sartre, he did accept it).

The letters published in this volume demolish such stereotypes. They reveal that Beckett was keenly and affectionately interested in a wide network of friends and relations, longing for news of and from them. Also, even though he could not resist frequent disparaging or dismissive remarks about his literary output, it is clear that he felt a sense of urgency about having his work read and evaluated. Moreover, he yearned fervently to see each manuscript through to publication, writing constantly to far-flung friends and acquaintances who might have been able to facilitate that process. Beckett's letters show that, like his mentor Joyce's fictional alter ego Stephen Daedalus, he had a growing conviction that he was meant to embrace the vocation of writer.

Also like Joyce, Beckett was intoxicated with language, and he would not confine his use of language to his mother tongue. He was fluent in French and very nearly fluent in both Italian and German. He wrote most of his letters in English, but quite a number of them are in French or German. He frequently peppered his letters with phrases and brief passages from the languages he loved, often inserting lines from his beloved Italian poet Dante.

In addition to introductions from the editors, this volume of letters includes prefaces from the French and German translators. These will prove most helpful to readers, as will the informative notes supplied by the editors. These notes set the context for specific letters and give useful but never excessive doses of information.

Beckett's letters of 1929-1940 were written primarily to friends, fellow writers, and persons in the publishing profession. He stayed in touch with friends in Ireland and regularly paid his respects to James Joyce and members of the Joyce family. For many years, Beckett was the object of unwelcome amorous attention from Joyce's mentally disturbed daughter Lucia, a predicament that sometimes caused strained relations between Beckett and the Joyces.

Many of Beckett's letters were directed to his good friend and literary agent George Reavey (1907-1976). Thomas McGreevy (1893-1967), though, stands as the recipient of by far the greatest number of letters. Like Beckett, he was an Irish writer and a passionate Francophile. Their friendship began when they met as fellow instructors at the École Normale Supérieure. To McGreevy especially, Beckett poured out his heart where his literary ambitions were concerned. McGreevy was also an art historian and would later become the director of the National Gallery of Ireland. Accordingly, Beckett often wrote to him of the galleries and art museums he visited in his travels.

Especially when writing to McGreevy, Beckett's considerable erudition is on impressive display. His letters virtually constitute a university course in Western civilization. His ability to recall and describe paintings he has seen is quite remarkable. Beckett regaled McGreevy with commentary on the Flemish painting he especially loved, as well as Italian Renaissance and eighteenth century French painting. His letters also contain frequent mention of their mutual friend, the artist Jack Butler Yeats (1871-1957), younger brother of poet William Butler Yeats. Beckett especially enjoyed visits to Yeats's studio when he was in Dublin.

Beckett was no less passionate when discussing music. He himself studied piano during these years, devoting himself especially to the music of Mozart. It was as a reader, however, that Beckett's restless intellect ranged most widely. The word "voracious" does not begin to do justice to his appetite for books, and when his personal library arrived from Dublin in 1938, it served as a dramatic confirmation that he had decided to take up permanent residence in Paris.

While it is not surprising that Beckett was vastly well read, some of the opinions he expresses in his letters about authors and certain works may come as a shock, especially those regarding authors one might expect him to revere. Marcel Proust, for example, comes in for his share of ridicule in the letters. Beckett registers particular scorn for Charles Darwin's *On the Origin of Species by Means of Natural Selection: Or, The Preservation of Favoured Races in the Struggle for Life* (1859), a book he professed to find tedious in the extreme.

As is true of his discussions of many topics, Beckett's mordant wit comes into play when he assesses certain authors. He mischievously reworks celebrated titles, often converting them into obscene puns. Beckett's letters to close friends give full rein to his penchant for scatological humor, more often than not directed at himself and his writings, as he compares his literary output to excrement. Coming across as something of a hypochondriac, he comments repeatedly on the state of his digestive tract, as well as other bodily functions and conditions. McGreevy received far more information of this kind than he is likely to have wanted. Readers of Beckett's novels and plays will be reminded of the physical afflictions and complaints associated with many of his characters. One thinks of the title characters of *Murphy* and *Molloy* (1951; English translation, 1955), as well as of Vladimir and Estragon from *En attendant Godot* (pb. 1952, pr. 1953; *Waiting for Godot*, 1954).

Beckett's correspondence became especially prolific from 1936 through 1938, years marked by frequent travel and, most important for his literary career, by the long campaign to find a publisher for *Murphy*. Expressions of discouragement appear quite often in these letters, as do words of gratitude to McGreevy for his encouraging comments on the manuscript. Reading these letters gives one the sense that Beckett's career itself hung in the balance and that he would have walked away from his literary vocation if he had not been able to get his book published. At times, his letters profess weariness and even complete indifference to the question of *Murphy*'s publication. More often, however, he makes it clear that he will pursue every avenue toward that end.

Beckett's frequent letters to Reavey contain many suggestions of publishers to try. Finally, Routledge of London accepted the work, and it appeared in early 1938. *Murphy* was a pivotal book for Beckett. While it is redolent of Irish wit and the influence of James Joyce, it prefigures in many ways the fiction Beckett would write during the following decade, when he made the bold move to begin writing in French.

Perhaps in part because Beckett stipulated that the only letters to be published should be those that have bearing on his work, the ominous political developments of the 1930's receive scarcely any comment in the published correspondence. Considering the amount of time the writer spent in Germany, this omission seems particuarly astonishing. Once in a great while, Beckett lets slip a reference to the Nazis, for example referring disparagingly to the virulent anti-Semite Julius Streicher in a letter to McGreevy dated March 7, 1937. Especially given his later activities on behalf of the French resistance, Beckett's sentiments seem clear enough.

The writer's letters do touch upon most other aspects of his life, since, as the editors argue, quite a broad range of topics can be understood to have bearing upon his work. The letters to his great friend McGreevy cover the gamut, from literature to his personal life, a brief glimpse of which Beckett offers when first mentioning (in his letter of April 18, 1939) his growing fondness for the French woman who would become his wife, Suzanne.

All in all, this volume of letters represents a substantial achievement, and it will be welcomed heartily by all admirers of Samuel Beckett. The editors supply very detailed and informative introductions, as well as helpful footnotes where needed. In nearly all cases, they include translations of the many foreign-language passages in the letters. The translators of the letters in French and German (George Craig and Viola Westbrook, respectively) also shed light on the specific challenges posed by Beckett's letters in those languages. *The Letters of Samuel Beckett: Volume I, 1929-1940*, ending as they do at the threshold of such a decisive decade both for the writer and for the world, will leave readers with appetites whetted for the volumes yet to appear.

James A. Winders

Review Sources

Library Journal 134, no. 4 (March 1, 2009): 72.
London Review of Books 31, no. 15 (August 6, 2009): 14-20.
The New Republic 240, no. 8 (May 20, 2009): 32-36.
The New York Review of Books 56, no. 7 (April 30, 2009): 13-16.
The New York Times, March 5, 2009, p. C23.
The New York Times Book Review, April 5, 2009, p. 1.
The New Yorker 85, no. 7 (March 30, 2009): 64-68.
The Spectator 309, no. 9418 (February 28, 2009): 28-29.
The Times Literary Supplement, March 13, 2009, p. 3-7.
The Washington Post, April 2, 2009, p. CO2.

LIFE IN SPACE
Astrobiology for Everyone

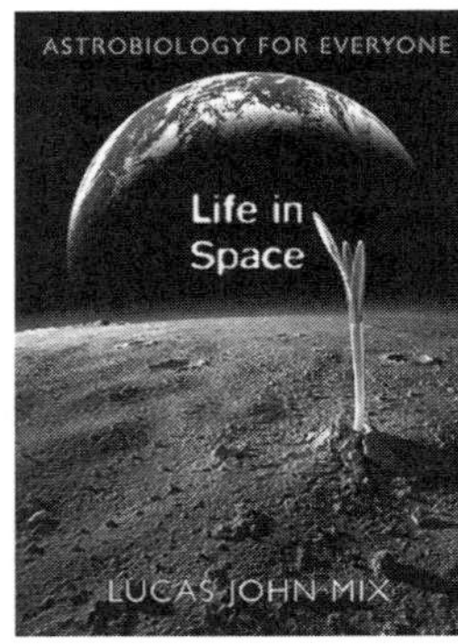

Author: Lucas John Mix
Publisher: Harvard University Press (Cambridge, Mass.). 331 pp. $29.95
Type of work: Science

Mix explains how astrobiology, drawing from the discoveries of many physical sciences, addresses such fundamental questions as the nature of life and its role in the universe

Extraordinary claims require extraordinary proofs. That observation from Scottish philosopher David Hume applies nowhere better than to speculations about the origin and evolution of life and whether it exists elsewhere in the universe. There is, after all, only a single example to judge by: life on Earth. The relatively new discipline of astrobiology nevertheless takes up those matters from a strictly scientific viewpoint, and Lucas John Mix explains how it does so in *Life in Space: Astrobiology for Everyone*. That subtitle seems tongue-in-cheek, given the complexities of the science involved, until one realizes that, even if astrobiology is not really for everyone, its findings will be. As Mix patiently, clearly, and humbly argues, how people define life influences how they look for life, and how people look for life reflects humanity's deepest assumptions and aspirations. Mix possesses a notable ability to guide readers, if not to an outright understanding of astrobiology's aims and methods, at least to a constructive appreciation.

Astrobiology studies life by drawing on many scientific disciplines—including biology, physics, astronomy, geology, oceanography, paleontology, and climate science—in order to treat it as an Earth-wide phenomenon. Astrobiologists hope thereby to learn where they might best look for life on other planets. This project is less straightforward than it sounds. Mix first sets out the assumptions behind the discussion and then methodically surveys the contributions of science.

Among those assumptions is the belief that reductionism is a useful method of investigation. Reductionism holds that simple phenomena give rise to more complicated phenomena. It works very well for physics and chemistry, which have posited basic laws and forces, but less well for biology. Still, Mix points out, when regarded as one method rather than as an end in itself, reductionism provides insights useful to assembling a coherent picture of life.

Another assumption of astrobiology is that it is possible to define life clearly. There are many approaches to formulating such a definition. Mix discusses five approaches and shows the weaknesses of each. These five include the "pornographic" definition of life ("I can't define it, but I know it when I see it"), the biochemical definition, the antientropic definition, the replication definition, and the evolutionary definition.

Yet another crucial set of assumptions is that the universe is well-ordered and that humans are capable of understanding it. In the first five chapters of *Life in Space*, Mix ably argues that science (and philosophy) have much of value to say about life. Thus, he asserts, astrobiologists should proceed with cautious confidence.

Lucas John Mix received a doctorate in biology from Harvard University. He lives in Redmond, Washington, serving as an Episcopal priest at a Seattle-area church and teaching courses on religion and science.

It is in chapter six, "Life in the Cosmos," that Mix grows specific. It and following chapters rely on physical laws and, especially, chemical formulae to make their case. Readers with no knowledge of science, or patience with it, will likely founder, but a high-school-level acquaintance with astronomy, chemistry, and physics easily suffices to follow Mix's argument. The effort will be rewarded not only with insights but, as important, with the assurance that even the most abstruse and seemingly intractable matters are accessible to an open mind.

In short order, Mix lists the circumstances of life on Earth: It needs a watery environment, is based on carbon, functions through reduction-oxidation (redox) chemistry and proton gradients, requires a few basic elements in sufficient quantity (carbon, hydrogen, nitrogen, oxygen, phosphorous, and sulfur), and subsists on an influx of energy (mostly sunlight, but in some cases geochemical reactions). Given these terrestrial (curiously, astrobiologists use "terrean") specifications, scientists logically can start their search for life elsewhere by locating places that seem to have the same characteristics. "In short," Mix concludes, "we are looking for a rocky planet or moon, close, but not too close to a star": A rocky planet (as opposed to a gas giant) will have the right variety of chemicals. It must be close but not too close to a star so that water can exist there as a liquid.

This formulation helps narrow astrobiologists' search somewhat. As it turns out, two very good candidates for their search exist in Earth's solar system: Mars and Jupiter's moon Europa. Saturn's giant moon Titan may represent a third candidate. These are not the only places where scientists might look, but they are the best places to start.

The solar system is only one planetary system in one arm of a big galaxy. Already, only twenty years after the discovery of the first "exoplanet," or planet outside the solar system, some 350 planets are now known to orbit stars other than the Sun just in the solar system's galactic neighborhood. It is reasonable to assume, considering the difficulty of spotting such planets, that this number represents only a small fraction of all the exoplanets nearby—and a tiny fraction of those in the Milky Way. Most exoplanets do not qualify as potential life-cradles if judged by Earth standards. Mix explains why this is so: They orbit the wrong kind of star, are too big, or are too cold or too hot.

Stars have a relatively narrow belt of space around them, the habitable zone, where life might arise on a rocky planet. Only a small percentage of planets would find their way into this zone, yet space is vast, so astrobiologists reasonably assume that if a planet has the right conditions, life may be found there. Mix devotes several chapters to planetary science and how astronomers detect exoplanets, a fascinating account in itself.

Mix's real enthusiasm shows in his discussion of the history and mechanisms of life, to which he devotes the last seven chapters of his book. He presents life as a kind of reprieve from the inexorable, inescapable desolation of entropy. Entropy is essentially the underlying tendency in nature toward disorder. The second law of thermodynamics holds that, in any energy system, entropy always increases. That is, disorder increases and energy is lost. The Earth and Sun together form such a system, yet the planet's surface hosts organisms with the antientropic capacity to trap energy and use it to expand order. They do so by reproducing, by evolving into more complex, efficient organisms, by filling every available niche that supports them, and by participating in the "web of life," the ecosystems of interdependent organisms.

All organisms are part of these communities. The biosphere itself is the grand community of these communities. There is competition among organisms, to be sure, but the overall direction for life is to exist in interconnectedness and to build from simplicity to complexity. This occurs, Mix points out, in the overall context of entropy: Disorder still increases in the Earth-Sun system. Nevertheless, the ages-long profusion and variety of life increases. To humanity, this fact is, or should be, value-creating and beautiful.

Mix considers the magnificent tree of life, from life's precursors (such as prions and viruses) to the largest and oldest living things, from the beginning of life on Earth to the present, and always with an eye toward what these observations might teach science about life elsewhere. A great many basic mysteries remain, which is precisely what makes science so exciting. For instance, the origin of life is a matter of speculation, but it is increasingly informed speculation as scientists discover more about microbiology, genetics, and ecosystems. According to Mix, a promising theory holds that the first ecosystems appeared around deep-sea volcanic vents, where organisms fed from chemical energy. Only later did they evolve the ability to convert solar energy through photosynthesis.

Such matters as the origin and age of life and whether it exists outside Earth are culturally sensitive. They frequently divide science from religion, as well as one religion from another. Mix takes great care not to characterize the results of science as in any way complete or final. Indeed, as he remarks, to do so would not be scientific. Moreover, he is as careful not to present his own speculations based on scientific results as anything other than a personal viewpoint. His viewpoint is modest yet compelling in how it views life. Mix suspects that humans can only know symptoms of life, not any essential character, and that it may be more productive to define life as a process rather than as the attribute of an individual. An organism may exist only in relation to its ancestors and to its offspring. That view insists on the historical journey of life, as well as any given organism's immediate environment.

Intelligence is probably the most sensitive of all topics related to life. It is difficult to define intelligence as a strictly human characteristic, as Mix makes plain. Still, the characteristic is central to humanity's definition of itself as a species (*Homo sapiens*, the thinking branch of the genus *Homo*). It underpins the idea of civilization and forms a basis for the doctrine of exclusiveness in religions. Accordingly, the possibility that intelligent beings might live on other planets is inherently disturbing. It is perplexing, too. If life is the rule and intelligent races are common, why has there been no solid evidence of contact?

One supposition is that intelligence is rare. This hypothesis is supported by the fact that the decades-long effort by the Search for Extraterrestrial Intelligence (SETI) program to detect artificial signals from outer space has thus far been unsuccessful. Another, less complimentary supposition is that intelligent aliens exist but find humanity not worth contacting. Mix's own viewpoint about extraterrestrial intelligence is as refreshing as it is sensible. Whether common or rare, awe-inspiring or diminishing, such beings would offer an opportunity. "For many of us," he writes of fellow astrobiologists,

> the greatest motivation to find life elsewhere comes from a hope that such life should provide perspective. It would help us step outside of ourselves and discover something fundamental about how we see the world.

Throughout *Life in Space*, Mix's tone is of that tenor: earnest, judicious, and guiding. There are occasional sparks of humor, albeit nerdy humor ("Only eukaryotes have sex"), but readers will mainly encounter in Mix a reasonable man intent on taking up an extremely complex discipline on the frontiers of science in order to offer it as a wholly rational, salutary enterprise. He soft-pedals religious qualms about scientific enquiry, especially reductionism, and avoids secular mysticism. For example, he does not discuss James Lovelock's concept of Gaia, a superintelligence that emerges from the biosphere as a whole. Such belief systems, while they may bear on the larger implications of life, do not directly clarify the methods and findings of astrobiology. Mix also barely alludes to human-caused environmental degradation, species extinctions, and climate change. Maybe he does not have to. *Life in Space*, by showing how wonderful life is, teaches readers to cherish it and seek it out. It is in this respect that *Life in Space* has a claim to being extraordinary.

Roger Smith

Review Sources

Chronicle of Higher Education 55, no. 25 (February 27, 2009): B16.
Library Journal 134, no. 4 (March 1, 2009): 96.
New Scientist 201, no. 2702 (April 4, 2009): 45.
Science News 175 (April 11, 2009): 30.

THE LIFE YOU CAN SAVE
Acting Now to End World Poverty

Author: Peter Singer (1946-   )
Publisher: Random House (New York). 207 pp. $22.00
Type of work: Ethics, economics

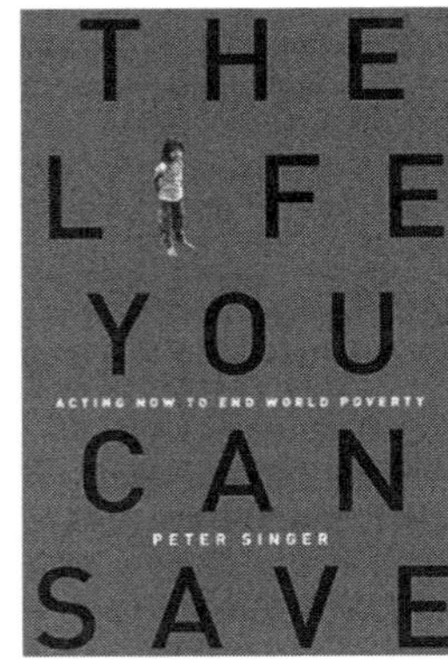

Singer deploys powerful ethical arguments to support the view that many Americans could and should increase their donations to save and improve the lives of people in low-income areas of the world, presenting information to help make such donations cost effective

Princeton philosopher Peter Singer has demonstrated awesome gifts for self-promotion and controversy. His *The Life You Can Save* is mostly uncontroversial, however, while Singer's skill at self-promotion is admirably harnessed to a thoroughly worthy cause. Around the world, millions of people (especially children) die every year from causes that would be preventable at comparatively low cost if appropriate resources were available to them. Singer's book is a call to action for Americans to elevate their giving, and it is working. A Web site based on the book records a steady escalation in the amount of funds donated or pledged since its publication. The book is being translated and published all over the world.

Singer confronts many potential objections and obstacles to his project. He feels that most Americans are not hopelessly mired down in the hedonistic pursuit of supposed self-interest. Indeed, research on happiness consistently finds that generous givers tend to be happier. After all, Christian teachings, and those of most other major faiths, strongly advocate for the poor. Singer's iconoclasm surfaces a bit when he challenges the common conviction that one's family comes first, but he sensibly concludes that this principle need not be an obstacle to generous giving. (The classroom examples he cites in this context, intended to discomfit his students, seem overdone).

Singer might have done better to stress that much of the expenditure made by the rich on their children may be damaging to those children's moral and emotional well-being. (Is a Princeton University education, for example, worth its price in comparison to the price of attending nearby Rutgers University?) He does point to the success of the "default option," where payroll deductions for a favored objective are taken automatically unless an employee explicitly opts out. This example establishes the extent to which Americans' spending is influenced by the path of least resistence.

Singer raises the question of why most Americans do not support overseas relief more generously, given their apparently generous inclination. One might respond that governmental foreign-aid programs, paid for with taxpayers' money, have not worked very well. Singer rejoins that the U.S. government spends relatively little on foreign aid, little of that spending goes to the lowest-income countries, and what does go to such countries is often impaired by "buy America" programs and other distractions. He strongly opposes dumping farm surpluses on poor countries, a practice that often harms those countries' abilities to develop their own food production systems.

Peter Singer is Ira W. DeCamp Professor of Bioethics at Princeton University. He has published more than thirty books, individually or cooperatively. He is considered one of the founders of the animal rights movement.

Singer could have spoken even more harshly against government-to-government aid programs and shown more systematically why private efforts are more likely to succeed. Among the obstacles to more giving, economists cite lack of information and the transaction costs of giving. The lives of the truly poor are so remote from U.S. experience that most Americans cannot identify with them. Singer acknowledges that generous giving is often forthcoming when the beneficiary has a name and a face and is "someone like us."

Singer also acknowledges that Americans may be less likely to respond to the needs of others if the only way to do so is by giving money. Money gifts are often the most efficient because they can support a cadre of specialists and can permit expenditures in the locality of need, drawing on the resources of that area (and paying the providers). For Americans with more time than money, volunteer activities such as serving in a food bank or senior center can offer face-to-face contact and sociability with other volunteers. For a man, being a blood donor can bolster a macho sense of self-esteem, partly because of the discomfort being overcome.

Singer effectively marshals evidence about the costs of saving lives. World Health Organization (WHO) programs directed against malaria, diarrhea, respiratory infections, and measles have cost about $300 for each life saved. Problems now faced in the developing world will probably more expensive to address. The comprehensive relief organization Population Services International (PSI) saves lives at a cost somewhere between $650 and $1,000 each. Perhaps more important is the fact that these programs have improved quality of life for many more than those who would have died.

Early WHO campaigns, though successful in their direct goals, were somewhat vitiated by the resulting population increases. Singer addresses this issue by citing the evidence that rising incomes tend to reduce birth rates. However, it is not evident that his proposals will increase incomes.

Singer is at his best in addressing the hard-boiled issue of cost effectiveness: He determines which organizations do the best work toward saving and improving lives per dollar spent. To begin, he alerts readers that many charitable organizations do not report data that permit cost-benefit calculation, and many do not even do a respectable job of self-evaluation. One of the hoped-for benefits of the charitable involvement of billionaires such as Bill Gates and Warren Buffett is greater attention being paid to such project evaluation. Singer himself strongly supports Oxfam; he also gives eloquent testimonials to the work of Partners in Health and Interplast.

The book provides moving descriptions of programs dealing with obstetric fistulas, surgery against deformities, and remedies for blindness. However, the discussion of fistulas illustrates an underlying systems problem: Some societies neglect women's rights and force girls into marriage and childbearing before their bodies are ready. The book's complementary Web site provides an updated directory of organizations that perform cost-effective work for the very poor. By highlighting these organizations, Singer is performing a service in institution building, helping drive financial support toward effective organizations. His data might lead some donors to redirect their contributions so as to increase the benefit derived from a given level of giving.

As an ethicist, Singer devotes much attention to why Americans should follow his recommendations. He uses one of economists' favorite bits of analysis in arguing that each person should donate up to the point where the personal expenditures sacrificed are nearly as important as the benefits obtained. Admittedly, entrepreneurs whose profits are plowed back into creating more capital and more jobs may be creating more social benefit than if they donated to even the most cost-effective charities. Singer urges that people forgo drinking bottled water, a singularly wasteful and environmentally unfriendly activity, and donate the cash they save. He notes that donating may contribute as much to one's self-esteem as would purchasing a lavish home or a fancy car.

Conceding that Americans are relatively generous givers, Singer remains skeptical about vast philanthropic support for the arts and cultural activities, leading readers on a scornful tour of the numerous donor identifications that adorn the new home of the Shakespeare Theatre Company in Washington, D.C. For potential donors with a propensity toward competition, the book's Web site offers donors the opportunity to receive publicity. As befits an ethicist, Singer finds many opportunities to berate the conspicuous excesses of the really rich, a topic developed by economist Robert Frank.

Singer has fun providing a suggested-giving chart with a progressive rate structure such as that used to determine income taxes. In the current recession, he might have added that people who have adjusted their lifestyles to generous giving are well placed to absorb income decrease without needing to make painful reductions in consumption.

Singer's book provides a scholarly and persuasive foundation for a commendable humanitarian cause, but the subtitle "acting now to end world poverty" is inappropriate. Most of the philospher's emphasis is on measures to improve health and schooling. The microcredit enterprises he praises have raised some people from being very poor to being merely poor. However, ending world poverty means raising people's productivity and their earned incomes. This is largely a systems problem, as dramatized by China's skyrocketing economic advance since emerging from Mao Zedong's oppressive regime. It requires entrepreneurship, capital, technology, organization, and favorable government. Singer momentarily stumbles on this matter when he gives credence to a crude calculation by Jeffrey Sachs of how much money it would take to raise everyone above the poverty line. Grassroots measures that raise agricultural productivity may worsen the level of surplus labor in rural areas—still a major problem in China.

In other sections of his book, Singer acknowledges the importance of systems elements such as the rule of law, property rights, and honest and effective government. He points to the systems approach embodied in the Millennium Villages Project, led by Jeffrey Sachs and sponsored by the United Nations. Besides health, education, and women's rights, the program stresses increasing productivity in agriculture and other appropriate village activities. By 2008, the program covered eighty African villages with a total population of more than 400,000 people. The program has targeted countries that are reasonably peaceful and law-abiding.

Such programs offer the prospect of complementarity with government aid to develop highways and other infrastructure. The greatest obstacle to economic improvement in Africa is bad government, as in Zimbabwe and Somalia, or absence of any effective government. The efforts of the United States government to upgrade the quality of government by direct action, such as in Iraq, have not met with great success.

U.S. foreign-aid policies now give more attention to recipient government quality. As private aid organizations gain support, they can also gain influence toward better indigenous government and toward better U.S. government aid policies. Such economic and political leaders as Gates, Buffett, Bill Clinton, and Rick Warren are acting on that assumption.

Singer recognizes that the policies of developed countries regarding international trade have powerful adverse effects on low-income countries, but he is pessimistic about prospects for overcoming the special-interest pork-barreling behind them. Unfortunately, he neglects the fact that the single most effective way to raise the income of persons in low-income countries is to enable them to migrate to the United States.

Singer's book has saved lives and will save many more. Not many authors can make such a claim.

Paul B. Trescott

Review Sources

The Age (Melbourne), April 11, 2009, p. A2-25.
Chronicle of Philanthropy 21, no. 11 (March 26, 2009): 24.
The Globe and Mail (Toronto), March 14, 2009, p. F11.
Kirkus Reviews 76, no. 24 (December 15, 2008): 1298.
The New York Times, March 11, 2009, p. 6.
Publishers Weekly 255, no. 50 (December 15, 2008): 42.
Quadrant Magazine 53, no. 5 (May, 2009): 67-69.
Times Higher Education, March 19, 2009, p. 51.
Wall Street Journal, March 5, 2009, p. A15.

LIT
A Memoir

Author: Mary Karr (1955-   )
Publisher: Harper (New York). 386 pp. $25.99
Type of work: Memoir
Time: 1972-2009
Locale: California; Texas; Massachusetts; New York

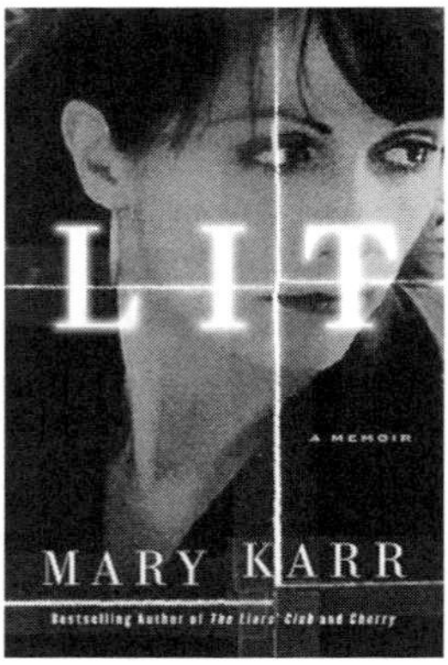

The third of Karr's memoirs describes her battle with alcoholism, as well as her unraveling marriage and her experience of motherhood

Principal personages:
MARY KARR, a writer, wife, and mother struggling with alcoholism, depression, and a volatile relationship with her mother
CHARLIE KARR, her mother, an artist and recovering alcoholic whose unpredictable behavior traumatized her children
LECIA KARR, Mary's older sister and confidant
WARREN WHITBREAD (a pseudonym), Mary's husband
DEV, Mary's son

Seven years in the making, *Lit* is the third of Mary Karr's memoirs. *The Liar's Club* (1995), her first, was principally about her childhood, and *Cherry* (2000) focused on Karr's teenage years. In *Lit*, Karr attends college in the 1970's, meets her future husband in graduate school, and becomes a mother while battling depression and alcoholism.

In the letter to her son that begins this memoir, Karr tells him, "Any way I tell this story is a lie" and asks him to forget that she is fifty to his twenty and that her brain is "dimmer" so that she can tell him the "whole tale" as she knows it. Karr describes how she hurt her son, not only by divorcing his father when he was five but also with the shouting and slamming doors that accompanied the end of her marriage. She expresses guilt for "vanishing" into the "madhouse" for a period and recounts her mother's psychotic episode when she stood over Karr and her sister Lecia with a carving knife before she herself was taken away to the madhouse. When Karr asked her why she had done it, her mother said, "I just couldn't imagine bringing two girls up in a world where they do such awful things to women. So I decided to kill you both, to spare you." Karr explains to her son that she always tried to protect him from the "knife-wielding goddess of death" who had also set a pile of her children's toys on fire.

Part 1 of the memoir begins in California, where Karr spends time with some "extremely stoned surfers." At "age seventeen," she is "stringy-haired and halter-topped, weighing in the high double digits and unhindered by a high school diploma." Thinking of her father makes her feel more rooted in the itinerant, unsanitary conditions in which she lives. She ponders the nights that he would go into the garage and drink from the bottle that he kept under his truck seat, as well as the times that he would come home at dawn after a long day of work in the oil fields and ask Karr to walk barefoot across his back.

Mary Karr's The Liar's Club *(1995) won the PEN prize. Her second memoir,* Cherry *(2000), was a* New York Times *Notable Book. Karr has received a Guggenheim Fellowship and Pushcart Prizes, as well as a Bunting Fellowship.*

After a hitchhiking incident in which a man high on crystal meth picks her up and she jumps out of the car and runs off, Karr realizes that she wants a more stable life than she has with the surfers. She goes to college at "a small midwestern school," where she decides to reinvent herself for that "leafy place" and the "college folks" who would not know how to speak to someone like her father, "who'd graduated grade six and spent days off cleaning his squirrel gun." In her father's absence, Karr seeks the favor of her male professors, one of whom—a "white-haired psychology prof, Walt Mink"—becomes her mentor. He helps her figure out how to improve her grades and possibly get some scholarship money, as well as offering her a job cleaning rat and pigeon cages to free her from the food service's "vile hairnet."

In the meantime, despite her reluctance to take a literature class because she feels outclassed by better-read students, Karr recognizes her affinity for poetry. She remembers that, in high school, she had "fallen in love with the visionary antiwar work of Bill Knott, who'd become a cult figure partly through a suicide hoax." Impressed with the way he read his poems, drawing them from a wrinkled bag stuffed with pages and then discarding them as if they were trash, she decides to take a poetry workshop with Etheridge Knight. Knight describes poetry as an oral art and impresses Karr with his support of her work, despite also telling her it is pretentious and incomprehensible.

As Karr explains it, Knight runs his workshops from his house with a forty-ounce bottle of Colt malt liquor between his knees, wearing "a string T-shirt and dark pants of a stiff material that I swear to God looked prison issue." When Walt Mink and his wife arrange a job for Karr teaching at a group home for "fairly functional retarded women," she is amazed at the women's ability to tell the good poetry she reads to them from the bad and their enthusiasm in doing so. The women's reactions remind Karr of her own visceral response to poetry. Karr also realizes at this time that she has "an appetite for drink, a taste for it, a talent."

Karr begins sessions with a therapist, and he encourages her to talk about her "complicated mother" and "absent father." As a result, she has what she calls "nonalcoholic blackouts," when she goes blank after being asked to recount memories of her mother, Charlie. At her therapist's suggestion, she invites her mother to a session, but neither of the women shows up for the appointment. Both of them claim that they forgot. After another session alone with her therapist, Karr flies home to Leitchfield, Texas, where her mother tells her that Karr's father was her fifth husband. Karr discovers that she has a half sister, a "blowsy L.A. blonde" with a taste for pills whom she sees only once, as well as an "easygoing" half brother, Tex, whom she takes to "right off."

Soon afterward, Karr is accepted on probation at a low-residency graduate school in Vermont—thanks to references from Mink and Knight, she thinks. Although the college is approaching bankruptcy, it remains open until the year she graduates. She describes herself as drinking "like a fish" during her residencies but staying sober between them, while she lives and teaches in Minneapolis, sobriety being "the only way to shovel through the heaps of work."

During one of her grad-school residencies, Karr meets her future husband, Warren Whitbread, who is rumored to be "the star of genius Robert Lowell's last class at Harvard," while he is touring the Vermont grad school for a week. Karr is impressed with his "shy smile and decorous bearing," which she later decides has been bred into him by his patrician family, who live in mansion called Fairweather Hall. She is struck by how different Warren's family is from her own, with their polite conversation, self-control, and apparently effortless entertaining, thanks in part to their domestic help. Years later, she will realize that she never really knew them.

Despite the conflicts that Karr and her husband have in their marriage, which increase as her drinking becomes more frequent, Karr describes herself as drawn to Warren's differences, finding in his "cool certainty" a counterbalance to her "ragtag—intermittently drunken—lurching around." Their love of poetry also draws them together. Karr admires Warren's self-discipline in keeping himself on a regular writing schedule, while she writes in fits and starts. In the meantime, her father's health is deteriorating, so she divides her time between Massachusetts and Texas, watching her father die. It is only after four years, when her father is on the verge of death, that Warren finally meets him.

Although she does not drink every day, Karr says, she finds herself "unpredictably blotto at inopportune times." When she discovers that she is pregnant, though, she swears off alcohol for the duration of the pregnancy. After twenty-two hours of labor, she is struck with a feeling of joy that she has never felt before, fascinated with her newborn son, Dev. Her mother says that Karr will "stare the skin off him" when she visits to help care for the baby. It turns out that Dev is not an easy baby to care for, and Karr later credits his frequent ailments for preventing her from getting as drunk as she might have otherwise.

At the age of thirty-four, Karr takes a job teaching six classes as an adjunct instructor, freeing herself from a "deeply respectable but non-writer-esque telecom consulting" job. As she and her husband speak less and less, Karr feels as if she is "circling" her marriage and "being erased with each rotation." Her drinking increases. Karr says that when Warren does speak to her, "the airspace is sandpapered and abraded, spiked as a bondage collar." They attend counseling sessions but cannot seem to contain the rage that they feel toward each other.

One night, when the room is "swirling" with their "invectives" and Karr sees Dev standing in the doorway, "naked and gap-mouthed," she realizes that she needs help and seeks it at a local support group for alcoholics. Karr is impressed with the diversity of the people who attend this meeting, noting that they do not fit her stereotype of such groups. She has a hard time, however, believing that she has anything in common with them, and she scoffs at the idea of a higher power. Nevertheless, with the help of her sponsor (whom she calls Joan the Bone), Karr maintains sobriety and concedes that a higher power might exist. She remains reluctant to pray.

After a poetry reading at Harvard College, Karr gets drunk and narrowly misses skidding into a concrete divider. Miraculously, to her, she and her car emerge unscathed, and she walks home. As Karr reconnects with her support system, she decides to give prayer a try, and within about a week she receives a call from the Whiting Foundation telling her that she has been awarded a thirty-five-thousand-dollar prize for which she had not applied. An "anonymous angel" nominated her. Although her initial response is guilt because Warren did not win the prize, Karr starts to believe in the power of prayer.

Karr and her husband continue to grow apart, however, and she realizes that prayer will not heal her marriage. She finds that the grant she has received paralyzes her writing rather than aiding it: She still feels guilty for receiving the award and for being underemployed while her husband is doing more and more editing and teaching. Feeling "dark and dead," sometimes going "days without obsessing about a drink," she begins to have suicidal thoughts. After a sleepless night of driving around with a garden hose in the back of her car and images of herself swerving into a telephone pole, tree, or ramp, she checks herself into a mental health institution famous for having had "blue-blooded 'Mayflower screwballs,'" including Robert Lowell, among its residents. After this experience, Karr decides to surrender herself to God, stating that, before, she feared that surrender would "sand" her "down to nothing." Now, she says, "I've started believing it can bloom me more solidly into myself."

Karr develops a support system so strong that she does not want to leave it for Syracuse University, so she initially turns down a professorship she is offered there. However, the university eventually makes her a better offer that she feels unable to refuse. Shortly after moving to Syracuse, Karr and her husband divorce. She begins not only dating but also "God Shopping," as she titles chapter 39. She eventually decides to become a Catholic after being surprised at the open-mindedness of a Catholic priest when she confesses her doubts about the existence of God. She also confesses to readers that, despite her newfound faith, she does not "much care to see God in all things." In fact, she says, "I prefer to find God in circumstances I think up in advance, at home in my spare time—circumstances God will fulfill for me like a gumball machine when I put the penny of my prayer into it."

The irreverence evident in this statement permeates *Lit.* Karr's voice expresses a skepticism not only about a higher power but also about her own power to overcome her alcoholism and finally consider herself a good wife, mother, sister, and daughter. She admits to failure in some aspects of her life and finds both frustration and salvation in writing, taking the pages and her journey to sobriety one day at a time.

Holly L. Norton

Review Sources

Kirkus Reviews 77, no. 15 (August 1, 2009): 81.
Library Journal 134, no. 16 (October 1, 2009): 77.
Los Angeles Times, November 8, 2009, p. E8.
The New York Times, November 6, 2009, p. C25.
The New York Times Book Review, November 15, 2009, p. 12.
The New Yorker 85, no. 38 (November 23, 2009): 113.
Publishers Weekly 256, no. 31 (August 3, 2009): 36.
The Wall Street Journal, October 31, 2009, p. W5.
The Washington Post, November 10, 2009, p. C01.